Systematic
Political
Geography

Harm J. de Blij

Systematic Political Geography

Second Edition

John Wiley & Sons, Inc.
New York London Sydney Toronto

Library of Congress Cataloging in Publication Data:

De Blij, Harm J
   Systematic political geography.

   Includes bibliographies.
   1. Geography, Political. 2. Geopolitics.
I. Title.
JC319.D4 1973   320.1'2   73-5665
ISBN 0-471-20053-0

Printed in the United States of America

10–9 8 7 6 5 4

*For my parents
with deep respect
and affection*

Preface

This revision and reorganization of *Systematic Political Geography* results from the advice, suggestions, and commentary of the book's users—students and faculty. The original formats of text and readings has been retained, but the volume is now divided into four parts, each with a particular focus. Part I views the development of the state and its salient spatial characteristics; Part II considers the state in systematic and processual terms; Part III focuses upon certain theories and models in political geography; and Part IV examines in detail prevailing policies and practices.

In the First Edition, articles drawn from the journal literature were photographically reproduced in the book. In the present Edition those articles have been printed in the same type as the remainder of the book, but against a slightly gray background to set them apart from the text.

I must reemphasize the aims of this book and state what it does *not* purport to do. It is intended to be an introduction to political geography—a beginning overview of this subfield. Political geography is such a wide-ranging area of geography that it is difficult to provide a representation of each topic with really great depth. Political geography is often introduced at the sophomore or junior level. This book was prepared for such a course. For advanced undergraduate seminars and graduate courses, volumes are available that serve admirably in that context. *Systematic Political Geography*, however, is designed for the initial phase of the sequence.

Coral Gables, Florida, 1972   *Harm J. de Blij*

Preface
to the
first edition

This book was developed over a period of six years, during which time I taught the senior-level political geography course in the Department of Geography at Michigan State University no less than twelve times to classes varying in size from under two dozen to more than two hundred students. The problems with which I was confronted while trying to increase the effectiveness of my political geography course led to my first attempt to put together a set of materials, and many readers of the present volume will recognize in it elements of its experimental predecessor, *Political Geography*, which was published in 1964 by the Continuing Education Service of Michigan State University and widely distributed for comments and criticisms. The completion of the present work has been the direct result of the encouraging response to the latter volume—a response which was supported by the results of a trial period of classroom use.

Systematic Political Geography consists of two kinds of material. First, there is a large body of original text, which constitutes an introduction to the field of political geography, approached along systematic lines. Second, a number of professional papers have been included, by direct reproduction from the journals in which they first appeared. These articles are used in two ways. Those that form a part of the progression of thought within a chapter are placed in the appropriate position in that chapter. Other articles are, in effect, case studies and are placed at the end of the chapter to which they are relevant, where they may be read as an illustration of what has just been considered.

The core of this book remains in the original text. The articles are supportive and illustrative, but this is *not* an extensively annotated volume of readings. The original text does not "introduce" the articles. The articles chosen have neither determined nor affected the direction of the original commentary.

An attempt is made, then, to do several things that seem important in the study of political geography—and, for that matter, in any kind of geography. Primarily, I have tried to develop a progression from the first to the last chapter. The initial chapters deal with elements, the middle chapters with system and function, the last chapters with evolving patterns. I have tried to confine my regional examples to those cases in which they are called for as illustrative devices. The use of the original papers will suggest to the student, even at this comparatively early level, the importance of an acquaintance with the professional periodicals in his field.

There is, of course, a further advantage to the inclusion of original articles. My experience, and, I am sure, that of many of my colleagues, is that the pressure on library materials increases every year, and the problem of rendering the contents of the professional journals available to students grows constantly. Several years ago I began to combat this difficulty by distributing a set of mimeographed materials, but eventually this too became prohibitively time-consuming and costly. After having experimented with *Political Geography*, which included text as well as salient readings, I decided on the present solution—which, I recognize, has some drawbacks. One limitation lies in the choice of the incorporated articles. Some will no doubt argue, and legitimately too, that I have been rather conservative in my selections. I suppose one can debate almost indefinitely the merits of the various contributions; one happy circumstance is that a replacement is easily made available. Certainly most political geographers would agree that a majority of the articles included in this volume are useful. In any event, I felt that I should include those articles that have, since their appearance, remained the object of more or less permanent attention on the part of political geographers, such as those of Mackinder, Hartshorne, Jones, and Kristof; at the same time I felt obliged to collect a sample of papers in the various subject matters of political geography.

As readers of this volume will perceive, *Systematic Political Geography* has undergone a good deal of modification during the writing of its various drafts. It does, of course, reflect my own preference in teaching in this field; I have found the modified systematic approach suggested by the Table of Contents to be more effective than the regional method. Nevertheless, there is a multitude of specific references to regional cases throughout the volume, and with them one of the incidental drawbacks of regional discussions comes to the fore: the problem of changing names. Literally dozens of names have changed during the writing of this final draft; some will change before it sees type. I do hope that readers will not find their entire train of thought disturbed by seeing Guiana instead of Guyana, Southern Rhodesia instead of Rhodesia, Bechuanaland instead of Botswana. I have rectified those I caught, but there will be other changes I may somehow have missed—and still others will occur before publication.

I am in debt to many people as this book is completed, for colleagues as well as students have been most generous in giving me assistance and advice. It obviously would be impossible to thank them all individually on these pages; one way or another, one is constantly influenced by one's colleagues, and although specific instances may be forgotten, ideas remain and may blossom. Professor Arthur E. Moodie introduced me to the field in courses and seminars at Northwestern University ten years ago, and my first research work in political geography was done under his direction; his enthusiasm has been an inspiration ever since. Professor Stephen B. Jones of Yale University read and commented extensively on an early draft, and I am most grateful for his many useful suggestions. Since 1960 graduate students have given me their reactions to my efforts, and many will recognize their suggestions embodied in the present text.

I am grateful also to Mr. D. L. Capone, who did the cartographic work that forms part of the original text in this volume and who aided materially in the research work involved. Miss K. Fuess did some initial work on the bibliography, and I am indebted to Mr. S. Birdsall for performing the major task of putting the bibliography in final form—sorting, alphabetizing, checking omissions, selecting additions, and typing. Miss K. Phelps and Miss C. Corwin typed the second draft of this volume, and Mrs. B. Naedele and Mrs. A. Zwick, secretaries in the Department of Geography, worked on parts of the third draft. The major share of the work on the final drafts was done by Mrs. V. Franks of the African Studies Center.

I also should like to thank the authors of the professional papers included in this book, and the editors of the journals from which they were taken, for their kind permissions to reproduce their work; many of the authors in their letters added words of advice and encouragement which were a source of great pleasure as the work progressed. I also appreciate the permission granted by the University of Chicago for the use of the *Goode World Base Map.*

East Lansing,   Harm J. de Blij
Michigan October 1966

Acknowledgments

This revision of *Systematic Political Geography* is the result principally of the numerous constructive and helpful commentaries received since the 1967 appearance of the first edition. Some of these responses have developed into a more or less permanent correspondence, an unexpected but delightful by-product of the effort. Thus I owe a great deal to many people, and I acknowledge an indebtedness of long standing to Professor Edward J. Miles of the University of Vermont, whose exhaustive review of an early, experimental version of this book had much to do with its eventual structure and content. I am also indebted to Professor Alfonso J. Freile of the University of Pittsburgh, who reviewed the manuscript of the present edition in detail. Again, I am grateful to my colleague Dr. D. L. Capone of the University of Miami for his work on the maps. Mr. Alan F. Ryan, also of the University of Miami, reviewed the chapters relating to territorial waters and maritime political boundaries.

I especially thank the authors of articles, all or part of which were included in this volume, for their kind permission to use their material, and the journal editors for taking the time for the necessary paper work. I am grateful to Professors S. S. Ball, S. S. Birdsall, D. L. Capone, S. B. Cohen, F. C. German, R. Hartshorne, J. H. Herz, S. B. Jones, L. K. D. Kristof, N. J. G. Pounds, L. D. Rosenthal, K. W. Robinson, A. F. Ryan, O. H. K. Spate, and to those who enabled me to include the work of H. J. Mackinder and D. Whittlesey.

In addition to those who were helpful in the preparation of the first edition, I acknowledge with much gratitude the work of my editor, Joseph F. Jordan, and members of the staff at Wiley, especially Stanley Redfern. Finally, I thank the students at the University of Miami and elsewhere for commenting candidly on aspects of the first edition and for suggesting many of the changes incorporated here.

H.J. de B.

Contents

1. An Introduction to Political Geography 1

PART I
TEMPORAL AND SPATIAL ATTRIBUTES OF THE STATE

2. The Focus: the Emergence and Structuring of the State 17
3. The Elements of the State: Territory and Population 36
4. The Elements of the State: Organization and Power 55

PART II
THE STATE: SYSTEM AND PROCESS

5. The Heart of the State: the Core Area 83
6. The Focus: the Capital City 116
7. Frontiers, Boundaries, and Buffer Zones 127
8. Boundaries: Concept and Classification 160
9. The concept of the Territorial Sea 189

10. Maritime Boundaries 201
11. Landlocked States: the Problem of Access 220

PART III
THEORIES AND MODELS

12. Lineages and Kinships 235
13. Exhortations and Prescriptions 267
14. Definitions and Models 296
15. New Directions 325

PART IV
POLICIES AND PRACTICES

16. Unitary and Federal States 343
17. Colonialism and Resurgent Nationalism 385
18. Supranationalism: from States to Blocs 425
19. Emerging Politicogeographical Realities 448

Author Index 467
Subject Index 477

Articles

D. Whittlesey   6
*The Impress of Effective Central
Authority upon the Landscape*

F. C. German   61
A Tentative Evaluation of World Power

N.J.G. Pounds S.S. Ball   87
*Core-Areas and The Development of
the European States System*

O.H.K. Spate   123
*Factors in the Development of
Capital Cities*

L. K. D. Kristof   136
The Nature of Frontiers and Boundaries

S. B. Jones   162
*Boundary Concepts in the Setting of
Place and Time*

D. L. Capone & A. F. Ryan   215
*The Regional Sea: A Theoretical
Division of the Gulf of Mexico
and the Caribbean Sea*

R. Hartshorne   241
*The Functional Approach in Political
Geography*

H. J. Mackinder   271
The Geographical Pivot of History

S. B. Jones   298
*A Unified Field Theory of Political
Geography*

H. J. de Blij & D. L. Capone   307
*Wildlife Conservation Areas in East
Africa: An Application of Field
Theory in Political Geography*

S. B. Cohen & L. D. Rosenthal   317
*A Geographical Model for Political
Systems Analysis*

S. S. Birdsall   327
*Preliminary Analysis of the 1968
Wallace Vote in the Southeast*

K. W. Robinson   369
Sixty Years of Federation in Australia

H. J. de Blij   413
*Cultural Pluralism and the Political
Geography of Decolonization:
the Case of Surinam*

J. H. Herz   454
Rise and Demise of the Territorial State

Maps

Prepared by Donald L. Capone

France: Paris is the Focus	4
Diffusions of the State Idea	22
The Roman Empire	31
Shapes of States	41
Exclaves	44
Age-Sex Pyramids	51
General Agreement on Tariffs and Trade, 1972	75
Suez Canal	76
Panama Canal	76
Core Areas: Europe	85
Core Areas: North America	104
Core Areas: South America	105
Core Areas: Africa	109
Core Areas: Asia	112
Core Areas: Australia	114
Capital Cities	118
Antarctica: a Last Frontier	128
Antarctic Treaty	130
The China-India Boundary	152
A Buffer Zone in Africa: Development and Decay	153
Buffer Zones and Shatter Belts	155
Physiographic-Political Boundaries: Zambia-Rhodesia in the Zambezi River	176
Physiographic-Political Boundaries: Czechoslovakia-Germany-Poland	176
Physiographic-Political Boundaries: Spain-France in the Pyrenees	178
International Boundaries in Lakes: United States-Canada	179
International Boundaries in Lakes: East Africa	179
Geometric Boundaries on Land	180
Antecedent Boundaries: United States-Canada	182
Subsequent Boundaries: Belgium-France	183
Superimposed Boundaries: West and East Germany	183
Relic Boundaries: Somali Republic	186
Offshore Zones	196
Continental Shelf	197
Submerged Shallow Areas	198
Bays and Low-Tide Elevations	203
Maritime Boundary Delimitation	205
Median Lines	206
Offshore Claims	209
The North Sea Divided	212
The Gulf and Caribbean Allocated	216–217
Landlocked States	221
Exits: Rivers	224
Exits: Corridors	226
Exits: Transit Lines	227
The Cycle Theory Applied Today	239
Mackinder and the Heartland	287
Spykman and the Rimland	288
The Airman's View	290
World Geostrategic Regions	293
Federal States	351
Federation, Mutual Interest: Switzerland	354
Federation, Mutual Interest: Brazil	356
Federation, Compromise: India	358
Federation, Compromise: Nigeria	359

Federation, Centralized:
Yugoslavia   363
Federation, Imposed:
Central Africa   365
A Doomed Federation   367
The German Colonial Empire   388
Black Africa: Colonial Evolution,
1890–1910   390
Portuguese Colonial Empire   393
France and Its Modern
Colonial Sphere   397
Great Britain and Its Modern
Colonial Sphere   399
Black Africa: Colonial Changes,
1940–1950   402
Black Africa: the Wind of Change,
1958–1972   406
Somali Irredentism   408
The Ewe Problem   409
Irredentism: Sudetenland   410
The League of Nations   427
The United Nations, 1972   428
Western Strategic Alliances   431
Organization of American States   433
Arab League   434
Commonwealth   436
French Community   439
Organization of African Unity   440
Europe and Economic
Supranationalism   444

Systematic
Political
Geography

CHAPTER
1
AN INTRODUCTION
TO POLITICAL GEOGRAPHY

Political geography is a varied and wide-ranging field of learning and research. Essentially, political geographers concern themselves with the ways in which man's political behavior and systems find spatial expression. We are all familiar with one kind of political system as it is spatially expressed: the *state*. Most of the people on this earth are inhabitants of one of its many states. Sometimes we tend to view our particular state—the United States of America, or Canada, or Brazil—in institutional terms, so that we equate the term with such establishments as the Senate and Congress, the State Department, and the many other governmental agencies and tentacles. Certainly these are important parts of the state system, but no state is made of institutions alone. All state systems also have a territorial or *areal* component: to exist, they must occupy a part of the surface of the earth. And it is with the manner in which they are organized on this piece of land that we are concerned here.

It is easy to see that the political institutions of the state constitute a system. There are parliaments, senates, congresses, upper and lower chambers, and there is representation from provinces, states, districts, and municipalities. We might conceive of this as the *vertical* component of the state system. But what makes the *horizontal* (or spatial) component? How are the institutions expressed on the ground? Some of these expressions are quite evident. States have boundaries, and they have frameworks of internal subdivision shown on maps by lines that separate counties from other counties and states from states, or provinces from provinces. States have capital cities, and many states have true *core areas* or heartlands, where a large percentage of the people and much of the productive capacity are concentrated. There are other spatial manifestations of the state's political organization: school districts, conservation areas, incorporated and unincorporated urban areas,

judicial districts, irrigation districts, and many similar spatially expressed subsystems that are, in one way or another, subject to the political process. And in the persistence of racial segregation, in the isolation and poverty of certain parts of rural America, in the Berlin Wall, in the location of military and industrial complexes, and in countless other ways, we print the evidence of our political instincts on the map.

There is more to political geography than the study of the spatial properties of the state alone. The state is but one manifestation of the efforts of human societies to organize themselves territorially. We are familiar, today, with a world political map that shows a boundary framework that delimits states from Finland to South Africa and from France to China. Still, there is a great deal that map does not tell us. In the desert there are groups of people who are constantly on the move in search of survival; their nomadic existence pays a minimum of heed to the political boundaries that meaninglessly cross their domain. But make no mistake; these nomadic or seminomadic people are no strangers to political activity, and just because they move from place to place does not mean that they have no sense of territoriality. And the map of Africa may show the political boundaries of several dozen states, but it does not show the homelands of several hundred tribal peoples, many of whom would put their own territory first and the state second in their scheme of priorities. From the abode of the Andean Indians of Peru to that of the Ainu of Japan, there are regions within states that have their own identity—an identity that may be far from the familiar image we may have of the state itself. The state, thus, is an aggregate of fragments.

In the other direction, too, there are circumstances our political map conceals. Groups of states in our world share certain interests, and they have shown a tendency to band together

1

to further their aims and to improve their security. Our familiar political map does not show it, but states on both sides of the Atlantic have joined in a North Atlantic Treaty Organization; there is an Organization of African Unity, an Arab League, a Warsaw Pact. We cannot be sure yet to what this international type of cooperation will lead; some political geographers speculate that the state as we know it will prove to be only a phase in our large-scale organizing process.

Political geographers, then, study nations and states, they are concerned with what we might call "subnational" units, and they look at "supranational" blocs, as well. But that is not all. Much—perhaps most—of the research political geographers have done has focused on the anatomy of the state: on boundaries and frontiers, enclaves and exclaves, corridors and transit routes. Those with a historical preference have tried to discern rules that might govern the emergence of states from lower-order units. Others have described and catalogued the territorial, demographic, and resource attributes of states. Still others have gone into the business, explicitly or implicitly, of evaluating the power of states and even of prescribing their courses of political action.

Thus political geography as a field of study is characterized by several different methods of approach and analysis and by numerous individual topics and subjects of interest. But whether the problems are small scale (as in the case of a meticulous, almost microscopic look at a small section of an international boundary) or of larger dimensions (as in a study of supranationalism), the *spatial* dimension is the vital ingredient in the political geographer's work. This is true also in some specialized areas not yet mentioned, such as *electoral* geography, the geography of urban politics, the political geography of resource management and development, studies in political decision making as it relates to the organization or "ordering" of the political area, and studies in the field of spatial perception.

Political geography has its share of theorists too. But that share has been rather small compared to some other fields of geography, and anyone who reads at all widely into the literature of political geography will find that political geographers themselves have often expressed dismay that their discipline has not produced a more solid theoretical foundation. All that is changing now, however, as political geography, along with other social sciences, is modernizing quite rapidly. We will explore some of the newer directions as well as the milestones of development of political geography in the past.

THE APPROACH

A field as varied as political geography is obviously open to numerous approaches. In this book we shall use as our frame of reference that familiar element of the politico-geographical world, the state. One advantage to this approach lies in our existing fund of general knowledge about states, which we will immediately begin to refine and from which we will select the fundamentals that we need in order to proceed. Another advantage relates to the fact that the vast majority of research in political geography is in one way or another relevant to the functioning of state systems. Whether it is a study of voting patterns or urban politics, resource management or even spatial perception, in one way or another it will relate to the state system as a whole. Several of the theorists whose work we will study have used the state as their unit of reference.

This is not to say that there are no disadvantages to a preoccupation with the state. The state is so complex and multivaried a system that it hardly seems possible to find out anything new about it by studying it as a whole. Many political geographers in recent years have been urging their colleagues who are involved in research to concentrate on smaller-scale topics and problems. By learning more about voting patterns in multiracial urban areas, the impact of expressways upon those sections of the city through which they are constructed, decision making with reference to limited resources (water supplies, for example), and similar subjects, political geographers will come to know much more about human behavior in a politicogeographical context than by studying states and nations in toto. And at the same time, the knowledge gained through such smaller-scale studies accumulates toward a better understanding of the state.

We will see some examples of this detailed kind of study, but in this introduction to political geography the state will often be our frame of reference. It is important to place what is studied in a familiar context and, as indicated earlier, there are other advantages to this procedure. But anyone who decides to continue in this field of study will undoubtedly find him- or herself concentrating on a particular aspect within this broad and challenging discipline.

In this book, our survey is divided into four parts, not counting this introductory overview. In Part One we consider some of the temporal and spatial characteristics of the state system. Here we recognize that the state as we know it, and as we see it every day on maps in newspapers and in televised news programs, is in large measure a legacy of the *Europeanization* of the world. In Middle and South America, in Africa, and in Asia, the states we have learned to identify and the boundaries that separate them are mainly the products of decision making by Europeans. We should not forget that political processes were going on in those parts of the world before the Europeans arrived, and that indigenous political systems were in formative, stable, or degenerative stages when the impact of Europe came. Thus we keep coming back to the same questions. What would have happened had the Europeans not destroyed or contributed to the destruction of those indigenous political entities? What would have grown out of the Aztec and Inca realms in the Americas? The savanna states of West Africa? The Indian subcontinent? We will never know with certainty. But we can learn a great deal about political behavior by studying the ways in which the modern successors to those ancient empires practice their statecraft now that the European influence has waned.

Also in Part One we look at the so-called four pillars of the state: its territory, population, organizational qualities, and power. There is more to this than meets the eye. A brief view of the world political map shows that states differ enormously in size (or, put another way, in their share of the available territory on this earth). Moreover, the states' individual territories have different *shapes*. Some states consist of only one contiguous area. Others are dispersed over many islands. In terms of political geography, these differences matter a great deal. And how the people of a given state have managed to organize themselves, to maximize their advantages and to minimize their disadvantages in the competition with other states, is one crucial issue in political geography. Man's organizational efforts are etched on the landscape and revealed by every politicogeographical map.

And one result that comes from organization is strength—power.

Part Two discusses the anatomy of the state. We now consider in detail such features as the core areas of states, to see what constitutes them, how they have come to exist, and how they function as the heart of the state. Next our attention focuses on the capital city of the state, and other cities as well. The capital is the hub of the state; it is the seat of government. Here the decisions are made that guide the state toward its national goals and objectives. But the capital city represents more than that. It often is the personification, the epitome, the "best foot forward" of the state. Certain states, seeking to redirect national goals, have even abandoned old and honored capital cities and have built new cities in new areas. We will study this phenomenon along with others relating to national headquarters.

Perhaps the most interesting property of the state is its boundary. Along boundaries, states make contact with other states; across such boundaries flow traffic and trade, and often ideas, as well. Political geographers have written a great deal about boundary problems, and the middle section of Part Two is devoted to a discussion of boundaries and frontiers. Special attention is given to an aspect of national boundaries that is of growing significance: the state's ownership of the adjacent seas. States are extending their control over these waters, and over the ocean floor as well. For some states, it is literally true that the maritime boundaries are more vital than the land boundaries. We ought to know why this is so, and where some of the problems of the future will lie.

Some states do not have coasts at all. They lie surrounded by other, more fortunate states, without direct access to the ocean trade routes of the world. They depend on treaties and promises and the good will of their neighbors, whose ports and railroads they must share. We close Part Two with a look at these countries and the solutions that have been devised to safeguard their access to the outside world.

Part Three examines some of the theoretical and conceptual directions in political geography. Now that we have an idea of the kind of data in which political geographers are interested, we should outline the development of this field of study, its origins and history, and the directions it has taken in the past. We will soon see that this is no simple matter. Political geography had practitioners in the days of ancient Greece and Rome; the field's modern development may be said to have begun in the nineteenth century. Modern times brought with them several conspicuous false starts, notably those that had to do with an ill-defined subfield called *geopolitics*. Geopoliticians combined their fervor as global strategists (on behalf of their home state) with the respectability deriving from their positions (as university professors, for example) and got into the business of advising governments on international strategy and the manipulation of power. But there were always political geographers who remained aloof from the strategic arena and who concerned themselves with theory for its own sake. They, too, did some exhorting—but not to their governments. Instead, they addressed themselves to their colleagues in political geography, suggesting ways in which common problems might be conceptualized, what models might be helpful in the search for solutions, and which directions in the field might be profitable and unprofitable. We should acquaint ourselves with some of this writing, for it tells us how political geography is now developing, what it has learned from the other social sciences, and where there are still gaps to be filled.

Part Four takes us back to some real-world manifestations of political geography. So far we have looked at the elements and the anatomy of the state, and we have considered political geography in the abstract. Now comes the time to ask, "How are these concepts expressed on the ground?" The people of a state and their decision-making leaders perceive the contents of the state-domain in certain ways. These ways are in part reflected by the manner in which they have organized their territory. Take, for example, one of those states mentioned previously, that have not one, but two capital cities. Why should this be so? Obviously there is or has been competition, either between two regions of that state or between two power groups within the state, for example, royalty and the church. Naturally you should be on the alert any time such a situation occurs. Then again, the degree of centralization of a state may to some extent be revealed by the map. We all know the expression that "all roads led to Rome"—a reference to the strong focus that was Rome in the heyday of the great empire of two millenia ago. But there are countries in this day and age that are equally strongly centered on one capital. Look at the map of modern France. More roads lead to Paris than ever led to old Rome. Does this have any

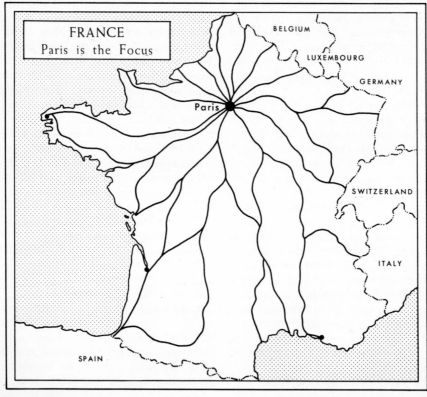

FRANCE
Paris is the Focus

BELGIUM

LUXEMBOURG

GERMANY

Paris

SWITZERLAND

ITALY

SPAIN

All roads lead to Paris.

politicogeographical meaning? It certainly does. France, by design, is a centralized *unitary* state.

On the other hand, some states are far less tightly unified and centralized. Some nations decided to give certain degrees of autonomy to regions or provinces within the state. Of course, this cannot always be read off the map. But the politicogeographical map surely is an aid in any understanding of the concept and practice of federalism.

Another question discussed in some detail in Part Four has to do with a waning practice, European colonialism. We will consider this phenomenon in just the terms described previously, and ask, "Did the colonial powers transfer their principles of politicoterritorial organization to their former dependencies, and if so, can we see evidence of this process on the map?" Here is an interesting case in point. In Africa, all but one of the former French dependencies have become unitary states, strongly focused on a single capital, very much in the image of the "motherland." Several of the British dependencies, however, became federal states upon independence. Since the United Kingdom is a unitary state, this seems to suggest that *this* European power, at least, tried a new tack in Africa. But before we jump to this conclusion, consider the United Kingdom compared to France—is it not much less centralized; is there not a Wales, a Scotland, an Ulster; did not the roots of federalism lie here? Perhaps the colonial map tells us much

more than we might have believed!

Also in Part Four we consider some of the principles and practices of supranationalism. Ours is the half-century of international "blocs," "treaties," "leagues," "pacts," and "communities" of states. Is this only a phase, or does it portend the end of the state as we have known it and the coming of the superstate? This question, among others, is discussed in the closing chapter of the book, in which we seek to discern some lasting and significant trends in the politicogeographical world.

THE IMPRESS OF AUTHORITY

The first article from the geographic literature to be included in this book is also one of the oldest (written in 1935) and most durable. In this paper, Whittlesey addresses himself to the very question we asked earlier: "How does politics modify the landscape?" He discusses this topic in four contexts: expressions of security, properties of boundaries, expressions of governmental activity, and manifestations of the legal system. Here, then, we see how a political geographer some four decades ago viewed the significant questions to be researched in this discipline. Whittlesey raises literally dozens of questions, leaving many of them unanswered. This is one reason why this article is still quoted so frequently; it is full of ideas and, as a call for action, it still has relevance today.

The Impress of
Effective Central Authority
upon the Landscape

Derwent Whittlesey

Harvard University
October, 1934.

Political activities leave their impress upon the landscape, just as economic pursuits do. Many acts of government become apparent in the landscape only as phenomena of economic geography; others express themselves directly. Deep and widely ramified impress upon the landscape is stamped by the functioning of effective central authority.

By "central authority" is meant sovereignty over an area of marked diversity. To be "effective" the central government must exert more than nominal control over its area. Today "effective central authority" is a function of the national state.[1]

EXPRESSIONS OF SECURITY

Security is one of the most valued products of effective central authority—the guarantee against molestation with the state and the assurance of resistance to invasion from without.

In the state which feels itself secure habitations are disseminated wherever this mode of settlement suits the economic life. In new countries (by "new" is meant those which have been settled in the current age of central authority) farmsteads are dispersed in most types of agricultural occupance. Even where the agricultural mode favors clustering, as in irrigated districts and on plantations and market gardens, the farmsteads commonly line up as stringtowns along roads, so that each may be centrally located in the midst of its farm land. This is in marked contrast to the

farm villages in similar agricultural units of old countries. There the houses may cluster in tight knots. A good many are perched on defensible hills or protected by water, and are therefore inconveniently remote from the farm land. A comparison of the settlement patterns of Southern California and Southern Italy illustrates this distinction. In countries which were settled in eras of insecurity, defense points have now been to some degree abandoned in favor of more convenient sites. Crowded hills are deserted for open plain, as at Les Baux in Provence. Or hill villages expand downhill, but retain their ancient centers on the defense point; Spain supplies numerous examples of this shifting. In extreme cases the crest is denuded of buildings and reclaimed for gardening (*e.g.*, Loudon, France). Sicilian villages which formerly hugged the coast and its protecting waters are pushing tentacles of farmsteads into the rolling, open uplands, now that the Mafia has been deprived of its threat to life and property. Where artificial defenses were formerly maintained, moated granges and villages free thenselves for expansion by filling their encircling waters with their encircling walls. Where the agricultural system cogently favors scattered habitations, isolated farmsteads appear, concomitant with security.

Urban centers are precluded by their function from dispersing in the way farm villages may do, but they may and do spread out. Security not only permits them to occupy more space, but it stimulates both trade and manufacturing, their two chief reasons for existing. Flourishing economic life demands land for port facilities, rail and road terminals,

---

[1] Unless capitalized, "state" is used throughout in its generic sense of "sovereign power."

Views of an ancient African headquarters—Zimbabwe. Top: In a hill-rimmed lowland lies the "Temple" surrounded by the ruins of many structures which fell before fortune hunters. Perhaps a religious and political focus for the Shona peoples of South-Central Africa, Zimbabwe experienced contact with the outside world, as revealed by the contents of the terrain—Chinese objects have been found here. Bottom: A detail of one of the entrances to the "Temple" shows the construction of the walls, which reach several dozen feet in height and, though without mortar, are very strong (Harm J. de Blij).

and wide thorofares; space must be provided for retailing on a large scale and for wholesaling; professions and other services multiply; new largeness of ideas sets up new space requirements for residence and for recreation. All these call for acreage undreamed of in days of straitened insecurity.

Trade follows security, and trade has forced walled seaports to burst their bonds. All of La Rochelle but its port lies on land which was outside the walls in the 17th century; so also with San Juan, Puerto Rico. The easily defended *calanque* which has fixed the Rhone Valley seaport of Marseilles for at least 2800 years has been turned over to the fishing fleet, and a new commercial port filched from the open Mediterranean by jetties. London, Antwerp, Rotterdam, Hamburg, and many another estuary city has dug a new harbor in soft alluvium adjacent to but below the ancient constricted port. To obtain space for new business nearly every commercial city in continental Europe, and the larger ones in Japan, have converted their moated walls into boulevards. Paris and Vienna are the most famous examples, but Toulouse, Cologne, Seville, Milan, and hundreds of others, large and small, disclose the same history in their street pattern. Less spectacular, but more costly, is the widening and straightening of countless streets, and the substitution of modern buildings for medieval rookeries. Of all the square miles pierced only by ten- or fifteen-foot streets and still narrower culs-de-sac which made up fourteenth century Paris, only one small fragment survives today. The dead-end and zigzag alleys of Japanese cities are giving way to more regular plats of streets. Three centuries ago hardly a cathedral in Europe stood free from a parasitic congeries of habitations; today their plazas are open. The cluttered and congested urban landscape which expressed the day when political security lagged behind expanding business has all but disappeared. New functions, particularly large-scale manufacturing and the manifold business of rail terminals, have grown up outside the "ring" boulevards which mark ancient fortifications.

The spacious residential suburb is likewise the product of an age of security as well as an age of fast transport. It has nothing but location in common with its precursor, the medieval faubourg, which was a slum huddled for protection against the walls of a city. Residences in most European and Asiatic cities retain the walled-in character of their predecessors. In the new countries of British origin, and even in Great Britain itself, dwelling houses are likely to face the street across open lawn, with no barrier except rarely a fence of wood or wire, or at most a low wall. The spacious habit of building each town house detached and not walled-off from its neighbors, seems to be the ultimate landscape expression of generations of security, beginning in Europe and transplanted to the colonies. At any rate it is practiced almost exclusively in English-speaking new countries, and most prevalently in the newer parts of them. But even there some time has generally elapsed between the abandonment of the stockade and the adoption of the detached house. The residential streets of little cities along the Atlantic seaboard of North America, such as Portsmouth (N.H.) and Charleston (S.C.), as well as the older sections of all the large seaboard centers, present solid ranks of abutting façades. West of the Appalachians only the most congested sections of the largest cities are built in solid blocks; in small cities and in residential sections of large ones the detached dwelling reigns, even where it is built with the intention of housing two or three families in "flats."

SPECIAL FEATURES OF BOUNDARIES

Expansiveness does not everywhere accompany security. Along international boundaries the landscape may be strewn with features intended by central authority to maintain security. At the least a custom-house and immigration post (often housed in the officer's home) stands sentinel at every major route crossing. On some European borders a gate, usually a heavy balanced pole, stands ready to be lowered at night and for any emergency. On minor roads a single military official is in sole charge. On main thorofares several men are stationed, often both civilian and military authorities. Even the undefended border between the United States and Canada is studded with official buildings where a few men are kept on duty. Along boundaries where acute tension is felt, either because of smuggling, antipathy between political systems which face each other across the line, or recent boundary displacements, the soldier guard may mount to a military encampment, although only at crucial passways. At the exit of the Vall d'Aran in the Pyrenees, where the temptation to smuggle is powerful, the border is controlled by a small company of soldiers. On the Carso the new frontier between Italy and Yugoslavia near the strategic Peartree Pass is marked by a made-to-order garrison city, regiments of soldiers, ariplane landing fields, ammunition dumps along the railroad, and freshly made military roads—all in a karst region almost bare of vegetation and apparently devoid of human inhabitants other than the garrison and its entourage. Even the St. Gotthard Pass on the border of peaceable Switzerland is heavily fortified.[2]

At railroad crossings there are, in addition to the usual officials, terminal facilities for trains which technically do not cross the border. In practice the terminal is generally in the town nearest the boundary, and not on the line. Whether the gauge differs or not, the terminal exists, because only a few of the trains go through, and in any event the locomotives and crews are changed. Many boundaries are closed to aircraft, except along specified lanes, which are as definite routes as roads or rails, although they are invisible.

Definition of boundary lines, *i.e.* replacement of boundary zones by boundary lines, follows upon the establishment of effective central authority. When central authority is weak, border districts, even if legally subordinate, are in practice at liberty to carry on their life pretty much as they please. They usually work out intimate economic reciprocity with neighboring political units, which themselves may be independent or nominally subordinate to some other inclusive state. Inhabitants of such harmoniously functioning border regions feel foreign to the people of their respective distant capitals, but not to their neighbors across the political boundary. When power is concentrated in a central locus, border zones are subordinated. Whenever the local interests clash with interests of the state as a whole, the border interests suffer. Central authority, to be effective, must proclaim fixed linear boundaries which can be defended against military aggression and economic penetration. Where political borders coincide with population deserts, such as oceans or large lakes, expanses of dunes without oases, perpetual ice, or dense forests, local life is little or not at all affected

by fixing a linear boundary. In new countries, where a linear boundary has been drawn antecedent to settlement, the economic life conforms to it without strain, although tariffs often induce branch factories in border towns, and thus modify the landscape. Where manufacturing plants are built beyond the line to take advantage of tariffs, workers commute from their established homes across the boundary, or if distance prevents this, they may move to new "line" towns on the frontier of their homeland. Rarely, a double town bestrides the line. In most regions the substitution of linear for zonal boundaries cuts off kinsmen from each other, parts business associates, and severs chorologic units. This is true even along mountains which are commonly thought of as barriers (*e.g.*, the Pyrenees), and populous plains such as Flanders, Lorraine, Posen, Silesia, have repeatedly seen towns lopped off from part of their upland, and have occasionally suffered the arbitrary dissection of cities.

Boundaries recently displaced are likely to mark zones of personal risk. On borders of the Polish Corridor and Upper Silesia transgression without the proper papers makes one liable to arrest and confinement, even though the culprit has not left his own property. Since boundaries are often arbitrarily drawn cross-country through farms and even through towns, this surveillance annoys the individual and so adds increments of personal hatred to the general enmity.

To guard against aggression many boundaries are lined with defenses, *e.g.*, the Franco-German border. Such defenses are linked by strategic roads and railroads, such as the Stelvio Pass road, the high-level bridge across the Kiel Canal, and certain railroads in pre-war Poland (many of which are now useless). The land thus used is withdrawn from other occupance. Towns along the boundary are semi-military, being differentiated from ordinary commercial towns by barracks, fortifications, and a general air of being supported by government rather than by business.

Boundary displacements may be followed by political acts which directly or indirectly modify the landscape. Slight changes, such as the substitution of one language for another on public buildings and street signs, are common. Even stores and offices may be required by law to display only the official language. Perhaps the extreme case at the moment is the Lower Vistula Valley. There an important railroad

[2]For details of border phenomena, especially those along the Franco-German boundary, see Hassinger, H.: "Der Staat als Landschaftsgestalter," *Zeitschrift für Geopolitik* 9 (1932), 117–22, 182–7.

bridge across the river was first closed, and later moved to another site. A fishing hamlet among the dunes has been elevated into a modern port by the construction of costly harbor works, and linked to the interior of Poland by new stretches of railroad. Indirect pressure, such as government contracts, is exerted to deflect goods and people into this new all-Polish channel of ingress and egress. As a result Danzig, the ancient port city of the Vistula Valley, has to share the trade with its politically fostered rival. By treaty Danzig has accepted the smaller share—45 per cent to Gdynia's 55 per cent.[3] Routes and other communication patterns are frequently altered after a boundary displacement; at first certain connections are closed or so restricted by inspections at the border that they fall into disuse, then new connecting links, suited to the new alignment of territory, are built. All this in the name of security.

EXPRESSIONS OF GOVERNMENTAL ACTIVITY

Central authority usually undertakes to act for the whole of its territory in specified matters. This tends to produce uniformity in cultural impress even where the natural landscape is diverse.

Public buildings of uniform function and form are commonplace examples. The post-offices in France, the army posts in all countries, the state capitols in the United States (these by imitation rather than prescription), are easily recognized types. In a very heterogeneous country, such as the United States, regionalism may be given recognition. Generally nowadays the federal government builds its post-offices in conformity to local tradition. In New England they are "colonial"; in California, Spanish; in the Middle West, either classical or modernistic.

In many new countries a uniform land survey, including routes, has been sketched upon the landscape antecedent to settlement. This is notably true of English-speaking North America, except for the colonial settlements and the Old South. It also applies, but much more locally, to parts of Latin America and other new countries, including settlements made centuries ago in eastern Germany, when it was "new." Perhaps the system of Roman

roads, still conspicuous features of the route pattern in Romanized Europe, may be cited as an additional and still earlier example of a pattern of communication ordained by central authority.

In the Roman permanent "camps" of Western Europe, and in towns laid out by Germans as they pushed eastward after the tenth century, rectilinear street patterns within circular or elliptical walls are common, although blocks are likely to be unequal and streets not quite straight. Modern national governments began to sponsor fiat towns early in the seventeenth century. The gridiron pattern of streets was seized upon as convenient, since the new towns were generally laid out on plains and defense was not necessary.[4] Richelieu in western France, laid out by an officer of the Church, and Mannheim on the Rhine, laid out by a military officer of the state, are samples. The grid proved to be an equally handy pattern for mushroom towns in new countries. Nearly every municipality of the Pampa, except Buenos Aires, is an example. Philadelphia is an early case (1682) in North America. The Dutch followed the scheme in Batavia. In these cases the orientation is rarely due north-south and east-west. Compass orientation of city streets fits naturally into the coarser grid of the rectilinear survey, adopted in many new countries. Melbourne is an example from the antipodes. Chicago is the outstanding case of the very large city oriented north-south and east-west, and monotonously and regularly extended. The almost featureless lacustrine plain on which it lies has neither compelled nor encouraged deviation from the ideal plan. The offsets which accommodate the straight-line survey to the spherical earth appear as jogs in the street pattern. Numerous new suburbs of old cities throughout the world have been similarly platted. Where no rectilinear survey exists, grids may have any conceivable orientation, e.g., along streams, country roads, or railroads, or hinged to a stretch of fortification-turned-boulevard.

Most gridiron street plans have not been directly imposed by governments. The appeal of convenience, however, has been irresistible in an age when new cities and new suburbs of old cities have been multiplying on open

---

[3]Other modifications of Germanic border regions since 1914 are discussed by Hassinger, op. cit.

[4]As compared to a jig-saw pattern shot through with a few radial lines, the gridiron city is difficult to defend. Ambush, barricades, and central command are handicapped.

plains, thanks to increased trade and manufacturing made possible by powerful government.

Governments often stimulate migration into newly acquired areas by offering landholdings larger than those current in regions from which settlers are drawn. This distinction tends to disappear in time unless it is reinforced by the natural environment. In the Pampa large holdings, originally stock ranches, persist because they carry social prestige, but much of the land is now under the plow, being tilled by tenants on short-term leases. Eastern Germany, wrested from Slavs, was blocked out by the invaders from the west in large, uninterrupted units, strikingly in contrast to the crazyquilt of both holdings and fields in parent Germany. These very large units persist today chiefly in rugged, marshy, sterile districts where small farmers can not make a living and horse raising affords a genteel occupation.

As the United States approaches demographic maturity, the average size of landholdings is undergoing progressive change toward harmony with the environment. In the Corn Belt the typical patent from the government granted 160 acres, a figure not far from the unit which in that region can most effectively be worked by a single farm family. Farther west, in the semi-arid and desert country, this unit early proved too small, and homestead allotments double and later quadruple this size came to be permitted by law. Where grazing or dry-farming dominates, even 640 acres is too small a unit, and holdings are being merged to form adequate ranches. In the irrigable areas of "Mediterranean" California and "Egyptian" Arizona, on the contrary, the original large holdings, many of them stock ranches dating from Spanish times, are being morselled into twenty-, ten-, and even five-acre lots.

The existence of effective central authority implies the power to collect taxes and distribute funds throughout the whole territory of the state. Notable modifications of the landscape have resulted from the habit governments have of distributing to backward and to pioneer sections money collected from prosperous districts. This is, in other terms, a transfer from regions favored by the natural environment to regions laboring under temporary or permanent environmental handicaps. The Tennessee Valley Project of the moment is a spectacular example, but the principle has long been in operation in the United States,

thanks to loose construction of the Constitution. Much of the irrigation of land in western States has been paid for from federal funds; the federal government provides aid in building roads, especially in sparsely populated regions; and many of the railroads in North America (and in every other continent) have been similarly aided, wherever they have been trajected through difficult or unpeopled territory. In North America and Australia, at least, the States and the Provinces have carried this redistribution of funds further. The southern half of Michigan, Wisconsin, Minnesota, and Ontario each supports schools and roads in the northern quarters; in like fashion the eastern part of each Great Plains State contributes to the maintenance of its western part, and humid Australia to the arid ends of the several States. Lowlands in mountainous middle latitude countries spend a part of their taxes for objects which make habitation of the highlands possible. Forests and recreational preserves in handicapped regions are likely to be maintained by central government. From this view-point the study of pioneer areas as undertaken recently by the American Geographical Society resolves itself into these problems: first, how much government aid is needed; and second, how much it is socially wise to disburse in any given area.

A number of regions, prosperous enough to support themselves in local affairs, can benefit greatly if given aid from the central government on specific problems which transcend a single region. Flood prevention in the Mississippi Basin is too comprehensive a task to be dealt with effectively by any existing political unit smaller than the United States. Reclamation of the Zuyder Zee by the Netherlands, reforestation in Alpine Europe and elsewhere, the construction of *autostrade* by the Italian state and similar national road systems wherever automobiles are important, the Canadian policy of supporting intersectional railroads, hydro-electric installations in Ireland and Russia—all these are examples of comprehensive undertakings which only central authority can handle.

Public funds available for regional redistribution may be misdirected. Some unwise expenditure results from necessary experimentation, since governments have had relatively little experience in enterprises of this nature. Political favor and log-rolling cause other and lamentable leaks. The federal appropriation for "rivers and harbors" in the United States has been notorious for a century. Every country no doubt has counterparts of our pork barrel. An abuse hard to eliminate arises naturally, as useful institutions become antedated or cease to satisfy the needs of the community. Vested interest, often supported by law, prolongs customary expenditure for indefinite periods. The continuance of army posts in the United States Indian Country, the support of the established church in England, are cases in point.

Government lays hands in a special way upon its capitals. The focussing of roads, railroads, and canals upon the seat of government is partly the result of economic evolution, but it is often encouraged by political aid. Berlin, for instance, is not the center of Germany to the degree indicated by its hub of communication lines. The location of some capitals has been shifted in harmony with migrating political power. Nearly every one of the original United States moved its capital from the seaboard to the interior, as population increased in the back country. The reverse process occurs when overseas powers impose their rule upon settled communities. The seat of administration may then be brought to the coast, as from Cuzco to Lima, from Kandy to Colombo, and from Delhi to Calcutta.

Once fixed, capitals become the pets of government. On them public money is frequently lavished beyond present needs, even beyond the natural desire of the people to dress up their capital city. Delhi, Peiping, Berlin, Rome (both ancient and modern), are notable examples of generous expenditure. All these cities are splendid to look at, and each looks very different from the ordinary commercial city. Minor capitals have been garnished in proportion to their funds. Every German quondam state has an imitation Versailles, and the forty-eight democratic United States of America have spent staggering sums to house their governments. Washington and Canberra, as purely political fiat towns, are the clearest beneficiaries of political favor, but even London, primarily a world port and the leading manufacturing city of Britain, is impressively the capital of a nation and an empire. The spaciousness of modern capitals —"Washington, city of magnificent distances," Paris with its broad boulevards, Rome, roomy enough to accommodate both the modern capital and its exhumed predeces-sor of antiquity, are made possible by the security which central authority affords. Some governments which have spent overmuch on dressing up their capital cities have been overthrown not long after. Athens of Pericles and Versailles of the later Bourbons by their very splendor contributed to the undoing of their sponsors.

Outside the capital city the hand of government puts its stamp on many places. Universities may form the nuclei of small cities. Prisons strikingly modify the landscape and in places, as at Princetown on Dartmoor, dominate it. Experimental farms may occupy large acreage. All these are exceptional. Most government agencies are housed in buildings more or less lost in ordinary towns and cities—district courts and police registration bureaus, central banks, port headquarters, and the like. Yet they are likely to bear clear evidence of their official character. If built of costly materials in a massive or a pretentious style, as is commonly the case, they stand out among their neighbors. The site too is likely to enhance their distinction. It may be a conspicuous hill, a plaza, or a park, such as only government can afford. On the other hand it may be an out-of-the-way spot or an obscure block on a mean street which people would never search out but for government compulsion. A government building erected in a poor neighborhood improves surrounding values. Conversely, if the site happens to be in a retail shopping section, the government building, lacking show windows and shops, no matter how fine a piece of architecture, serves as a damper to trade, and surrounding land values are thereby lessened.

LAWS RESULTING IN LANDSCAPE MODIFICATIONS

Tariffs imposed by central authority set their mark on widely separated regions. The incidence of tariffs is determined largely by economic geography. Those which fence out foreign manufactured goods lead to the creation of new manufactural districts, as in Montreal, Toronto, Hamilton, and Windsor, in Canada. Budapest and Ljubljana are creating factory districts to supply peoples formerly served by Vienna. Tariffs or subsidies applying to agricultural produce favor agricultural systems different from those which would exist with free trade. Examples: the large acreage of wheat in France, a cool, moist land; the intensive spots of tobacco and sugar beets in nearly every country of Western Europe; sugar-cane as the dominant crop in Hawaii, Puerto Rico, the Philippines, and a crop of moderate importance in Louisiana.

Embargoes of other sorts alter the location of items in the landscape. The refusal of the State of Maine to permit the exportation of its water power leads to the building of a large pulp-mill on the Lower Penobscot to use Kennebec power and imported pulpwood. Power developed in New Hampshire on the Upper Connecticut in the same year is shipped to populous Boston and vicinity for miscellaneous manufacturing and lighting. Dissatisfaction with Mexican participation in an irrigation canal which crosses the international boundary in the Imperial Valley spurs on the construction of an all-American canal on less advantageous terrain.

Laws affect both the tempo and the direction of settlement in all new countries, although in the process the law itself is much modified, or where it conflicts too stridently with its new-found environment, abrogated.

The early European settlements in the New World, made in the fifteenth century, were launched under franchise from European governments; in many cases the present political subdivisions are bounded by the terms of those franchises. Sea-to-sea grants in British North America account for the east-west boundaries of several States on the Atlantic seaboard and in the Middle West, boundaries which run counter to the grain of the country. The Papal Line of Demarcation of 1493–4 accounts for Portugese Brazil in Spanish America and for four centuries of Spanish rule in the Philippines.

As settlement progressed inland from toeholds on harbors, it was protected or hampered or deflected by the aegis of the law. At the outset the seigneurial system dominant throughout Europe was transplanted to the new continents. It suited the plantation system of agriculture and has never been much modified where that mode of land use still prevails. For centuries it suited the Pampa, a remote grassland where livestock ranching paid better than any other agricultural system. With increasing demand for grain, all the more humid Pampa has recently become potential wheat or mixed farming country. Thus far the social prestige of immense estates, fortified by the law, has retarded their subdivision, although more and more land is being tilled under a wasteful system of tenantry. In contrast to the Pampa stand Canada and the United States. In New England particularly, the seigneurial system never took root; elsewhere, except in the plantation South, it was abandoned because the small farm better fitted the environmental conditions. As settlement swept inland from the humid seaboard into the humid Middle West, homestead laws fixed the size of individual's claims to unappropriated public land at a figure which had proved satisfactory in the parent States. In sub-humid regions, where tillage has to be extensive, and still more in regions so dry that only grazing can prosper without irrigation, application of these laws predestined homesteaders to hopelessly inadequate holdings. The common practice of alloting alternate sections of the land to railroad companies as an inducement to extend the rails, further complicated the pattern of land holdings. Successive laws increased the acreage allowed, but they came too late to benefit most of the stock raising country. It has been found difficult, often impossible, to piece together from abandoned claims and the rigid checkerboard of railroad holdings, enough land with the proper balance between winter and summer pasture and with suitably spaced waterholes, to make a successful stock ranch. As a result some land is overgrazed while other land is not used to its capacity, or is occupied without legal right.

The general progression of settlement in new countries of British origin has been from humid to arid. The English Common Law did not require much modification to serve for the humid parts of the United States and the British Dominions, but when it began to be applied indiscriminately to dry regions some sections of the code were found to run so sharply counter to local needs that they had to be abrogated. To cite a notable example: riparian rights if adhered to would have prevented the installation of irrigation works, without serving any useful purpose in regions devoid of navigable streams. Conversely, laws had to be drafted to safeguard the rights of irrigation farming, since the Common Law, a native of the humid English climate, incorporated no such rules. In the San Joaquin Valley of California litigation between landholders who wished to maintain riparian rights and those who desired to divert water for irrigation, retarded the evolution of "Mediterranean" agriculture for decades. Even today not all the irrigable land is under ditch, and in each irrigated district the crops grown are dominantly those which promised profit at the time when legal controversies happened to be settled.

Laws affecting the use of land and natural resources are not confined to new countries. Every considerable social revolution produces its crop of laws affecting land holdings. Generally such laws are calculated to break up or to prevent the rise of large estates, to restrict holdings to small acreage, and to limit the agricultural occupance to those modes in which small holdings pay. In Rumania, Russia, Ireland, and other parts of Europe where estates have been subdivided during and since the World War, subsistence farming has generally replaced commercial farming, crude tools have replaced machinery, fields have been reduced in size, the percentages of crops grown and stock reared have changed, and in places soil fertility has decreased. In general small holdings in Europe favor stock raising at the expense of grain production, since the small proprietor can pay careful attention to his animals, whereas he may not be able to afford the machinery needed for economical grain growing on a commercial scale.

In the Philippines plantations large enough to attract foreign capital may not be owned by outsiders. In Java laws imposed by the Dutch have the effect of maintaining a fixed ratio in the acreage of the major crops. This restricts unbridled planting of commercial crops and reserves adequate acreage for the food crops on which the natives subsist. In Cuba and Brazil laws forbid or limit new plantations of certain cash crops produced in excess of the market demand.

GOVERNMENT AND REGIONAL GEOGRAPHY

Examples of cultural impress of effective central authority upon the landscape can be multiplied indefinitely. The cases cited suffice, however, to point to a group of geographic phenomena often overlooked. Each deserves more detailed study, particularly in its regional setting. Phenomena engendered by political forces should have a recognized place as elements in the geographic structure of every region.

Part
I
Temporal and Spatial
Attributes
of the State

CHAPTER
2

THE FOCUS:
THE EMERGENCE AND STRUCTURING
OF THE STATE

The world political map of the 1970's shows the earth's living space parceled out among more than 140 countries. Apart from some sections of the Arabian Peninsula and the south polar continent of Antarctica, all the land—and some of the water—on this globe has been appropriated by the governments of our 147 states and is now enclosed by their boundaries. Some governments still own distant possessions such as colonies or protectorates, but the age of colonialism is coming to a close. Almost every year, colonial dependencies that have been prepared for independence are awarded their sovereignty, and the list of the world's states grows longer.

So familiar has the world political map become that it is difficult to imagine a world without that framework of boundaries we see time and again. Even a quarter of a century of decolonization has hardly changed it; when Africa's many colonies became independent states, only very few boundary changes took place. Even substantial territorial conflicts, such as the Arab-Israeli struggle, have produced boundary changes which, viewed against the world map as a whole, seem of but minor consequence. There are numerous unresolved boundary disputes in Middle and South America, Africa, and Asia. Real change, however, comes but rarely and usually after a prolonged contest.

Thus it is difficult to perceive of a world not subdivided and allocated for all to see. And yet, so complete a boundary framework as exists today is a very modern phenomenon when the thousands of years that have gone into man's search for a satisfactory political order are taken into account. Just a century or so ago there were still areas of uncertain disposition in Europe, the African boundary framework as we know it today had barely begun to be laid out, that of the Middle East was similarly embryonic, and many parts of

Asia still were not integrated in any state. In fact, the boundary layout with which we have become so well acquainted is largely a product of the past 100 years. This leads us to some questions. Why did this framework emerge as it did? And in view of its recency, how lasting is it likely to be?

THE STATE

Today, 147 countries are peopled by the vast majority of the world's 3 1/2 billion inhabitants (the rest find themselves in one of the remaining dependencies). These 147 countries are more properly referred to as *states*. The state is more than a piece of the world's living space enclosed by a boundary; it is a concept of politicoterritorial organization, a functioning system that serves the population, the *nation*. From the present world political map we might conclude that practically all the world's peoples have decided to adopt the state system as the most promising means of governing themselves. Wherever colonies have become independent states, they have opted for the state system in one form or another, and most frequently on the pattern of the colonial power that controlled them. Thus they imitated the means of government and spatial organization that have evolved in the western hemisphere, first in Western Europe and later elsewhere.

The modern boundary framework and the omnipresence of the state system in the political world is still another of the many manifestations of the Europeanization of the world over the past several centuries. Europe's revolutionary progress in industrial, technical, agricultural, and other spheres was tangibly conveyed to the Americas, Africa, and Asia during the age of colonial expansion; along with this process went the export of European philosophies of state organization.

This is not to suggest that the concept of the

state is uniquely European, and that European influences produced states in areas where there had previously been no such development at all. Quite the opposite is true. In many non-European areas of the world—in Middle and South America, in black Africa, in North Africa and Southwest Asia, and in East and Southeast Asia—states had been developing for thousands of years. Some of these ancient states collapsed almost immediately in the face of the European onslaught, but others, such as Ashanti in West Africa, held out until early in the twentieth century. We will never know what sort of a boundary framework South America and Africa would have produced without the European imposition. But it is worth remembering that the boundaries we see today in these as well as other areas of the world were the products of alien forces. And it is appropriate for us to know something of the indigenous states that fell before the European transformation of the world.

EARLY BEGINNINGS

Where lie the roots of the state system? How have states emerged? Are there consistencies and similarities in the patterns of emergence of the ancient, indigenous states of the Americas, Africa, and Asia? These questions arise quite naturally in any discussion of the evolution of the state. But it is not easy to discern all the forces and stimuli that contributed to the development of the first true states. Many plausible explanations have been given to account for the growth of the states that have left their marks on history, such as ancient Egypt, the Aztec state in Mexico, early China, and others. Such explanations usually involve factors of soil productivity, opportune location, natural protection against enemies, advantageous climate, and similar assets supposedly possessed by those ancient human agglomerations that managed to forge states out of their habitats. But what is not explained is why, in other places where conditions were the same or even more attractive, states failed to emerge.

Clan and Tribe

One way to approach the whole question of man's territorial organization is to look for the most uncomplicated example that can be found. *Homo sapiens* is a gregarious individual, and he has always wanted to live in a society, in a community. While hunting and gathering were his mainstays, however, such communities could not have been very large. Early man found that the numbers of people who could associate closely were limited by mode of life and environmental circumstance. Can we still see such a situation existing today? We can—and in more than one part of the world. In Southern Africa live a people, the Bushmen, who face just such limitations. Having been driven into dry, inhospitable country by their enemies, the Bushmen continue to subsist on hunting and collecting. They do so mainly in groups or *clans* of about 60 individuals. Life for the Bushmen revolves around the tenuous supply of the water hole, which must draw the animals they trap and kill while providing them with this essence of life in the Kalahari Desert and Steppe.

But does this mean that the Bushmen wander aimlessly, without having a sense of domain and without a feeling of ownership over such territory as sustains them? Quite the contrary:

Although Bushmen are a roaming people and therefore seem to be homeless and vague about their country, each group of them has a very specific territory which that group alone may use, and they respect their boundaries rigidly. Each group also knows its own territory well; although it may be several hundred square miles in area, the people who live there know every bush and stone, every convolution of the ground. . . .[1]

Not only do the Bushmen have an attachment to their living space, but there are also some interesting kinds of organization within the clan itself. Certain fuctions are performed according to the age and sex of the individual, and often (though not always) the band has a leader. There is nothing ceremonial about this leader's position. Normally he is an older man who knows the clan's domain especially well; other than his age there may be nothing at all to distinguish him from others in the band. Nevertheless, here is a manifestation of government; the leader makes decisions concerning the breaking and moving of camp, and the group acquiesces and acts upon them.

Undoubtedly there is much in the Bushmen's existence that mirrors the condition of man at a very early stage in history. What is remarkable is these people's strong attach-

[1]Elizabeth Marshall Thomas, *The Harmless People*, New York, Knopf, 1959, p. 10.

ment to their territory, and their sense of its finiteness. These same characteristics also have been associated with a people whose mode of life resembles that of the Bushmen, but in an entirely different part of the world: the Australian aboriginal population. When the Europeans first entered Australia, there were perhaps somewhat over 300,000 black Australians. This number declined until the 1930's, when some 50,000 remained. Since then, some growth has again been recorded.

Like the Bushmen, the Australian aborigines live in clans, frequently numbering four or five dozen individuals. Like the Bushmen, they are hunters and gatherers and are limited in their searches by the availability of fresh water. The clans experience periods of want and times of plenty, and when there is adequate food they tend to join together. But during times of hunger the individual bands separate and trek into their own domain (averaging perhaps over three hundred square miles) to hunt and collect food.

The domain of the Australian aboriginal clan has as its focus the all-important water hole. This source of fresh water is of more than life-giving significance, for here, according to belief, did the ancestors of these people first settle and here the spirits of these ancestors now reside permanently. The retention of control over this area is thus a matter of material and spiritual survival for the clan.

In indigenous Australia, some of the boundaries between clan territories were very well defined, while others took on the character of frontiers. An area of barren plateau between two clan-controlled lakes was rarely if ever a matter of dispute between clans; rather, it formed a useless and unoccupied stretch of land through which no definite boundaries were drawn. Elsewhere, near the more productive coast, for example, boundaries were known with great precision, and trespass lines were carefully guarded. Like the Bushmen, the Australian aborigines did not possess the organization required to resist a challenge from more advanced competitors, and except in their reserve areas, nothing remains today of such political institutions as did exist when the Europeans arrived. Had Australia experienced the evolution of strong and well-organized tribal states, some influence would no doubt have been exerted in the sequence of events that led to the formation of the modern Australian federation. What might have happened is well illustrated in Africa, where the

Bushmen suffered a fate similar to that of their Australian contemporaries, but many of the more advanced tribal states in other parts of that continent resisted the European advance for some time. Indeed, while these states were eventually overthrown, their political and economic organization not only withstood the European impact, but to some extent channeled it. And after the termination of the colonial period, many of the characteristics of the precolonial African tribal states were reflected in the emergent modern black African states.

The fate that befell the Bushmen in Southern Africa and the black inhabitants of Australia presumably also overcame other peoples living under similar circumstances elsewhere; they were challenged and ousted from much of their habitat by more numerous, more highly organized competitors. In the case of the Bushmen, it was the Hottentots who posed this challenge initially. Whereas the Bushmen hunted and collected, the Hottentots were pastoralists. While the Bushmen's most permanent shelter was a windbreak and some skins, the Hottentots' villages were of a more permanent nature and included sizeable, well-constructed huts. While some of the Bushmen's clans may have been fairly large because of the superior hunting grounds they occupied, the mode of life of the Hottentots permitted them to agglomerate in far larger numbers. And the Hottentots' institutions included a powerful chieftainship, a number of headmen, and well-organized means of warfare.

The Hottentots, who later were themselves to fall victim to the onslaught of still more powerful African peoples, were members of a more complex form of politicoterritorial organization, namely the *tribe*. It is difficult to define this concept comprehensively; there are very large tribes and very small ones. But comparing it to the Bushmen's clans, several important differences emerge. The power of the tribal leader (there always is one or more) is greater. Personally given laws emerge. Territorial limits are even more jealously guarded. Hundreds of thousands of people may pay allegiance to the tribal chief or king. And it is especially important to note that the concept and reality of the *central place* exist at this level. Thus the tribal habitat will center on a headquarters (possibly with several subsidiary, minor foci), a seat of government in the real sense. Such a central place may be positioned according to some of the same rules that governed the beginnings of some towns that grew into capital cities of world importance: a defensible site, a place at the center of an area rich in resources, a location especially favorable as a market, a point that has significance on historical or religious grounds. Long before the coming of the white man in Africa and many other parts of the world, important capital cities had developed in tribal-organized areas. Many a European traveler described with awe the qualities of those early cities.

The Central Place as Stimulus

Undoubtedly many of the headquarters of indigenous tribal states were villages, and no more—and they remained so throughout their existence. But certain of these places found themselves endowed with particular advantages, and they grew into real urban centers. As such, they achieved significance far beyond the limits of the tribal territory in which they were located, and functioned as foci for interregional trade. This was the case, for example, with towns located in the "savanna belt" of West Africa. As the strength and wealth of the Arab world to the north increased and the demand for goods there grew, these towns found themselves between one of the major sources of supply—the forested regions of coastal West Africa—and this north African region of demand. Soon the markets of these savanna towns were among the busiest in the world as people and goods moved northward and items of trade came from the north in return. In response, the towns grew into cities, complete with markets, suburbs, religious shrines, places of learning, governmental buildings, and so forth.

In turn, these oversized cities now played a role in transforming tribally organized territory into something more complex than that. Historical geographers do not hesitate when they point to West Africa between 300 A.D. and about 1600; here were true states in an African tradition, with political influences from the Nile Valley, religious influences from Mecca, but with a population welded from the characteristic heterogeneity of tribal Africa. It was the wealth concentrated in the cities, the stability of the rule that was based there, the effectiveness of the military force based there, the effectiveness with which taxes and tribute were collected, and the unprecedented degree of circulation and cohesion generated by the

power at the center that provided the stimulus toward statehood in this part of the world.

Elsewhere in the precolonial world, large cities similarly passed a certain threshold of self-perpetuation and became, in effect, the pulse of the indigenous state. In Aztec Middle America, it was Tenochtitlan. It was Cuzco in the Inca empire, Babylon in Mesopotamia, Mohenjo Daro in the Indus valley, Anyang in China, and many others. Some of these cities possessed attributes that permitted them to sustain the impact of the transition to the era of European domination with undiminished strength. Thus Tenochtitlan, though largely destroyed in the conflict with the white man, was rebuilt and is today Mexico City, capital of the successor state. Cuzco still remains a town of some importance. Others, however, have failed; there is little left of Timbuktu's old splendor.

ANCIENT STATES

We noted earlier that it is appropriate to remind ourselves of the progress toward statehood made in several parts of the world before—in some places *long* before—the advent of Europe. Here we should consider (1) the Middle East and adjacent areas, (2) East Asia, (3) West Africa, and (4) Middle and South America.

The Middle East

In the Middle East, for thousands of years progress was made that overshadowed all else on the globe. In the Fertile Crescent, man learned to domesticate certain plants. By 5000 B.C. the small farming villages on the lower slopes of the hills were showing the effects of improving farming techniques and higher yields; they were growing larger than they had ever been. Irrigation, metal working, writing, planning, organization—innovations multiplied in numerous spheres and were transmitted to the Nile region, to Mesopotamia, and to the lowland of the Indus River. By 3000 B.C. urban life had become a reality in the Middle East, and unprecedented political consolidation was taking place.

Despite the fact that Mesopotamia probably was ahead of Egypt and the Indus region in the earliest times (the wheel and chariot, for example, were in use in Mesopotamia shortly after 4000 B.C., and were not used in Egypt until 2000 years later) it was ancient Egypt that was destined to have the most lasting impact upon the politicogeographical world. The political philosophies and practices of pharaoic Egypt were diffused to West Africa's savanna kingdoms and to many of black Africa's tribal states; to this day there are tribal ceremonies as far away as southern Africa that bear the unmistakable imprint of Egyptian origins. Egypt forged security and stability out of the protection nature provided, but Egypt was nevertheless a cosmopolitan state. Phoenician ships brought timber and tribute to Egyptian ports, Asian and African slaves were numerous in the cities, mercenaries from Aegean coasts served in the armed forces, and Greek merchants settled permanently in the country. And the advantages of isolation notwithstanding, Egypt sent its armies as far as Turkey and Syria in the north, Mesopotamia in the east, and Nubia and Cush in the south.

Thus there were plenty of avenues of contact through which Egyptian modes of governmental and administrative organization were learned by foreigners. Indeed, there are those who believe that Egyptians themselves crossed the Atlantic Ocean in papyrus boats and contributed directly to the cultural evolution of Middle America. The Phoenicians brought many of the elements of the Egyptian order to Aegean shores, where they were readily embraced, transformed, improved, and subjected to experimentation. It was this contribution to Greek civilization that was ultimately to constitute a critical link in the chain that connects ancient Egypt to the modern state.

What were the particular attributes of ancient Egypt, other than its pivotal location, felicitous protection, and productive capacity? Remarkable is the state's longevity. Historians often identify the period of "true" empire to have extended from 2650 to 1100 B.C., but there were many centuries of consolidation prior to 2650 and although subjected to invasion and defeats, the state hardly ceased to exist during the last millenium B.C. At a time when territorial organization was just beginning (in a world context), Egypt rose and survived longer than any other political entity ever. In the process, the state changed from a theocratic to a militaristic one, and, in common with some other states we know, it developed an incredibly complex bureaucracy. Egypt's armies were well disciplined and used with great effectiveness; the cities were skillfully fortified. Subjugated peoples were relentlessly exploited in the interests of the state. Egypt was no paradise for those who were unfortunate enough to find themselves in serfdom to the relatively small ruling elite. The peasants, workers, and slaves all fell victim to a most ruthless use of manpower. When the power of the state finally began to fail, and conquering, alien enemies rode in triumph through the streets, they were welcomed by the masses as liberators, as were the Persians in 525 B.C.

Nevertheless, in Egypt and Mesopotamia lay the roots of "western" civilization, and among those roots are those of statecraft. Innumerable innovations were made in the cultivation of cereals, vegetables, and fruits, in the domestication of farm animals, in irrigation, calendrics, mathematics, astronomy, engineering and metallurgy, and, importantly, in administration and government. The productive capacity of Mesopotamia and Egypt generated the first substantial, urban-based wealthy classes that could afford the luxury of leisure, the arts, and philosophy. What the ancient Egyptians thought and wrote about in politics was not lost upon their successors.

East Asia

Middle Eastern contributions may even have reached China as early as 2000 B.C., and perhaps even before that. From Mesopotamia and the Indus area, it is thought, innovations in agriculture, techniques of irrigation, metal working, and even writing were diffused to the valley of the Hwang Ho (Yellow River), in the vicinity of its confluence with the Wei River. Whatever the sources of ancient China's stimuli, there is a record of Chinese civilization some 5000 years in length, and from 2000 B.C. on that record is continuous, quite reliable, and positive proof of China's cultural individuality.

Out of those beginnings in northern China, in the lowland of the Hwang-Wei Rivers, rose a series of dynasties. The oldest of these about which there is substantial knowledge is the Shang (Yin) Dynasty, which lasted from about 1900 B.C. until 1050 B.C. Centered upon the ancient capital of Anyang, this dynasty secured the consolidation of China as a true state. The Bronze Age reached China during this period; walled towns developed. Gradually there came improvements in irrigation and flood control, in farming techniques (the water buffalo came into use), and metallurgy (iron

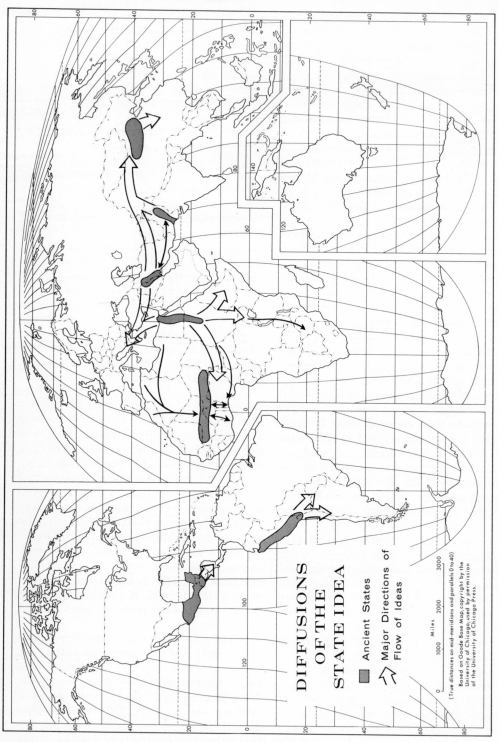

DIFFUSIONS
OF THE
STATE IDEA

■ Ancient States

☖ Major Directions of
   Flow of Ideas

0   1000   2000   3000
        Miles
(True distances on mid-meridians and parallels 0 to 40)
Based on Goode Base Map, copyright by the
University of Chicago; used by permission
of the University of Chicago Press.

Ancient States   Major directions of flow of ideas.

tools appeared during the last several centuries B.C.). Coupled with this were innovations in political organization and control, administration, and the use of military forces; the original core was ready to expand and absorb adjacent frontiers.

Such expansion was both easiest and most profitable in a southward direction, and during the Ch'in Dynasty the lands of the Yangtze Kiang were integrated in the Chinese state. Canals linked natural waterways to facilitate the transporting of food from the productive southern areas to the original heart of the state; this increased circulation did much to consolidate the growing Chinese empire. During the Han Dynasty ancient China experienced a crucial period of growth and further consolidation. Between 202 B.C. and 220 A.D., the Han rulers brought unity and stability to their state, and they also organized the extension of the Chinese sphere of influence to include Korea, Manchuria, and Mongolia (to the east, north, and west of the original core area, respectively), as well as distant Sinkiang and Annam.

The Han period was a critical time in the life of the Chinese state. Not only was there military might and great territorial expansion, but the country's internal order changed decisively. The old feudal system of land ownership broke down and individual property was recognized. Internal circulation had unprecedented effectiveness. Towns grew into cities; internal trade intensified. The silk trade grew into China's first regular external commerce. Along the silk route across Asia came ideas, innovations—China was being transformed. To this day the people of China, recognizing the germinal character of the Han period, call themselves the People of Han.

Like Egypt, Mesopotamia, the Indus area, and so many other great ancient states and cultures, China faced a conquering enemy. But there was a difference. In 1280 A.D. the Mongols captured control of China and made the state a part of a vast empire that stretched all the way across Asia to Eastern Europe. It was not the Mongols who imposed a permanent new order upon China, however, but the Chinese whose culture was imprinted upon the Mongols. The Mongol period ended in 1368, and history recognizes the Mongol conquest as but an interlude in the continuity of Chinese life. Egypt and Mesopotamia fell, but China managed to shake off its severest challenge. And so today, with China still focused upon its ancient northern heartland, this is the only major ancient state whose lineage traces back—spatially as well as temporally—directly to its oldest origins.

West Africa

The savannas of West Africa lie between the desert to the north and the tropical rain forest to the south. For many centuries the peoples of the desert have traded goods with the people of the forests. The forest dwellers needed salt; the desert people could easily provide it. The forest people could produce ivory, gold, spices, hides and skins, and certain kinds of wood; from the desert they got metal goods, many kinds of cloth, dried fruits, and even goods the desert traders had obtained from European markets.

West Africa's economic mainstays, then, were gold and salt, and the West African savanna peoples found themselves positioned very advantageously between the traders (not unlike the old Swiss and their Alpine passes between Adriatic and northwestern Europe). From the Nile Valley these fortunate savanna dwellers received some political ideas about the divine kingship, about the power inherent in a monopoly over the use of iron, and about the use of military forces to exact tribute and maintain control. And so the cities of West Africa grew into great market centers, and they generated wide realms of control—here was a form of the *city-state*. But West Africa was also a place of invention and innovation. There are anthropologists who argue that West Africa, along with Southwest Asia, Southeast Asia, and Middle America, was one of the four major agricultural complexes of the ancient world, where crops were domesticated and farming techniques invented and refined.

In West Africa a series of states of impressive strength and amazing durability arose. The oldest of these about which much is known is ancient Ghana, located in parts of present-day Mali and Mauritania. The Niger River bisected Ghana, and from its headwaters the Ghanaians got a great deal of the gold that helped make their state powerful and wealthy. For perhaps more than 1000 years (the first millenium A.D.) ancient Ghana's rulers managed to weld many diverse groups of people into a stable state. The capital city had extensive markets, suburbs for foreign merchants, religious shrines, public buildings, and, some miles from the city center, a fortified royal retreat.

Ghana eventually fell to its northern competitors, and it was succeeded in the savanna belt by the state of Mali, centered on Timbuktu on the Niger River. Mali received the impact of Islam, and its prosperity was reflected by the splendor of Mecca-bound pilgrimages joined by tens of thousands of people. Timbuktu in its heyday was a university city, a place of learning of international significance. Mali, too, eventually collapsed. Its initial successor was the state of Songhai, slightly to the east; still later the center of power shifted farther east again, to the region that is today northern Nigeria and western Chad. But by then the European impact was being felt along the West African coast, and the era of the slave trade was soon to upset the patterns of development of nearly two millenia in this part of the world.

Middle and South America

In the Americas prior to the European invasion there were also large, stable, and well-organized states. Toward the end of the fifteenth century various sectors of the American Indian realm were at different stages of politicoterritorial organization. In the southern part of South America lived peoples who subsisted by hunting and gathering. This economy prevailed also in parts of what is today Canada and the western half of the United States (though not the southwest). In the Amazon Basin rainforests, in southeastern North America, and in some other parts of the Americas some agriculture accompanied the practices of hunting and gathering, but the practice of agriculture was not always accompanied by a more advanced form of politicoterritorial organization. In the forests of South America, for instance, where shifting, "patch" agriculture was carried on along with hunting and fishing, political integration had hardly begun. Each semipermanent village formed a complete and self-sufficient unit, and often the only contact between adjacent, independent villages was during armed hostilities.

In some parts of equatorial South America, the pattern described above occasionally was changed by the exceptional abilities of a village chief. Such a chief might gain the allegiance of surrounding villages through his

[2] It is important to distinguish between indigenously conceived "federal" associations and those of the kind that developed after the European impact was felt. The latter were the result, directly, of common enmity toward the European invader and conceived as a better means of defense.

successes during war, his powers of magic, his wealth, and oratorical abilities. Temporarily he might unify under his control a large region including several dozen villages, but eventually such an embryonic political unit would again fall apart.

In other parts of the Americas, tribal organization was achieved by many Indian peoples, who established permanent villages, practiced more intensive agriculture, and developed considerable technological skill. The idea of a form of federation also came to the leaders of these peoples, and many multicommunity tribal states developed through voluntary alliance and through conquest (north of the Rio Grande, only the Iroquois achieved a confederacy prior to the European invasion), though such alliances were often short-lived.[2] Nevertheless, these tribal political entities represent a major advance in the quest for the state: here, the society was beginning to create the necessary excess energy needed for progress in various social spheres. The main difference between many of these societies and their contemporaries in the equatorial forests lay in the percentage of the population engaged in the search for and production of food. Among the hunters and gatherers who also practiced some agriculture, practically everyone in the scattered villages was occupied in this manner—and it is still true in those societies in this category which can be observed today. But with more intensive agriculture came technological development, the production of surpluses, and the liberation of a section of the population for other pursuits. This population sector grew as the general population increased, and the division of labor in the society became more and more marked. Inevitably, the increasing complexity of the society would produce clashes of interest between various groups; those who verbalized the positions of the opposing groups were often specialists in the field of politics. Thus there arose, in these societies, a number of political theorists who, like the artists and the craftsmen, were able to devote their lives to the direction of political affairs in the growing state. Now, the securing of the allegiance of surrounding villages was no longer merely a matter of a chief's exceptional qualities. States that produced agricultural surpluses produced social surpluses, and those that produced social surpluses produced the central place. As in Africa, such growth as described above

. . . begins to draw the villages and towns of its periphery like a magnet. Its growing population offers an ever increasing market of ready consumers for the produce of the countryside; its craft specialists need raw materials to convert into finished products; its elite, hungry for surpluses, begins to look beyond the confines of its domain to other domains.[3]

Aztec State and Inca Empire. The culmination of indigenous political evolution in the Americas, so closely bound up with the development of organized agriculture, was achieved in Middle America and in the Central Andes. Although the Mayan civilization, which flourished in Yucatan and adjacent areas between A.D. 300 and 900, was a forerunner to the significant events later to take place in what is today Mexico, there are important differences between the Mayan societies and those of the Toltecs and Aztecs. The Mayan societies were theocratic, controlled by priest-rulers; Toltec and Aztec society was militaristic and structurally much more complex. The main centers of Mayan culture lay in the forested sections of Yucatan, to the north of the mountain slopes of Guatemala and El Salvador. From what has been said about forest peoples who practice patch agriculture, it would appear that the Mayan leaders would scarcely have been able to control extensive areas; yet they did. Their central places, however, were not central places in the usual sense. They were ceremonial centers (perhaps comparable to the Zimbabwes of Shona societies in south-central Africa) and served as markets, but did not contain large permanent populations. It has been surmised that the Mayans, in order to have achieved such stability and progress in the fields of arithmetic and astronomy, must have possessed methods of agriculture other than those of slash-and-burn. Whatever the answer may be, the momentum of Mayan civilization carried on for over a thousand years; and although there may be doubt concerning the manner of control that was exercised over so wide an area, the achievements in the sciences attest to the permanency of their governmental system.

Ultimately one ceremonial site, Mayapan, did become a true central place, albeit after the decline of Mayan power and organization had begun. Mayapan was a walled city, the location of a despotic authority, the home of

thousands of residents, and the heart of all Yucatan. But by this time the area that had been unified by Mayan civilization was breaking into warring tribal states, with a corresponding decline in the arts and other fields of achievement.

Elsewhere in Middle America, the strands of progress remained intact, ultimately to lead to the formation of one of the most impressive states to develop anywhere in the world at any time prior to the rise of modern Europe. Again, the Aztec state had its forerunners (most important among them, the Toltec state centered upon Tula), but its rise was extremely rapid, as was its decline, resulting directly from contact with the Europeans. In fact the Aztec state was achieved by a relatively small number of Indians who were acquainted with Toltec technology, scattered by the disastrous breakup of Toltec society, and finally regrouped in a very fortuitous location. The choice of headquarters proved a permanent one: the site of the Aztec capital, Tenochtitlan, also was to become the capital of an empire, the seat of government for New Spain, and finally the focus for the modern state of Mexico. The end of Mayan civilization saw the decline of the theocratic state and the priest-ruler; the Toltec states had been militarist in nature, and the Aztecs were to perfect this form of politicoterritorial control to unprecedented levels. Indeed, the areas in which military units of the Aztec state forayed and exacted tribute far exceeded the margins of the actual empire. Military prowess brought the soldiers fame and fortune at home—where a complex class system developed in which they held favored positions—and produced a commodity needed in vast quantities for sacrifice: human beings. Rather than subdue and incorporate certain peripheral areas into the Mexica Empire (as the Aztec state came to be called), the armies perpetuated hostilities purposely, so that human beings could be taken under the pretense of continuing enmity.

Meanwhile, the government in Tenochtitlan was attempting to organize the state into provinces, allotting certain production requirements to each. A highly complex bureaucracy developed in the capital, and there were systems of tax collection, law enforcement, mail delivery, rapid messenger communication, and provincial administration with governors and district commissioners. In the Valley of Mexico the Aztecs had found the

[3]E. Wolf, *Sons of the Shaking Earth*, Chicago, University of Chicago Press, 1959, p. 20.

Top: Unearthing the past. Increasingly, archaeological evidence is revealing the story of Man's
past—political as well as cultural. Largely because
of archaeological research and new directions in the
study of oral historical evidence, vast gaps in our
knowledge regarding the development of early
organized societies are being filled in. In the
photograph above, the archaeological research site
at Novgorod, U.S.S.R., is shown at a depth of
about twenty feet. Bottom: More recent evidence
exists on the shores of Loch Ness, Scotland, where
the remnants of a castle form a reminder of a former
political age (Harm J. de Blij).

pivotal geographic feature to Middle America;
agricultural productivity was high, and technology, including irrigation practices, had
been developing for centuries. Population was
relatively dense, the region at that time
perhaps containing over two million inhabitants. Central places grew rapidly and to sizes
that were remarkable for any part of the world:
Tenochtitlan had well over a hundred thousand inhabitants, as did a number of other
centers of trade and administration. Surrounding the Valley of Mexico in various directions
were areas producing diverse commodities, so
that expansion could take place first under the
aegis of legitimate trade, this to be followed by
military conquest and the levying of taxes and
tribute. Furthermore, the situation of Tenochtitlan along a lake system within the Valley of
Mexico added to its function as the core of the
Empire. The city could be served by craft using
these lakes and artificial canals dug to connect
them: in the absence of the wheel, this was a
major element in its prosperity and eminence.
When the Spanish arrived in this area, there
may have been as many as two hundred
thousand such craft in use.

Thus geographical factors played a major role in the rise of Mexica; the psychological condition of the population of the Empire and its relationships with its neighbors and subjects directly contributed to its downfall. The Aztec's cult of the sun, with the belief that ever increasing numbers of human sacrifices were necessary in order to ensure the survival of man, ensured the permanent hostility and mistrust of those who might be victimized for this purpose. Thus the European invaders found ready support for their campaign, quite apart from their fortune in having been at first viewed as "White Gods" whose arrival was predicted by an Aztec prophecy. But while the Empire fell, the advantages of the Valley of Mexico remained—and played their part in the momentous events that have marked the evolution of the modern state in Middle America.

The American region marked by the culmination of indigenous politicoterritorial organization is the Central Andes. Here, over a distance of 2,500 miles from Ecuador to central Chile, evolved the Inca Empire. The Inca Empire was itself preceded by earlier civilizations; notably that centered upon Tiahuanaco in the area of Lake Titicaca. Better integrated, more stable, less violently militaristic, and generally more benevolent than the Aztec sphere of influence, the Inca domain in many ways was the only real empire to develop in the Americas, Aztec achievements notwithstanding. The Inca Empire was centered upon Cuzco, a city located some 11,000 feet above sea level, two hundred miles from the ocean, and with a population of over a quarter of a million. Here the Inca rulers built the mighty fortress of Sacesahuaman, the Temple of the Sun (for the Incas too were sun worshippers), and other huge megalithic structures. Cuzco was located in the center of a densely populated, well-watered, fertile valley, but unlike Tenochtitlan, its site has not witnessed the rise of a modern capital upon the ruins of the old. Cuzco did not become a permanent European center of government and population agglomeration: its population to this day is largely Indian.

Cuzco and its surrounding region formed the core area for a vast state with far-flung possessions and an intricate politicoterritorial organization which may with justification be called its major achievement. At the height of its power the Empire contained perhaps as many as eleven million subjects, each of

whom had an assigned task of supplying certain tax or tribute to the central authority, the king. In view of the contrasts in terrain within the domain over which the Inca rulers held sway, the permanency and stability of the Empire is a matter for admiration, and it could not have been accomplished without a system of central places and efficient communication lines:

In these places there were large houses and more resources than in many of the other towns of this great empire, so that they were in central positions or capitals of the provinces; for the tribute was brought into these centres from certain distant places at so many leagues distance to one, and at so many to another. The rules were so clear that every village knew to which centre it had to send its tribute.[4]

A system of roads connected these central places, and along these roads were a number of supply stations at regular intervals, staffed by professional messengers; in relay fashion an order issued in Cuzco would reach outlying districts in the shortest possible time. There were two main north-south highways, one along the mountain ranges, the other along the coast. Transverse and secondary roads formed a grid which focused upon Cuzco. When European visitors first arrived in this area, they wondered

. . . how and in what manner they can have made such grand and admirable roads as we now see, and what a number of men would suffice for their construction, and with what tools and instruments they can have levelled the mountains and broken through the rocks to make them so broad and good as they are.[5]

The states of the Americas are reminiscent of several that arose in Eurasia and Africa. The Mayan societies may have resembled the megalithic societies which arose in Subsaharan Africa after the Cushitic impregnation. The Aztec state has been compared to that of the Assyrians in the Middle East.[6] The Inca Empire in certain ways resembled that of the

[4]Pedro Cieza de Leon, The Second Part of the Chronicle of Peru, translated by C.R. Markham, London, the Hakluyt Society, 1883; quoted from H.E. Driver (ed.), The Americas on the Eve of Discovery, Englewood Cliffs, N.J., Prentice Hall, 1964, p. 107.

[5]Ibid., p. 98.

[6]Wolf, op. cit., p. 149.

Romans. It secured the allegiance of many varied tribal peoples. In practice Inca systems of administration were superimposed upon conquered areas, but local leaders were permitted to remain in their positions and normal modes of worship were allowed to continue. Hence there was a decree of retention of regional autonomy not unlike that granted outlying Roman areas in return for ultimate allegiance to the central authority. Like the Romans, the Incas depended upon an advanced system of communications in order to keep their empire intact, and both empires made efforts to mark their boundaries on the ground—a feature that was ultimately to become one of the hallmarks of the modern nation-state.

THE STATE IN EUROPE

The sequence of events that led to the emergence of the European state system began in pre-Christian times. A major factor in the transmission of early stimuli from the Middle East to southeast Europe lay in the growing need for raw materials in the advanced societies of the Nile Valley and the lowland of the Tigris and Euphrates. They wanted metals, textiles, and oils, and their search for these and other commodities brought contact with southeast Europe. Greek traders were active in Egyptian towns, Phoenician ships linked Aegean and Mediterranean shores. The traffic was by no means confined to copper and tin; the political ideas of Middle Eastern states filtered into Europe as the trade grew.

Ancient Greece

During the first millenium B.C. the Greeks created what in many respects is the foundation of European civilization. Prior to that time, the Greek peninsula had gone through a formative period of immigration, adjustment, and the beginnings of a stable civilization known as the Mycenaean. But the Mycenaean period was comparatively short as it was disrupted by another period of population movement and relocation. This brought onto the scene the Hellenic peoples, who expanded rapidly and dispersed widely over a vast part of Southeast Europe.

The Hellenic peoples occupied much of Southeast Europe, but they had to adjust to the landscapes of the region, which are characteristically rugged, peninsular, and insular.

Hellenic settlements were founded in river valleys and on estuaries, on the narrow littorals of peninsulas, and on islands. They were in contact with one another, but mostly by sea—water often provided a better avenue than did the land. Thus the Hellenic civilization was extensive—but it was not contiguous.

This situation produced another version of the city-state. Individuality and independence were strong features of the ancient Greeks, and in their comparative isolation they experimented with government and politics. At times several of the city-states would join together in a *league* to promote common objectives, but never would the participants give up their autonomy altogether. And just as the Greek city-states competed with each other individually, so there were rival leagues; Athens, Sparta, and Thebes each headed powerful and competing leagues.

Ancient Greece has been described as a microcosm of the Europe that was to follow it. During the Mycenaean period, kings ruled in ways reminiscent of the theocratic states of earlier Middle Eastern times. Then followed a period of feudal disarray, and out of this chaos the comparative stability of Hellenic civilization emerged. Now a push to more democratic forms of government began, although an oligarchy of landowners and a wealthy, privileged nobility sought to delay the emergence of democratic types of government. But eventually (though not everywhere to the same degree, of course) the general population, except for the slaves, became involved in the running of the state. Mass participation of this kind was achieved in several of the ancient Greek states, though not all; others remained under autocratic rule. And to complete the analogy, groups of city-states bound themselves together in leagues—as modern states have joined in blocs, communities, treaties, and pacts.

During Greek times, political philosophy and public administration became sciences, pursued by the greatest of practitioners. Plato (428 to 347 B.C.) and Aristotle (384 to 322 B.C.) are two of the most famous philosophers of this period, but there was a host of other contributors to the greatness of ancient Greece. What they wrote has influenced government and politics ever since, and the constitutional concepts that emerged at that time are still being applied in one form or another today.

The Roman Empire[7]

The Romans succeeded where the Greeks had failed. Theirs was not a nation dispersed through a string of city-states but a contiguous and unified empire in the true sense of the word, strongly centralized in one unrivalled city, Rome. But Rome itself had not achieved supremacy overnight. Italy around 400 B.C. (about the time of Greece's greatest glory) was a territory of many tribes and nations. Well-fortified hilltop towns dotted the area; these were the centers of power and protection for local groups. As in Greece, but on a smaller scale, towns entered leagues of mutual defense, and as time went on places whose natural protections were less than adequate were abandoned as their inhabitants moved to larger and safer centers. Gradually the regional influence of Rome increased. Its original populations had been largely Italic (the name given to a people whose first representatives entered Italy across the Eastern Alps and who settled in Latium before 1000 B.C.), but an ever-wider variety of nationalities entered the place. The great achievements of Rome lay in its successful absorption of this influx, the stability of its political institutions, and an effective campaign of Roman colonization in outlying districts. The great empire that was to come had its local predecessor: by the middle of the third century B.C. there was a true Roman Federation extending from near the Po Valley in the north to the Greek-occupied south.

Having achieved unification on its peninsula, Rome now was a major force in the entire Mediterranean area. Its commercial interests and trade connections widened and Rome made friends—and enemies. Naturally there was competition with the Greeks, but there were challenges elsewhere as well. Carthage on the North African coast managed to resist the Roman thrust for decades. Nevertheless, the Roman Empire continued to spread. The defeat of Carthage removed the major obstacle to westward expansion, and to the east the Greeks were forced to recognize Roman superiority. But Greek culture had a major impact on the Roman civilization, and Greek identity survived despite the strength of the Roman invasion. In the eastern Mediterranean borderlands, for example, Greek remained the

dominant language, while almost everywhere else in the Roman Empire the language of common use became Latin. It is more accurate to speak of a Roman-Hellenic civilization than of a Roman civilization alone, for the Romans provided the vehicle to disseminate Greek cultural achievements throughout Mediterranean and Western Europe.

Greek culture was a major component of Roman civilization; but the Romans made their own essential contributions. The Greeks never achieved politicoterritorial organization on a scale accomplished by the Romans. In such fields as land communications, military organization, law, and public administration the Romans made unprecedented progress. Comparative stability and peace marked the vast realm under their domination, and for centuries these conditions promoted social and economic advances. The Roman Empire during its greatest expansion (which came during the second century A.D.) extended from Britain to the Persian Gulf and from the Black Sea to Egypt. In North Africa the desert and the mountains formed its boundaries; in the west it was the sea, and to the north tribal peoples lived beyond the Roman domain. Only in Asia was there contact with a state of any significance. Thus the empire could organize internally without interference. But its internal diversity was such that isolation of this kind did not lead to stagnation. The Roman Empire was the first truly interregional political unit in Europe. In many ways the Roman Empire was centuries ahead of its time. It was also the first true empire by modern criteria, with outlying colonies and diverse racial groups under its control. Many political experiments which were to become normal practice in the modern state were tried for the first time in the Roman Empire. Geographers have attempted to explain the rise of this great empire in a variety of ways. Some have invoked the idea of climatic conditions being at their optimum. Others have pointed to the location of Rome and its obvious "geographical" advantages. Still others pointed out that the time was ripe for a combination of the lessons history had taught by that time:

The possibility of combining the lessons taught by these empires was equally due to geographical controls. So far we have seen three empires—Egypt, Chaldea, Assyria—entirely based on land. Then we saw a succession of three peoples powerful on sea—the Phoenicians, Greeks and Carthaginians . . . for a brief moment a man arose who

[7]Parts of this section are drawn from Harm J. de Blij, *Geography: Regions and Concepts*, New York, John Wiley & Sons, 1971, pp. 22–26.

understood the value of both land and sea . . . [thus it is not surprising that] the next development should take place in a land which projected far into the sea, and in a land, too, which was exposed to the action of forces which had made history. It is natural, from the very shape and position of Italy, in touch with, but separated from, the older civilizations, that here should arise a new great centre.[8]

Whatever the impetus was, the Roman Empire stood out from all its predecessors and contemporaries, especially in the area of organization. Almost everything else—its power, its size, its longevity, its internal variety—was a function of the Romans' dedication to organize their land and possessions. One aspect of this organization was the effort to build a network of communications. The concept was totally new, and the scale of its execution was grand. The *Via Appia* linked the very "heel" of Italy to the city of Rome, and soon several other great roads led from the center of power to the empire's outlying districts. Nor was such road-building confined to the heart of the state. Recognizing the immense value of the road in the moving of goods and armies and the exercising of control, the Romans built roads even in Britain, where some of the old routes are still in use today. Naturally the network was not dense, by modern standards, but it was carefully planned to meet the needs of the state.

Though highly centralized, the Roman Empire's political structure contained elements of the federal as well as the unitary state of today. Peace—and a certain amount of autonomy—was granted to areas west of the Rhine and east of the lower Danube. A true *body politic* had evolved, and

. . . here the Pax Romana allowed of the growth of a civilization over very different and widely scattered areas, which had no natural cohesion except that which was due to their common dependence upon the Roman power and administration. Their peoples were able in peace, without spending their energies in war, to turn to useful account such advantages as their positions gave them.[9]

Feudal Europe

Feudalism. Europe during the period from about the middle of the eighth century to the end of the twelfth was dominated by feudal

[8]J. Fairgrieve, *Geography and World Power*, London, University of London Press, 1932, pp. 73–75.

[9]Ibid., p. 90.

institutions. Roman judicial processes and other institutions that protected individual rights had weakened. The new kings ruled by private law, personal power, influence, and wealth, and through the allegiance of counts, barons, dukes, and other representatives. Although some kings were successful in forging and maintaining states of considerable size (Charlemagne was foremost in this respect), the framework of government was not sufficiently strong, and there was not enough contact and communication within the country to withstand disorder and disorganization. Great as it was, Charlemagne's empire was inherently weak because it required a person of the power and stature of Charlemagne to maintain it. And although he managed to hold his dominions together for a long time, even Charlemagne was compelled to grant increasing powers to local lords.

In this way feudalism served the kings. In order to secure their allegiance, feudal rights were granted to counts and dukes in outlying parts of the state. There the royal agent was in charge of practically every aspect of life, from the peasantry to the military. These old units can still be seen in the locations and names of the political subdivisions of certain countries of the Old World, such as the *county*, the *duchy*, and the march or *mark*. And when the larger political unit disintegrated through the death of a king, a weak succession, or an invasion, the feudal counts and barons were quick to assert complete hegemony over their local domains, including all land and people within them.

Thus, during the feudal period much of Europe was organized into dozens of such jigsawlike feudal units, each with its nobility and vassals, and its more or less tenuous connections with higher authority. The connectivity that Rome had brought to Europe was now at a minimum, and reforms were needed to rekindle economic as well as political progress. These began during the second half of the eleventh century and continued throughout the twelfth. In England the Norman invasion (1066) destroyed the Anglo-Saxon nobility and replaced it with one drawn from the new immigrants. William the Conqueror strengthened the feudal organization of England to such a degree that he became the most powerful ruler in Western Europe; at the same time he introduced changes in the system of governmental organization that were to outlast the feudal period.

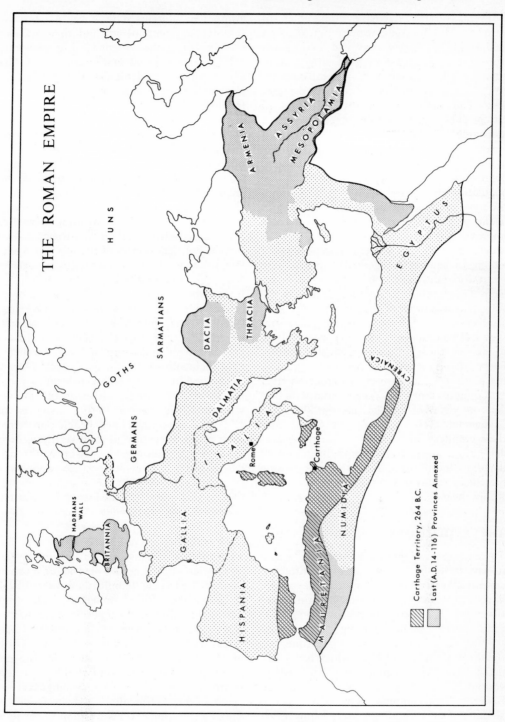

THE ROMAN EMPIRE

HUNS

GOTHS

SARMATIANS

GERMANS

HADRIANS
WALL

BRITANNIA

GALLIA

HISPANIA

ITALIA

Rome

DALMATIA

DACIA

THRACIA

ARMENIA

ASSYRIA

MESOPOTAMIA

EGYPTUS

CYRENAICA

Carthage

NUMIDIA

MAURETANIA

Carthage Territory, 264 B.C.

Lost (A.D. 14–116)   Provinces Annexed

Several of the dynastic monarchies of Europe's Middle Ages were outgrowths of feudal rule; a family that had maintained control for a lengthy period might have obtained the allegiance of a comparatively large number of subjects and controlled a large area. The emergence of this situation in Europe did not occur without a lengthy period of friction and hostilities, but the change was a positive one. The consequences for Europe's political evolution are all-important. Despite oppression and excesses perpetrated on the population under the divine rights of kings, the roots of modern European nationalism lie in this period. There was a slow but noticeable improvement in communications and circulation, especially in western Europe, and a feeling of belonging together within a state framework developed among the peoples. Even though this feeling of participating in the state still was in reality servitude to the king of that state, people began to recognize that they had common interests and were willing to defend those interests against enemies. Eventually they began to perceive certain of the physiographic features of Europe—a river or mountain range—as "their" country's borders. By virtue of the fact that the kings had amalgamated diverse groups of people into their empires, the peoples within those borders often were quite varied in terms of language and religion. But if the state or king provided a stronger common interest, a nation was in the making.

THE REVOLUTIONS: STATE AND NATION

The emergence of modern Europe may be said to date from the second half of the fifteenth century. Western Europe's monarchies, as we have seen, began to represent something more than mere authority; increasingly they became centers of an emerging national consciousness and pride. At the same time, the trend toward fragmentation, which had dominated the feudal period, was reversed as various monarchies, through marriage, alliance, or both, combined to promote territorial unity. Feudal privileges were being recaptured by the central authority, and there was progress in the parliamentary representation of the general population. Renewed interest was shown in Greek and Roman philosophies of government and administration. Europe was ready for change.

Change did come to Europe, and in many forms. The emerging states engaged in intense commercial competition, and mercantilism was viewed as the correct kind of economic policy to serve the general interest of all. The search for precious metals, the standard of wealth, sent the ships of several countries traversing the oceans to lands that lay open for discovery—and appropriation. Kings and noblemen sent many of those ships on their way, but in the growing cities a new class of influential men was on the rise: the merchants. Their capital strength increased by leaps and bounds, and before long the merchants and businessmen in the Western European states were demanding a greater voice in the politics of their countries.

"The political history of the Modern Age is largely the story of the successful struggle to wrest . . . omnipotence from an individual or from a privileged few and, through the growth of Parliamentary Government and the extension of the franchise, to bestow self-government."[10] Europe's revolutions in industry, commerce, and agriculture were paralleled by a sociopolitical revolution as well. During the second half of the eighteenth century and much of the nineteenth century, Europe witnessed the rise of *nationalism* as an all-pervading political force. People transferred their prime allegiance to their territory, their state—a state they often helped create through participation in a revolution that swept away the old order. The prime example of this process undoubtedly is the French Revolution, the revolution that ended the czarist era in Russia is also considered a case.

Thus the nations of Europe were forged. But what, precisely, constitutes a *nation?* Must a population attain a certain size before it can be identified as such? Should there be cultural, religious, and ethnic homogeneity? Or is any person who finds himself permanently within the boundaries of a certain state automatically a member of that country's "nation?" These are far-reaching questions, and they are not easily answered. The word *nation* is a very common one in the English language; we speak of our "nationality" and the French or Brazilian "nation." Yet definitions of the term (for such it is) vary widely, and one only has to check some of the world's major dictionaries to prove the point. One, for instance, defines nation as "a distinct race or people . . . hav-

---

[10]A.E. Moodie, *Geography Behind Politics*, London, Hutchinson, 1957, p. 24.

ing a distinct history and political institutions." Another describes it as "a people inhabiting a certain extent of territory, and united by common political institutions . . .an aggregation of persons speaking the same or a cognate language." According to the first definition, there is either no American (United States) nation, or there is more than one—for the United States has a plural society. And according to the second, multilingual states have more than one nation, and one can therefore not speak of a Belgian nation or a Canadian nation.

Emotional and Legal Nationhood

Quite apart from the divisive factors just identified, there are other, less tangible but perhaps even more important qualities of nationhood. *Legal* nationhood, obviously, is membership in the nation of a particular state, proved in a number of ways: by birth certificate, military record, voting eligibility, and other attributes of citizenship. But there is also something we might call *emotional* nationhood, that is, the level of a people's commitment, collectively and individually, to the state as they perceive it. It is possible, for example, for some Canadian citizens living in, say, Montreal to feel much stronger allegiance to their province (or even to distant France) than to the state of Canada itself. They seek a sovereign Quebec, and promote the principle of secession from Canada. From their standpoint, the state of Canada has not functioned satisfactorily and their commitment to the Canadian nation as a whole is very low.

In this respect Canada is by no means unique. There are French-speaking Belgians who feel stronger emotional ties with France than with their own country, English-speaking South Africans who still prefer to speak of the United Kingdom as "home," and Bangladeshiani who felt that they had more in common with their neighbors across the border in India than with their own countrymen in West Pakistan. These people's commitment to the state of which they are legal citizens is not very great.

There is another aspect to this. As the flow of information and communication gets better, people—"the nation"—are better informed about what their state is doing in the world. There are states in which this flow of information is inhibited by official means, but even in such places it becomes more difficult by the day to stop unwanted news from spreading. There is evidence that many Soviet citizens resent the treatment of some artists and intellectuals in that country. During the Nazi advent in the Germany of the 1930's, the Nazis succeeded in securing the commitment of the overwhelming majority of Germany's nation, but a minority resisted the course of events; thousands left the country rather than acquiesce. In the United States in the 1960's and 1970's, the nation was torn by an ill-fated campaign in Indochina, with incalculable damage to the cohesion of the nation.

The Nation-State

In those countries where there is a close coincidence between the "legal" nation (that is, the state's boundaries) and the "emotionally committed" nation, the political geographer recognizes the *nation-state*. Many definitions of this concept have been written, all seeking to define a model against which all states can be measured. We define the nation-state as a political unit comprising a clearly defined territory and inhabited by a body of people, both of sufficient size and quality, and sufficiently well organized to possess a certain measure of power; the people considering themselves to be a nation with certain emotional and other ties that are expressed in their most tangible form in "law" and "government" or "ideology."

This is obviously a very broad definition. But broad as it is, several of today's more prominent states may not qualify as nation-states. And note that there is no attempt to be quantitatively precise in this model; we say "sufficiently" large, "a certain measure" of power, "the people considering themselves to be" a nation. Obviously there is not a state in the world where *all* the people consider themselves committed and emotionally a part of the nation—so we are saying that the vast majority of the people must feel this way. But whether it is 90 percent of the people, or 80 percent, the definition does not pinpoint. Nevertheless, it gives us a sense of what the ingredients of the nation-state must be.

These ingredients include the so-called "four pillars" of the state, which are discussed in some detail in Chapters 3 and 4. The definition suggests that the state must have (1) a clearly defined territory, (2) a substantial population, (3) certain organizational qualities, and (4) a measure of power. Thus a state must have a well-defined part of the earth's surface, marked by boundaries that are recognized by international treaty; it must have a population of considerable numbers (a few thousand people cannot constitute a nation), it should display organizational achievements (in government, communications, and education, for example), and it should reflect all these qualities by having some strength or power. Power in this context is not necessarily military in nature; it can be expressed in economic terms, in associations with politically powerful allies, and in other ways.

Clearly we should look into these criteria in greater detail, for the implications are far reaching. On the basis of what has been said in the preceding paragraphs, a considerable number of countries would not qualify as nation-states, and perhaps not even as states. There are several very small countries (called "microstates") with territories of just hundreds of square miles (sometimes less) and populations numbering tens of thousands of people, not millions. These do not satisfy the definition's requirements. And a number of the recently decolonized, emergent states have not yet achieved the levels of organization that would qualify them as nation-states. The concept of the nation-state constitutes a world-wide national objective for attainment, but it remains an elusive goal.

REFERENCES

Adams, Robert M., "The Origin of Cities," *Sci. Amer.*, 203, 3 (September 1960), 153–168.

Banks, A. Leslie (editor), *The Development of Tropical and Subtropical Countries, with Particular Reference to Africa*. London, E. Arnold, 1954.

Bowman, Isaiah, "The Valley People of Eastern Bolivia," *J. Geography*, 11 (1912), 114–119.

Brainerd, George W., "The Maya Civilization," *Masterkey*, 27, 3 (May-June, 1953), 83–96; and 4 (July-August, 1953), 128–133.

Brigham, A.P., *Geographic Influences in American History*. Boston, Ginn and Company, 1903.

Bryce, J., *The Holy Roman Empire*. New York, Macmillan, 1919.

Chakrabongse, Chula, Prince of Thailand, "The Political and Economic Background in Thailand," *J. Roy. Central Asian Soc.*, 42, Pt. 2 (April 1955), 116–127.

Clarke, John I., "Economic and Political Changes in the Sahara," *Geography*, 46, Pt. 211 (April 1961), 102–119.

Collingwood, R.G., and J.N.L. Myres, *Roman Britain and the English Settlements*. Oxford, Clarendon Press; New York, Oxford University Press, 1937.

Coulborn, Rushton, *The Origin of Civilized Societies*. Princeton, N.J., Princeton University Press, 1959.

Cunningham, J.K., "Maori-Pakeha Conflict, 1858–1885: a Background to Political Geography," *New Zealand Geographer*, 12, 1 (April 1956), 12–31.

Deutsch, Karl W., "The Growth of Nations: Some Recurrent Patterns of Political and Social Integration," *World Politics*, 5, 2 (January 1953), 168–195.

Emeny, Brooks, *Mainsprings of World Politics*. New York, Foreign Policy Association, 1956.

Febvre, L.P.V., and Lionel Bataillon. *A Geographical Introduction to History*. New York, Knopf, 1925.

Fleure, H.J., "The Geographic Study of Society and World Problems," *Scot. Geog. Mag.*, 48 (1932), 257–274.

Floyd, Barry N., "Pre-European Political Patterns in Sub-Saharan Africa," *Bull. Ghana Geog. Assn.*, 8, 2 (July 1963), 3–11.

Frank, Tenney, *Roman Imperialism*. New York, Macmillan, 1914.

Goad, H.E., *The Making of the Corporate State*. London, Christophers, 1932.

Hallowell, A. Irving, "The Backwash of the Frontier: The Impact of the Indian on American Culture," *Annual Report of the Smithsonian Institution* for the year ended June 30, 1958 (1959), 447–472.

Howells, William W., "The Distribution of Man," *Sci. Amer.*, 203, 3 (September 1960), 113–127.

Hyde, George E., *Indians of the High Plains, from the Prehistoric Period to the Coming of Europeans*. Norman, University of Oklahoma Press, 1959.

Kephart, Calvin, *Races of Mankind: their origin and migration; all recognized ancient tribes and nations identified and their migrations traced*. New York, Philosophical Library, 1960.

Kostelski, Z., *The Yugoslavs; the History of the Yugoslavs and Their States to the Creation of Yugoslavia*. New York, Philosophical Library, 1952.

Larus, J., *Comparative World Politics*. Belmont, Wadsworth, 1964.

Lattimore, Owen, "The Geographical Factor in Mongol History," *Geog. J.*, 91 (1938), 1–20.

———, *Inner Frontiers of Asia*. New York, American Geographical Society, Research Series No. 21., 1940.

———, "Origins of the Great Wall of China," *Geog. Rev.*, 27, 4 (October 1937), 529–549.

Marquis, R.V., "London's New City within the Old," *Geog. Mag.*, 31, 9 (January 1959), 448–455.

Martin, G.J., "Ellsworth Huntington and the Pace of History," *Connecticut Review*, 5, 1 (October, 1971), 83–123.

Morley, Sylvanus Griswold, *The Ancient Maya*. Stanford, Calif., Stanford University Press, 1946.

Niebuhr, R., *The Structure of Nations and Empires*. New York, Charles Scribner's Sons, 1959.

Roxby, P.M., "The Terrain of Early Chinese Civilization," *Geography*, 23 (1938), 225–236.

Roys, Ralph L., *The Political Geography of the Yucatan Maya*. Washington, Carnegie Institution of Washington, Publ. No. 613, 1957.

Smailes, A.E., *The Geography of Towns*. London, Hutchinson, 1957.

Sprout, Harold and Margaret, "Environmental Factors in the Study of International Politics," *J. Conflict Resolution, 1* (1957), 309–328.

Straker, Ernest, and Ivan Margary, "Ironworks and Communications in the Weald in Roman Times," *Geog. J., 92* (1938), 55–60.

Thompson, J.E.S., *The Rise and Fall of Maya Civilization*. Norman, University of Oklahoma Press, 1954.

Vaillant, G.C., *The Aztecs of Mexico*. New York, Doubleday, 1950.

Waterman, T.T., "North American Indian Dwellings," *Geog. Rev., 14*, 1 (January 1924), 1–25.

CHAPTER
3

THE ELEMENTS OF THE STATE:
TERRITORY AND POPULATION

Whatever the nature of the political entity referred to as the state—the degree of its internal unity, the size of its capital city, the variety of its products—it must possess three basic elements. Without a specific land area, inhabited and exploited by a certain number of people, there can be no state, and neither can a state function without being organized. These attributes—territory, people, and organization—would seem so obvious as to require no elaboration. But where are the limits? Just how many people must live in a state in order to justify the term, and what is the minimum size of the state in terms of area?[1] What is the degree of organization required in the state? After all, every group of people, however small, lives on a certain piece of the earth's available land, and even a clan is somewhat organized. Is Liechtenstein sufficiently populous to constitute a state? Does Gambia possess organization in a sufficient number of spheres to be so described?

Conversely, it is important to recognize that abundance in the preceding terms does not ensure statehood either. A certain country may have a very large territory, but that does not mean that its resources are therefore similarly sizable. A large population does not guarantee high productivity and great power. The West African State of Mauritania is larger in area than any state in Western Europe, but its population is barely one million and its capital has less than ten thousand inhabitants. Spain has almost three times as many people as the Netherlands, but a glance at world trade figures indicates that numbers alone do not mean much.

[1]This problem has been of concern to several leaders of emergent states. Former President Nkrumah of Ghana proposed in a speech some years ago that any colonial territory achieving independence should have at least three million people in order to be permitted to exist separately, and that emergent territories with fewer people should be merged with neighboring states.

TERRITORY

The most basic tool of the political geographer is the world map showing all political boundaries, international as well as internal. These boundaries, as we have seen, are superimposed upon a world population which has many different languages, religions, and cultures. Sometimes boundaries separate peoples that are similar in many respects, and unite vastly different and differing peoples. Such boundaries may have peculiar histories, and they may themselves become the object of study in political geography.

Boundaries, however, do more than divide and unify various peoples. They determine also the exact land area of the state, its physical base. Within these boundaries lie the resources with which the state must work in order to survive: soils for agriculture, minerals for industry and trade. And again, the boundary pattern often seems to have no relation to the physical world. Sometimes boundaries run along rivers or mountain ranges, but frequently they divide areas of physical homogeneity among several political entities, while at other times they seem determined to give one state all the resources in a certain area, and none to its neighbors.

Detailed boundary study is the subject of a subsequent section of this book. Presently we should confine ourselves to a consideration of the world boundary framework and the conclusions that can be drawn from it. The areas of states, like their populations, vary greatly in size. And as was the case with population, it is easy to misinterpret the effects of great size. A very large state is not necessarily one that possesses more mineral resources than a smaller state, nor is it always stronger and more powerful that its smaller counterpart. Along with size, a number of factors such as location, physiography, and shape come into play. A very large state which is sparsely populated may experience internal division, especially if the areas intervening between the populated regions are difficult to cross and are unproductive. Australia's central desert, the Soviet Union's vast eastern domain, and Canada's Rocky Mountain belt all exemplify the barrier effect of vastness, although in each there is greater political unity than there is in many smaller states that do not have size problems. Nevertheless, very large states can be observed attempting to diminish the "empty" aspect of their sparsely populated regions by encouraging settlement in those areas (as witnessed by Brazil's westward relocation of the capital) or by practicing population policies aimed at rapid growth as well as encouraging migration (as the case of the Soviet Union). In the African state of Sudan the problem of size is directly related to the forces of fragmentation which have confronted that country almost constantly since its attainment of independence. The Sudan is so large that it extends from Arab Africa into black Africa. Thus it contains an Arab population in the north, focusing upon the capital of Khartum, while the southern provinces are occupied almost exclusively by peoples who are more closely related to black Africa—racially, culturally, historically. As it happens, the two "heartlands" of the state are separated by desert and swamp, so that communication has always presented problems. The young state has had to expend much of its energy in controlling the divisive forces that have come to the fore, distance complicating virtually every aspect of the matter.

Size

The size of a state—the amount of earth space it incorporates—is related in many ways to problems of effective national control and organization. Many of the states that evolved in various parts of the world ultimately broke up because their frontiers extended too far outward to be sufficiently integrated with the central area of the state. Continued growth meant growing strength—up to a certain point, after which it meant increasing vulnerability. This was one of the reasons for the collapse of the Aztec Empire, the ancient state of Ghana, and the Roman Empire. It also has been a major factor in the breakup of more recent colonial empires. And in such states as India and Sudan, it is a critical matter today.

On the other hand, it is obvious that size can present advantages. If some attention is also paid to location (relative location, with reference to environmental regions, mineralized belts, trade routes), a generalization regarding size might even be possible. After all, the United States fits comfortably within the Sahara Desert, and its size there would be meaningless. But the United States lies in middle latitudes, in a world zone of many

The element of size: Australia's vastness (the state is almost as large as the contiguous United States of America) should be seen in terms of the extensive arid and nonproductive central regions of the country. For many years, the Australian railroad network (the means by which the obstacle of distance could be overcome) was beset by many problems, including the use of different gauges in different sections of the Commonwealth. This, however, is now largely a thing of the past, and a Commonwealth Railways train is shown here traversing the flat, treeless null-arbor plain which extends between South and Western Australia. As in the United States, the "piggy-back" system of transporting loaded road vehicles is employed (Australian News and Information Bureau).

transitions (in terms of soils and climate, to name but two), and fronting two oceans. Depending upon location, then, size and environmental diversification are indeed related. One way to consider this would be as follows. The total land area of the world is limited, and it contains the bulk of the resources upon which progress is based. A state that has a larger area than another obviously has a chance to find a greater percentage of such resources within its borders. But these known resources themselves are not evenly distributed; they are scattered in patches across the globe. They are concentrated in certain areas, apparently absent in others. The soils of the lowland tropics are often incapable of sustaining sedentary agriculture; those of the highest latitudes are not useful for other reasons. The climates of the polar regions are not conducive to agriculture; those of the low-latitude regions are often excessively dry or excessively moist. A series of maps of mineral resources indicates the remarkable concentrations of significant deposits in rather well-defined belts. Taking these world distributions into consideration when evaluating the effects of size upon the wealth and self-sufficiency of the state, we see why some of the largest states are comparatively poor, while others are incomparably rich.

The Problem of Terminology. With such an enormous range in the territorial size of states, it would be useful to have some terms to identify states within certain size categories. For example, the very smallest states such as Luxembourg (998 square miles), Liechtenstein (60 square miles), San Marino (24 square miles), and Monaco (about six-tenths of a square mile) are referred to as *microstates*. States somewhat larger than these smallest units, such as Brunei (2,226 square miles), Gambia (4,360 square miles), and Cyprus (3,572 square miles) often are called *ministates*. But neither term has any precise connotation.[2]

Generally, states exceeding 1 million square miles are described as very large, while those

[2]Pounds puts the upper limit of the microstate as high as 25,000 kilometers, as a result of which no less than twenty-five states fall into this category, including El Salvador, Jamaica, Cyprus, Israel, and Lebanon. These would seem, however, to form a group distinctly different, in terms of their approach to nation-state characteristics, from that listed above for Europe. See N.J.G. Pounds, *Political Geography*, New York, McGraw-Hill, 1972, p. 35.

under 10,000 square miles are referred to as very small. Small states range from 10,000 to 60,000 square miles, and medium-size states from 60,000 to 140,000 square miles. Those over 140,000 but under 1 million square miles are referred to as large. Thus the following would apply:

Very small	Cambodia	Lebanon
Small	Netherlands	Liberia
Medium	United Kingdom	Poland
Large	France	Mexico
Very large	U.S.S.R.	Canada
Very small	Israel	El Salvador
Small	Ceylon	Panama
Medium	Ecuador	Uganda
Large	Nigeria	Pakistan
Very large	China	Brazil

One of the remarkable aspects of the group of very large states is the clustering of several of these states around the 3-million-square mile mark:[3]

Canada	3,851,113
China	3,767,751
U.S.A.	3,615,210
Brazil	3,286,344
Australia	2,974,581

Shape

The states of the world have not acquired their territorial properties overnight. They have attained their present areas through a long sequence of adjustment and readjustment, loss and gain of territory. Poland's boundaries have shifted so many times that it is difficult to imagine that the process is really over; everyone knows of the numerous readjustments of Israel's boundaries with its Arab neighbors. Nevertheless, there is a certain apparent permanence in the overall world boundary framework, and on maps in textbooks, in newspapers, and on television we see all or part of that framework so frequently that it begins to look familiar. And there is a certain value in that familiarity. Thus we automatically know Spain as a larger state

[3]Figures from *Goode's World Atlas*, Rand McNally and Co., eleventh edition (1960), p. 170.

than Portugal—it occupies a much larger share of the Iberian Peninsula. And a reference to Norway immediately brings to mind a long, strongly indented stretch of land on the seaward side of a great northern peninsula. In fact, so obvious is this aspect of political geography that it is easy to miss the lessons that can be learned from a close look at the *shape* of states. We described Norway as a strip of land lying along a peninsula; we might also have described Chile as a narrow belt of territory between the Andes and the ocean. Both of these states are, in fact, elongated or attenuated in shape—very long and very narrow. Now the question is whether Chile and Norway share any problems of a politico-geographical nature that can possibly be related to that shape characteristic, and whether there are other elongated states that display similar features.

Thus it is advisable to determine the categories of shape that are repeated across the world map and to group the world's states, as far as possible, on this basis. Then, perhaps, some recurrent themes will emerge. An *elongated* or *attenuated* state may, on the basis of the Chilean example, be defined as one that is at least six times as long as its average width. Thus Norway, Sweden, Togo, Gambia, Italy, Panama, and Malawi are among the states in this category. Depending to some extent upon the state's location with reference to the world's cultural areas, elongation may involve internal division. The north-south division of Italy is one that permeates life in that country, and is related to the different exposures of the two regions to European mainstreams of change. The Norwegian administration of the Laplanders is a regional matter, involving the northern parts of that state. The Ewe of southern Togo have political views with reference to their state which differ from those of other tribal peoples.[4] Furthermore, the physiographic contrasts within the elongated state may accentuate other divisions. Chile, for example, possesses at least three distinct environmental regions. The central region is Mediterranean in nature, while the south is under Marine West Coast conditions, and the north is desert. The country's headquarters lie around the capital city, in the central (Mediterranean) part, and

the effects of distance and remoteness are very evident on the Peruvian-Bolivian borders in the north and on Tierra del Fuego in the south. On the other hand, the internal diversification of the state resulting from its straddling of several environmental or cultural zones may be advantageous. Again, as in the case of size, much depends upon location. The elongation of Malawi, within Bantu Africa, is an altogether different matter culturally from the attenuation of Togo, with its contrasting influences from south and north. Physiographically, also, location plays its role. Chile lies astride the Tropic of Capricorn; Norway is bisected by the Arctic Circle. The resulting differences are obvious.

Many states appear to lie spread about their central area and are nearly round or rectangular in shape. Again, some generalizations are possible. Theoretically, since all points of the boundary of such a *compact* state lie at about the same distance from the geometrical center of the state, there are many advantages. First, the boundary is the shortest possible in view of the area enclosed. Second, since there are no peninsulas, islands, or other protruding parts, the establishment of effective communications to all parts of the country should be easier here than under any other shape conditions (unless there are severe physiographic barriers). Third, and consequent to the second point, effective control is theoretically more easily maintained here than in other countries. Of course, additional factors should be considered. In many compact states, the capital city is located along the periphery rather than at or near the geometric center of the state. Often the area of greatest productive capacity lies in one of the quadrants of the state rather than at the center. Finally, a compact state, no less than an elongated one, may be located in a zone of transition—cultural or physiographic, or both. Thus internal divisions may still occur. Examples of the type are not difficult to find: Uruguay in South America, Belgium and Poland in Europe, Sudan in Africa, and Afghanistan in Asia fall into this category.

Certain states are in nearly every way compact—but they possess an extension of territory, in the form of a peninsula or a "corridor," leading away from the main body of territory. Such *prorupt* states and territories often face serious internal difficulties, for the proruption frequently is either the most important part of the political entity or is a

---

[4] This is an *irredentist* problem, the nature of which will be discussed in a subsequent chapter; as will be seen, elongated states are theoretically especially vulnerable to irredentist problems.

distant problem of administration. Perhaps the best example is that of Zaïre (formerly Congo) in Africa, which consists of a huge, compact area with two proruptions, both of which are vital to the country and in many ways its most important areas.[5] The capital city itself, and the administrative headquarters, lie on the western proruption, which also forms a corridor to the ocean via the Zaïre port of Matadi. The most important area of revenue production, on the other hand, is the Katanga, itself a proruption in the far southeast. Separating the two areas lies the vast Congo Basin, in many ways more a liability than an asset to the state. Another African example is that of South West Africa (now officially known as Namibia), whose proruption extends to the Zambezi River. Long a useless area, this belt of land has recently become of great strategic importance, as the South African government has decided to establish a major military base there. In Asia, the example of Burma and its neighbor, Thailand, is relevant. Both states have large territories, fairly compact in shape, but they share a section of the Malayan Peninsula along a boundary which runs almost down the middle of this narrow strip of land.

Other states consist of two or more individual parts, separated by land or by international water, and are therefore *fragmented*. Such fragmentation brings with it obvious consequences. Contact between the various population sectors is more difficult than in a contiguous state, and the sense of unity so necessary in the forging of a nation may be slow to develop. Because any state must have a capital, it will be located on one of the fragments, the choice of which may itself be a source of friction. Governmental control can be rendered ineffective by distance, as was proved repeatedly by the case of Indonesia, where the Java-based government had great difficulty putting down revolts in Sumatra. Despite its claims to all intervening waters, Indonesia remains an example of one type of fragmented state: the insular type. Japan and the Philippines are two others in this category. In contrast, the fragmented state may lie entirely upon land. While it existed, Pakistan (West and East) exemplified the continental type. Pakistan's two "wings," the West and the East, were united by a common religious

faith—but divided by numerous cultural contrasts. As happens frequently with fragmented states, one part of the state, in this case the East, felt itself the victim of political discrimination. Charges of "domestic colonialism" abounded, and in the end the state broke up as East Pakistan—now Bangladesh—fought for independence, aided by neighboring India. The problems of territorial separation are indeed many. A third type of fragmented state is that which lies partly on a continental landmass and partly on one or more islands. The recently founded state of Malaysia consists of a mainland section on the Malayan Peninsula, a host of smaller intervening islands, and a sizable portion of the large Indonesian island of Borneo. Technically Italy, with its island territories of Sicily and Sardinia, fits this category, as do many other states with island possessions.

Finally, scrutiny of the world map will prove that there are a few, very few, states that completely enclose other states. Such states are *perforated*, and it is impossible to reach the perforating state without crossing the territory or air space of the perforated state. This means, obviously, that the perforated state is in a strong position with reference to the landlocked perforator. Usually these terms refer to tiny enclaves such as San Marino (which perforates Italy; hence Italy is the perforated state), which have little if any political significance. But in Southern Africa, the case of the Republic of South Africa is in a different class. South Africa is perforated by a former British dependency long known as Basutoland. In common with other British African colonies, Basutoland attained its sovereignty and is now known as Lesotho. A state of 11,716 square miles and with a population of about 1 million, Lesotho is no San Marino. Politically, its black nationalism contrasts sharply with South Africa's white rule. In a size category shared with such states as Belgium and Costa Rica, Lesotho is a substantial impediment to the territorial integrity of the South African Republic.

Some states, when analyzed on the basis of the preceding criteria, will be seen to have more than one shape characteristic. Italy, for example, is an elongated state, with considerable contrasts between north and south. But the state is also fragmented, since it includes island territories, and perforated as well. Usually only one of the shape characteristics plays a really major role in the political

[5]For a detailed discussion of Zaïre on this basis see "Lowland Africa: Problems of Development in the Congo Republic," in H.J. de Blij, *A Geography of Subsaharan Africa*, Chicago, Rand McNally and Co., 1964, pp. 185 ff.

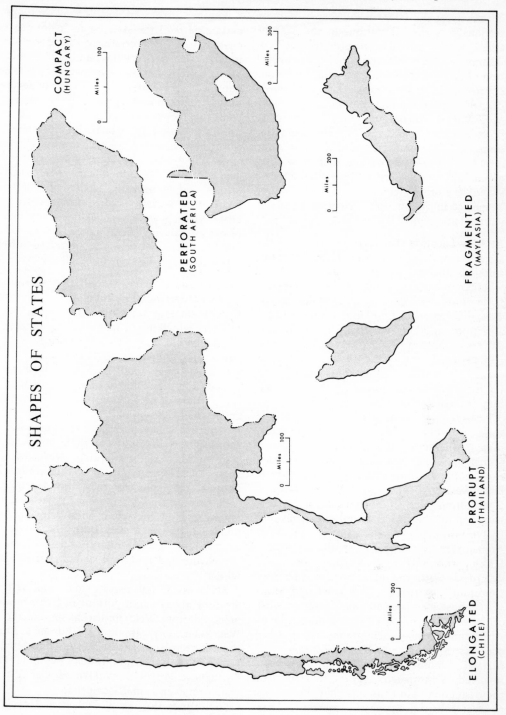

SHAPES OF STATES

COMPACT
(HUNGARY)

PERFORATED
(SOUTH AFRICA)

FRAGMENTED
(MAYLASIA)

PRORUPT
(THAILAND)

ELONGATED
(CHILE)

geography of the state. In the case of Italy, it obviously is the elongation; in the case of Chile, which is also fragmented—certain islands lie beyond the territorial sea—elongation likewise is the major shape phenomenon. South Africa's compactness is far more significant than its perforation, and the compactness of France exceeds in importance the existence of the island of Corsica. On the other hand, the impression of compactness of Zaïre is soon dispelled by a study of the distribution of population and resources. Thus the factor of shape, like other elements of the state, must be viewed in conjunction with other factors of political geography.

Relative Location. The relative location of the state is a multifaceted issue. There are many sides to the matter of a state's location: whether it lies far or near the world's major trade routes, whether it extends (as Sudan does, for instance) from one ethnic-cultural area into another, whether it has coastal outlets, and so on. Historical political geography often concerns itself with the proximity of a state to the main avenues of historic change. Environment and resources can be discussed from the standpoint of location.

Probably the most obvious feature of the state, as seen on a basic politicogeographical map, is whether it has access to the sea or not. States that do not have such access are referred to as *landlocked;* and in Europe, only Switzerland, Austria, Czechoslavakia, and Hungary (apart from the microstates) are in this situation. In the Americas only Paraguay and Bolivia are deprived of coasts, and in Asia, Afghanistan, Nepal (and its smaller neighbors Sikkim and Bhutan), and Laos can be so described—with the exception of currently Communist territories like Tibet and Mongolia whose identities are not the same. Most of the world's landlocked states, in fact, lie in Africa, and most of them are emergent states such as Mali, Chad, Niger, Zambia, and Malawi. Landlocked states have often been involved in campaigns seeking to terminate their isolation, and thus this characteristic is of great politicogeographical interest. Bolivia has warred over its outlet westward; more recently, Mali and its western neighbor, Senegal, joined in a federation known as the Mali Federation (at that time Mali was known as Soudan), thus acquiring exit rights. But the federation collapsed. In East Africa Uganda is landlocked and in need of secure access to the sea, and some problems loom there.

Another aspect of location focuses upon certain parts of the state, or its major city or cities. Often when a state has a large territory, much of that territory lies far from the world's major trade routes. But that state may possess one city located at the focal point of several busy avenues of trade. The whole country may come to depend upon that city and its immediate vicinity. Goods and ideas move through it, most of the people may live and work there, and the country more or less depends upon the money made there. Such a city is said to have the quality of *nodality*. Some of the ancient empires arose first around cities that possessed nodality: they were places of exchange, markets, and they grew rapidly in size and power. Modern cities often thrive on much the same principle.

Exclave and Enclave. One or two additional aspects of territorial morphology are relevant. Certain states possess a medium-size or large territory which might appear to be compact on a small-scale map. Close scrutiny of the boundaries, however, indicates that these states also have small pockets of land lying outside the main territory, as islands within the territory of neighboring states. These tiny areas are far too small to render the state fragmented. They may be less than a dozen square miles in area, and their populations may number a few hundred. Nevertheless, these *exclaves* are of some importance in political geography, for they may depend for their survival upon their connections with the "homeland." Hence their boundaries may be under great stress, and from the study of exclaves may come a greater understanding of the nature and functions of boundaries elsewhere.

Exclaves are not always small, and neither are they always unimportant in terms of area or population. West Berlin, as an exclave of West Germany, is one of Europe's most important urban centers and is considered a vital part of the German Federal Republic. The Portuguese Angolan exclave of Cabinda is visible on even a small-scale map.

Sometimes the terms exclave and *enclave* are confused. The correct usage depends upon the point of reference. When an outlying, surrounded area is considered in connection with the homeland of which it forms a part, it is described as an exclave. In this sense, West Berlin is an exclave of West Germany. On the other hand, a state that has such a small territory within its borders (though not necessarily surrounding it) would view the entity as an *enclave*. West Berlin, then is an enclave in East Germany. The former Portuguese Overseas Province of Goa was an enclave in the state of India.

Exclaves can be classified according to their degree of separation from the "homeland."[6] *Normal* exclaves are parts of certain states completely and effectively surrounded by the territory of other states. Such normal exclaves are usually small. Those in Europe are all under 10 square miles in area and have populations under 2,000. There are small Belgian exclaves within the Netherlands, and there is Dutch territory within Belgium. *Pene*-exclaves are "parts of the territory of one country that can be approached conveniently—in particular by wheeled traffic—only through the territory of another country."[7] In other words, these are proruptions, barely connected to the main territory of the state, the connecting links being so narrow or difficult that the only transport lines lie through neighboring territory. *Quasi*-exclaves are those that are technically separated from the motherland, but in reality they are so completely connected with it that they do not function as exclaves. *Virtual* exclaves are areas treated as the exclaves of a country of which they are not legally an integral part. Finally, *temporary* exclaves result from the fragmentation of a state through an armistice; occupation zones or demilitarized areas may create temporary exclaves. West Berlin is such a temporary exclave.

These, then, are some of the territorial properties of states. Others will emerge later, as we consider in detail the anatomy of the state system.

POPULATION

If there is a great range in the territorial size of states, the range of their populations is even greater. As everyone knows, the most populous state on earth is China, whose population is approaching 900 million and which, at a growth rate of just 1 percent, will reach 1 *billion* people in the 1980's. This means that one-quarter of all mankind forms the nation of one state—for China, as we will see, is indeed a nation-state. But China is not the world's only state with a huge population. India now counts well over 500 million citizens, the Soviet Union some 250 million, and the United States of America, nearly 210 million. At the other end of the scale there are states with minipopulations just as there are territorial ministates. Iceland, for example, has just over 200,000 inhabitants, Guyana not many more than three-quarters of a million, and Liberia fewer than 1 1/2 million. Between these extremes are the populations of such states as the United Kingdom (56 million), Mexico (nearly 40 million), and Thailand (35 million). It would be difficult to categorize the population totals; China is obviously in a class by itself, as is India. The United States and Soviet Union stand alone between 200 and 250 million, and clustered about the 100 million figure are Pakistan, Indonesia, Japan, and Brazil.

Density and Distribution

Among the basic features of any state's population of interest to the political geographer are density and distribution. But again, there is what we might call the danger of the average. If we are told that the land area of the Netherlands is 12,500 square miles and the population is 12,500,000 it is clear that the average density per square mile is 1,000. But this figure is not much more revealing than the total by itself, for we do not know whether all the people depend for a living upon a small part of the state and are agglomerated there, leaving the rest of the state sparsely occupied, or whether most of them live in a few scattered cities. Egypt, for example, has an average population density of about 70, and so does the state of Georgia. Egypt has seven times as many people as Georgia, and it is about seven times as large as Georgia. But in Egypt, most of the people are huddled together in an area perhaps half as large as that of Georgia, so that population densities here run into the thousands per square mile while other parts of the country are deserted. Thus, what meaning does the average really have?

Along with density, therefore, details concerning population distribution are required. Here, now, we have the beginnings of data that may be useful in political geography. Certain states have populations that are concentrated heavily in one area; this area may be the zone of greatest productive capacity, it may be the most heavily industrialized, or it may focus upon the largest city. Other states, whose

---

[6]G.W.S. Robinson, "Exclaves," *Ann. A.A.G.*, 49, 3 (September, 1959), 283–295.

[7]Ibid., p. 283. For examples, see the detailed maps in this article.

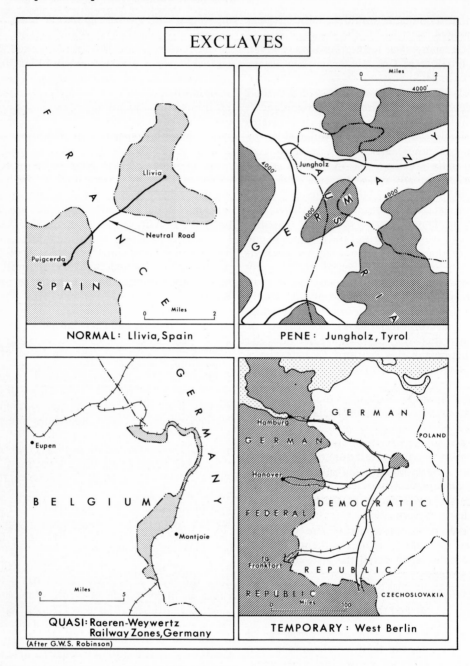

EXCLAVES

NORMAL: Llivia, Spain

PENE: Jungholz, Tyrol

QUASI: Raeren-Weywertz
Railway Zones, Germany

TEMPORARY: West Berlin

(After G.W.S. Robinson)

population totals and average densities may be about the same, may have more than one such area of population agglomeration; in other words, such states possess more than one focal point. It may be that these areas of population concentration are separated by zones which may form barriers to contact; perhaps there are deserts between them, or mountain ranges. And perhaps the people of one such area speak a language that differs from that spoken in the other. If such is the case, there are obviously divisive elements present in the state. Peoples with distinct characteristics tend to desire a certain amount of autonomy; they may want to foster their "own" culture. In fact, they may feel more strongly about their small area than they do about the state of which they form a part. We might suggest a model; the state that has only one "heart," other things being equal, enjoys a greater degree of internal unity than a state that possesses several such foci.

This idea was one employed by Napoleon, and by the Romans before him. "All roads lead to Rome" is exactly this principle: there shall be one central area to the state, whose focus shall be the capital city. Napoleon saw a divided France, with various semiautonomous "provinces," and he reorganized the road system of the country in such a manner that all major roads ultimately led to Paris. It was one of the major steppingstones in the evolution of the centralized state of France. It is, in addition, a lesson that is repeated with the emergence of the ex-colonial territories to statehood. Those states that possess more than one area of population concentration or productive capacity (Zaïre, Nigeria, Sudan, Pakistan, Malaysia), all have faced serious internal difficulties.

The Problem of Quality

The political geographer must concern himself with matters in addition to population density and distribution. Thus there are demographic questions to be considered, such as literacy and education, health and age structure, skills and abilities. And once more, the range of conditions defies the imagination. All of these have something to do with the people's mobility, awareness, and political consciousness. The problem of illiteracy has been a major one facing the emergent ex-colonial states, for it is impossible to transfer allegiances from the tribe and the region to the nation and the state without the tools of understanding. Thus many of these emergent

states are spending much of their annual revenues on education budgets, which always seem insufficient nevertheless. Unfortunately, the consequences are not always salutary; increased education in the village often causes an emigration from rural areas to the urban centers, where thousands of unemployed must be accommodated, for jobs are few. Such unemployed form a major political threat, and several countries have taken steps to limit the migration to the cities.

Of equal or even greater importance is the health condition of the population, and this question is related directly to that of food supply. Comparisons between western European states and some Asian countries in terms of life expectancy, daily calories of food available, dietary balance, and incidence of disease quickly indicate why available energies differ in quantity and are expended in different directions. A population that is largely engaged in day-to-day survival under a subsistence form of agriculture cannot be expected to make any great contribution to the state, economically or otherwise. The struggle for food is a major factor in political geography, affecting as it does the internal condition of the state as well as its international relationships.

When we established our nation-state "model," we argued that the nation-state must possess a people "of sufficient size and quality . . . (and) . . . considering themselves to be a nation. . . ." Our reference to quality, then, included considerations of health and well-being, education and skills. But there are other qualities that have much to do with the forging (or failing) of a nation. We in North America, and especially in the United States, only need to look around ourselves to see the detrimental impact of racial differences and related inequities upon this nation. Millions of people have come from eastern and western Europe to become United States citizens in the real sense of the word, emotionally as well as legally. But the people who came from other continents, especially Africa, have been assimilated far less completely and effectively. As a result, many are Americans neither legally (being still deprived of some of the privileges theoretically belonging to all citizens of the state) nor emotionally, for obvious reasons. This is the sort of situation that fosters what might be called "retribalization," and there are examples in world history to emphasize the dangers to any state inherent in such a situation.

Racial diversity probably is the greatest obstacle of all; people can never shed it, they are constantly reminded of it, and they become deeply involved emotionally when something happens to someone of their own racial group. The survival of racial identity is the survival of an element of tribalism, and tribalism and nationhood are opposites. But there are other obstacles. A prominent one is religion. In the early 1970's the United Kingdom's Ulster (Northern Ireland) teetered on the brink of civil war; the issue was centuries old, namely conflict between Protestants and Catholics. Northern Ireland, in effect, is a substantial, Protestant-dominated enclave in overwhelmingly Catholic Ireland. Catholic residents of Northern Ireland have charged that the Protestant majority has discriminated against them and has deprived them of their civil rights; the Protestants, in turn, charge the Catholics with subversion, sabotage, and even terrorism. British armed forces have had to intercede. It is worth remembering that these are Christian opponents confronting each other—this is no clash with Islam or Hinduism. The hatreds that can be aroused, unfortunately, are no less intense. In the Netherlands in 1964, a member of the traditionally non-Catholic royal family decided to marry a Catholic, Spanish prince. So deep-seated were the roots of the crisis that followed that the Queen could not afford to attend the Rome wedding of her own daughter. The Netherlands government would not permit the compromise whereby a Catholic ceremony would have been held in a non-Catholic church. And we Westerners accuse Africans of hangups about tribalism and ritual!

Still another quality that has much to do with the building of nations is that of language. After skin color, language marks its man so effectively: who has not imitated the drawl of a Southerner? Indeed, a mere accent can arouse animosities. But at least, in the United States, almost everyone speaks English. Certainly there are Spanish-speaking minorities and some others as well, but the overwhelming majority of the people speak a version of the same basic language. Many countries are not so fortunate. In Canada, for example, the language issue has a great emotional charge. Canada is a bilingual country—that is, it has two official languages. Unfortunately, this bilingualism is also regionally expressed. The Province of Quebec is the historic, cultural, and of course the linguistic stronghold of Canada's French-speaking minority. As minorities tend to be, the French Canadians are very proud of their heritage, and they often express the view that their culture is negated by the English-speaking majority. Of course the issue involves

The use of a single language may be a strong unifying factor in the state. A number of states, such as Belgium and South Africa, suffer from internal division in which language plays an all-pervading role. The press and other media of mass communication, education, and parliamentary exchange are all complicated by the language issue. This road sign, in Italian and German, reflects the linguistic complexity of the Austrian-Swiss-Italian border regions (Robert Janke).

more than linguistic matters alone, but language is the focus of a problem that has afflicted Canadian nation-building for generations. And Canada is not alone. Belgium, South Africa, India, Guatemala, and many other states face similar problems.

The test of the state in its effort to forge a national spirit lies in its ability to outweigh these inevitable liabilities with greater tangible assets. The pace of progress in modern Yugoslavia appears to have accomplished there what some historians predicted would not be done in this century; a stable state seems to be developing. Multilingual Switzerland survives, as does multiracial Brazil. There are alarming signs in the latter, but they are economic rather than racial. If a large population sector in any state begins to express the feeling that it would rather strike out on its own than continue its allegiance to the state, the system has failed. In some states, the nation has been held together by force, and the differences have lessened with time. Some of the emergent states are being held together in this way. And occasionally internal differences are submerged by outside interference or attack, and the population may emerge from the hostilities with a newfound sense of national pride and unity. This is a lesson that has not been lost on some of the leaders of the newly independent states, who have actually appeared to precipitate armed conflicts in order to rally their peoples. The reference, of course, is to certain southeast Asian states.

As states emerge, their territory well defined and limited by boundaries, their populations being forged into nations, and their economic development in progress, political geographers are able to observe some of the essential binding forces that hold states and nations together. All states have divisive forces within their boundaries—perhaps in the form of physical barriers to contact and communication, racial or other minorities, religious division, or possibly economically lagging areas. The degree to which a state succeeds in overcoming these centrifugal forces depends to a large extent upon its internal organization. Not only does governmental organization play a role here, but organization in practically every other sphere also. The power of a state is largely a function of its organization—military, economic, and otherwise. Its internal unity has much to do with organization in the field of education. Thus political geographers, in studying the evolution of the modern nation-state, must concern themselves not only with basic matters such as population numbers, densities, and skills, and territorial location, shape, and size, but also with the relevant aspects of the state's internal organization.

Environmentalism: Another View of Quality. Almost from the very first time man began to record his thoughts in writing, scientists and philosophers have expressed their interest in the relationships between human capacity and environmental quality. Do the cold climates of polar areas and the hot climes of tropical regions in some way inhibit man's capacity for thought or work—and break his will to have a hand in the kind of government to which he is subject? Do nations have greater difficulty forming in steppe or forest areas than in, say, open grassland country in the middle latitudes? Does the variable weather of the middle latitudes tend to stimulate mental and physical activity?

These are large questions, and there are no simple answers. The ancient Greeks and Romans thought, quite naturally, that *they* possessed environmental circumstances in such a combination that they were destined to achieve and maintain superiority. Later, writers in Western Europe attributed the ascendancy of the North Sea countries to the stimulus provided by the environment—principally the climate—of that region. And the twentieth century, too, has had its proponents of *environmental determinism*: the idea that man's behavior, including his ability to perform mentally and hence produce ideas in the field of politics, is in large measure determined by his natural environment.

The problem with the environmentalist philosophy (and it has had a considerable impact in political geography) lies in the deceptively easy and apparently obvious solutions that so frequently seem to present themselves. Western Europe's weather is varied, but neither extremely hot nor extremely cold, and here lies the cradle of the modern nation-state and the source of so much of the world's progress. In the tropics the climate is hot, humid, and debilitating. Is this why people subjected themselves to despotic regimes and succumbed to slavery? Here is how one geographer put it in 1940:

. . . The people of the cyclonic regions rank so far above those of other parts of the world that they are the natural leaders . . . the . . . contrast between the energetic people of the most progressive parts of the temperate zone and inert inhabitants of the tropics and even of intermediate regions, such as Persia, is largely due to climate.[8]

What of those parts of the world where such a favorable climate as western Europe's did not exist but where, nevertheless, great civilizations arose? Again there is a ready answer, and one not too difficult to conjure up: the climate must have been different when those societies made their great progress.

. . . Thus the whole of this area, from Persia to Egypt and from Arabia to the Caucasus, while it may not have been much cooler thousands of years ago than today, certainly had a heavier rainfall. Mesopotamia may also have had a less extreme range of temperature owing to the greater water expanse of the period. . . . This region, therefore, must have presented at that period of the world's history a well-watered, fertile plain with a less extreme but more rainy climate than today. . . .[9]

The early civilizations of the Americas, too, can be accounted for on environmental grounds:

. . . It is noteworthy that the Inca civilizations were born at an elevation of over 8,500 feet in average temperatures of 58 F. or less; the Aztec civilizations developed at 7,000 feet in a mean temperature of about 60 , and the Maya civilizations developed in areas over 4,000 feet high in average temperatures (as far as one can estimate) of between 65 and 68 F.[10]

Does all this mean that states in climatic areas of unsuitable character have little or no hope of making substantial progress, achieving nationhood, and developing a high level of civilization (whatever that may involve)? Not necessarily. Obviously there are certain relationships between man's natural environment and his individual and collective behavior. At least to that point, Huntington and Markham and others were on the right track. But whether these relationships involve *determinism*—that question is far from proved. Those who believed in the old environmentalist philosophy did not shun research; Ellsworth Huntington was the most prolific

[8]E. Huntington, *Principles of Human Geography*, New York, Wiley, 1940, pp. 339 and 471.

[9]S.F. Markham, *Climate and the Energy of Nations*, London, Oxford, 1947, p. 16.

[10]Ibid., p. 65.

geographer-author ever, and he obtained his data through field observation, the distribution of questionnaires, and an enormous correspondence. But the deceptive simplicity of the determinist solution conceals a very complicated interaction of factors, an interaction whose exact nature is still not known. Predictably, the determinist concept led to ideas about master races and natural inferiors, ideas that were unacceptable to a world rendered sensitive to racism by World War II and its aftermath. But today, there is a renewed interest in questions about man and his environment, and scientists are trying again to gain some insights into the ecology of man. This time, however, they are asking the questions more carefully, and large-scale, "obvious" solutions are no longer accepted out of hand.

Population Growth. World population, which is growing at an increasing rate and presently totals well over 3½ billion, is undergoing a cycle of expansion in which several distinct stages can be recognized. Various states are at different stages in this cycle, which is closely related to the introduction of modern amenities in such fields of health and education, and is reflected by the state's degree of urbanization, industrial development, literacy rates, and so forth. Basically, the sequence is this: During the first stage (in which most of the world found itself prior to the revolutions of the late 1700's) both birth rates and death rates are high, resulting in a fluctuating population which increases but slowly. In time of famine and plague, severe setbacks occur, and then the population gains again for a period of time. During the second stage, as various aspects of development take effect, death rates are reduced. Health conditions improve, sanitary standards are raised, diseases and epidemics are fought successfully. The result is an ever-increasing excess of births over deaths and an "exploding" population. This is largely true because while health conditions get better, socioeconomic conditions remain virtually unchanged. It is still desirable to have a large family to help in the farm work and to bring in wealth. In many of the colonial areas the Western world brought better hygienic conditions, but could not stimulate social change. The third stage, as exemplified by several Western European countries, is one of renewed stability, a "leveling off" of the rate of increase. As people become educated and urbanization and industrialization take effect, there are social and financial restraints to having a large family. In the case of France, these factors and a considerable amount of emigration by younger people caused such a slowdown in births that the government became alarmed and began to support family increase by offering tax reductions and other incentives.

Although it is difficult to classify the world's states according to the growth stage in which they find themselves—and various regions of states may actually be at different stages in the cycle—the matter is nevertheless a crucial one in political geography. It is probably true that every group of people who became united in a state—either in recent centuries in Western Europe or thousands of years ago in the Middle East—underwent changes in this respect. Probably the most dramatic changes ever to occur took place as a result of the technological revolutions of Europe, but it is worth remembering that rapid technological progress also took place in the Indian states of the Americas and the indigenous states of Africa. Unfortunately we have no censuses to prove the point, but those early heartlands of political development probably also experienced a mushrooming of population. The Inca Empire, for example, was able to send tens of thousands of residents from the central parts of the state to newly incorporated, outlying districts, with the aim of pacifying the local peoples and introducing modern agricultural techniques. If the conditions of the first stage (as we view it) of the population growth cycle had prevailed in that region at that time, such emigration could not have been sustained.

When today a state experiences the impact of modern change, of "development," are the changes that occur similar to those recorded in Europe after 1700? Can the lessons of geography and politics be applied in the presently emerging world? The answer may well be no. Those states that are today still in the first stage of the cycle (some African and Asian states) are in many ways unlike preindustrial Europe. Population densities are higher today than they were three centuries ago, so that these emergent states have a different point of departure. Europe's mortality rates declined relatively slowly as the changes caused by the industrial revolution took effect; the Western contribution to its colonial realms brought far more sudden declines in death rates. Thus the

rates of population increase (the "explosion") in developing, urbanizing, industrializing western Europe in its second stage were probably less than they are and will be in many developing states now experiencing these conditions. If these arguments are valid (that conditions during western Europe's first and second stages both differ importantly from the same stages currently prevailing elsewhere), then there is reason to believe that the third stage in, say, India may not be identical to that of France or Great Britain. In other words, the thesis that the ultimate fate of the population growth cycle is stability, based upon the European experience, may well be invalid.

Demographic data are vitally important to political geography, but they also present some of the greatest problems. In many parts of the world, few or no censuses have been taken, and those that have been taken may be unreliable and inadequate. In order to evaluate such factors as those discussed above in any consideration of a state such as Pakistan or Nigeria, detailed information regarding wage levels, schooling, terms of residence in towns and villages, and many other data are necessary. More often than not, such data are not available, and interpretations and conclusions become subjective and doubtful. Not long ago, Nigeria's population was usually listed in geography texts and elsewhere as about 36 million, based on the last census. Then the first census after independence revealed that the figure was 55 million. This meant that the political balance sheet in this country required complete review, as will be seen in a later chapter. But clearly, if errors of such magnitude can prevail in the relatively simple matter of counting heads, the reliability of any other data concerning wages, taxes, religious preferences, languages spoken, etc., must be open to question.

The Age-Sex Pyramid

One manner in which the population of any state can be quickly characterized is by means of the age-sex pyramid.[11] The figures indicate the number of persons within various age groups for both sexes living in the country at a given time, so that the ratios can be recognized at a glance. The pyramid representing France,

[11]For a discussion of this and related matters see D.H. Wrong, *Population and Society*, New York, Random House, 1961.

for example, shows a top-heavy population including a great number of older people, while Japan is marked by losses sustained during the last war. The war also shows its effect upon the population of the United Kingdom. Although these pyramids do not reveal anything regarding the spatial distribution of the people involved, they do indicate much concerning longevity, changing male-female ratios (which can be severely disturbed by war or migration), and perhaps the effects of migration. They do not provide much help in detail, but they do form one of those tools used by the political geographer who wishes to gain an insight into the problems of any state as a whole.

Population Policies. Finally, several states have population policies that may reveal much concerning their internal demographic conditions. Those states that have *expansive* population policies desire an increase in the growth rate, and reward large families by tax reduction and even elimination, birth premiums, loans and allowances, and even public praise. The Soviet Union, which desires growth in view of the vastness of its territory and the need for eastward spread of effective occupance, is a case in point. Bulletin boards in Soviet cities often display photographs of local women who have given birth to their tenth child, with a commending caption and an announcement of an award.

A *restrictive* policy, aimed at the reduction of birth rates, may be reflected by government-sponsored education of the public in methods of contraception, the rendering available of contraceptive equipment, and an absence of financial reward (low tax reductions per child, for example) for growing families. Some of the emergent states are seeking the assistance of Western countries in the spread of information regarding contraceptives, and are establishing clinics to make such materials available to their people. The impact to date can only be described as minimal, but the very existence of the practice in these countries is of great significance. And the developed world, too, desires a reduction of the population growth rate; in the United States, policies that at first sight seem expansive in nature are actually restrictive, for the tax relief granted to parents for each child is minimal compared to the immense cost of adequately clothing, feeding, and educating that child.

Eugenic population policies, finally, are those that seek to support one racial group within a country over others. The prime example is the Nazi effort on behalf of the "superior race;" current policies in Australia, aimed at the exclusion of races other than the "European," may be so described. Perhaps the most important current case is that of South Africa, where government projects involve the relocation of Africans and other nonwhites to certain restricted "homelands," while the major part of the country is made available to the whites. Meanwhile the immigration of Europeans is encouraged while that of other races is either forbidden or severely controlled.

Subsequently it will be seen that all these factors play their role in the study of political geography. Among the several distinct approaches within the field, there is one that attempts to determine the degree of internal cohesion of any given state—that is, it weighs the unifying elements of the state against those that tend to divide. In this area of political geography, obviously, such demographic matters as considered above are of major importance.[12]

It is difficult to recognize in a politicogeographical map which was itself the result of a very unorderly sequence of events. One way to begin is to establish a terminology for those features that show some repetition. Another way is to remember that all states are moving along a continuum toward an ideal—the nation-state—of which there may be different versions in various parts of the world, but versions that are coming closer and closer together. Some states are failing and are retrogressing, while others are forging rapidly ahead. Certain states are far developed in several spheres, only to lag behind in others; the most powerful state in the world, and the most developed economically, faces a critical problem of racionational unity. In terms of the two elements of the state here discussed, however, there are two major conditions prevailing today that never did mark the majority of the many ancient states of history. First, all states have "legal" nations (if not "emotional" nations) and the time of the uncertain frontier has come to an end; and second, all states have clearly defined and fixed territories, with exact size and permanent shape.

---

[12]For a study containing useful materials in this connection see K. and A.F.K. Organski, *Population and World Power*, New York, Knopf, 1961. See especially pp. 183 ff. Also see P.E.P. (Political and Economic Planning), *World Population and Resources*, London, Allen & Unwin, 1962.

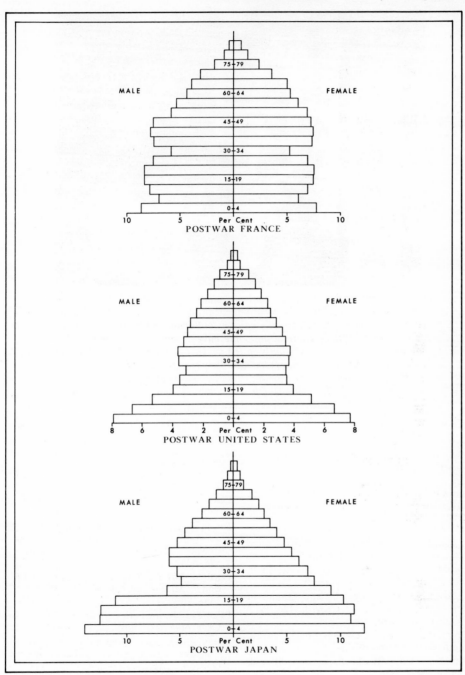

MALE   75-79   FEMALE
              60-64
              45-49
              30-34
              15-19
               0-4
10   5   Per Cent   5   10
POSTWAR FRANCE

MALE   75-79   FEMALE
              60-64
              45-49
              30-34
              15-19
               0-4
8   6   4   2   Per Cent   2   4   6   8
POSTWAR UNITED STATES

MALE   75-79   FEMALE
              60-64
              45-49
              30-34
              15-19
               0-4
10   5   Per Cent   5   10
POSTWAR JAPAN

In every Soviet town, bulletin boards are placed in prominent positions and carefully maintained to reflect current local and national events. In some cities these boards carry the daily editions of Pravda and Izvestia as well as cultural and political information; some have "permanent" corners where certain people are kept constantly in the public eye, such as Cuban Premier Fidel Castro. Among local individuals publicly honored are the mothers of ten or more children, as the Soviet Union is engaged in an expansionist population policy. This photograph was taken in Leningrad in 1964, when Premier Nikita S. Khrushchev was still in power (Harm J. de Blij).

REFERENCES

Ahmed, Anis-Ud-Din, "A Geographer's Approach Towards the Problem of National Language of Pakistan," *Pakistan Geog. Rev.*, 10, 1 (1955), 17–24.

Bogue, Donald J., *The Population of the United States.* Glencoe, Ill., The Free Press, 1959.

Bone, Robert C., "Will Indonesia Disintegrate?" *Foreign Policy Bull*, 36, 16 (May, 1957), 125–127.

Caroe, Sir Olaf, "The Geography and Ethnics of India's Northern Frontiers," *Geog. J.*, 126, Pt. 3 (September, 1960), 298–309.

Carrington, C.E., *Gibralter.* London, Royal Institute of International Affairs, 1956.

Carr-Saunders, A.M., *World Population.* Oxford, Clarendon Press, 1936.

Chidell, Fleetwood, *Australia—White or Yellow.* London, Heineman, 1926.

Clarke, J.I., *Population Geography* (2nd ed.), Oxford, Pergamon Press, 1972.

Condominas, Georges, "Aspects of a Minority Problem in Indochina," *Pacific Affairs*, 24, 1 (March, 1951), 77–82.

Crawshaw, Nancy, "The Republic of Cyprus; from Zurich Agreement to Independence," *World Today*, 16, 12 (December, 1960), 526–540.

Cunningham, J.K., "A Politico-geographical Appreciation of New Zealand Foreign Policy," *New Zealand Geographer*, 14, 2 (October, 1958), 147–160.

Davis, Kingsley, "Population," *Sci. Amer.*, 209, 3 (September, 1963), 62–71.

Eason, Warren W., "The Soviet Population Today; an Analysis of the First Results of the 1959 Census," *Foreign Affairs*, 37, 4 (July, 1959), 598–606.

Fairfield, Roy P., "Cyprus: Revolution and Resolution," *Middle East J.*, 13, 3 (Summer, 1959), 235–248.

Faladreau, Jean-Charles, "French Canada Today," *Geog. Mag.*, 32, 3 (July, 1959), 107–120.

Farran, C. d'Olivier, "International Enclaves and the Question of State Servitude," *Int. and Comp. Law Quar.*, 4, 2 (April, 1955), 294–307.

Flugal, Raymond R., "The Palestine Problem; A Brief Geographical, Historical, and Political Evaluation," *Social Studies*, 48, 2 (February, 1957), 43–51.

Gann, Lewis H., and Peter Duignan, *White Settlers in Tropical Africa.* Harmondsworth, Penguin Books, 1962.

Ginsburg, Norton, "Natural Resources and Economic Development," *Ann. A.A.G.*, 47, 3 (September, 1957), 197–212.

Gregory, J.W., *Race as a Political Factor.* London, Watts and Company, 1931.

Harding, Sir John, "The Cyprus Problem in Relation to the Middle East," *Internat. Affairs, 34,* 3 (July, 1958), 291–296.

Haupert, J.S., "The Impact of Geographic Location upon Sweden as a Baltic Power," *J. Geography, 58,* 1 (January, 1959), 5–14.

Hauser, Philip M., and Otis Dudley Duncan, *The Study of Population; and Inventory and Appraisal.* Chicago, The University of Chicago Press, 1959.

Heenan, L.D.B., "The Population Pyramid: a Versatile Research Technique," *Prof. Geog., 17,* 2 (March, 1965), 18–21.

Herman, Theodore, "Group Values Toward the National Space: the Case of China," *Geog. Rev., 49,* 2 (April, 1959), 164–182.

Hertz, F., *Nationality in History and Politics.* London, Kegan Paul, Trench, Trubner & Co., 1944.

Huntington, Ellsworth, "The Arabian Desert and Human Character," *J. Geography, 10* (1912), 169–175.

———, *Civilization and Climate.* New Haven, Conn., Yale University Press, 1924.

———, "The Geography of Human Productivity," *Ann. A.A.G., 33,* 1 (March, 1943), 1–31.

———, "The Relation of Health to Racial Capacity: The Example of Mexico," *Geog. Rev., 11,* 2 (April, 1921), 243–264.

———, "Season of Birth and the Distribution of Civilization," abstract, *Ann. A.A.G., 27,* 2 (June, 1937), 109–110.

Huxley, Elspeth, and Margery Perham, *Race and Politics in Kenya.* London, Faber and Faber, 1956.

Jones, Emrys, "Problems of Partition and Segregation in Northern Ireland," *J. Conflict Resolution, 4,* 1 (March, 1960), 96–105.

Krenz, Frank E., *International Enclaves and Rights of Passage.* Geneva and Paris, E. Droz and Minard, 1961.

Kurganov, Ivan, "The Problem of Nationality in Soviet Russia," *Russian Rev., 10,* 4 (October, 1951), 253–267.

Lambert, Richard D., "Factors in Bengali Regionalism in Pakistan," *Far Eastern Survey, 28,* 4 (April, 1959), 49–58.

Lee, D.R., and G.T. Sallee, "A Method of Measuring Shape," *Geog. Rev. 60,* 4 (October, 1970), 555–563.

LePage, R.B., *The National Language Question.* New York, Oxford University Press, 1964.

Lijphart, Arend, "The Indonesian Image of West Irian," *Asian Survey, 1,* 5 (July, 1961), 9–15.

Losch, August, *The Economics of Location* (trans. by William H. Woglom). New Haven, Conn., Yale University Press, 1954.

Lorimer, F., *The Population of the Soviet Union.* Geneva, League of Nations, 1946.

Lowenthal, David, "Population Contrasts in the Guianas," *Geog. Rev., 50,* 1 (January, 1960), 41–58.

Lowry, M., "Racial Segregation: a Geographical Adaptation and Analysis," *Jour. Geog., LXXI,* 1 (January, 1972), 28–40.

Markham, S.F., *Climate and the Energy of Nations.* London, New York, Oxford University Press, 1944.

Maron, Stanley, "The Problem of East Pakistan," *Pacific Affairs, 28,* 2 (June, 1955), 132–144.

Martin, Howard H., "A Geographic Interpretation of the Japanese Population Curve," abstract, *Ann. A.A.G., 25,* 1 (March, 1935), 48–49.

Martovych, Oleh R. (pseud. for John F. Stewart), *National Problems in the U.S.S.R.* Edinburgh, Scottish League for European Union, 1953.

Melamid, Alexander, "Partitioning Cyprus; A Class Exercise in Applied Political Geography," *J. Geog., 59,* 3 (March, 1960), 118–122.

Mudd, Stuart (ed.-in-chief), *The Population Crisis and the Use of World Resources.* Bloomington, Indiana University Press, for World Academy of Art and Science, 1964.

Murray, R. Allan, "Two Brazils," *Geog. Mag., 25,* 2 (June, 1952), 94–104; 25, 4 (August, 1952), 157–166.

Nel, A., "Geographical Aspects of Apartheid in South Africa," *Tijdschrift voor Economische en Sociale Geografie, 53,* Jaarg., 10 (October, 1962), 215–217.

Newbigin, Marion I., *The Mediterranean Lands.* New York, Knopf, 1924.

Odell, Clarence B., "Significance of Population Studies in International Problems," abstract, *Ann. A.A.G., 37,* 1 (March, 1947), 56.

Organski, Katherine, and A.F.K. Organski, *Population and World Power.* New York, Knopf, 1961.

Osborne, Harold, *Bolivia, a Land Divided.* London, New York, Royal Institute of International Affairs, 1954.

Pakatas, Kazys, "Changing Population in Lithuania," *Lithuanus, 1,* 10 (March, 1957), 16–19.

Parker, Mary, "Race Relations and Political Development in Kenya," *African Affairs, 50,* 198 (January, 1951), 41–52.

Planhol, Xavier de, "Geography, Politics, and Nomadism in Anatolia," *Internat. Social Science J., 11,* 4 (1959), 525–531.

Robinson, E.A.G. (ed.), *Economic Consequences of the Size of Nations.* London, Macmillan, 1960.

Robinson, G.W.S., "Exclaves," *Ann. A.A.G., 49,* 3 (September, 1959), 283–295.

———, "West Berlin: the Geography of an Exclave," *Geog. Rev., 43,* 4 (October, 1953), 540–557.

Roxby, Percy M., "The Distribution of Population in China: economic and political significance," *Geog. Rev., 15,* 1 (January, 1925), 1–24.

Ryan, C., "The French-Canadian Dilemma," *Foreign Affairs, 43,* 3 (April, 1965), 462–474.

Scofield, John, "Jerusalem, the Divided City," *National Geographic, 115,* 4 (April, 1959), 492–531.

Seawall, F., and Jerome Clemens, "A Population Profile," *Prof. Geog., 16,* 2 (March, 1964), 20.

Smith, Wilfred Cantwell, "Hyderabad: Muslim Tragedy," *Middle East J., 4,* 1 (January, 1950), 27–51.

Spate, O.H.K., "Toynbee and Huntington: A Study

in Determinism," *Geog. J., 118* (1952), 406–428.

Stephenson, G.U., "Pakistan: Discontiguity and the Majority Problem," *Geog. Rev., 58,* 2 (April, 1968), 195–213.

Swan, Michael, *British Guiana; Land of the Six Peoples.* London, H.M. Stationery Office, 1957.

Sweet, John V., "The Problem of Nationalities in Soviet Asia," *Ukrainian Quart., 10,* (1954), 229–235.

Thomas, Franklin, *The Environmental Basis of Society.* New York, Century, 1925.

Turner, F.J., "Geographical Influences in American Political History," *Bull. Amer. Geog. Soc., 46* (1914), 591–595.

Van der Kroef, Justus M., "Disunited Indonesia," *Far East Survey, 27,* 4 (April, 1958), 49–63; *27,* 5 (May, 1958), 73–80.

———, "Indonesia: Sources of Disunity," *Orbis, 2,* 4 (Winter, 1959), 478–491.

Van Heerden, W., "Why Bantu States?" *Optima, 12,* 2 (June, 1962), 59–65.

Walker, P.C. Gordon, "The Future of 'City and Island States,'" *New Commonwealth, 29,* 8 (April, 1955), 369–371.

Ward, R. De C., "Primitive Civilization and the Tropics," *J. Geog., 6* (1908), 224–226.

Weihl, Alfred, "Altitude and Settlement in North America," *Geog. Rev.,* note, *16,* 1 (January, 1926), 136.

Whebell, C.F.J., "Models of Political Territory," *Proceedings,* A.A.G., 2 (1970), 152–156.

Wheeler, Geoffrey, *Racial Problems in Soviet Muslim Asia.* London, Oxford University Press, 1960.

Wheeler, Raymond H., "History Cycles and Climate," abstract, *Ann.* A.A.G., *29,* 1 (March, 1939), 99–100.

Whitbeck, R.H., and O.J. Thomas, *The Geographic Factor, Its Role in Life and Civilization.* New York, Century, 1932.

Whittlesey, Derwent, "Lands Athwart the Nile," *World Politics, 5,* 2 (January, 1953), 214–241.

———, "Southern Rhodesia—an African Compage," *Ann.* A.A.G., *46,* 1 (March, 1956), 1–97.

Woytinsky, W.S., and E.S. Woytinsky, *World Population and Production: Trends and Outlook.* New York, Twentieth Century Fund, 1953.

Wrong, Dennis H., *Population and Society.* New York, Random House, 1961.

Zelinsky, W., "Beyond the Exponentials; the Role of Geography in the Great Transition," *Econ. Geog., 46,* 3 (July, 1970), 498–535.

CHAPTER
4

THE ELEMENTS OF THE STATE: ORGANIZATION AND POWER

All states—and indeed all political entities on the world map—possess a certain degree of organization. Practically every kind of organization, in whatever sphere of life, has some relevance in political geography. The manner in which a state has organized the exploitation of its resources is a partial determinant of its power. One of the great strengths of the United States of America lies in the availability of higher education to so many citizens. This, too, is an aspect of organization. Tax collection and boundary control, the power of religious organizations, the strength of local, traditional organizations—all these have bearing upon the political geography of any state.

Power is largely a function of organization, and in any discussion it is impossible to separate one from the other. This is true in the case of internal power (which is largely institutional) as well as external power. Studies of internal power concern themselves mainly with the effectiveness of governmental control—for example, the ways in which a state has dealt with the problem of isolated or outlying areas that must be integrated into the framework of the state. By external power is meant the amount of influence a state has in the political world, which depends, of course, upon its proven ability to enforce its desires through economic or military activity. Thus by studying organization under four headings —governmental, economic, military, and various other forms—a measure is obtained of the internal (governmental, institutional) power of the state as well as its external (political) power, its economic power, its war power, and its power over opinion in the outside world.

GOVERNMENTAL ORGANIZATION

Government plays a large part in the internal and external relationships of the state, more today than ever before. Thus the type of government a state has adopted is an important factor in political geography. In the older states, the present-day politicoterritorial organization reflects a long period of trial and adjustment, and the emergent states are adopting similar forms of internal organization, some of which seem destined to change radically. Several different aspects of governmental organization are relevant here. With the exception of the microstates, all modern states are divided, for purposes of administration, into subunits. At times these subunits (provinces, states, or other entities) have aims and desires that are at odds with national goals, and friction may occur. But once an administrative pattern is established and has been in operation for some time, it becomes very difficult to change. Lines of demarcation have been drawn, and many governmental agencies' operations within the state are based upon this geographical framework. Hence such internal difficulties are often resolved through institutional rather than geographic change.

This subject will be discussed again in Chapters 16 and 17, for it involves the entire issue of choice of government, individual freedom, and regional autonomy. Several political geographers have attempted to relate the degree of national strength and cohesion of a state to the quality of its democratic institutions. Van Valkenburg, in his discussion of the fortunes of democracy in states at various stages in their politicogeographical evolution, argued that

The number of democracies has declined within recent years, not because of the failure of the democratic form of government as such but because it was applied in many instances to countries politically immature. Only countries in the mature stage of development are able to use democracy to advantage, and it is up to them to preserve that most precious possession, liberty, until others will mature enough to use it as a base of government.[1]

[1]S. Van Valkenburg, *Elements of Political Geography*, New York, Prentice-Hall, 1939, p. 308.

Politicoterritorial organization and the landscape. While the boundaries visible on these two photographs are not political boundaries, they nevertheless tell us much about the politicohistorical development of the regions involved. Left: In the central parts of the United States, the Township and Range System has not only produced the unmistakable, regular pattern of fields and roads, but has to a considerable extent also controlled the county subdivision of the region, which shows similar straight-line characteristics. Right: In Western Ireland, on the other hand, the pattern is less regular—it shows subsequent rather than antecedent characteristics (see Chapter 7). The lower photograph is quite representative of the English or French countryside, and reflects a very different sequence of development than that of Illinois (Harm J. de Blij).

Actually, this is only one aspect of governmental organization—the extent to which the individuals in the nation participate in politics and government. Describing the effect of the nature of government upon the degree of a state's power as difficult to assess, Stoessinger adds: "It is tempting to assume that a democratic form of government provides greater national strength than a dictatorship. Yet though the historical record does not invalidate this assumption, it certainly places it in question."[2]

Certainly modern totalitarianism has proved capable of persuading large numbers of people to subscribe to it, through indoctrination programs, youth movements, and isolation from the outside world (depriving the governed of opportunities to compare). Widespread consent now marks the attitude of the populations of several totalitarian states. But the greatest advantage appears to lie in the totalitarian government's capacity to turn the entire economic and military effort into a certain desired direction, without fear of argument, strikes, or lack of public support: ". . . geography is turned to strategic advantage, and population and natural resources become twin pillars of power—military preparedness and industrialization."[3]

Thus there are three areas of emphasis under the present heading. One is the politicogeographical framework, literally, of the state: the manner in which it is delimited on maps, demarcated on the ground, and operative administratively. The second is the degree of centralization of government and the effect of governmental organization and practices upon

[2]J.G. Stoessinger, *The Might of Nations*, New York, Random House, 1961, p. 22.

[3]Ibid., p. 24.

The administrative divisions of states, represented by lines on political maps, are fixed by a variety of markers on the ground. In the United States, whenever one leaves or enters a county or state along any major artery, one is reminded by road signs. The slow evolution of the British politicoterritorial framework has produced a framework very different in its appearance on the map as well as in terms of structure. Top Left: the shire denotes county status, and frequently appears in county names. Counties comprise three types of district —Top Right: The borough. Left: Urban district; and rural district. All of these are themselves subdivided into parishes (Robert Janke).

the exploitation of the resource base and the use made of raw materials. The third includes the study of problems associated with governmental administration: tax collection in peripheral areas, erection of tariff barriers to protect local industries, official action to implement legislation, and so forth.

ECONOMIC ORGANIZATION

All states have resources. Some have very few such resources, while others have a major share, but no state can exist without any resources at all. Some states, however, have mobilized their limited resource base very diligently and, in so doing, have reaped rich rewards in terms of progress and stability and, incidentally, in the acquisition of power. Other states, on the other hand, have failed to exploit much of their resource base, for which a wide variety of reasons can usually be found. But however rich the subsoil may be known to be, the power of a state can only be measured in terms of resources actually available or available almost immediately, after only a brief period of adjustment.

One aspect of economic organization lies not only internally, but also externally. This is related to the ability of a state to command resources in other parts of the world in times of need. The United States today, for example, has trade agreements for raw materials with dozens of countries, and has paid for the exploitation of those overseas resources it desires. It imports petroleum from Venezuela and iron ore from Liberia, and its influence in both those countries is undeniably considerable. For some of its strategic projects, the United States requires certain scarce commodities, and its ability to acquire those commodities (like alloys, uranium, etc.) is one indication of its power. In addition, this country is aware of the possibility that certain strategic materials now being imported may be temporarily unavailable at some future time. Thus, supplies are stored for such emergencies, and the ability of a state to devote capital to such activity is another piece of evidence of its economic strength. Furthermore, the United States is capable of aiding allies by supplying them with necessary strategic commodities, while it also has the capacity, because of its influence in so many countries, to deny critical goods to its enemies. Sometimes it is not capable of isolating an actual or potential enemy as completely as would be desired, as the case of Cuba proved.

Organization in agriculture: a Soviet collective farm near Kharkov. Soviet efforts to increase the annual output of agricultural products have focused upon the collective, where various inducements (including slogans, exhortations, public praise, and prizes) are employed to ensure the maximum effort of every worker. Top: The central office of this particular collective is a virtual notice board for these purposes: posters, slogans, honored names, and prizes all are visible. Bottom: The results are often satisfactory, as constantly higher yields are sought and achieved. Two workers show the photographer the size of sugar beets grown on the collective farm (Harm J. de Blij).

But a great deal of influence over the world movement of essential commodities is a major indicator of economic power, and, of course, requires a complex organization to achieve.

Reference was made previously to the degree of availability of resources. S.B. Jones has categorized the state's resources in order to clarify the weight such actual and potential resources should carry in any evaluation of the state's power.[4] Five groups are recognized:

1. *Power resources available immediately.* These include the standing army, stockpiled ammunition, mines that are operating, factories producing equipment of immediate use.

[4]S.B. Jones, "The Power Inventory and National Strategy," *World Politics,* VI, 4 (1954), 421 ff.

2. *Power resources available after activation.* The reserve army, military equipment that has been temporarily stored (such as mothballed ships and aircraft), factories and mines not operating but capable of operation within at most a few weeks.

3. *Power resources available after conversion.* A factory producing passenger cars could turn to the production of army equipment, but only after the entire assembly line has been converted, a process which may take several months. Untrained but eligible men for army duty also are included here.

4. *Power resources available after development.* Mineral and fuel deposits which are known to exist but have as yet not been

mined. Materials which are known to be useful but which have not been mass-produced, like synthetic rubber prior to 1942.

5. *Hypothetical resources.* Deposits whose existence is conjectured but has not been proved. These resources do not have any power value, but any urgent need might lead to vigorous exploration and exploitation in areas where such important resources might lie.

Some idea of the "have" and the "have-not" states of the world can be gained from the simple exercise of placing an overlay showing the international boundaries on top of maps indicating major fuel and mineral deposits and reserves, and further insights can be obtained by doing the same with maps of productive capacity of soils, actual agricultural production, and density of population. But such maps do not tell the whole story; they do not reveal the important element of organization. Anyone who has seen the network of American roads and railroads, its ports, the complexity of its cities' industrial distircts, the rapid and efficient movement of goods, and the labor-saving machinery constantly being introduced, will be aware of the significance of organization in the economy of any state. A map of world transport systems gives some indication, but there is much more to be considered than that.

MILITARY ORGANIZATION

Stoessinger has defined power as "the capacity of a nation to use its tangible and intangible resources in such a way as to affect the behavior of other nations."[5] The most obvious way to affect such behavior is through military intervention, and this can be done only if a state possesses a sufficient quantity of Jones' "immediately available resources" to permit the deployment overseas of a military force.

Most states possess military forces and thus have some form of military organization. Some countries spend little annually to maintain a skeleton force; in the absence of actual or potential enemies, such an army is used mainly to assist the police in keeping internal control. But other countries, possessed of ideological drive and in support of economic motives, maintain huge armed forces the like of which the world has never seen. Other countries, in the face of actual and/or potential

enemies, are in the process of building armies well beyond the average for their size. South Africa's armed forces are already the largest and best equipped in Africa, and the country is pouring more resources into its army, navy, and air force each year. For South Africa, this is a matter of security in the face of an increasingly hostile black Africa. Israel's armed forces already have had occasion to prove that they are unusually strong for a state of its size. In other parts of the world, the army in effect rules the country, directly or indirectly.

The state with the most far-flung armies in the world (and, in terms of quantity, in world history), of course, is the United States. Very few years go by when Americans do not get an illustration of the nature of military power. Korea, Lebanon, South Viet Nam—each of these cases fits the Stoessinger definition of United States power. Again, the key to such an effective military arm is organization. Armies require a constant supply of manpower, ever improving equipment which is the result of constant research, and never-ending supplies of fuel. Occasionally the returns to the state and its people are in the form of combat, but more often the very existence of such armed might does exactly what, according to our definition, power should do: it causes other states to act in ways that evince a recognition of United States desires.

POWER ANALYSIS

In 1950, R. Hartshorne, writing about the field of political geography and its methodology, suggested that four distinct approaches could be recognized.[6] Chapter 3 deals to some extent with one of these approaches: the so-called *morphological* approach, which involves the study of patterns, structures, and shapes as they exist. Two of the other approaches, namely the *historical* approach and the *functional* approach, will be utilized later in this book. The historical approach, though not frequently employed, is a very fruitful one and formed one of the bases for a famous work in the field of political geography.[7] The functional approach concerns itself with the cohesive

[5]J.G. Stoessinger, op. cit., p. 31.

[6]R. Hartshorne, "Political Geography," in Preston E. James and Clarence F. Jones (eds.), *American Geography: Inventory and Prospect*, Syracuse University Press, 1954, pp. 174 ff.

[7]D. Whittlesey, *The Earth and the State*, New York, Holt, 1939.

and divisive forces within the state and their effects upon the interacting parts of the territorial system making up the state.

The remaining approach emphasized by Hartshorne is that of *power analysis*. This approach involves the weighing of many factors, geographical and nongeographical, in an attempt to arrive at an index of national power for each state. Environment and resources, circulation and communication, quality and quantity of population, and state organization in all its forms are included here. Clearly such an approach remains to a considerable extent subjective, and no two geographers would probably agree on the exact procedures to be followed. Nevertheless, the results of such efforts are often significant.

The article that follows is an example of power analysis. Although written more than a decade ago, it remains of substantial interest today. Note in the section entitled *Explanatory Notes to Table 1* how the author coped with the problems of converting basic data on the area and population of states into meaningful indices. You may disagree with his decisions and wish to substitute other information; certainly the derivations Professor German makes are not necessarily of absolute validity. On the basis of his 1960 analysis, the major powers of the world and their point scores (see Table 1 of article) ranked as follows:

1.	United States	6459
2.	Russia	6321
3.	United Kingdom	1257
4.	China	999
5.	West Germany	663 1/2
6.	Canada	498
7.	Japan	410 1/2

Today, the situation might be substantially changed. Look into Professor German's sources for the most recent years you can obtain (the United Nations Yearbooks for the early 1970's should be available to you at the library) and see whether the situation has changed at all. Intuitively, would you feel that China's relative position has improved? Would Japan still rank behind Canada? Have factors emerged since 1960 that you feel should be included now in the tabulation of criteria? The article follows.

A Tentative Evaluation
of World Power

F. Clifford German

Cambridge University

Throughout history the decisive factor in the fates of nations has usually been the number, efficiency, and disposition of fighting forces. This power has been in the hands of a few military leaders and has generally been used for direct military domination. Now, however, we are faced with a new situation. In spite of the existence of the hydrogen bomb and the perfected guided missile, the weapons of the nations are not overwhelmingly military, for the two major camps are unlikely, short of desperation, to seek a solution in war. Instead, these two groups are now engaged in a tactical, economic, and ideological conflict on a world-wide scale aimed at achieving paramount economic and political influence rather than at conquest. It follows that the weapons of the struggle are now more varied and depend on much more than major military and diplomatic leaders. It does, however, remain largely true that national influence bears a direct relationship to gross national strength; without that, the most exquisite statesmanship is likely to be of limited use. Even without nuclear war the outcome of the present rivalry will have a decisive, far-reaching, and possibly irrevocable effect on the lives of billions of people, now and far into the future. Consequently, the evaluation of the sources of any nation's strength deserves careful consideration.

The writer has attempted, therefore, to compile a blend of admittedly selected statistics and judgments to summarize and compare the over-all past, present, and future strength of various nations by giving a numerical value to all factors considered relevant, whatever their origin. The difficulties and shortcomings involved are obvious; although experts can describe a nation's military disposition, or its confidence and determination, or the nature

F. Clifford German, "A Tentative Evaluation of World Power," *Journal of Conflict Resolution*, Vol. 4 (1960), 138–144.

and volume of production, or population trends in general terms with considerable accuracy, it is necessary to combine and compare different qualities by applying selective and subjective criteria in order to reach the desired over-all impression. Since it is impossible to claim absolute scientific detachment, it is pointless to complicate the statistics too far or to give a false impression of accuracy and attention to detail. With these reservations, certain key elements have been selected as representative indexes of productivity, industrial power, defensibility, and self-sufficiency. They have been chosen within the limitations of available statistics to come as close as possible to the general truth in all cases and places rather than as a summation of each and every complex modifying factor. Statistics themselves present a problem; the latest figures for some countries and some factors may not be immediately available, and it may be necessary to go back some while to get absolutely contemporaneous material. Some sacrifice of either realism or immediacy is unavoidable. As a compromise, and to allow comparisons to be carried further than the scope of the present article, the source material is derived from two sources only—the United Nations *Statistical Yearbooks*, principally for 1958, and the *Statesman's Yearbook* for 1959, where this contains additional or significantly more recent information.

Four basic dimensions have been selected and then modified and added in order to show the interplay of other factors and to obtain a sum total representing an estimate of total national strength. The four are: (1) national economy, which includes the resources of agriculture, minerals, raw materials, and industry; (2) land and (3) population (both used advisedly to avoid the implications of *Raum* and *Volk*); and (4) military power. Together, these four factors cover the field of natural and human resources, but for most practical purposes, of course, they are interdependent.

Land is the simplest to consider. Sheer area is undeniably a potent factor; it contributes as much to the strength of the Soviet Union at the present time as it did to the weakness of Nazi Germany between 1942 and 1945. Room for dispersal and maneuver are considerable assets, and their value is enhanced if they are facilitated by the possession of adequate communications; empty space and inaccessible areas are virtually liabilities. For the purposes of this article, the basis of calculation is the national area in thousands of square kilometers. This figure is divided by 5, 10, or 20, according to the effectiveness of national occupancy, represented by a scale of population density, and still further reduced in most cases by a third, a half, or two-thirds, according to the excellence or otherwise of communications. This is measured by the proportion of railroad mileage to area. This is probably the fairest simple measure, since in many parts of the world roads do little more than feed or duplicate rail facilities.

Population in terms of manpower is another basic factor but not a simple one. Total numbers are only significant in that they include young people, the next working generation; this is generally a significantly smaller proportion in western Europe than elsewhere. Only those people between fifteen and sixty, the active working population, are considered here. Then, since food is literally a vital commodity, the number of the total population surplus to home-produced food supply is deducted, or the hypothetical number of people who could be fed by a food surplus is added.

A further set of factors is brought to bear, loosely termed "morale." Certain countries, through corruption, apathy, or poverty, do not mobilize their human resources effectively, while it seems certain, for example, that the momentum of Russian and Chinese industrial advance gains much from the single-mindedness of their peoples' desire for progress, and a similar effect is produced in most capitalist countries by the operation of economic incentive. Up to 50 per cent of the total working population may be added to represent this.

We should note that the vastly greater productivity of most workers in the Western, and in parts of the Communist, world is partly balanced by the fact that a much greater per capita consumption of food and goods is considered essential, working hours are shorter, and much wealth is diverted into consumer goods of little worth in increasing the strength of a nation. (In this category must be included much of the United States annual automobile production.) Similarly, the ability of much of the population of underdeveloped countries to subsist on much less than would be demanded as a minimum elsewhere is considered part compensation for the lower yields per annum and in assessing the extent of overpopulation reckoned above. In spite of this, however, technical efficiency has now reached such a level of achievement in some parts of the world that a considerable further factor has been applied to the active working population on the basis of consumption of energy per year per head of the population, and measured in terms of tons of coal equivalent, to bridge the gap between the productivity of, say, an Indian peasant beset by all the difficulties of economic and social backwardness and, say, a Stakhanovite steelworker whose labor is assisted by the ultimate in capital, organization, and machinery. Consequently, the working population has been increased in some cases up to five times. Since industry is usually more productive and powerful than agriculture, the numbers employed in manufacturing are counted five times more. For this purpose, employment in service industries has been excluded, since this may mean anyone from a businessman to a barber.

Significant though it is in itself, it is clear that population need bear little relationship to resources, developed or latent. Perhaps the best guide to industrial strength is the production of steel and energy; either or both must be considered fundamental for most industry. Little can be accomplished without them, and they are essential for industrial expansion and diversification. Crude steel production in hundreds of thousands of tons per annum is added to coal and oil production in millions of tons and to hydroelectric energy converted into millions of tons of coal equivalent. Naturally, it is almost impossible to ascertain with any degree of accuracy the enormous strategic gain of the Communist countries, or of any efficient and determined dictatorship, in dispensing with supply and demand and the free-market economy, liberating for them an immense amount of capital, skill, labor power, and steel to produce capital goods such as trucks, tractors, and machine tools. As a rough makeweight, Communist industrial production, as defined above, has been doubled. If, as is probably true, more than double goes into strategic production, it must compensate for much basic construction such as railroads and bridges and for pioneer development still taking place in most Communist countries.

While absolute industrial production is a considerable asset, relative abundance is as important for industrial goods and raw materials as for food. Middle East oil is of great international significance because it is available for export to deficit countries, which in turn must be considered weakened by their dependence on an outside source. For each of four strategic materials—steel, oil, metallic minerals, and engineering products—a figure equal to 5 or 10 per cent of the combined steel and energy total given above may be added to or subtracted from that total to account for deficits or surpluses to present needs. In this way, the strategic advantages of self-sufficiency and industrial diversification, great sources of strength to the United States and the U.S.S.R. and of weakness to the European industrial powers which rely greatly on trade for most raw materials and many industrial goods, are taken into account.

The sum totals so far represent the contributions of the physical, human, and economic resources of a nation to its power and may show the particular sources of any nation's strength or weakness, balance or disbalance, in times of peace. But, whether we like it or not, national strength must still be considered enhanced by military preparedness. Ten times a nation's total military personnel in millions should be added to the non-military total. This is not in itself a very considerable factor and truly reflects the relative unimportance of conventional weapons in assessing differences between the medium-sized powers, especially in different areas of the world. But, for the purpose of assessing true political power, the possession of nuclear weapons and the means of delivering them has been considered as at least doubling the sum total of all other factors taken together. In practice this really affects only three powers at the present time, but it is a useful method of emphasizing the great gap in world importance between the two leading powers and all other contenders and of illustrating the theoretical independence of action which the United Kingdom derives from its nuclear weapons. It can also be taken as giving as indication of what might happen to the balance of world power if one nation's means of delivering nuclear weapons were to become so obsolescent as to be virtually ineffective.

Table 1 shows two giant powers, each at least five times as strong as its closest rival. The United States is still in first place, with the Soviet Union second but incomparably closer than she would have been even five years ago; such has been the increase in her industrial and military potential. The secondary powers are the United Kingdom, by virtue of her industrial strength and her strategic bases overseas which make possession of nuclear weapons effective at the moment, and China, whose sheer area and numbers are being enhanced by controlled heavy industry growing at a startling speed. In the third rank are West Germany, industrially slightly ahead of Great Britain but without her strategic advantages; Canada, as yet a pale reflection of the United States but not yet at her zenith; Japan, severely circumscribed by population pressure and a lack of raw materials and markets; France, whose only hope of regaining a higher place in the hierarchy of world powers seems to lie not in industry but in the possession of nuclear weapons and a successful pacification and reorganization of her colonial territories; India, whose lack of industrial progress has prevented her not only from preceding but even from emulating China as the great mainland Asian power in spite of her compact and populous area and good communications; and Poland, the third Communist power. The fourth-class nations are Australia (a kind of isolated and underequipped Canada), Brazil (the chief Latin-American power), Czechoslovakia, Italy (in some ways the Japan of Europe), and East Germany. Still farther down the scale come Argentina, the Union of South Africa, Sweden, and Belgium.

These figures are only an approximation to the absolute and comparative power of any nation as viewed in the light of present-day circumstances. Thus they take little direct note of high standards of living or of textile industries. No attempt has been made to add up total Communist or non-Communist strength or to predict decisive margins. The method has the merit of flexibility (the dissatisfied reader can construct his own scale of values) and of adaptability (as soon as new statistics become available, it can be revised). The extent to which sweeping changes will have to be made must depend upon the effectiveness of any further moves toward European integration and the spread of nuclear weapons and missiles to such nations as Germany, Sweden, Turkey, Pakistan, or Australia.

Table 1

Key	Source	U.S.A.	U.S.S.R.	United Kingdom	China	West Germany	Canada	Japan	France	India	Poland
1. Area in square kilometers (thousands)	U.N., *Yearbook* (1958)	(7828)	(22403)	(244)	(9761)	(248)	(9974)	(370)	(551)	(3182)b	(312)
2. Area corrected for population density	U.N., *Yearbook* (1958)	(391½)	(1120)	(49)	(976)	(50)	(499)	(74)	(55)	(318)	(31)
3. Area further corrected for rail density	*Statesman's Yearbook* (1959)	*391½*	*373*	*49*	*325*	*50*	*250*	*74*	*55*	*212*	*31*
4. Working population in millions	See Explanatory Note 2	(67½)†	(75)*	(23½)†	(200)*	(23)‡	(5¾)†	(43½)†	(19½)‡	(110)*	(13)‡
5. Above, corrected for technical efficiency	U.N., *Yearbook* (1957)	(337½)	(225)	(117½)	(200)*	(92)	(28½)	(87)	(58½)	(110)	(39)
6. Plus five times manufacturing population	See Explanatory Note 3	(78)†	(60)*	(45)†	(20)*	(40)‡	(7½)†	(40½)†	(27½)†	(9)†	(12½)†
7. Plus factor for "morale," based on row 4	Estimated	(34)	(37½)	(8)	(100)	(11½)	(3)	(22)	(6½)		(4)
8. Plus or minus food supply factor	U.N., *Yearbook* (1958)	(+22)		(−22)		(−6)	(+8)	(−14)		(−20)	(−3)*
9. Total population factor (rows 5, 6, 7, & 8)		*471½*	*322½*	*148½*	*320*	*137½*	*47*	*135½*	*92½*	*99*	*52½*
10. Steel production in metric tons per year (millions)	U.N., *Yearbook* (1958)a	(1022½)	(549)†	(220)	(52½)	(280)	(46)	(126)	(141)	(17½)	(53)
11. Coal production in metric tons per year (millions)	U.N., *Yearbook* (1958)a	(468)	(348)†	(227)	(124)	(151)	(10)	(52)	(57)	(44)	(94)
12. Lignite production (5,000,000 metric tons per year)	U.N., *Yearbook* (1958)a		(29)†			(20)					(1)
13. Crude oil production (million metric tons per year)	U.N., *Yearbook* (1958)a	(354)	(113)†		(1½)	(4)	(24½)		(1½)		
14. Hydroelectricity in million tons coal equivalent	U.N., *Yearbook* (1958)a	(203)	(61)	(4)		(20)	(119)	(87)	(38)	(9)	(1)
15. Total industry (provisional) (rows 10, 11, 12, 13 & 14)		(2047½)	(1100)	(451)	(178)	(475)	(199½)	(265)	(237½)	(70½)	(149)
16. Additional factor for directed economy			(1100)		(178)						(149)
17. Indexes of surplus or deficit: steel	Estimated	(+102)				(+24)	(−10)	(−13)		(−7)	
18. Indexes of surplus or deficit: oil	Estimated			(−45)	(−37)	(−48)		(−26½)	(−24)	(−7)	(−30)
19. Indexes of surplus or deficit: minerals	Estimated	(+102)	(+220)	(−23)	(+37)	(−24)	(+20)	(−26½)	(+12)	(+7)	(−15)
20. Indexes of surplus or deficit: engineering	Estimated	(+102)		(+45)	(−37)	(+48)	(−10)			(−7)	(−15)
21. Total surplus or deficit factor (rows 17–20)		(+306)	(+220)	(−23)	(−37)			(−66)	(−12)	(−14)	(−60)
22. Revised industrial total (rows 15, 16, & 21)		*2353½*	*2420*	*428*	*319*	*475*	*199½*	*199*	*225½*	*56½*	*238*
23. Military personnel (millions)	*Statesman's Yearbook* (1959)	*2.6*	*4.5*	*0.6*	*3.5*	*0.1*	*0.15*	*0.2*	*0.1*	*0.55*	*0.3*
24. Total civil factors (rows 3, 9, & 22)		(3216½)	(3115½)	(625½)	(964)	(662½)	(496½)	(408½)	(373)	(367½)	(321½)
25. Additional factor for nuclear weapons		*3242½*	*3160½*	*631½*							
26. Grand total (rows 3, 9, 22, 23, & 25)		*6459*	*6321*	*1257*	*999*	*663½*	*498*	*410½*	*383*	*373*	*324½*
RANKING		1	2	3	4	5	6	7	8	9	10

[a]Rows 10, 11, 12, and 13 for U.S.S.R. are from the *Statesman's Yearbook*. Recession elsewhere makes United Nations figures (a year earlier) more suitable.
[b]Excluding part of Kashmir, de facto part of Pakistan.

Table 1—Continued

Key	Source	Australia	Brazil	Czecho-slovakia	Italy	East Germany	Argentina	Union of South Africa	Sweden	Belgium
1. Area in square kilometers (thousands)	U.N., *Yearbook* (1958)	(7704)	(8514)	(128)	(301)	(108)	(2778)	(2047)	(450)	(30)
2. Area corrected for population density	U.N., *Yearbook* (1958)	(385)	(426)	(13)	(30)	(11)	(139)	(102)	(22½)	(6)
3. Area further corrected for rail density	*Statesman's Yearbook* (1959)	*128*	*142*	*13*	*30*	*11*	*92*	*51*	*22½*	*6*
4. Working population in millions	See Explanatory Note 2	(4)‡	(18)‡	(6)*	(21½)‡	(8)*	(6½)‡	(5½)‡	(3¼)‡	(3¾)‡
5. Above, corrected for technical efficiency	U.N., *Yearbook* (1957)	(16)	(18)	(24)	(43)	(32)	(13)	(16½)	(13)	(15)
6. Plus five times manufacturing population	See Explanatory Note 3	(5½)‡	(11)†	(6)*	(25)‡	(14)*	(7½)‡	(4½)†	(5½)‡	(7½)‡
7. Plus factor for "morale," based on row 4	Estimated	(1½)		(2)	(7)	(3)			(2)	(1½)
8. Plus or minus food supply factor	U.N., *Yearbook* (1958)	(+5)	(−7)	(−2)*	(−3)	(−1)*	(+8)	(+2½)		(−2)
9. Total population factor (rows 5, 6, 7, & 8)		*28*	*22*	*30*	*72*	*48*	*28½*	*23½*	*20½*	*22*
10. Steel production in metric tons per year (millions)	U.N., *Yearbook* (1958)a	(28)	(16)	(52)	(68)	(29)	(2½)	(17½)	(25)	(63)
11. Coal production in metric tons per year (millions)	U.N., *Yearbook* (1958)a	(20)	(2)	(24)	(1)	(3)		(35)		(29)
12. Lignite production (5,000,000 metric tons per year)	U.N., *Yearbook* (1958)a	(2)		(10)		(43)				
13. Crude oil production (million metric tons per year)	U.N., *Yearbook* (1958)a		(1½)		(1½)		(5)			
14. Hydroelectricity in million tons coal equivalent	U.N., *Yearbook* (1958)a	(5)	(21½)	(3)	(49)		(1)		(41)	
15. Total industry (provisional) (rows 10, 11, 12, 13, & 14)		(55)	(41)	(89)	(119½)	(75)	(8½)	(52½)	(66)	(92)
16. Additional factor for directed economy				(89)		(75)				
17. Indexes of surplus or deficit: steel	Estimated		(−2)		(−6)		(−1)			(+9)
18. Indexes of surplus or deficit: oil	Estimated	(−5½)	(−4)	(−18)	(−12)	(−15)		(−5)	(−6½)	(−9)
19. Indexes of surplus or deficit: minerals	Estimated	(+11)	(+4)	(−9)	(−12)	(−15)	(−1)	(+5)	(+6½)	(−9)
20. Indexes of surplus or deficit: engineering	Estimated		(−2)			(−7)	(−1)	(−5)	(+6½)	
21. Total surplus or deficit factor (rows 17–20)		(+5½)	(−4)	(−27)	(−30)	(−37)	(−3)	(−5)	(+6½)	(−9)
22. Revised industrial total (rows 15, 16, & 21)		*60½*	*37*	*151*	*89½*	*113*	*5½*	*47½*	*72½*	*83*
23. Military personnel (millions)	*Statesman's Yearbook* (1959)	*0.05*	*0.25*	*0.2*	*0.1*	*0.2*	*0.15*	*0.05**	*0.05*	*0.1*
24. Total civil factors (rows 3, 9, & 22)		(216½)	(201)	(194)	(191½)	(172)	(126)	(122)	(115½)	(111)
25. Additional factor for nuclear weapons										
26. Grand total (rows 3, 9, 22, 23, & 25)		*217*	*203½*	*196*	*192½*	*174*	*127½*	*122½*	*116*	*112*
RANKING		11	12	13	14	15	16	17	18	19

See Explanatory Notes to Table 1 on following page.

EXPLANATORY NOTES TO TABLE 1

1. The area in thousands of square kilometers is divided by 5 if the population density exceeds 201 per square kilometer, by 10 if the density is between 30 and 200 per square kilometer, and by 20 if below 30 per square kilometer. The resulting figure (row 2) is not changed if each kilometer of rail net serves 30 sq. km. or less of the national area; it is reduced by one-third if the service is between 31 and 75 sq. km. per kilometer; by one-half if between 76 and 150 sq. km. per kilometer. If the ratio is over 150 sq. km. for every kilometer of railroad, row 2 is reduced by two-thirds. The resulting figure (row 3) represents the effective contribution of area to national strength.

2. Row 4 represents the national work force in millions. Some totals (*) have been estimated since, for China and the U.S.S.R., statistics are not available; others (†) are derived from the *Statesman's Yearbook* (1959), where these are clearly more recent and significantly in excess of the older data in the United Nations *Statistical Yearbook* (1957), much of the material for which is derived from censuses of the early 1950's. In cases where the *Statesman's Yearbook* figures are deficient or not comparable (some omit employers, etc.), the United Nations figures are employed (‡) with a suitable correction based on total population increase since the date of the United Nations figures. Errors are likely to be below 5 points either way in the ultimate reckoning (i.e., even after further calculations).

3. Row 5 represents the above total (row 4) multiplied by 1 if the national consumption of energy is less than 0.5 ton of coal equivalent per head per year; by 2 if between 0.5 and 1.5 tons; by 3 between 1.5 and 3.0 tons; by 4 between 3.0 and 5.0 tons; and by 5 if above 5.0 tons. Row 6 represents the national work force engaged in manufacturing industry (in millions) multiplied five times. Its derivation is similar to that of row 4. Row 7 shows for some nations an increase of one-third or one-half of the figure in row 4, to represent "morale." This is a highly subjective factor, but few will question the intense application of the German and Japanese worker, for example, or the relative purposefulness of workers in many highly developed states, capitalist or communist. Row 8 indicates the compensation allowed on total population (not shown here) for food deficits or surpluses. The figure is based entirely on the United Nations *Yearbook* tables showing proportion of home-produced supply of wheat, rye, rice, "other grains," and potatoes. Owing to the elasticity of human stomachs, food supplies tend to equal consumption, but deficit countries occur in Europe and Asia, surpluses in Australia and the Americas. Row 4 is a basis for calculation and is not itself added. Rows 5, 6, 7, and 8 together comprise the total population sector—row 9.

4. Rows 10–14 inclusive are relatively straightforward and together form row 15, a provisional total

for industrial power. Row 14 has been derived from hydroelectric production in millions of kilowatt-hours by assuming the calorific value of coal to be 10,000 Btu. per pound, and consequently 1 million tons of coal representing 656 million kw-h. Row 15 is added again (row 16) for highly centralized (communist) economies.* Rows 17–20 inclusive represent arbitrary additions or subtractions of 5 or 10 per cent of rows 15 and 16 to account for unduly rich or poor resources. There is no single source for such information; that shown here has been derived from inspection of production and consumption figures, trade balances, and economic atlases. Iron ore is the principal mineral taken into consideration. Row 21 shows the sum total of these surpluses or deficits. Taken together with rows 15 and 16, it shows the revised total industrial contribution.

5. Row 23 shows total military personnel in hundred thousands; row 24 represents the sum total for civil factors. Rows 23 and 24 together give the grand total, except for three countries, for which this total is added again (row 25) to take the possession of nuclear weapons into consideration. In all cases, row 26 represents the completed evaluation of power on the basis of the writer's terms. It consists of the gross totals of rows 3, 5, 6, 7, 8, 10, 11, 12, 13, 14, 16, 17, 18, 19, 20, 23, and 25. This addition can be abbreviated to rows 3, 9, 22, 23, and 25. For clarity, these figures are italicized; other figures are in parentheses to show that they form part of the running calculation.

Table 1 may now be read as follows (e.g., for Japan):

The basic area in thousands of square kilometers is 370, to the nearest whole number; a high population density (246 per square kilometer) and good communications (28,000 km. of track, or about 1 km. to every 13 sq. km. of area) give a total area contribution of 74. The work force, here taken as 43½ (millions) is doubled, as Japan uses 1.08 tons of coal equivalent per head (1956 figures). The industrial labor force is about 8 (millions); this gives a corrected total of 40½. A full half of the original work force is added again (22) to indicate the diligence of the Japanese worker. But since Japan can feed only a little over 80 per cent of her total population (1954–56 average), the appropriate proportion (14) is subtracted. Steel production and fuel of all kinds, suitably weighted, total 265. But Japan is reckoned to have a 5 per cent deficit on steel supplies (chiefly imported scrap, since even poorly endowed countries like Japan tend to build steel industries almost up to needs on the basis of scrap). On minerals (chiefly iron ore) and oil, the maximum deficit, 10 per cent, is awarded. This reduces the effective contribution of Japanese industry by 66—to 199. Japanese military power in hundred thousands currently amounts to about 2. The area, population, and industry figures taken together amount to 408½. In the absence of nuclear weapons, Japanese total over-all strength is reckoned on this basis at 410½. Its derivation, strengths, and weaknesses are readily apparent from reference back to unit totals.

OTHER FORMS OF ORGANIZATION

In addition to governmental, economic, and military organization, a number of other types of organization affect the power of the state. Mention was made above of transportation networks. Of course, in most countries, transportation is in the hands of government and thus becomes an aspect of governmental organization. But where it is not, the effectiveness of the transport networks must be studied as a separate form of organization. In the United States, with its highly developed communications systems, private railroads are nevertheless subject to federal scrutiny. The federal and state governments build roads. Airlines are also subject to government regulations. In the Soviet Union, all transport is in government hands; one major airline serves most cities; buses and trains are government-operated, and comparatively few cars are privately owned. Roads are built to serve as truck routes between cities and supply areas, and many of them are not fit, by Western standards, for car travel. But whereas this is a major American concern, it is a minor matter in the U.S.S.R., where the aim is toward mass transportation rather than individual travel by car. The differences reflect the ideological contrasts between the two states.

Another form of organization of significance here is the educational system. Here a wide range of conditions occurs among the states. In Africa, there is a vigorous drive to increase literacy and extend educational opportunities; the governments are treating this matter with priority. For obvious reasons the task has fallen on the government; in areas of poverty and subsistence there is not a large market for private schools. But the aim is exactly that of private and public education in America: to reduce the loss of human resources that occurs when students cannot find a place to learn. In totalitarian states, the educational system is used for purposes of indoctrination. In all cases, again, this is a state-wide form of organization of great relevance to the political geographer.

There is one other form of power and organization (among several remaining) to be touched on here, and it concerns the matter of power over the minds of people in other states. This is not the same type of power produced by a strong military force. It is the kind of ideological penetration that is made when, in another state, there is a minority which is known to be dissatisfied with local conditions and seeks a new allegiance. Such instruments as the Voice of America, Radio Free Europe, Radio Cairo, Radio South Africa, and other media of this sort perform the function of distributing information that may strengthen the (sometimes antistate) opinions of those minorities. The Soviet Union, the United States, and China have used such minorities successfully in their ideological struggle with their adversaries, as did the Nazi Germans during the war years. Minorities have come to be recognized and identified much more strongly in recent years than they possibly ever have been before, and as an element in the political power struggles in the world they have attained new importance.

THE LANDSCAPE OF POWER

The measurement of power, then, involves scrutiny of the contents of state areas. A critical reading of German's article no doubt produces many arguments regarding the most appropriate procedure for such measurement; many will disagree with some of the criteria employed. But the additions or alternatives may in the end be no more useful. This remains one area in which a great deal of speculation and guesswork is required.

Previously in this chapter, the state's natural resources were indicated as a major determinant of national power, and the suggestion was made that a simple map analysis could give us an initial idea of the power potential of a state. Indeed, no consideration of the international position of any state would be complete without reference to its resource content. However, such an analysis could also be misleading. While the actual possession of raw materials is obviously a prime requisite for power, perhaps even more important is the state's capacity to use those resources. A world map showing the available fuels and energy sources in the present-day world indicates that many Caribbean and Middle East states possess vast petroleum reserves, and that many African states have magnificent hydroelectric sites and even uranium deposits. And yet none of these states is particularly powerful in the world sense. Those resources have not automatically endowed the state with power.

A number of reasons can be enumerated to account for this situation, among them the accessibility of territorial resources, the world demand, actual or potential strategic significance, and so forth. But the most important of all refers to the degree of industrial develop-

Power over opinion: the ruins of a ruler's memorial. The post-Stalin era in the Soviet Union saw the progressive erosion of the former dictator's image, a process that was directed from the top and was culminated during the rule of Khrushchev. The completeness with which Stalin's memory has been eradicated is suggested by these two photographs, taken in Kiev (Top) and Yerevan (Bottom). Magnificent statues of Stalin marked these sites; that of Yerevan overlooked the entire city. Both have been toppled and destroyed; the sites have been left unattended and are marked by posters and scribblings. Still, such places can only suggest the turnabout that was required of the Soviet citizen who had lived through the decades of Stalin's rule and who had been trained to believe in Stalin as the personification of the state (Harm J. de Blij).

ment of the state within which such resources occur. Middle East countries sell their oil to overseas consumers because local needs are comparatively minor; African states do not develop much of their hydroelectric potential because the market for the electric power supply does not yet exist. In fact, it may be argued that the capacity to make use of raw materials is, in the final analysis, more important than the possession of such domestic resources: witness the rise of Japan to world military power during the second World War without a great wealth of local strategic materials. The United States has the capacity to use more petroleum than is produced internally, and this very capacity implies a technological development that enables this country to import what is required. It means that the United States is able to purchase, transport, and distribute vast quantities of petroleum. Foreign trade, transport systems and equipment, and industrial consumers all reflect the power of the state.

INDUSTRIAL DEVELOPMENT

Industrialization, thus, is the cornerstone of power. The advantages of an industrialized state over one that is not are obvious and many. Mechanization means higher production ratios; an individual worker capable of operating a machine can outproduce one working by hand. The advantage, furthermore, is cumulative. Not only do industrialized states outproduce nonindustrialized countries, but the labor force, acquainted with the necessary skills, is able bit by bit to keep pace with advancing technology as machinery becomes ever more sophisticated and production costs go down. Every day the industrialized state goes farther ahead; every day the gap between the "have" and the "have-not" states grows larger.

What industries are determinants of state power? All are, to a greater or lesser degree, for all contribute to strength in helping raise standards of living and improving the economic condition of the nation. But clearly some industries are more important than others. "Guns or butter" was the cry in Germany of the 1930s (it was heard in the United States at the height of the drive for victory in Viet Nam in the mid-1960s), and guns are manufactured of steel. A steel industry, then, is a prime power industry, and no state that has in recent decades risen to world status has done so without steel mills. Two major necessities for a steel industry are iron ore and coal. As it happens, iron ore is rather widely distributed throughout the world. Many states have such deposits, though the quality varies. Many major ore deposits are only just being opened up, such as those of Mauritania, Swaziland, and a new field in Liberia.[8] As a result, many countries have steel mills, although the United States (20 percent of the world total), the U.S.S.R. (19 percent), Japan (16 percent), West Germany, and the United Kingdom produce the bulk.

[8]For an examination of the impact of such opening up of iron ore reserves in a developing country, see Alan C.G. Best, *The Swaziland Railway: A Study in Politico-Economic Geography*, East Lansing, African Studies Center, Michigan State University, 1966.

A steel industry, in addition, requires deposits of usable coal. Here we have a partial explanation for the fact that while the United States and the U.S.S.R. are the world's major steel producers, India (about 30 percent) and Brazil 20 percent) have the greatest iron ore reserves. The United States, Soviet Union, and China each produce about 20 percent of the world's coal. The United Kingdom and the German Federal Republic rank next in order.

Apart from limestone, steel industries require alloys. Alloys are essential in the production of steel of certain qualities; qualities that may be essential in times of war. Hence a number of alloys, such as manganese, nickel, tungsten, vanadium, chrome, and cobalt, may be of strategic importance. Sudden changes in the desired properties of steel may render various alloys of great importance at certain times. During the second World War, efforts were made to keep certain vital alloys out of German hands, thus hindering the German war effort.

Five major concentrations of heavy manufacturing, with steel industries at the core, can be observed in the world today. The northeastern United States, including the Chicago-Gary area as well as the Appalachian and East Coast regions, dominates the Americas. The other four all lie in Eurasia: northwestern Europe, including the United Kingdom, France, and the Federal Republic of West Germany; the Ukraine-Urals area in the western U.S.S.R., which, as we shall see later, is expanding eastward, toward Lake Baikal; the northern China-Manchuria area; and central and west Japan. Of these, only the Soviet and Chinese regions are supplied totally from domestic sources. The United States imports almost half of its annual iron ore needs, and Japan more than three-quarters. The world distribution of alloys is such that industrialized countries depend for several critical minerals upon "developing" suppliers.

Heavy industries, then, reflect and sustain state power. These are the industries that fall in Jones' first category—they are available immediately for the production of war equipment in the event of national need. A journey through the Chicago-Gary complex, the Krivoy Rog, and the Ruhr traverses the very core of American, Soviet, and German strength. Such a journey cannot fail to impress, with miles of congested manufacturing, transport links, power lines, converging and dispersing labor shifts, arriving raw materials and departing finished products. This, indeed, is the landscape of power.

If the metal manufacturing and associated industries (including shipbuilding, airplane construction, general engineering, and construction) form the main bulwark of the state's power, other industries nevertheless are of great importance as well. The so-called chemical industries, including those manufacturing explosives and others producing fertilizers, also make a critical contribution to the state's welfare, as do the electronics, textile, and food processing plants. In the industrialized states, all these industries are represented. Developing states are attempting to industrialize, sometimes by making tremendous investments apparently simply to join the industrial age, without the proper economic justification. No doubt the hope is, in part, to impress neighbors and hence to improve the state's power status, but in the present-day world of super-powers, this hardly appears a sound philosophy.

Two countries that have, in the postwar period, plunged headlong into industrialization as a means to achieve possibly attainable goals are China and South Africa. Any observer wishing to gauge the effects of industrialization in power politics should follow closely the fortunes of these two states, which have embarked upon these programs with specific aims: in the case of China, world power status and extension of the Asian sphere of influence, and in the case of South Africa, survival in the face of black African (and world) hostility. While China's road will be a hard one, it may be shorter than many have supposed, and the fore-shadowing of Chinese nuclear capability has come faster than anticipated. South Africa's success in breaking an economic boycott lies in part in that country's rapid move toward self-sufficiency in critical areas; from timid beginnings in the 1930's the steel industry is now making a vital contribution to state power. Vehicles, oil (manufactured from coal), explosives, and weapons are produced internally, and the state appears capable at present of withstanding any combined African assault.

The preceding reference to self-sufficiency leads us to an aspect of states which, in any discussion of power, quickly comes to mind. Does the state—and should it—attempt to direct its economic development in such a way that it will ultimately become completely self-sufficient, thus requiring nothing from other states and being in a position, if desired, to bow out of world politics? In fact, such self-sufficiency is practically impossible, even for the best-endowed states. Not without major reductions in living standards could the majority of the industrialized states even approach self-sufficiency. In modern times, self-sufficiency obviously does not bring with it the security it brought three decades ago, perhaps with the single exception of South Africa, which faces a regional, "conventional" confrontation. For the United States, the United Kingdom, France, or the Soviet Union, total self-sufficiency is neither possible nor a workable policy. Of course, countries strive to reduce dependence upon others for critical supplies, and Soviet failures in this area are reflected by recent and repeated overseas wheat purchases. United States imports of fuels and ores that *could* be produced at home by more intensive exploitation of known reserves is involved with the retention of such domestic reserves in the event of an emergency—which could cut the country off from its overseas sources.

Another vital aspect of the question of resources and power is that of *balance.* Many states, as we have seen, possess a great deal of one single resource or raw material, but little or nothing of others. Included here are such necessities as cultivable soils, climates producing adequate moisture and permitting a sufficiently long growing season (soil and climate, indeed, are resources), a supply of energy (from such sources as coal, petroleum, hydroelectric sites, or radioactive minerals), as well as metalliferous and other ores. No country has all it would desire, but some states are endowed with a much better balance than others. A state that possesses large and good-quality coalfields, a sizable, high-grade iron ore reserve, but few necessary alloys can more easily import the needed alloys than a state that happens to have the alloys can import both iron ores and coking coal. Hence the underdeveloped country possessing only a single alloy (or an iron reserve, oilfield, or copper deposit) can expect at best to see plants established to refine the product somewhat; it alone will not draw an industrial complex to the site. This, really, is what the "have" countries possess. Not only do they have the basic ingredients in the right quantities for an industrial base; they have a share of the many other resources that are essential for state progress—and power.

POLICY

States, and the leaders of states who make the essential decisions, desire national strength and power on the international scene. The industrial development and exploitation of resources to which I have just made reference are naturally affected in great measure by the economic policies of the governments of the states involved. In one way or another, governments have sought to involve themselves in the economic efforts of their subjects for many centuries. During the Renaissance, Europe's monarchies, in their rivalry with each other and their search for self-sufficiency, developed a policy known as *mercantilism*. The objectives of mercantilist policies were the accumulation of as large a quantity of gold and silver as possible and the promotion of foreign trade and colonial acquisition to achieve this end. Mercantilism was a *state* policy, thought to be in the general interest of all citizens. It would produce a favorable balance of trade; home-produced products (from raw materials obtained cheaply elsewhere) could be sold profitably overseas. The governments protected their home industries by imposing high duties on imported goods. But later the pendulum swung the other way, when the now-wealthy merchants in Europe's cities became disenchanted with government interference. They demanded an end to government interference and a laissez-faire policy—a hands-off policy by the government and a termination of state protection and control.

The pendulum is still swinging. States with planned economies, notably the Soviet Union, have plunged headlong into industrialization programs whose economic foundations, by free-enterprise yardsticks, are not always sound. Other states have tried to balance state control with a measure of capitalism; still others maintain as much free enterprise as possible. Among states to have undergone radical changes in direction in recent decades have been Cuba, Chile, and Libya.

It is reasonable to assume that all states desire accelerated development, and that their policies are designed to promote this aim. In a recent volume, Professor J.R.V. Prescott points out that some political geographers have failed to take adequate note of such policies.[9] Prescott states that these tend to take three main directions: (1) policies that attempt to increase existing production, (2) policies that will stimulate new forms of production, and (3) policies that seek to prevent losses of production and the maintenance of existing output levels.[10] Of course, he emphasizes that such policies need to be viewed in light of the actual *intentions* of the government involved (does it want to favor one particular sector of the economy, or one region of the state?) and the degree to which *other* governments may be affected by them. And, Prescott continues, political geographers must take account of the *motives* behind various policies, the *processes* by which the policies are implemented, the *economics* of the situation, the degree of *authoritarianism* of the government involved, and the impact of economic *plans* that have effect in various states.

With these cautions in mind, Professor Prescott proposes that four groups of policies can be recognized: (1) *general unilateral* policies which seek to promote the development of the state as a whole, (2) *general multilateral* policies, in which the government decides to join with another—or several others—to create favorable conditions for development, (3) *specific unilateral* policies, which are aimed at the development of a particular sector of the economy or a specific region within the state, and (4) *specific multilateral* policies, whereby a government decides to ask another, or several others, to assist the state's development.[11] It is not difficult to identify policies in each category. In the first instance, the general welfare is promoted by taxation measures, interest rates, exchange controls, and so forth. Professor Prescott analyzes in detail the manner in which fiscal policies of the government of South Africa during the period 1961 to 1966 withstood and countered a crisis of confidence that had to do with the apparently explosive racial situation in that country. In the second case, when a government decides to join with others, it does so in customs unions, economic communities, and trade blocs. The United Kingdom's determined bid to enter the "Common Market" is a case in point. Third, a government can structure freight rates to help isolated industries, it can protect home industries through tariffs, it can stimulate the development of a region whose potential is recognized but

[9]J.R.V. Prescott, *The Geography of State Policies*, Chicago, Aldine Publishing Co., 1968. See especially pp. 140–190.

[10]Ibid., p. 141.

[11]Ibid., pp. 143–145.

unfulfilled, and finally, it can request an aid program from a stronger, wealthier state.

As Professor Prescott states, it hardly seems that these considerations have much geographic relevance. But consider the impact of South Africa's fiscal policies during the 1960's; cityscapes were transformed as skyscrapers shot up, the valley of the country's major river, the Orange, was transformed by one of the world's greatest river-control projects, which was vigorously pursued (eventually a TVA-like scheme will result). Consider the effect of the Soviet Union's assistance in the building of the Aswan High Dam upon various aspects of the regional geography of Egypt, or the impact of Tanzania's Chinese-built railway to Zambia. The policies themselves may not be geographical, but their consequences are patently so. And this is Professor Prescott's point.

FOREIGN TRADE

Another indicator of the power of states is the quantity of foreign trade they carry on. Obviously any single country controlling all international trade—by possessing the equipment to carry the goods as well as the sources of the goods themselves—would dominate the world. No state is in such a position today, but foreign trade and control over the avenues to overseas wealth certainly promoted the early rise to power of Portugal, Spain, the Netherlands, and Britain. We saw how government protected home industries and encouraged the hoarding of gold and silver during the mercantilist period, when self-sufficiency was the objective; but later, mercantilist policies became oppressive to the successful merchant class. Change was bound to come, with increased and improved circulation and com-

Foreign trade and national power. The amount of trade carried on by a state is an indication of its power in the world. The case of South Africa serves as a good example. South Africa's foreign trade, by value and volume, is far larger than that of any other state in Africa south of the Sahara. While South Africa's total population is only about one-third that of Nigeria and two-thirds that of Ethiopia, it possesses many more overseas trade connections than they do. In fact, virtually all overseas trade is in the hands of the small minority of white residents of the country, who by virtue of their economic power have managed to retain their ruling position in the multiracial state. South Africa's resources and products (gold, diamonds, wool, lobster, fruits, etc.) permit the acquisition of those goods that have helped create an island of Western life in black Africa. Shown here is the loading of an American-made electric locomotive aboard a freighter forming part of a government-subsidized fleet in the port of New York. Not shown (but equally important) is the large-scale importation of arms equipment, including jet fighter aircraft, armored vehicles, and various weapons—all of which have been bought in return for trade revenues and which have greatly strengthened the South African government's control over its diverse population groups (Harm J. de Blij).

munications. It came during the nineteenth century, and was supported most strongly by Great Britain, which had most to benefit from the liberalization of trade. British industries were strong and ahead of most of the competition. British goods were cheaper than those of its commercial rivals. The range of products from British colonies was greater than that of any other colonial power. The British merchant fleet far outstripped any competitors. British power, indeed, had been built on trade.

The liberalization of trade did not take place without difficulties, and the process is far from completed. Certain states were forced to continue their protection of local industry or agriculture and kept their tariff walls up. Others joined in trade agreements which lowered the barriers between them, but not with states outside the agreement. The postwar attempts at European economic unification indicate the difficulties involved in the matter, however attractive the rewards of solution might be. Perhaps the most significant step in recent decades has been the General Agreement on Tariffs and Trade, ratified (in 1970) by some seventy-seven states which are together responsible for well over 80 percent of the world's trade tonnage. The aims of G.A.T.T. include the regularizing of international trade, the lowering of tariffs, the prevention of sudden "dumping" of goods on the world market, the reduction and elimination of restrictive quotas, and the general lowering of the many remaining obstacles to interstate commerce.

With the liberalization of trade, merchants found themselves less controlled and more assisted by their home governments. For the state, the returns were often handsome, for these merchants often performed functions beyond those of the trader; he spread the influence of his country in unclaimed areas, established fortifications, raised his state's flag, and at times even financed the occupation of territory in the name of his homeland. Today, the trend appears again in the direction of government control; not only does government play a major role in the economic affairs of many developing countries such as Ghana, Algeria, and Indonesia, but in the Communist states it is the sole economic policy maker. Communist governments have pursued economic policies whose objective is the progress of the state; in the process they have at times placed the state in a straitjacket from which no escape may be possible. Poland, for example, has encountered a self-imposed obstacle in its effort to liberalize its trade somewhat—its entire economic orientation is toward the Soviet Union, not only in terms of goods exchanged but also, and more importantly, in terms of its permanent transport network.

Recent events in the political world notwithstanding, the politicogeographical map still reflects the location of power during the nineteenth century. The bulk of world trade tonnage is, and has always been, carried by oceangoing vessels. Hence security on the seas is of prime importance to the states that engage in much international trade. As we shall see later, the freedom of the seas and the retention of very narrow territorial waters are principles that have always been adhered to by trading nations. Many of the natural (i.e., physiographic) obstacles to maritime trade, such as straits and narrows, were claimed by the dominant powers of the nineteenth century in order to protect the lucrative overseas avenues. Britain gained control over the Strait of Gibraltar, at the western entry to the Mediterranean, as well as Bab-el Mandeb, the southern strait leading into the Red Sea, the latter through the occupation of Aden. The possession of Singapore assured a strong position in the Strait of Malacca. The acquisition of the Falkland Islands permitted the British to command the Straits of Magellan. Elsewhere, vital points were likewise placed under British control: Cape Town and the Cape of Good Hope, the Niger Delta, Hong Kong, as well as a number of actually or potentially useful islands: Malta, Cyprus, Zanzibar, the Seychelles, Ascension, and St. Helena. The last two territories remain under British jurisdiction today.

Two important straits over which Britain did not gain jurisdiction are those connecting the "interior" seas of Europe, the Baltic and the Black, to the High Seas. The Baltic Sea is linked to the North Atlantic Ocean by the Danish Straits, consisting of three individual waterways. Danish control over these waters brought the Crown a great deal of revenue, for ships were forced to pay tolls as they traversed them. After growing friction between the states whose vessels used the Straits and the Danes, the mid-nineteenth century saw the elimination of toll collection here and the opening of the Straits to international navigation. The Turkish Straits, linking the Black Sea to the Mediterranean, actually consist of two narrows (the Bosporus and the Dardanelles) and the intervening Sea of Marmora. Again, Turkey restricted (for a long time it actually prohibited) non-Turkish use of the Straits, but with the rise of Czarist Russia and later the Soviet Union, Turkey has been forced to surrender its monopoly over these waters.

Two Lifelines?

No discussion of the politicogeographical aspects of international trade would be complete without reference to two critical bottlenecks of this trade; the Suez and Panama Canals. Their origins reflect the great power of each of the states most directly involved in their creation; Britain, the United States, and France. British control over the Suez Canal —built by a concern that was largely French —was formally acquired in 1875 and not relinquished until three-quarters of a century later. Great Britain was then at the height of its power, made greater use of the Suez Canal than any other state, and thus depended to a very great extent upon its functioning. Even when Britain terminated its control over Egypt, it retained a foothold along the Canal Zone, benefiting from its bases at the south and north end of the Canal, Suez, and Port Said. That hold was eventually broken by Egypt during the events in 1956, when a combined British-French-Israeli military operation failed—unaccountably, in view of subsequent developments. At that time, Britain's prime minister went on radio and television and, in justifying his government's decision to intervene in the Suez area, spoke of the Canal as "Europe's Lifeline," which must continue to function at all costs.

In 1967, the "June War" did what the British government had feared; a conflict in the area led to the closure of the Canal. The conflict, of course, was Israel's massive retaliation against real and potential threats to shipping in the Gulf of Aqaba (and other pressures as well). Israeli troops marched across the Sinai Peninsula and reached the Canal; Egypt held the west bank. Ships were sunk in the Canal, and with the two hostile powers facing each other across the narrow waterway, traffic was no longer possible.

Here, then, was the situation so feared in the mid-1950's; the Canal was closed and the only open route lay around the Cape of Good Hope—around Africa. Did the closure of Suez strangle Europe? Hardly. Enlarged tankers sailed the ancient routes from the Persian Gulf to the Atlantic; pipelines carried increased quantities of oil across the desert to eastern Mediterranean ports. The capacity to mobilize the necessary systems and equipment evinced once again the power of Western Europe.

The Panama Canal was cut more recently than the Suez Canal, and unlike Suez it remains under the control of its creator, the United States. Indeed, the whole emergence of the state of Panama itself relates to North American involvement; once a part of Colombia, Panama was severed from that country and its separateness was sustained by United States guarantee. This was no unselfish generosity on the part of the United States; the Canal Zone is a strip of land, approximately 10 miles wide, and with Panamanian approval it was placed under United States sovereignty. In effect, the Panamanians agreed to the fragmentation of their national territory.

Like the Suez link, the Panama Canal was built to eliminate a lengthy and costly journey around a southern continent. Britain was the major user of the Suez Canal; the United States sends the largest tonnage each year through the Panama Canal. But in recent years a wind of change has reached even Panama. Although the economic benefits of the Canal are acknowledged, there is rising Panamanian opposition to the United States presence, and some resentment over the alienation of the Canal Zone. There has been talk of alternatives; another canal in Panama, which, unlike the current version, would lie at sea level and would not require the elaborate system of locks now operating there. Without the locks and with a new and more favorable international agreement, such a canal might be more acceptable to Panama than the old. It has also been suggested that the Panamanian experience ought to induce the United States to look elsewhere for a site for a new canal. Whatever the outcome, Britain's capacity to outflank the Suez Canal and the United States' continued presence in its Canal Zone reflect the organizational capacities and power position of these two states.

TRANSPORTATION AND POWER

If foreign trade is a measure of a state's power, so must be the quantity of equipment available for the efficient transportation of large numbers of men and large amounts of materials. One reason for the United States govern-

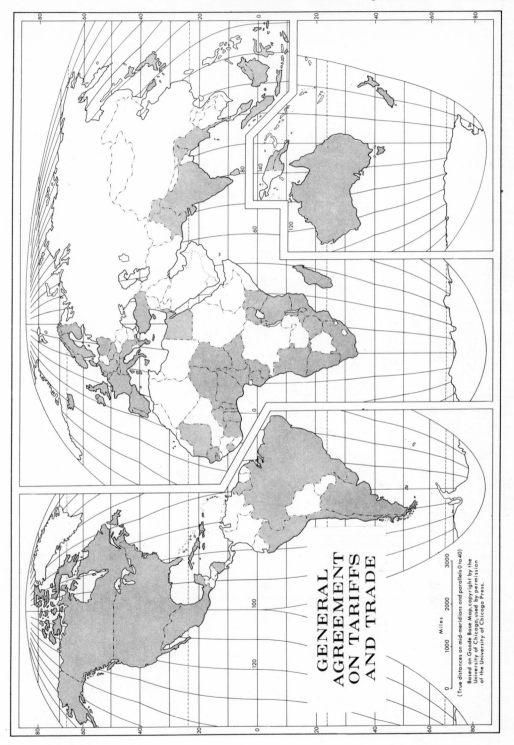

GENERAL
AGREEMENT
ON TARIFFS
AND TRADE

Miles
0   1000   2000   3000

(True distances on mid-meridians and parallels 0 to 40)

Based on Goode Base Map, copyright by the
University of Chicago, used by permission
of the University of Chicago Press.

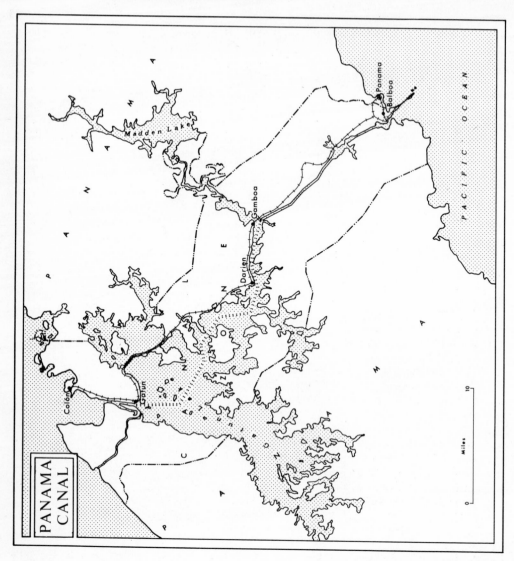

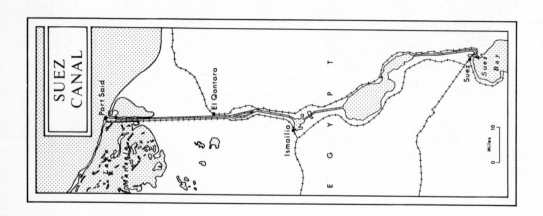

ment's subsidizing of domestic airlines lies in their potential usefulness in an emergency situation; their combined equipment constitutes a huge resource. Similarly, a large merchant marine not only reflects economic power but is a factor in military power as well. During the second World War several great ocean liners, originally designed for passenger transport, were quickly converted into troop carriers and played their role in the Allied victory.

While we have examined some aspects of international trade above, we have not dealt with the role of the internal transport network of the state as an indicator of power. Perhaps, here, the better word is "strength," for a good system of communications obviously enchances the cohesion of the state, the circulation of goods and ideas within it, and the feeling on the part of the people that they belong together. This aspect of the state is particularly significant since it can be clearly represented cartographically. We can gain an initial impression of the state's strength and unity from an examination of maps of transport routes; later we shall see that transport lines tend to focus upon the heart of the state, the so-called core area.

In a subsequent chapter we shall examine the view of a leading American political geographer, R. Hartshorne, who has suggested that we should, in our politicogeographical consideration of the state, pay attention to the factors promoting unity within the state territory and those causing division and separation. Clearly, the state's transport network is a unifying factor when well developed. But when such a network covers only one part of the state, leaving other sections far removed from these mainstreams of progress and change, we may recognize a divisive element. In the underdeveloped world, new emergent states have shown an awareness of the inadequacy of their transport systems which, more often than not, served the European colonial power's economic interests rather than the local territorial interests. Hence road building and railroad construction are given priority in development plans. The new governments, like their colonial forerunners, are well aware that effective transport ties promote effective national control, and such control promotes strength and unity.

A good transport network not only increases the cohesion of the state, it also renders it more easily capable of self-defense. The success of insurgent elements in Viet Nam is directly related to the difficulty in moving combat equipment over the difficult terrain; the impunity with which China acted in the Indian border areas is related to the scarce and difficult communications facing Indian defenders. In many countries, the United States included, certain highways are clearly marked as closed during a national emergency, which means that they are strategic arteries required for military operations.

It is obviously difficult, if not impossible, to identify exactly the contributions made by all the elements of the state in the total power situation. The same network of internal transport lines that promotes state strength and cohesion also facilitates the distribution of goods arriving and departing at ports on the coasts and hence facilitates foreign trade. Thus this feature of the organized state, a feature we can observe on the map, creates security internally and is a major factor in the external power relationships of the state.

REFERENCES

Ackerman, Edward A., "Population and Natural Resources," in P.M. Hauser and O.D. Duncan (eds.), The Study of Population. Chicago, University of Chicago Press, 1959, 621–648.

Aitken, H.G.J. (ed.), The State and Economic Growth. New York, Social Science Research Council, 1959.

Alcock, N.Z., and A.G. Newcombe, "The Perception of National Power," Journal of Conflict Resolution, XIV, 3 (September, 1970), 335–344.

Angell, Sir Norman, Raw Materials, Population Pressure and War. New York, National Peace Conference, 1936.

Apthorpe, Raymond, "The Introduction of Bureaucracy into African Politics," J. African Admin., 12, 3 (July, 1960), 125–134.

Barnett, H.J., "The Changing Relation of Natural Resources to National Security," Economic Geography, 34, 3 (July, 1958), 189–201.

Brandt, Karl, Europe, The Emerging Third Power; Phenomenon and Portent. New York, City News Publishing Co., 1958.

Carr, E.H., "The Forms of Political Power," in H.H. Sprout and M. Sprout (eds.), Foundations of National Power. Princeton, N.J., Princeton University Press, 1945, 31–38.

Coleman, James S., "Problems of Political Integration in Emergent Africa," Western Political Quart., 8, 1 (March, 1955), 44–57.

Cressey, George B., Soviet Potentials; A Geographic Appraisal. New York, Syracuse University Press, 1962.

De Bunsen, B., "Higher Education and Political Change in East Africa," *African Affairs*, 60, 241 (October, 1961), 494–499.

Delf, G., *Asians in East Africa*. London, Oxford University Press, 1963.

DeMille, John B., *Strategic Minerals*. New York, McGraw-Hill, 1947.

Deutsch, Karl W., "Social Mobilization and Political Development," *Amer. Political Sci. Rev.*, 55 (1961), 493–514.

Dunn, John M., "American Dependence on Materials Imports the World-wide Resource Base," *J. Conflict Resolution*, 4, 1 (March, 1960), 106–122.

Elegant, Robert S., *The Dragon's Seed; Peking and the Overseas Chinese*. New York, St. Martin's Press, 1959.

Frazier, E. Franklin, "Urbanization and its Effects Upon the Task of Nation-Building in Africa South of the Sahara," *J. Negro Educ.*, 30, 3 (Summer, 1961), 214–222.

German, F. Clifford, "A Tentative Evaluation of World Power," *J. Conflict Resolution*, 4, 1 (March, 1960), 138–144.

Gilliland, H.B., "An Approach to the Problem of the Government of Nomadic Peoples," *South African Geog. J.*, 29, 2 (April, 1947), 43–58.

Hagen, Everett E., "Population and Economic Growth," *Amer. Econ. Rev.*, 49, 3 (June, 1959), 310–327.

Hance, William A., "The Zande Scheme in the Anglo-Egyptian Sudan," *Economic Geography*, 31, 2 (April, 1955), 149–156.

Harbeson, Robert W., "Transportation: Achilles Heel of National Security," *Political Sci. Quart.*, 74, 1 (March, 1959), 1–20.

Hayton, Robert D., "Polar Problems and International Law," *Amer. J. Internat. Law*, 52, 4 (October, 1958), 746–765.

Helin, R.A., "The Volatile Administrative Map of Rumania," *Annals, A.A.G.*, 57, 3 (September, 1967), 481–502.

Hinsley, F.H., *Power and the Pursuit of Peace*. London, Cambridge University Press, 1963.

Hodgkins, Jordan A., *Soviet Power: Energy Resources, Production and Potentials*. Englewood Cliffs, N.J., Prentice-Hall, Inc., 1961.

Hoffman, George W., "The Role of Nuclear Power in Europe's Future Energy Balance," *Ann. A.A.G.*, 47, 1 (March, 1957), 15–40.

Horne, Alistair, *Return to Power; A Report on the New Germany*. New York, Praeger, 1956.

Janowsky, Oscar I., *Nationalities and National Minorities*. New York, Macmillan, 1945.

Jones, Stephen B., "The Power Inventory and National Strategy," *World Politics*, 6, 4 (July, 1954), 421–452.

———, *Theoretical Studies of National Power*. New Haven, Conn., Yale University Press, 1955.

Khrushchev, Nikita S., "On Peaceful Coexistence," *Foreign Affairs*, 38, 1 (October, 1959), 1–18.

Kieffer, John E., *Realities of World Power*. New York, D. McKay Co., 1952.

Kissinger, Henry A., *Nuclear Weapons and Foreign Policy*. New York, Harper and Brothers, 1957.

Knorr, Klaus, "The Concept of Economic Potential for War," *World Politics*, 10, 1 (October, 1957), 49–62.

———, *The War Potential of Nations*. Princeton, N.J., Princeton University Press, 1956.

Koch, Howard E., Jr., Robert C. North, and Dina A. Zinnes, "Some Theoretical Notes on Geography and International Conflict," *J. Conflict Resolution*, 4, 1 (March, 1960), 4–14.

Krengel, Rolf, "Soviet, American and West German Basic Industries; A Comparison," *Soviet Studies*, 12, 2 (October, 1960), 113–125.

Landheer, B., "Interstate Competition and Survival Potential," *J. Conflict Resolution*, 3 (1959), 162–171.

Laswell, H.D., and Abraham Kaplan, *Power and Society: A Framework for Political Inquiry*. New Haven, Conn., Yale University Press, 1950.

Leith, C.K., *World Minerals and World Politics*. Washington, Brookings Institution, 1931.

Lewis, W. Arthur, "Education and Economic Development," *Soc. & Econ. Studies*, 10, 2 (June, 1961), 113–127.

Lincoln, G.A., *Economics of National Security*. Englewood Cliffs, N.J., Prentice-Hall, Inc., 1954.

Livermore, Shaw, "International Control of Raw Materials," *Ann. Amer. Ac. Pol. & Soc. Sci.*, 281 (1951), 157–165.

Maas, Arthur (ed.), *Area and Power; A Theory of Local Government*. Glencoe, Ill., The Free Press, 1959.

Melamid, Alexander, "The Economic Geography of Neutral Territories," *Geog. Rev.*, 45, 3 (July, 1955), 359–374.

Mellor, Roy, "Trouble with the Regions: Planning Problems in Russia," *Scot. Geog. Mag.*, 75, 1 (April, 1959), 44–47.

Neumann, Franz L., "Approaches to the Study of Political Power," *Political Sci. Quart.*, 65, 2 (June, 1950), 161–180.

North, Geoffrey, "Poland's Population and Changing Economy," *Geog. J.*, 124, Pt. 4 (December, 1958), 517–527.

Orchard, John E., "Industrialization in Japan, China Mainland, and India—Some World Implications," *Ann. A.A.G.*, 50, 3 (September, 1960), 193–215.

Organski, A.F.K., "Population and Politics in Europe: Demographic Factors Help Shape the Relative Power of the Communist and non-Communist Blocs," *Science*, 133, 3467 (June 9, 1961), 1803–1807.

Organski, Katherine, and A.F.K. Organski, *Population and World Power*. New York, Knopf, 1961.

Parker, Albert, "The Fuel and Power Industries and National Prosperity; Three Cantor Lectures," *J. Roy. Soc. Arts*, 118, 5045 (April, 1960), 316–353.

Potter, E.B. (ed.), *The United States and World Sea Power*. Englewood Cliffs, N.J., Prentice-Hall, Inc., 1955.

Pounds, Norman J.G. *The Geography of Iron and Steel*. London, Macmillan, 1959.

Pounds, Norman J.G., and W.N. Parker, *Coal and*

Steel in Western Europe. Bloomington, Indiana University Press, 1957.

Pye, Lucian W. (ed.), *Communications and Political Development.* Princeton, N.J., Princeton University Press, 1963.

Read, M.H., "Education in Africa: Its Pattern and Role in Social Change," *Ann. Amer. Ac. Pol. & Soc. Sci.,* No. 298 (1955), 170–179.

Richards, J. Howard, "Changing Canadian Frontiers," *Canadian Geographer, 5,* 4 (Winter, 1961), 23–29.

Riggs, F.W., "Public Administration: A Neglected Factor in Economic Development," *Ann. Amer. Ac. Pol. & Soc. Sci.,* No. 305 (1956), 70–80.

Schurr, Sam H., "Energy," *Sci. Amer., 209,* 3 (September, 1963), 110–126.

Shabad, Theodore, "The Population of China's Cities," *Geog. Rev., 49,* 1 (January, 1959), 32–42.

Shimkin, D.M., *Minerals: A Key to Soviet Power.* Cambridge, Harvard University Press, 1953.

Siegfried, Andre, *Canada; An Internatiokal Power.* London, J. Cape, 1949.

Sprout, Harold H., and Margaret Sprout (eds.), *Foundations of National Power.* Princeton, N.J., Princeton University Press, 1945.

Spykman, Nicholas J., "Geography and Foreign Policy," *Amer. Political Sci. Rev., 32,* 1 (February, 1938), 28–50; No. 2 (April, 1938), 213–236.

Stahl, Rudolf, "Power Supply, Today and Tomorrow," *Universitas, 1,* 3 (1957), 247–254.

Steiner, H., Arthur, "Communist China in the World Community," *Internat. Conciliation,* No. 533 (May, 1961), 387–454.

Stevens, Georgiana G., "Reform and Power Politics in Iran," *Foreign Policy Reports, 26,* 19 (February 15, 1951), 214–223.

Stoessinger, J.G., *The Might of Nations.* New York, Random House, 1963.

Thomas, S.B., "Government and Administration in China Today," *Pacific Affairs, 23,* 3 (September, 1950), 248–270.

Wiens, H., *Pacific Island Bastions of the United States.* Princeton, N.J., Van Nostrand, 1962.

Wilson, Curtis M., "The Geographical Basis of National Power," *Ohio J. Sci., 50,* 1 (January, 1950), 33–44.

Wittfogel, Karl A., *Oriental Despotism; A Comparative Study of Total Power.* New Haven, Conn., Yale University Press, 1957.

Wolfe, R.I., *Transportation and Politics.* Princeton, N.J., Van Nostrand, 1963.

———, "Transportation and Politics: the Example of Canada," *Ann. A.A.G., 52,* 2 (June, 1962), 176–190.

Part II

The State: System and Process

CHAPTER
5

THE HEART OF THE STATE:
THE CORE AREA

Every adequately functioning state system has a nucleus; a central, essential, enduring heart. It was probably the German geographer Ratzel who first tried to define this reality in politicogeographical terms. He stated that states tended to begin as "territorial cells," which would then become larger through the addition of land and people, and eventually evolved into states or even empires. The American geographer, Whittlesey, has typified the state as "crystallized about a nuclear core that fostered integration . . . in nearly all states the nuclear core is also the most populous part—its ecumene."[1] While it is easy to understand the idea of the core area as the heart of the state, it is not quite so easy to define the term exactly. Whittlesey has called it "the portion of the State that supports the densest and most extended population and has the closest mesh of transportation lines . . . it is more richly endowed by nature than the rest of the State."[2] From the historical politicogeographical viewpoint he defines it as "the area in which or about which a State originates."[3] The capital city of the state, he argues, will normally be positioned within the core area. Thus we could describe the French core area as the region around Paris, and that of the United Kingdom as the basin of the Thames River. But when we are confronted with the task of actually putting the core area on the politicogeographical map, we need criteria that are more precise than that. How close does the mesh of transportation lines have to be? How densely populated should a true core area be? What determines where the limits of the core area are—agricultural or industrial productivity, proximity to transportation lines, ethnic homogeneity—what?

In fact, it may be argued that these criteria vary from state to state. If we describe the core area of the United States as comprising the megalopolis along the eastern seaboard and the intensively industrialized and agriculturally productive interior adjacent to it, and then try to look for something similar in Iran or Tanzania, we would not be very successful. In some states a single railroad leading to the only port which also functions as the capital and only airport, where most of the literate people live and where the largest market is—that may constitute the core area for that particular state. Thus when core areas are studied, the level of development of the state system (not just politically, but economically, socially, and otherwise) must be taken into account. It is not possible at the moment to establish criteria that would be universally applicable.

But the absence of generally applicable criteria should not cause us to lose sight of the fact that we do look for certain specific geographical factors in every state whose core area we study. No core area exists today that is not served by communication lines, whether these lines be high-speed electrified railroads or dirt tracks, or, for that matter, a navigable river. Communication lines from outside converge upon the core area, and within the core area there are interconnecting routes, whatever the means of transportation. No core area exists without a certain degree of urbanization which is normally greater than elsewhere in the state. In Chapter 2, the rise of American and African states was described as closely associated with the evolution of sizable urban centers. Sometimes the heart of the state is still formed by a single, large urban center, which may also be the capital city; immediately surrounding the city begins a rural landscape which does not vary much from there to the border. Several African states possess such city cores. Elsewhere, a number of cities may form part of the core area.

[1] D. Whittlesey, *The Earth and the State*, New York, Holt, 1939, p. 2.
[2] Ibid.
[3] Ibid., p. 597.

Western Nigeria and the eastern United States are cases in point.

Core areas, also, tend to be more productive than other parts of the state. At times this is due to the fortuitous location of mineral resources, and at other times the productive capacity of the soil is greater here than elsewhere. Occasionally it is a combination of both. Thus, in defining the core area, we must pay attention to the source of the state's income—what are the roles of industry, agriculture, and mining in the national economy? The core area of Argentina is marked not only by several great urban centers, but by an expanse of fertile soil, flat land, and suitable climate. This is a deceptively large area when mapped and compared to, say, the industry-and-mining core of South Africa, focusing upon the relatively narrow Witwatersrand.

As Whittlesey has pointed out, the capital city often lies within the core area, so that the functions of government are generally performed within this region. New ideas applied elsewhere in the state originate in the core area and are distributed from it; decisions regarding the political posture of the state on the international scene are made here. Thus the core area is usually the most cosmopolitan part of the country, with representatives of foreign governments and other agencies in evidence. In that part of the world affected by European colonialism, present-day core areas can be seen often to lie along the coasts. The new ideas that came from Europe tended to spread from the coastal settlements sometimes founded and developed by the Europeans; modern schools, medical facilities, the money economy, and other European contributions first took hold here. The coastal peoples were "Europeanized" more rapidly than those of the interior; they gained political advantages over their more isolated countrymen, and these political advantages are today expressed in the newly independent governments of the emergent world. The core areas and capitals of Ghana, Peru, Algeria, and many other formerly colonial territories reflect all or part of this sequence of events.

DEFINITIONS

Although it is not difficult, then, to form a sort of subjective image of what the concept of core area involves, political geographers have not been able to agree entirely on specific definitions and appropriate usage of the term. This was pointed out by Professor Burghardt in an article published in 1969, in which he suggests that we begin to solve the problem by distinguishing between different *types* of core areas.[4] The concept of Ratzel and Whittlesey he identifies as the *nuclear core*. This is the case in which a small territory grows into a larger state, perhaps over a period of centuries, by intermittent absorption of land and people. But, Burghardt argues, there are other kinds of core areas. The *original core*, for example, was never the "kernel" of the state around which the accretion of territory took place; instead, it always was the area of greatest political and possibly also economic importance within an already larger framework. Third, Professor Burghardt recognizes the *contemporary core*, the area which is at present the area within the state that is of greatest political and/or economic significance. This contemporary core may have superseded the nuclear core of a state; in other words, a state's core area can shift and relocate over long periods of time.

Whenever the subject of core areas is discussed, European cases come to mind, for here arose many of the earliest core areas to develop into nation-states. In an article entitled "Core Areas and the Development of the European States System," Professors Pounds and Ball trace the evolution from nuclear and original cores of the modern states of the European continent.[5] Although their article is designed to review the territorial growth of some 25 European states, they, too, are concerned with typology. In their conclusion, the authors take a functional view of the problem; they recognize (1) states with *distinct* core areas, such as France, Czechoslovakia, and Russia, (2) states with *peripheral* core areas, including Yugoslavia and Portugal, and (3) states *without* distinct core areas, such as Albania and Belgium.[6]

It is also possible, of course, to seek a spatial solution to the problem of classification. In certain states, such as France and South Africa, the core area is *centrally* positioned. In other countries, including Brazil and Australia, the core areas are locationally *marginal* —that is, they lie on the margins, near the edges of those states. In the article by Pounds and Ball, there is mention even of *external*

[4]A. Burghardt, "The Core Concept in Political Geography: a Definition of Terms", *Canadian Geographer*, XIII, No. 4 (October, 1969), 349–353.

[5]Norman J. G. Pounds and Sue Simons Ball, "Core-Areas and the Development of the European States System," *Annals of the Association of American Geographers*, 54, No. 2 (March, 1964), 24–40.

[6]Ibid., p. 39.

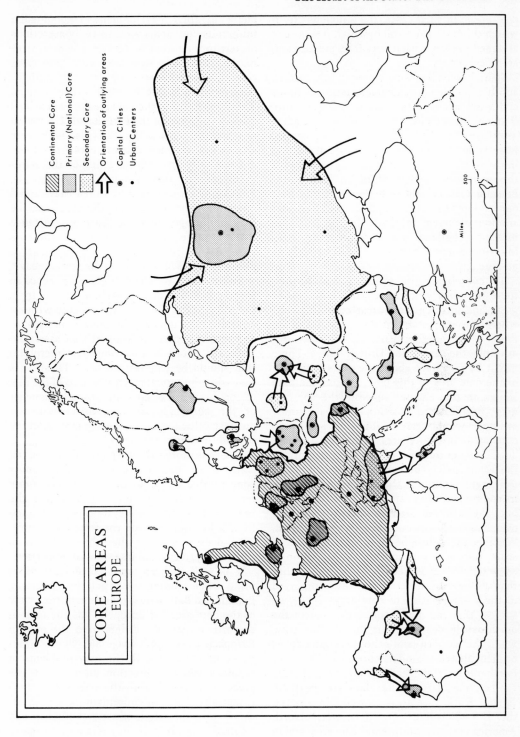

CORE AREAS
EUROPE

Continental Core
Primary (National) Core
Secondary Core
Orientation of outlying areas
Capital Cities
Urban Centers

Miles
500

core areas. In such cases, the "nucleus" from which the state arose and to which it was once attached has since been cut off by politicogeographical events.

Spatial considerations immediately lead to another problematic characteristic of states and core areas; certain states possess more than one such focus. Thus we might recognize multi-core, single-core, and no-core states. Nigeria, for example, has three core areas: one in the southwestern part of the country, one in the southeast, and a third in the north. Ecuador may be said to have two core areas: one centered upon Guayaquil on the coast, and another focusing on Quito in the highland interior. Thailand has a single core area; Mauritania and Chad might well classify as no-core units.

To complicate the problem still further, there are states which have quite distinct core areas *and* incipient core areas emerging elsewhere. Are such states multicore states or are these of a different variety? Consider, for example, the case of the United States. There might be argument about the exact boundary of the core area of this country, but the map shown in this chapter suggests the approximate northeastern position of what almost everyone would agree is this state's national core area. But core area characteristics are developing to the west of this core, notably on the west coast. The urban-industrial-population agglomeration in the west is large enough to constitute a core area in almost any state but the United States—where it is still overshadowed by the northeastern core region. What is the solution? It is probably one of *scale*, the same solution we alluded to on p. 83 when we suggested that national rather than universal criteria ought to be employed in the determination of core areas. Thus we suggest that the major core area, that of the northeast, be designated as the *primary* core, while the western (and other emerging areas) be identified as *secondary* core areas. Professor Burghardt suggests that this criterion of scale can be carried farther, that there are *continental* and *world* core areas as well.[7] In a sense, the U.S.–Canadian core in eastern North America is such a continental core area, and in Europe a developing continental core area can be recognized as well.

CORE AREAS AND CITIES

In Chapter 2, we noted that some states began as cities, and passed through a "city-state"

phase in their development. Undoubtedly, numerous core areas were initially accretions of territory around a central place, a large market town, or a defensible site. Thus most core areas—nuclear, original, or contemporary—include one or more urban centers. The Paris Basin is the core area of France, and Paris is the focus of the Paris Basin. The region of which Moscow is the focus also is the core area of Russia. Such cities in core areas, then, are normally the *capital* cities of the states involved. But this is not always the case. Professor Lewis Alexander noted that capital cities may relocate outside the core area; the map of Europe shows at least one instance where a state's capital lies outside the core area, and, as we will see later, there are a number of these instances in the world today.[8]

To Professor Burghardt's question, posed in his previously quoted article, "but in a functional sense can one have a core without an included capital?" the answer is "yes"— and there are cases to support that assertion. Two aspects of core areas and their interpretation should be emphasized here. The first is that while historical interpretations of the role of core areas are of great interest, the concept of the *contemporary* core area holds the greatest value for political geography. And the second involves the term "functioning;" a core area is more than the political heart of the state, it is the most productive, the most concentrated region in the state in economic terms, as well. It is indeed possible for the functioning of the state system to be directed from a location outside the state's core area. This does not mean that the core area is thereby deprived of all its essential properties.

It is well to keep these considerations in mind when reading the article by Professors Pounds and Ball, which takes a historical view of the core areas of Europe. Thus the map in the article (page 92) differs from the map of European Core Areas (page 85). These differences have to do with the very problems of typology and classification discussed in the preceding pages. Again—the map in the text is essentially a map of contemporary core areas; the map in the article illustrates *nuclear and original core areas* as they relate to European state development. The core area concept is a useful one, but its utility is still afflicted by definitional problems.

[7]Burghardt, op. cit., p. 351.
[8]1. M. Alexander, *World Political Patterns*, Chicago, Rand McNally, 1963, p. 55.

Core-Areas
and the Development of
The European States System

Norman J. G. Pounds and Sue Simons Ball

Indiana University

"There is no little provincial state," wrote Lucien Febvre in 1932, "which has not had its germinal, its geographical starting-point."[1] Among the 130 or so sovereign states which today decorate the political map of the world, it is perhaps legitimate to distinguish two broad categories: those which have been created arbitrarily to fill some preconceived geographical frame, and those which have grown slowly and over a long period of time from some nuclear, germinal, or core-area. This division is not rigid or absolute. Some states, such as France, which are commonly thought of as growing by a process of accretion around a core-area, nevertheless came to think of themselves as filling out a prescribed physical framework.[2] To these two generalized categories we have given the names of "arbitrary" and "organic" states. If they may be typified by their extremes, perhaps Jordan and Tsarist Russia may serve as examples. The purpose of this paper is to examine the physical nature of and the geographical role performed by the core-area in the formation of a particular group of states, namely those of Europe.

The geographical pattern of the states of Europe had, in general, taken shape before the age of modern nationalism, and it is difficult to discover among the forces which brought the states into being during the Middle Ages those same forces which gave impetus to their policies and shaped the boundaries in the 19th and 20th centuries. It cannot be denied, however, that a state system, once established, profoundly influenced the emergence of national feeling within the political boundaries already drawn. There are several instances—the Netherlands is an example—of national feeling coming within a very short span of years to fill out the geographical framework that had been defined arbitrarily, like new wine poured into an old bottle.[3] Examples are no less numerous of the territorial expansion of neighboring states into the political no-man's land which once separated them, and of the competition of neighboring national ideologies for the adherence and loyalty of the peoples who inhabit it. However profoundly they may have been modified and their expansion influenced by the forces which make up modern nationalism, most European states grew in fact by a process of accretion from germinal areas which have come, after Derwent Whittlesey, to be called "core-areas."[4]

A core-area must have considerable advantages in order to permit it to perform this role. Simply put, it must have within itself the elements of viability. It must be able to defend itself against encroachment and conquest from neighboring core-areas, and it must have been capable at an early date of generating a surplus income above the subsistence level, necessary to equip armies and to play the role in contemporary power politics that territorial expansion necessarily predicates. In terms of the Middle Ages, with which we are primarily

[1]Lucien Febvre, *A Geographical Introduction to History* (London: Kegan Paul, Trench, Trubner and Co., 1932), p. 310.

[2]Norman J. G. Pounds, "The Origin of the Idea of Natural Frontiers in France," *Annals*, Association of American Geographers, Vol. 41 (1951), pp. 146–57.

[3]G. J. Renier, *The Dutch Nation: an Historical Study* (London: George Allen and Unwin Ltd., 1944), p. 10.

[4]Derwent Whittlesey, *The Earth and the State* (New York: Henry Holt and Co., 1944), p. 597: "core, or nuclear core—the area in which or about which a state originates."

N.J.G. Pounds and S.S. Ball, "Core Areas and the Development of the European States System" *Annals of the Association of American Geographers*, Vol. 54 (March, 1964) 24–40.

concerned in this paper, this means a fertile soil, well cultivated within the limits of contemporary technology, a population dense enough to derive the maximum advantage from local resources, and, generally, a long-distance commerce to enable it to obtain materials not locally available.[5]

The question has been raised whether those who initiated the process of state expansion had any clear concept of the future geographical limits of the state, and whether they strove consciously to reach them. In nineteenth-century France, a school of historians, led by Albert Sorel, argued that from the first the French kings conceived of a France bounded by its "historic" or "natural frontiers."[6] It is difficult to accept such a view either for France or for any other country. Geographical concepts of space, distance, and direction were in general indefinite and unrefined. Maps were in some degree schematic, and rarely gave even an approximation to a true picture of the land. When the sons of the Emperor Louis the Pious met at Verdun in 843 to divide their father's lands between them, they discovered, not without some sense of shock, that they did not know what it was that they were dividing. In the words of the contemporary chronicler, Nithard:

And when those who had been sent by Ludwig and Charles to divide the kingdom had arrived, it was asked whether any among them had any conception of the extent of the whole empire. When no one was found with this knowledge, it was suggested that messengers should be sent to all parts to record what was there.[7]

It is inconceivable that, when the states system of Europe began to take shape, people could have had any clear concept of the geographical ends to which their expansion might be directed. Until the eighteenth or even the nineteenth century the territorial expansion of states was contingent and empirical, and only when the process of growth had made considerable progress did ideas both of nationalism and of a kind of geographical predestination enter in and attempt to impose a final shape upon the boundaries of states.

[5]Karl W. Deutsch, "The Growth of Nations: Some Recurrent Patterns of Political and Social Integration." *World Politics*, Vol. 5 (1952–1953), pp. 168–95.

[6]See Albert Sorel, *L'Europe et la Révolution française* (Paris, 1897).

[7]Nithard, *Monumenta Germaniae Historica, Scriptores*, Vol. 2, p. 671.

The medieval Kingdom of Hungary, it has recently been claimed by Andrew Burghardt, is an exception to the generalization that the state, in Europe at least, was never preordained and given, complete and clearly defined by the hand of nature. "The state idea bequeathed to his nation by King Stephen," he wrote,[8] "was at that time unique in Europe, in that it dealt with a territorially completed state. In terms of area, the Kingdom of Hungary was fully grown when it was born. . . . In Hungary no growth from a central, vital core was necessary. . . . The great contribution of the Magyars to Europe was the organization of the Carpathian Basin, and this was possible as an entirety, or not at all."

This echoes the traditional Hungarian argument, which has always asserted the basic physical and historical unity of the Pannonian Basin, and denied the validity of the contrary claim that the Hungarian Kingdom grew from a relatively small core-area near the Danube until it had embraced unrelated ethnic groups in the surrounding region of hills and mountains. To quote Burghardt again, "In Hungary no growth from a central vital core was necessary. The Kingdom had been established within an area eminently suitable to the creation of one state." Without examining at this point the historical validity of this claim (see below page 33), some doubt may nevertheless be expressed whether King Stephen (977–1038 A.D.) had any clear concept either of the geographical extent or of the physical unity of the Pannonian Basin, nor is it at all clear that he made any attempt to dominate and control it.

FRANCE THE PROTOTYPE

France is so often cited as the type case of the expansion of a state by territorial accretion around a nucleus or core-area, that it is worth-while to examine this process somewhat more closely. Some unity was given to the area now known as France by the Roman Conquest in the first century B.C. Its boundary was established along the Rhine, as a result in large measure of the contingencies of war. Its administrative focus lay in the middle Rhône valley, at Lugdunum (Lyon), from which the Roman road system radiated over the country. Roman authority was either withdrawn or

[8]Andrew F. Burghardt, *Borderland: A Historical and Geographical Study of Burgenland, Austria* (Madison: University of Wisconsin Press, 1962), pp. 71–72.

overthrown in the course of the Germanic invasions, and a congeries of small states emerged in its place, changing shape in a kaleidoscopic fashion until they were again united under the Carolingian rulers. Under the later Carolingians not only was the territory over which they ruled fragmented politically, but political authority itself became so attenuated that the local regions of France—the countries and duchies—became, under their counts and dukes, for practical purposes independent of the central authority.

The theoretical unity of most of what is today France was perhaps never in question, but this purely national unity ceased to be translated into the practical terms of political authority and control. The so-called unification of France consisted not in the extension over the whole area of the titular authority of a king of France—that was already admitted —but rather of the extension of the practical power of a government whose seat was in the country's capital. This could only be done by replacing the quasi-regal power which local dukes and counts had assumed, by the royal power itself. It was a question of the French king stepping into the place of the local territorial lord, and of adding to his own titular authority the latter's practical power. It is evident that the French kings succeeded by the end of the Middle Ages in doing just this. It is no less evident that this is what the Holy Roman emperors failed to do in either Germany or Italy. The French kings annexed to themselves the power of the local aristocracy by a variety of means: marrying their heiresses, overthrowing them in war, or even buying out their pretensions.

How it was done is, in the present context, less important than the definition of the nuclear area from which it was done. The Paris region was of no exceptional importance under the Romans, and provided a permanent residence for none of the later Merovingian and Carolingian rulers. The Carolingians more often made their home in northern France, the Low Countries, or the Rhineland. Charlemagne's favorite residence was Aachen, and the last of his successors in France made his home in the hilltop city of Laon, in Champagne. The rise of Paris to preeminence would seem to have owed little to environment or to tradition, and everything to the personality of its local rulers, the Counts of Paris of the Capet family. The enfeeblement of the last Carolingians, the personal strength and vigor of the early rulers of the House of Capet, and the success with which they held their small island in the Seine against the Norsemen, all led in 987 to Hugh Capet attaining the empty honor of being elected king of France. His real power was as wide, and no wider than the lands which he personally controlled. These lands surrounded Paris, and extended, with interruptions, beyond Senlis to the northeast and southward beyond the Loire. This was the *domaine royale*, and the royal power was later extended only by accessions to this area of direct royal control (Fig. 1).

It was entirely accidental that this *domaine royale*, the nucleus around which the Kingdom of France, as distinct from the geographical concept of France, was built, lay, for the greater part, in the fertile soils of Beauce and Brie. The Polyptiques[9] of the ninth and tenth centuries are evidence of the prosperity and dense population of these areas. Irminon's Polyptique demonstrates the high degree of organization of the manors,[10] and Ferdinand Lot has argued[11] that its population in the ninth century was greater than the rural population of the same area in the nineteenth. It is highly probable that it was the greater wealth and population of this nuclear area that gave the early Capets the influence and the material power which allowed them to extend their authority. This expansion was neither continuous nor regular;[12] nor can it be related to the facts of physical geography, such as the convergence of rivers on the Paris region.[13] Its course was at every stage contingent upon the exigencies of birth and death, succession and war.

The French example is far from typical of the territorial accretion of a state from a nuclear or core region. Expansion was not continuously outward, and it consisted not in the extension of the limits of the state *per se*, but rather of a particular kind of governmental control over it. Nevertheless, the boundary of France remained at the end of the Middle Ages

[9]Surveys or inventories of estates, which normally included lists of manors and the numbers of their inhabitants.

[10]See Auguste Longnon, *Polyptique de l'abbaye de Saint Germain des Prés* (Paris, 1895), and M. B. Guérard, *Polyptique de l'Abbé Irminon* (Paris, 1844).

[11]Ferdinand Lot, "Conjectures démographiques sur la France au IX siecle," *Le Moyen Age*, 2 Serie, Vol. 23 (1921), pp. 1–27; 109–37.

[12]See Albert Mirot, *Manuel de Géographie historique de la France* (Paris: Éditions A. et J. Picard et Cie., 1948).

[13]James Fairgrieve, *Geography and World Power* (London: University of London Press, 1921), p. 157.

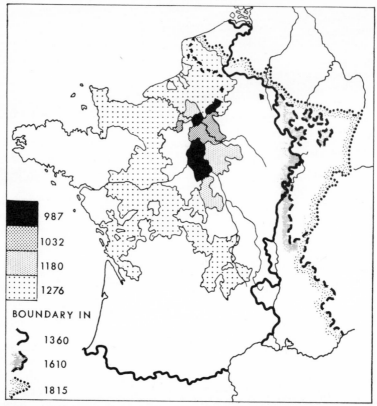

FIG. 1. *The core-area of France, and the territorial expansion of royal authority.*

approximately where it had theoretically been for centuries, along the lines of the rivers Scheldt, Meuse, Saône, and Rhône, with some local departures from this line. Between the sixteenth century and the period of the French Revolution, the limits of the state were physically advanced to the Alps, the Jura, and the Upper Rhine. This latter expansion accords more closely with the generalized concept outlined at the beginning of this paper, of the territorial expansion of a state by the extension of its authority into areas which it had not hitherto possessed either in theory or in practice.

NORTHWEST EUROPE

Fifteen of the major political units which at present make up Europe may be said to have expanded to their present limits from a clearly conceived core-area, and in most of them the political capital remains today in the nuclear area from which expansion took place. The most clear-cut examples are:

United Kingdom. The Roman occupation of the British Isles stopped short of the Scottish Border and faded out along the Marches of Wales and in the Celtic Southwest. The states

of the Saxon Heptarchy had each a small nucleus for its own tribal territory, but wars between them and the invasion and settlement of Norsemen and Danes in the northern and eastern parts of Britain led in time to the emergence of Wessex which during the last two centuries of Anglo-Saxon history became the dominant power in Britain, extending its authority northward and northeastward. It was to the ancient Kingdom of Wessex that the Norman rulers in effect succeeded in 1066, and they were obliged to reconquer much of the north of England themselves. Their core-area, the material base from which expansion and reconquest took place, was the Thames Valley. Here, Domesday Book shows us, was a region of relatively dense population, intensive agriculture, and high land values.[14] There were isolated areas of greater wealth and prosperity outside this nuclear-area, as there were also areas of small population density within it, but the former were isolated, and the

[14]H. C. Darby, *The Domesday Geography of Eastern England* (Cambridge: The University Press, 1952); H. C. Darby and I. B. Terrett, *The Domesday Geography of Midland England* (1954); and H. C. Darby and E. M. J. Campbell, *The Domesday Geography of South-East England* (1962).

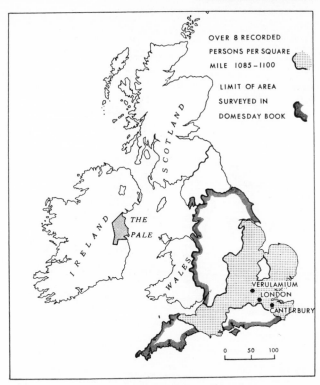

FIG. 2. The core-area of Great Britain and the expansion of sovereignty.

latter easily circumvented. Foremost among the outlying areas of high population was East Anglia, broadly the counties of Norfolk and Suffolk. If one asks why this area never became the core-area from which an English state was built, the answer—the contingencies of history aside—may lie in its high degree of physical isolation, with the Fenland to the west and the forested,[15] lightly settled London clays to the south.[16] The limit of Anglo-Norman power is roughly defined by the boundary of the territory surveyed in Domesday Book.

Wales was slowly penetrated by Anglo-Norman influences, and at the end of the thirteenth was conquered, though not formally absorbed into the Kingdom of Britain until the sixteenth. The map (Fig. 2) shows the chief lines of Anglo-Norman penetration into the Highland Zone of the British Isles. Scotland was subjected to a number of abortive invasions, before it in 1603 came to share its king with the rest of Britain, and in 1707 was joined with England in a parliamentary union.

[15]H. C. Darby, "The Fenland Frontier in Anglo-Saxon England," Antiquity, Vol. 8 (1934), pp. 185–201.

[16]S. W. Wooldridge and D. J. Smetham, "The Glacial Drifts of Essex and Hertfordshire, and Their Bearing Upon the Agricultural and Historical Geography of the Region," The Geographical Journal, Vol. 78 (1931). pp. 243–69.

Scandinavia. Both Sweden and Denmark developed from core-areas which differentiated themselves at an early date, while Norway presents a special case which is discussed below. For Sweden the archeological evidence shows a dense population even in the Middle and Late Iron Age (about 400–800 A.D.) in the lowland region which encloses Lake Malaren. Almost all the important Late Iron Age finds are from the area of Uppsala, or Uppland;[17] the seat of the earliest recognizable Swedish state was at Old Uppsala, and from this area one can trace at least the broad lines of a political expansion. This core-area, defined in Figure 3 in terms of Late Iron Age settlement, was not outstandingly fertile, though far more productive than the hilly regions to north and south. The branching waterway of Lake Malaren became a commercial focus relatively early, and the Uppland region, furthermore, enjoyed some degree of physical protection during the period of the Völkerwanderung. In the pre-Viking age (seventh century and earlier) Swedish rule had probably been extended from this area southward into the hills of Gothland, and throughout the medieval period it was slowly extended northwestward and north-

[17]Marten Stenberger, Sweden: Ancient Peoples and Places (London: Thames and Hudson, 1962), pp. 152 ff.

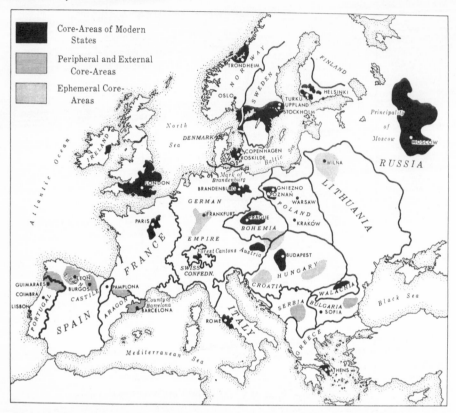

FIG. 3. Core-areas of modern European states. (Boundaries are shown as of the late 15th century.)

ward into the thinly peopled forest region of Norrland. In the early Viking age, the maritime connections of the Uppland region led to Swedish settlement along the eastern shore of the Baltic Sea and to the penetration of Swedes into and even across the territory that was later to become Russia. This expansion and settlement were not, however, followed by the establishment of political control from the core-area itself until the early years of the seventeenth century. The hills of Gothland formed a southern frontier to the Swedish state, and not until 1660 was Swedish rule extended to the southern and southwestern provinces of modern Sweden, Skane, Blekinge, and Halland.

The territory which today comprises Denmark was until the tenth century occupied by several tribes, whose boundaries shifted as their power rose and declined. At first a kind of paramountcy was exercised by the Danes of southern Jutland, in what is today Schleswig-Holstein. There the profits of the trade carried on by Danes and Frisians between northwest Europe and the Baltic contributed to the wealth and power of the local rulers. But the hegemony of this area was not permanent. The

country was in fact united in the tenth century by a ruling family whose seat and power rested at Jelling in northern Jylland (Jutland). The tendency was at first for the young Danish state to expand westward, across the North Sea, to Great Britain. In the mid-eleventh century this "sea-state" collapsed, and, after a period of division and anarchy, the Danish state turned its attention eastward and extended its authority through the Danish archipelago to the Halland, Skane, and Blekinge provinces of southern Sweden. With this change in the geographical outlook of the state, there came a shift in the location of its capital, from Jylland to Roskilde, which lay on the island of Sjaelland and was already the seat of the Danish archbishop.

Sjaelland, with the neighboring island of Fyn and the territory of Skane in southern Sweden, had far greater agricultural potentialities than Jylland. The wealth of this, the second Danish state, allowed it to engage in extensive maritime adventures, and its location astride the Danish straits permitted it not only to engage in trade but also to tax the trade carried on by others, primarily by the Hanseatic merchants, between the Baltic and the North seas. The importance of maritime trade led in the later Middle Ages to the rise of the commercial city of Copenhagen and to the transferrence there in 1445 of the seat of the Danish kings.

Despite the shifts in the center of Danish rule, it is difficult not to see in Sjaelland and neighboring Fyn and Skane, the core-area of the modern Danish state.

Switzerland, though clearly growing by a process of accretion around a core-area, departs in one important respect from the general pattern of states which grew in this way. The Confederation originated in 1291, when the four Forest Cantons of Uri, Schwyz, and Ob- and Nidwalden united in opposition to the feudal restrictions from which they suffered. The success of their cause attracted other areas which became in turn cantons in the confederation. The difference between the core-area of Switzerland—the original cantons—and that of other states examined thus far lies in the fact that, whereas the latter were fertile, prosperous, and relatively densely peopled, the Swiss area was essentially poor. The documents show, in the area of the Forest Cantons a sparse and primitive population, whose ideas of political organization were rudimentary in the extreme. The paradox is explained by the fact that, whereas other core-areas derived their political power and their capacity to expand in part at least from their productive agriculture and relatively dense population, the core-area of Switzerland derived both wealth and political ideas from the trade and the merchants who came from Italy to Germany by the newly opened St. Gotthard route.[18]

EAST AND SOUTHEAST EUROPE

The Slav countries present what are perhaps the clearest examples of territorial expansion from nuclear areas. Indeed, it is possible to discover more incipient core-areas than were able ultimately to expand and to become nuclei of separate states. Some, especially in the Danube basin and Balkan peninsula, after serving for a time as the core-areas of primitive or tribal states, lost their primacy or were extinguished by invasion and conquest. It thus became the role of historical forces to choose from among the several areas of increment in this area those which were to develop as the

[18]Charles Gilliard, "Problèmes d'histoire routière: I—L'Ouverture du Gothard," *Annales d'Histoire Economique et Sociale*, Vol. 1 (1929), pp. 177–82.

foci of their respective states. Curiously most of these core-areas had appeared by the end of the tenth century as centers of relatively dense population, foci of trade, and centers of some form of political power.

The Polish and the Russian cases are the simplest, along with the non-Slav Hungarian state. The Czech example is somewhat more complex and those of the Balkans are of a degree of complexity which excludes them from this category of states growing from simple core-areas.

Poland

The Polish state emerged a thousand years ago in the area of relatively good soil and early settlement (Fig. 3) which is bounded on the three sides by the River Warta and its tributary, the Noteć. The intrinsic advantages of soil were reinforced by the commerce between the Baltic region and southern Europe, which followed the lakes and navigable rivers characterizing this region. The seat of the earliest Polish kings as well as of the first archbishop was Gniezno. The political capital was later shifted to Poznań, still within the core-area, and later to Krakow and in 1596 to Warsaw, which lay a short distance outside it. Gniezno remained the ecclesiastical capital until this function was also taken over by Warsaw.

This Polish core-area was protected by the flat, wide, and marshy valleys of the rivers which enclosed it on most sides. The surplus which derived from its agriculture and commerce was in part invested in the Romanesque churches which still distinguish this region, and in part furnished the armies with which the early kings extended their rule westward approximately to the line of the lower Odra (Oder) River and eastwards to the Prypeć marshes and the "cities" of Ruthenia. During the following centuries, the Polish state lost territory on the west, and expanded farther to the east. Its original core-area became eccentric without however ceasing to be part of prepartition Poland. One is, however, still reminded of the early primacy of the Gniezno-Poznań region by its name: Wielkopolska, or Great Poland.

Russia

The Russian case is too familiar to require, or to deserve, any extended discussion. The first Russian state had its focus in the Steppes, where it had every advantage except that of natural protection. The second grew up amid the mixed forest of the Muscovy region, around the headwaters of the Volga and Oka rivers, and here it enjoyed some degree of natural protection, without, however, the sources of agricultural and commercial wealth which had distinguished the Kievan state.

Muscovy spread outwards from the Moscow region with the same apparent constancy of purpose which characterized the extension of royal power in France from the Paris region. And, like the "expansion" of France, that of Muscovy has also been attributed to a kind of grand design, a compulsion to expand outward until the sea set a limit to expansion. Although it is as erroneous to see such a *Leitmotiv* in Russian history[19] as it is in that of France, the formation of the Russian state is marked by an almost continuous outward movement from the sixteenth to the nineteenth centuries. It was not "an insatiable thirst for salt water," as has been convincingly discussed by John Morrison,[20] but local and immediate contingencies which led to the phenomenon of Russian expansion to the seas. The Russian core-area of Muscovy had the advantages of protection from the raiders of the Steppe; it lay at a focus of routes which tended to follow the Russian rivers, and it possessed a natural fertility which, though less than that of the Steppe region to the south, was probably as high as that of the Polish core-area.

The Danube Valley

The valley of the middle and lower Danube, together with the Czech lands of Bohemia and Moravia, is made up of a series of basins, generally level and relatively fertile, ringed by hills or mountains. One can distinguish the plains of northern Bohemia and of Moravia, the small basins along the Danube, especially those between Melk and Tulln, and below Vienna; the larger plain between the Leitha-Little Carpathian ridge and the Bakony Forest; the Transdanubian region, or Dunántúl, and the Sava valley in Slovenia and Croatia. Here, as in Poland and Russia, lived a number of tribes, many of which were listed and briefly described by the anonymous Bavarian geographer of the ninth century[21] and by the Arab traveler and merchant, Ibrahim Ibn Jakub.[22] We do not know how primacy among these tribes was achieved, but it is tempting to attribute it to the area, the agricultural productivity, the population density, and the commercial relations of those core-areas which came to be dominant. Unquestionably such environmental factors were little more than permissive; the contingencies of history played the major role in this process of selection.

If we exclude the nebulous state of Samo of the seventh century, the earliest Danubian state to emerge was "Great Moravia," to which the missionaries, Cyril and Methodius, were sent in the ninth century. Its core was made up of the plains of southern Moravia and southwestern Slovakia, and its capital may have been the city of Nitra, 45 miles to the northwest of Bratislava. The Moravian state was extinguished in the late ninth and early tenth century by the Magyar invaders, and its core-area became a disputed borderland between Germans, Czechs, and Hungarians.

The valley of the River Elbe in northern Bohemia was more fortunate in its history. Two separate political units, perhaps tribal in origin, developed here, based respectively in the western and eastern parts of the region. Whatever their origin, the conflict between them came to be focused in the rivalry of the Premyslids of the Prague area and the Slavniks of the area lying to the east around Libice (Fig. 4). In the course of this conflict the Premslids were victorious, and united first the lowlands around Prague, and later extended their authority first to all Bohemia and then to Moravia and Silesia. It is from this Czech state of Greater Bohemia that modern Czechoslovakia derives, in part at least, its boundaries and traditions.

Austria constitutes an exception to this pattern of state building in east-central Europe, and will be examined below. In the meanwhile, another state began to emerge in the southwestern corner of the Pannonian Basin. There the rivers Drava and Sava, discharging from the Alps of Carinthia and Carniola, are separated only by a low, broken, and easily traversed divide. Into this region Croat tribes came in the seventh century.

[19]Robert J. Kerner, *The Urge to the Sea: The Course of Russian History* (Berkeley: University of California Press, 1942).

[20]John A. Morrison, "Russia and Warm Water," *United States Naval Institute Proccedings*, Vol. 78 (1952), pp. 1169–79.

[21]Geograf Bavarski, *Monumenta Poloniac Historica*. Vol. I (1864), pp. 10–11.

[22]Relatio Ibrahim Ibn Ja'kub de Itinere Slavico, *Monumenta Poloniae Historica*, new series, Vol. I (1946).

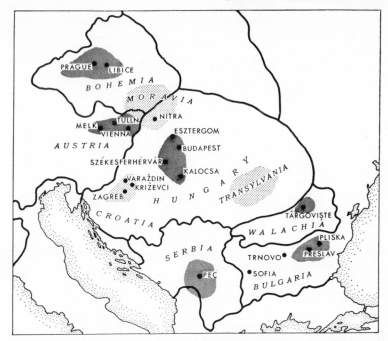

FIG. 4. Core-areas in the middle Danube valley; for key to symbols see Figure 3.

Until the tenth century the region remained one of loosely organized tribes. Then part of it became united politically under King Tomislav, and during the following century the Croat state expanded to the Adriatic, into the hills of Bosnia and Serbia, and eastward into the forested plain of Slavonia. Its core lay in the Sava and Drava valleys, and corresponded approximately with the three *Zhupaniya* (administrative districts) of Varazhdin, Krizhevats,[23] and Zagreb, which were created soon after the year 1100 by King Koloman. There was reputedly some road building between the Drava and Sava to the east of Zagreb at this time, and a bishopric was established in Zegreb. But already Croatia was beginning to fall under the control of the Hungarian state, and a Croat state based upon this core-area failed to maintain itself.

Hungary

The Hungarians, or Magyars, had entered the plain that has since borne their name about the year 896. They were made up of a number of tribes, of which that of Arpad seems to have been dominant and may have been the largest. Arpad's horde crossed the Danube and settled the region still known as Transdanubia, or Dunántúl. The center of his power was near Szekesfehervar, which was the Hungarian capital until, in 1247, this was moved to the hill of Buda, overlooking the Danube, 40 miles to the northeast.[24] The Hungarian tribes, which seem to have spread widely over the plain, were a loosely organized group, over which the authority of Arpad and of his successors was gradually established. The core-area of this state was the land which Arpad settled in Dunántúl, though it probably extended across the ridge of the Bakony Forest to the Little Alföld, where it embraced part of the area of the former Great Moravian state. Within this area the two archiepiscopal sees, Esztergom and Kalocsa, not to mention a number of monasteries, were established.

It may be suggested that the early Hungarian kings had no concept of the unity of the great plain, and did not identify themselves with it. They may, however, have visualized some unity among the Magyar and related tribes, and thus have gradually established their own authority over the plain. But it was not until the end of the eleventh century that they established their rule over the southwestern or Croatian parts of the plain. Their authority over the surrounding hills and mountains came much later, and Hungary, like its

[23]The modern Krizevci, to the northeast of Zagreb. See Francis R. Preveden, *History of the Croatian People* (New York: Philosophical Library, 1955), p. 95.

[24]C. A. Macartney, *Hungary, a Short History* (Edinburgh: The University Press, 1962), p. 9.

neighbors, seems to fall into the category of states which grew by a process of accretion around a core-area.

Romania is perhaps the marginal example of a state that has been derived by a process of accretion from a nuclear-area. Romanian historians claim a historical continuity from the province of Dacia, which the Romans held in the second and third centuries A.D.[25] The future state of Romania emerged, however, outside the limits of the Roman province, in the plains of Walachia and Moldavia, which lay beyond the curving line of the Carpathian Mountains and Transylvanian Alps. It is difficult to say whether its Romance-speaking, or Vlach, population came from beyond the Danube to the south or from beyond the mountains to the north and west. Walachia emerged under the dominance in turn of Hungarians, Bulgars, and Turks; Moldavia, under that of Turks, Tatars, and Poles. The focus of power in the Walachian principality lay in the loess-covered plains of the center, where Târgoviste became its capital during the Middle Ages, and was subsequently replaced by the city of Bucharest, 45 miles away. Moldavia was in general poorer because more exposed to the raiding Tatars from the Russian steppe. The best soil and the densest settlement lay toward the north of the province, amid the loess-covered hills around Iasi. This focus of political power in Moldavia was separated by a distance of some 200 miles, as well as by the marshes along the lower Pruth, Siret, and Danube, from the Walachian core-area. It may be that political power did, in fact, extend outward from each of these core-areas to cover their respective provinces during the Middle Ages, but of this process there is no unambiguous record. The boundaries of the provinces themselves were the result of wars and treaties between the Turks (who retained a jurisdiction that was at times only nominal until 1858) and their northern neighbors. The Romanian state was created in 1859, when these two provinces were merged under a single ruler, and it increased its territory during the following half century, with the incorporation of southern Dobrodgea, Transylvania, the eastern border of the Hungarian Plain, and Bessarabia.

[25]R. W. Seton-Watson, *A History of the Roumanians* (Cambridge: The University Press, 1934), pp. *ibid.*, "Roumanian Origins," *History*, Vol. 7 (1922–1923), pp. 241–55.

SOUTHERN EUROPE

The modern states of Italy and Greece were established during the nineteenth century. They were shaped by the current spirit of nationalism, but their boundaries had in some degree been influenced by memories of the *Italia* and *Hellas* of classical times.

Italy

A lasting shape was given to the concept of Italy by the expansion of the Roman Republic to cover the whole peninsula. Its nucleus was the city of Rome and the Surrounding Campagna (Fig. 5). The record of the invasion and conquest of the hill country to the east and southeast and of Etruria to the northwest is a matter of legend rather than of history. It was followed by the conquest of southern Italy from the Greeks and Carthaginians, and of the Po Valley, or Cisalpine Gaul. The unity of Italy in the geographical sense was thus effected in classical times. The Germanic invasions undid this work and the Middle Ages perpetuated the chaotic political pattern which then evolved. Commercially, Florence, Vernice, and Genoa came to surpass the city of Rome, but in an ideological sense Rome never lost its primacy; nor the concept of a united Italy, its fascination for at least an educated minority of Italians. The events of 1860–1918 restored by a series of quick strokes the geographical pattern of the late classical period.

Greece achieved unity in ancient times, but not through the efforts of the Greeks themselves. Though the commercial primacy of Athens was as clear-cut as its cultural dominance, its sovereignty was restricted to Attica, and the "Athenian Empire," even when its control by Athens was least disputed, remained something of a misnomer. Political unity was imposed on the Greek peninsula from outside, in turn by the Macedonians, Romans, Byzantines, and Turks. Whatever the rulers, the primacy of Attica was undisputed, and it remained the seat of a local government until it became in 1832 the capital of an independent Greece. The boundaries of Greece were extended by stages to enclose the whole peninsula, the northern littoral of the Aegean Sea, and the Aegean islands. Greece is, like Romania, a marginal case, where the focus of economic and political power had long been apparent, but around which the state was not built by a process of accretion.

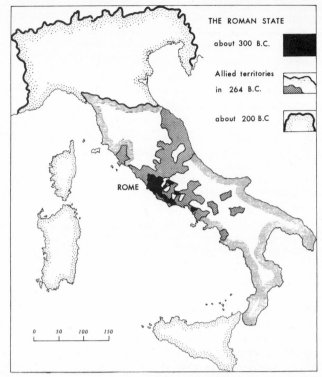

FIG. 5. The core-area and expansion of Roman authority in Italy.

CORE-AREAS OF DEPENDENT TERRITORIES

At least four states of the European states system began as dependent territories which developed nevertheless around a definite and clearly defined core-area. Only after expansion from this nucleus was almost complete, did the territory thus unified, become politically independent.

Republic of Ireland

The unity of the island of Ireland was achieved from the late twelfth century onwards, by conquering immigrants from England, who made the Dublin region the basis of their activities. The core-area from which English authority spread out over the island may be roughly equated with the so-called "Pale," an area of some 1,200 square miles, forming the hinterland of Dublin (Fig. 2). The political and economic dominance of this area became so secure, that no attempt was ever made by independent Eire to move it. In the meanwhile, however, English and Scottish settlement in the seventeenth century had created in the northeast of the island a second core-area in the lowlands that surround Lough Neagh and extend down the Lagan valley to

Belfast. Today, and probably for the last three centuries, the Belfast and Dublin areas have been the most densely peopled areas in Ireland. But the marked difference between the Protestant tradition and the industrial economy of Belfast and its hinterland, and the Catholic and rural traditions of the Dublin hinterland led in 1922 to the partition of the island into the Irish Free State (now the Republic of Ireland) and Northern Ireland, which has since remained an integral part of the United Kingdom, with its political and economic focus in Belfast.

Finland

The Finnish case fits the model closely. Political unity was imposed on the area by Swedish settlers who occupied the southwestern littoral, where the climate is less severe than in other parts of the state and agricultural land is more extensive and of a higher quality than elsewhere in the country. The making of the later Finnish state came about, not so much by conquest, as by the process of pioneer settlement in almost virgin country.[26]

[26]See map of the expansion of settlement in W. R. Mead, *Farming in Finland* (London: The Athlone Press, 1953), p. 10.

The core-area of Finland is roughly the hinterlands of Helsinki and Turku, today the largest cities, and in the early Middle Ages probably the only area with a settled population.

Austria

The Republic of Austria began its political history as a frontier dependency of the Duchy of Bavaria, to which it stood as the Ostmark, the Eastern Borderland. Its political center moved gradually down the Danube valley, as Austria fulfilled its historic function of protecting south Germany from invasion and then extended its authority eastward into the Pannonian plain. The capital of the Ostmark was established first on the Danube at Melk. About 1100, the capital was moved to Tulln, and later in the twelfth century to Vienna. At about the same time the Ostmark terminated its dependence on Bavaria, and became—what it remained until 1806—the Duchy of Austria. In this instance the filling out of the territorial limits of the state was completed after Austria had ceased to be a dependency of Bavaria, but the process had begun while it was still a "colony."

Norway

During the early Middle Ages, a group of tribal kingdoms came gradually to be dominated by the one which centered in the Trondheim area. The growing population of this fjord coast sought, like the early Danes, adventure, wealth, and new lands to settle westward beyond the sea, in the British Isles, Iceland, and even Greenland. Trondheim remained the Norwegian capital and the seat of the archbishop until 1380. Thereafter, Norway was ruled by Danish kings; the functions of capital were transferred to Denmark, and no attempt was made to build a cohesive state around the Trondheim core-area.

In 1814, rule over Norway was transferred to the king of Sweden, and the Oslo region, which in the early Middle Ages had constituted the important tribal kingdom of Vestfold,[27] now began to assume the role formerly played by Trondheim. Oslo lay close to the Swedish boundary, and had easy communications with Stockholm, which other areas more traditionally Norwegian did not have. In 1906 the union between Sweden and Norway was terminated. By this date the governmental functions were so well established in Oslo, that no attempt was made to transfer them to any site more closely identified with Norwe-

gian history and culture. Instead, the name of the capital was, in 1925, changed from the Danish name of Christiania, to the now familiar Norwegian name of Oslo.

Summary

In the previous pages we have examined fifteen European states which can be said in some sense to have grown by a process of accretion around a core-area. We have also mentioned some areas, which during the early Middle Ages had some of the characteristics of core-areas, but whose independent existence was terminated by the growth of others. With the exception only of that of modern Switzerland, these core-areas have certain features in common. All are regions of good soil and, in early times, of relatively high agricultural productivity. They were, in Fleure's phrase, "regions of increment." Most were centers of prehistoric population and culture, and archeological evidence, dating in some instances from as far back as the Neolithic, shows them to have been relatively densely populated.[28] Several were colonized by various of the Neolithic Danubian cultures. This is especially true of the Paris region, central Poland, and the various core-areas already in existence along the middle and lower Danube valley. Attica and the Roman Campagna came to be intensively settled and cultivated in early classical times. All showed during their formative period in the early Middle Ages —roughly from the eighth to the twelfth centuries—a very heavy investment in art and architecture, itself an indication of the surplus which these areas yielded, and most became the seat, not only of civil administration, but also of ecclesiastical.

Most of these core-areas lay also at the focus of routes. Relatively little is known about the volume or even of the direction of the trade carried on by the core-areas which emerged during the ninth and tenth centuries. The scanty finds, in central Poland, in Bohemia and Moravia, in the neighborhood of Paris, in southeastern England, in Muscovy, and in central Sweden, taken together with the literary sources, are evidence that it was, for

---

[27]Wilhelm Keilhan, Norway in World History (London: Macdonald & Co., 1944), p. 58.

[28]See particularly V. Gordon Childe, The Prehistory of European Society (Harmondsworth, Middlesex: Penguin Books, Ltd., 1958); ibid., Prehistoric Migrations in Europe (Oslo: Instituttet for Sammenlignende Kulturforskning, 1950); J. G. D. Clark, Prehistoric Europe: The Economic Basis (London: Methuen and Co., 1952); Marija Gimbulas, The Prehistory fo Eastern Europe (Cambridge, Mass.: American School of Prehistoric Research, Peabody Museum, 1956).

its age, both vigorous and important. The wealth gained from trade must in every instance have contributed to the political power of the core-area, and, in the case of Switzerland, provided the chief source of income for the incipient state.

Lastly, most core-areas possessed in some degree a natural means of defense which gave them some protection during this early, formative period. In some instances the core-area lay away from contemporary invasion routes. In others a physical barrier was provided by forest, such as gave some protection to the Paris and London regions, or of wide, marshy valleys such as enclosed the core-area of Poland, or of mountain and waste such as enclosed the core-areas of Sweden and Switzerland.

ECCENTRIC AND EXTERNAL CORE-AREAS

The political geography of the Balkan countries and of Spain and Portugal differs from that of the European countries already discussed, insofar as the original core-areas from which they grew either lapsed into relative insignificance or were later abandoned. In other words, expansion was in these instances a one-sided or unidirectional movement, and the focus of political power moved with the advance of the boundary. The core-area today is thus marginal to, or even outside the boundaries of the state.

Spain and Portugal

The Iberian Peninsula had been part of the Roman Empire, and its political and economic foci had been along the shore of the Mediterranean Sea. Most of the penninsula succumbed to the Moorish invaders in the eighth century, but remnants of the local population maintained themselves in the northern mountains, where, in quasi-independence, they perpetuated a system of petty states of their own. From the valleys of the Cantabrian Mountains and the Pyrenees they spread southward, creating at one time a tier of no less than half a dozen small states. As these states expanded southward into a region of more genial climate and, in general, of better soil, their capitals were also moved south. Portugal severed its connection with the Galician mountains from which it had sprung, and its capital city was first Guimaraes, then Coimbra, and finally, after 1256, Lisbon.[29]

In the Spanish part of the peninsula the city of Madrid, chosen in 1561 by Philip II to epitomize the new-found unity of the peninsula, succeeded to the functions formerly performed by a group of more northerly capital cities of the "Five Kingdoms": Burgos, Leon, Pampluna, Saragossa, and Barcelona. Castile, indeed, had never had a fixed seat of government, "the capital being," in typical medieval fashion, "wherever a peripatetic court happened to find itself, with Valladolid and Toledo as preferred centers in the two previous reigns."[30] The several core-areas from which modern Spain derived, unlike that of Portugal, still lie wholly within the boundaries of the state but are today peripheral to it.

Balkan Peninsula

The comparable development in the Balkan countries has been complicated and interrupted by war, invasion, and conquest. Yugoslavia, Bulgaria, and even Romania were represented during the Middle Ages by states, each having a distinct core-area, which it retained for centuries, however much its peripheral regions may have fluctuated with the vicissitudes of war. The medieval Serb state thus had its nucleus in the basins (polja) of what is today Kosovo-Metohija and neighboring areas. Here the flat-floored polja, with their covering of residual clays, provided a region of modest increment. Today it is distinguished by a rich legacy of early medieval churches, built in a Byzantine style well adapted to local materials and needs.[31] One of them, the church of Peć, became the seat of the Serb archbishop and patriarch. It was within this, its own core-area, that the medieval Serb state, in 1389, suffered the disastrous defeat of Kosovo, which led to its extinction early in the following century.

When, early in the nineteenth century a Serb state again emerged, its nucleus lay in the forested Sumadija region, in northern Serbia, where the successful revolt against Turkish rule first broke out. It was not until 1913 that the Serb state again came to embrace its original core-area, now largely deprived by migration of its Serb inhabitants, and settled by Albanians.

Bulgaria

The Bulgarian state was created by an invading

[29]H. V. Livermore, A History of Portugal (Cambridge: The University Press, 1947), p. 134; J. B. Trend, Portugal (London: Ernest Benn Ltd., 1957). pp. 57–59.

[30]William C. Atkinson, A History of Spain and Portugal (Harmondsworth, Middlesex: Penguin Books, 1960), P. 153; also Harold Livermore, A History of Spain (London: George Allen & Unwin Ltd., 1958), pp. 101–18.

[31]Cecil Stewart, Serbian Legacy (London: George Allen and Unwin Ltd.), p. 18.

Ural-Altaic people, who entered the Balkan peninsula from the South Russian Steppe. They crossed the lower Danube and settled in the open loess-covered region between the Balkan Mountains and the Danube. Their number, and the rapidity with which they were assimilated by the local Slav population, are a matter of dispute. There is no question, however, that the Bulgarian Empire continued to be ruled from the area where they first settled.[32] Here were their earliest capitals, Pliska and Preslav, and in this area recent excavations have revealed extensive remains of the earliest Bulgarian Empire.[33] From this nuclear region, the first Bulgarian state spread south across the Stara Planina and even to Serbia and Macedonia, and beyond the Danube into Walachia and even the Hungarian Plain.

After a period of eclipse and conquest by the Byzantine emperors, the Second Bulgarian Empire arose from the ashes of the first. Its core-area was again on the fertile platform which slopes down from the Stara Planina to the Danube, and its capital was established at Trnovo, about 60 miles west of the sites of the earlier capitals. From this area the Tsars of the Second Bulgarian Empire (1185–1393) extended their rule to cover an area similar to that held by the First Empire.

The third Bulgaria did not appear until 1877–1878, when the Turkish Empire suffered military defeat and was obliged to recognize the Bulgarian state. Although this new Bulgarian state embraced the Danubian platform and had pretensions no less extensive than either of its predecessors, its capital was established at Sofia, south of the Stara Planina. This choice demonstrated a new orientation in Bulgarian politics. Bulgaria no longer linked itself with the region from which the Bulgars had come; instead, it looked for territorial advancement to the south, and the expense of the Turk. The site of the capital of Bulgaria, like those of Portugal and Spain, moved south with the territorial expansion of the state.

STATES WITHOUT CORE-AREAS

This survey of the states of modern Europe leaves only three major states unmentioned: Germany, the Netherlands, and Belgium. The

formation and growth of each of these differed in certain respects from that of other European states. The Netherlands and Belgium were formed, not in response to the urgings of nationalism, but as a result of war and the European power balance. The Netherlands were created almost overnight by the successful revolt against Spain of some of the Hapsburg possessions in the Low Countries. In the words of G. J. Renier,[34] the Dutch people "found themselves overnight where it had taken the people of other national states centuries to arrive." Once the state had been created, its focus of political and economic power came to be established in the Province of Holland, where it has since remained, but the state did not grow up around this nucleus.

Belgium is a yet more arbitrary creation. It remains substantially what was left of the Spanish Low Countries after the Dutch revolt, trimmed and modified in detail by subsequent treaties and agreements. From the late Middle Ages until 1815 it was a dependency first of Spain and then of Austria. Linked with the Netherlands in 1815, it broke away in 1831, and became the Kingdom of Belgium. It remains divided between two culture groups, the Flemings and the Walloons, each with a sort of core-area in respectively the cities of Flanders and the rolling plains of central Begium, but in neither instance did this focus of power serve as a nucleus around which a state was built.

To this list should be added six other states: Albania, an arbitrary creation of the London Conference of 1912–1913,[35] which, though justified by its ethnic composition, owed both its origin and its boundaries to the complex power balance in Europe at that time; and Luxemburg, Liechtenstein, Monaco, San Marino, and Andorra, feudal units which are individually too small to have had distinct nuclei from which they developed.

THE GERMAN CASE

It is impossible to fit Germany into any one of the categories previously discussed in this paper. Its ultimate unity was not the result of a gradual expansion from any recognizable core-area, nor was it arbitrarily imposed from

[32]Steven Runciman, The First Bulgarian Empire (London, 1930).

[33]Stantcho Stantchett, "L'archéologie slave en Bulgarie de 1945–1947," Slavia Antiqua, Vol. 2 (1949–1950), pp. 522–35.

[34]G. J. Renier, The Dutch Nation (London: George Allen & Unwin,Ltd., 1944), p. 10

[35]Lord Grey of Falloden, Twenty-five Years, 1892–1916 (New York: Frederick A. Stokes Co., 1925), Vol. I. pp. 255–67.

without. It was achieved almost suddenly by the strongest of the many small states which made up nineteenth-century Germany, acting in the name of German nationalism. "The internal physical structure of Urdeutschland is inimical to unity," wrote Derwent Whittlesey,[36] attributing to nature what was essentially the result of the contingencies of history. The original Germany of the early Middle Ages was made up of a number of tribal dutchies. "The tribes did not set in the mold of stem dutchies because of tribal coherence, but because each group settled down in a core of arable lowland separated from its neighbors by wooden hills, marshy lowlands, or sandy heaths and forests." There were, in other words, some half dozen core-areas, not one of which "possessed clear superiority of power based on either agricultural or commercial resources." A kind of balance was preserved between them, and the imperial title was tossed from Saxon to Swabian, to Franconian, to Bavarian dukes. The nuclear-region of Lorraine, consisting of the fertile plains of the upper Meuse and Moselle, was too close to France and too exposed to French territorial claims and to invasion by French armies for it ever to have had a good chance of becoming a nucleus of a German state. The same is true of Burgundy whose political and economic focus lay in the Saone valley. The four remaining German duchies, Swabia, Bavaria, Franconia, and Saxôny, had a greater potential. Swabia centered in the fertile loess-covered plains that lie amid the rolling hills of the upper Neckar and upper Danube valleys. Bavaria had as its core-area the scattered areas of good farmland which lay on each side of the Danube from Donauwörth down to Passau, separated by more extensive areas of forest and marsh. Franconia, which included the Rhine plain from Bingen up to Heidelberg, as well as the Wetterau and the loess lands along the middle Main valley, was potentially richer in its agricultural resources, was a focus of early commercial activity, and was almost centrally placed in medieval Germany. If one could conceive of the German emperors of the Franconian dynasty (Conrad II, 1024, to Henry V, d. 1125) as playing a role similar to that performed in France by the House of Capet, a progressive unification of Germany might have been achieved. Franconia was the economic focus of the medieval German Reich; it

was probably the most densely peopled;[37] it contained many of the larger commercial centers, and its leading cities: Frankfurt, Mainz, Worms, and Speyer were by far the most frequent meeting places of the medieval German Diet of the Holy Roman Empire.

The most significant rival to Franconia would have been Saxony, whose core-area spread over the loess belt, between the hills of central Germany and the marshy and thinly peopled northern plain. Throughout most of the tenth century and into the eleventh the German Empire had the Saxon dukes as its titular head. But the Saxons, like the Lorrainers, lay on the border of medieval Germany and eastward conquest and settlement in the Slav lands occupied their energies, just as expansion down the Danube valley did that of the Bavarian dukes.

Yet is was around none of these nuclei that Germany was in the end united, but instead around a relatively poor and backward area which was even outside the limits of the early German Empire. The rise of Brandenburg, first to an equality with the older power centers of Germany, and then to a position of supremacy was achieved in defiance of the factors of physical geography. It was, in the words of A. J. Toynbee, "an unprepossessing country . . . with its starveling pine-plantations and its sandy fields,"[38] and he attributed the Brandenburg-Prussia into its position of supremacy to the stimulus of this "hard country." The fact is that the Hohenzollerns of Brandenburg proved to be able to organize and develop the modest resources of their realm and to build so efficient a military machine, that they acquired the power to extend it by conquest and ultimately to draw the whole of Germany into an empire ruled by themselves.

There thus proved to be in Germany two separate core-areas, the middle Rhineland and Brandenburg. As late as the mid-nineteenth century the historical, cultural, and economic dominance of the middle Rhineland was still apparent. The "Parliament," which reflected the strivings of Germans for political unity in the early nineteenth century, met in 1848 in Frankfurt. Only with the political failure of

---

[36]Derwent Whittlesey, The Earth and the State (New York: Henry Holt and Co., 1944), p. 181.

[37]Julius Beloch, "Die Bevolkerung Europas im Mittelalter," Zeitschrift für Sozialwissenschaft, Vol. 3 (1900), pp. 405–23; Wilhelm Abel, "Wachstumsschwankungen mitteleuropäisher Völker seit dem Mittelalter," Jahrbücher für Nationalokonmie und Statistik, Vol. 142 (1935), pp. 670–92.

[35]A. J. Toynbee, A Study of History (Oxford: The University Press, 1934), Vol. II, p. 58.

this movement, did the ultimate triumph of the more easterly core-area become assured. It is not without significance that, with the division of Germany into East and West, their respective capitals are Berlin, in Brandenburg, and Bonn, only about 85 miles downstream from Mainz, and thus on the fringes of the more westerly core-area.

Table 1

A	B	C
Distinct Core-Area	Peripheral or External Core-Area	No Distinct Core-Area
England	Spain	Netherlands
Ireland[1]	Portugal	Belgium
France	Yugoslavia	Albania
Switzerland	Bulgaria	Luxembourg
Sweden		Germany
Norway[1]		
Finland[1]		
Denmark		
Czechoslovakia		
Austria[1]		
Hungary		
Russia		
Romania		
Italy		
Greece		

[1]The core-area in these instances emerged when the state possessed some form of dependent or colonial status.

CONCLUSIONS

In this paper the territorial growth of about 25 European states has been reviewed. Fifteen of them have achieved their present limits by a process of accretion around a nuclear- or core-area. In every instance, the core-area was itself a region of increment; they were foci of trade routes and, with the exception only of Switzerland, were regions of some agricultural surplus during the early periods of this territorial growth. In most instances also—since territorial expansion began during the Middle Ages—the seat of the archbishop or patriarch lay also in the core-area. Lastly, the core-area is usually distinguished by its medieval architecture, itself a consequence of the surplus production of the region.

A second group of states grew from core-areas which are today peripheral or even outside their present territory. The reasons for the abandonment of the initial core-area vary from one state to another. In the case of the states of the Iberian Peninsula, the original centers were strongholds and refuges from the Moslem invaders, offering little advantage beyond a degree of military security, and were abandoned as soon as the Moslems weakened and withdrew. In the case of the Balkan examples—Serbia (Yugoslavia) and Bulgaria, there was a long hiatus, marked by foreign conquest, between the medieval state and its reappearance in modern times. The new state emerged with a new center for its political activities, determined by the political and military exigencies of the time.

Lastly, we have the small number of states which were established, as it were, at a blow, by a sudden creative act, either of external powers, as in the cases of Belgium, Luxemburg, and Albania, or of internal forces suddenly mustered to resist external pressures, as in the case of the Netherlands.

It remains to examine the significance of this argument to the conditions of today, and to ask whether the different ways in which the territory of each of the European states was put together has any relevance to their coherence and viability. The territorial evolution of a state is only one among many factors in national unity, but it would appear from an examination of list A in Table 1 that those states which grew by a process of accretion around a central, or eccentric but nonetheless internal core-area, have a higher degree of unity and cohesion than the others. France, the United Kingdom, Switzerland, Sweden, and Denmark clearly belong to this category of highly cohesive and politically and socially united countries.

In most of the states in list A, the cohesiveness or sense of unity diminishes outward from the core-area toward the borders of the state, as might, of course, be anticipated from a theoretical model of their formation. The actual degree of cohesiveness depends to a large degree on whether the actual boundaries have been cut back, as in Hungary, to eliminate areas and peoples not fully attuned to the ideals of the country, or, as in Czechoslovakia, expanded to embrace peoples who could not be expected fully to share these ideals within a measurable period of time.

In general, a much smaller degree of unity and cohesion characterizes both states with peripheral or external core-areas and also those which were created arbitrarily without ever having experienced a process of territorial growth. Of both it may be said that they lack a specific focus, epitomizing national values and perpetuating the earliest memories of the nation. Yet generalization is difficult. A state, created arbitrarily by an act of war and its concluding truce, such as the Netherlands, may nevertheless develop the most intimate sense of cohesion, and another, like Italy, which first acquired unity by a steady outward expansion from the plains of the lower Tiber, may still today, mainly for social and economic reasons, lack such cohesion and unity.

CORE AREAS ELSEWHERE

The development of core areas in the Americas, Africa, and Australia has taken place over a shorter period than several of those discussed in the preceding article. In some African states the evolution of true core areas is still in the initial stages, reflecting the youthful character of the various state systems. In Australia and North America, on the other hand, well-defined core areas have developed in relatively short periods.

North America's core area has been identified recently by Philbrick.[9] The northeastern core area of the United States merges with the core area of Canada, located in the southeast of that state. "The core regions of the United States and Canada are the primary manufacturing concentrations of the Americas . . . [they] contain less than 10 percent of the total areas of the United States–Canada, but . . . half the total population and nearly three-fourths of the industrial employment."[10] While Philbrick has employed specifically economic criteria in his cartographical representation of the North American core area, the use of other factors relevant in political geography would not significantly alter the conclusions he has drawn. The United States–Canadian core area forms the cultural, political, as well as economic focus for two states which are very closely related in many ways. The state idea originated here; territorial expansion into the western frontier took place from here; the capital cities of the states that emerged are today situated here. This northeastern core area lies on the shores of an ocean across which so many of the ideas implemented in America have come, and the fortuitous juxtaposition of a wide range of resources produced a core area that is, in many respects, without rival.

The United States, like several other states, possesses a number of subsidiary core areas, of which the most important is that along the West Coast. The size and importance of the cities that form part of this core area notwithstanding, the western subsidiary core area of the United States is still far overshadowed by the attributes of the continental eastern core.

The emergence of core areas and the state-idea in Latin America have been analyzed by Platt[11] and later by James.[12] The origins of several of these cores go back to pre-European patterns of political organization. "The two outstanding centers of Spanish colonization were Mexico City and Lima, each reflecting in its location the presence of one of the two major concentrations of Indians in Latin America."[13] The Mexican core region is indeed well defined by the concentration of population on the southern Central Plateau, where more than half the population, the major urban centers of the state, its densest communication networks, much of the best agricultural land, and most of the manufacturing plants are located. The capital itself, Mexico City, contains nearly a quarter of the state's entire population, and several other major urban centers, including Guadalajara (1 million) lie within the Mexican core.

Veracruz, the early contact point for Europe on the Caribbean coast, did not become the focus for the modern state of Mexico. The indigenous political organization already existent in the interior Plateau, the advantages of the region focusing upon Mexico City, and the wealth to be found in the Mexico Empire all drew the Spanish invaders into the interior. When modes of life began to change, the advantages of the plateau continued to attract

[9]For a summary see A. K. Philbrick, *This Human World,* New York, Wiley, 1963, pp. 285 ff. An earlier statement by the same author is "Principles of Areal Functional Organization in Regional Human Geography," *Economic Geography,* 33, 4 (October, 1957), 299–336. See Map on p. 333.

[10]Philbrick, op. cit (1963), p. 285.

[11]R. A. Platt, *Latin America: Countrysides and United Regions,* New York, McGraw-Hill, 1942. Maps showing the core areas of all Latin American states are included in this volume.

[12]P. E. James, "Latin America: State Patterns and Boundary Problems," pp. 881–897, and "Latin American States: Four Case Studies," pp. 922–941, in W. G. East and A. E. Moodie (eds.), *The Changing World,* New York, World Book Co., 1956.

[13]James, op. cit., p. 883.

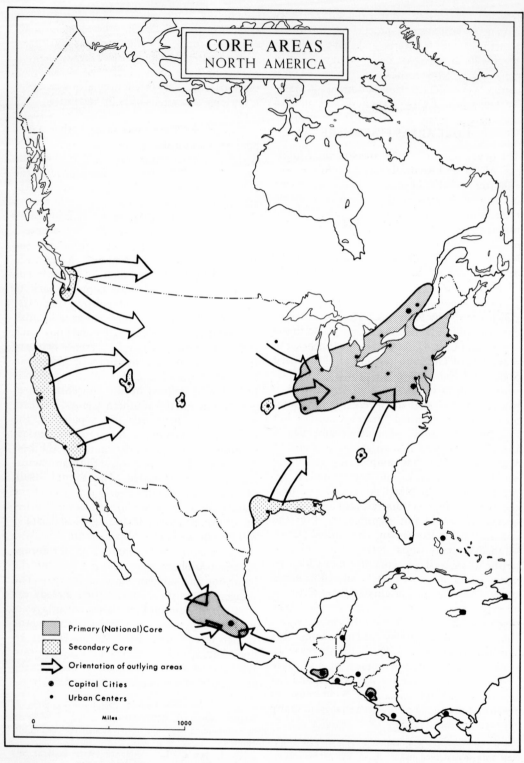

CORE AREAS
NORTH AMERICA

Primary (National)Core

Secondary Core

Orientation of outlying areas

Capital Cities

Urban Centers

Miles

0   1000

settlement. This historical momentum has continued ever since, and today the main stage of Mexico is still the Plateau, "clearly the heart of the country, the national center of gravity."[14] Although Mexico has several outlying, coastal cities, these do not form foci even for subsidiary core areas today.

[14]Platt, op. cit., p. 21.

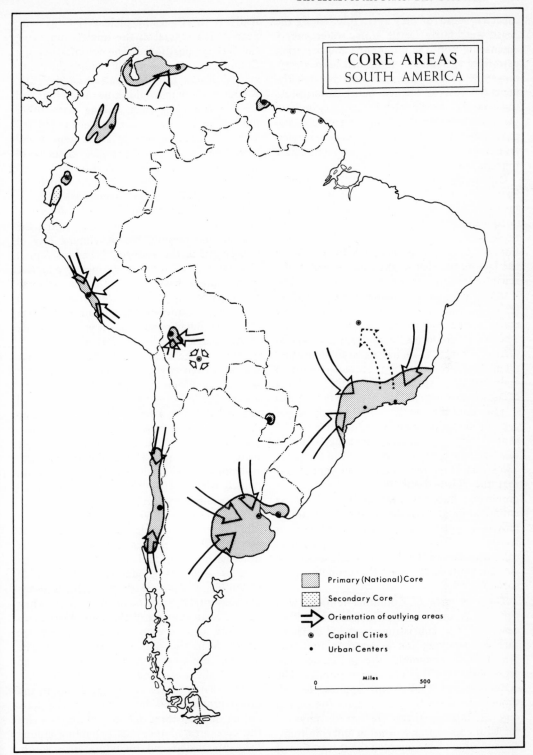

CORE AREAS
SOUTH AMERICA

▨ Primary (National) Core

▦ Secondary Core

➜ Orientation of outlying areas

◉ Capital Cities

• Urban Centers

Miles
0   500

The evolution of the core area about Lima, capital of Peru, has a very different background. The Inca Empire was no less wealthy and no less attractive than the Aztec state on the Mexican Plateau, and initially the Peruvi- an coastal lowlands formed only a gateway to the riches of the Andes. But when those riches were exhausted, which did not require a very long time, the factors of inaccessibility of the interior and the limited areas of productive capacity began to play their role. Along the coast were fairly fertile soils; water supply emanating from the mountains and irrigation permitted agriculture. Lima had been a steppingstone to the Andes; it now became the focus for western, Spanish South America. As the capital of the Spanish Viceroyalty of Peru, the city functioned as the seat of colonial government for a vast and disconnected region far exceeding the Inca Empire in its immediate hinterland.

Ultimately the initially politically unified Spanish South American realm fragmented into several units, each focusing upon an area of concentrated European settlement. Some of these settlements were coastal. Remoteness from the Peruvian center of control was one of the factors that led to the establishment of a separate political unit around the central Chilean population cluster. The elongated state of Chile has one of the world's most concentrated and clearly defined core areas. The state "conforms to the familiar general plan of countries, in having a populous and productive central region, secondary provincial districts, sparsely populated outlying areas, marked regional variety, and boundaries in unfruitful regions."[15] Indeed, nearly 90 per cent of the population of Chile live in the central (largely Mediterranean) zone, which in turn focuses upon the capital city of Santiago. "So strong is the focus on a single central city that the political subdivisions of Chile, the provinces, have no significance except as enumeration areas of the census. There are no provincial police, no provincial governors or legislatures. This centralization of the political structure of Chile is matched with a similar centralization of the economic and social life."[16]

The core area of Colombia remains well defined. A quarter of a century ago Platt described it as consisting of several districts, each as populous and as separate from the others as, for example, the individual core areas of the republics of Central America. The statement essentially still applies, for although the country focuses upon the capital city of Bogota, there are severe physical impediments to transportation and communications which have retarded the integration of the state around this focus. In fact, several cities in Colombia rival Bogota in population, and the pivotal geographic feature of the state really is the Cauca-Magdalena river system, near which several of the nuclei composing the core are positioned. The delimitation of a Colombian core area would require the inclusion of Bogota, Cali, Manizales, and Medellin. A large-scale map would show these cities and their surrounding areas, along with other productive and relatively densely populated areas, all forming part of a fragmented and interrupted heartland. The insular character of Colombia's developing areas is further exemplified by several coastal regions which are attaining subsidiary core characteristics.

Between Colombia and Peru, Ecuador's core area consists of two segments, of which the coastal one (around the developing city of Guayaquil) is the younger. Ecuador's capital city, Quito, lies in one of the most productive intermontane basins of the Andes, although the altitude imposes certain limitations upon agriculture. Quito was and remains the center of a large Indian population; it was the capital of Atahoalpa, and before that was the headquarters of the kingdom of Chiris (or Caras). Unlike Cuzco it was chozen as a permanent seat of government by the Spanish immigrants. The growing importance of the coastal region has led to a fragmentation of the core area, with Quito functioning as the administrative center and Guayaquil as the economic focus of the state. The exploitation of petroleum reserves in the vicinity of Guayaquil (which is also Ecuador's only important port) has intensified this division.

The core area of Venezuela has developed rapidly in recent decades, which is reflected by the growth of the capital, Caracas. Platt describes the Venezuelan core region as much smaller and less productive than that of Colombia, and not clearly dominant in terms of either total population or productivity when compared to the rest of the state. Platt maps the core area as extending along the *tierra templada* in the vicinity of the capital. The historic core areas of Venezuela were around Coro in the west, and Cumana in the east. Today, that core area looks very different, and much progress has been made in the state during the past three decades. Philbrick maps the core area of today as extending around Lake Maracaibo and including areas southward and eastward of those composing the core as delimited by Platt.[17]

Despite the fact that Bolivia lost its outlet to the Pacific Ocean during the Pacific War, the

[15]Platt, op. cit., p. 330.
[16]James, op. cit., p. 931.
[17]Philbrick, op. cit. (1963), p. 286.

state would still focus upon the highlands of the interior even if it had retained its corridor to the sea. Bolivia, like Colombia, has a core area that consists of a number of scattered nuclei, but unlike Colombia, the productive capacity of these areas is limited. Apart from individual mining towns and scattered areas of productive agriculture, subsistence modes of life dominate even near the capital city. Administrative functions are shared by La Paz and Sucre, the traditional rival cities of Bolivian history.

Paraguay, with a total population that is reminiscent of Central American figures, has one sizable urban center, Asuncion, which forms the heart of the state's limited core area. Surrounding this city, which is also the capital of the country, lies a farming area that is fairly densely populated.

The core area of Argentina developed rather late, and quite rapidly, into one of the major regions of its kind in the Americas. The absence of mineral deposits or accumulated wealth, together with the presence here of Indians who long resisted effective occupation by the Europeans, long retarded the emergence of this core area. European settlement remained confined to the Plata estuary, and Buenos Aires was a relatively insignificant center of Spanish influence, until the assets of the Pampa were recognized. Then, European control was finally extended across the country, and large cattle ranches laid out. The demand for food in industrializing western Europe, and the invention of refrigeration, supplied the impetus for the development of an agriculturally based core area which today forms the heart of the state of Argentina. A railroad network second to none in Latin America was created, and Buenos Aires grew rapidly. Few core areas are as clearly defined as this, with its great productive capacity, its dominant role in the economy of the country, the density of its transport network, and the inclusion of several large cities.

The core area of Argentina, when represented on a map, may be misleading in terms of its size. When this core area is compared to others, however, it should be remembered that this is an entirely agriculturally based core, unlike others that may be based upon other criteria. In addition, the Pampa is not interrupted by the omnipresent Andes of western South America, and is in fact one of America's largest uninterrupted productive regions.

Uruguay is a medium-sized and compact state. It faces Argentina across the Plata estuary and in effect shares the economically productive area straddling this waterway. Its core area occupies a greater percentage of the entire state's territory than does any other in Latin America, and in many ways the core itself resembles that of Argentina. Uruguay does not have distant areas not effectively integrated in the state, and its capital city, Montevideo, is one of South America's largest urban centers. It forms the focus of one of the most effectively functioning state systems in Latin America.

Both mining and agriculture are carried on in the core area of Latin America's largest state, Brazil. Along the coast, this core region extends from beyond Vitoria in the north to Curitiba in the south, and inland it includes Belo Horizonte, the steel-producing center, and most of the *tierra templada* of the east. Thus this core region includes a number of important urban centers, of which Rio de Janeiro and São Paulo are the chief; until recently the functions of the capital city were performed by Rio de Janeiro. With the establishment of a new capital some five hundred miles westward, Brazil indicated its desire for the penetration of the interior. Until now, the state has focused heavily upon its coastal, eastern heartland, with its productive agriculture and mining. The vast majority of surface communications, cities, towns, farms, mines, schools, and other assets still are located here. But the interior is by no means incapable of productive occupance. The more central location of the capital, it was thought, would be an important factor in causing Brazil to look west, inland, rather than eastward, to the coast.

AFRICA

African core areas, in a number of the emergent states of that continent, are still developing. Without doubt the most significant, in terms of productivity, degree of development, variety of activities and intensity of urbanization, among other factors, is the core area of South Africa. This consists of an east-west axis extending from the coal-mining town of Springs in the east to the gold-mining town of Klerksdorp in the west, along the Witwatersrand. Johannesburg forms the focus of this east-west belt, where manufacturing has begun to replace mining as the most important economic activity. A north-south axis marks the core area along a line running from the administrative capital of the state, Pretoria, to Vereeniging on the Vaal River, where important iron and steel industries are located.[18] This core area contains between one quarter and one-third of the South African population of 19 million.

South Africa, by far the most developed state in Africa, possesses a number of secondary core areas. The most significant of these economically is that around the port city of Durban, where an important industrial-agricultural complex forms the heart of the province of Natal. Historically, the most significant core lies at Cape Town, long the only major European settlement in Southern Africa. Finally, minor core developments exist at East London and Port Elizabeth.

Among the states of Africa, most possess a single core. That of Kenya is situated in the Highlands, and the capital of Nairobi is the focus. Agriculture and dense occupance are the characteristics of this European-developed zone. The core area of Uganda lies in the province of Buganda, along the shores of Lake Victoria. Zambia's core region is situated along the Zaïre border, and is known as the Copperbelt. In Lusaka, Zambia has an external capital. The core area of Sudan focuses upon the Gezira-Khartum region, incorporating at the same time the most important agricultural producing zone and the largest urban agglomeration of that country. Along the west coast, Ghana has one of the most strongly defined core areas in the Sekondi-Kumasi-Accra triangle, and Liberia's core comprises the iron-producing, rubber-afforested belt spread in various directions around Monrovia.

Most of the former French territories, now independent republics, also possess one core region. In West Africa, Ivory Coast focuses upon its capital, Abidjan, and environs, while Senegal possesses the largest urban center in all of former French Africa, Dakar (500,000). Mali, Niger, Dahomey, and Togo all focus upon their capital cities, while Upper Volta, Guinea, and Chad have even less clearly identified cores. Upper Volta has two distinct foci in its capital, Ouagadougou, and the second city, Bobo Dioulasso, and their contrasting ethnic backgrounds. Guinea's capital, Conakry, lies on the coast, but the interior, in and beyond the Futa Jallon, is economically

important. Chad has developing areas around Lake Chad and Fort Lamy, its capital, and also in the south, on the border with the Central African Republic.

In French-influenced Equatorial Africa, Cameroun and Congo both focus upon coastal cities and the interior to which they are connected by railroad; and especially in the former case, a core area may be said to be emerging. This is less true in Gabon and the Central African Republic, neither of which are yet served directly by a single railroad.

Along the North African coast, the core area of Egypt requires no elaboration, as it is one of the best defined in the world. Westward, such core areas as have developed are positioned on or near the shore. Tunisia's core region focuses upon Tunis and incorporates much of the northern part of the state, while the core area of Algeria is attenuated along the Mediterranean coast. Morocco's heartland lies between the western Atlas and the Atlantic Ocean.

Among those territories still under the control of Europeans, Rhodesia and Angola possess clearly defined, developing core areas. That of Rhodesia is by far the most conspicuous, lying as it does along the Great Dyke, a mineralized belt which also forms the physical backbone of the country. The capital, Salisbury, and most of the other important urban centers of Rhodesia, lie along this ridge, and the best agricultural land lies spread about it. Communications focus upon the cities of the Great Dyke, and this is one embryo state that has, theoretically at least, a number of distinct assets: a compact shape, centrally located core area, and a diversified economy. It also has some liabilities, as we shall see later.

A number of African states posses more than one core area, and since several of these states are also among the most important and populous of the continent, they deserve special attention. These do not fall into the category of Chad, Guinea, or Upper Volta, where core areas are still developing. Here the core areas are well defined, the countries involved are large, and the significance of their multicore character is far-reaching. These states are Zaïre (Congo) (Leopoldville, now called Kinshasa), Tanzania, Ethiopia, and Nigeria.

Vast Zaïre has two major core areas, whose functions as parts of the state system differ greatly. In the west, where the proruption connecting the country to the ocean lies, is

---

[18]For a discussion of this region see T. J. D. Fair and E. W. N. Mallows, "The Southern Transvaal," *Town Planning Rev.*, 30, 2 (July, 1959), 125–138.

what may be described as Zaïre's administrative core area. The capital city, also the largest city in the country, is located here, as are a number of small urban centers. The main army training base is not far from Kinshasa, which for a half century functioned as the seat of the Belgian governor's authority. Several of the major waterways of the Congo Basin (now the Zaïre Basin) focus upon Kinshasa: the city lies on the river, which is joined by the Kasai,

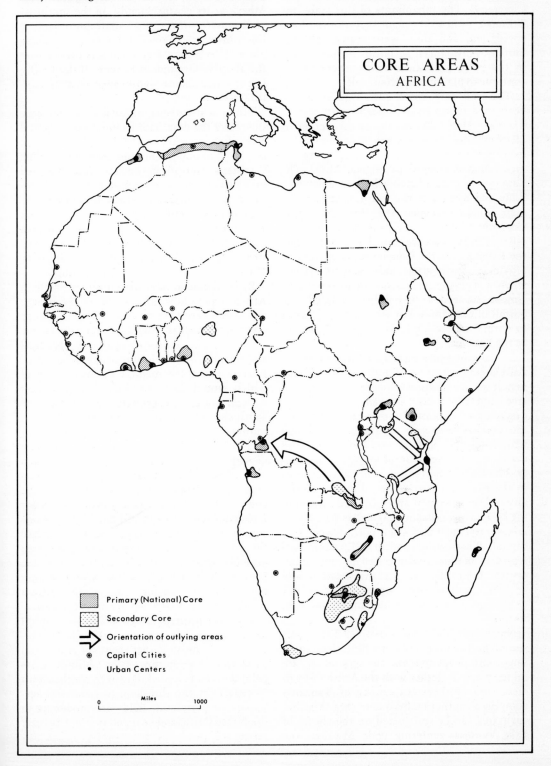

CORE AREAS
AFRICA

☐ Primary (National) Core

☐ Secondary Core

➜ Orientation of outlying areas

◉ Capital Cities

• Urban Centers

Miles
0   1000

and a railroad connects it to the ocean port of Matadi. For the Belgian colonial administration this was the obvious place from which to rule, and in addition, this area is the site of a once-powerful African indigenous state (see Chapter 2). The inhabitants of this state, the BaKongo, form a dominant sector of the local population, and they were drawn into the European-introduced activities in this region. In the politics of Zaïre today, these people continue to play an important role.

The other core area of Zaïre is its economic heart, and it lies in the distant southeast, in Katanga. Here the major urban center is Elizabethville (now known as Lubumbashi), focus for one of the largest European settlements that developed in tropical Africa. The Katanga is a mineral-rich belt divided between Zaïre and Zambia to the south. Copper is the main product (hence the Zambian name Copperbelt for its core region), but a number of other minerals also are mined. For many years the Katanga was the Congo's most productive province, until after independence (1960) when a secessionist movement in the region almost succeeded. Instability reduced the output of the mines, but when Zaïre returned to normal its economic focus again proved to be the Katanga.

The case of Tanzania is very different. While Zaïre's core areas are significant on a continental scale and are well defined in terms of area and functions, Tanganyika has been described as a country without a core. In fact the country possesses a number of nuclei which may all develop into core areas, and every one of these nuclei is located peripherally. The most important, in political terms, lies in the east, and is constituted by the capital city of Dar es Salaam and a limited surrounding area. Dar es Salaam (150,000) is Tanzania's largest city, most important port, as well as its capital. What limited industry Tanzania possesses is mainly concentrated in this urban center. Railroads connect the western and northern parts of the state to this city, but development in its immediate hinterland is in its initial stages.

Northward, along the coast, lies Tanzania's second port, Tanga, and in its hinterland some important developments in agriculture are taking place. Together with the Arusha-Moshi area, this northeastern corner of Tanzania comprises another embryo core area. Another such area can be recognized on the shores of Lake Victoria, centering upon Mwanza, the lake port. Mwanza is served by rail and lake steamer, and farming as well as mining are carried on in its vicinity. In the southwest of the state, at the northern end of Lake Nyasa (Malawi), is yet another developing area, with Mbeya at its center. Finally, in the southeast of the state, in the immediate hinterland of Lindi-Mtwara, some development is taking place. This southeastern area was the scene of the abortive Groundnut Scheme of the 1940's, but it retains some significance as an agricultural zone today.

Ethiopia also displays multicore characteristics. Here the dominant element is the capital city of Addis Ababa (400,000), the seat of government and the headquarters of the ruling Christian minority in the state. Two hundred miles eastward, an economic core is developing around Diredawa, which is located near the traditional Moslem center of Harar. Union with Eritrea brought another embryo core area into the Ethiopian sphere of influence. Eritrea's capital, Asmara, and its main port, Massawa, form the focus of that territory.

By far the most important multicore state in Africa is populous Nigeria. Not only are the core areas here very clearly defined, but they also are individually unique in terms of ethnic characteristics, economic activities, historical associations, and a wide range of other aspects. Nigeria has three major core areas, each of which would do justice to any single West African state. The primary core lies in the southwest of the state, and and includes a number of major urban centers such as Ibadan (1 million), Ife, Abeokuta, and Oyo. This is one of Africa's most highly urbanized regions, and one third of the population resides in towns exceeding 20,000. In the southeast of the country is the core area whose desire for independence led to the ill-fated Biafra recessionist movement of the late 1960's. Unlike the cocoa-producing western core, this area depends upon the oil palm and its products. Despite the fact that this area is very densely populated (the region counts 12 million inhabitants on 30,000 square miles) urbanization is very limited. Enugu, the former capital of the region, has only about 100,000 inhabitants, and only 7 per cent of the total population live in towns. In addition to its palm-derived revenues, however, southeastern Nigeria is at the threshold of a mineral age. Important petroleum fields are producing in the Niger Delta, and coal and iron ore also are mined.

Nigeria's third core area lies in the north. Unlike the southern cores, this area is landlocked, and depends for its contact with the outside world upon the southern ports. Religion, tradition, and history have produced a region of great individuality. Despite the existence of great, old cities such as Kano, Kaduna, and Zaria, only 4 per cent of northern Nigeria's 30 million people live in urban centers. Subsistence modes of life predominate, but in the core area the production of peanuts and cotton is of significant proportions. A Moslem area whose modes of life were left essentially intact during the period of British colonization, the north in Nigeria is a world apart from the south, and this is nowhere more true than in the core · area between and around Kano and Kaduna.

ASIA (INCLUDING THE SOVIET UNION)

Core areas in Asia show a great deal of variety. The core area of the Soviet Union displays some of the characteristics also encountered in North America. There is an overlap between regions of agricultural productivity and industrial development. A dense transport network serves a number of major cities, and Moscow is the focus of the whole. Leningrad forms the northern outpost of this core area, while the shores of the Black Sea are the southern limits. Eastward the core region extends to the Urals. It may be argued that the Moscow industrial-agricultural region forms the only contiguous core area of the Soviet Union, and that such areas as the Ukraine, the Leningrad nucleus, and the eastern industrialized zones are in fact outliers resembling the western subsidiary core of the United States. Pounds' map reflects this view.[19] On the same basis, the Novosibirsk and Irkutsk areas of the eastern interior may be considered subsidiary secondary core areas.

The core area of mainland China lies in the northeast, and comprises mainly the four provinces of the coastal region. Nearly one third of the total population of these provinces live in cities, and these major cities of the core area contain some 50 million people. In fact the Chinese core area extends along the coast from Shanghai in the south to the Korean border in the north, so that it includes Chinese cities such as Nanking, Tsinan, Tientsin, and

[19]N. J. G. Pounds, *Political Geography*, New York, McGraw-Hill, 1963, map, p. 181.

Peking as well as Manchurian cities such as Shenyang (Mukden) and neighboring Fushun. Some two thirds of the manufacturing industries of the state are located within this heartland, and the large cities are the main industrial centers of the country. The North China Plain has long been the central region of China, but it has become much more clearly the core of the newly emergent Communist state since the takeover of the present regime. Expansion of industry, tighter integration of the state territory and population from the capital, growth of urban centers, increased control over all means of production, and considerable improvements in the communication systems have all contributed to the accelerated emergence of this region.

While China has a single and well-defined core area, India does not. Several areas of India have core characteristics, of which the leading one extends from Delhi (3 million) along the Ganges to the border with East Pakistan, and thence south to Calcutta (6.5 million). This constitutes India's greatest population concentration, and the region is served by a communication network that is somewhat denser than that of any other area in the country of similar size. The coastal cities of Madras (3 million) and Bombay (5.5 million) both form foci for regions of considerable size. The Bombay-Ahmedabad area, especially, is of significance. In terms of the location of the capital city, the number of sizable urban centers, population concentration, transport networks, and productive capacity, the northern (Ganges) sector satisfies more core requirements than other areas of India today. But industry is quite dispersed through the country, and as industrialization takes effect, the center of gravity may shift.

Japan's core area covers a considerable percentage of the national territory. Its northern limit lies just north of Tokyo, and it extends southward to include the cities of Yokohama, Nagoya, Kobe-Osaka, Kyoto, and Kitakyushu. Thus the core area includes the northern margins of the island of Kyushu. The whole belt is served by an intensive transport network, and in every other way it displays the characteristics of the well-functioning heart of the state. Tokyo (12 million) is the focus; it is the headquarters of the Japanese state from every conceivable point of view. With Yokohama it is the chief industrial complex of the country, and within sixty miles of this megalopolis live about 30 per cent of the

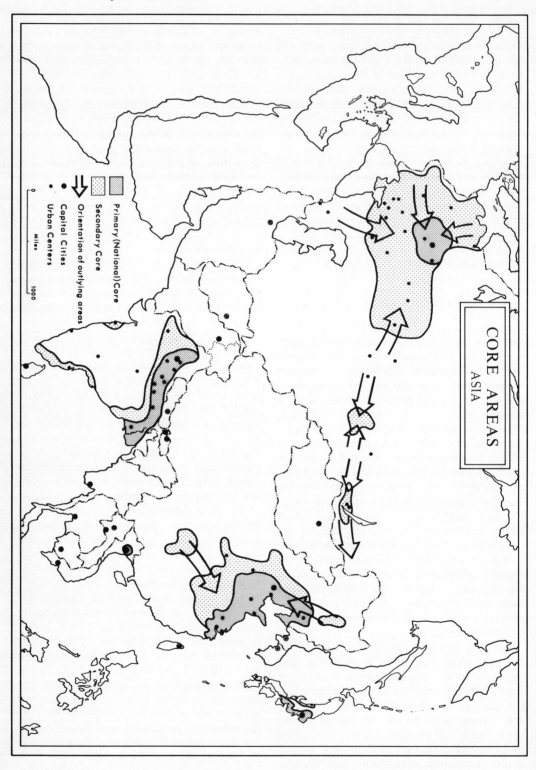

In the core area of a federal state: the Kremlin, Moscow, U.S.S.R. This side view of the famous Kremlin—where Lenin shaped much of the future of the state, and where many a struggle for power since has reached its culmination—reminds us that Moscow was a part of the Russian heartland before the Bolshevik takeover. Churches such as that marked by a series of golden domes (foreground) now function largely as museums, but in the days of the Czars they themselves were centers of splendor and power (Harm J. de Blij).

Japanese population. Practically all these people are in one way or another directly affected by the presence of the great city, which forms a huge market for agricultural products, requires a vast labor force for its industries, and dominates cultural and political life.

The core areas of the archipelago states of the Philippines and Indonesia lie on the most productive and densely populated islands of each. In both cases, the capital city also is situated there: Manila lies on Luzon, and Djakarta on Java.

AUSTRALIA

The Australian core area is located in the southeastern part of that state, with the two ports of Melbourne and Sydney forming the focal points of the region. Good agricultural land, the vast majority of manufacturing establishments, the bulk of the Australian population, and the capital city (Canberra) all are found within this zone. Beyond its margins there are several nuclei which are developing into subsidiary cores: Brisbane in the north and Adelaide to the west are so near the core area that eventual incorporation is not impos-

sible. The other outlying nucleus is the area of Perth in the far west.

In considering the relevance and importance of core areas in political geography, a number of questions are to be answered. Only a few of the core areas of the states of the world have been briefly outlined above, but it is clear that core areas must be seen in two ways: first, on a world scale, second, on a state scale. We have seen that we cannot apply the same criteria to define the core areas of the United States and Chad. But we can use the same criteria in determining the core areas of the United States, Argentina, the Soviet Union, China, the United Kingdom, Japan, and Germany. Comparisons between these states, therefore, are possible. When considering the core areas of individual states, our attention is focused upon the contrasts between conditions within the core and those in the remaining parts of the country. Here we must vary our judgments, although the factors of significance remain the same (population density, productivity, communications, etc.).

The most important question regarding core areas, and the most difficult one to answer, is whether the core functions satisfactorily as the binding agent for the state. This depends

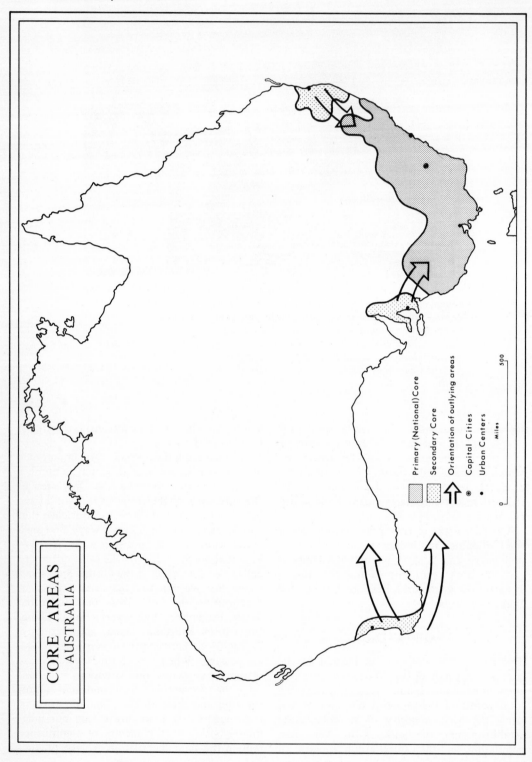

CORE AREAS
AUSTRALIA

Primary (National) Core
Secondary Core
Orientation of outlying areas
Capital Cities
Urban Centers

Miles
0   500

on a number of factors, including the adequacy of the capital city, its position with reference to the population distribution within the state, its ethnic content and the values held, the efficacy of various core-centered organizations in areas outside the core, and many more. This matter will be stressed in Chapter 16, when the role of core areas in the development of the politico-territorial organization of a number of states is examined.

REFERENCES

Bascom, William, "Urbanism as a Traditional African Pattern," *Sociol. Rev.*, n.s., 7, 1 (July, 1959), 29–43.

Cole, Monica M., "The Witwatersrand Conurbation: A Watershed Mining and Industrial Region," *Trans. and Papers, Inst. Brit. Geographers*, Publ. No. 23, 1957, pp. 249–265.

Dickinson, R. E., *City Region and Regionalism.* New York, Oxford University Press, 1947.

Duncan, Otis Dudley, and others, *Metropolis and Region.* Baltimore, The Johns Hopkins Press for Resources for the Future, Inc., 1960.

East, W. G., *An Historical Geography of Europe.* London, Methuen, 1935.

Fair, T. J. D., "A Regional Approach to Economic Development in Kenya," *South African Geog. J.*, 45 (1963), 55–77.

Gottmann, Jean, *Megalopolis.* New York, The Twentieth Century Fund, 1961.

———, "Megalopolis, or the Urbanization of the Northeastern Seaboard," *Economic Geography*, 33, 3 (July, 1957), 189–200.

Green, L. P., and T. J. D. Fair, *Development in Africa; a Study in Regional Analysis with Special Reference to Southern Africa.* Johannesburg, Witwatersrand University Press, 1962.

Haig, Robert Murray, "Toward an Understanding of the Metropolis: Some Speculations Regarding the Economic Base of Urban Concentration," *Quart. J. Economics*, 40 (1926), 179–208.

Hooson, David J. M., "The Middle Volga: an Emerging Focal Region in the Soviet Union," *Geog. J.*, 126, Pt. 2 (June, 1960), 180–190.

———, "A New Soviet Heartland?" *Geog. J.*, 128, Pt. 1 (March, 1962), 19–29.

Isard, Walter, *Location and Space Economy.* New York, The Technology Press of Massachusetts Institute of Technology and John Wiley & Sons, Inc., 1956, Chap. 11.

Lösch, August, *The Economics of Location*, trans. by William H. Woglom. New Haven, Conn., Yale University Press, 1954.

Lonsdale, R. E., and John H. Thompson, "A Map of the U.S.S.R.'s Manufacturing," *Economic Geography*, 36, 1 (January, 1960), 36–52.

Mallows, E. W. N., "Planning Problems of the Witwatersrand," *South African Geog. J.*, 43 (December, 1961), 41–48.

Martz, John D., *Central America: the Crisis and the Challenge.* Chapel Hill, The University of North Carolina Press, 1959.

Masai, Yasuo, and Allen K. Philbrick, "A Geographic Comparison of the Sizes of Great Cities, Examples from New York, Tokyo and London," *Japanese J. Geology and Geography*, 34, 2–4 (October, 1963), 45–61.

McManis, D. R., "The Core of Italy: the Case for Lombardy–Piedmont," *Prof. Geog.* 19, 5 (September, 1967), 251–257.

Murphey, Rhoads, "The City as a Center of Change: Western Europe and China," *Ann. A.A.G.*, 44, 4 (December, 1954), 349–362.

North, Douglas, "Locational Theory and Regional Economic Growth," *J. Political Economy*, 63, 3 (June, 1955), 243–258.

Nowland, John L., "The Port of Istanbul," *Scot. Geog. Mag.*, 77, 2 (September, 1961), 67–74.

Pearson, Norman, "Conurbation Canada," *Canadian Geographer*, 5, 4 (Winter, 1961), 10–17.

Petterson, Donald R., "The Witwatersrand, a Unique Gold Mining Community," *Economic Geography*, 27, 3 (July, 1951), 209–221.

Philbrick, Allen K., "Principles of Areal Functional Organization in Regional Human Geography," *Economic Geography*, 33, 4 (October, 1957), 299–336.

Platt, Robert S., *Latin America; Countrysides and United Regions.* New York, McGraw-Hill, 1942.

Roxby, P. M., "The Terrain of Early Chinese Civilization," *Geography*, 23 (1938), 225–236.

Russell, Josiah C., "The Metropolitan City Region of the Middle Ages," *J. Regional Sci.*, 2, 2 (Fall, 1960), 55–70.

Schmieder, Oscar, "The Brazilian Culture Hearth," *Univ. Calif. Publications in Geography*, 3 (1928), 159–198.

Sjoberg, Gideon, *The Preindustrial City; Past and Present.* Glencoe, Ill., The Free Press, 1960.

Stanislawski, Dan, "The Political Rivalry of Patzcuaro and Morelia, an Item in the Sixteenth Century Geography of Mexico," *Ann. A.A.G.*, 37, 3 (September, 1947), 135–144.

Steel, R. W., "The Copperbelt of Northern Rhodesia," *Geography*, 42, Pt. 2 (April, 1957), 83–92.

Ullman, Edward L., "Regional Development and the Geography of Concentration," *Papers and Proc. Regional Sci. Ass.*, 4 (1958), 179–198.

Vance, James E., Jr., "Areal Political Structure and Its Influence on Urban Patterns," *Yearbook, Ass. Pacific Coast Geographers*, 22 (1960), 40–49.

Whittlesey, Derwent, *The Earth and the State.* New York, H. Holt & Co., 1939.

———, "The Impress of Effective Central Authority upon the Landscape," *Ann. A.A.G.*, 25 (1935), 85–97.

Withington, William A., "Medan: Primary Regional Metropolis of Sumatra," *J. Geog.*, 61, 2 (February, 1962), 59–67.

CHAPTER
6

THE FOCUS:
THE CAPITAL CITY

Many states originally grew around urban centers which possessed nodality and attained strength and permanence. Many were market centers for large tributary areas; others were fortifications to which the population retreated every night after farming the surrounding lands. As the influence of those cities expanded, far-flung territories came under the control of the political authority located there. Rivalries between "city-states" occurred, in which the largest and best-organized center had the greatest chance of survival and of absorbing its competitors.

Some cities in existence today trace their history back to exactly such a sequence of events. The high percentage of urbanized population in Western Nigeria, to which reference was made in the last chapter, derives from the days when the cities of the Yoruba peoples were walled, protective forts. Ultimately they combined, and today they are part of a state that includes not only most of the original Yoruba cities but also the people against whom they were defending themselves. The city of Kano, one of the market centers of Northern Nigeria, once was a great trading metropolis with immense influence over vast reaches of West Africa. The city-state of Athens continues to function today, not as a city-state, but as a capital of a modern nation.

Capitals, then, have often evolved as centers of trade and government because of their fortuitous situation. But not all capitals can claim such a past. In simpler as well as complex societies of history, the ruler and his entourage moved about within their realm, not by preference, but because supplies could be stored for him at various places which he visited at regular intervals; it was simpler to take the ruler to his food than food to the ruler. Such rulers may have expressed a liking for one of his temporary abodes over others, and ultimately arrangements were made to permit the chief of state to occupy such a place permanently.

Whatever the origins of the capital, it is destined to become "an epitome of the national life, in which their history and traditions are enshrined . . . its . . . authority is buttressed by increasing size and wealth which accompany multiplication of administrative business and concentration of trade and industry at the political center."[1] Capital cities, adds Whittlesey, embody and exemplify the nature of the core areas of states, and are a reflection of the wealth, organization, and power of the political entity. And indeed, they sometimes are more than that. Some states have poured money into their capital cities in order to create there an image of the state as it will be in the future, a goal for the people's aspirations, and a source of national pride. Anyone who has seen the shining capitals of some Latin American states and the abject poverty of areas within sight of the rooftops of the skyscrapers will attest to this phenomenon; Addis Ababa, capital of Ethiopia, has been described as "a mask, behind which the rest of the country is hidden."[2] Certain states have poured considerable resources into the creation of wholly "new" capitals which are constructed with specific aims. Brasilia was built at tremendous expense in large part to draw the Brazilian nation's attention toward the interior. Here the functions of the capital, long performed by Rio de Janeiro, were actually taken out of the core area and placed elsewhere.[3] Other motives underlie Pakistan's decision to replace Karachi as its capital with Islamabad, in what may still be described as a northern frontier. Islamabad lies close to areas

[1]D. Whittlesey, *The Earth and the State*, New York, Holt, 1939, p. 196.

[2]D. Mathew, *Ethiopia*, London, Longmans, Green, 1947, p. 5.

[3]For a discussion of Brasilia from the point of view of both form and function see D. E. Snyder, "Alternate Perspectives on Brasilia," *Economic Geography*, 40, No. 1, 34–45.

disputed with India, and thus the government will be in a critical position to determine policy. Emergent, formerly colonial states have at times decided to replace their European-developed capital with another town possessing either traditional importance or a more fortuitous location from the point of view of the new government. The Europeans built their administrative centers in such a manner that contact could be maintained with Europe as well as the colonized realm; the objectives of the present governments differ. Hence the state of Malawi decided in 1964 to move its capital from the town of Zomba to more centrally located Lilongwe.

FUNCTIONS AND TYPES

Capital cities perform certain distinct functions. Some of these are obvious: this is the place for parliamentary and legislative gatherings, and the residence of the chief of state. Here is a prime place for the state's reception of external influences, for other states which have relations with the state locate their embassies here, international organizations of trade have representations here, and the turnover of foreign visitors is likely to be greater than anywhere else. In most states, the capital city is also the most "cosmopolitan" city of the country.

Capital cities must also act as binding agents, for example in a federation such as Brazil or Nigeria. In a federal state of great internal diversity the capital city may be the only place to which all the people can look for guidance, for they as well as everyone else have representatives in the capital who participate in governmental decision making. Often, in such a state, a territory is separated from the

A panoramic view of the new capital city of Brazil, Brasilia. Planned in every detail this ultra-modern metropolis was designed to represent the country's forward strides—the major outlines of the plan represent a giant airplane. Located west of Brazil's core area, the city forms a new focus for a developing region, and its interior location was intended to stimulate the country's "inward" look. In many ways, Brasilia is a unique capital city. Most capitals, even new, planned cities, have a central assemblage of impressive governmental buildings, but the surrounding city has been left to grow by accretion, as cities have always grown. Thus the image-making governmental headquarters often are submerged in a sea of urban sprawl. But Brasilia was planned in every last detail, and while critics soon saw it as an "atmosphere-less" city and a vast, incredibly expensive monument, others hailed it as the city of the future (Brazilian Government Trade Bureau).

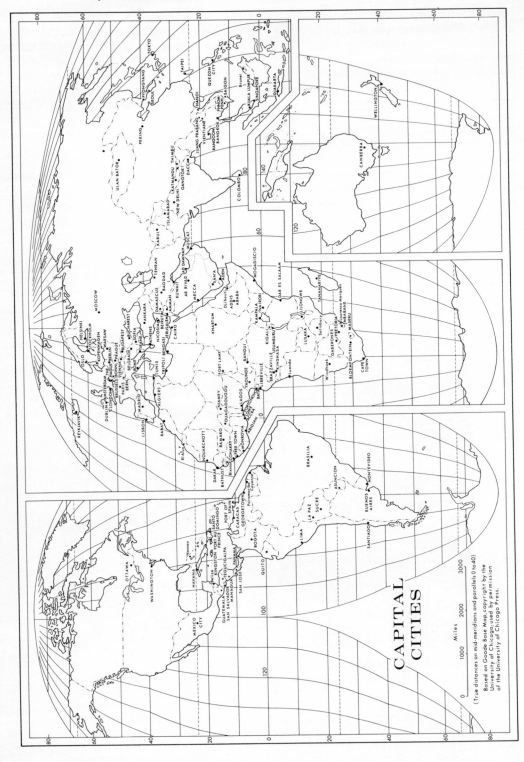

CAPITAL CITIES

(True distances on mid-meridians and parallels 0 to 40)

Based on Goode Base Map, copyright by the
University of Chicago; used by permission
of the University of Chicago Press.

Miles
0   1000   2000   3000

rest of the country and made into "federal territory," so that none of the other entities in the federation can claim bias in the location of the state capital. In the United States, the District of Columbia serves such a function.

Capital cities must also be a source of power and authority, either to ensure control over outlying and loosely tied districts of the state or to defend the state against undesirable external influences. In the changing strategic situation of the world, this function is diminishing, reminiscent as it is of city-state times. But the capital is most frequently located in the economic heart of the country, from which much of the image of strength of the state emanates.

The functions of capital cities have changed much over time. The case of London provides a good example; after the Roman conquest in the first century A.D. it was the trade center of the Roman Province of Britain, but not the capital, which was located about twenty miles away at Verulamium. Under Norman influence it became the capital, and after the conquest of Wales and Scotland those territories fell under its jurisdiction also. The city's salutary location became an even greater asset during the years of increasing overseas trade and empire building. Thus once a local center, then a regional capital, London became the capital of a state and then the headquarters of an empire.

Types

Study of capital cities quickly leads to the conclusion that there are several distinct types of capitals, so that classification may be possible. But caution is needed here. Some geographers, for example, have argued that there are are "natural" (that is, evolved) capitals and "artificial" capitals. This categorization would suggest that certain capitals have emerged and developed as the state system grew increasingly complex, while others have been simply the result of arbitrary decision. In a paper to which we will refer in some detail later, Professor O. H. K. Spate attacked this whole concept, arguing that any decision leading to the establishment of an "artificial" capital is itself the result of pressures created within and by the system.[4] Thus Spate would suggest that Brasilia is no less "natural" a

capital than Rome, since the need for Brazil to penetrate its Western interior generated the creation of Brasilia just as the complexity of the Roman Empire generated multifunctional Rome.

The Primate City

Another approach might be based upon Jefferson's Law of the Primate City: "A country's leading city is always disproportionately large and exceptionally expressive of national capacity and feeling."[5] This may still be the rule in a majority of states, but there are many more exceptions now than Jefferson was able to identify. The states that have selected new capital sites, such as Brazil and Pakistan, are states where the "law" does not apply. Certain federal states, such as Canada, Australia, and Nigeria, similarly have cities larger and culturally more expressive of their nations than their capitals. In some other states the rule does not hold for other reasons: in Ecuador, where Guayaquil is larger than Quito, in South Africa, where Johannesburg is the largest city but not the capital, in West Germany, where several cities are larger than the capital, Bonn.

A MORPHOLOGICAL APPROACH

Perhaps the most productive approach is a morphological one. Here we view capital cities in relation to their position with reference to the state territory and the core area of the state. This results in three classes of capital cities:

1. Permanent Capitals. Permanent capitals might also be called historic capitals; they have functioned as the leading economic and cultural center for their state over a period of several centuries. As we will see in a later chapter, the life cycle of a nation state can be divided into at least four phases, and when a capital has retained its leading position through at least two of these stages, it may be classed as permanent. Obvious examples are Rome, London, Paris, and Athens, the leading cities in their respective states for many centuries and through numerous stages of history. The Japanese capital, Tokyo, however, is not in this category. It has been the Japanese headquarters for just over a century—the century, in fact, spanning the emergence of the modern nation-state of Japan. A whole new

[4]O. H. K. Spate, "Factors in the Development of Capital Cities," Geographical Review, 32, No. 4 (October, 1942), 622–631.

[5]M. Jefferson, "The Law of the Primate City," Geographical Review, 29, No. 2 (1939), 226.

cycle began in the life of the Japanese state in the late 1860's, and with it the old capital of Kyoto gave up its primacy. Tokyo symbolized the new Japan, and although the city seems destined to become the permanent Japanese capital, it does not yet rank with Rome and Paris (or Peking) as such a headquarters of continuity.

2. *Introduced Capitals.* Tokyo, in fact, was *introduced* to become the focal point for Japan when the revolutionary events referred to as the Meiji Restoration occurred. Kyoto had been an interior city, but the new Japanese leadership wanted a capital that looked out over the sea, the sea that was to become Japan's lifeline of survival and prosperity. Recent history has seen similar choices made in other countries, but while Tokyo (then called Edo or Eastern City) was already a substantial urban center, other capitals were created, literally, from scratch. They replaced older capitals in order to perform new functions—functions perhaps in addition to those normally expected of the seat of government. Thus Spate's argument against the concept of the "artificial" capital is not contradicted; it is very natural for a state to periodically reassess its capital city's functions, effectiveness, and service. Capital cities tend to become congested by the accumulation of bureaucracies and their parasitic agencies; such congestion may begin to impede the functioning of the government. An escape to a new site may be desirable.

Over long periods of time (as we have observed) core areas of states may shift. Such a shift, for example that which occurred in Switzerland, may lead to the decision to move the functions of government to a more appropriate site.

It was Professor Whittlesey who astutely observed that

. . . Government lays hands in a special way upon its its capitals. The focussing of roads, railroads, and canals upon the seat of government is partly the result of economic evolution, but it is often encouraged by political aid . . . Once fixed, capitals become the pets of government. On them public money is frequently lavished beyond present needs, even beyond the natural desire of the people to dress up their capital city . . .[6]

His commentary implies that people tend to look upon their capital city in a special way,

[6]D. Whittlesey, "The Impress of Effective Central Authority upon the Landscape," *Annals of the Association of American Geographers,* XXV, No. 2 (June, 1935), 93.

and that their attention finds a considerable response in governmental action. In turn, government has also capitalized on the special national visibility of the national headquarters. It was argued that Rio de Janeiro's congestion and inefficiencies had led to a deterioration of governmental efficiency, but the major reason the Brazilian government chose to build a gleaming new capital deep in the interior had to do with the realization that the nation's eyes would be diverted in that direction—a direction the nation had long and excessively ignored. Just another city where Brasilia lies would have meant very little, but the *capital*—that, it was hoped, would indeed start a new era for an inward-looking Brazil. Whether the experiment succeeds is yet in the balance, but the statement by Professor Whittlesey about the lavishing of monies on capitals is certainly borne out by Brasilia, where huge, multistory structures and planned, ultramodern living quarters rose from a previously sparsely settled plain, where statues to national heroes were erected and where the first automobile to reach the site overland stands—bronzed—as a symbol of the pioneering spirit the interior needs.

Introduced capitals have also come about by less lofty actions. Intense interstate rivalries between Australia's individual states made it impossible to select one of that country's several large cities as the permanent national capital, and a compromise had to be reached. That compromise is the new capital of Canberra, built on federal territory carved out of the State of New South Wales.

One other factor must be taken into account in connection with introduced capitals. In recent decades, numerous former colonial dependencies have attained sovereignty, in many cases with capital cities whose sites were chosen by alien powers. Such capitals were built for the purposes of the European administrations, often with little regard for the future. In the 1920's and 1930's, who would have guessed that just a few decades later, Bangui, Bamako, Ouagadougou, and Mbabane would have to serve as the capitals of independent states? But despite the general absence of planning for a time when the colonial city in Africa would serve as a national capital, the vast majority of the emerging states have retained the former European headquarters as the national capital. Some of these capitals are really quite embryonic, such as Mbabane (Swaziland), Libreville (Gabon), and Kigali (Rwanda), but others have

Canberra, capital of Australia, is also the largest inland city of the Federation. The grand design was conceived by Chicago architect, Walter Burley Griffin, in 1911; building began in 1913. Artificial Lake Griffin was filled in 1964, and final plans were laid for the location of major structures. The photograph shows various government buildings (foreground) surrounding the focus, City Hill. The two recently completed bridges link the northern and southern sections of the city across the lake, while the empty spaces ringing the Hill are reserved for future retail development (Australian News and Information Bureau).

been converted, with just the kind of enthusiasm Professor Whittlesey reported, into modern symbols of the nation's aspirations. Former President Nkrumah of Ghana so sought to transform his capital of Accra, and it has been done in Abidjan (Ivory Coast), Dakar (Senegal), Kinshasa (Zaïre), and elsewhere. Only three African states in the early 1970's were building new capitals, and all for different reasons. When the British Protectorate of Bechuanaland attained independence, it had —incredibly—no capital, since the territory had for 80 years been administered from a town called Mafeking, located *outside* its boundaries. Thus Gaberone was chosen as a new, internal (and introduced) capital of Botswana, and construction of the necessary facilities begun.[7] In the case of the former British protectorate of Nyasaland (now the state of Malawi), the government was dissatisfied with the location within the rather

elongated national territory of the capital, Zomba. With obvious awareness of the problems of territorial elongation and the role a more centrally positioned capital could play in national integration, the Malawi government decided to select a new site. The new capital will be at Lilongwe, well to the north of Zomba. Finally, the new capital of Nouakchott, of Mauritania, can be classed as an introduced capital. With barely more than 1 million people inhabiting a territory of over 400,000 square miles, Mauritania at independence needed an urban center with facilities for administration. Previously, the territory had been a low-priority item in the French administration of West Africa. The capital now reportedly has a population of over 15,000.

3. *Divided Capitals.* In certain states the functions of government are not concentrated in one city, but divided among two or even more. Such a situation suggests—and often reflects—compromise rather than convenience. In the Netherlands, a kingdom, the

[7]For a discussion of the sequence of events see A. C. G. Best, "Gaberone: Problems and Prospects of a New Capital," *Geographical Review*, LX, No. 1, (January, 1970), 1–14.

parliament sits in The Hague, the legislative capital. But the royal palace is in Amsterdam, the "official" capital. In Bolivia, intense rivalry between the cities of La Paz and Sucre produced the arrangements existing today, whereby the two cities share the functions of government. In South Africa, following a war between Boer and Briton, a Union was established in which the Boer capital—Pretoria—retained administrative functions, while the British headquarters, Cape Town, became the legislative headquarters. As a further compromise, the judiciary functions were placed in Bloemfontein, capital of one of the old Boer Republics that fought in the Boer War. There are other states in which the primacy of one capital city is uncertain, for example Libya and Laos.

THE SEARCH FOR CONCEPTUAL UTILITY

The capital city, thus, is the focus of the state system, the node, often, of the core area. As a search of the literature soon proves, political geographers have described many capital cities, they have made attempts at classification, and they have explained why certain cities became capitals while others did not. But as in the case of the core area concept, it has not been easy to define exactly *how* the capital functions in the integration of the total state system. Among the first geographers to consider this whole subject was Vaughan Cornish. About a half century ago Cornish published a book entitled *The Great Capitals*, and it is still worth a careful reading, its environmentalist overtones notwithstanding. Cornish discusses the origin and evolution of capital cities in many parts of the world, and suggests that

. . . they fall into three categories of *Natural Storehouses, Crossways,* and *Strongholds.* The first is the original and fundamental character, the second and third dependent upon it, for easy movement and natural barriers are only important if there be inducement to develop or obstruct traffic. It is therefore the world's Storehouses of natural wealth which sooner or later determine the importance of Crossways and Strongholds. . . .[8]

Following an elaboration of this theme, Cornish adds still another category:

. . . The initial capital of a federation of sovereign States is at a connection between the States themselves, not of the whole territory with foreign

countries, but when the States consolidate the capital is in a *Forward Position* . . . as every civilized country is engaged in foreign as well as home trade, the same conditions determine the site of the best commercial centre. In time of war the government has to be in a forward position in order to keep in touch with operations, but the presence of a large urban population is an embarrassment. This drawback has attracted more popular attention than the advantage of a great junction of roads not far from the principal frontier (ensured by the forward position of the capital) which assists strategic concentration. The doctrine of the *Forward Position* of the capital, which it is hoped this book will establish, is, however, not theoretical but historical. . . .[9]

Cornish's idea of the forward capital has indeed, gained hold in political geography. There is no doubt that some governments are today using capital cities for purposes over and above those having to do with administration. As national foci they enjoy the attention of the nation—an attention that can be manipulated through the manipulation of the capital itself. The frontier-like position of newly completed Islamabad, Pakistan's capital, underscores that state's determination to confirm its presence in nearby, still-contested areas.

Professor O. H. K. Spate also comments on the forward capital, calling Cornish's concept "a great advance; it introduces dynamic and historical elements."[10] But he has little sympathy for the distinction between "natural" and "artificial" capitals:

. . . Such a crude distinction completely begs the question; it may be more natural, more appropriate, to build a new city than to take over a going concern with its own vested interests. . . . It is entirely "natural" for a federation to construct a new—hence so-called "artificial" capital free of bested sectional interests that might attach to a city whose historic traditions or economic ties were with one of the components rather than with the country as a whole. Washington is really a more "natural" capital than New York, Canberra than Sydney or Melbourne, Ottawa than Toronto or Montreal. . . .

Professor Spate, too, struggles with the problem of defining the functional qualities of the capital in the state system. He proposes the idea of the *Head-Link* function, whereby the capital is viewed as the primary link in a chain representing the organizing direction of the state.

"Functionally, the task of capitals varies in

[8]V. Cornish, *The Great Capitals*, London, Methuen, 1923, p. vii. Italics added.

[9]Ibid., p. viii. Italics added.
[10]Spate, op. cit., p. 624.

time no less than their location varies in space. They may be designed specifically to act as binding centers in a federation, or some regional center may come to assume that role, gradually consolidating the state it serves. The capital is often the link through which the state in process of formation receives the vital external influences that impregnate its internal potentialities; for, as Vidal de la Blache remarks, "no civilized state is the sole architect of its own civilization." Finally, it often guards a dangerous frontier, gathering behind it the not yet united components of the state, organizing them into a whole in the face of some external menace to their common culture, perhaps finally taking the offensive and becoming the forward capital of an advancing empire; such was the role, for example, of Vienna before 1700. Besides the indefinite combinations that prevail in any one city at one time, it may be said that any great capital in its time plays many parts. Thus we have seen London as local center, regional focus, border depot and fortress, but above all as the "head-link" that provides the organizing direction of the state, at the same time acting as a receiving chamber through which pass external influences, to be there translated into stimuli of the local culture. The part played by Canterbury in ecclesiastical affairs was taken by London in society and politics: here came the merchants of Venice and the Hanse, knightly poets and chroniclers from France, reformers and scholars from Germany; and in the eighteenth century the Thames from Hampton Court to Greenwich was the focus of literary and social life of the day to an extent scarcely paralleled by any more classic stream, the avenue whereby the predominantly French culture of the age entered England. In modern times London still has far closer continental links than any other of England's great cities.

THE "HEAD-LINK"

Examples of the importance of this organizing "head-link" function are numerous. Calcutta's existence as a capital was due to its position at the entrance of the English seaways into India, especially before the Suez Canal gave Bombay an advantage in distance to England. These were the gates by which Western concepts entered to destroy and to build; the return to Delhi—New Delhi—partakes curiously both of "historical imitation" and of the creation of a new federal capital. A

similar part was played by Rangoon.[11] It has been suggested that one of the reasons for the decline of the Burmese monarchy was the abandonment of the forward capital Pegu, in touch with oversea influences, for a situation in the heartland of the country, whereas Thailand, with its capital nearer the sea, was able to absorb external influences without being swamped by them. There is value in the suggestion, but it is evident that it leaves out some larger considerations, such as the position of Burma relative to India and of Thailand relative to British and French power in Indochina.

Washington, again, chosen for centrality, became eccentric almost at once territorially, though not with regard to the distribution of population, by the addition to the United States of all the territory between the Mississippi and the Rockies. It may be regarded as fortunate for the world at large that, after the center of population had shifted, Washington remained the capital by historical inertia. From a narrowly American viewpoint, Chicago or St. Louis might be a better center, but there have been periods when the continental environment of the Middle West, with its sentiment of detachment from "corrupt and effete Europe," has exercised a powerful influence on the mass mind; the Atlantic slope has had a greater measure of European comprehension. During the perilous years of the Civil War, Washington was a "forward capital" in the fullest sense.

Turin, the capital of the Kingdom of Sardinia, which led the movement for Italian unity, was at once the link for nationalist ideology—the seed of the French Revolution—and the frontier town against Austrian domination, cementing behind it the fragmentary materials of the Italian state. When unity had been attained, however, undoubted nodal advantages, but, above all, the great prestige of the Eternal City, transferred the capital to Rome—one of the classic examples of historical imitation. Other factors in the choice of Rome were the lack of unity between north and south and the strong regional feeling that still existed in the various components of the state—Sardinia looking to Turin, Lombardy to Milan, the center to Florence, and the south to Naples. A relatively neutral site was an obvious advantage. Even Paris, the very type of a centralizing capital, evolved to some extent

[11] O. H. K. Spate and L. W. Trueblood: Rangoon: A Study in Urban Geography, *Geogr. Rev.*, Vol. 32, 1942, pp. 56–73.

as a link between the Rhenish lands, whence came the Franks, and the more Romanized south. And, as Toynbee points out, Dublin, although associated with an alien ascendancy, has been retained as the capital of Eire simply because it is the geographical point of contact with the outer Western world. . . ."[12]

Spate then analyzes the cases of Belgrade and Prague, the capitals of Yugoslavia and Czechoslovakia, two states which, at the time this article was written, were still extremely youthful. Belgrade become a "head-link" capital for several reasons: its preemptive position (it was already a regional capital), the role played by Serbia, the "active organizing principle in the creation of the new state." In Czechoslovakia, Prague was the regional center of Bohemia (one of the regions merged into that eastern European state), and, as Spate points out, the city was "the very flower of Slav civilization, enriched by western contacts." The choice of Prague was inescapable; although "the geographical center of Czechoslovakia would have been somewhere near Brno . . . there could be only one political center, and that was eccentric Prague; centrally focal to Bohemia, to Czechoslovakia as a whole it was the link with western cultural and social influences, the type of a 'head-link' capital."

Summarizing the functions of capital cities, Spate concludes that they must be the keystones of federations or complex states, the frontier organizers of victory and union ("forward capitals"), or "head-links," through which the states receive nourishment during their formative phase and vivifying influences for indefinite or recurrent periods.[13]

An especially interesting article relating to capital cities—and a very valuable one in the search for utility—was written by Professor David Lowenthal about the selection of a capital city for a state that did not survive: the West Indies Federation. This Federation was to have been put together from most of the many pieces of Britain's colonial empire in the Caribbean Sea. There was a plan to weld Jamaica, Trinidad and Tobago, Windward Islands including Grenada, Barbados, and Dominica, and Leeward Islands such as Antigua and St. Kitts into a West Indies Federation. Such an island Federation would have to have a capital city, and Dr. Lowenthal reports

on the candidates, the competitors, and the behavior of those involved in making the final decision. Indeed, it is this very quality of the article—its scrutiny of local behavior, attitudes, images, and decision-making processes—that render it so valuable.[14] As Dr. Lowenthal writes, "the nature and intensity of local self-consciousness are the heart of regional inquiry . . . to understand what makes a place live, one must know not only its terrain and climate, economy and population, society and culture, but also what both its own inhabitants and outsiders think about it. Men behave in accordance with their own images of themselves, of others, and of their surroundings."[15]

What is written about the West Indies applies to much of the politicogeographical world, although the parochialism and individualism of the several competitors for the capital's functions were made worse by the insular character of the federal state that was being created. The three major aspirants were Jamaica, Trinidad, and Barbados, and for a while there was the possibility of a small-island compromise:

. . . After a prolonged deadlock, the delegates agreed on provisional headquarters in St. George's, Grenada, the picturesque, solidly built, red-brick capital (population 8000) of the nutmeg-and-cacao island north of Trinidad. Delighted Grenana regarded its election as a compliment . . . but the other territories had led Grenada up the garden path. Barbadians warned against placing the capital on an "island which must be approached in a punt and where the drinking water for the federal legislators must be carried in barrels" . . . Trinidad likewise rejected the London decision.[16]

Thus the compromise solution was negated, and that negation was confirmed by a special commission that argued that certain minimal service and living conditions were to be met by the town or city chosen as capital. This eliminated all but three of the proposed Federation's cities: Bridgetown, Barbados; Port of Spain, Trinidad; and Kingston, Jamaica. The commission then itemized some of its impressions: the generally heard accusation that corruption was rife on Trinidad, and that the black-Indian racial division on Trinidad was a detriment; the distance and excessive size of Jamaica. Thus the commission chose Barbados.

[12]O. H. K. Spate, op. cit. (1942), pp. 418–420.

[13]The foregoing quotations are all from the article identified in footnote 4.

[14]D. Lowenthal, "The West Indies Chooses a Capital," Geographical Review, XLVIII, No. 3, (July, 1958), 336–364.

[15]Ibid., p. 337.

[16]Ibid., p. 343.

All this emanated from a London—and still colonial—commision, of course. But in the West Indies, it was received with anger almost everywhere except Barbados. Dr. Lowenthal reports how accusations multiplied and animosities were intensified; in editorials in newspapers, on radio stations—everywhere the report was condemned and insults exchanged. When, finally, the Standing Federation Committee met to consider the Barbados proposal, it rejected it outright. In the subsequent balloting, Jamaica was first eliminated, and in the second ballot Trinidad was selected by eleven votes to five over Barbados.

As we now know, the West Indies Federation survived a mere four years (1958 to 1962). Perhaps the intensity of the islands' ethnic and religious diversity and their very scattered distribution made a working framework a very unlikely achievement. But there can be no doubt that the animosities aroused by the competition for the capital functions helped minimize the chances for success. Dr. Lowenthal's article details much of this diversity—in terms of West Indian beliefs and attitudes, as he points out, rather than his own. From what he writes about the atmosphere in the component parts of the short-lived Federation, we can learn much, not only about the West Indian case, but about the circumstances and motivations that have played a part in the selection of some of the world's capitals.

REFERENCES

Acquah, Ioné, *Accra Survey; A Social Survey of the Capital of Ghana* . . . London, University of London Press, 1958.

Alger, C. F., and S. J. Brams, "Patterns of Representation in National Capitals and Intergovernmental Organizations," *World Politics*, XIX, 4 (July, 1967), 646–663.

Augelli, J. P., "Brasilia: The Emergence of a National Capital," *J. Geog.*, 62, 6 (Sepetmber, 1963), 241–252.

Best, A. C. G., "Gaberone: Problems and Prospects of a New Capital," *Geog. Rev.* 60, 1 (January, 1970), 1–14.

Bird, J., "The Foundation of Australian Seaport Capitals," *Econ. Geog.* 46, 3 (October, 1965), 283–289.

Boateng, E. A., "The Growth and Functions of Accra," *Bull. Ghana Geog. Ass.*, 4, 1 (January, 1959), 9–13.

Chang, S., "Peking: The Growing Metropolis of Communist China," *Geog. Rev.*, 55, 3 (July, 1965), 313–327.

Chapin, Helen B., "Kyongju, Ancient Capital of

Silla," *Asian Horizon*, 1, 4 (Winter, 1948), 36–45.

Chapman, Brian, "Paris," in *Great Cities of the World*, William A. Robson (ed,). New York, Macmillan, 1957, pp. 451–486.

Chiarelli, Giuseppe, "Rome," in *Great Cities of the World*, William A. Robson (ed.), New York, Macmillan, 1957, pp. 517–546.

Conditt, Georg, "Vienna: the History of an Urban Landscape," *Landscape*, 5, 3 (1956), 3–14.

Cornish, Vaughan, *The Great Capituals: an Historical Geography*. London, Methuen; New York, George H. Doran Co., 1923.

Craig, John Keith, "Vienna; A Geographical Analysis," *Tydskrif vir Aardrykskunde—Journal of Geography*, 1, 6 (April, 1960), 10–21.

Dale, Edmund H., "The West Indies: A Federation in Search of a Capital," *Canadian Geographer*, 5, 2 (Summer, 1961), 44–52.

Dickinson, R. E., *The West European City*. London, Rutledge and Kegan Paul, 1951.

Foran, W. Robert, "Rise of Nairobi: from Campsite to City," *Crown Colonist*, 20, 220 (March, 1950), 161–165.

Fryer, D. W., "The 'Million City' in Southeast Asia," *Geog. Rev.*, 43, 4 (October, 1953), 474–494.

Hance, William A., and Irene S. Van Dongen, "Dar es Salaam, the Port and Its Tributary Area," *Ann. A.A.G.*, 48, 4 (December, 1958), 419–435.

Haupert, J. S., "Jerusalem: Aspects of Reunification and Integration," *Prof. Geog.*, 23, 4 (October, 1971), 312–319.

Holford, William, "The Future of Canberra," *Town Planning Rev.*, 29, 3 (October, 1958), 139–162.

Hookham, Maurice, and Roger Simon, "Moscow," in *Great Cities of the World*, William A. Robson (ed.), New York, Macmillan, 1957, pp. 383–410.

Hoppé, E. O., "Australian Capitals," *Canadian Geog. J.*, 44, 3 (March, 1952), 97–107.

Horvath, R. J., "The Wandering Capitals of Ethiopia," *Jour. of African History*, X, 2 (1969), 205–219.

James, Preston E., and Speridião Faissol, "The Problem of Brazil's Capital City," *Geog. Rev.*, 46, 3 (July, 1956), 301–317.

Jarrett, H. R., "The Port and Town of Freetown," *Geography*, 11, Pt. 2, 188 (April, 1955), 108–118.

———, "Some Aspects of the Urban Geography of Freetown, Sierra Leone," *Geog. Rev.*, 46, 3 (July, 1956), 334–354.

———, "Bathurst, Port of Gambia River," *Geography*, 36, Pt. 2, 172 (May, 1951), 98–107.

Jefferson, Mark, "The Law of the Primate City," *Geog. Rev.*, 29, 2 (April, 1939), 226–232.

Keith, Bertram, "Canberra's Changing Scene," *Walkabout*, 19, 7 (July, 1953), 10–19.

Kirk-Greene, A. H. M., and M. J. Campbell, "The Capitals of Northern Nigeria," *Nigeria*, No. 54 (1957), 243–272.

Knight, D. B., "Gaberones: a Viable Proposition?" *Prof. Geog.* 17, 6 (November, 1965), 38–39.

Kureshi, Kahalilullah, "Choice of Pak Capital; A Politico Geographical Analysis," *Pakistan Geog. Rev.*, 5, 1 (1950), 13–25.

Linge, G. J. R., "Canberra After Fifty Years," *Geog. Rev.*, 51, 4 (October, 1961), 467–486.

Lowenthal, David, "The West Indies Chooses a Capital," *Geog. Rev.*, 48, 3 (July, 1958), 336–364.

Miller, J. M., *Lake Europa: a New Capital for a United Europe.* New York, Books International, 1963.

Moscoso Cárdenas, Alfonso, "Between the Earth and the Sky; Quito, Capital of Ecuador," *Américas*, 10, 5 (May, 1958), 14–19.

Murphey, Rhoads, "New Capitals of Asia," *Econ. Devel. and Cultural Change*, 5, 3 (April, 1957), 216–243.

Orico, Osvaldo, *Brazil Capital: Brasilia.* New York, Brazilian Government Trade Bureau, 1958.

Platt, Robert S., "Brazilian Capitals and Frontiers," *J. Geog.*, 53, 9 (December, 1954), 369–375; 54, 1 (January, 1955), 5–17.

Roberts, W. Adolphe, *Havana, the Portrait of a City.* New York, Coward-McCann, 1953.

Ruddock, G., "Capital of East Pakistan," *Pakistan Quart.*, 7, 1 (Spring, 1954), 49–58.

Ruiz Cardénas, Alberto, "Jungle Capital: Iquitos on the Amazon," *Américas*, 7, 3 (March, 1955), 15–18.

Siddall, William R., "Seattle: Regional Capital of Alaska," *Ann. A.A.G.*, 47, 3 (September, 1957), 277–284.

Simey, T. S., "A New Capital for the West Indies," *Town Planning Rev.*, 28, 1 (April, 1957), 63–70.

Simpich, Frederick, "Honolulu, Mid-ocean Capital," *National Geographic*, 105, 5 (May, 1954), 577–624.

Singh, Ujagir, "New Delhi—Its Site and Situation," *National Geographic J. India*, 5, Pt. 3 (September, 1959), 113–120.

Smailes, A. E., *The Geography of Towns.* London, Hutchinson, 1957.

Snyder, D. E., "Alternate Perspectives on Brasilia," *Economic Geography*, 40, 1 (January, 1964), 34–45.

Spate, O. H. K., "Two Federal Capitals: New Delhi and Canberra," *Geographical Outlook*, 1, 1 (January, 1956), 1–8.

————, and L. W. Trueblood, "Rangoon: a Study in Urban Geography," *Geog. Rev.*, 32, 1 (January, 1942), 56–73.

Sutherland, Mason, "Mexico's Booming Capital," *National Geographic*, 100, 6 (December, 1951), 785–824.

White, H. L. (ed.), *Canberra, A Nation's Capital.* Sydney, Angus and Robertson, 1954.

Willson, Betty, "Brasilia, Brazil; Carving a Capital out of the Wilderness," *Américas*, 10, 8 (August, 1958), 2–8.

Winch, Michel, "Western Germany's Capital," *Geog. Mag.*, 31, 1 (May, 1958), 32–41.

Wiskermann, Elizabeth, "Berlin Between East and West," *World Today*, 16, 11 (November, 1960), 463–472.

CHAPTER
7

FRONTIERS, BOUNDARIES, AND BUFFER ZONES

Many studies in political geography have dealt with frontiers and boundaries. Boundaries, on the map and on the ground, mark the limit of the state's jurisdiction and sovereignty. Along boundary lines states make physical contact with their neighbors. Boundaries have frequently been a source of friction between states, and the areas through which they lie are often profoundly affected by their presence. In many ways boundaries are the most obvious politicogeographic features that exist, for we are constantly reminded of them—when we travel, when we read a newspaper map or an atlas, and in many other ways.

Discussions of boundary problems sometimes treat the word "frontier" as though it were synonymous with "boundary." We read of the boundary between Portugal and Spain in one paragraph, and of the Spanish-Portuguese frontier in the next. Both references are to the same phenomenon, represented on the map by a line separating these two states. But are both terms correctly applied? Perhaps the answer can be arrived at through a consideration of their respective functions. What are, and have been, the functions of the frontier, as compared to those of the boundary?

THE FRONTIER

In Chapters 2 and 3, the expansion of states from their heartlands or core areas was briefly described. Such states as the Aztecs' Mexica Empire or the Empire of the Incas were able to expand into areas that were unable to resist their power. At times in history, several states grew to local power and prominence simultaneously, but never made effective contact. Separating them were natural impediments to communication: lakes, swamps, dense forests, mountain ranges. These states, with very few exceptions, possessed no boundaries in the modern sense of the word, but they were nevertheless separated from their neighbors.

Whatever the separating agent—it might have been sheer distance—it functioned effectively to prevent contact.

This situation prevailed throughout history, and in various degrees on all populated continents, until very recently. The modern map showing all states bounded by thin lines that can be precisely represented on maps is, in the politicogeographical world, a very new phenomenon. Although some of the old states, like the Roman Empire, attempted to establish real boundaries by building stone lines across the (in this case, British) countryside, and natural features such as rivers served as trespass lines, the present, almost total framework of boundaries is a recent development. Maps representing the situation one, two, three, or more centuries ago show vast areas which are either unclaimed, unsurveyed, or merely spheres of influence. And man's political evolution has been going on for thousands of years, not just hundreds.

Thus the states and embryonic states of the past were separated, not by lines, but by areas. Still, they were separated, and they were either not in contact or only sporadically and ineffectively so. And here it is possible to recognize that this intervening area functioned—it functioned to prevent contact. Today's boundaries do not prevent contact; along them states *make* physical contact!

This, then, is perhaps the best way to view the frontier: as a politicogeographical area lying beyond the integrated region of the political unit, and into which expansion could take place. It is not surprising that Kristof, in a paper reproduced at the end of the chapter, describes the frontier as "outer-oriented," for after all, states becoming stronger and more powerful were able to expand into the peripheral frontier, and gain control over more and more of it. It is the same principle we use when we speak of the "frontiers of science": obviously we mean an ill-defined outer belt, vague, and unknown, but into which we are penetrating. So it was with the geographical frontier. In Southern Africa, the European-settled core area forming after 1652 around Cape Town grew stronger, unaware of the powerful Zulu state which was developing in Natal. The frontier functioned to separate these two political units, until penetration of this intervening belt began in the 1830's. Then, finally, a confrontation occurred, and the frontier was replaced by uneasy (and, as it turned out, impermanent) truce lines.

Thus we see the frontier as an area, but it was not always an area separating two or more states. Sometimes it was invaded by a state without any serious obstacles until its natural limits were reached. So it was with the westward expansion of the American state, and the invasion of the Australian "frontier." But although that invasion may have led to minor hostilities only, the function of the frontier remained the same. Ratzel would have argued that it formed the life-giving element to the culture which was growing and expand-

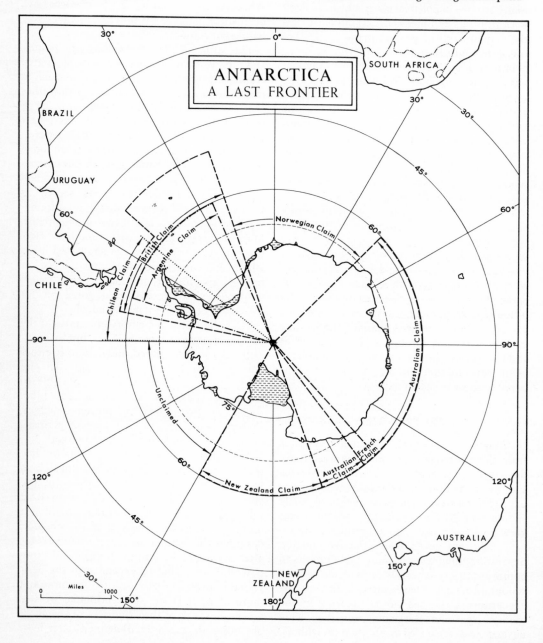

ing, and that once the limits of the frontier were reached, the decay of the state would be sure to follow. Today we would suggest that the frontier was an area, as Kristof puts it, of darkness, of unknown, of dawn. The partition of Antarctica is a modern case in point. Little is yet known about the subsoil of this continent, but a number of states have staked claims, supported by a treaty arrangement.

Through frontiers, boundaries were often drawn. Expanding states or spheres met; sometimes they fought over the area involved, and sometimes they settled the disputed area by boundary treaty. The colonial invasion of Africa is full of examples of the latter. Thus states made contact, and the boundary just established began to function. The frontier, in the original sense of the word, is no more, for the space into which the states had been expanding has been fully occupied. Going from the core of the state into the frontier meant looking outward, pioneering, working outward; reaching the boundary now means that the limit has been set, and that the effective control of the central government prevails here, all the way up to the line. Hence the boundary, a manifestation of integration, is inner-oriented.

Why, then, are the terms boundary and frontier sometimes still used interchangeably? Is it entirely wrong to speak of a frontier in an area where a boundary has been established? Acutally, the use of these terms reflects a reality in political geography—namely, that it is often still possible to recognize frontier characteristics in an area where a boundary does exist. Among the functions of boundaries, as we shall see, is that of division, separation—not physically, but in other ways, such as in economic terms. A tariff wall (which takes effect at the boundary of any state) causes a price differential in certain goods on either side of the boundary, which in turn affects the location of retail outlets for these goods. When a boundary shift takes place, the area through which the boundary is placed may become depressed, for great adjustment in economic activity is necessary.[1] On either side of an international boundary,

[1]For several valuable studies of this nature, see A. Lösch, *The Economics of Location*, translated from the second revised edition by W. B. Woglom and W. F. Stolpler, New Haven, Yale University Press, 1954, especially pp. 192 ff. For a discussion of an internal situation which has international significance see J. R. Mackay, "The Interactance Hypothesis and Boundaries in Canada," *Canad. Geograhper*, No. 11 (1958), pp. 1–8.

therefore, there may be a discernible zone suffering from the interruptive effects of the boundary. This zone, obviously, has spatial characteristics, and hence the word frontier may come into use.

Another reason for the continued use of the word frontier in areas where boundaries have been established involves the fact that such boundaries often run through relatively empty, sparsely populated land. In view of the processes of boundary establishment (see below) this is not surprising. Least friction was encountered if, in a disputed area, the boundary were located through useless land. Hence such a boundary may not even be marked on the ground, even by a line of stones. Such is the case along sections of the Portuguese-Spanish border, so that one cannot, off the beaten path, be sure exactly where one is—in Portugal or in Spain. In the absence of a clearly marked boundary, in empty, barren territory, it is not surprising that the word frontier comes to mind, the theoretical existence of a boundary notwithstanding.

THE BOUNDARY

Boundaries appear on maps as thin lines marking the limit of state sovereignty. In fact a boundary is not a line, but a plane—a vertical plane that cuts through the airspace, the soil, and the subsoil of adjacent states. This plane appears on the surface of the earth as a line, because it intersects the surface as is marked where it does so. But boundaries can be effective underground, where they mark the limit of adjacent states' mining operations in an ore deposit they may share, and they can be effective above the ground, for most countries jealously guard their airspace.

Before proceeding to a discussion of the criteria for boundary creation and the functions performed by boundaries, it is necessary to define certain terms which, like the frontier, have been subject to misuse. The ideal sequence of events in the establishment of a boundary is as follows. The first stage involves the description of the boundary and the terrain through which it runs. This description identifies, in words, as exactly as possible, the location of the boundary being established. Reference may be made to hilltops, crestlines, rivers, and even to cultural features such as farm fences and roads. The more detailed the description, the less likely is there to be subsequent friction. As will be seen

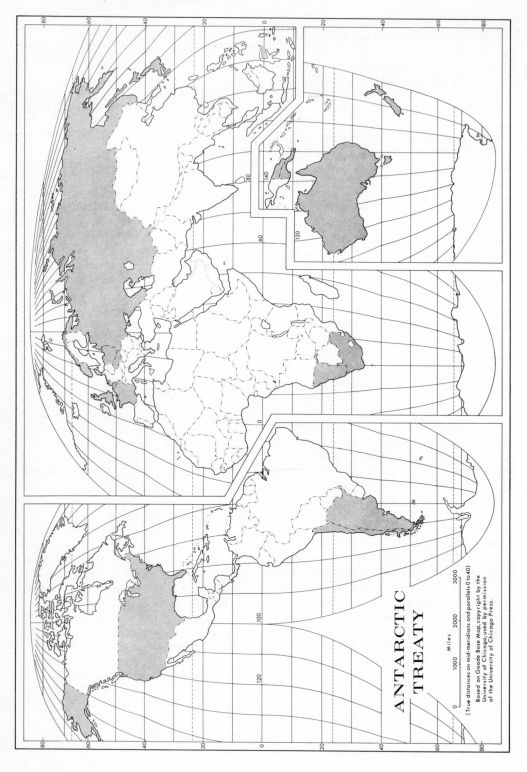

ANTARCTIC TREATY

0   1000   2000   3000
Miles

(True distances on mid-meridians and parallels 0 to 40)

Based on Goode Base Map, copyright by the
University of Chicago, used by permission
of the University of Chicago Press.

later, even the most prominent physical features in the landscape—mountain ranges, rivers, etc.—have given rise to serious disputes when used as political boundary lines. This first stage, represented by the language found in many treaties, is referred to as the *definition* of the boundary.

When the treaty makers have completed their definition of the boundary in question, their work is placed before cartographers who, using large-scale maps and air photographs, locate the boundary as exactly as possible. The period of time separating this stage of *delimitation* from the initial stage of definition may amount to decades: for example, several of the emergent African states whose boundaries were defined at the end of the last century are only now in the process of exactly delimiting their borders. Some of them are discovering that the original work of definition was done rather crudely and imprecisely, so that many difficulties are now experienced.

Finally, there remains the task of marking the boundary on the ground. For this purpose, both the actual treaty as well as the cartographic material are employed. Boundary *demarcation*, as this process is called, has by no means taken place along every boundary defined and delimited: only a minority of the many miles of the world's boundaries are actually marked on the surface. When they are demarcated, a wide variety of methods may be employed. A mere line of poles or stones may suffice. Cement markers may be set up, so that from any one of them, the two adjacent ones on either side will be visible. Fences have been built in certain delicate areas where exact demarcation is required, and, as we know, on rare occasions walls have been built. Boundary demarcation is an expensive process, and when states do not face such problems along their boundaries as to absolutely require demarcation, they often delay this stage permanently.

Political geographers have been interested in several types of boundary research, among

Until the early 1960's, this sign (and a cattle gate) was all there was to tell the traveler that he was leaving South Africa and entering another political entity, Swaziland. At that time, Swaziland was still a British dependency (one of the so-called High Commission Territories), and there was a possibility that these countries would be yielded to South African administration and Bantustan regulations. But the future held a different course for Swaziland; with its 6,700 square miles and population of about 400,000, it was given independence. In common with other formerly British African territories, Swaziland's society became a multiracial one—thus directly opposed to South Africa's separationist philosophies. With a rather antagonistic radio station in the capital of Mbabane and the specter of political refugees crossing this boundary, it was soon demarcated. This has become a border post, and all formalities must be completed.

them studies of boundary definition, disputes, shifts, and so on. In the past, there was a great deal of concern with the criteria upon which boundary definition should be based, but subsequently interest has focused upon the functions of boundaries as parts of the system that is the state.

CRITERIA

Political geographers, among others, have engaged in the search for the "ideal" criteria for boundary definition, in hopes of reducing the world tensions created by boundary disputes. This activity was especially common during the interwar period, and led to intense debate regarding the merits of "artificial" boundaries as opposed to "natural" (physical). In fact, no discussion of criteria is possible without at the same time referring to functions. A boundary is one of the parts of the state system, and by speaking of criteria for their establishment we speak, also, of the effect the use of these criteria will have. And by effect we mean function. An example will clarify this. Some political geographers have felt that ethnic criteria may be the most appropriate for the definition of international boundaries. In other words, boundaries should be drawn so as to separate peoples who are racially unlike, and to unify peoples who are racially uniform.[2] Behind this, of course, is the idea that the boundary will therefore separate peoples who are culturally so different that a minimum of stress will be placed upon it.

Of course, world population is too heterogeneous and interdigitated to permit the definition of boundaries that completely and exactly separate peoples of different racial character (not to speak of the difficulty in always correctly identifying "race"). There are minorities in practically every state. Occasionally, rather than altering boundaries, states have attempted to exchange such groups: once, some hundreds of thousands of Turks were moved into Anatolia, from where Greeks were expatriated. In 1964 there was talk of repatriating the Cypriot Turks from Cyprus, leaving the island entirely Greek. Another view of the Cyprus problem was that

[2]This is one of the bases for the South African Bantustan Scheme, whereby the racial elements of the very heterogeneous South African population are being assigned their own "homelands" (Bantustans for the African peoples). Repatriation of the population to these homelands is in progress, and one; the Transkei, had achieved limited self-government by 1964. See H. J. de Blij, Africa South, Evanston, Northwestern University Press, 1962, pp. 247–291.

of partition—the demarcation of an ethnic boundary separating the Turkish minority from the Greek majority. Note, again, that while the criterion in this case is race, the expected function of such a boundary is to minimize friction between adjacent peoples and their institutions.

The criterion of language, also, might be proposed as a basis for boundary definition. But a map of the world's languages shows a patchwork of great complexity which would immeasurably compound the boundary framework existing today. Many states are multilingual and would be fragmented in any such effort; furthermore it is impossible to reconcile the language criterion at all times with that of race. This brings up a question that kept political geographers at odds for some time—namely, whether a boundary should be a barrier or a bond between adjacent states. In its simplest form, we might put it this way: if a boundary separates people who speak different languages, they are not likely to understand each other well, with the result that relations will remain potentially hostile across their mutual boundary. On the other hand, a boundary running through a region of linguistic homogeneity would ensure that people on either side would have, at least, a language in common, and as a result could communicate more easily. This common language across the border, then, would act as a cement between the two states involved. The point can also be put differently, in terms of physical criteria: a mountain range performs the barrier function, with divisive consequences; a river, with its two banks close together, would form a bond.

One of those criteria that do not overlap with language or race is religion. Peoples of widely varied races and tongues have accepted the same faith—and peoples speaking the same language have adopted different religions. Nevertheless, in areas where religion has been a strong source of internal friction, this has been a major basis for boundary definition. A recent example is the partition of the Indian subcontinent into (mainly Hindu) India and (mainly Moslem) Pakistan. The latter state, as a result, became a fragmented state, and has shown the ill effects of its condition.

Inspection of the world framework of boundaries will indicate that many political boundaries lie along prominent physical features in the landscape. Such boundaries, based upon physical features, have become known as physiographic political boundaries, a term not to be confused with the physiographic boundary as used in physical geography. In physical geography this term implies the edge of a physiographic region or province—an area of physiographic homogeneity. In political geography it refers to any prominent physical feature paralleled by a political boundary—a river, mountain range, or escarpment. These would seem to be especially acceptable criteria, since pronounced physical features often also separate culturally different areas. But in practice such boundaries have also produced major problems. No state corresponds exactly to a physiographic province, and very homogeneous physiographic regions are sometimes divided by boundaries based upon some insignificant feature such as a small stream or a low divide. In the early days of boundary establishment, physiographic features were useful in that they were generally known and could be recognized as the trespass line. But this function has ceased now, and the most divisive and obvious physical features have created major difficulties between states. For instance, it would be difficult to imagine a more obvious divider than the Andes between Chile and Argentina, and yet the boundary running along the great divide was the subject of a half-century's bitter wrangling, mainly because the original treaty (1881) did not adequately define the boundary it intended to establish. Any mountain range has recognizable crestlines, but they rarely coincide with the watershed. As a result, water flowing from one side of the state boundary (which coincides with a physiographic, but not with a hydrographic feature) feeds the streams of the state on the other side of the boundary. If the state that possesses the source areas decides to dam those waters, it may impede the water supply of the other state, and friction may result. There are many other examples—transhumance, the use of passes, the need for tunnels—each has produced its own problems.

Rivers, too, seem obvious and useful boundary features, but again many problems attend their use as boundaries. The use of the water by the riparian states is one major issue for debate. Furthermore, rivers tend to shift their course, producing new circumstances which require a redefinition of the boundary, which may lead to friction. Thus physical features, which seem almost to be nature's own provision for boundary establishment, are at times as problematic as boundaries based upon the other criteria enumerated.

While such criteria as have been considered

above, among others, have played a role at the time of boundary definition, the most important recurring element is one that cannot be mapped and which changes with time: power. Often states have been able to dictate to others where boundaries should be drawn: after both the first and the second World War this occurred ubiquitously. Many boundaries, first drawn as temporary truce lines, became permanent international borders. Such boundaries have appeared on the map since the end of the second World War: the present partition of Germany, Korea, and Viet Nam resulted from power struggles and has little or nothing to do with the cultural realities within those territories. Only time will tell whether these boundaries, like so many truce lines of the past, will attain permanency.

FUNCTIONS

The functions of boundaries, as Boggs has pointed out, change over time.[3] This is perhaps best illustrated through a consideration of the role of the boundary as a line of defense. Until quite recently, it was conceivable for a state to attempt to fortify its boundary to such an extent that it would be invincible. French hopes until 1940 were pinned on the Maginot Line, a belt of fortifications constructed along its northeastern boundary. Germany rapidly transformed the Atlantic coasts in its possession during the second World War into another line of forts and obstacles to invasion. The idea is as old as the Chinese Wall, and the principle is the same. Plateaus with sheer escarpments have afforded protection to societies which used these natural barriers to their advantage and considered the scarps to mark the limit of their domain: the histories of Lesotho and Ethiopia illustrate the case.

But advancing technology has diminished the importance of the defensive function of boundaries, and states no longer rely upon fortified borders for their security. In some parts of the world, where guerrilla activities short of open warfare occur, a river or mountain range may still present strategic advantages: northern Mozambique is a case in point. To the major powers of the world, however, and those states possessing modern military equipment, the naturally or artificially fortified boundary is no longer an asset.

Thus the once-important function of the boundary as a line of defense has all but

[3] S. W. Boggs, "Boundary Functions and the Principles of Boundary Making," *Ann. A.A.G.*, 22 (March, 1932), p. 48.

disappeared. On the other hand, this should not suggest that the boundary as a mark of territorial inviolability has thereby also vanished: fortified boundaries served the dual purpose of defense and unmistakable demarcation: many states are presently demarcating their boundaries without intending or attempting to fortify them. Rather, the aim is to mark the limit of state sovereignty, which may have become necessary as a result of emerging friction. The government of India has recently been demarcating its northern boundaries with China, and the government of Kenya has not only demarcated its border with Somalia (the Somali Republic) more clearly, but also cleared a belt of adjacent land of all settlement, in order to reduce infiltration by Somali herdsmen. The tension-ridden boundaries between Israel and its Arab neighbors, and between Haiti and the Dominican Republic, all serve to illustrate the uselessness of fortification but the undiminished function of the boundary as the mark of state inviolability, not only on the ground, but above it as well.

The boundary, then, is one of the interacting parts of the state system. It has an impact upon many of the forms of organization within the state, and in turn the way in which the state's various arms of organization function affects the nature of the boundary. The first case is exemplified by the commercial function of the boundary. The government can erect tariff walls against outside competition for its market and thus assist internal industries. These industries may prosper, and owe their prosperity to the protection thus afforded. However, as we have seen, the price differential on either side of the boundary will affect the location of outlets for the products of the various industries affected by tariff provisions; and while the industry may prosper, the area under the shadow of the boundary may not. The second case can best be envisaged in terms of contrast. Some boundaries due to the close and positive relationship between the societies they separate, do not mark great changes in modes of government, prosperity, etc. The United States–Canadian border is an excellent example of the kind. Some other borders, on the contrary, mark lines across which contrasts are severe and prominent. The societies they separate may have different institutions, different levels of development, and different ideological ties. Such a boundary may be very interruptive in every way. The boundary between East Germany and West Germany functions in this manner. Compare it to the German-Netherlands border on the one hand, and the East German-Czechoslovakian boundary on the other!

The boundary, of course, also has a legal function. State law prevails to this line. Taxes must be paid to the government by anyone legally subject to taxation, whether he resides

A border station on the boundary between Austria and Liechtenstein. Here is a boundary which does not separate peoples whose ways of life differ greatly; it is a mere formality, and the boundary line itself is not demarcated (Robert Janke).

one or one hundred miles from the border. Even though a resident living within sight of the border may have closer linguistic, historical, and religious ties with the people on the other side, he is subject to the regulations prevailing on his side of the boundary, including compulsory education to a certain age, selective service enlistment, and so forth. Furthermore, the state government is capable of controlling emigration and immigration at points along the border.

Perhaps it is useful to look at boundary functions as consisting of two distinct kinds. First, there is the set of functions performed by all boundaries marking the limits of states (as opposed to dependent territories), and they are related to those parts of the functioning state system which all states have in common. All states, for instance, have laws. All boundaries mark the limits of territory where such laws apply. All states have economic policies. All boundaries in some degree have economic importance. All states are theoretically sovereign. Thus all boundaries mark limits of sovereignty. Second, there is a set of functions which derives from the particular state system of which the boundary is a part, and from the conditions prevailing in the adjacent state. Some boundaries, as we have seen, do not separate strongly contrasted states. The functions of the dividing boundaries are very different from those that separate states possessing vastly contrasting internal conditions.

Political geographers long discussed the question of whether boundaries should be bonds or barriers, and whether very divisive borders such as mountain ranges and lakes are "better" than artificial, "unnatural" boundaries. Changing conditions have brought changes in emphasis. In the first place, the world boundary framework, apart from relatively minor adjustments, is not likely to be changed, however salutary the criteria that might be "discovered" to be best. Secondly, the evolution of supranationalism in many spheres of human activity has provided some new hope that the interruptive and divisive nature of boundaries may ultimately be reduced. Peattie long ago argued that boundaries with few functions served man better than those with many important functions;[4] this would derive directly from what was said in the preceding paragraph, for the fewer the functions, the fewer the contrasts across the border. But boundaries tend to reflect the increasing complexity of society: their functions increase in number and importance. To reverse the trend, then, would require a reversal in the very process of man's political evolution—not a likely event. Hence, as Jones has expressed it,[5] the hope lies in eventual changes in the concept of state sovereignty with the emergence of supranationalism. And indeed, states have given up a small degree of their sovereignty in order to participate in economic and cultural blocs. This subject will be discussed in Chapter oo.

One of the most significant articles to appear on the subject of frontiers and boundaries, and a wide range of associated aspects, was published in 1959. Before developing the matter of boundary functions further, this paper, by L. K. D. Kristof, is worth examining. Note the emphasis upon the frontier and the boundary in terms of their respective functions: the question of separation or assimilation, which has kept political geographers in debate for a half century, remains a major issue.

[4]R. Peattie, Look to the Frontiers: A Geography of the Peace Table, New York, Harper, 1944, p. 103.

[5]S. B. Jones, Boundary Making: A Handbook for Statesmen, Treaty Editors and Boundary Commissioners, Washington, D. C., Carnegie Endowment for International Peace, 1945, pp. 19 ff.

The Nature of Frontiers and Boundaries

Ladis K. D. Kristof[1]

University of Chicago

There exists a quite extensive literature dealing with the subject of frontiers and boundaries.[2] There have been also successful attempts at classification and development of a proper terminology.[3] Few writers have, however, tackled the problem from a more theoretical point of view.[4] This study is more particularly concerned with the problem of clarifying, and disentangling for the purpose of theoretical understanding, the two elements which combine in what we commonly call frontiers and boundaries: the physical (or nonhuman geographical, or "natural") and the political, i.e., moral and legal, element.

THE ORIGINS AND EVOLUTION OF TERMS

In common speech we use the words "frontier" and "boundary" with the implication that these have not only a quite well-defined meaning but also that they are (or almost) interchangeable. However, it does not take much reading in pertinent literature to discover that the problem is not simple.[5]

Frontier

Historically, the word "frontier" implied what it suggests etymologically, that is, that which is "in front."[6] The frontier was not an abstract term or line; on the contrary, it designated an area which was part of a whole, specifically that part which was ahead of the hinterland. Hence it was often called the foreland, or borderland, or march.[7] For the purpose of our discussion it must be stressed that in its historical origin the frontier was (1) not a legal concept, and (2) not, or at least not essentially, a political or intellectual concept. It was rather a phenomenon of "the facts of life"—a manifestation of the spontaneous tendency for growth of the ecumene. In antiquity, and later too, the frontier was on the margin of the inhabited world, but each particular ecumene, for instance, that of the agricultural society as opposed to the nomad society, also had a frontier. The *limes* of the Roman empire were those of the ecumene of Western civilization.[8]

With the development of patterns of civilization above the level of mere subsistence strictly adapted to particular environmental conditions, the frontiers between ecumene became meeting places not merely of different ways of physical survival, but also of different concepts of the good life, and hence increasingly political in character.[9] But even at this stage the frontier was something very different from what a modern boundary is. It had not the connotation of an area or zone which marks a definite limit or end of a political unit. On the contrary, given the theory that there can (or should) be only one state—a universal state—the frontier meant quite literally "the front": the *frons* of the *imperium mundi* which expands to the only limits it can acknowledge, namely, the limits of the world. Thus the frontier was not the end ("tail") but rather the beginning ("forehead") of the state; it was the spearhead of light and knowledge expanding into the realm of darkness and of the unknown. The borderlands—the marches —were areas of dawn; they were frontiers in the sense of Turner's agricultural frontier: pioneer settlements of a forward-moving culture bent on occupying the whole area.[10]

Boundary

The etymology of the word "boundary" immediately points to the primary function of

L. K. D. Kristof, "The Nature of Frontiers and Boundaries," **Annals of the Association of American Geographers**, Vol. 49 (1959), 269–282.

the boundary: the boundary indicates certain well established limits (the bounds) of the given political unit, and all that which is within the boundary is bound together, that is, it is fastened by an internal bond.[11]

"Boundary" is a term appropriate to the present-day concept of the state, that is, the state as a sovereign (or autonomous) spatial unit, one among many. Since the transition from tribal law to territorial law[12] the essentials of statehood, both from the functional and legal point of view, are: territory, people, and a government in effective control internally, independent externally, and willing and able to assume obligations under international (or federal) law.[13] Sovereignty is territorial; hence it must have a certain known extent: a territory under exclusive jurisdiction limited by state boundaries. The borderlands, the old marchlands, are defined more and more exactly until there is, in principle, an exact borderline.[14] The modern sovereign state is bound within and confined to its legal limits. The boundaries bind together an area and a people which live under one sovereign government and law and are, at least presumably, integrated not only administratively and economically but also by means of a state idea or "crede."[15] At the same time "the state is marked off from its neighbors by political boundaries."[16] In an age in which we (with exceptions) do not think in terms of universal empires but accept the co-existence of many credes and states, it is important to have the spheres of the several centripetal, integrating forces legally delimited.[17]

THE DIFFERENCES BETWEEN FRONTIERS AND BOUNDARIES

There are some difficulties in trying to distinguish between frontiers[18] and boundaries First, not all languages have separate words for the two.[19] Then, the historical transition from one to another in many regions tends to diminish the awareness of the essential differences.[20] Still, this does not change the fact that frontiers and boundaries are in their very nature two different things.[21]

The *frontier is outer-oriented*. Its main attention is directed toward the outlying areas which are both a source of danger and a coveted prize. The hinterland—the motherland—is seldom the directing force behind the pulsations of frontier life. As history, Ameri-

can, Russian, or Chinese, well illustrates, the borderlands often develop their own interests quite different from those of the central government.[22] They feel neither bound by the center nor binding its realm. Rather, they represent runaway elements and interests of the state's corporate body.[23]

The *boundary*, on the contrary, is *inner-oriented*. It is created and maintained by the will of the central government. It has no life of its own, not even a material existence. Boundary stones are not the boundary itself. They are not coeval with it, only its visible symbols. Also, the boundary is not tied inextricably to people—people teeming, spontaneous, and unmediated in their daily activities on, along, or athwart the border. It is the mediated will of the people: abstracted and generalized in the national law, subjected to the tests of international law, it is far removed from the changing desires and aspirations of the inhabitants of the borderlands.

While the frontier is inconceivable without frontiersmen—an "empty frontier" would be merely a desert—the boundary seems often to be happiest, and have the best chances of long survival, when it is not bothered by border men.[24] Yet, the boundary line is not merely an abstraction. Still less can it be a legal fiction. It must be reality, or , rather, reflect reality. In other words, it must be co-ordinated with an empirical force actually present and asserting itself in the terrain. The boundary is, in fact, the outer line of *effective* control exercised by the central government.[25]

The *frontier* is a manifestation of *centrifugal forces*. On the other hand, the range and vigor of *centripetal forces* is indicated by the *boundary*. True, the frontier has, and always had, also a strategic meaning—the defensive line which keeps enemies out—and in this it depends on support from the hinterland. But precisely in order to be able to maximize its strategic forces the central government must mobilize and integrate all the available resources. All efforts and loyalties must be concentrated and co-ordinated under the banner of the state idea and interest. Consequently, the frontier lands, too, have to be controlled and bound to the state; they must be subordinated to the imperative and overriding demands of the sovereign *raison d'etre* of the state as a whole. In other words, an effort is made to draw somewhere a line of effective control over both ingress and egress: not only the enemy has to be kept out but one's own citizens and resources have to be kept in. It is in the interest of the central government to substitute a boundary for the frontier.[26]

The *frontier* is an *integrating factor*. Being a zone of transition from the sphere (ecumene) of one way of life to another, and representing forces which are neither fully assimilated to nor satisfied with either, it provides an excellent opportunity for mutual interpenetration and sway. Along the frontier life constantly manipulates the settled patterns of the pivotally organized socio-political and cultural structures. It is precisely this watering down of loyalties and blurring of differences that the central governments attempt to forestall by substituting the semi-autonomous frontiers with a controlled and exact borderline.

The *boundary* is, on the contrary, a *separating factor*. "[It is the] boundary [that] impinges on life. . . . Few natural obstacles restrict the movement of persons, things, and even ideas as completely as do the boundaries of some states."[27] The boundary separates the sovereign (or federal, or autonomous, or any other) political units from one another. However much physical—geographical, cultural, or certain political factors may tend to make it inconspicuous, it remains always a fixed obstacle; it impedes integration across the borderline.[28] To propose, as one writer does,[29] the drawing of boundaries in such a way as to make them meeting places for people and thus rather an assimilative than a dissimilative factor is a misconception as to what a boundary is and what are its purposes and functions. Any assimilation, hence integration, cannot be stimulated by the drawing of a line which separates and delimits the spheres of the integrating forces, but, on the contrary, by the removal of such obstacles to interpenetration. Every confederation, federation, or merger of states must always begin with a (total, or at least partial) elimination of the limiting and separating factors inherent in the boundary, and thus a withering away of the boundary itself.

In general, discussing the differences between frontiers and boundaries, one faces a grave dilemma: to what degree is it possible to generalize about the frontier? The boundary is defined and regulated by law, national and international, and as such its status and characteristics are more uniform and can be defined with some precision. But the frontier is a phenomenon of history; like history it may repeat itself, but, again like history, it is always unique. It is difficult to pinpoint essential features of the frontier which are universally valid. For instance, the degree to which the frontier is an integrating factor depends on the attractiveness to the frontiersman of the way of life of his opposite number. This way of life usually seems attractive if the adoption of it promises better chances of survival in the given environment or if it appears generally "superior." On the American frontier both the white settler and the Indian were willing to learn from each other certain techniques, but on the broader cultural level each considered his way of life as definitely preferable ("superior"). Consequently, the integrating process along the American frontier touched only upon the externals—the internal lives of the two social groups remained incompatible, witness the fact that intermarriages were rather rare and almost no white American ever really "became" an Indian or vice versa. The Spanish and the native Mexican culture were relatively more compatible; hence much more integration occurred along the frontier in Mexico, and the result is a genuinely composite culture, especially outside the cities.

The importance of the relative compatibility of cultures which meet on a given frontier can be illustrated by comparing the advance of the Russian and the northern Chinese frontier. Both of these frontiers have been biting into the heritage of the Mongol Empire. But the Russian way of life, based on an extensive agriculture, was much less different from that of the pastoral nomad subjects of the Mongol khan than was the Chinese culture which was based on an intensive and irrigated agriculture. This helps to explain why the Russians succeeded in taking such a lion's bite of the Mongol Empire, and in integrating, even absorbing to a large extent, the natives, while the Chinese pushed their frontier only a few hundred miles or less into Extra-Mural China. Since the Russians did not, like the Americans, steam-roll the native cultures, or even the natives themselves, out of existence, the Russian expansion was not merely a *frontier of conquest* but also a *frontier of integration:* the new culture was the result of a fusion.[30] There are historians who think that the Russians paid a heavy price for integrating so many "barbarians": in the process they ceased to be Europeans and became Eur-Asiatics.

BOUNDARIES AS LEGAL-POLITICAL PHENOMENA
PAR EXCELLENCE

We have said that boundaries are fixed by law. There is, however, often confusion as to what a law is and what kind of laws determine the limits of states. The misunderstandings which arose from the use of the terms "natural boundaries" and "artificial boundaries" are at least partly due to this confusion. Thus, it will be helpful if we make the distinction between three types of law:

(1) *Law of nature, i.e., scientific law,* is a creature of facts. *Ex facto jus oritur.* It is ruled by the empirical world. We observe the natural phenomena (or reproduce them in a laboratory) and deduce from our observations certain generalizations about the behavior of elements and call them laws, e.g., the law of gravity. But these laws have no coercive power over nature. On the contrary, if facts do not conform to the laws, the latter are adjusted to conform to reality. The concordance between what *is* and the law must be absolute.

(2) *Natural law,*[31] *i.e., moral law,* is as strict as the scientific law but in an exactly opposite sense. It is not the *is* but the *ought* which is sovereign. The status of the moral law is not affected by the facts. All Jews and Christians ought to obey the Ten Commandments, yet even if not a single one of them did, the Law would still be there; unchanged, categorical, and as binding as ever. The moral law exists in itself, that is, in the justice of "thou shalt" and not in the empirical world in which it may or may not be observed. While in the natural world a law which does not conform to facts is no law at all, in the moral world only that is a "fact," i.e., a moral fact, which conforms to the moral law.[32]

(3) *Jural law (lex)* is a formal verbalization and particularization of the moral standards of a given socio-political order in respect to the practical (or at least observable) behavior of the members of the society. It is an attempt to bring the spiritual and empirical realms together, to make the moral standards "efficient." Three characteristics of jural law are important for our discussion: it is coercive, it may be violated,[33] and its ultimate source is public opinion about values.[34] Imperfect both in its moral substance and enforcing procedure, the jural law is, as all political phenomena are, the result of compromises reflecting the complexity of the social forces interacting on the given scene.

Boundaries are supported by jural laws.[35] They are one of the spatial expressions of the given legal order. As distinguished from "boundaries" between phenomena of the physical geographical or natural history world, they are man-made geographical occurrences. A boundary does not exist in nature or by itself. It always owes its existence to man.[36]

True, the "boundary" in the natural world,[37] e.g., an orographic line, or the limit of the habitat of certain species of flora and fauna in the desert, steppe, or forest zone, also may occasionally be man-fixed, but it is not man created. It *is* in nature, and all man does is to shift and reshuffle it in space as he transforms the natural environment into a cultural environment.

The limit in the political world is not a matter of *is;* like everything political it is of the domain of *ought.* Man chooses between certain priorities and values—of faith, philosophy, or civilization—and decides according to them where the boundary ought to be: follow the line of religious divisions, extend to where "might made it right," or separate the peoples according to their tongues and customs. And the life span of the boundary is coeval with the pre-eminence of the forces stemming from the given "ought," for it is a function of human will.[38] Human will brings it to life and must sustain it continuously in the terrain or at least within the legal framework on which it rests.

The "boundaries" in the natural world rest on physical laws which are self-enforcing and cannot be broken. A water divide always conforms to the law of gravity, and it must always exist in nature. It does not need to and cannot be willed because it is independent of human will. Man may want to know where it is, but he does not create it. In any given environment the watershed is automatically traced by immutable physical laws.[39] The boundaries in the political world are, on the contrary, built on jural laws, and thus, in the ultimate instance, on the moral laws accepted by the lawmakers. Given certain values the boundary ought[40] to be here or there, but it may be elsewhere. Moral laws are not absolute rulers. They are, like all wisdom, only advisory.

If we understand the political nature of boundaries we shall never commit the mistake of speaking, like Lapradelle, of an objective as opposed to a subjective (that is, one leaving room for choices and preferences) conception of boundary-making.[41] Even if we reject the currently fashionable theories of cultural relativism and adhere to the classic philosophical concept of objective truths, problems of boundaries will always remain a matter of the particular—an application of general principles to specific cases—and thus *par excellence* political. To say that there is an "objective conception" of politics which eliminates choices[42] reminds us of the often advocated "depoliticised politics."[43] Politics without alternatives and choices is a contradiction in terms; like dehydrated water.

In fact, not only boundaries but all limits ascribed to an area—any compound area,[44] also a non-political purely physical geographical and wholly uninhabited area—are always subjective. They are defined anthropocentrically: both the area and its limits are viewed through the eyes of man and conceived in terms of human concepts of life. "Any attempt to divide the world involves subjective judgment. . . . A map of 'natural regions' or of 'regions based solely on natural elements' with reference to mosquitoes, would be entirely different from one made with reference to sequoias. . . . Needless to say, all such divisions by geographers have been made with reference to man's point of view—nature as man is concerned with it."[45] Moreover, man's judgments of areas are colored by his particular culture. The criteria of definition for "natural" regions or landscapes are of one kind in an industrial society, of another in a society of primitive food gatherers, and again different among pastoralists, peasants, etc.[46]

The political nature of boundaries, and the nature of politics itself, is much better understood by Haushofer than by Lapradelle. We may disagree with Haushofer's classification of boundaries and boundary problems, or with the solutions he envisages,[47] but this is a political disagreement, one which has its roots in the values we cherish and the concepts of state we hold. It is not possible to deny the validity of his assertion that boundaries are zones of frictions.[48]

The boundary is a meeting place of two socio-political bodies, each having its particular interests, structure, and ideology. Each generates loyalties and also imposes duties and constraints for the sake of internal harmony and compactness and of external

separateness and individuality. Two neighboring states do not need to be engaged continuously, or at any time, in a struggle for life and death. They may compete peacefully and, in general, minimize their conflicts of interest. Still, the very existence of the boundary is proof that there are some differences in ideology and goals, if not of a virulent present-day character then at least imbedded in the historical heritage. The French–Swiss boundary is certainly very peaceful. Yet, the political ideas and ideals, the ways of life, and the structure of society are very different in the two countries, and consequently no one advocates a Franco–Swiss merger or even federal union. If two neighboring political units pursue both theoretically and practically identical goals then the intellectual and physical communication across the boundary will be so intensive as to sweep it away. When Malta voted to join Great Britain, or Syria and Egypt merged, the community of thought and interest was able to overcome even geographical separation. The two Germanys are, in their own political will, one, but remain separated by a boundary which is that of superimposed political entities and supranational integrating forces.

FRONTIERS IN THE CONTEMPORARY WORLD

The example of Germany brings us face to face with the problem of the current reappearance of the phenomena of frontiers and frontier lands, but in a novel, less earth-bound form. Whether we like it or not, boundary disputes, so dominant in international politics a generation ago, are fading away from diplomatic agenda.[49] They are replaced in both urgency and importance by problems of a new kind of frontiers—frontiers of ideological worlds.[50]

During the Middle Ages the development of clear-cut concepts of political entities and boundaries was hampered by two factors: one, the hierarchical system of feudal authority with its overlapping, divided, and often conflicting loyalties,[51] and, two, the still lingering idea of the supremacy of a universal *imperium* (or *sacerdotium*) over the particular *regnum*—the lingering hope for a Christian *Monarchia*, a true *Civitas Maxima*. But after the fiasco of the religious wars the idea of sovereignty, combined later with the rising tide of nationalism, favored the emergence of national states with sovereign territory bound by an internationally recognized and inviolable boundary.[52] With the adoption in 1918 of the principle of national self-determination, it was hoped that a stable international order with rule of law might be realized. However, any legal order is possible only if a certain socio-political maturity is attained, that is, if there is a general understanding as to the underlying values. Laws reflect the crystallization of the political community around a value system.

The Versailles-created system of quasi-law-regulated international order was based on a Western concept of justice, and, among others, on the assumption that loyalty to the nation and the nation state is *the* overriding loyalty.[53] But new ideas sprang up and generated new values and new loyalties. Today, not only is the old consensus undermined, but the very concept of territorial law is challenged. "Proletarians have no fatherland" and "proletarians of all countries unite" are the best known but not by any means the only ideas which try to transgress on the territorially organized socio-political order. In the resulting confusion friends are sought in enemy territory, and enemies discovered among fellow citizens of the homeland.[54]

Under such circumstances the whole situation on the international scene, and often even on the national scene, retrogresses from a state of relative maturity,[55] indispensable for the rule of law, into a state of unpredictability and fluidity.[56] The concepts of sovereignty and boundary often become meaningless. The French Communist parliamentarians openly boast that "France is our country, but the Soviet Union is our fatherland."[57] The Soviet Union exercises, for all practical purposes, full sovereign rights in certain, not even contiguous, territories, e.g., Albania. Just as in pre-modern times all members of a tribe obeyed their tribal law regardless of which and whose territory they inhabited, so today all adherents of an ideology are urged to obey their ideological, and not the territorial law. Our national and international law system was possible because *jus sanguinis* was superseded by *jus soli*. It cannot survive if allegiance to a *jus ideae (jus idealogi)* takes roots.[58]

One of the great difficulties of American foreign policy is that it tries to enforce clear-cut loyalties and territorial divisions in a world which is in flux. Those who accuse the State Department of being legalistically minded point out that law and order do not precede but follow from a certain general agreement as to the desired legal order. As long as such a consensus is wanting, politics are necessarily in a more primary, that is, pre-rule of law stage. Given the existing conditions, it is wiser to recognize that between the two great ideological ecumene certain "grey areas" of frontier lands, equivocal loyalties, and undefined allegiances, are unavoidable; perhaps not only unavoidable but even desirable: they permit mutual influencing and interpenetration in a broad border zone in which either of the two centripetal forces is too weak to integrate. The detachment of Yugoslavia or India is an offspring of centrifugal forces reacting against colonialism—of the Eastern and Western variety, respectively—but the two countries, having integrated into their systems certain characteristics from both camps, are areas of transition often much more valuable in our quest for international peace than the old buffer states.

Buffer states were a purely mechanical device of international politics: they separated physically two potential warriors, making it more difficult for them to exchange blows. The "grey areas" of the ideological frontiers of today are capable of a more sophisticated intellectual-political role. In contact with and willing to internalize currents from both poles, they are not merely transitive but also transformative: like an electrical transformer they adjust the tensions of the two political voltages to permit at least some flow of current without danger that flying sparks will fire the whole house.[59]

A clear-cut boundary between East and West would, on the contrary, accentuate and underline the differences and divisions, and tend thus to heighten the existing tensions. Besides, it could not prevent ideological influences from jumping a border line, however well-armored. The chain of military alliances from Greece to Pakistan—the so-called southern tier—was intended to seal off all of the Middle East from the Russians. But it has not. Sparks between Moscow and Cairo jumped our earth-bound defense line and established Soviet influence right in the center of the area.[60] It is for this reason that the British would like to substitute for our legalistic and centralizing "boundary-seeking" foreign policy, a more pragmatic and looser "frontier-tolerating" foreign policy.

The present American attitude . . . is to regard

all Communists as undifferentiated and untoucha-
ble, resolve to make the best of freedom in half a
world, and man a *rigid boundary,* permanently
vigilant. . . . To this conception Great Britain is
bound to offer an alternative, less clear-cut but also
less pessimistic. We have to look at fixing of the
frontier, not as a final solution of our dispute with
Communism, but as a step to the attainment of
tolerable relations. . . .[61]

The British are "less pessimistic" because
they believe that a zone of interpenetration—a
frontier of mutual influence—will not necessarily lead to Soviet gains; it may also work to
our advantage. The British seem to have
greater faith in the vigor and potential strength
of the West, and in the attraction it may
exercise.

Soviet leaders boast that Communist ideology spreads throughout the world "without
visas and fingerprints" and that "revolutionary ideas know no boundaries."[62] This may be
true, but, as we know, it does not mean that
the Soviets do not have to face knotty
problems on the frontiers of their own
ideological ecumene. The case of Tito is most
obvious. It is also most illuminating of the
dilemma frontier *versus* boundary.

Though frontier conditions may sometimes
be deliberately created by governments, the
state tends to view frontiers and frontiersmen
as a temporary expedient; as appropriate to a
period of transition. The ultimate goal is a
boundary, not a frontier.[63] This is what the
Chinese frontier policy of keeping the Chinese
in and the barbarians out aimed at.[64] Since
frontier conditions affect, and unsettle, the
internal order and quiet, the state must,
ultimately, *either* make an effort to integrate
the frontier lands within its socio–economic
–political system—to enclose them within the
state boundary—*or,* if it cannot be done
economically or at all, to exclude them from
its realm: put them beyond the pale of its
community. This is something of the dilemma
that has confronted the Soviet Union in its
dealings with the satellites China and, especially, Yugoslavia.

On the one hand, it was desirable to keep
Tito within the bounds of the Communist
camp; on the other, given the fact that he was
not willing, and could not be forced, to
consider himself integrated within and bound
to this camp, it was not possible to include
him.[65] Hence, despite all the disadvantages of
having such a "barbarian" with ways of life
(or, rather, ways of thinking) "Chinese"

enough to attract not too loyal border elements, he had to be shut without the "Great
Wall." Putting him outside the "boundary"
Moscow acknowledged that Tito is a chieftain
with whom one has to negotiate: he is beyond
the line of control and command.[66] In relation
to the Iron Curtain, the Yugoslavians are like
the semi-nomadic and semi-Chinese tribes
which did not fit either within or without the
Great Wall: they are the Hsiungnu of the
Soviet empire.

CONCLUSION

The nature of frontiers differs greatly from the
nature of boundaries. Frontiers are a characteristic of rudimentary socio–political relations;
relations marked by rebelliousness, lawless-
ness, and/or absence of laws. The presence of
boundaries is a sign that the political community has reached a relative degree of
maturity and orderliness, the stage of law-abi-
dance. The international society in a frontier
era is like the American West during open-
range ranching: limits, if any, are ill-defined
and resented; there is little law and still less
respect for law; and men afield do not always
worry on whose territory or under whose
jurisdiction they nominally are. Under a
boundary regime the international society
resembles rather fenced ranching: each ranch-
er holds a legal title to his land, knows and
guards its limits, and manages and surveys it
with a view to some over-all end.

Both frontiers and boundaries are manifestations of socio–political forces, and as such are
subjective, not objective. But while the former
are the result of rather spontaneous, or at least
ad hoc solutions and movements, the latter
are fixed and enforced through a more rational
and centrally co-ordinated effort after a conscious choice is made among the several
preferences and opportunities at hand.

Boundaries are not boundaries of all political
power. They are the limits of *internal* political
power, that is, of the power which integrates
the given political unit in the name of certain
values and loyalties within the bounds of its
territory as delimited under international law.
External political power does not know territorial limits; it operates on the international
scene. However, orderly international inter-
course is possible only if it is, on the whole, a
relation between legal governments: an encounter between the external governmental
political powers. In other words, in order to

have some stability in the political structure, both on the national and international level, a clear distinction between the spheres of foreign and domestic politics is necessary. The boundary helps to maintain this distinction.

It is a characteristic of contemporary, so-called ideological politics that it deliberately tends to blur the difference between foreign and domestic territory, and between internal and external politics, weakening thus the status and importance of boundaries.[67] Governments, and nongovernmental organizations, bypass the legal channels in order to deal directly with peoples inhabiting territories under the jurisdiction of other governments. Supranational, non-national, and other loyalties and interests are promoted which integrate socio–political forces into unofficial or semi-official groupings and blocks transgressing upon the existing formal territorial arrangements.[68]

These groupings and blocks are neither fully incadrated by, nor responsible for, the upholding of law. On their fringes—the edges of communities of thought and culture—there are borderlands, frontiers, and frontiersmen. On the fringes of the ideological ecumene of our divided world unintegrated elements occupy shifting frontier zones. These zones are not the cause of international instability; they reflect the unsettledness of the contemporary human society.

[1]The author, a political scientist and student of geopolitics, wishes to express gratitude to two geographers, Professors Norton S. Ginsburg (University of Chicago) and Stephen B. Jones (Yale University), for a very careful reading of the manuscript and critical remarks which helped to clarify certain points. All responsibility for the views expressed remains, of course, with the writer.

[2]Major references (in chronological order): George Nathaniel Curzon, Frontiers (Oxford: Clarendon Press, 1907); Thomas Hungerford Holdich, Political Frontiers and Boundary Making (London: Macmillan and Co., Ltd., 1916); Charles B. Fawcett, Frontiers: A Study in Political Geography (Oxford: Clarendon Press, 1918); Vittorio Adami, National Frontiers in Relation to International Law ([translated from Italian by T. T. Behrens] London: Oxford University Press, 1927); Karl Haushofer, Grenzen in ihrer geographischen und politischen Bedeutung (Berlin-Grünewald: Kurt Vowinckel Verlag, 1927); Paul de Lapradelle, La Frontière: Étude de Droit International (Paris: Les Éditions Internationales, 1928); Otto Maull, Politische Grenzen (Weltpolitische Bücherei, Vol. 3) Berlin: Zentral-Verlag, 1928); S. Whittemore Boggs, International Boundaries: A Study of Boundary Functions and Problems (New York: Columbia University Press, 1940); Stephen B. Jones, Boundary-Making: A Handbook for Statesmen, Treaty Editors and Boundary Commissioners (Washington: Carnegie Endowment for International Peace, 1945).

[3]Major references: Robert Sieger, "Zur politisch-geogra-

phischen Terminologie," Zeitschrift der Gesellschaft für Erdkunde (Berlin, 1917, pp. 497–529, and 1918, pp. 40–70); Johann Sölch, Die Auffassung der "natürlichen Grenzen" in der wissenschaftlichen Geographie (Innsbruck: Universitätsverlag Wagner, 1924); Richard Hartshorne, "Suggestions on the Terminology of Political Boundaries," Mitteilungen des Vereins der Geographen an der Universität Leipzig, fascicle 14/15 (1936), pp. 180–92, abstracted in the Annals, Association of American Geographers, Vol. XXVI, No. 1 (March, 1936), pp. 56–57.

[4]As this study proceeds, reference will be made to pertinent works.

[5]It may be of interest to cite the following definitions on which the British Association Geographical Glossary Committee has agreed: "Frontier. 1. A border region, zone, or tract which forms a belt of separation, contact, or transition between political units. 2. A delimited or demarcated boundary between States (more properly a frontier line). — Boundary. 1. Synonymous with frontier (in sense 2). 2. The line of delimitation or demarcation between administrative units or between geographical regions of various types, whether physical or human." "Some Definitions in the Vocabulary of Geography," The Geographical Journal, Vol. CXVII, No. 4 (December, 1951), pp. 458–59, on p. 459. One must note with surprise that G. Taylor's Geography in the Twentieth Century (3d ed; New York: Philosophical Library, 1957), does not even mention in Chap. XXIX, "A Concise Glossary of Geographical Terms," either term, "frontier" or "boundary," even if it lists such "geographical" terms as Pax Romana and cephalic index.

[6]The English word is derived from the Latin frons (and more directly from the French front) meaning "forehead," that is, "forehead of a man," but figuratively it means the forehead of anything, be it material (e.g., the front of an approaching cold air wave) or spiritual (e.g., the frontiers of a new intellectual or artistic movement). Cf. Webster's New International Dictionary, 2d ed., 1947.

[7]The Ukrainian (and Russian) equivalent of the English "march" (French: marche; German: Mark) is ukraina, meaning literally "borderland." Krai (or kraina) means in Ukrainian "land" or "country," but krai (or ukrai) means also "border" or "margin." U kraia (or na kraiu) means "on the margin," and ukraiaty (or ukroity) is to "cut off," especially to cut off a smaller piece (e.g., margin) from some larger entity. Ukraina (like the several German Mark) was originally not a proper name of a specific country, the Ukraine of today, but a general description of the lands on the periphery of Russ or Lithuania (later Poland). Cf. Yury Šerech, "An Important Work in Ukrainian Onomastics," The Annals of the Ukrainian Academy of Arts and Sciences in the U. S., Vol. II, No. 4 (Winter, 1952), pp. 435–44.

[8]The Greek oikumene designated the areas of the inhabited world known to the Greeks.

[9]Lapradelle (op. cit., pp. 9–11) distinguishes three types (or three stages of evolution) of the frontier: (1) the concept of the frontier in "pure geography" (i.e., "geography as a pure science applied to the study of the physical aspects of the earth") in which it designates zones under the influence of several physical phenomena; for instance, the estuary is subject to two different and contradictory forces, those of the river and those of the sea; (2) the concept of the "geographic frontier of the second degree," that is, the anthropo-geographical concept of the frontier between particular ecumene; and (3) the concept of the political frontier.

[10]The Russian ukraina was also an advancing frontier, a

spearhead directed against the "dark" and unchristian Tartary, and the Cossacks were not a nation or ethnic group, but a social group: pioneer settlers and conquerors of the advancing borderlands, men not unlike the American frontiersmen.

[11]Cf. Richard Hartshorne, "Political Geography," in Preston E. James and Clarence F. Jones, eds., *American Geography: Inventory and Prospect* (published for the Association of American Geographers by Syracuse University Press, 1957), p. 200; also *idem*, "Geographic and Political Boundaries in Upper Silesia," *Annals*, Association of American Geographers, Vol. XXIII, No. 4 (December, 1933), pp. 195–228, on p. 199.

[12]Tribal law is sometimes identified broadly with primitive law—the law of primitive societies—and in this case it may also be territorial. Caesar described how German tribes used territorial jurisdiction in their internal affairs in times of peace and tribal law (one authority for the whole tribe irrespective of territory) in case an external war threatened (*De Bello Gallico*, Bk. VI, Chap. XXIII, 29–34). But some authorities have pointed out that the essence of the tribal system is "a theory of blood relationship" (E. Sidney Hartland, *Primitive Law* [London: Methuen & Co., 1924], p. 43). I am using tribal law in this more restricted sense of "right of blood" (*jus sanguinis*), especially as related to citizenship and international relations: not territory but blood relationship is the basis of the tribal "state"; citizenship is acquired only by right of blood, irrespective of place of birth or residence, and the tribal political rights and duties extend to all with a right of blood and only to them.—Modern international law is based on the principle of territorial sovereignty (impenetrability) of states but some concessions to *jus sanguinis* are made in questions of citizenship. The Nazi government attempted to revive tribal Germanic law and granted full political rights only to citizens by right of blood (*Reichsbürger*) while reducing the status of territorial subjects (*Reichsangehörige*).

[13]Cf. Herbert W. Briggs, ed., *The Law of Nations* (2d ed.; New York: Appleton-Century-Crofts, Inc., 1952), p. 66.

[14]In practice there is never merely a line but a zone which for different political, strategic, or administrative reasons may be broader or narrower, or even graduated in the restrictions it imposes and limitations it creates. Cf. Otto Maull, *Politische Geographie* (Berlin: Safari-Verlag, 1956), p. 56.

[15]Hartshorne, "Political Geography," *op. cit.*, pp. 192–99; *idem*, "The Functional Approach in Political Geography," *Annals*, Association of American Geographers, Vol. XL, No. 2 (June, 1950), pp. 95–130; on pp. 110–12. Recently, Johannes Steinmetzler published an interesting study related to this subject: *Die Anthropogeographie Friedrich Ratzels und ihre ideengeschichtlichen Wurzeln (Bonner Geographische Abhandlungen*, fascicle 19, Bonn: Geographische Institut der Universität Bonn, 1956).

[16]Derwent Whittlesey, *The Earth and the State* (New York: Henry Holt and Co., 1939), p. 5.

[17]Since communists do think in terms of a universal empire and do not, ultimately, accept the co-existence of many creeds and states, they deny the importance of, or even the need for, boundaries within their orbit. Speaking in Leipzig, on March 7, 1959, Soviet Prime Minister N. S. Khrushchev stressed that boundary questions in Eastern Europe could be safely ignored: "We consider that to us communists the question of boundaries is not of major importance and that there can be no conflicts about it between Socialist countries. . . . With the victory of Communism . . . state boundaries will die off." *East Europe*, Vol. VIII, No. 5 (May, 1959), p. 43. Incidentally, the

Politicheskii Slovar (Political Dictionary), ed. by B. N. Ponomarev (2d ed.; Moscow: Gospolitzdat, 1958), does not even list the term *granitsa* (boundary).

[18]The term "frontier" is used here, and throughout the paper, in its "borderland of an ecumene" meaning as described above. See also below, note 46.

[19]The French commonly use *frontière* both for frontier and boundary, but they could distinguish between *frontière* and *limite*. The Germans, however, have only one word: *Grenze*.

[20]Historical memories play a role in the choice we make between the two words. We speak of the boundaries of Massachusetts, or Boston, or of this or that county. We do not refer to them as frontiers because they have never been associated in our memory with fronts, frontiersmen, and the whole expansionist and beyond-the-legal atmosphere of life in frontier lands. But we do (although less and less as time passes) sometimes speak of the U.S.-Mexican, or U.S.-Canadian frontier, and still more about the frontiers of Russia and China. This because we associate past frontier conditions with the areas through which these present-day boundaries are drawn.

[21]Adami (*op. cit.*, p. 3, note) observes that most Italian writers use the word boundary (*confine*) and not frontier (*frontiera*) to indicate the legal limits of a state. An interesting discussion of the differences between frontiers and boundaries can be found in Owen Lattimore, *Inner Asian Frontiers of China* (New York: American Geographical Society, 1940), pp. 233–42, 480–83, 496–510.

[22]"There grows up a nexus of border interests which resents and works against the central interest. This phenomenon of the border society, differing in orientation from the bulk of the nation, recurs in history at all times and in many places." Lattimore, *op. cit.*, p. 244. The conflict of interests between the foreland and the hinterland may be so acute as to become the dominant political factor and reverse the geographical orientation of defensive attitudes. Students of Chinese affairs have pointed out that the Manchurian problem was (perhaps still is), for many centuries, not that of an expanding Chinese frontier—a frontier conflict with neighboring Mongolia, Russia, or Japan—but, essentially, a problem of Chinese–Manchurian relationship, that is a clash between the authority of the motherland and a self-assertive regionalism. The more important frontier in Manchuria was not the "outward-facing frontier" of the North, but the "inward-facing frontier" of the South along the Great Wall. In Lattimore's words, "the frontiersman [of Manchuria] still has his back to the frontier . . . [because] the policies of the inward-facing frontier of regionalism still take precedence over the outer frontiers of the nation." See Owen Lattimore, "Chinese Colonization in Manchuria," *The Geographical Review*, Vol. XXII, No. 2 (April, 1932), pp. 177–195 (quotation on p. 181) and Norton S. Ginsburg, "Manchurian Railways Development," *The Far Eastern Quarterly*, Vol. VIII, No. 4 (August, 1949), pp. 398–411 (especially pp. 398–401 on inward- and outward-facing frontiers).

[23]This does not mean that the frontiersmen are not willing, at an opportune occasion, to rely on or even request the support of the motherland. But, basically, the frontiersmen do tend to insist on a degree of detachment, autonomy and differentness which sets them apart and is incompatible with the state interests and the rule of law as seen by the central government. Of course, in concrete cases the pattern varies. Frontiers are offsprings and reflections of particular historical conditions. The Cossacks were culturally less different from the "barbarians" they faced than the American colonists from the Indians, and the *Zaporozhskaia Sich* (an autonomous quasi government of the

Dnieper Cossacks) had to fear the absolute and centralizing tsar more than the American frontiersman ever needed to fear his federal and *laisser-aller* government. Consequently, the Russian frontier had, on the whole, a much more anti-motherland attitude (it was more of an "inward-facing frontier") than its American counterpart (which was primarily an "outward-facing frontier"), but even in Russia the foreland–hinterland relationship oscillated widely as circumstances changed in time and space. We may also choose, as one historian does (Walter Prescott Webb, *The Great Frontier* [Boston: Houghton and Mifflin, 1952]), to consider the American frontier as the frontier of Euro-America, and see Europe in the role of the motherland and all Americans as a type of frontiersmen. In this case, we shall have little difficulty in discovering signs of an anti-motherland attitude in America (e.g., the Revolutionary War, the Monroe Doctrine, isolationism), and American foreign policy vis-à-vis Europe up to 1917 could then be viewed as conditioned by the apprehensions of an "inward-facing frontier."

²⁴Cf. Haushofer, op. cit., Chap. V; also p. 155.

²⁵"The boundaries of the state are determined according to the principle of effectiveness, which plays an important part in international law. The exclusive validity of a national legal order extends according to international law just as far as this order is firmly established, i.e., is, on the whole, effective; as far as the national legal order is permanently obeyed and applied." Hans Kelsen, *Principles of International Law* (New York: Rinehart and Co., Inc., 1952). p. 213.

²⁶Lattimore (*Inner Asian Frontiers* . . ., pp. 238–42) points out that Intra-Mural China has developed a certain socio-political organization based on a specific type of economy (intensive agriculture) which was possible only within its area. Any Chinese settling further north (that is, beyond the ecumene of the "Chinese life" properly speaking), was necessarily adopting alien ways of life and thus becoming, in the long run, un-Chinese and an asset to the economy and power potential of the "barbarians," and not that of the Chinese emperor. The Great Wall had to prevent such loss resulting from dispersion of resources beyond the range of the Chinese cultural and economic centripetal forces. It marked also the limits of the area which, given the *raison d'être* of the Chinese state, was susceptible to integration at a cost not exceeding the possible returns.—See also below, note 65.

²⁷Jones, op. cit., p. 11. The Germans, who have no separate words for "frontier" and "boundary" sometimes use the terms of *Zusammenwachsgrenzen* and *Trennungsgrenzen* which indicate a similar confrontation of characteristics as that in our analysis of frontiers as stimulating a "growing together" and of boundaries as a divisive (separating) element. For a case study of *Trennungs-* and *Zusammenwachsgrenzen* see M. Schwind, "Die Aussengrenzen Niedersachsens und Schleswig-Holsteins," *Festschrift der Geographischen Gesellschaft Hannover*, 1953, pp. 262–81. One British geographer distinguishes between "frontiers of contact and frontiers of separation" and notes that "hitherto states have always sought frontiers which foster separation from, rather than assimilation with, their neighbors." W. G. East, "The Nature of Political Geography," *Politica*, Vol. II, March, 1937, pp. 259–86; on p. 279.

²⁸One German geographer speaks even of *Grenzzerreissungsschäden*: of "damages" that occur when a boundary is drawn that cuts through a previously culturally homogeneous area. Peter Schöller, "Wege und Irrwege der politischen Geographie und Geopolitik," *Erdkunde*, Vol. XI, No. 1 (February, 1957), pp. 1–20; on p. 17.

²⁹Lionel William Lyde, *Some Frontiers of Tommorow: An Aspiration for Europe* (London: A. and C. Black, 1915), p. 2. Cf. Boggs, op. cit., p. 11, note.

³⁰The American frontier was, of course, also an integrating factor—the proverbial "melting pot." It integrated *on* the frontier, it "melted" into a new nation all those Europeans who came into contact *with* the frontier, but it did not promote an *across-the-frontier* integration. In the writings of Frederick Jackson Turner the American frontier is not viewed as a borderland between two ecumene, between two different types of human societies. It is primarily a meeting place between man and nature, "the meeting point between savagery and civilization." True, the "savagery" includes the Indian and his civilization, but it is not, or at least not primarily, under the influence of the natives and their way of life that the settler changes. It is "the wilderness [that] masters the colonist. It finds him a European in dress, industries, tools, modes of travel, and thought. . . . It strips off the garments of civilization and arrays him in the hunting shirt and the moccasin. . . . In short, at the frontier the environment is at first too strong for the man." The European is Americanized in the process of responding to the challenge of the environment. "The stubborn American environment is there with its imperious summons to accept its conditions." "The frontier is the line of most rapid and effective Americanization." Thus, in Turner's opinion, the significance—the historical uniqueness—of the American frontier is that it creates a new civilization—"a new product that is American"—which springs not from an encounter between man and man, but between man and nature. (Quotations are from F. J. Turner, *The Frontier in American History* [New York: Henry Holt and Co., 1920], pp. 3–4, 38. Turner's concept of nature and the man–nature relationship is interestingly discussed by a Norwegian scholar, Per Sveaas Andersen, *Westward Is the Course of Empires, A Study in the Shaping of an American Idea: Frederick Jackson Turner's Frontier* [Oslo: Oslo University Press, 1956].)

³¹Natural law *(jus naturale)* in the sense of an eschatological norm of human behavior, that is, behavior based on the metaphysical and teleological nature of man, and not on the physical nature of man which is animalic and governed by the amoral law of nature *(jus naturae)*.

³²It is in this sense of necessary conformity between facts and laws in the spirtual realm that Hegel declared that "what is real is rational and what is rational is real." Similarly, in Kant's philosophy the possibility of a bad will is denied. In the noumenal world, i.e., in the world of pure reason, freedom, and morality, there can be only good will. A bad will would be a self-contradiction; it would not be a will at all, but only an impulse guided by the deterministic forces dominating the phenomenal world.

³³In the realm of the scientific law the automatic relationships leave no room for an "ought." In the realm of the moral law, which is based on the principle of free will, it is coercion which has no place. In the realm of the jural law the standing of both the "ought" and the free will are depreciated by the factor of coercion, but they are not eliminated. We do not obey the law mechanically. We either can follow the "ought" and be law-abiding, or let our free will brave the threat of sanctions and become lawbreakers. "It is the essence of a jural law that it may be violated, whereas a scientific law cannot be violated." Quincy Wright, *Contemporary International Law: A Balance Sheet* (Garden City, N. Y.: Doubleday and Co., Inc., 1955), p. 53.

³⁴"[The source of jural law] lies not in the behavior of the society and its members, but in the prevailing opinion of what that behavior ought to be." *Ibid.* It is to be noted that

the jural law is always merely a derivative norm of behavior concerned with specific places and timebound situations, and as such it is only the *opinion about* morals and their practical applications and not, like the moral law, *the* moral standard. Politics is the process of choosing among several opinions in order to make one of them a legally binding norm.

35 "The boundaries of a state have always a legal character, whether or not they coincide with such 'natural' frontiers, as, e.g., a river or a mountain range." Kelsen, *op. cit.*, p. 213. Obviously, boundaries depend on both national and international law, but for our purposes, and given our definition of the jural law, we do not need to distinguish between the two.

36 "The fixing of boundaries is not a problem of geography; it will always remain a task of the political decision makers." Schöller, *op. cit.*, p. 19.

37 The Germans have a good term for "boundary" in the natural world: *Natur Grenze*. It should, however, not be confused with *natürliche Grenze*, the so-called "natural boundary" which, as Adami (*op. cit.*, p. 4, note) correctly points out, is a seminatural (or, rather, mixed and confused) concept of boundary. On *Natur* and *natürliche Grenze* see Sölch, *op. cit.*, especially p. 14.

38 A boundary may survive the forces that located it, but only if new social forces arise in the same area and the decision is taken, for historical, economic, or other reasons, to sustain a boundary running along the same demarcation line. A boundary drawn by the will of an absolute king can survive him, his dynasty, or even the institution of monarchy, provided a new will, e.g., that of the sovereign nation, is substituted for the old. The change may be imperceptible to contemporaries. The old boundary becomes slowly obsolete—it disappears gradually as one political phenomenon and re-emerges simultaneously as a new, geographically perhaps identical but politically and functionally different, phenomenon. No boundary survives as a pure relict, that is, merely by the dead weight of inertia, but its impress upon the human landscape may, in the long run, contribute to the crystallization of cultural patterns that will have a vested interest in it. See the discussion of "persistence in relict boundaries" and of "concurrent persistence and obsolescence" of boundaries in Eric Fischer, "On Boundaries," *World Politics*, Vol. I, No. 2 (January, 1949), pp. 196–222.

39 Obviously, man may change the landscape and thus alter the course of the watershed. But whatever cultural environment man creates it will be inescapably governed by the same law of gravity which rules all physical environments.

40 "In the rule of law the connection between condition and consequence is characterized by the term 'ought,' in order to emphasize that the rule of law has not the meaning of a law of nature." Kelsen, *op. cit.*, p. 6.

41 Lapradelle, *op. cit.*, pp. 89–96, speaks of two "principles —types of delimitation of boundaries: the objective and subjective conception. He does not seem to see any fundamental difference between a watershed, i.e., a physical geographical "boundary," and a boundary properly speaking, for instance, one based on the ethnological principle. He thinks there is a transition between the two (cf. pp. 9–11) and each may, according to circumstances, be considered the objective boundary of a state. Where the border zone is not, or only little, populated and thus "the physical element of the soil predominant" the watershed is the "ideal limit," while in areas where the human element predominates it is the plebiscite which is "the *only* objective criterion of political origin" (p. 90; emphasis added).

42 "While in the objective conception of delimitation two confronting states *have to* accept a limit-type, in the subjective theory they choose freely." *Ibid.*, p. 95; emphasis added.

43 It seems that it is precisely this that Lapradelle advocates. He thinks that international law should apply the "objective thesis" and divorce itself from the "political point of view" (*ibid.*, p. 96). Lapradelle forgets that international law is both in its origin and essence political; it is not a technical or otherwise scientific and objective law. Jural laws are objective criterions only given our agreement as to the underlying philosophy. There was a time, in the early 1930's, when the U.S. Congress and different protectionist lobbies labored on a scheme for a "scientific tariff." However much it was "scientifically" calculated, the tariff, and the statute establishing it, was nonetheless not above subjectivity; it was a matter of choices between values and alternatives, and the result of direct political pressures.

44 In defining the limits of a compound (complex, "total") area we take into consideration all, or at least several, factors present in it and affecting its homogeneity; hence we act as the arbiter who decides how much weight should be given to any particular factor. The limits of a simple area, e.g., a drainage basin, are by definition monistically defined. Nature does not make value judgments; hence it cannot be an arbiter over the limits of a compound area. The "boundaries" in the natural world can be only delimitations of simple (one element) regions of homogeneity.

45 Richard Hartshorne, *The Nature of Geography* reprinted by the Association of American Geographers from the *Annals*, Association of American Geographers, Vol. XXIX, Nos. 3 and 4 [1939]), pp. 296, 300. See also Jean Brunhes and Camille Vallaux, *La Géographie de l'Histoire* (Paris: Felix Alcan, 1921), pp. 61–62: "A river or a mountain are frontiers [boundaries] only in so far as we have this or that economic and political conception of the frontiers—conception which is subject to change with the course of history. . . . There are in nature only those frontiers which we seek. . . . According to times and places the same phenomena of nature have been, or have ceased to be limits." See also Sölch, *op. cit.*, 20, 40. For a recent, very exhaustive, discussion of the problem of subjectivity in man's concept of landscape—subjectivity conditioned by value systems, specific scientific interest, or individual preference, see Otto Wernli, "Die neuere Entwicklung des Landschaftsbegriffes," *Geographica Helvetica*, Vol. XIII, No. 1 (March, 1958), pp. 1–59, especially pp. 17–22, 35–46. See also Hans Carol, "Zur Diskussion um Landschaft und Geographie," *Geographica Helvetica*, Vol. XI, No. 2 (June, 1956), pp. 111–33.

46 It is this cultural (technological or ideological) differentiation and subjectivity of judgments which, in this writer's opinion, justifies the use of the terms "ecumene" and "frontiers of ecumene" not only in all-human but also in a particular human sense: it may be sometimes meaningful to speak of the ecumene of the human race as a whole, but it may, at other times, be equally meaningful to differentiate between the ecumene of the Pygmies, of the Eskimos, of the Chinese civilization, of the Islamic faith, etc. In fact, such differentiation was already at least implied in the use of the term by the Greeks and early Christians when they contrasted their *oikumene* with the lands of the barbarians or the *partibus infidelium*. Contemporary writers who speak of cultural blocs are also implying such a differentiation. See Donald W. Meinig, "Culture Blocs and Political Blocs: Emergent Patterns in World Affairs," *Western Humanities Review*, Vol. X, No. 3 (Summer, 1956), pp. 203–22.

[47]Haushofer, op. cit., Chap. XV.

[48]Ibid., Chap. II. Cf. Nicholas John Spykman, "Frontiers, Security, and International Organization," Geographical Review, Vol. XXXII, No. 3 (July, 1942), pp. 436–47, on p. 437.

[49]Boundary disputes, characterized by such a wealth of legal technicalities, played a major role only between the Congress of Vienna and 1914 (or 1933), that is, after Russia became Westernized and before the African and Asiatic (except for Japan since 1905) countries were accepted as equal members of the "civilized" family of nations. With the rise of Bolshevik and Nazi ideologies, and the emergence of new states with a non-Western cultural background, the community of thought, on which the voluntarily accepted rules of nineteenth century diplomacy rested, was wrecked. International politics abandoned legal and diplomatic finesses for a rather Hobbesian understanding of life, and it is interesting to note that while the Convenant of the League of Nations leaned on Locke's more peaceful and harmonious concept of society, the Charter of the United Nations is closer both to Hobbes' pessimistic understanding of human nature and to his concept of peace guaranteed by a powerful policeman. For a historical review of the East-West division and frontier in Europe prior to the Congress of Vienna, see Werner J. Cahnman, "Frontiers between East and West in Europe," Geographical Review, Vol. XXXIX, No. 4 (October, 1949), pp. 605–24; see also H. Duncan Hall, "Zones of the International Frontier," Geographical Review, Vol. XXXVIII, No. 4 (October, 1948), pp. 615–25.

[50]For instance, the present-day problem of the German-Polish boundary is overshadowed by the East-West ideological struggle although the territory in dispute is much larger than any which the Germans contested after the Versailles peace treaty. Even the classic contemporary case of a boundary dispute, the dispute between India and Pakistan over Kashmir, cannot escape being weighed on the international scene primarily in terms of its impact on the over-all competition between the Soviet and Western world view.

[51]See the interesting study by Norman J. G. Pounds, "The Origin of the Idea of Natural Frontiers in France," Annals, Association of American Geographers, Vol. XLI, No. 2 (June, 1951), pp. 146–57.

[52]Out of the religious wars emerged the belief that matters of faith and religious toleration should be an internal affair of the state: cujus regio ejus religio. This, on the one hand, strengthened the hand of the sovereign in enforcing loyalty and a certain homogeneity of outlook among all the inhabitants of the realm, and, on the other, was a milestone toward the establishment of the principle of impenetrability of the state's territory which is the cornerstone of the concept of sovereignty and of the modern international system. And once this principle of impenetrability was recognized, it became possible for each state to develop its national law, the law of the land.

[53]"In our complex society, there is a great variety of limited loyalties, but the overriding loyalty of all is to our country. . . ." Chief Justice Fred M. Vinson, United States v. United Mine Workers, March 6, 1947.

[54]See Ladis K. D. Kristof, "Political Laws in International Relations," Western Political Quarterly, Vol. XXI, No. 3 (September, 1958), pp. 598–606; on p. 606.

[55]The maturity of a political system does not depend on its being classified "modern," "progressive," or "advanced." A political system is mature when it develops to the point that, given the material framework and the values of the society, it is able to cope with normally arising problems in a predictable way making use of generally acceptable procedural techniques and substantial judgments. At times and in places theocracy or feudalism can be more mature than enlightened absolutism or democracy. No system of government is intrinsically more mature than another, though, in terms of ethics, one may be superior to the other.

[56]If all aspects of international politics were to reach a state of maturity, that is, if a general consensus on fundamentals of politics were achieved, then all international disputes would become, sooner or later, justiciable. The distinction which is made today between the so-called justiciable (legal) and non-justiciable (political) disputes is based on the fact that only in respect to a certain limited range of international conflicts is there some agreement as to the principles which should guide their solution. For the other ones ad hoc political solutions must be sought because no prior understanding, obligation, or institution exists to deal with them in a preconceived, i.e., legal, way. For a review of the concept of justiciable and non-justiciable international disputes see Lincoln Bloomfield, "Law, Politics, and International Disputes," International Conciliation, No. 516 (January, 1958).

[57]This is an old Communist slogan used in France already prior to World War II. On March 3, 1950, a Communist deputy, A. Musmeaux, said in the French National Assembly: "And when you tell us that the Soviet Union is our fatherland we do not consider this an insult. We glorify ourself with it and are proud of it."

[58]To be sure, religious wars, for instance, were also ideological conflicts. But, as noted above (note 52), they took place prior to the crystallization of the principle of territorial law, and it was precisely their end that made possible this crystallization. Then, too, the contemporary ideological struggle is much more all pervading. Modern means of communication make it impossible, especially in our closed-space world, to seek isolation. A contemporary Puritan could not sail to a New World, settle on a terra nullius, and live his way of life protected by distance from "corrupting" influences. See also below, note 60.

[59]The "grey area" ("third") countries of today should not be confused with either buffer states or old style neutrals. Buffer states were not only de facto not independent but often lacked a de jure sovereign status and seldom maintained direct diplomatic relations with the world at large. They were a "local affair"—a "private" geopolitical arrangement among the neighboring powers and as such not members of, or protected by, the international community as a whole. The old style neutrals, on the contrary, were full members of the international community but chose, of their own vioition, to withdraw from active politics on the world scene. Such a withdrawal was officially announced and taken note of, and the neutrals' status was protected and guaranteed under international law by all the states. The "third" countries of today are neither subordinate nor really neutral. They are powers actively engaged in international politics, and, though uncommitted ("neutralist") in the East–West conflict, they have not withdrawn from—to the contrary, are active in—politics that affect that conflict. While an old style neutral, Switzerland, has refused to even join the United Nations, India and Yugoslavia strive to play an important role in that body.

[60]F. Ratzel and R. Kjellén have stressed that all politics are erdgebunden (earth-bound). This is true. However, ideological politics are less so than politics based on a concept of sovereignty derived from property rights of the monarch or from a national group's "right" to "rights" and cultural roots in the soil. Ideas are, essentially, philosophical concepts abstracted from their empirical setting. Consequently, ideological frontiers are also less of a geographical (spatial) phenomenon than traditional fron-

tiers were. They have been, so to speak, squeezed upward from the ground level to a less earth-bound level. Moreover, modern man is, in general, more literate and sophisticated, and as such less "geographical" and more intellectual. And "to the intellectual the frontier is not the land but the mind, and the Soviet leaders seem to understand this." Jerome Wiesner, "Are Research and Technology the Soviets' Secret Weapon?" in *Soviet Progress vs. American Enterprise* (Garden City, N.Y.: Doubleday and Co., 1958), p. 78.

[61]"Co-existence; Two Conceptions of a Frontier," *The Round Table* (London), Vol XLIV, No. 176 (September, 1954), pp. 323–25, on pp. 324–25. (Emphasis added.)

[62]Lazar M. Kaganovich in a speech, on November 6, 1955, in Moscow's Bolshoi Theatre, at a gathering of Soviet leaders commemorating the Bolshevik Revolution. *New York Times*, November 7, 1955.

[63]In terms of the ideological frontier of the Communist Party the Popular Front and fellow travelers are such a temporary expedient; they are semi-integrated and semi-independent border elements that belong only to the period of transition. The ultimate aim is complete integration within the bounds of the Party, or of the obedient citizenry of the communist state, while the unassimilable elements will be eliminated or literally bound (coerced physically).

[64]Cf. Lattimore, *Inner Asian Frontiers . . . .*, op. cit., pp. 470–73. See also above, note 26.

[65]Lattimore points out that every empire must ponder what effects different frontier policies—of strict integration or laxity and concessions—may have on the hinterland. Marginal imperial growth reaches the point of diminishing returns where the special interests of the borderlands can be neither cheaply overridden by, nor reconciled with, those of the imperial center. Further expansion will result not in centripetal gain but in centrifugal loss of resources. *Ibid.*, pp. 242–43.

[66]"The very act of drawing a boundary is an acknowledgment that the peoples excluded are not under control and cannot be ruled by command. They must be dealt with by negotiation" *Ibid.*, p. 243.

[67]It is characteristic that the importance and "strength" of a boundary—the degree to which it restricts and "impinges on life"—today depends largely on whether or not it coincides with the limits of an ideological ecumene. For instance, the Bulgaro-Rumanian or Soviet-Rumanian boundary is at present a rather unimportant and "weak" (permeable) boundary. But the Bulgaro-Greek and the Soviet-Turkish boundary is a formidable obstacle: it is the Iron Curtain. And in Germany it is more difficult to cross the "boundary" between East and West Germany—*de jure* it is not even a boundary, only a demarcation line—than to cross the Franco-German or Belgian-German boundary.

[68]Boundaries may be today better defined, marked, or even guarded, than at any other time in history. This is an outgrowth of the general technical, administrative and legal development. Private property boundaries and rights are also today better defined and delimited than a century ago. However, in this writer's opinion, the state boundary tends today to be less of a boundary than a few decades ago because, on the one hand, it *binds less*, and, on the other, it makes the state territory *less impenetrable*. Ideological and/or functional integration of foreign *and* domestic policies of different states transgresses upon boundaries. Franz Gschnitzer, Foreign Minister of Austria and professor at the Salzburg University, argues that boundaries in Western Europe have outlived their usefulness, that is, that they must disappear in so far as they are lines of division—walls between fully sovereign states—and can remain only as demarcation lines between administrative units similar to boundaries between countries, fiscal districts, parishes, etc.: ". . . europäische Binnengrenzen als Grenzen zwischen vollsouveränen Staaten sind längst überholt. Als trennende Schranken müssen sie verschwinden, nur noch als Ordnungs-, als Verwaltungsgrenzen sind sie berechtigt." F. Gschnitzer, "Gibt es noch Grenzen?" *Aussenpolitik*, Vol. IX, No. 2 (February, 1958), pp. 70–77; on p. 77. Compare with Khrushchev's statement (above, note 17) on the status of boundaries in East Europe.

BUFFER ZONES:
HIGHER-ORDER FRONTIERS?

Earlier, reference was made to frontiers and their function of separating emerging power cores. States enlarged and expanded, and were able to do so because the frontier was, by definition, a yet unclaimed region awaiting penetration and occupation. But, as we saw, all frontiers were ultimately invaded and replaced by linear boundaries. Today, with the exception of the Antarctic (which is rapidly being divided among interested powers), the classic frontier no longer exists. It may be true that there are border zones in which state control is little more effective today than it was when such areas were parts of frontiers; the point is that these areas have been claimed, bounded, and legally absorbed. States today can no longer enlarge their territories into available land without thereby violating the sovereignty of other states.

The present world map, then, consists of a mosaic of contiguous states, and there are few areas being contested by adjacent powers. And even the exceptions are well defined in terms of their boundaries: the Kashmir dispute involving India and Pakistan does not concern some ill-defined tract of land but a political entity of precise delimitation. The question now before us is whether those functions once performed by the frontier are no longer needed now that boundaries form the universal dividers between states, or whether a new kind of frontier actually does exist although we cannot recognize it as an unclaimed area on the map.

SUPRANATIONALISM

The latest stage in the politicogeographical evolution of the world appears to be dominated by a desire on the part of states to align themselves in groups or blocs based upon strategic, economic, ideological, and cultural considerations. This matter, which will be discussed in detail in Chapter 18 of this book, is relevant here, for it has produced an entirely new power situation on the globe. Several decades ago, the application of the power analysis approach to the world scene would have produced a group of perhaps a half dozen or more powers whose actual and potential strength was, within a certain range, quite similar. Germany, the United Kingdom, France, Italy, Japan, and the United States formed part of this group. Today, however, the power cores of the United States and the Soviet Union, as German's article reprinted in Chapter 4 showed, are vastly superior to any other state or group of states. Although this power situation is likely to change, with the entry of China and perhaps a united Western Europe in the not too distant future, it remains a fact that many states, several dozen emergent states among them, do not form part of any of these power structures. On a global scale, therefore, we see a large number of "neutral" or "nonaligned" states for which there is, among the great powers of today, considerable competition. Are these states and territories the frontier of the modern day? And do they, consequently, face the same fate as did the frontier areas of the past: absorption?

It is not only the neutral or unaligned states that face the pressure of Soviet-American competition. Such supranational groupings as the Organization of African Unity and the Arab League themselves have aims that may include expansion, and Southern Africa and the Arabian Peninsula are the scenes of their efforts. A similar situation exists and is further developing in Southeast Asia. Here, Laos has been a separating agent between the (Chinese) Communist sphere and member states of the American-dominated Southeast Asia Treaty Organization.

Since the term frontier applies to undefined areas, political geographers have used several other terms to describe states and dependencies caught in zones of contest between power blocs. Among them, *shatter belt* and *buffer zone* (also buffer state) are the most common. Both terms indicate what is meant. "Shatter" refers to the breakup of the force of impact in the cushion of separation provided by the intervening state. "Buffer" has a similar meaning: the reduction of impact as a result of physical separation of the competing powers. Thus the buffer zone is in fact a higher order frontier, and states within it may well face absorption by rival forces.

BUFFER ZONES

The process whereby frontiers were penetrated and divided still takes place—but in another form. With virtually the entire habitable world allocated by boundaries, powerful states and supranational blocs of states can further their territorial aims by (1) absorbing adjacent entities and integrating them, and (2) precipitating boundary disputes that lead to shifts in boundary delimitation.

The process of absorption can take different courses. Estonia, Lithuania, and Latvia are no longer on the map as states—they are parts, today, of the Soviet Union. Eastern European states were also absorbed by the Soviet power bloc, though in a different way; they still retain their territorial and national identities. The absorption of Czechoslovakia, Poland, and Bulgaria by the power core of the Soviet Union, and the partition of Germany, eliminated the possibility of the development of a European buffer zone in one of the major theaters of Communist-Capitalist competition. Only Austria, and to some extent Yugoslavia, might be described as performing buffer functions in this part of Europe: Austria is theoretically neutral following its temporary partition; Yugoslavia has chosen a separate direction as a Communist state. The serious confrontations that have taken place at the East-West boundary in Germany, the need for the Berlin Airlift, and the establishment of the Berlin Wall, all exemplify the tensions produced by border contact between great powers and ideologies.

In Southeast Asia, also, the attempt at absorption can be observed. The state of Laos, which was created artificially out of the former French Indo-Chinese realm, was to serve the purpose of acting as a buffer between Communist and non-Communist spheres of influence. Internal opposition to the status quo existed, and enmities were fanned by outside support given to pro-Western elements as well as pro-Communist elements. Infiltration from the north and arms shipments from Western powers led to a crisis in the late 1950's, but although actual warfare did occur its scope remained limited. Despite the absence of a permanent solution for Laos and the continuation of its uneasy existence, the buffer state did fulfill its function. While supporting infiltration, China did not openly invade the country; Western powers supported anti-Communist activities but did not strike

The fragmentation of Germany and calls for a demilitarized zone across this country reflect a desire on the part of Western and Communist power cores to develop here a buffer zone and to avoid the re-emergence of Germany as a major military power. Despite the Berlin crises, from the airlift to the wall, and despite Western moves to rearm West Germany, the country has to some degree functioned as a buffer in postwar Europe. Western pressure has long held off the proposed separate peace treaty between the Soviet Union and the (East) German Democratic Republic; Communist pressure helped delay (West) German participation in a multilateral nuclear force. Within Germany, calls for reunification are often heard: all over West Germany signs such as this serve to remind the people of their country's current division. But the decision lies with the major powers, and their ends have been best served, until now, by the retention of the lines of fragmentation agreed upon after the end of the second World War (Robert Janke).

China. As Spykman has said, buffer states survive "because they separate States that would otherwise be powerful neighbors and because the attempt to conquer them would be met, not by the relatively weak resistance of the buffer, but by the much stronger opposition of the other neighbor."[6] The attempt in Laos was not to conquer, but to test the internal political structure; it could be resisted by limited force, and it probably was not the last test to be made by the Communist elements involved.

The case of Viet Nam, as a contrast, shows what the absence of a token buffer state can mean. The eastern part of former French Indo-China was not rendered neutral by conference and treaty, but was divided, with a boundary defined and delimited between a Communist (northern) section and a non-

Communist (southern) "state." Again, it might be argued that the two Viet Nams in fact constitute a buffer zone because their strength is very much less than that of China in the north or the Southeast Asia Treaty Alliance in the south. But the north-south boundary did represent a contact zone between the two ideological opposites, and serious trouble was not long in coming. Strong pro-Communist elements remained in South Viet Nam, where the central authority also failed either to win the support of the majority of the population or to institute the reforms that the termination of colonialism was expected to bring. Religious division and a lack of effective national control also contributed to instability, which was immediately fanned by support from the north. Here, once again, was an opportunity for absorption: without actually invading South Viet Nam, it seemed possible to destroy such internal order

[6]N. J. Spykman, "Frontiers, Security, and International Organization," *Geog. Rev.,* 32 (1942), 436.

as did exist and replace it with one paying allegiance to the north. This time, one powerful force did strike the suspected invader, and the possibility of escalation of the hostilities into a major conflict became real.

The increasing separation in terms of ideology between China and the Soviet Union has brought into focus another potential buffer zone, that extending along the Sino-Soviet boundary in Mongolia and, possibly, Manchuria. Reference was made in Chapter 3 to the desire on the part of the Soviet Union for a population migration eastward, into Siberia. This drive has objectives other than just the economic, for the Soviet Union has long desired to render the occupation of its eastern "frontier" more effective. China's claims to ethnic and historical affinities with the peoples of this border region of the U.S.S.R., and Soviet aid and propaganda programs in Mongolia, all may be viewed as a prelude to competition for a buffer zone. Again, note that the boundaries of the political entities are defined and delimited; the goal is not penetration and partition, but the control and allegiance of the central authority. Furthermore, China's overthrow and absorption of authority in Tibet, and its boundary disputes with India, all serve to focus attention upon expansionist tendencies which may not remain confined to non-Communist spheres.[7]

The second vehicle for expansion on the part of states and power blocs (short of open warfare) is the boundary dispute. A number of these, actual or potential, remain to be settled, but many of them involve minor and relatively unimportant land, so that settlement is either delayed or agreed upon through arbitration. Serious cases, on the other hand, involve major powers and have far-reaching consequences. They may reflect the whole posture of a state in the international scene, and may reveal to what extent it is prepared to abandon any search for peace to which it may give lip service.

The most significant dispute in recent years has, again, involved China, this time with India over the McMahon Line of 1914. China not only claimed a different boundary, but supported its claims with limited aggressions in difficult terrain. Chinese dissatisfaction is not wholly without cause:

With regard to the boundary . . . known as the McMahon Line . . . there was . . . little or no conference discussion. Unfortunately the formal proceedings of the [Simla] Conference, which might clarify this point, have never been released by the British Government. What is known is that on 14 March, 1914, as the result of conversations between the Tibetan and British representatives, a line was drawn on a General Staff map [India] of the India-Tibetan border titled 'North East Frontier.' It consisted of two sheets and was in the scale of one inch to eight miles. The map was signed A. H. McMahon and the seal and signature of the Tibetan plenipotentiary appear immediately below the Englishman's signature. Delhi is given as the place name. Neither the initial nor the signature of the Chinese plenipotentiary appear on this map.[8]

The McMahon Line, never demarcated, and defined in the most broad and imprecise terms, was in all probability established to function as an administrative convenience within a colonial empire; it ran through an area best described as a frontier, in physiographic as well as anthropogeographic terms. It was not designed to withstand the stresses and strains of an international boundary, especially not in an emergent, "adolescent" area of the world. China's sphere of influence includes Tibet, and it is a fact that the boundary, rather than running along the foothills of the Himalayan Mountain ranges in this part of Asia, lies well inside these ranges and separates people of Tibetan ties and traditions from one another. On linguistic, ethnic, historic, and other cultural bases, the border certainly would seem to be ill-positioned—but so are many other boundaries over which no aggressions are taking place. Certainly the contents of the disputed area do not appear to justify China's vigorous expansionist actions. Why, then, the friction over this particular zone?

The answer appears to lie in the field of geopolitics. From the Chinese point of view, much was to be gained from the initiation of aggressive policies with reference to this area, and little to be lost. There are real justifications for China's demands, for when the McMahon Line was established Tibet was considered to lie within a Chinese sphere of influence, as evidenced by China's invitation to the Simla Conference. But China did not

---

[7]For a discussion of South and Southeast Asian politico-geographical conditions see D. W. Meinig, "Heartland and Rimland in Eurasian History," *Western Political Quart.*, 9 (1956), 553–569.

[8]A detailed study of the problem is E. Burke Inlow, "The McMahon Line," *J. Geography*, 63, 6 (September, 1964), 261–272. Quotation is from pp. 264–265. Also see P. P. Karan, "The India-China Boundary Dispute," *J. Geography*, 59 (January, 1960).

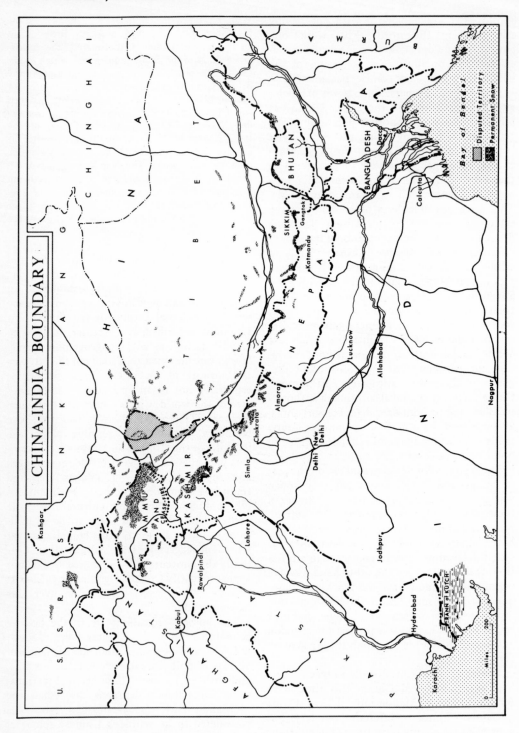

sign any treaty. India had occupied the disputed area with a police force, and it had published maps showing the McMahon Line as its northern boundary. This afforded China the opportunity to support its argument that no defined boundary exists here (only a traditional one: the foothills of the Himalayas) by making penetrations into the border area, testing Indian reactions. The geopolitical advantages were several: firstly, it asserted

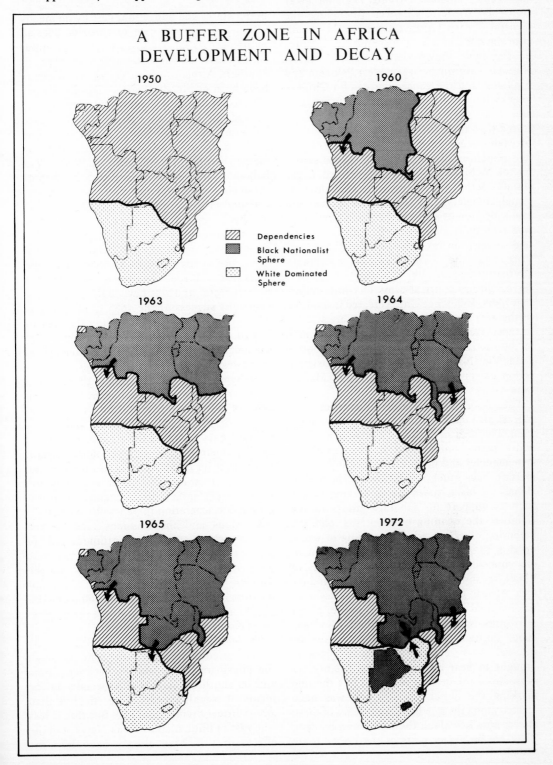

A BUFFER ZONE IN AFRICA
DEVELOPMENT AND DECAY

1950   1960

Dependencies

Black Nationalist
Sphere

White Dominated
Sphere

1963   1964

1965   1972

Chinese strength in Asia; secondly, the terrain is too difficult for a major conflict; thirdly, the expected Western support for India would aggravate the lingering disharmony between India and Pakistan. Driving Pakistan away from its Western alliances (including the Central Treaty Organization) would constitute a major Chinese victory in Asia. A glance at the map shows that a corridor exists through Kashmir between West Pakistan and Sinkiang, and the consequences of a Chinese axis to Karachi would be difficult to exaggerate.

In a way, then, the zone associated with the McMahon Line could be viewed as one of very few remaining frontiers in the classic sense, for the McMahon Line, though defined, never actually performed the functions of an international boundary. But the dispute is over the exact location of a line rather than a two-way war over unclaimed territory. India has inherited its position from the British Empire, and China has indicated where an acceptable alternative would lie. The actual friction serves the geopolitical aims of China rather that India, and hence China created instability in the area involved. The motives are similar to those exemplified by Chinese involvement in the internal situation of the Laotian buffer state, Viet Nam, and Mongolia; the basis for action exists in the nature of the McMahon Line.

The absorption of political entities is a process also reflected by events in Africa since 1960. The African nationalist drive to oust the white man from control in the remaining dependencies and in South Africa does not, at present, have much military power behind it. Hence the black states are employing tactics such as support for sabotage efforts in the colonies, the training of saboteurs, and the harboring of exiles, while appealing to world opinion to support the principle of one-man-one-vote, which in the Portuguese colonies, in Rhodesia, and in South Africa would produce local African governments. These tactics were not required in the case of two former buffer territories, Nyasaland and Northern Rhodesia. Here, political changes—brought about by internal and external political pressure brought to bear by the Africans themselves —produced the desired results. Thus the line marking the buffer zone, which was once located along the northern boundaries of these states, now lies along their southern borders. They are no longer parts of the buffer zone:

they have been absorbed by the black African sphere of influence.

THE BUFFER ZONE IN HISTORY

Buffer states and buffer zones are by no means unique to the past two or three decades of politicogeographical history. Some buffer zones have slowly emerged (like that in Southern Africa in recent years), while others have been artificially created. During periods of tension between France and Germany in Europe, the Low Countries (the Netherlands, Belgium, and Luxembourg) served as buffers between these powers; the Netherlands remained neutral during the first World War. Balkan states have functioned as buffers between Soviet and European power cores. Colonial powers, realizing that the expansion of their spheres of influence might bring warfare unless some separating agent could be established, sometimes voluntarily desisted from occupying certain regions. Thailand separated a British Empire in Asia from a French realm and was never subjugated. King Leopold's success at the 1885 Conference on Africa (when he claimed much of the present Congo as his "Free State") was partly due to the location of the Congo and its interruption of the designs of rival colonial powers.

Perhaps the best illustration of the function of buffer states can be found in the nineteenth century, when Britain possessed a vast coastal sphere of influence in southern and southwestern Asia and faced the growing power and expansionism of Russia to the north. Britain feared that its Asian realm might become the object of this Russian drive, and thus the British were intent on protecting whatever geographic separation there was between their possessions and the Russians'. Indeed, the British helped sustain a continuous belt of political entities (of which the cornerstone was Afghanistan) which cordoned off the Russian empire. Afghanistan is a prorupt territory, and its eastern proruption (connecting the territory to China) formed the narrowest of dividers, but an effective one.

Eastward, Nepal, Sikkim, and Bhutan may be seen as constituting a buffer zone, although the physiographic separation between China and its southern neighbors (especially in the region of Nepal) appears more effective than any political divider could be. But this is less true east of Bhutan and west of Nepal, and the effects of this have already been felt: the

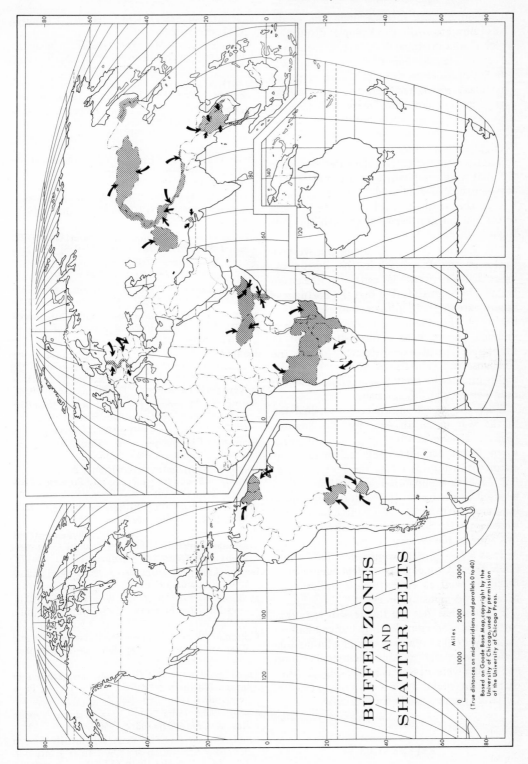

BUFFER ZONES
AND
SHATTER BELTS

Miles

0   1000   2000   3000

(True distances on mid-meridians and parallels 0 to 40)

Based on Goode Base Map, copyright by the
University of Chicago, used by permission
of the University of Chicago Press.

McMahon dispute focuses upon the border east of Bhutan, while the Kashmir dispute, to which China might well ultimately become a party, involves the region west of Nepal.

In South America, also, states and territories exist today which had their origins at least in part in buffer roles. The Treaty of Tordesillas (approximately the 50th meridian west) was designed to separate the rival Spanish and Portuguese spheres. In the north, where contact was not effective, the three European Guianas were established, separating sections of (Spanish) Venezuela and (Portuguese) Brazil. But in the south, toward the Plata estuary, direct competition between Spanish and Portuguese did develop.

The Spanish center lay along the western banks of the Plata, while the Portuguese focused upon what is today southeastern Brazil. The Spanish feared that the Portuguese might extend their influence to the eastern banks of the Plata, and Montevideo was founded (in 1726) as a Spanish outpost to counteract Portuguese influence. In fact the Portuguese did establish a number of settlements directly on the Plata, an effort in which they were aided by the British.

When the British influence diminished due to the war in North America, the Spanish position in the conflict improved. In 1822, when Brazil declared itself independent, it claimed territory as far as the Plata estuary. But Argentina supported a rebellion which resulted in the ouster of the Brazilians, and a long and fluctuating war might have ensued were it not for renewed British involvement, this time in the interests of political stability. In 1828 a peace treaty went into effect which established Uruguay as independent from Brazil as well as Argentina—a buffer state between the opposing forces.

It is possible that the future will see other parts of the world develop into buffer zones. In the early 1970's there was talk of a buffer area between Israel and its Arab enemies; Lebanon and Jordan were viewed as possessing qualities that might make such a function possible. Certainly the potential conflicts exist.

REFERENCES

Adami, Vittorio, National Frontiers in Relation to International Law (1919), trans. by T. T. Behrens. London, Oxford University Press, 1927.

Alexander, L. M., "Recent Changes in the Benelux-German Boundary," Geog. Rev., 43, 1 (January, 1953), 69–76.

Alexander, Lewis M., "The Arab-Israeli Boundary Problem," World Politics, 6, 3 (April, 1954), 322–337.

Anderson, Albin T., "The Soviets and Northern Europe," World Politics, 4, 4 (July, 1952), 468–487.

Arciszewski, Franciszek, "Some Remarks about the Strategical Significance of the New and Old Soviet-Polish Border," Polish Rev., 1, 2–3 (1956), 89–96.

Arden-Clarke, Sir Charles, "The Problem of the High Commission Territories," Optima, 8, 4 (December, 1958), 163–170.

Armstrong, Hamilton Fish, "Where India Faces China," Foreign Affairs, 37, 4 (July, 1959), 617–625.

Austin, D. G., "The Uncertain Frontier: Ghana–Togo," J. Modern African Studies, 1 (1963), 139–146.

Barton, Sir William, "Pakistan's Claim to Kashmir," Foreign Affairs, 28, 2 (January, 1950), 299–308.

Bennett, George, "The Eastern Boundary of Uganda in 1902," Uganda J., 23, 1 (March, 1959), 69–72.

Betts, R. R. (ed.), Central and South East Europe, 1945–1948. London, Royal Institute of International Affairs, 1950.

Bianchi, William J., Belize; The Controversy Between Guatemala and Great Britain over the Territory of British Honduras in Central America. New York, Las Americas Publishing Co., 1959.

Billington, Monroe, "The Read River Boundary Controversy," Southwestern Historical Quart., 62, 3 (January, 1959), 356–363.

Birdwood, Christopher B. B., Two Nations and Kashmir. London R. Hale, 1956.

Boggs, S. Whittemore, International Boundaries: A Study of Boundary Functions and Problems. New York, Columbia University Press, 1940.

Brecher, Michael, The Struggle for Kashmir. New York, Oxford University Press, 1953.

Brown, David J. L., "Recent Developments in the Ethiopia-Somaliland Frontier Dispute," Int. and Comp. Law Quart., 10, 1 (January, 1961), 167–178.

Buday, Laszlo, Dismembered Hungary. London, Grant Richards, 1923.

Busk, C. W. F., "The North-West Frontier; Pakistan's Inherited Problem," Geog. Mag., 22, 3 (July, 1949), 85–92.

Cahnman, Werner J., "Frontiers between East and West in Europe," Geog. Rev., 39, 4 (October, 1949), 605–624.

Caroe, Sir Olaf, "The Geography and Ethnics of India's Northern Frontiers," Geog. J., 126, Pt. 3 (September, 1960), 298–309.

———, "The India-Tibet-China Triangle," Asian Rev., n.s., 56, 205 (January, 1960), 3–13.

Child, Clifton J., "The Venezuela-British Guiana Boundary Arbitration of 1899," Amer. J. Internat. Law, 44, 4 (October, 1950), 682–693.

Christie, E. W. Hunter, The Antarctic Problem; An Historical and Political Study. London, G. Allen & Unwin, 1951.

Connell, John, "The India-China Frontier Dispute,"

Roy. *Canadian Asian J.,* 47, Pt. 3–4 (July–October, 1960), 270–285.

Curzon, Lord, *Frontiers.* London, Oxford University Press, 1908.

Day, Winifred M., "Relative Permanence of Former Boundaries in India," *Scot. Geog. Mag.,* 65, 3 (December, 1949), 113–122.

Dickinson, Robert E., "Germany's Frontiers," *World Affairs,* n.s., 1, 3 (July, 1947), 262–277.

East, Gordon, "The Concept and Political Status of the Shatter Zone," in *Geographic Essays on Eastern Europe,* Norman J. G. Pounds (ed.). Bloomington, Indiana University Press, 1961, pp. 1–27.

East, W. Gordon, "The New Frontiers of the Soviet Union," *Foreign Affairs,* 29, 4 (July, 1951), 591–607.

Fall, Bernard B., "The Laos Tangle," *Internat. J.,* 16, 2 (1961), 138–157.

Fawcett, C. B., *Frontiers: a Study in Political Geography.* London, Oxford University Press, 1918.

Feer, Mark C., "India's Himalayan Frontier," *Far Eastern Survey,* 22, 11 (October, 1953), 137–141.

Fifield, Russell, "The Postwar World Map: New States and Boundary Changes," *Amer. Political Sci. Rev.,* 42, 3 (June, 1948), 533–541.

Fischer, Eric, "On Boundaries," *World Politics,* 1, 2 (January, 1949), 196–222.

Fishel, Wesley R., *The End of Extraterritoriality in China.* Berkeley, University of California Press, 1952.

Fisher, Margaret W., and Leo E. Rose, "Ladakh and the Sino-Indian Border Crisis," *Asian Survey,* 2, 8 (October, 1962), 27–37.

Fiske, Clarence, and Mrs. Clarence Fiske, "Territorial Claims in the Antarctic," *U.S. Naval Inst. Proc.,* 85, 1 (January, 1959), 82–91.

Fraser-Tytler, Sir W. Kerr, *Afghanistan; A Study of Political Development in Central Asia.* London, Oxford University Press, 1950.

Freshfield, D. W., "The Southern Frontiers of Austria," *Geog. J.,* 46, 4 (December, 1915), 413–435.

Friters, Gerard M., *Outer Mongolia and Its International Position.* Baltimore, Johns Hopkins Press, 1949.

Hagen, Toni, Friedrich Traugott Wahlen, and Walter R. Corti, *Nepal, the Kingdom in the Himalayas,* trans. by Britta M. Charleston. Berne, Kümmerly & Frey, 1961.

Hall, H. D., "Zones of the International Frontier," *Geog. Rev.,* 38, 4 (October, 1948), 615–625.

Hammond, Thomas Taylor, *Yugoslavia—Between East and West.* New York, Foreign Policy Association, 1954.

Hanessian, John, Jr., "Antarctica; Current National Interests and Legal Realities," *Proc. Amer. Soc. Internat. Law,* 52 (1958), 145–164.

Hanna, A. J., *The Story of the Rhodesias and Nyasaland.* London, Faber and Faber, 1960.

Harrison, John A., *Japan's Northern Frontier; A Preliminary Study in Colonization and Expansion with Special Reference to Relations of Japan and Russia.* Gainesville, University of Florida Press, 1953.

Hartshorne, Richard, "The Franco-German Boundary of 1871," *World Politics,* 2, 2 (January, 1950), 209–250.

———, "Geographic and Political Boundaries in Upper Silesia," *Ann. A.A.G.,* 23, 4 (December, 1933), 195–228.

———, "A Survey of the Boundary Problems of Europe," in *Geographic Aspects of International Relations,* C. Colby (ed.). Chicago, University of Chicago Press, 1938. pp. 161–213.

Haupert, J. S., "Political Geography of the Israeli-Syrian Boundary Dispute, 1949–1967," *Prof. Geog.* 21, 3 (May, 1969), 163–171.

Haupert, John S., "Some Aspects of Boundaries and Frontiers of Israel," *Calif. Council Geography Teachers,* 4, 3 (June, 1957), 2–6.

Hay, Sir Rupert, "The Persian Gulf States and Their Boundary Problems," *Geog. J.,* 120, Pt. 4 (December, 1955), 433–443.

Hayton, Robert D., "Polar Problems and International Law," *Amer. J. Internat. Law,* 52, 4 (October, 1958), 746–765.

Held, Colbert C., "The New Saarland," *Geog. Rev.,* 41, (October, 1951), 590–605.

Hertslet, Sir Edward, *The Map of Africa by Treaty,* 3 vol. London, printed for H. M. Stationery Office by Harrison & Sons, 1909.

Hill, J. E., Jr., "El Chamizal: A Century-Old Boundary Dispute," *Geog. Rev.* 55, 4 (October, 1965), 510–522.

———, "El Horcon: a United States-Mexican Boundary Anomaly," *The Rocky Mountain Social Science Journal,* IV, 1 (April, 1967), 49–61.

Hoffman, George W., "The Shatter-Belt in Relation to the East-West Conflict," *J. Geography,* 51, 7 (October, 1952). 265–275.

Holdich, Sir Thomas H., *Political Frontiers and Boundary Making.* London, Macmillan, 1916.

House, J. W., "The Franco-Italian Boundary in the Alpes Maritimes," *Transactions and Papers, The Institute of British Geographers,* Publ. No. 26, 1959, pp. 107–131.

Humphreys, R. A., "The Anglo-Guatemalan Dispute," *Internat. Affairs,* 24, 3 (July, 1948), 387–404.

Huttenback, R. A., "A Historical Note on the Sino-Indian Dispute over the Aksai Chin," *China Quart.,* 18 (April–June, 1964), 201–207.

Hyde, Charles Cheney, "Maps as Evidence in International Boundary Disputes," *Amer. J. Internat. Law,* 27, 2 (April, 1933), 311–316.

Inlow, E. Burke, "The McMahon Line," *J. Geog.,* 63, 6 (September, 1964), 261–272.

Innis, H. A., "Canadian Frontiers of Settlement; A Review," *Geog. Rev.,* 25, 1 (January, 1935), 92–106.

Ireland, Gordon, *Boundaries, Possessions and Conflicts in South America.* Cambridge, Mass., Harvard University Press, 1938.

Jackson, W. A. Douglas, *Russo-Chinese Border-*

lands. Princeton, N.J., Van Nostrand, 1962.

John, I. G., "France, Germany and the Saar," *World Affairs*, 4, 3 (July, 1950), 277–293.

Jones, Stephen B., *Boundary-making, a Handbook for Statesmen, Treaty Editors, and Boundary Commissioners*. Washington, Carnegie endowment for international peace, Division of International Law, 1945.

Kapil, R.L., "On the Conflict Potential of Inherited Boundaries in Africa," *World Politics*, XVIII, 4 (July, 1966), 659–673.

Karan, Pradyumna P., "The Fringes and Frontiers of India and Pakistan," *Geography*, 4, 1 (May, 1951), 6–14.

Karan, Pradyumna Prasad, "The Indo-Chinese Boundary Dispute," *J. Geog.*, 59, 1 (January, 1960), 16–21.

———, and William M. Jenkins, *The Himalayan Kingdoms: Bhutan, Sikkim, and Nepal*. Princeton, N.J., Van Nostrand, 1963.

Kerner, R. J., *The Urge to the Sea: the Course of Russian History*. Berkeley, University of California Press, 1942.

Khan, Fazlur R., "The Geographical Basis of Pakistan's Foreign Policy," *Pakistan Geog. Rev.*, 7, 2 (1952), 90–101.

Kingsbury, Patricia, and Robert C. Kingsbury, *Afghanistan and the Himalayan States*. Garden City, N.Y., Doubleday, 1960.

Kirk, W., "The Inner Asian Frontiers of India," *Trans. and Papers, Inst. Brit. Geographers, Publ. No. 31*, December, 1962, pp. 131–168.

———, "The Sino-Indian Frontier Dispute: A Geographical Review," *Scot. Geog. Mag.*, 76, 1 (April, 1960), 3–13.

Kohn, Hans, *The Future of Austria*. New York, Foreign Policy Association, 1955.

Kozicki, Richard J., "The Sino-Burmese Frontier Problem," *Far Eastern Survey*, 26, 3 (March, 1957), 33–38.

Kuhn, Delia, and Ferdinand Kuhn, *Borderlands*. New York, Knopf, 1962.

Kureishy, Khalil Ullah, "The Natural Frontier of Pakistan," *Pakistan Geog. Rev.*, 7, 1 (1952), 35–52.

Lamb, A., *The China-India Border*. London, Oxford University Press, 1964.

Lamb, Alastair, "The Indo-Tibetan Border," *Australian J. Politics and History*, 6, 1 (May, 1960), 28–40.

Lattimore, Owen, *Inner Asian Frontiers of China*. Boston, Beacon Press, 1962.

———, "The New Political Geography of Inner Asia," *Geog. J.*, 119, Pt. 1 (March, 1953), 17–30.

———, *Pivot of Asia: Sinkiang and the Inner Asian Frontier of China and Russia*. Boston, Little, Brown, 1950.

Lenczowski, George, *Russia and the West in Iran, 1918–1948*. Ithaca, N.Y., Cornell University Press, 1949.

Lessing, O. E. (ed.), *Minorities and Boundaries*. New York, Van Riemsdyck, 1931.

Levi, Werner, "Bhutan and Sikkim: Two Buffer States," *World Today*, 15, 12 (December, 1959), 492–500.

———, "Nepal in World Politics," *Pacific Affairs*, 30, 3 (September, 1957), 236–248.

Lewis, I. M., "The Problem of the Northern Frontier District of Kenya," *Race*, 5, 1 (1963), 48–60.

Low, D.H., "The Kingdom of Serbia: Her People and Her History," *Scot. Geog. Mag.*, 31, 6 (June, 1915), 303–315.

Macartney, C.A., "The Slovak-Hungarian Frontier," *Geog. Mag.*, 20, 8 (December, 1947), 293–295.

Maillart, Ella, "Nepal, Meeting-Place of Religions," *Geog. Mag.*, 29, 6 (October, 1956), 273–288.

Mayfield, Robert C., "A Geographical Study of the Kashmir Issue," *Geog. Rev.*, 45, 2 (April, 1955), 181–196.

Mazour, Anatole Grigorevich, *Finland Between East and West*. Princeton, N.J., Van Nostrand, 1956.

Mead, W. R., "Finnish Karelia: an International Borderland," *Geog. J.*, 118, Pt. 1 (March, 1952), 40–57.

Meinig, Donald, "Colonization of Wheatlands; Some Australian and American Comparisons," *Australian Geographer*, 7, 5 (August, 1959), 205–213.

Minghi, J. V., "Boundary Studies and National Prejudice," *Prof. Geog.*, 15, 1 (January, 1963), 4–8.

Misra, S. D., "The Sino-Indian Dispute; A Geographical Analysis," *Indian Geog. J.*, 34, 3 & 4 (July–September, and October–December, 1959), 59–64.

Missakian, J., *A Searchlight on the Armenian Question (1878–1950)*. Boston, Hairenik Publishing Co., 1950.

Monroe, Elizabeth, "The Arab-Israel Frontier," *Internat. Affairs*, 29, 4 (October, 1953), 439–448.

Moodie, A. E., "The Cast Iron Curtain," *World Affairs*, 4, 3 (July, 1950), 294–305.

———, *The Italo-Yugoslav Boundary, a Study in Political Geography*. London, G. Philip & Son. Ltd., 1945.

Moodie, A. E., "States and Boundaries in the Danubian Lands," *Slavonic and East European Rev.*, 26, 67 (April, 1948), 422–437.

Mukerji, A. B., "Kashmir: a Study in Political Geography," *Geog. Rev. India*, 17, 1 (March, 1955), 19–32.

Murdoch, Richard K., *The Georgia-Florida Frontier, 1793–1796; Spanish Reaction to French Intrigue and American Design*. Berkeley, Calif., University of California Press, 1951.

Nadan, Ram, "Jammu and Kashmir," *Focus*, 13, 1 (September, 1962).

Nijim, B.K., "Conflict Potential and International Riparian Dispute: the Case of Jordan," *The Iowa Geographer*, 28, (Fall 1971), 8–14.

Nugent, W. V., "Geographical Results of the Nigeria-Kamerun Boundary Demarcation Commission, 1912–13," *Geog. J.*, 43 (1914), 630–648.

Ogilvie, Alan Grant, *Europe and Its Borderlands*. Edinburgh, T. Nelson, 1957.

Pelzer, Karl J., "Micronesia—A Changing Frontier," *World Politics*, 2, 2 (January, 1950), 251–266.

Platt, Robert S., "Coffee Plantations of Brazil, A Comparison of Occupance Patterns in Established and Frontier Areas," *Geog. Rev.*, 25, 2 (April, 1935), 231–239.

——, *A Geographical Study of the Dutch-German Border*. Munster-Westfalen, Selbstverlag der Geographischen Kommission, 1958.

——, "The Saarland, An International Borderland," *Erdkunde*, 15, 1 (March, 1961), 54–68.

Pounds, Norman J. G., "France and 'Les Limites Naturelles' from the Seventeenth to the Twentieth Centuries," *Ann. A.A.G.*, 44, 1 (March, 1954), 51–62.

——, "History and Geography: A Perspective of Partition," *J. Internat. Affairs*, 18, 2 (1964), 161–172.

——, "The Origin of the Idea of Natural Frontiers in France," *Ann. A.A.G.*, 41, 2 (June, 1951), 146–157.

Rao, K. Krishna, "The Sino-Indian Boundary Question and International Law," *Int. and Comp. Law Quart.*, 11, 2 (April, 1962), 375–415.

Raup, Philip M., "The Agricultural Significance of German Boundary Problems," *Land Economics*, 26, 2 (May, 1950), 101–114.

Rawlings, E. H., "The India-China Border," *Asian Rev.*, n.s., 58, 213 (January, 1962), 21–26.

Reilly, Sir Bernard, and J. C. Morgan, "South Arabian Frontiers," *Corona*, 10, 3 (March, 1958), 88–91.

Richards, J. Howard, "Changing Canadian Frontiers," *Canadian Geographer*, 5, 4 (1961), 23–29.

Roucek, Joseph S., "The Geopolitics of Afghanistan," *Social Studies*, 48, 4 (April, 1957), 127–129.

Rubin, Alfred P., "The Sino-Indian Border Disputes," *Int. and Comp. Law Quart.*, 9, 1 (January, 1960), 96–125.

Russell, Frank M., *The Saar, Battleground and Pawn*. Stanford, Calif., Stanford University Press, 1951.

Schoenrich, Otto, "The Venezuela-British Guiana Boundary Dispute," *Amer. J. Internat. Law*, 43, 3 (July, 1949), 523–530.

Scott, John, *Africa, World's Last Frontier*. New York, Foreign Policy Association, 1959.

Sen, D. K., "China, Tibet and India," *India Quart.*, 7, 2 (April–June, 1951), 112–132.

Shute, J., "Czecho-Slovakia's Territorial and Population Changes," *Econ. Geography*, 24, 1 (January, 1948), 35–44.

Solomon, R.L., "Boundary Concepts and Practices in Southeast Asia," *World Politics*, XXIII, 1 (October, 1970), 1–23.

Spate, O. H. K., "The Partition of India and the Prospects of Pakistan," *Geog. Rev.*, 38, 1 (January, 1948), 5–29.

Spykman, N. J., "Frontiers, Security and International Organization," *Geog. Rev.*, 32, 3 (July, 1942), 436–447.

Stacey, C. P., "The Myth of the Unguarded Frontier, 1815–1871," *Amer. Historical Rev.*, 56, 1 (October, 1950), 1–18.

Stern, H. Peter, *The Struggle for Poland*. Washington, Public Affairs Press, 1953.

Stoneman, Elvyn Arthur, "The Partition of Ireland," *Clark University, Abstracts* of dissertations and theses, 22 (1950), 22–26.

Strang, Sir William, "Germany Between East and West," *Foreign Affairs*, 33, 3 (April, 1955), 387–401.

Sullivan, Walter, "Antarctica in a Two-Power World," *Foreign Affairs*, 36, 1 (October, 1957), 154–166.

Swann, Robert, "Laos, Pawn in the Cold War," *Geog. Mag.*, 32, 8 (January, 1960), 365–375.

Szaz, Zoltan Michael, *Germany's Eastern Frontiers; the Problem of the Oder-Neisse Line*. Chicago, H. Regnery Co., 1960.

Taylor, Griffith, "Frontiers of Settlement in Australia," *Geog. Rev.*, 16, 1 (January, 1926), 1–25.

Tayyeb, Ali, "A Note on the Political Geography of the India-China Border," *Canadian Geographer*, No. 16 (July, 1960), 22–26.

Teal, John J., Jr., "Europe's Northernmost Frontier," *Foreign Affairs*, 29, 2 (January, 1951), 263–275.

Thomas, H. B., "The Kagera Triangle and Kagera Salient," *Uganda J.*, 23, 1 (March, 1959), 73–78.

Turner, F. J., *The Frontier in American History*. New York, H. Holt, 1921.

Vevier, Charles, "American Continentalism: An Idea of Expansion 1845–1910," *Amer. Historical Rev.*, 65, 2 (January, 1960), 323–335.

Ward, Michael, "The Northern Greek Frontier," *Geog. Mag.*, 21, 9 (January, 1949), 329–335.

Weigend, Guido G., "Effects of Boundary Changes in the South Tyrol," *Geog. Rev.*, 40, 3 (July, 1950), 364–375.

Wilber, Donald N., "Afghanistan, Independent and Encircled," *Foreign Affairs*, 31, 3 (April, 1953), 486–494.

Wiley, S. C., "Kashmir," *Canadian Geog. J.*, 62, 1 (January, 1961), 22–31.

Williams, M. H., "Russia and the Turkish Straits," *U.S. Naval Inst. Proc.*, 78, 5 (May, 1952), 479–485.

Wiskemann, Elizabeth, *Germany's Eastern Neighbours; Problems Relating to the Oder-Neisse Line and the Czech Frontier Regions*. London, Oxford University Press, 1956.

——, "The Saar Moves Towards Germany," *Foreign Affairs*, 34, 2 (January, 1956), 287–296.

Wright, L. A., "A Study of the Conflict between the Republics of Peru and Ecuador," *Geog. Jour.*, 98, 5–6 (November–December, 1941), 253–272.

Wulff, H. E., "Laos," *Australian Geographer*, 7, 4 (February, 1959), 141–148.

Zartman, I. W., "The Sahara: Bridge or Barrier," *Internat. Conciliation*, No. 541 (1963), 3–62.

CHAPTER
8

BOUNDARIES:
CONCEPT AND CLASSIFICATION

In an article published recently in *World Politics*, Robert L. Solomon makes the following observation:

> . . . All peoples divide up the space they inhabit in some distinct and customary fashion. In spite of the existence of international legal and diplomatic standards, which have in some respects influenced political behavior in the region, it is as wrong today as it was in the heyday of imperialism to assume that Western concepts invariably have the same meaning for Southeast Asians as they do for statesmen in the West. . . . [1]

What Dr. Solomon said about Southeast Asia applies to other non-Western parts of the world as well. He points out that when the European colonizers arrived in Southeast Asia with their ideas of partitioning the region by a framework of boundaries, "there were no stable, delimited, or demarcated boundaries (and) even the concept of a boundary line was alien to the Southeast Asian experience. Within the region, the functional equivalent of borders consisted of zones of contact and intermittent postional warfare, within which the limits of extension of the 'sovereignty' of each kingdom or principality were determined by a power-relation that was always subject to change."[2] In Chapter 2, we wondered what might have become of some of the ancient states, such as the Inca and West African entities, if the European invasion had not taken place. Would boundary concepts have emerged similar to those that accompanied the rise of modern Europe? Or would frontier-like transition zones have come to be recognized as legally acceptable "cushions" against competing pressures?

As a matter of fact, it is necessary for us to realize that Western views of boundary creation and the partitioning of earthspace are quite unusual and, indeed, are ethnocentric and biased—notwithstanding their export to the non-Western world. Westerners see territorial space as capable of being owned, parcelled out, bought and sold. This attitude toward earth space is reflected by the familiar world boundary framework, which suggests that all territory is—or at least ought to be—allocated in the first instance to nation-states. The fact is that there are areas in the world where those boundaries are barely defined, not exactly delimited, and not at all demarcated, and where some other form of territorial accommodation exists. Many African peoples, for example, see territorial space as something as communally owned as, say, the air we breathe. To cut it into parcels for exclusive exploitation is unthinkable, to sell and trade it even more so. In Asia, Africa, and the Americas, land was the central issue of colonial conflict—it was not the Europeans' sharing, but their aggrandizement of it that led to so many conflicts.

Yet, in Chapter 2, we said that there were non-Western peoples who did mark or know their boundaries with some precision. Certainly the European practice was not unique; those ancient boundary makers interest us because they may be able to teach us something about the processes whereby we Westerners came to treat territorial space as we do. And while it is true that Europe's nation-state system was exported to virtually all of the rest of the world, let us not forget that the system has, in most instances, been forced upon local societies through colonial-imperial decision making. It has worked better in some areas than in others; some societies have adjusted to it and capitalized upon it with considerable success. But elsewhere the state system is no more than a veneer as yet, and traditional society is still strong.

A second set of questions concerns the various types of boundary that can be recog-

[1]Robert L. Solomon, "Boundary Concepts and Practices in Southeast Asia," *World Politics*, XXIII, No. 1 (October, 1970), 8.

[2]Ibid., p. 3.

nized. Geographers often attempt to classify data before them, for out of classifications emerge valuable insights. In the previous chapter, for example, reference was made to truce lines as power-determined boundaries. Presumably it would be possible to locate every boundary that originated from a truce line, and from studies of prevailing conditions in the border areas generalizations may emerge concerning the long-range efficacy of such boundaries. Some boundaries were defined, delimited, and demarcated well before the present pattern of settlement developed, whereas others were drawn through areas that were already densely populated and functioning as units. There are other criteria: some boundaries are drawn along lines of latitude and longitude, whereas others lie exactly along physical features. Thus it is possible to classify boundaries according to their appearance on the map as compared to other features on the map, without any reference to the time element, and boundaries can also be classified according to their relationship with the evolving pattern of settlement.

Let us turn our attention, first, to boundary concepts in various parts of the world and at various times in history. In one of the most carefully documented studies in historical political geography available, S. B. Jones addresses himself to these very questions. It will be noted that reference is made to practically every major subject discussed in the first seven chapters of this book, but without losing sight of the central concern —namely, the role of the boundary in the minds of men and in the state systems the world has seen.

Boundary Concepts
in The Setting
of Place and Time[1]

Stephen B. Jones

Yale University

The theme of this address is simply that ideas about boundaries are related to their geographical and historical milieu. This theme is implicit in many writings about boundaries. It has been clearly exemplified for a particular area and era in Norman Pounds's two papers on the concept of natural frontiers, which appeared in the *Annals* of this association five and eight years ago.[2] It is my aim to extend the study backward and forward in time and expand it in space and to a variety of boundary concepts.

To develop my theme fully would demand a great deal more time than I have had in which to prepare this paper, and a great deal more time than I have in which to deliver it. It would have been impossible to complete even this limited survey without the generous help of many friends.[3] Indeed, so many have helped me that I feel like that editor of symposia who was introduced to an audience as "a man you all know; you have either read his books or written them."

In surveying boundary concepts from pole to pole and from the age of the slingshot to that of the sputnik, I have deliberately chosen breadth over depth. The choice of breadth has revealed to me how little I know about long periods of time and wide sweeps of space. Eight months of study have not been enough to make up these deficiencies. In most parts of this paper I have had to rely on secondary materials, and on only a sampling of those. I only hope that the very faults of this paper, its obvious gaps, its possible errors, will be a challenge to critics to do more and do it better.

I am focussing on boundaries rather than frontiers, but anyone who has delved into the subject knows that it is impossible completely to separate the two. I am dealing with both external and internal boundaries, partly in response to the availability of materials, partly because, for some times and places, it is difficult to distinguish the two kinds sharply.

TRIBAL BOUNDARY CONCEPTS

I begin with the boundary concepts of people we call "primitive," whose political systems we loosely call "tribal." One might call this the study of anthropological political geography, though I am tempted by "geoanthropolitics." This is a field in which political geographers have trod only lightly. It is easy to assume that primitive men have primitive ideas about boundaries, and that these are more or less alike around the world. A common assumption has been that primitive men have no linear boundaries but only zones. As Ratzel neatly puts it, "Not lines but positions are the essentials for this concept."[4] He describes many such cases,[5] and they undoubtedly are common, but there certainly are exceptions. Forde says that the Boro, a people of the western Amazon, may set up fences and other boundary marks in the forest and use stream courses to delimit territories.[6] Both the Maidu of California and the Vedda of Ceylon had boundaries that were sometimes patrolled by sentries, according to Lowie.[7] Sharp describes the region of the Cape York peninsula of Australia inhabited by the Yir Yoront and their neighbors as divided into thousands of small, named tracts. These are clan property, the clan being "the only corporate entity," and are clustered to form larger, unnamed tracts, "the boundaries of which are well defined."[8] Pospisil spent a year in a part of New Guinea where European influence was virtually nil. Politically, the

S.B. Jones, "Boundary Concepts in the Setting of Place and Time," *Annals of the Association of American Geographers*, Vol. 49 (1959), 241–255.

people among whom he lived formed a confederacy with four subdivisions. Boundaries, both internal and external, were clear-cut.[9]

Definite boundaries are compatible with depopulated defensive zones. Ratzel cites examples described by Barth and others from the Sudan, while Fischer mentions similar sharply bounded no-man's-lands between Germanic tribes.[10]

Barton's book on the Kalingas is an interesting anthropological study that touches on political geography.[11] This people of the Luzon mountains inhabits much the same sort of environment as do the Ifugaos, and makes its living in much the same way. But the Kalingas developed the more definite concept of territory and boundaries. The Ifugaos have a zonal concept. The home region is surrounded by a neutral zone, with the people of which there is generally peace and intermarriage. Around this is a feudist zone with which there is more strife and less marriage. Outside all is a war zone, where hostility is the normal expectation. The Kalingas, on the contrary, present "a hard crustacean shell with respect to foreign affairs." "The bounds are vague and shifting in Ifugao, definite and stable in Kalinga."[12] Barton further states that, although kinship is more often in the people's consciousness than is territory, territorial units are dominating the kinship groups, a process "considerably more advanced among the Kalingas than among the Ifugaos."[13]

Kinship and territory have been major principles of political organization, sometimes competing, sometimes cooperating or compromising. Lowie argues convincingly that the territorial principle is never absent, even where kinship appears to be of overwhelming importance.[14] The territorial principle has tended to dominate as political development has progressed, though relics of kinship appear, as in the conflict of jus sanguinis and jus soli. It is permissible, I think, to say that the problem of racial segregation in the United States today is a form of kinship–territory conflict. The issue can be stated as, Shall there be two grades of citizenship based on so-called "blood" or only one based on territory? Residential segregation is a more or less conscious attempt to maintain the racial system by forcing it into the more viable territorial form. But if there is anything in historical trends, one should bet on the ultimate triumph of the territorial principle pure and simple.

Barton's study of the Kalingas illustrates the kinship–territory interaction in another way. Two men of different Ifugao home regions may enter into a trading partnership, which involves ceremonies and obligations, even to avenging the death of the partner's kin if it occurs in certain places. These Ifugao partnerships are usually not stable. Among the Kalingas, similar pacts have developed into "one of the most admirable and efficient primitive institutions I have ever seen or read about."[15] These peace pacts, as they are called, are "held" by an individual and his kin and can be inherited. Only a man with numerous kin can muster the strength to enforce such a pact. The people of a region sometimes speak of themselves as "owned" by the pact-holders, although there is general social equality. As a mere hypothesis, I suggest that, in the absence of outside forces, Kalinga peace pacts might presage the development of a sort of feudalism and the emergence of strong territorial concepts. They could represent the incipient merger of the kinship and territorial principles, with the commoner's kinship bonds politically sublimated, so to speak, to those of the pact-holding families.

The foregoing are only samples of the possibilities that are open to the political geographer who delves into anthropology. The man who enters this field will find, however, that anthropologists have by no means supplied all the data he desires. The anthropologist who studies the politics of primitive peoples is likely to stop just where the political geographer becomes most interested. Tribal customs are described in detail, but the areal aspects of politics are likely to be given only vaguely, if at all.[16] There may be more on what may be called political ecology—for example, on the relation of customary law to agriculture—but even here, the things the geographer wants to know in detail are often the things that the anthropologist records only generally. This is of course no criticism of anthropologists. They do their research in terms of their own disciplinary goals. Rather it is an appeal to political geographers to do field work among primitive peoples. The results may be highly significant, for the political geography of tribes may shed light on that of national states.

SOME ASIAN BOUNDARY CONCEPTS AND PRACTICES

China can hardly be said to have had international boundaries, in the strict sense, until modern times. Like the Romans, the Chinese considered themselves to be surrounded by barbarians, not by nations of equal rank.[17] The Chinese did, according to Lattimore, conceive of and desire precise limits between themselves and the barbarians. "The idea of a stable and exact Frontier—a Great Wall Frontier —was inherent in the structure of China as a whole. What could not be included must be excluded."[18] This was especially true on the north, vis-à-vis the peoples of the steppes. China's southern frontier was one on which the Chinese mode of agriculture could expand; that on the north could be crossed only by adopting another mode of life.[19] The Chinese state was built on the base of irrigated agriculture. In Wittfogel's terminology, it was an agromanagerial despotism, ruling a hydraulic society.[20] Its organization was inapplicable to the steppes. But the ideal of a linear boundary between China and the steppes was never fully realized in practice. "That which was politically conceived as a sharp edge was persistently spread by the ebb and flow of history into a relatively broad and vague margin."[21]

Wall-building, according to Lattimore, was an expression of the desire for linear frontiers. It was, he says, a characteristic of the age. There were many Chinese walls before the Great Wall was built.[22] He calls the concept of a Great Wall "a product of the kind of state created within China"[23]—a centralized state based on irrigated agriculture. In this connection, it may be noted that the steppe frontier of China parallels and flanks the irrigated valley of the Hwang Ho, exposing it to invasion at many points. In contrast, Egypt's steppe frontier is transverse to the Nile.

Americans, conditioned by their own westward expansion, commonly think of frontiers as advancing and eventually disappearing. But only in recent times has Chinese expansion beyond the Great Wall been of that character. The historical purpose was to control the frontier rather than to obliterate it. The wall itself is evidence that further conquest was not strongly desired. Expansion beyond it was essentially defensive, to control border peoples, to suppress embryonic march-states.

In the steppes, the Chinese could not use their power in a normal way.[24] At the risk of a strained analogy, one may suggest that this expresses a difficulty facing the United States along its "ideological frontier"[25] today. The normal American way combines what we call "democracy" and "free enterprise." We understand that these words are simplifications of a complex way of life that has grown up in Europe and North America, chiefly, over many generations. We have found it difficult to operate in this way in lands of very different histories. At times even the most liberal of us must dream of a Great Wall—military, political, and economic—shutting out those whose ways we do not understand. It is fortunate that orbiting sputniks remind us of the impossibility of such a boundary concept in this age.

China's southern frontier has been studied by my colleague, Herold Wiens.[26] In this region, a sort of indirect rule was maintained over some border peoples. Wiens quotes a statesman of the Ming Dynasty as follows:

These barbarians are like the wild deer. To institute direct civil administration by Han-Chinese magistrates would be like herding deer into the hall of a house and trying to tame them. . . . On the other hand, to leave these tribal chieftains to themselves to conduct their own alliances or split up the domains, is like releasing deer into the wilderness without enclosing fences. . . . However, to fragment these domains under separate chieftains is to follow the policy of erecting restraining fences and is consonant with the policy of gelding the stallion and castrating the boar.[27]

But the Ming Court did not consistently follow this policy and the Ch'ing Dynasty was even more negligent. "Far from maintaining peace in the frontier area, [the chieftains] became the instigators of strife, and their capacity for protecting the frontiers was negligible."[28]

One would expect to find waterpartings in common use as internal boundaries in lands of irrigated agriculture, to preserve the unity of drainage basins. Such in fact is often the case, Japan and Hawaii being exceptionally good examples. But the relationship of boundary to waterparting is incompletely explained by the assumption that it is inevitable. One must consider the relative role of pastoralism, for instance. Pastoralism was lacking in Japan and Hawaii.[29] Where it is important, as in Tibet, waterpartings may not be the obvious boundaries. Kingdon Ward says of the Tibetan: "His frontier is the verge of the grassland, the fringe of the Pine forest, the 50-inch rainfall contour beyond which no salt is. . . . The barrier may be invisible; but it is a far more formidable one to a Tibetan than the Great Himalayan range."[30]

Chinese statesmen, many centuries B.C., recognized the virtues of highlands and the defects of rivers as boundary sites, for their civilization.[31] The ideal of waterpartings as boundaries can be found in Japanese writings of the eighth century, A.D.[32] Indeed, the Japanese word for boundary is *sakai*, which means crest or divide. Where the Japanese boundaries cross or follow streams, they nearly always do so in parts of the course where there is little or no irrigated land.

In the third century, B.C., China first became a unified state and was divided into districts. The formal subdivision of Japan into provinces or *kuni* dates from the seventh and eighth centuries, A.D. The Chinese and Japanese languages use several of the same characters for territorial subdivisions, though the size of the division to which a given character applies may be quite different.

The general uniformity in size of the subdivisions of Japan is notable. This bespeaks not merely a naive use of waterpartings as obvious features but also a concept and a plan. The basic pattern is long-lived. The modern prefectures resemble the ancient *kuni* very closely, though consolidations have reduced the number. In the intervening centuries, the *kuni* boundaries were much used, though at times they "served merely as a geographical frame of reference."[33]

The pattern of water control in present-day Japan is exceedingly complex, says Eyre, with over one hundred thousand irrigation cooperatives and no general code of water law.[34] There is little central control; indeed there is marked aversion to it, though the central government has in recent years taken over some major constructions. The small size of the river basins favors local control. Moreover, there is generally a good deal of rain in Japan. Eyre quotes an old saying, "When rain falls, water disputes turn to bubbles."[35] Wittfogel holds that the absence of large-scale irrigation works was a reason that a full-fledged hydraulic society, with its agromanagerial bureaucracy, did not develop in Japan.[36]

For India, "from Asoka to Aurenzeb," Spate has synthesized much information in the form of a map of boundary permanence.[37] The "skirt of the hills," both along the northwest frontier and in the jungles below the Himalayas, shows up prominently on this map, as does the line of the Narbada River across the northern Deccan. The *Arthasástra*, a manual of Indian statecraft perhaps dating from the fourth century, B.C., recommends strong boundary defenses, with fortifications on sites naturally fitted for the purpose.[38] There appears to be a mine of rich ore, little touched as yet, from which significant geography can be smelted, in the historical records of India.

Spate's chapter on "Historical Outlines" gives one an idea of both the possibilities and the difficulties.[39] The linguistic obstacles are great, but some day our graduate schools may consider the mastery of one difficult language at least equivalent to a smattering of two easier ones. If so, the learning of an Asian tongue may prove more attractive to language-shy Americans.

The partition of India in 1947 is described by Spate as "the expression of a new economic nationalism that has inevitably taken into its hands the immensely powerful weapon of immemorial religious and social differentiation."[40] It left in its wake problems of water supply. The land drained by the Indus and its tributaries is one of the most ancient homes of a hydraulic society, and the great modern irrigation works have likewise been directed by the central government. Water supply is an immediate issue in the Punjab and potentially one in Kashmir.[41]

ROMAN BOUNDARY CONCEPTS

As suggested above, there was considerable similarity between the frontier problems and policies of Rome and China. "The Roman Republic," wrote Pelham, "can scarcely be said to have had any frontiers. It had certainly no system of frontier delimitation or defence."[42] (It is obvious that "frontier" is here used in the sense of "boundary.") The Roman of the Republic "disdained to set any bounds to Roman dominion." The Rhine and the Euphrates were first suggested as boundaries not by the Romans but by barbarian rulers, and the suggestions fell on deaf ears.

The foundations of a frontier system were laid by Augustus. It was he who organized the Roman army as a standing force, who stationed the greater part of it in the frontier districts, and who first established permanent camps; and though in the earlier years of his reign the old ideas of universal empire found expression in literature, and were possibly shared by himself, he left as a legacy to his successors the advice "to keep the bounds of the empire within fixed limits."[43]

The centralizing and organizing zeal of the emperors, coupled with increasing anxiety about the barbarians, led to the elaboration of a frontier administrative and defensive system. Although the immensely long boundary cannot properly be treated as a unit, the basic desire seems to have been security within definit limits. Adami says that the Romans habitually laid down natural boundaries—rivers, mountain tops, watersheds. "Large rivers make essentially the best military boundaries. The Romans knew this well."[44] Given the military technology of the time, this was probably true. Moreover, the rivers were natural lines of communication along the frontier.[45] And, of course, the Roman state was not based on irrigation, as was the Chinese; so river boundaries were less inconvenient.

But there were stretches of the Roman frontier where no rivers or other strong natural lines existed, and other stretches where, for one reason or another, the Romans overpassed the natural lines that did exist. Although the Romans did dig ditches and erect palisades and even walls in such places, they were less inclined to continuous fortifications than were the Chinese. *Limes*, the word commonly applied to such frontiers, originally meant a road along a property line. It came to have the military meaning of a fortified road in a frontier zone and, by extension, the frontier zone itself.[46] It was "a zone where all is organized for the protection of the empire."[47] The general map in Poidebard's atlas shows well the network of forts, watchtowers, and roads on the Syrian frontier. In North Africa, many miles of trench and wall exist, but Baradez believes these did not delimit the territories of Romans and barbarians but were rather the last line of a defense in depth.[48]

One of the best known of the Roman *limes* was that across the re-entrant formed by the upper courses of the Rhine and Danube. In this area, according to Pelham, a true barrier was erected only near the end of Roman rule, earlier constructions having been apparently for administrative convenience rather than defense. One stretch of nearly forty-eight miles was laid out in a straight line—perhaps the earliest example of a major straight-line boundary. Farther north, in the Taunus, a chain of posts was built beyond the Rhine in order to surround and isolate a formidable German tribe.[49]

The Romans, like the Chinese, sought to stabilize frontiers and cut military costs by means of self-sustaining border forces. In the rear of the Roman defense lines was a zone called *terra limitanea* or *agri limitanei*. Those given land here were in general obligated to assist in defense. The system developed faults, however. The frontier militiamen became inferior in status to the soldiers of the regular army and were relatively immobile, "many of them indeed being little better than armed peasants."[50]

BOUNDARY CONCEPTS OF MEDIEVAL EUROPE

The Middle Ages in Europe, speaking very generally, saw feudalism evolve into absolute monarchy, though, to be sure, there were kings in the feudal system and noblemen under the monarchies. The basic change, of course, was in the degree of central power. The salient characteristic of these ages, in respect to territory, was inheritance, not by the group but by individuals, and especially by eldest sons. Church lands were of course not transmitted in this wise, but we do observe the association of church lands with individuals for their lifetimes.

Yet, oddly, European feudalism did not begin as a hereditary system.[51] Neither kinship nor territory was an original principle. Rather, feudalism began as a personal bond between two individuals, a lord offering protection and favor, a vassal offering loyalty and service. But this personal bond acquired both hereditary and territorial nature in many cases. Technically, the death of either lord or vassal ended the bond, but it became common practice to renew the bond with the successor, until this became customary. As Bloch puts it, the ties of kinship tended to pattern themselves after those of the feudal relationship.[52]

Since the lord was responsible for the maintenance of his vassals, he commonly granted them land, and these fiefs tended to become hereditary. The combination of territorial and hereditary principles eventually obscured the purely personal bond. A nobleman might hold fiefs from a number of lords. The Count of Champagne held lands from the King of France, the German Emperor, the Duke of Burgundy, two archbishops, four bishops, and the Abbot of St. Denis.[53] Obviously, he could not pledge complete loyalty to all of them. The concept of *liege homage*, or first loyalty, arose, but it was clear that the purity of feudal tenure was gone.

In the feudal system, each noble was largely autonomous at his own level. The power of the king was restricted. The obligations of inferior to superior were definite and limited. The limited nature of feudal rule was, Pounds points out, a reason that river boundaries often functioned smoothly. "The life of market and farm was one thing; the hommage of the seigneur another."[54]

A well-known feature of feudalism is that it produced a patchwork political map. Discontinuous holdings were common, and were tolerable because of the decentralized nature of feudal rule and warfare. Some of this discontinuity persisted into the period of monarchies, but with increasing dissatisfaction. The discontinuous nature of Brandenburg–Prussia is a well-known case. The two principal parts of this domain were separated by a band of Polish territory for a century and a half. This was slowly whittled away. Frederick the Great, who made Prussia a major power, was concerned for the unification and "rounding out" of his territory.[55] By his time, of course, government and defense were strongly centralized.

The hereditary principle remained powerful after the feudal system had effectively been swallowed by centralism. Louis XIV, the monarch who did so much to emasculate feudalism in France, went to great pains to justify his territorial designs by claiming hereditary rights. Such claims were a factor in the War of Devolution (1667–68), the War of the League of Augsburg (1688–97), and the War of the Spanish Succession (1701–14).

Relics of feudalism still exist in Europe. Andorra's autonomy is legally a dual feudal tenure.[56] The continued independence of Monaco hinged on the birth of an heir. This in the age of nationalism and ideology rampant!

THE CONCEPT OF
NATURAL BOUNDARIES

Perhaps the clearest example of my theme in all history is the rise of the concept of natural boundaries, discussed by Pounds in the two papers already mentioned.[57] Some, perhaps many, of those who read this address were taught in school that there are two kinds of boundaries, natural and artificial. The concept of natural boundaries retained enough vitality to stimulate critical discussion at least as recently as 1940.[58]

Natural marks were of course used for boundaries for millenia before there arose a doctrine about them. They are still being adopted—for example, the Oder–Neisse line. The virtues and defects of natural boundaries and the several meanings of the term have been well discussed by Broek[59] and need not be recapitulated here. It is the rise of the *doctrine* that concerns us, for it accompanied a change in *Zeitgeist*.

The doctrine of natural boundaries was a product of the Age of Reason and of nationalism chafing at old restraints. Its origin, according to Pounds, was largely French. Philosophers of the Age of Reason appealed to

Nature for guidance, at least when it was convenient. Pounds quotes Grégoire on the annexation of Savoie in 1792: "Before considering whether you should, in accordance with the freely expressed wish of Savoie, incorporate it in the French Republic, you should consult the Law of Nature and see what it permits and requires in this respect."[60] The speaker of course went on to show that the Law of Nature required annexation.

When the revolution swept away the remnants of French feudalism, the concept of natural boundaries took predominance over historical claims. But such claims were not completely dropped, especially if they could be identified with those of natural law. Thus Carnot is quoted as desiring "the ancient and natural boundaries of France," combining the appeals of history and of nature.[61]

NATIONALITY AND
BOUNDARY CONCEPTS

A German reaction to the concept of natural frontiers was the concept of boundaries based on folk or nationality. Actually, nationality was often confused with the related but not identical fact of language. Fichte said that one born where German was spoken could consider himself not only a citizen of that state but of "the whole common fatherland of the German nation."[62] But most interestingly, Fichte did not discard the notion of natural law. He simply said that common language and culture constitute a natural law higher than that of rivers and mountains. The French reply, Pounds says, was to emphasize culture rather than language. ". . . what marks out a nation is neither race nor language. Men feel it in their hearts that they are a single people when they have in common thoughts and interests, affections, remembrances and aspirations."[63] With this, most would now agree, but we know how difficult it is to determine such facts objectively and to translate them into boundaries.

It is understandable that the Germans of the early nineteenth century, not having attained a national state, should idealize it, and needing a criterion for German nationality, should turn to the seemingly simple one of language. We see something similar currently at work in India. Leaders of that federal republic have had to yield to the demand for states based on language, though fearing the divisive effect.[64] The problems of the near but imperfect correlation of speech and nationality, of dovetailing along linguistic frontiers, and of imperfect censuses of languages plagued boundary makers after both World Wars.

Cobban states that national self-determination is inherent in nationalism—"the Divine Right of Peoples."[65] But the problem of determining nations by self-determination has been a difficult one. Its application has proved to be an art rather than a science. It has been particularly difficult to apply this concept to the drawing of boundaries; yet this is precisely where nationality is a most acute question.

The theme of self-determination was heard in chorus in the fateful years of 1917 and 1918. The Central Powers, the Provisional and the Bolshevik governments of Russia, and the Western Powers all sang in praise. Wilson made a most broad and explicit statement on July 4, 1918, calling for "the settlement of every question, whether of territory, of sovereignty, of economic arrangement, or of political relationship, upon the basis of the free acceptance of that settlement by the people immediately concerned."[66]

The Paris treaties reflected Wilsonian idealism in part, in part power-politics. The statesmen at Paris felt themselves competent to determine "self-determination" in most cases. Plebiscites were held in a number of questionable areas, with varied success. All in all, it is one of the surprises of history that the map of Europe of today bears so much resemblance to that established at Paris in 1919. But some of the resemblance is superficial. There has been wholesale transfer of populations, making peoples fit boundaries instead of boundaries fit peoples.

Although nationality is basically a "we-feeling" in a group of people, it embodies a strong territorial bond. The desire for territorial contiguity seems to be intensified by nationalism. After Waterloo, France was reduced to its pre-Napoleonic bounds, but, significantly, the Avignon enclave was not taken away. Of all the territorial clauses of the Treaty of Versailles, none angered the Germans more than that establishing, or re-establishing, the Polish Corridor, even though there was some ethnic basis for it.[67] The increasing activity of central governments in all phases of life may be a reason for this dislike of discontiguity, but sometimes it seems almost mystical. One occasionally hears Canadians object to the odd but inconsequential projection of Minnesota north of the forty-ninth parallel. Discontiguity was used as an argument against statehood for Alaska and Hawaii.

IMPERIALISM AND BOUNDARY CONCEPTS

European overseas imperialism followed the voyages of discovery that, to use Whittlesey's phrases, gave a world-wide sense of space and opened up an immense exploitable world.[68] It was late in this era of imperialism—when, however, European flags still floated bravely over much of the world—that Friedrich Ratzel promulgated his seven laws of state expansion.[69] Ratzel's laws refer to the growth of states as well as of empires, but because the emphasis is on expansion, and expansion has usually at least a flavor imperialism, I am mentioning them at this point.

Only one of Ratzel's laws deals specifically with frontiers or boundaries. This is the fourth: "The frontier is, as a peripheric organ of the state, the bearer of its growth and its security, conforming to all changes of the state organism."[70] Not feudal tenure or natural law is the principle, but the character of the state as an organism. It is true that Ratzel used organismic terms as analogies and felt the state to be incomplete as an organism. Semple in fact said that the organismic aspect of his thought was only a scaffolding that could be removed without injuring the main structure.[71] There is certainly much that is substantial in Ratzel's work.[72] Nevertheless, the organismic aspect exists, and the geopoliticians later made use of it.[73]

The organismic concept sees an analogy between such biological frontiers as timberline and the frontiers between human groups.[74] As a descriptive device this may be effective, but an analogy is neither analysis nor proof. Stripped of its organismic terminology, Ratzel's fourth law is little more than a truism so far as it refers to territorial growth. Moreover, it is difficult to keep analogies in the role of servant. It is easy to use them as props for further analogies. This is what happened in the writings of Maull and Haushofer, acquiring with the latter a dynamism that is well-known. With the geopoliticians, boundary stability was denigrated, as an effort to limit the growth of a living thing.

Lord Curzon's ideas on boundaries are well-known through his lecture on frontiers.[75] In this lecture, Curzon set forth his own frontier conditioning:

It happened that a large part of my younger days had been spent in travel upon the boundaries of the British Empire in Asia, which had always exercised upon me a peculiar fascination. A little later, at the

India Office and at the Foreign Office, I had had official cognizance of a period of great anxiety, when the main sources of diplomatic preoccupation, and sometimes of international danger, had been the determination of the Frontiers of the Empire in Central Asia, in every part of Africa, and in South America. Further, I had just returned from a continent where I had been responsible for the security and defence of a Land Frontier 5,700 miles in length, certainly the most diversified, the most important, and the most delicately poised in the world; and I had there, as Viceroy, been called upon to organize, and to conduct the proceedings of, as many as five Boundary Commissions.[76]

Curzon looked upon his career as an imperial administrator with satisfaction. The peroration of his lecture is too long to quote, but it extolled the courage and skill of the frontier officer and called upon the English universities to furnish such men. Here, then, was a most explicit statement of the political climate as Curzon felt it, in which his boundary concepts grew. A similar feeling of successful work on the frontiers permeates the writings of Thomas Holdich, the great demarcator of about the same period.[77]

Curzon did not sharply distinguish between "frontier" and "boundary," but he recognized the process by which a frontier may become a demarcated line. In contrast to the organismicists, he regarded this as progress, not as an artificial restraint. Curzon spoke respectfully of Science, which by this time had replaced Nature and Reason as an object of veneration:

It would be futile to assert that an exact Science of Frontiers has been or is ever likely to be evolved: for no one law can possibly apply to all nations or peoples, to all Governments, all territories, or all climates. . . . But the general tendency is forward, not backward; neither arrogance nor ignorance is any longer supreme; precedence is given to scientific knowledge; ethnological and topographical considerations are fairly weighed; jurisprudence plays an increasing part; the conscience of nations is more and more involved. Thus Frontiers, which have so frequently and recently been the cause of war, are capable of being converted into the instruments and evidences of peace.[78]

Curzon stood somewhere between what I shall call the power-political and the contractual concepts of boundaries. He knew the need for force along frontiers. He described the use of protectorates and spheres of influence in bland words but with callous realism.[79] But he at least dreamed of boundaries as "instruments and evidences of peace." I think anyone will agree, after reading the lecture, that the imperialist was the core of the man. Boundary-making, to him, was to a great extent unilateral—a strong, wise, just, imperial power establishing good boundaries. He speaks of "what is known as the Scientific Frontier, i.e., a Frontier which unites natural and strategical strength, and by placing both the entrance and the exit of the passes in the hands of the defending Power, compels the enemy to conquer the approach before he can use the passage."[80] Science is thus military science and the Scientific Frontier gives an advantage to one side that obviously cannot be given to both. If frontiers were to be "the instruments and evidences of peace," preferably it was *Pax Britannica.*

THE CONTRACTUAL CONCEPT OF BOUNDARIES

The theory that government is, or should be, a contract between rulers and ruled has a long history and has been used to explain or justify a wide variety of institutions, from absolutism to democracy. This theory of government, in its democratic form, has been congenial to Americans, whose Declaration of Independence holds that governments derive their just powers from the consent of the governed.[81] The American faith in written constitutions reflects the contractual concept.

The essence of the contractual concept of boundaries is that two countries should agree on a line and stick to it, as individuals agree on property lines. In contrast, an organismic state could hardly consider its "peripheric organ" to be the proper subject of a contract. Please note that, in distinguishing between power-political and contractual concepts of boundaries, I do not mean that practices necessarily follow one or the other. The contract may be a mere façade to hide power-politics.

Although I shall, for convenience, illustrate the contractual concept mainly with American examples, it would be hypocritical as well as incorrect to call it the American concept. American territorial expansion was basically power-political. Yet the steps in acquiring much of this territory had also some of the nature of real-estate transactions. Many of the Atlantic seabord colonies began essentially as land ventures. Louisiana, Florida, Alaska, and the Gadsden strip were purchased and a payment was made to Mexico after the Mexican War. These steps seem to show a desire to establish a sort of contractual title. That the Indians might claim a prior title was seldom considered seriously, though some-times this title was expunged, to American satisfaction at least, by purchase or treaty. That these treaties were repeatedly broken shows that the contractual concept was not allowed to stand in the way of "destiny." Yet it is possible that lip-service given this concept in time affects practice.

The increasing divergence between the usage of "frontier" and "boundary" is congru-ent with the contractual concept. Other languages than English permit a distinction between the two ideas, but in American usage the difference is now so great that they are essentially unrelated. In the United States and other new lands, a framework of boundaries was laid down before the land was densely settled or even effectively controlled in many cases. "Frontier" came to mean the advancing fringe of settlement rather than of territorial acquisition. Indeed, "frontier" has come to mean the locus of a way of life rather than a specific geographical location. There was still a frontier long after the Pacific Ocean became the western boundary of the United States. The Mexico–United States boundary lies in what most Europeans would call a frontier, but I have never heard an American so describe it.

We are not justified in attributing superiori-ty to the contractual concept just because it has seemed to work with us. Perhaps this concept, if raised to the level of a general principle, would be an attempt to apply "one law," and that law based heavily on the unusual American experience, to "all nations and peoples." Americans have quite correctly been charged with not understanding Euro-pean politics. In an article in *Life* that began as a study of boundary-making but turned into a "profile" of Isaiah Bowman, we are told of Bowman's irritation with "overemotional Eu-ropeans" who remembered injustices that were centuries old.[82]

The contractual concept has certainly col-ored the views of American writers on boundaries. We find it expressed in S. W. Boggs's *International Boundaries*.[83] Boggs was both idealistic and practical. He sought to reduce friction along boundaries by changing functions rather than locations—by functional contracts, so to speak. Your present speaker mentioned the boundary concepts of Curzon, Haushofer, and Spykman in the opening chapter of his book, *Boundary-Making*, but it is clear that he thought the contractual

concept was the desirable one.[84] This book was written during the war, expressly for use in postwar treaty-making and boundary de-marcation. With the wisdom of hindsight, it can be called a case of "preparing for the last peace." We thought in terms of formal peace conferences. We hoped the victors would unite in seeking a lasting peace and would frame territorial settlements with that in view. We were strangely blind to the tumult of forces—the madness of the Nazis, the Communists' vested interest in disorder (outside their own domain), and the power vacuums created by destruction.

THE CONCEPT OF GEOMETRICAL BOUNDARIES

There is in the United States, Canada, Aus-tralia, and to a lesser degree in some other parts of the world, a massive simplicity in boundary pattern. Probably any governments occupying or claiming vast, poorly mapped, lightly settled areas would be inclined to adopt simple boundaries. The common use of rivers as boundaries in such cases was not respect for "the Law of Nature" but for the practical matters of exploration, transportation, and cartography. Rivers were conspicuous and seemingly precise on maps that showed mountains only vaguely.[85]

The use of long geometrical lines as bound-aries required some geodetic sophistication. Their application to America was of European origin. The Papal Line of Demarcation—really a "line of allocation" and not a boundary—was the earliest. The charters of English colonies specified geometrical boundaries in many cases. The conflicting western land claims of these colonies arose largely from the extrapo-lation of their geometrical boundaries.[86] The parallel of forty-nine degrees was first suggest-ed by the Hudson's Bay Company, as a boundary between French and English posses-sions in eastern Canada, as early as 1714.[87]

Thomas Jefferson played a leading part in applying geometry to the American landscape.[88] A neo-classical love of order, symmetry, and simplicity permeated his ca-reer. In 1784, Jefferson chairmanned a congres-sional committee to plan for the western lands, between the Appalachians and the Mississippi, that had become federal property when the seaboard states gave up their conflicting claims. This committee presented a plan for fourteen new states.[89] Lines of latitude and longitude were to be boundaries wherever possible. The Ohio River was admitted as a boundary for part of its length, with the apology that it nearly coincided with the parallel of thirty-nine degrees. This is indeed an about-face from the concept of natural boundaries! Needless to say, this plan was not followed literally. Only a few state boundaries in this area conform to the committee's recommendations; yet the general pattern certainly reflects the geometrical ideal. In the new west, across the Mississippi, the geometers came into their own, creating two rectangular and many nearly rectangular states, with sublime disregard for mountains and canyons. That Americans and Canadians adapted themselves to such boundaries with relative ease reflects their acceptance of the contractual concept.

POWER-POLITICAL BOUNDARY CONCEPTS

Boggs's *International Boundaries* and the second edition of Haushofer's *Grenzen* appeared at about the same time.[90] Boggs's America and Haushofer's Germany were divergent in their climates of political thought. The environment in which Haushofer evolved his boundary concepts needs little description. He was an officer in a proud army that had suffered defeat. His country had been forced to accept peace terms that he and many of his fellow citizens felt to be humiliating. Economic depression led him to think that Germany lacked *Lebensraum*. He read widely, drawing on such writers as Kjellén, Mahan, and Mackinder. His knowledge was vast but he "overinterpreted" it.

Haushofer's basic boundary concept is perhaps best summed in his own words: "a biological battlefield in the life of peoples."[91] To be more precise, this was his concept of frontiers, the boundary being but a truce line in the battlefield. If we grant his organismic postulate, his frontier concept follows as the night the day. To be sure, few of us have ever granted the postulate, even in the heyday of American interest in *Geopolitik*. But the mistake we made was failing to see that many in Germany did accept such a postulate or at least acted as if they did. The climate of thought that produced *Geopolitik* produced Nazism. Many of us believed Hitler when he

said that the Sudetenland was his last territorial demand and felt that Chamberlain's scrap of paper was a valid contract.

The full impact of *Geopolitik* did not hit the United States until the war years. Then there was some truth in *Life's* gibe that "on campuses all over the country musty old geographers are blossoming out as shiny new geo-politicians."[92] Actually, nearly all of those who played prominent roles in familiarizing Americans with *Geopolitik* were strongly critical. Gyorgy, Mattern, Strausz-Hupé, Walsh, Weigert, and Whittlesey come to mind. Spykman wrote critically of Haushofer's "geographical metaphysics" but said that "the fact that certain writers have distorted the meaning of the term geopolitics is no valid reason for condemning its method and material."[93]

Spykman had been, in the nineteen-twenties, a supporter of the League of Nations. In the disillusionment of the thirties, he found a rationale for world politics in power and geography. He was one of the ablest proponents in America of a frank view of the role of power in world politics. His most notable work along this line was *America's Strategy in World Politics*.[94] For years afterwards, writings on international politics oozed "power" at every pore, those of your present speaker being no exception.

Spykman's concept of boundaries was derived from his ideas on power. A boundary is not only a line demarcating legal systems but also a line of contact of territorial power structures.[95] "Specific boundaries at any given historical period become then merely the political geographic expression of the existing balance of forces at that period."[96] Now and then Spykman came close to organismicism: The power of a state is "like the dynamic force of every organic entity" and "other things being equal, all states have a tendency to expand."[97] There is no doubt that his boundary concept is power-political rather than contractual. He would not have denied this or apologized for it.

Spykman evaluated power in terms of resources and strategy, both on a grand scale. Peacemakers, he argued, must think of the geography of power, for "interest in the frontier is now no longer in terms of the strategic value of the border zone but in terms of the power potential of the territory it surrounds."[98] In the United States of 1941 this was a more starling statement than it seems today.

BOUNDARIES SINCE THE SECOND WORLD WAR

I shall not attempt to discuss the climate of political thought of recent years but will call attention to some aspects of it that are pertinent to the theme of this address. One is the concern with national power or, as the Sprouts have suggested, state capabilities.[99] National power has been conceived as having two dimensions, inventory and strategy, or what one has and what one does.[100] Thoughts on the power inventory have considered population, natural resources, and industries, primarily. Thoughts on strategy have been dominated by spectacular advances in nuclear weapons and space technology, but the importance of diplomacy and economic activity and the possible menace of "limited wars" are now of widespread concern. Population and resources have been of concern not only as factors of state capability but also in respect to the maintenance of existing industrial civilization and its spread to the underdeveloped areas.

Important among the intangible aspects of the postwar Zeitgeist is the strength of nationalism and its spread to new parts of the world. Accompanying this is an increasing feeling of the need for international or even supranational organizations that is finding expression in a number of ways. Then there is, of course, the ideological factor that, with the concomitant activation of the resources of the Soviet Union and China, has divided the world into hostile camps of relatively equal power.

An awareness, though somewhat myopic, of the problem of power led to the focussing of much thought in the last years of the war on the containment (a word not then used) of Germany and Japan. Mackinder and Spykman were rather optimistic about Soviet–Allied cooperation for the control of unruly "Rimland" countries.[101] In fact, of course, Soviet –Allied cooperation was a bit mythical even during the war and dissolved completely soon after. Welles and Morgenthau advocated the reduction of German power, the former by partition, the latter by both partition and de-industrialization.[102] Germany and Japan were temporarily de-industrialized by air attack and Germany was partitioned by the freezing of occupation zones, but this negative approach to power backfired. It was the Communist Bloc, not the erstwhile enemies, that had to be contained, and both Germany and Japan have re-industrialized and are slowly rearming, with the blessing of former conquerors. A more positive approach to the power needs of the present has been the system of alliances that the United States, once wedded to the doctrine of "no entangling alliances," has taken the lead in forming, though some of these may still be no more than "Paper Curtains."

Some actual boundary settlements after the war were a restoration of the status quo ante. Some conformed to a degree with linguistic borderlands. Considerations of power underlay most of these decisions. The ideal of self-determination, which had been reaffirmed in an article of the Atlantic Charter, was not much heard in the actual war settlements but has influenced the postwar devolution of overseas empires.

As is well known, population transfers took place on a colossal scale, both during and after the war. My book on boundary-making mentioned exchange of populations but called it a last resort.[103] During and after the Second World War it was almost a first resort. There is no major sector of the "Crush Zone" from Finland to Sakhalin that has not seen some population transfer and the resulting sores are far from being healed.

In the first draft of my book, I wrote that transfer of populations indicated the bankruptcy of nationalism as a form of human organization. In the final draft, "bankruptcy" was replaced by "inadequacy"—a fortunate change, for nationalism at the moment shows no signs of bankruptcy. Its hold on the human mind is stronger than that of ideology. Nevertheless, it is possible that nationalism is near its zenith. As the national map of the world approaches completion, its colors may begin to lose their luster.

What may emerge is anybody's guess. A pessimist may predict the total collapse of organized society—thus ending boundary problems. But unless the human race is exterminated, organized society will persist and so will some sort of boundaries. An optimist may predict world federation, and so an end to international boundaries and their problems. The world needs idealists, even if they are far ahead of their time, but the flaw in some discussions of world federation is that defense is assumed to be the only vital function of international boundaries. Replace national armies with a supranational police force and there will be peace. But a federation in which tariff, fiscal, and immigration laws remained under the control of individual states would simply not be a federation. It would be a difficult and probably an impossible task to establish a common loyalty and to pool the control of force in such an organization.

But one need not be a complete pessimist or a complete optimist. If Utopia is a long way off, so may be Hell. Boggs's belief in the possibility of changing boundary functions has had more illustrations than we may realize. NATO, Benelux, and the European Economic Community are examples, though it remains to be seen how they survive the stress of events. Perhaps the pressure on boundaries may diminish if population growth tapers off and economic status becomes more equal among states.[104] Nuclear explosives and intercontinental missiles may eventually favor a contractual approach to international problems, since the consequences of war are so catastrophic. These things could lead to a better world within the general frame of national states. This is not a prediction. It is only guarded optimism, based on the hope, and the possibility, that mankind may make the right choices at the most crucial crossroads.

[1]Address given by the Honorary President of The Association of American Geographers at its 55th Annual Meeting, Pittsburgh, Pennsylvania, April 1, 1959.

[2]Norman J. G. Pounds, "The Origin of the Idea of Natural Frontiers in France," Annals, Association American Geographers, Vol. 41 (1951), pp. 146–57, and "France and 'Les Limites Naturelles' from the Seventeenth to the Twentieth Centuries," ibid., Vol. 44 (1954) pp. 51–62.

[3]The following have supplied information and suggestions. I hope I have omitted no name: Edwin H. Bryan (Bishop Museum), Cheng-siang Chen (National Taiwan University), John D. Eyre (University of North Carolina), Eric Fischer (George Washington University), Ralph Fisher (University of Illinois), Otto E. Guthe (U. S. Government), Andrew Gyorgy (Boston University), Arthur R. Hall (U. S. Government), Robert B. Hall (Asia Foundation), Richard Hartshorne (University of Wisconsin), James M. Hunter (Georgetown University), Kōzō Iwata (Tokyo Gakugei University), Mrs. Marion Kelly (Bishop Museum), E. S. Kirby (University of Hong Kong), George Kish (University of Michigan), Ladis K. D. Kristof (University of Chicago), Owen Lattimore (Johns Hopkins University), Alexander Melamid (New York University), Leopold Pospisil (Yale University), Norman J. G. Pounds (Indiana University), David N. Rowe (Yale University), O. H. K. Spate (Australian National University), Joseph E. Spencer (University of California at Los Angeles), William L. Thomas (University of California at Riverside), Richard Walker (University of South Carolina), C. Bradford Welles (Yale University), Herold J. Wiens (Yale University), Robert L. Williams (Yale University), Karl A. Wittfogel (University of Washington). Messrs. Fischer, Hartshorne, Kristof, and Pounds read the manuscript and made very valuable suggestions. The author of course assumes full responsibility for the published paper.

[4]Friedrich Ratzel, "Die Gesetze des räumlichen Wachstums der Staaten," Petermanns Mitteilungen, Vol. 42 (1896), p. 103.

[5]Friedrich Ratzel, Politisch Geographie (München und Leipzig: Oldenbourg, 1897), pp. 458–63.

[6]C. Daryll Forde, Habitat, Economy and Society, A Geographical Intruduction to Ethnology (New York: Harcourt, Brace, 1934), p. 145.

[7]Robert H. Lowie, Social Organization (New York: Rinehart, 1948), p. 139.

[8]R. Lauriston Sharp, "People Without Politics," in Systems of Political Control and Bureaucracy in Human Societies, Proceedings, American Ethnological Society (Seattle: American Ethnological Society, 1958), pp. 3–4.

[9]Leopold Pospisil, Kapauku Papuans and Their Law, Yale University Publications in Anthropology, No. 54 (New Haven: Department of Anthropology, Yale University, 1958), pp. 96–97.

[10]Ratzel, "Die Gesetze des raumlichen Wachstums der Staaten," op. cit., p. 103; Eric Fischer, personal communication.

[11]R. F. Barton, The Kalingas, Their Institutions and Custom Law (University of Chicago Press, 1949).

[12]Ibid., p. 138.

[13]Ibid., p. 137.

[14]Robert H. Lowie, The Origin of the State (New York: Harcourt, Brace, 1927), pp. 51–73.

[15]Barton, op. cit., pp. 144 ff.

[16]In the index to the contents of the Human Relations Area Files, "boundary" appears but once, and that refers to property lines. George P. Murdock et al., Outline of Cultural Materials (3rd ed.; New Haven: Human Relations Area Files, 1950).

[17]Theodore Herman, "Group Values Toward the National Space: The Case of China," The Geographical Review, Vol. 49 (1959), pp. 165–67. Also personal communications, E. S. Kirby and David N. Rowe.

[18]Owen Lattimore, Inner Assian Frontiers of China (2nd ed.; New York: American Geographical Society, 1951), pp. 482–83.

[19]Ibid., pp. 38–41.

[20]Karl A. Wittfogel, Oriental Despotism, A Comparative Study of Total Power (New Haven: Yale University Press, 1957).

[21]Lattimore, op. cit., p. 238.

[22]Owen Lattimore, "Origins of the Great Wall of China: A Frontier Concept in Theory and Practice," The Geographical Review, Vol. 27 (1937), pp. 529–49.

[23]Lattimore, Inner Asian Frontiers, op. cit., p. 434.

[24]Ibid., p. 474.

[25]The term "ideological frontier" is from Ladis K. D. Kristof, "The Nature of Frontiers and Boundaries," pp. 269–82, present issue of Annals. The author has generously permitted me to refer to his manuscript.

[26]Herold J. Wiens, China's March Toward the Tropics (New Haven: The Shoestring Press, 1954).

[27]Ibid., p. 219.

[28]Ibid., pp. 220 and 240.

[29]Pasture is the largest single category of land-use in Hawaii today, exceeding cultivated land four-fold (John Wesley Coulter, Agricultural Land-use Planning in the Territory of Hawaii [Honolulu: University of Hawaii, 1940], p. 57) but the internal boundaries are still essentially those established along interfluve ridges in Polynesian days, forming sectors based on the coast and reaching back into the main mountain masses. (Robert D. King, "Districts in the Hawaiian Islands," in John Wesley Coulter, A Gazetteer

of the Territory of Hawaii [Honolulu: University of Hawaii, 1935], pp. 214–30. Stephen B. Jones, "Geography and Politics in the Hawaiian Islands," The Geographical Review, Vol. 28 [1938], pp. 206–208. Also personal communications, Edwin H. Bryan, Jr., and Mrs. Marion A. Kelly.)

30F. Kingdon Ward, "Explorations on the Burma–Tibet Frontier," Geographical Journal, Vol. 80 (1932), p. 469.

31Personal communication, Cheng-siang Chen.

32Personal communication, Kōzō Iwata.

33Personal communication, John D. Eyre. For maps of kuni, see J. and R. K. Reischauer, Early Japanese History (Princeton University Press, 1937), Part B, pp. 10–37.

34John D. Eyre, "Water Controls in a Japanese Irrigation System," The Geographical Review, Vol. 45 (1955), pp. 197–216.

35Ibid., p. 213.

36Wittfogel, op. cit., pp. 197–200.

37O. H. K. Spate, India and Pakistan, A General and Regional Geography (2nd ed.; New York: Dutton, 1957), p. 147.

38Kautilya's Arthasastra, translated by R. Shamasastry (4th ed.; Mysore: Sri Raghuveer Press, 1951), pp. 45–50. Also V. R. Ramachandra Dikshitar, Hindu Administrative Institutions (University of Madras, 1929), pp. 275–76.

39Spate, op. cit., pp. 144–70.

40Spate, "The Partition of India and the Prospects of Pakistan," The Geographical Review, Vol. 38 (1948), p. 5.

41Kazi S. Ahmad, "Canal Water Problem," The Oriental Geographer, Vol. 2 (1958), pp. 31–46. F. J. Fowler, "Some Problems of Water Distribution Between East and West Punjab," The Geographical Review, Vol. 40 (1950), pp. 583–99. Robert C. Mayfield, "A Geographical Study of the Kashmir Issue," The Geographical Review, Vol. 45 (1955), pp. 181–96. Newspaper reports at the time of writing suggest that these water disputes may be approaching settlement.

42Henry Francis Pelham, Essays, collected and edited by F. Haverfield (Oxford: The Clarendon Press, 1911), p. 164.

43Ibid., pp. 165–66.

44Vittorio Adami, National Frontiers in Relation to International Law, translated by T. T. Behrens (Oxford University Press, 1927), pp. 4 and 13.

45Jean Gottmann, La Politique des États et leur Géographie (Paris: Armand Colin, 1952), p. 122.

46A. Poidebard, La Traee de Rome dans le Désert de Syrie (Paris: Librairie Orientaliste Paul Geuthner, 1934), p. 18 The aerial photographs of Roman frontier fortifications in the atlas volume of this work, and also in the work of Jean Baradez, cited below, are extremely interesting.

47Jean Baradez, Fossatum Africae (Paris: Arts et Métiers Graphiques, 1949), p. 134. Cf. Ratzel, Politische Geographie, op. cit., pp. 497–98.

48Ibid., p. 358.

49Pelham, op. cit., pp. 183–204.

50Ibid., pp. 172–76. George Kish, in a personal communication, remarks that Austria–Hungary established a military zone in the seventeenth century, after the Turks were pushed from the Hungarian Plain. The men given land in the boundary zone were liable for military duty on a few hours' notice. This zone was not finally abolished until 1873.

51Marc Bloch, "European Feudalism," Encyclopedia of the Social Sciences (New York: Macmillan, 1931), Vol. 6, pp. 203–10.

52Ibid., p. 204. Cf. Owen Lattimore, "Feudalism in History," Past and Present, No. 12 (1957), p. 52.

53G. B. Adams, "Feudalism," Encyclopedia Britannica (11th ed.; Cambridge University Press, 1910–11), Vol. 10, p. 301.

54Pounds, "The Origin of the Idea of Natural Frontiers in France," op. cit., p. 151.

55J. Ellis Barker, The Foundations of Germany (London: Smith, Elder, 1916), pp. 81, 101, 233–34.

56Derwent Whittlesey, "Andorra's Autonomy," The Journal of Modern History, Vol. 6 (1934), pp. 147–55.

57See footnote No. 2.

58Jan O. M. Broek, "The Problem of 'Natural Frontiers'," in Frontiers of the Future (Berkeley and Los Angeles: University of California Press, 1941), pp. 3–20.

59Ibid.

60Pounds, "France and 'Les Limites Naturelles'," op. cit., p. 54.

61Ibid., p. 55.

62Ibid., p. 57.

63Ibid., p. 60.

64Hans W. Weigert et al., Principles of Political Geography (New York: Appleton–Century–Crofts, 1957), pp. 385–88.

65Alfred Cobban, National Self-Determination (University of Chicago Press, 1951), pp. 5–6.

66Samuel Flagg Bemis, A Diplomatic History of the United States (New York: Holt, 1936), p. 635. For statements by the Central Powers, see Cobban, op. cit., p. 11, and by the Russian governments, see John W. Wheeler-Bennett, The Forgotten Peace, Brest–Litovsk, March 1918 (New York: Morrow, 1939), pp. 46 and 117.

67Richard Hartshorne, "The Polish Corridor," The Journal of Geography, Vol. 36 (1937), pp. 161–76.

68Derwent Whittlesey, The Earth and the State (New York: Holt, 1944), pp. 78–85, and "The Horizon of Geography," Annals, Association of American Geographers, Vol. 35 (1945), pp. 9–15.

69Ratzel, "Die Gesetze des räumlichen Wachstums der Staaten," op. cit., pp. 97–107.

70Ibid., p. 102.

71Ellen Churchill Semple, Influences of Geographic Environment on the Basis of Ratzel's System of Anthropogeography (New York: Holt, 1911), p. vii.

72Jan O. M. Broek, "Friedrich Ratzel in Retrospect," abstract in Annals, Association of American Geographers, Vol. 44 (1954), p. 207.

73It has been argued that Kjellén, not Ratzel, is the source of the organismic ideas in Geopolitik, but the geopoliticians regard Ratzel as ancestral to Kjellén. See Karl Haushofer et al., Bausteine zur Geopolitik (Berlin–Grünewald: Vowinckel, 1928), pp. 3, 32, and 49. Also Otto Maull, Politsche Geographie (Berlin: Bornstraeger, 1925), p. 23.

74Ratzel, Politische Geographie, p. 452.

75Lord Curzon of Kedleston, Frontiers, The Romanes Lecture, 1907 (2nd ed.; Oxford: The Clarendon Press, 1908).

76Ibid., pp. 3–4.

77For bibliography, see S. Whittemore Boggs, International Boundaries, A Study of Boundary Functions and Problems (New York: Columbia University Press, 1940), pp. 253–54.

78Curzon, op. cit., pp. 53–54.

79Ibid., p. 47.

80Ibid., p. 19. Adami (op. cit., p. 68) attributes the origin of the term "Scientific Boundary" to Lord Beaconsfield and its strategic definition to General Hamley, both in 1878.

81The Declaration also invokes "the laws of nature and of nature's God."

82Robert Coughlan, "Isaiah Bowman," Life, Oct. 22, 1945, pp. 118–29.

83Boggs, op. cit.

[84]Stephen B. Jones, *Boundary-Making, A Handbook for Statesmen, Treaty Editors, and Boundary Commissioners* (Washington: Carnegie Endowment for International Peace, 1945), pp. 4–11.

[85]Pounds suggests that the concept of natural boundaries may have been influenced by the prominence of rivers on sixteenth century maps. ("The Origin of the Idea of Natural Frontiers in France," op. cit., p. 155).

[86]C. O. Paullin, *Atlas of the Historical Geography of the United States*, edited by John K. Wright (New York and Washington: American Geographical Society and Carnegie Institution, 1932), pp. 34–36 and plate 47. New York was exceptional, since its claims were based on those of its allies and dependents, the Iroquois.

[87]Max Savelle, "The Forty-Ninth Degree of North Latitude as an International Boundary, 1719, The Origin of an Idea," *The Canadian Historical Review*, Vol. 38 (1957), pp. 183–201.

[88]William D. Pattison, *Beginnings of the American Rectangular Land Survey System, 1784–1800* (University of Chicago, Department of Geography, 1957).

[89]Paullin, op. cit., p. 33 and plate 46.

[90]Karl Haushofer, *Grenzen in ihrer geographischen und politischen Bedeutung* (2nd ed.; Heidelburg–Berlin–Magdeburg: Vowinckel, 1939).

[91]Karl Haushofer, "Das Wissen von der Grenze und die Grenzen des deutschen Volkes," *Deutsche Rundschau*, Vol. 50 (1924), p. 237. Haushofer calls this a German concept of boundaries and attributes it to Ratzel.

[92]Joseph J. Thorndike, Jr., "Geopolitics," *Life*, Dec. 21, 1942, p. 115.

[93]Nicholas John Spykman, *The Geography of the Peace*, edited by Helen R. Nicholl (New York: Harcourt, Brace, 1944), p. 7. The present writer is dubious about this statement but is giving Spykman's views, not his own.

[94]Nicholas John Spykman, *America's Strategy in World Politics* (New York: Harcourt, Brace, 1942).

[95]Nicholas John Spykman, "Frontiers, Security, and International Organization," *The Geographical Review*, Vol. 32 (1942), p. 437.

[96]Nicholas John Spykman and Abbie A. Rollins, "Geographic Objectives in Foreign Policy," *American Political Science Review*, Vol. 33 (1939), p. 391.

[97]*Ibid.*, pp. 392 and 394.

[98]"Frontiers, Security, and International Organization," op. cit., p. 444.

[99]Harold and Margaret Sprout, "Environmental Factors in the Study of International Politics," *The Journal of Conflict Resolution*, Vol. 1 (1957), p. 310.

[100]Stephen B. Jones, "The Power Inventory and National Strategy," *World Politics*, Vol. 6 (1954), pp. 421–452.

[101]Halford J. Mackinder, "The Round World and the Winning of the Peace," *Foreign Affairs*, Vol. 21 (1942–43), pp. 595–605. Spykman, *The Geography of the Peace*, op. cit., pp. 57–61.

[102]Sumner Welles, *The Time for Decision* (New York and London: Harper, 1944), pp. 336–61. Henry Morgenthau, Jr., *Germany Is Our Problem* (New York and London: Harper, 1945).

[103]Jones, *Boundary-Making*, op. cit., p. 44.

[104]Lest this give the impression that equalizing economic status will be quick or automatic, I refer the reader to Gunnar Myrdal's *Rich Lands and Poor, The Road to World Prosperity* (New York: Harper, 1957).

CLASSIFICATION

The classification of boundaries, as we have seen, can be carried out on the basis of two different types of criteria. They can be grouped from the point of view of their static characteristics—for instance, their correspondence to physiographic features, their separation of ethnic regions, their straightness, and so forth. This, basically, is a descriptive classification. It utilizes the morphological approach in political geography, and the classification is known as the *morphological* classification of boundaries.

Boundaries can also be classified according to their relationship with the cultural landscape. Some boundaries were established prior to the permanent occupation of areas by the present inhabitants. Indeed, some frontiers were parcelled out long before the advancing state penetrated them, by agreement with other interested powers. In such cases, the existing boundary strongly influenced the pattern of settlement that eventually developed. Elsewhere the frontier was slowly absorbed, expanding states met, and the boundary was finally defined after much deliberation, competition, and perhaps even friction. But in such cases patterns of settlement were already developing, so that the boundary ultimately established has a different relationship to the cultural realities of the area involved. A classification based on considerations such as this is referred to as the genetic classification of boundaries.

A Morphological Classification

Any glance at the world politicogeographical map indicates that boundaries, especially in the older parts of the political world, are seldom straight and that they zigzag continuously. Further scrutiny, with the aid of a physiographic map, shows that much of the total length of these boundaries follows physiographic features, like the Spanish–French boundary in Europe, the U.S.A.–Mexican boundary in America, and the Zambia–Southern Rhodesian boundary in Africa. These are grouped under the heading of *physiographic* boundaries, but this term requires careful use lest it be confused with the same term applied to the edges of physiographic regions. Several kinds of physiographic boundaries exist. One example has been mentioned: mountain ranges, lines of hills, and other prominent features in the landscape. A second type is the boundary that runs through relatively open land such as desert

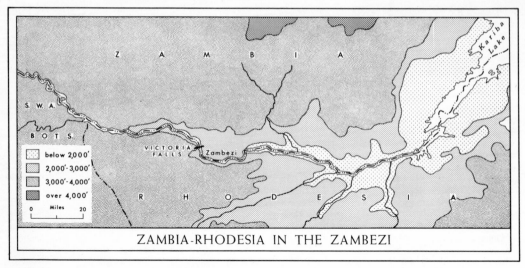

ZAMBIA-RHODESIA IN THE ZAMBEZI

country or swamps, marshes, or, in some cases, forests. Thirdly, there is the river boundary, and it presents special problems.

Physiographic-Political Boundaries. At first, rivers tended to act as divides, and performed their separating function especially well if floodplains were wide, increasing the difficulty of crossing them. As obvious, continuous, and permanent features in the landscape, they were protective barriers. But later in time, river valleys and floodplains came to perform different functions altogether. Transportation increased in volume, and river valleys form easy places for routes to be located; and the rivers themselves, if the gradient permits, can be very important arteries of trade and transport. Furthermore, the large rivers possess major basins, and economic (and often other cultural) development on both sides may be similar. Thus the divisive function be-

comes an artificial and inhibiting one for regional development. Many of the old core areas which included capital cities around which states were formed were located in river basins. With increased movement of men and goods, the place where the river reaches the sea became a very fortuitous one, with the whole surrounding region benefiting. The obstructive effect of a boundary located along such a river was well shown at the Italo–Yugoslav boundary in Fiume.[3]

Even when a river flows in a veritable canyon—few more divisive physiographic features could be imagined—problems may arise. Such was the case along the Tagus between Spain and Portugal and the Zambezi between Zambia and Rhodesia: hydroelectric power development created the difficulties.

[3] For a detailed examination of the Fiume problem see A. E. Moodie, *The Italo-Yugoslav Boundary*, London, Philip & Son, 1945.

CZECHOSLOVAKIA-GERMANY-POLAND

In addition to these general conditions, there is the question of the actual demarcation of the boundary along a river. Rivers have width. Any definition of a river boundary will have to be more specific than merely to state that it "runs along the river." There are, of course, three possibilities: (1) along one of the banks; (2) along the center line of the navigable channel; (3) along the median line. All three present serious difficulties.

The use of one of the banks is an unfair division of the river's attributes in terms of water supply (presumably the nonriparian state may not use water for irrigation or pumping) and transportation. The question of maintenance of the boundary bank cannot be solved satisfactorily. Furthermore, rivers have regimes; they are sometimes greater in volume than at other times. If the definition of the boundary states that it will "run along the contact between land and water on the right bank," then the boundary would shift with the changing volume of water of the river. This would be intolerable. If the boundary is fixed, then part of the nonriparian state is flooded and this would mean that it had right to water which, by definition, it cannot share. Certainly the use of one of the banks is not satisfactory.

Probably the most frequently adopted method has been that of the center line of the navigable channel. The Rhine and Danube have stretches where they perform this function. Again, the definition is not without problems. Navigable channels are the deepest parts of the rivers, and they are created by forces of river development which involve hydrology and physics. But simply stated, the navigable channel is rarely or never exactly in the middle of a stream, and second, a navigable channel is subject to constant modification. Thus although the buoys marking the international boundary stay fixed at the surface, the navigable channel may undergo such significant shifts that it is no longer possible to use it on both sides of the line of buoys. This requires constant adjustment. In addition, experience has shown that the buoy line degenerates and must be maintained, and some arguments have arisen concerning the state responsible for this maintenance.

The median line is a line equidistant from the river banks. The problems here are obvious from what has been said above. If the river is navigable, the navigable channel will swing from one side of the river to the other, and if the median line is the boundary this means that the navigable channel repeatedly crosses the international boundary thus established. In order to mark the median line, the exact location of the banks must be known or agreed upon, and this, in a river of changing volume and a wide floodplain, presents difficulties similar to those involved in the use of one bank as the boundary.

Finally, there is the boundary type that runs through lakes. Normally, the median line is used in these instances, as in the case of the U.S.A.–Canada boundary through lakes Superior, Huron, Erie, and Ontario. Although it would seem relatively unimportant to have boundaries within large water bodies, they are necessary in view of any urgent need for jurisdiction in cases of emergencies, fishing disputes, and the like. In East Africa, individual treaties were drawn up to satisfy the various countries bordering the Great Lakes there; there is a very uneven division of Lake Victoria between Uganda, Kenya, and Tanzania, based not upon a median line but upon lines of latitude and longitude drawn from the points where the international boundaries of these states reach the water.

Anthropogeographic Boundaries. The second major group of boundaries may be referred to as *anthropogeographic*. Again, this term has been used in other connections, and care should be taken with it. What is meant here by an anthropogeographic boundary is one that follows ethnic, linguistic, religious, and/or other dividing lines in the cultural landscape. No allusion is made to the manner in which this correspondence has come about; only its present existence plays a role. To recognize such boundaries, a map of the political boundaries of the world should be placed as an overlay over maps showing world regions of language, religion, race, and so on. On some occasions, cultural breaks and political boundaries will be seen to coincide. There will be evidence of the religious contrasts across the India-Pakistan boundary; ethnic differences exist across the boundaries between Israel and its Arab neighbors (though a sizable body of Arab population continues to live in Israel). Ethnic factors mark the internal boundaries of South Africa and a number of other African states: Zaire recently established more than twenty provinces on the basis of criteria that were largely ethnic

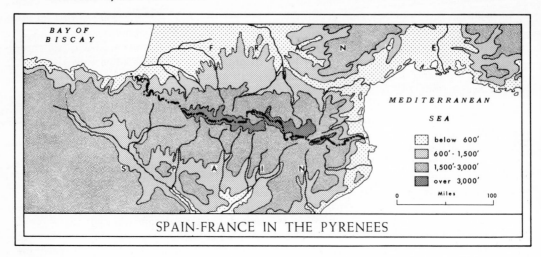

BAY OF
BISCAY

MEDITERRANEAN

SEA

below 600'
600' - 1,500'
1,500' - 3,000'
over 3,000'

0   Miles   100

SPAIN-FRANCE IN THE PYRENEES

(tribal). The United States-Mexico boundary falls into this category also.

Anthropogeographic boundaries sometimes coincide with physiographic boundaries. The boundary between Spain and France, for example, lying along the Pyrenees, is obviously physiographic in character, but there are several cultural constrasts across this border also. This may be a reflection of the historical role played by the physiographic feature in functioning as a barrier. A number of the trespass lines of history served to separate independently developing power cores, ·and some survived to become permanent, modern international boundaries.

Geometric Boundaries. A third group of boundaries is made up of those that can best be described as *geometric*. Most geometric boundaries appear on the map as ruler-stright lines drawn along parallels or lines of longitude. Another type of geometric boundary is represented by an arc, drawn by compass, from some point of definition. Examples of the first (straight) type can be found in North America, where the boundary between Canada and the United States west of the Great Lakes is mainly of the geometric variety; many of the boundaries of Africa, especially those traversing the desert regions, are straight lines also. The boundary dividing the island of New Guinea (Irian) into an Indonesian and an Australian sphere is geometric, as are most of the internal boundaries of Australia. Examples of the second (arc) type are harder to find, but one very small state in West Africa, Gambia, is entirely bounded by arcs drawn from the center of the river which gives the country its name—and shape.

Geometric boundaries were drawn either because the areas through which they lie were considered (at the time of boundary definition) to be useless wastes, or because rapid boundary delimitation was necessary for certain reasons. Many of the straight-line boundaries of Africa, for example, were defined at the 1884/1885 Berlin Conference, where the various colonial powers met to establish the limits of their hitherto ill-defined spheres of influence. Although it might be true that such boundaries are justified in areas such as the Sahara Desert and the Kalahari, where settlement of a permanent nature is either very limited or absent, there are other regions where geometric boundaries have become serious liabilities, for they correspond to none of the divisions existing, physiographic or anthropogeographic. The geometric boundary is today being used as a possible solution to the division of the Antarctic continent, where spheres of influence have begun to develop recently.

Indeterminate Boundaries. Finally, we should take account of boundaries that coincide neither with physiographic nor cultural breaks in the landscape, and which are *not* geometric. For want of a better term, we identify such boundaties as *indeterminate*. Examples would include much of the boundary between Tunisia nad Algeria, and sections of boundaries in the Amazon Basin between Brazil and its neighbors to the west and north.

A Genetic Classification

When relating a boundary to the cultural landscape through which it lies, we involve ourselves once again in a discussion of func-

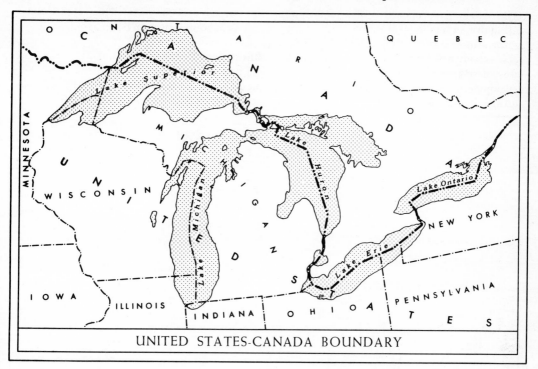

UNITED STATES-CANADA BOUNDARY

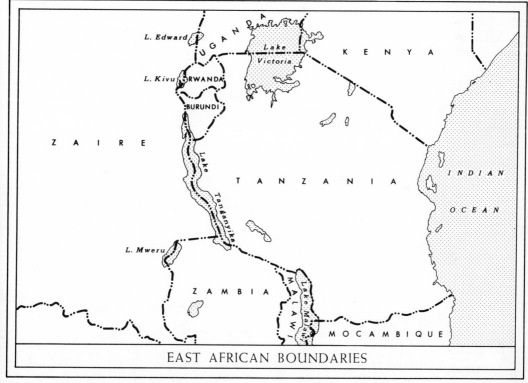

EAST AFRICAN BOUNDARIES

tions. Specifically, we are interested in the relationship between the boundary and the cultural landscape *at the time the boundary was established.* The original idea behind this approach is Hartshorne's,

and it was formulated in a paper read three decades ago.[4] Although some of the

[4]R. Hartshorne, "Suggestions on the Terminology of Political Boundaries," abstract, *Ann, A.A.G.,* 26 (March, 1936), p. 56.

terms originally proposed by Hartshorne are still in use, others have been replaced. Basically, the principle is as follows. Boundaries have been established either before the main patterns of settlement have evolved, during the development of the main elements of the cultural landscape, or after this development has already taken place. Thus three major groups of boundaries can be recognized.

Antecedent Boundaries. Boundaries that were defined and delimited before the main elements of the present-day cultural landscape began to develop are referred to as *antecedent*,

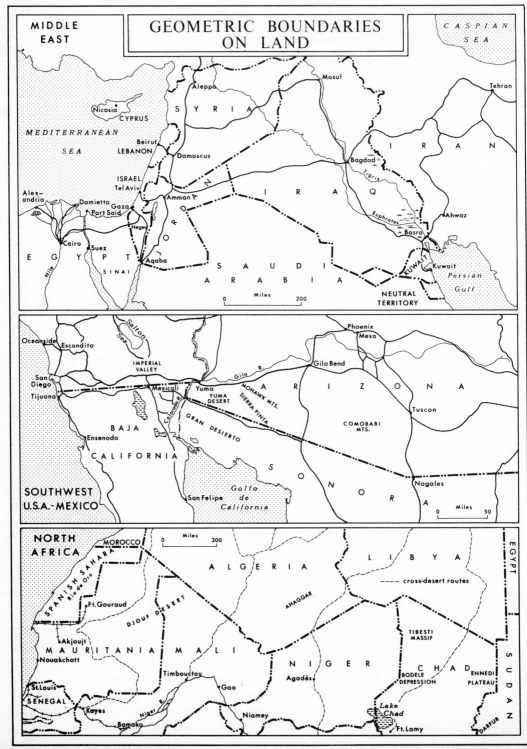

GEOMETRIC BOUNDARIES ON LAND

Concentrated activity in the desert. The discovery of resources (in this case, oil) under the desert sands may lead to a transformation of the barren countryside as a bustling hub of human activity develops. A nearby boundary, for decades undelimited and undemarcated, may suddenly acquire great significance, for the reservoir may extend under it. Now it may have to be demarcated with precision, and its antecedent characteristics will soon be relfected by the duplication of facilities on both sides—wells, pipelines, refineries, roads, and airfields (Standard Oil Co., New Jersey).

The boundary between Chile and Argentina was long the subject of a dispute which was eventually settled by arbitration. This photograph shows the marker erected to commemorate the settlement. In addition, it illustrates the difficult Andean terrain through which the boundaries lies. While the monument indicates the exact position of the boundary at one point, there is no barrier to divide the countries; some goods are seen temporarily stored at the customs shed at right. Weather data are also gathered at this point—see the small screen in the left foreground (Argentine Embassy).

...

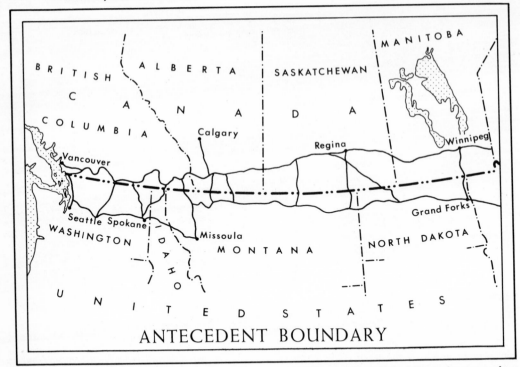

ANTECEDENT BOUNDARY

again a term used also in physical geography. A boundary might be drawn through a desert occupied only by some hundreds of wandering nomads, but a later discovery of petroleum can produce a completely new pattern of settlement. Thus, the boundary was there before the railroads, roads, airports, and other installations appeared on the scene. The boundary between the United States and Canada, west of the Great Lakes, was defined when the only representatives of the present-day majority population were some hunters, traders, and explorers. Today the boundary separates farms, towns, schools, all of which were established after the boundary, not before. Thus the boundary precedes the development of the main elements of the cultural landscape. Hartshorne recognized that it is possible to argue that even those few hunters and trappers, along with the Indian population of the border zone (in the U.S.-Canada example), might constitute at least a beginning in the evolution of settlement. Thus he differentiated between antecedent boundaries and *pioneer* boundaries, the latter running through absolutely unoccupied and undeveloped territory, which he described as "virginal."

Subsequent Boundaries. Some boundaries display a certain degree of conformity with the main and secondary elements of the cultural landscape through which they run. Having been established as the state systems evolving on either side expanded and met, these *subsequent* boundaries may lie along linguistic, religious, or ethnic breaks. The boundary upon which Chile and Argentina finally agreed (through the arbitration of King Edward VII) may be so classified. The religiously based Pakistan-India borders also fall into this category, as do a number of the boundaries of Europe. A subsequent boundary need not, however, always coincide with cultural breaks. The boundaries of Switzerland, for instance, which separate German-speakers from Germany and French-speakers from France, are nevertheless subsequent over the majority of their length. Here the major element in the formation and development of the state was the economic advantage of location, and the growth of the Swiss state shows how internal cultural heterogeneity need not always come about through the imposition of the will of an outside power.

Superimposed Boundaries. Truce lines are defined, delimited, and demarcated after the patterns of settlement have fully developed. Their existence may not be related to the local cultural landscape at all, but may result from confrontations between distant powers which have waged war in a particular area. Such boundaries, without any conformity to the cultural landscape, are *superimposed*. But truce lines are not the only type in this category. Colonial powers which divided

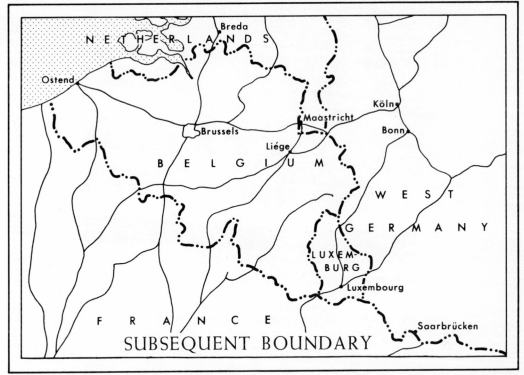

SUBSEQUENT BOUNDARY

among themselves the lands and peoples of Asia, Africa, and America established boundaries that split single tribes into two, three, or more political entities, often without the slightest concern for the cultural or economic conditions prevailing among the indigenous peoples. These boundaries have existed for so long that it is often forgotten how they came about. In many areas opposition to their functions of separation and division of related

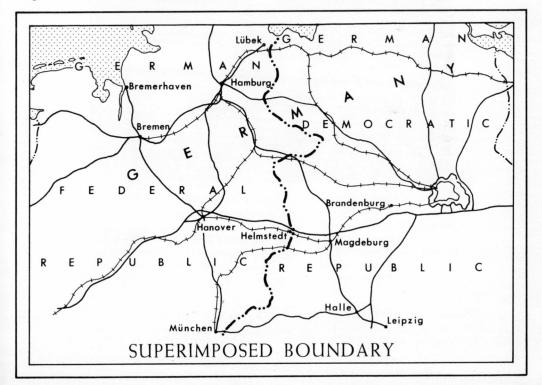

SUPERIMPOSED BOUNDARY

The demarcation of a superimposed boundary. In the Spree River, the Berlin Wall crosses several hundred feet of water. Shown here is the lowering of barbed-wire frames, designed to perform the same function as the Wall on land—the prevention of unauthorized crossing of the border (German Information Center).

A superimposed boundary cuts across railroad lines. This demarcated boundary separates West Germany from the German Democratic Republic. Here, it disrupts the railroad link between Bavaria and the industrial complex of Tettau. Those rails that lie astride the border have been left in position, marking the location of the formerly busy railroad, but those within East Germany have been removed and very little evidence of the former artery remains (German Information Center).

people continues and, with the emancipation of colonial areas, pressure on these borders has risen. The geometric boundary between Ethiopia and the Somali Republic, as we shall see later, is under severe stress, as is that between Kenya and Somalia. The Zaïre-Angola border divides a people who once formed part of an advanced political unit in the area of the lower Congo River—and the people have not forgotten their past. The geometric boundary be-

The Berlin Wall at the Brandenburg Gate. This is the eastern boundary of the West Berlin enclave, superimposed upon a city which for centuries has functioned as an undivided whole. The sign warning that one is now leaving West Berlin is a reminder of the days when the intra-Berlin boundary was demarcated only by markers and movable fences, and when traffic across it was so easy that visitors to the West often strayed into the East. Today, the Berlin Wall is perhaps the best example of a superimposed boundary: it separates people whose ties are those of a nation, it fragments a world metropolis, and exemplifies the division of a nation-state. But even after two decades, the contrasts across this boundary already are strong. Ideologically, economically, and perhaps even politically, intense differences are being engraved upon the once-united landscape—differences which time may prove to be ineradicable (German Information Center).

tween southern Angola and South West Africa, both still dependent territories, is a latent source of friction, for peoples here are divided as well. As long as the central authority is sufficiently strong to determine how effectively the boundary shall serve to separate, the boundary functions adequately. But with a weakening in this area, as has happened with the emergence of independent states in former colonies, the boundary fails and transgressions commence.

Truce lines such as the boundary between East and West Germany, the intracity boundary in Berlin now represented by the Wall, the 1953 cease-fire line in Korea, and the North-South Viet Nam border, all are recent examples in this category. The question is how long they will remain in place, for, as Fischer has pointed out, the longer a boundary exists and functions, the more difficult it is to alter in any way.[5] It is sometimes quite surprising to discover that a boundary of great permanency and familiarity was long ago established as a

[5]E. Fischer, "On Boundaries," World Politics, 1 (January, 1949), p. 196.

truce line with all the stresses and strains this entails. The boundary between the Netherlands and Belgium is such a case. Hartshorne used the term "entrenched" for the long-existing boundary, arguing that whatever the initial and intended functions of a boundary, it begins to affect the cultural landscape associated with it and ultimately becomes an inextricable part of that landscape.

Relic Boundaries. Occasionally boundaries do disappear from the map. With the emergence of recently decolonized territories as states, some amalgamation has taken place. In Africa the Somali Republic was created out of two former dependencies, British and Italian Somaliland. The Federal Republic of Cameroun consists of the former French trust territory of that name and the southern part of the former British Cameroons. Ghana consists of the British colony, the Gold Coast, and its eastern neighbor, former British Togoland, also a trust territory. Once, boundaries separated the political units involved, but when they joined in statehood, those boundaries disappeared. It

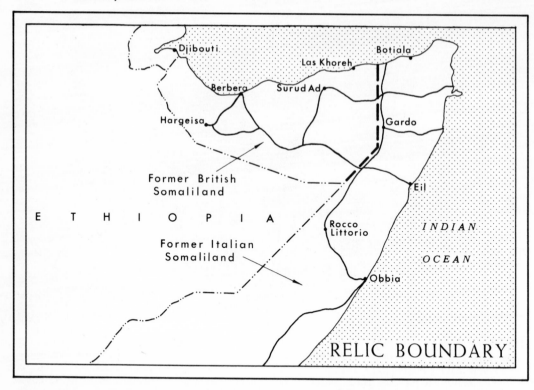

Djibouti

Botiala

Las Khoreh

Berbera   Surud Ada

Hargeisa

Gardo

Former British
Somaliland

Eil

E   T   H   I   O   P   I   A

Rocco
Littorio

INDIAN

Former Italian
Somaliland

OCEAN

Obbia

RELIC BOUNDARY

has happened in other parts of the world: European boundary shifts involving Germany and Poland, Ottoman influences in the Balkans, and Spanish elements in the cultural landscape of the southwestern United States, all mark a similar sequence of events. But although the boundaries may have disappeared from the map and may no longer have political significance, they often do remain noticeable on the ground. Sometimes it is possible to retrace the original border by paying attention to sudden changes in the cultural landscape: styles of architecture, layout of farms, place names, and other features may reveal the existence of the *relic* boundary. At times such boundaries continue to function as internal boundaries, reflecting the continued contrasts in the associated zones.

The use of these systems of classification greatly adds to the rapid communication of ideas in political geography. Boundaries may belong to a certain category in both the morphological and the genetic classification, and their identification in this manner tells us much concerning the nature of the state system of which they form a part. For example, a state whose boundaries can be described as mainly geometric and antecedent (Chad, Mauritania, Niger) is obviously in a condition that differs from one whose boun-

daries are geometric and superimposed (Korea of 1945; Somali Republic, Israel). Both, in turn, differ from states whose boundaries are anthropogeographic and subsequent (France, Pakistan, Thailand). Naturally there are sections that form exceptions to these generalizations, but this does not diminish the usefulness of the latter.

REFERENCES

Ahmad, Nafis, "The Indo-Pakistan Boundary Disputes Tribunal, 1949–1950," *Geog. Rev.*, 43, 3 (July, 1953), 329–337.

———, "The Revolution of the Boundaries of East Pakistan," *Oriental Geography*, 2, 2 (July, 1958), 97–106.

Alexander, Lewis M., "The Arab-Israeli Boundary Problem," *World Politics*, 6, 3 (April, 1954), 322–337.

———, "Recent Changes in the Benelux-German Boundary," *Geog. Rev.*, 43, 1 (January, 1953), 69–76.

Billington, Monroe, "The Red River Boundary Controversy," *Southwestern Historical Quart.*, 62, 3 (January, 1959), 356–363.

Bloomfield, L. M., *The British Honduras—Guatemala Dispute.* Toronto, Carswell Co., 1953.

———, and Gerald F. Fitzgerald. *Boundary Waters Problems of Canada and the United States.* Toronto, Carswell Co., 1958.

Boggs, S. Whittemore, *International Boundaries.* New York, Columbia University Press, 1940.

Bouchez, L. J., "The Fixing of Boundaries in International Boundary Rivers," *Int. and Comp. Law Quart.*, 12, 3 (July, 1963), 789–817.

Classen, H. George, "Keepers of the Boundary," *Canadian Geog. J.*, 65, 4 (October, 1962), 122–129.

Cumpstom, J. H. L., "The Story of the Boundaries," *Walkabout*, 17, 4 (April, 1951), 18–20.

Day, Winifred M., "Relative Permanence of Former Boundaries in India," *Scot. Geog. Mag.*, 65, 3 (December, 1949), 113–122.

Dayan, Moshe, "Israel's Border and Security Problems," *Foreign Affairs*, 33, 2 (January, 1955), 250–267.

Deutsch, Herman J., "A Contemporary Report on the 49° Boundary Survey," *Pacific Northwest Quart.*, 53, 1 (January, 1962), 17–33.

——, "The Evolution of the International Boundary in the Inland Empire of the Pacific Northwest," *Pacific Northwest Quart.*, 51, 2 (April, 1960), 63–79.

Fenwick, C. G., "The Honduras-Nicaragua Boundary Dispute," *Amer. J. Internat. Law*, 51, 4 (October, 1957), 761–765.

Fischer, Eric, "On Boundaries," *World Politics*, 1, 2 (January, 1949), 196–222.

Foulkes, C. H., "The Anglo-French Boundary Commission, Niger to Lake Chad," *Royal Engineers J.*, 73, 4 (December, 1959), 429–437.

Franck, Dorthea Seelye, "Pakhtunistan—Disputed Disposition of a Tribal Land," *Middle East J.*, 6, 1 (Winter, 1952), 49–68.

GilFillan, S. Columb, "European Political Boundaries," *Political Sci. Quart.*, 39, 3 (September, 1924), 458–484.

Goetzmann, W. H., "The United States-Mexican Boundary Survey, 1848–1853," *Southwestern Historical Quart.*, 62, 2 (October, 1958), 164–190.

Grey, Arthur L., "The Thirty-Eighth Parallel," *Foreign Affairs*, 29, 3 (April, 1951), 482–487.

Hale, Richard W., Jr., "The Forgotten Maine Boundary Commission," *Proc. Mass. Historical Soc.* (October, 1953-May, 1957), 71, (1959), 147–155.

Hall, Arthur R., "Boundary Problems in Cartography," *Surveying and Mapping*, 12, 2 (April-June, 1952), 138–141.

Hartshorne, Richard, "The France-German Boundary of 1871," *World Politics*, 2, 2 (January, 1950), 209–250.

——, "Suggestions on the Terminology of Political Boundaries," *Ann. A.A.G.*, 26, 1 (March, 1936), 56–57.

Hay, Sir Rupert, "The Persian Gulf States and Their Boundary Problems," *Geog. J.*, 120, Pt. 4 (December, 1954), 433–445.

Heslinga, M. W., *The Irish Border as a Cultural Divide. A Contribution to the Study of Regionalism in the British Isles.* New York, The Humanities Press, 1963.

Hirsch, Abraham M., "From the Indus to the Jordan; Characteristics of Middle East International River Disputes," *Political Sci. Quart.*, 71, 2 (June, 1956), 203–222.

Hodgkiss, A. G., and R. W. Steel, "The Changing Face of Africa," *Geography*, 46, Pt. 2, No. 211 (April, 1961), 156–160.

Hoffman, George W., "Boundary Problems in Europe," *Ann. A.A.G.*, 44, 1 (March, 1954), 102–107.

——, "The Netherlands Demands on Germany: A Post-War Problem in Political Geography," *Ann. A.A.G.*, 42, 2 (June, 1952), 129–152.

House, J. W., "The Franco-Italian Boundary in the Alpes Maritimes," *Trans. and Papers, Inst. Brit. Geographers*, Publ. No. 26 (1959), pp. 107–131.

Hutchison, Bruce, *The Struggle for the Border.* New York, Longmans, Green, 1955.

Jackson, W. A. Douglas, *The Russo-Chinese Borderlands.* Princeton, N.J., Van Nostrand, 1962.

Jones, Stephen B., *Boundary Making.* Washington, Carnegie Endowment for International Peace, 1945.

——, "The Cordilleran Section of the Canada-United States Borderland," *Geog. J.*, 89, 5 (May, 1937), 439–540.

——, "The Forty-Ninth Parallel in the Great Plains: the Historical Geography of a Boundary," *J. Geog.*, 31, 9 (December, 1932), 357–368.

Karan, Pradyumna P., "Dividing the Water: A Problem in Political Geography," *Prof. Geog.*, 13,) (January, 1961), 6–10.

——, "The India-China Boundary Dispute," *J. Geog.*, 59, 1 (January, 1960), 16–21.

——, "Indo-Pakistan Boundaries: Their Fixation, Functions and Problems," *Indian Geog. J.*, 28, 1–2 (January-June, 1953), 19–23.

Kelly, J. B., *Eastern Arabian Frontiers.* London, Faber and Faber, 1964.

Kingsbury, Robert C., "The Changing Map of Africa," *J. Geog.*, 59, 5 (May, 1960), 220–224.

Kusielewicz, Eugene, "New Light on the Curzon Line," *Polish Rev.*, 1, 2–3 (1956), 82–88.

Lloyd, Trevor, "The Norwegian-Soviet Boundary; A Study in Political Geography," *Norsk Geografisk Tidsskrift*, bind 15, hefte 5–6 (1956), 187–242.

——, "The Norwegian-Soviet Boundary in Lapland," *Internat. Geog. Congress*, 17th, Washington, D.C., 1952 (1957), pp. 533–538.

Lord, Robert Howard, "The Russo-Polish Boundary Problem," *Proc. Mass. Historical Soc.*, October, 1944-May, 1947, 68 (1949), 407–423.

McCune, Shannon, "The Thirty-Eighth Parallel in Korea," *World Politics*, 1, 2 (January, 1949), 223–232.

McKay, J. Ross. "The Interactance Hypothesis and Boundaries in Canada; A Preliminary Study," *Canadian Geographer*, No. 11 (1958), 1–8.

Moodie, A. E., "Some New Boundary Problems in the Julian March," *Trans. and Papers, Inst. Brit. Geographers*, Publ. No. 16, 1950, pp. 83–93.

Mosely, Philip E., "The Occupation of Germany: New Light on How the Zones Were Drawn," *Foreign Affairs*, 28, 4 (July, 1950), 580–604.

Nicholson, Norman L., *The Boundaries of Canada, Its Provinces and Territories.* Ottawa, Canada, Department of Mines and Technical Survey, Geographical Branch, Memoir No. 2, 1954.

Pitts, Forrest R., "The 'Logic' of the Seventeenth

Parallel as a Boundary in Indochina," *Yearbook of the Association of Pacific Coast Geographers, 18* (1956), 42–56.

Pounds, Norman J. G., *Divided Germany and Berlin.* Princeton, N.J., Van Nostrand, 1962.

———, "France and 'les limites naturalles' from the Seventeenth to the Twentieth Centuries," *Ann. A.A.G., 44,* 1 (March, 1954), 51–62.

———, "The Origin of the Idea of Natural Frontiers in France," *Ann. A.A.G., 41,* 2 (June, 1951), 146–157.

Prescott, J. R. V., "Africa's Major Boundary Problems," *Australian Geographer, 9,* 1 (March, 1963), 3–12.

———, "The Evolution of Nigeria's Boundaries," *Nigerian Geog. J., 2,* 2 (March, 1959), 80–104.

———, "The Evolution of the Anglo-French Inter-Cameroons Boundary," *Nigerian Geog. J., 5,* 2 (December, 1962), 103–120.

———, "Geographical Problems Associated with the Delimitation and Demarcation of the Nigeria-Kamerun Boundary 1885–1916," *Research Notes,* Ibadan University College, Department of Geography, No. 12 (February, 1959), 1–14.

Procházka, Theodore, "The Delimitation of Czechoslovak-German Frontiers after Munich," *J. Central European Affairs, 21,* 2 (July, 1961), 200–218.

Reyner, A.S., "The Case of an Indeterminate Boundary: Algeria-Morocco," *Duquesne University Institute of African Affairs,* No. 18, 1964, 1–7.

Savelle, Max, "The Forty-Ninth Degree of Latitude as an International Boundary, 1719: the Origin of an Idea," *Canadian Historical Rev., 38* (1957), 183–201.

Smit, P., "Recent Developments and Trends in Africa: Africa's Changing Political Pattern," *Tydskrif vir Aardrykskunde—Journal of Geography, 1,* 7 (September, 1960), 55–60.

Smith, S. G., "The Boundaries and Population Problems of Israel," *Geography, 37,* 177 (July, 1952), 152–165.

Stacey, C. P., *The Undefended Border; The Myth and the Reality.* Ottawa, Canadian Historical Association, 1953.

Thomas, Benjamin, "The California-Nevada Boundary," *Ann. A.A.G., 42,* 1 (March, 1952), 51–68.

Volacic, M., "The Curzon Line and Territorial Changes in Eastern Europe," *Belorussian Rev., 2* (1956), 37–72.

Weigend, Guide G., "Effects of Boundary Changes in the South Tyrol," *Geog. Rev., 40,* 3 (July, 1950), 364–375.

Whittam, Daphne E., "The Sino-Burmese Boundary Treaty," *Pacific Affairs, 34,* 2 (1961), 174–183.

U. S. Department of State. Office of the Geographer. *International Boundary Studies,* 1961 ff.

CHAPTER
9

THE CONCEPT OF
THE TERRITORIAL SEA

Less than 30 per cent of the Earth's surface is land area; more than 70 per cent of it is water. The oceans and what lies beneath them form part of man's life support system, and multiplying man, having already severely strained the terrestrial components of that system, is intensifying his search for wealth in and below the seas. Resources that once lay beyond our reach can now be exploited, for the technological advances that have been made in recent years allow us to drill for oil in water hundreds of feet deep and to search by completely new methods for minerals hidden in the floors of the oceans. Undoubtedly our capacity to do these things will grow enormously in the next several decades, and there may eventually be little left on this planet that is beyond our grasp.

So it has been with our "harvesting" of the oceans' fish resources. Decades ago there was little prospect that this harvest could be endangered by excessive exploitation; consider the vastness of the oceans, the volume of their waters, and the comparative minuteness of even a fleet of fishing trawlers. But in the 1970's things are different; floating canning factories and thousands of fishing vessels, automated systems, and new devices to locate fish schools have begun to seriously endanger the survival of several species. And so the states argue among themselves about who owns how much of the world's waters, who should sign treaties to limit annual catches, and who fails to live up to the treaty obligations. As the era of colonialism on land comes to an end, we seem to be entering a new period of competition among states for territorial supremacy: an era of maritime aggrandizement. Eventually, the spoils of this maritime competition may prove to be greater than those the colonial ventures ever produced. So may be the risks to all mankind.

THE BEGINNING

This is not to suggest that man's intense interest in the seas dates from the twentieth century, or that ancient seafarers such as the Phoenicians and the Greeks did not take a proprietary view of some of the waters they travelled. On the contrary; possession of the waters that separated these peoples' fragmented habitat was of greater importance than the acquisition of extensive hinterlands. The decline of ancient Greece was due, to a large extent, to an imbalance in military organization, and Greek preoccupation with the sea was linked to a vulnerability on land. The Roman Empire, on the other hand, managed to combine sea power with effective organization on land. The Mediterranean became what the Greeks had never been able to make it, an interior sea.

The Romans ventured far beyond the Mediterranean, for we have descriptions of Indian Ocean coasts written by Roman sea captains. But in the centuries that followed, the oceans remained an insurmountable barrier to Europe. Chinese vessels reached the eastern coast of Africa while the Dark Ages settled over the European continent. Not until the ascent to power of the Spanish and Portuguese Empires on the Iberian Peninsula, almost a dozen centuries after the fall of Rome, did the oceans begin once again to form a link between Europe and other parts of the world. Since then, the link has been permanent, and the oceans have carried European power to all parts of the globe. In search of land and resources, the Spanish and Portuguese vessels returned home with new knowledge of the earth. Soon, there were competitors for the domination of the ocean routes to spices, gold, and slaves. The Hollanders successfully challenged the Portuguese; the English challenged the Dutch. Once the oceans had contained Europe, and now they were the routes to wealth and power.

The development of overseas "spheres of influence" began almost immediately. So intense was the competition for control in the

Americas that Spanish and Portuguese interests were limited by the Treaty of Tordesillas even before the end of the fifteenth century. The treaty, in fact, constitutes a first attempt to define and delimit a geometrical boundary: known as the "Pope's Line," it divided the yet unexplored world into a Spanish and a Portuguese realm, the boundary lying along the meridian 370 leagues west of the Cape Verde Islands.[1] The Portuguese established themselves along the west coast of Africa, and made contact with the Arabs plying the eastern coasts. The Dutch laid claim to major portions of southeast Asia and established settlements and fortifications in a multitude of other places, including Cape Town. Danes, Brandenburgers, English, French, Germans, Italians—all entered the scramble for overseas possessions at one time or another.

While the oceans had thus become avenues of conquest and power, they also became a threat to coastal communities, not only in the colonized world but also in Europe itself. A powerful state that could invade the Americas, Africa, or Asia could also assert its strength in Europe by attacking actual or potential competitors. Hitherto frontiers had acted as separating agents on land, and it was never difficult to interpret the intentions of any army moving into such frontiers, whether such an army was one of occupation or conquest. But a group of vessels approaching offshore might simply be passing toward some distant land, or might suddenly attack, having approached unmolested to within a few hundred yards of the coast!

It is not a matter for surprise that the Dutch were among the first to recognize the need for a zone of water that was to belong to the state, and over which the state would possess sovereignty as though it were a piece of its land territory. Attacked during eighty years from land as well as from the sea by Spain (1568–1648), its subsequent Golden Age brought prosperity, envy, and, above all, many pirates along its coast. In previous centuries the Dutch had already been involved in disputes over fishing rights in the North Sea. Hence they were very interested in the acquisition of sovereignty over their adjacent waters. Their interests were strongly championed by a Dutch Jurist, Cornelius van Bynkershoek, whose name is among those most closely associated with the development of the legal concept of the territorial sea.

THE DEVELOPMENT OF CLAIMS TO TERRITORIAL WATERS

"Never have national claims in adjacent seas been so numerous, so varied, or so inconsistent," exclaimed Boggs in 1951.[2] Nevertheless, such claims are nothing new. In the thirteenth and fourteenth centuries, the Norwegians, Danes, English, and Dutch exercised control over various parts of the North Sea and North Atlantic Ocean. They did so by treaty or ordinance, and usually the areas claimed were not precisely defined. In the fourteenth century, activity in the North Sea greatly increased. The Dutch fishing fleet expanded, and fishing vessels from Flanders, France, and England joined in the search for the best fishing grounds. Sporadic friction occurred, but it was not until the end of the sixteenth century that the question of countries' rights on neighboring waters developed into a full-scale legal battle.

In the 1590's the Danes, to whom power had gone from Norway, decided to abandon the "closed sea" practice they had inherited from the Norwegians.[3] Instead, they announced that a belt of water, eight miles in width, lying around their possession of Iceland, constituted Danish territorial waters. Some of northwestern Europe's best fishing grounds lie off the Norwegian, Icelandic, and Faeroe coasts, and soon the Danish crown defined similar belts around all these possessions.[4] It was not long before they increased these widths: in the mid-seventeenth century they claimed as much as twenty-four miles.[5] The English, meanwhile, had drawn baselines along the British coast from promontory to promontory, cutting off large portions of the coastal waters; some of these baselines were more than fifty miles in length. Furthermore the English demanded that the Dutch and others fishing near their coasts obtain permits to do so.

[2]S. W. Boggs, "National Claims in Adjacent Seas," *Geog. Rev.*, 12, 2 (1951), 185.

[3]In the thirteenth century, Norwegian law included the stipulation that no foreign vessels were permitted to sail north of the latitude of Bergen without a Norwegian Royal License. Norway eventually became part of the Danish Realm, and the Danes maintained this practice.

[4]All measurements in this and the following chapter are in nautical miles. Once nautical mile is 1.151 statute miles.

[5]For details see H. S. Kent, "The Historical Origins of the Three-Mile Limit," *Amer. J. Internat. Law*, 48 (1954), 537.

[1]Hence Portuguese cultural influence dominates Brazil, while Spanish influences lie to the west. According to the treaty, land to the west of the meridian should go to Spain, land to the east should become Portuguese.

Thus began the legal debate that ultimately produced many of the principles to which states still adhere today. The Dutch, who did not have large coastal bays and identations, argued that the closing off of the sea constituted violation of "customary" international law. Early in the seventeenth century a Dutch jurist, Grotius, published a treatise, the significant part of which was called *The Free (Open) Sea*. The British legal expert Selden soon replied under the title of *The Closed Sea*. During these opening stages of the lengthy dispute, one idea emerged that kept the negotiators occupied for many decades to come: that the limit of the territorial sea should be determined not by arbitrary baseline drawing, but by the distance a cannon, standing on the shore, could fire a cannon ball.

As the seventeenth century wore on, the argument grew in intensity. Indeed, it was a major contributor to four naval wars fought between the English and the Hollanders, while the legal debate raged on in the intervening periods. The Dutch objected to restrictions of any kind other than a narrow belt of territorial sea perhaps determined by the cannon-shot rule; the British stood firm on the principle of extensive closed seas. But time was on the side of the Hollanders. Like the Dutch, the English came to depend to an ever greater extent on their growing merchant fleet, and they wanted that fleet to face as few obstacles as possible. Thus by the end of the seventeenth century the English had begun to realize that their policy of closed seas could not be reconciled with their dependence upon free oceanic trade. Thus they yielded to some extent to Dutch desires, and the debate now came to focus upon the problem of the manner by which the extent of any belt of territorial sea should be determined.

Again, two schools of thought existed. Whereas the question previously had revolved around "free" or "closed" seas, it now concerned the principle of effective occupation as opposed to that of a continuous (if narrow) belt of territorial sea along all coasts. This is the point where the name of Cornelius van Bynkershoek enters the legal controversy. Van Bynkershoek, the Dutch jurist, was probably the most vocal and energetic legal expert ever to become involved in this question, and as a result, many innovations are attributed to him which actually seem to have been thought up by others. But Van Bynkershoek had the ability to express himself so well and convincingly that his name has become inextricably attached to a number of rules and definitions—among them, the cannon-shot rule. In fact, he was *not* the inventor of that rule, as we have seen, but he was, without doubt, its most effective supporter.

Van Bynkershoek, while agreeing that states could indeed claim sovereignty over water just as they could over land, felt that such sovereignty should be recognized only if one of two conditions were satisfied. First, no state could claim adjacent waters over which it did not have control by force of arms—in other words, shore-based cannon. A fortification on a promontory would imply control over a surrounding stretch of water by virtue of the existence of means of enforcement. But where such means did not exist, he argued, the state could not claim any water at all. Thus an unguarded coast should not have territorial waters adjacent to it: only free and open water for all to use. If a state wished to control any part of such a coast, it should build fortifications and position cannons to support its claim.

Second, Van Bynkershoek produced the principle of "intended and continuous occupation." He did indeed feel that a state had the right to claim, for permanent possession, any part of the sea over which it exercised such effective control, whether adjacent to its coast or not. What constituted "intended and continuous control?" Only the presence of a fleet. Few states would be able or willing to secure any part of the sea permanently by placing a fleet there; hence, Van Bynkershoek reasoned, the only relevant question remained that of domination from shore.

Van Bynkershoek's *De Dominio Maris Dissertatio*, first published in 1702 and revised in 1744, summarized the entire question as it stood at that time, established a terminology that is still in use today, and brought the Dutch standpoint forcefully to the attention of the English. The English favored the concept of a continuous belt of equal width rather than Van Bynkershoek's shore-domination principle, and this time the English idea came to be generally accepted. The Danes, French, and Italians preferred the equal-width zone of territorial water also, and now the problem was one of determining the exact width of such a belt.

This particular problem—concerning the width of the territorial sea—is still the subject of world controversy today. Looking at west-

The North Sea waters have been fished by its coastal peoples for many centuries. As fishing techniques have improved and fish resources dwindled, competition has become more intense. The economies of some regions and even countries depend on the annual fish harvest to such an extent that armed confrontations have occurred over fishing rights. The photograph shows a part of the fleet of the Scottish port of Lossiemouth (Harm J. de Blij).

ern and northwestern Europe in the eighteenth century, the divergence of opinion seems minimal compared to that which prevails at present. The Danes in 1745 announced that they would claim a width of one league, equal to four nautical miles. The Dutch agreed to observe a belt of equal width, but they insisted upon using the cannon-shot as their determinant. Galiani, an Italian writer, is credited with the proposal that three miles be used as the generally acceptable standard width. In fact, just how the three-mile limit, which was the most generally accepted in the first half of the present century, came about is still a matter of research. Smith has attributed it to Galiani,[6] and Walker also has argued that Van Bynkershoek, to whom it has been credited, was not in fact the originator.[7] But Galiani himself apparently based his suggestion upon what he viewed as the maximum range of the cannon of that day—military experts have determined that the range of eighteenth century cannons probably did not exceed a mile. Whatever the origins of the three-mile limit, when the United States and Britain, around the turn of the nineteenth century, adopted this as their maritime boundaries, it

rapidly became the most common claim in many parts of the world.

During much of the nineteenth century and the first half of the twentieth, by virtue of European colonial control and the application of European claims to overseas possessions, the situation remained relatively stable. There were disputes over European fishing grounds and several separate treaties were signed among interested states, but until the second World War those states that thrived partly or largely on their overseas trade maintained the three- or four-mile limit. In 1951, 80 per cent of the merchant-shipping tonnage of the world was registered in countries that subscribed to the three-mile limit, and another 10 per cent to states adhering to the four-mile limit. Today, more and more states are claiming twelve and even more miles as their territorial sea, bays are being closed off, fishing disputes growing in number and intensity, and the range of claims and justifications is unprecedented. The problem has once again become one of major international concern.

IS SOVEREIGN POWER OVER ADJACENT WATERS NECESSARY?

The state territorial system, as we have observed, requires a number of elements to function properly. It needs territory, resources,

[6]H. A. Smith, *The Law and Custom of the Sea*, London, Stevens and Sons, 1948, p. 14.

[7]W. L. Walker, "The Territorial Waters: The Cannon Shot Rule," *Brit. Yearbook Internat. Law*, 22 (1945), p. 210.

a population with nation-characteristics, land boundaries, a capital city. Does such a state, located on a coast, require a maritime boundary as well? Is the maritime boundary an essential part of the state system of today, and are the conditions that led, centuries ago, to the practice of claiming territorial waters still facing the state?

Two factors affect the nature of the seaward edge of continents, and therefore states. Due to geological factors which have not been fully explained, the slope of the land surface of the continents is continued under the water of the oceans to a depth of on the average one hundred fathoms, after which a relatively sharp increase in angle of slope is noted. The relatively flat continuation of the continent is the continental *shelf*, and it is bounded by the continental *slope*. Continental shelves are found off coastlines of emergence as well as submergence, and also off compound shorelines, and there does not appear to be a direct relationship between the nature of the coastline and the adjacent shelf.

Along many coasts, thus, the water's depth increases gradually, and some miles out into sea the depth of the water may not exceed one hundred fathoms. On the other hand, there are coastlines that are marked by abrupt cliffs, stacks, and fault scarps (Madagascar's east coast is the classic example) and where the water a few hundred yeards offshore is many hundreds of fathoms deep. In other words, the continental shelf may vary in width from many miles to some yards, and it may even be absent. Its edge is not found at a uniform depth and may occur at less than one hundred or even two hundred fathoms.

However, irregularities do not occur only in depth, nor are they confined to the seaward edge of the shelf. The actual contact of the land and sea, one of the geomorphologists' greatest problems of definition, the shoreline, is rarely straight and never continuously so. Submerged coasts are marked by estuaries and bays, emerged coasts by offshore bars and lagoons. Elsewhere fiords have been carved by great glaciers, and these valleys are now inundated by water. The emerged coast is usually of the more straight variety; the submerged coast is embayed, and the fiorded coastline is marked by long, narrow peninsulas, small, rocky islands and penetrating tongues of water.

If the complexity of the coasts is so great, then, why do maritime states insist upon the extension of their sovereignty over the waters immediately adjacent to their shores? In attempting to list the causes for this action it is necessary to emphasize the stage of evolution of the modern state. Having absorbed all the habitable land on the earth, and having eliminated practically all the early frontiers of history, states are today bounded by vertical planes which are expressed on the surface of the earth by boundary lines. Such boundaries are marked on maps and demarcated on the surface with a greater or lesser degree of clarity. The most distinguishing factor of the twentieth-century political map is that each state is bounded by such lines, although these boundaries are not always permanent and some areas are still being contested.

Growth from the nucleus and expansion into the separating frontier zones has now ceased, although the Antarctic is still the scene of such activity. But today's frontier zones are the oceans, and even they are decreasing in their effectiveness as separating agents with the development of rapid means of transportation. Every year, an increasing number of ships sail the oceans, and the resources of the waters are won in larger quantities. As intercontinental trade increases, many previously isolated and land-oriented states (though not landlocked) are now turning toward the seas for trade, fishing, and expansion.

It is true that certain states which have recently acquired independence find their taste for expansion unsatisfied. In a later section it will be shown that the majority of the older and established states satisfy themselves with a less exorbitant seaward limit than such states as Indonesia, which wishes to establish sovereign power over all waters within twelve miles from the outer islands. Those states that suddenly recognize their power through independence, not having experienced the lengthy evolution of the European states, seem to expend their expansionist tendencies on the adjacent seas, not having had the oportunity to expand into frontier zones on land.

This alone, however, is not a reason for the establishment of a seaward boundary for maritime states. For an evaluation of these reasons we may return to the states of Western Europe, which have for centuries depended on the seas for some of their wealth and to whom order on the seas is of the greatest importance. The continental shelves alluded to previously are especially extensive under the North Sea, and here, along the Norwegian coast and near Iceland, are some of the richest commercial fishing grounds on earth. As long as Western Europe has harbored seafaring peoples, these fish resources have been exploited. Often it is true that the most favorable grounds occur very close to the shores of the continent, and it is natural that from the earliest times the people living along these coasts and depending for their livelihood upon the water have looked upon the adjacent seas as theirs to fish on. Very early in history, disputes arose between countries of Western Europe concerning the ownership of fishing grounds close to the shore, and the need for some suitable arrangement was obvious.

Wars have demonstrated the need for a maritime boundary repeatedly. Wishing to remain neutral, a state might have found this to be impossible without a protective territorial sea. In the Western Hemisphere during the early part of the second World War the Treaty of Panama was designed to maintain a security zone some three hundred miles wide along the American states.

In recent decades, the mineral potential of the continental shelf has been recognized, and its exploitation has contributed to the economic power of some states. The recovery of oil from the continental shelf has demonstrated better than any other factor the need for division of both the surface of the sea and the underlying rock. The drilling for oil near the very beaches of one state by companies of another state is an unacceptable situation, although a position not very different from this has recently existed off the east coast of Mexico.

Problems of sanitation, and pollution, the jurisdiction over bays and estuaries of great width, the fight against smuggling—all require that a maritime state extend its sovereign power over the seas. Indeed, if the matter were only one of territorial waters, it would be relatively simple. But there are many associated factors. A state that claims only a narrow belt as territorial sea may wish to establish the right of searching suspicious vessels farther out, before they have come so close to the shore. The exercise of that right immediately gives that coastal state a certain (if small) amount of influence in a belt beyond its maritime boundary. Another state may wish to prevent ships disposing of waste fuel or

Exploration and exploitation of the continental shelf and subsoil. Several man-made islands dot the High Seas off the North American coast. In the foreground is a crane-legged drilling barge, complete with permanent quarters and flight deck for helicopter shuttle of crews. Such structures, obviously, endanger navigation, and the coastal state has the responsibility for its protection. The appearance of such structures as these along the shore of a foreign state can lead to serious disputes (Standard Oil Co., New Jersey).

other pollution while they are still outside the territorial sea. Again, the state has some influence in the supposedly "open" high seas. Hence it has become necessary to recognize, in addition to the territorial waters, a series of contiguous zones marking the maritime borders of coastal states.

ZONES

Zones lying beyond the territorial sea have been defined for centuries, and it is important once again to realize that we are not here dealing with a new phenomenon in the international politicogeographical scene. Denmark and England, while claiming a narrow belt of territorial water in the late seventeenth century, nevertheless also insisted upon a wider belt of "neutrality" or "customs." Britain, for example, in 1736 announced that a twelve-mile customs zone existed; the Danes claimed a four-mile (one-league) neutrality zone. The United States, likewise, in 1790 claimed jurisdiction for purposes of customs inspection to a distance of twelve miles from shore, although a three-mile territorial waters boundary was recognized. During the period of prohibition, the U.S. signed a number of "liquor treaties" with other states, permitting this country to search vessels that were within one hour's sailing distance from shore. The Anti-Smuggling Act of 1935, subsequently, authorized the President to establish, in the event that it should become necessary, customs-control points located up to fifty miles beyond that twelve-mile limit.[8]

No less than five zones can now be distinguished along the coasts of maritime states. First, there are the *internal waters* of the state, consisting of lagoons, closed estuaries, river mouths, natural harbors, and bays which are indisputably part of the land area of the state, either because they are almost completely closed off by land or because they are filled by fresh rather than salt water (and thus could not be construed as part of the sea). The recognition of internal waters is important, as we shall see later, in the determination of the seaward boundary of the state. An internal water body may be closed off by a straight line (a baseline) drawn across whatever seaward opening it may have. The territorial sea, then, is measured from that baseline, and the internal waters are not technically part of that territorial sea.

The second zone, the *territorial waters*, is

[8]G. von Glahn, *Law Among Nations*, New York, Macmillan, 1965, p. 314.

that belt of sea water of which the outer edge legally constitutes the boundary of the state. Its width varies from state to state, depending upon the most recent internationally announced claim. Within the territorial waters, the state possesses exactly the same sovereign rights that it does on its land territory. Ships that arrive in port have already entered the state's domain, even though the port may lie exposed along the coast rather than inland along a river. A crime committed aboard while the ship was between the limit of the territorial waters and the port will be treated as though it occurred while the vessel was docked alongside a quay. A crime that occurred just outside the territorial waters may be treated differently.

Beyond the territorial sea lies the *contiguous zone*, in which the state may have certain powers, including, as we have noted, customs inspection. Here, the state may insist that certain regulations which apply within its territorial waters continue to be observed. In 1958, a conference was held by interested states in Geneva, known as the Geneva Convention on the Law of the Sea. Article 24 of the Convention on the Territorial Sea and the Contiguous Zone provides that a state may exercise, within the contiguous zone, controls pertaining to immigration, sanitation, and fiscal regulations, as well as general customs. But the Convention also stipulated that the contiguous zone should not exceed twelve miles from the points from which the territorial sea is also measured. Thus a state possessing a three-mile territorial water limit could, by that Convention, claim a nine-mile contiguous zone, but a state claiming twelve miles as its territorial sea could not, theoretically, claim a contiguous zone of any kind.

One important decision emerging from the 1958 Convention was the negation of a request of a number of coastal states that they be granted exclusive fishing rights in their contiguous zones. For these purposes, the Convention decided, the contiguous zone is in fact high seas, unless individual treaties are signed by all interested parties.

The fourth zone which has been recognized is the *zone of diffusion*.[9] This ill-defined zone

[9]For a detailed summary of these zones, and a general discussion of the maritime boundary problem, focusing upon the area where many of the basic concepts involved were formulated, see L. M. Alexander, *Offshore Geography of Northwestern Europe*, Association of American Geographers and Rand McNally, 1964. The zone of diffusion is discussed on pp. 67, 68.

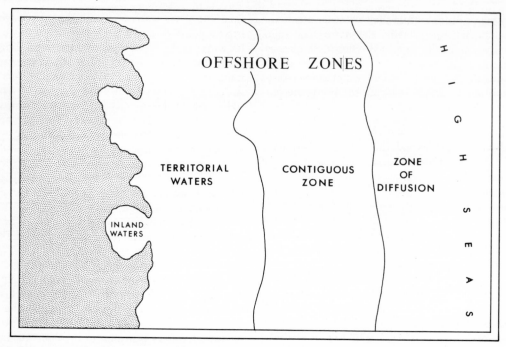

OFFSHORE ZONES

TERRITORIAL WATERS

CONTIGUOUS ZONE

ZONE OF DIFFUSION

INLAND WATERS

HIGH SEAS

includes such waters lying beyond the twelve-mile limit of the contiguous zone and within which certain states possess or claim some influence. The zone of diffusion does not have the international sanction of the contiguous zone, and, as its name implies, it is a belt of widely scattered and intermittent claims. The terms of the Anti-Smuggling Act of 1935, for example, help create this zone. Some states have stated that they will not permit navy maneuvers there by vessels of other states (except, of course, allied forces). Some of the claims to fishing monopoly made by certain states have gone beyond the twelve-mile limit. Furthermore, some states have arbitrarily selected parts of the seas and oceans for their purposes: the testing of missiles and other weaponry, for example. The basis for this, unlike the other zones so far discussed, is power. Any state that has the power to support is claims in the zone of diffusion can do so, for there is no legal machinery to stop it. And the very existence of the zone of diffusion emphasizes the fact that the problem of the freedom of the seas is a changing and growing one.

The fifth zone, then, is made up of those bodies of water to which no claims have been laid: the *high seas*. Actually, the contiguous zone and the zone of diffusion are technically parts of the high seas, but the influence of states in these zones is such that several of the freedoms of the high seas are seriously

abridged. Indeed, the high seas are in many ways the last frontiers on earth. Here, exploration and research are carried on without restriction, states compete with one another for resources of various kinds, vessels carrying every conceivable flag traverse uncontrolled spaces. And states are penetrating these frontiers, seeking to extend control over them, just as they did over the land frontiers of the past.

THE CONTINENTAL SHELF

Whereas the problems associated with the territorial sea are centuries old and have been the subject of legal debate since the seventeenth century, the question of the continental shelf has emerged only recently, in fact, since 1945. In that year, President Truman of the United States issued Proclamation No. 2667 (September 28), a far-reaching document which was to become known as the Truman Declaration. It claimed for the United States sovereignty over the "seabed and subsoil" of the adjacent continental shelf (though not over the waters lying above it), and within months several other states followed suit, claiming, in addition to the seabed and subsoil, the waters lying above the continental shelf, described as the *epicontinental sea*. In South America several states made unprecedented claims on this basis: Chile in 1947 and Ecuador and Peru in 1952 announced that they claimed sovereignty over two-hundred miles of adjacent waters. In subsequent years, other states, including Argentina (1966), Uruguay (1969), and Brazil (1970) claimed a maritime boundary 200 miles offshore. Maritime powers protested, but the claims have survived various tests. In 1954 the Onassis whaling fleet was arrested by Peruvian navy vessels within the two-hundred-mile territorial sea and not released until Peru had secured three million dollars in "damages." In 1971, United States fishing vessels were similarly arrested in the "territorial" waters of Ecuador.

The problem of the continental shelf became a most complex one in a very short span of time, and the United Nations called upon the International Law Commission to address itself to this question without delay. The Commission recommended that the continental shelf be defined as extending to a depth of two hundred meters, and that littoral states be recognized as exercising sovereignty over the shelf for the purposes of exploring and exploiting the resources it may contain. These rights, however, should not affect the waters lying above the shelf: these should remain high seas.

The 1958 Geneva Convention on the Law of the Sea produced a treaty embodying the above proposals, stipulating that any decision by a coastal state not to exploit such resources as

the continental shelf might contain would not mean that it thereby abandoned its sovereignty there: no other state could without permission exploit these resources. However, the coastal state possessing sovereignty over the shelf should not obstruct the laying or maintenance of cables and pipelines on the seabed, and its exploration and exploitation of the shelf's resources should not in any way interfere with navigation, fishing, or any other activity carried on in the high seas. The coastal state, in carrying on the exploitation of continental shelf resources, was permitted to build installations for that purpose, but would at the same time be responsible for the safety of shipping, and could not interfere with established shipping lanes. Such installations as were built would not have the status of islands, and they would therefore not possess their own territorial sea.

One problem related to the continental shelf involves marine organisms which live in the waters of the high seas but on the seabed in a sedentary fashion as, for example, oysters. The Convention determined that "living organisms belonging to sedentary species" belong to the coastal state and cannot be pursued by other states. Thus states with pearl fisheries saw their industries protected. Nevertheless, a minor crisis arose between Brazil and France over the interpretation of this language. French fishing vessels continued to fish for

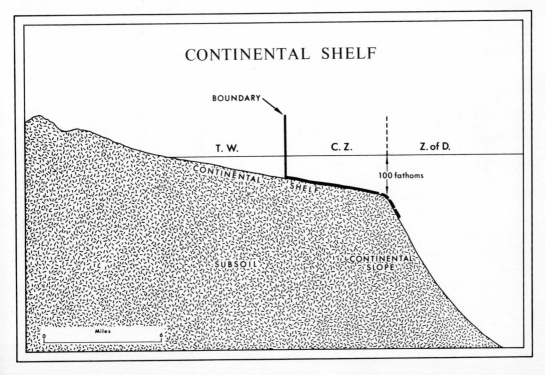

CONTINENTAL SHELF

BOUNDARY

T. W.   C. Z.   Z. of D.

CONTINENTAL SHELF

100 fathoms

SUBSOIL   CONTINENTAL SLOPE

Miles

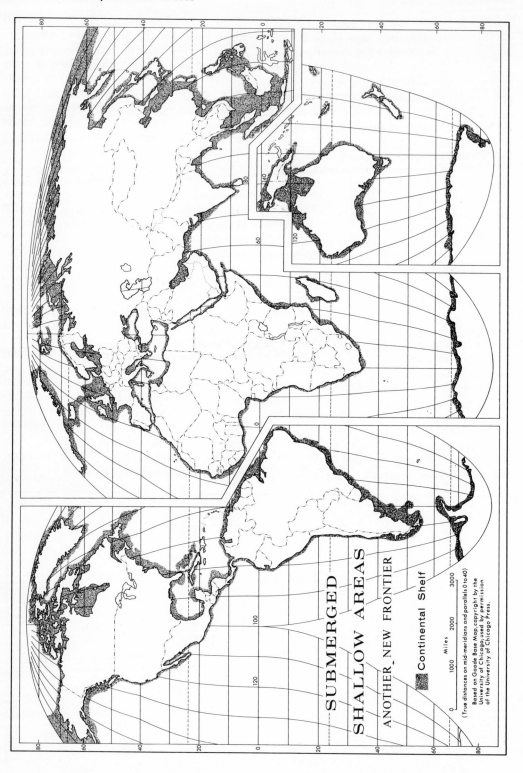

SUBMERGED SHALLOW AREAS

ANOTHER NEW FRONTIER

Continental Shelf

Miles

0   1000   2000   3000

(True distances on mid-meridians and parallels 0 to 40)

Based on Goode Base Map, copyright by the
University of Chicago, used by permission
of the University of Chicago Press.

Seven miles off the Louisiana shore in the Gulf of Mexico, this well, which belongs to Humble Oil Company, stands upon the continental shelf, in international waters. (Standard Oil Co., New Jersey).

lobsters on the Brazilian shelf, the French claiming that lobsters are not "sedentary" and rely on the waters of the high seas to a greater extent than they do on the seabed. The Brazilians took the opposite view, and warships confronted each other before the French yielded on the matter. In 1971 United States and Soviet lobster fishing off the U.S. Northeast coast led to a brief but telling conflict. The Soviets allegedly dragged their gear through U.S. lobster traps, breaking them.

The successful claims made by coastal states to the continental shelf have greatly complicated the offshore boundary problem in general. Whereas the maritime boundary, prior to this development, was a vertical plane cutting air, water, and subsoil, and thus was comparable in these respects to the land boundary, the absorption of the continental shelf means that states' maritime boundaries follow both a vertical and a near-horizontal plane. States may, in time, come to find that such boundaries do not function satisfactorily.

In the shallow waters upon the continental shelf, many of the oceans' resources are concentrated. A state that is technologically sufficiently advanced to establish a network of installations to exploit the resources of the underlying continental shelf must, in the same area and within sight of the coast, compete with other states for the resources of the water. If the trend of the recent past is continued, states may eventually claim the superjacent waters as well as the seabed and subsoil, just as several South American states have already done. In the general framework of expansion into a frontier, it is a logical step, in view of the fact that power and self-interest still tend to override adherence to international law.

REFERENCES

Alexander, L. M., "The Expanding Territorial Sea," *Prof. Geog.*, 11, 4 (July, 1959), 6–8.

Allen, Edward W., "Territorial Waters and Extraterritorial Rights," *Amer. J. Internat. Law*, 47, 3 (July, 1953), 478–480.

Amador, F. V. Garcia, *The Exploitation and Conservation of the Resources of the Sea.* Leiden, Sijthoff, 1959.

[1]For a discussion of this topic see R. Young, "Sedentary Fisheries and the Convention on the Continental Shelf," *Amer. J. Internat. Law*, 55 (1959), 359.

200 The State: System and Process

Anninos, P. C. L., *The Continental Shelf and Public International Law.* La Haye, Imprimerie H. P. DeSwart & Fils, 1953.

Archdale, H. E., "Territorial Waters; What are They?" *Australian Outlook,* 10, 1 (March, 1956), 42–45.

Baty, Thomas, "The Three-Mile Limit," *Amer. J. Internat. Law,* 22, 3 (July, 1928), 503–538.

Boggs, S. Whittemore, "Delimitation of Seaward Areas under National Jurisdiction," *Amer. J. Internat. Law,* 45, 2 (April, 1951), 240–266.

Brittin, B. H., "International Law Aspects of the Acquisition of the Continental Shelf by the United States," *U.S. Naval Inst. Proc.,* 74, 550 (December, 1948), 1541–1543.

Codding, G. A., Jr., and Alvin Z. Rubenstein, "How Wide the Territorial Sea, Pt. II: The Problems Left by Discord," *U.S. Naval Inst. Proc.,* 87, 2 (February, 1961), 74–77.

Colborn, Paul A., "National Jurisdiction over Resources of the Continental Shelf," *Bull. Pan American Union,* 82, 1 (January, 1948), 38–40.

Colombos, C. John, *The International Law of the Sea,* 5th rev. ed. London, Longmans, 1962.

Dean, Arthur H., "The Second Geneva Conference on the Law of the Sea: The Fight for Freedom of the Seas," *Amer. J. Internat. Law,* 54, 4 (October, 1960), 751–789.

Fulton, T. W., *The Sovereignty of the Sea.* Edinburgh, Blackwood & Sons, 1911.

Groom, Sidney M., "Our Newest Frontier: the Outer Continental Shelf," *Our Public Lands,* 5, 1 (January, 1955), 12 ff.

Grzybowski, Kazimierz, "The Soviet Doctrine of Mare Clausum and Policies in Black and Baltic Seas," *J. Central European Affairs,* 14, 4 (January, 1955), 339–353.

Hargreaves, Reginald, *The Narrow Seas.* London, Sidgwick and Jackson, 1959.

Jessup, P. C., *The Law of Territorial Waters and Maritime Jurisdiction.* New York, Jennings, 1927.

Johnson, Gilbert R., "United States–Canadian Treaties Affecting Great Lakes Commerce and Navigation," *Inland Seas,* 3, 4 (October, 1947), 203–207.

Kawakami, Kenzo, "The Continental Shelf and Its Geographically Controversial Points," *J. Geog.* (Tokyo), 63, 2 (1954), 53–59.

Kent, H. S. K., "The Historical Origins of the Three-Mile Limit," *Amer. J. Internat. Law,* 48, 4 (October, 1954), 537–553.

Kunz, Josef L., "Continental Shelf and International Law: Confusion and Abuse," *Amer. J. Internat. Law,* 50, 4 (October, 1956), 828–853.

Leonard, L. Larry, *International Regulation of Fisheries.* Washington, Carnegie Endowment for International Peace, Division of International Law, 1944.

McDougal, Myres S., and William T. Burke, "The Community Interest in a Narrow Territorial Sea: Inclusive versus Exclusive Competence over the Oceans," *Cornell Law Quart.,* 45, 2 (Winter, 1960), 171–253.

———, *The Public Order of the Oceans. A Contemporary International Law of the Sea.* New Haven, Conn., Yale University Press, 1962.

McFee, W., *The Law of the Sea.* Philadelphia, Lippincott, 1950.

Melamid, Alexander, "Legal Status of the Gulf of Aqaba," *Amer. J. Internat. Law,* 53, 2 (April, 1959), 412–413.

Moodie, A. E., "The Continental Shelf: Some Territorial Problems Associated with the Continental Shelf," *Advance. Sci.,* 11, 4 (June, 1954), 42–48.

Morgan, R., *World Sea Fisheries.* London, Methuen, 1956.

Mouton, M. W., *The Continental Shelf.* The Hague, M. Nijhoff, 1952.

Oda, Shigeru, "The Concept of the Contiguous Zone," *Int. and Comp. Law Quart.,* 11, 1 (January, 1962), 131–153.

———, "The Territorial Sea and Natural Resources," *Int. and Comp. Law Quart.,* 4, 3 (July, 1955), 415–425.

Pearcy, G. Etzel, "The Continental Shelf: Physical vs. Legal Definition," *Canadian Geographer,* 5, 3 (Autumn, 1961), 26–29.

———, "Geographical Aspect of the Law of the Sea," *Ann. A.A.G.,* 49, 1 (March, 1959), 1–23.

Powers, R. D., Jr., and Leonard R. Hardy, "How Wide the Territorial Sea, Pt. I: Background and the Vote," *U.S. Naval Inst. Proc.,* 87, 2 (February, 1961), 68–73.

Shalowitz, A. L., "Boundary Problems Associated with the Continental Shelf," *Surveying and Mapping,* 15, 2 (April–May, 1955), 189–211.

———, "Boundary Problems Raised by the Submerged Lands Act," *Columbia Law Rev.,* 54 (November, 1954), 1021–1048.

———, "The Concept of a Bay as Inland Waters," *Surveying and Mapping,* 13, 4 (October–December, 1953), 432–440.

Smith, H. A., *The Law and Custom of the Sea.* London, Stevens & Sons, 1948.

Sorensen, Max, "Lwa of the Sea," *International Conciliation,* No. 520 (November, 1958), 195–256.

Whiteman, Marjorie M., "Conference on the Law of the Sea: Convention on the Continental Shelf," *Amer. J. Internat. Law,* 52, 4 (October, 1958), 629–659.

Young, Richard, "The Legal Status of Submarine Areas Beneath the High Seas," *Amer. J. Internat. Law,* 45, 2 (April, 1951), 225–239.

———, "The Overextension of the Continental Shelf," *Amer. J. Internat. Law,* 47, 3 (July, 1953), 454–456.

———, "Recent Developments with respect to the Continental Shelf," *Amer. J. Internat. Law,* 42, 4 (October, 1948), 849–857.

CHAPTER
10
MARITIME BOUNDARIES

The maritime boundary is an essential part of the territorial state system. Every coastal state requires it for customs, fiscal, sanitary, and immigration control. However, maritime boundaries, though they perform several of the functions also performed by land boundaries, differ in at least one important respect. The land boundary affects two states, for a boundary can only separate two adjacent political entities. But the maritime boundary affects many states. It is the seaward limit of the state and at the same time divides it from the high seas, in which every state has a degree of interest. Thus the maritime boundary is a boundary between the coastal state and the interests of the remainder of the world. Any encroachment upon the high seas affects the world community of states, not just one neighbor.

Maritime boundaries, like land boundaries, may lie in economically important areas and they may lie in waters that hitherto have been worthless to the littoral state for any purpose other than navigation. Several of the offshore boundaries of western and northwestern European states cut through fishing grounds that are among the world's richest. Here, boundary delimitation and even demarcation are required with a precision equaling that on land. On the other hand, the maritime boundaries of many African and Latin American states run through waters beneath which there is no continental shelf, and temperature and salinity conditions may occur here which prevent the existence of an important fish fauna. In such areas, little purpose would at present be served by exact demarcation. And yet conditions might suddenly change. The oceans contain resources which will only be exploited in the future, and the share of every state of the seas of the world may at some time have to be precisely determined.

Two major problems are considered in this chapter. The first concerns the actual definition and delimitation of the maritime bound-ary. The second focuses upon the politicogeographic significance of the variety of claims to territorial waters currently made by different states. The problem of definition is reminiscent of similar matters encountered when land boundaries were discussed: everything depends upon the accuracy with which the terms employed are defined by the treaty makers. In some ways the difficulties are even greater, for land boundaries can at least be related to static features in the landscape, or features that are temporarily static. Nothing is static along shorelines. Tides cause the waterline to rise and fall; erosion rapidly changes landforms. Coasts vary tremendously in configuration, and yet rules of procedure must be established which will fit all. Bays, offshore islands, and innumerable other obstacles render the process of maritime boundary definition an extremely difficult one.

BASELINES AND INTERNAL WATERS

All maritime boundaries are geometric boundaries. The seas do not provide trespass lines or other points or lines of reference. Hence all measurements must be taken from the shoreline, the nearest fixed physical feature. The shoreline, however, is rarely sufficiently straight to permit measurement to be taken directly from it. Bays and estuaries indent it, river mouths interrupt it. Furthermore, the location of the shoreline may vary considerably as ocean tides change: high tide may inundate a belt of shoreline, and at low tide that belt will be exposed. Thus measurement taken from the coast at low tide would push the territorial sea farther out to sea than a measurement taken at high tide.

The question of the low-water baseline as opposed to the high-water baseline has been discussed at several international conferences dealing with the law of the sea. Conferences at Monaco in 1929 and The Hague in 1930 served to establish agreement on this and other matters.[1] The decision reached at The Hague was that measurement should take place from low watermark at spring tide. Later, that decision was overridden during the 1958 Geneva Conference, where *mean low water* was adopted as the baseline for measurement of the territorial sea. Actually, while the vertical range between normal high tide and low tide may be as much as fifteen or twenty feet, the tides show their greatest range along coasts that are marked by vertical cliffs. In such a case, the horizontal difference is, of course, minimal. And where coasts are gently sloping seaward, the tidal range is usually much less. Here a great vertical range would produce a wide belt of alternate inundation and exposure—but the range is small, and so the horizontal difference is limited to some dozens of feet.

Why, then, was mean low water adopted at all? The major reason is that the coastal charts published by the maritime state will always show minimum depths offshore, if soundings are taken from the low waterline. Thus a vessel using those charts will be able to rely on indicated depths, since they are taken from the low waterline and not during high tide. This simplifies the navigational problems that might otherwise hamper shipping, and eliminates the necessity for several series of charts to be published by the coastal state. Of course, there are other advantages as well. The admissibility of low watermarks as the basis for measurement eliminates any possible disputes that might arise in places where there are exceptions to the rule stated above concerning the steepness of coastal slopes and the vertical range of tides.

An associated problem is that of the *low-tide elevation.* Along very gently sloping coasts, there may be offshore sandbanks which are exposed at low tide, but covered by water at high tide. Of course, a state might claim that such elevations are part of the mainland, and, since they are exposed at low tide, that State might assert that it is entitled to measure from the edge of the sandbank rather than from its coast. The 1958 Geneva Convention stipulates that such low-tide elevations may only be used to extend the territorial sea

if they fall within the territorial sea as measured from the coast. Thus a state that claims three miles as its territorial sea and has a low-tide elevation two miles from its coast may extend the territorial sea three miles from that low-tide elevation—a total of five miles. On the other hand, if a state claims three miles and a low-tide elevation exists four miles from the coast, that low-tide elevation may not be used to extend the territorial waters.

The question of bays, estuaries, and other indentations of the coastline also has kept treaty makers busy. When, in the previous chapters, we described such inlets as internal waters, no effort was made to define the geographical term "bay." Obviously it is subject to many possible interpretations. At the 1930 Conference in The Hague, the American delegation proposed a complicated method for determining whether a bay is really a bay or merely a curvature in the coastline. It also proposed that no bay wider than 10 miles at its mouth should be claimed as inland water. From this evolved the present procedure, which is as follows. A baseline is drawn across the mouth of the bay. This is referred to as the line of closure. The length of this line should not exceed twenty-four miles, which is twice the maximum claim to territorial waters recognized under international law. When the mouth of the bay is more than twenty-four miles wide, its waters can be claimed only through the application of accepted methods of territorial waters delimitation. If the mouth of the bay is less than twenty-four miles in width, a semicircle is drawn with the closure line as its diameter. The area of the semicircle is now compared to the water area of the bay behind the line of closure. If the bay has an area smaller than that of the semicircle based on its closure line, it cannot be cut off by such a line. If the water area of the bay is larger than that of the semicircle, it is indeed a part of the inland waters of the state in question.

Again, a number of associated possibilities arise. What, for example, is done with a bay in whose mouth one or more islands are located? The width of the mouth may be forty miles, but the islands may make up twenty miles of that total. Here the rule applies that the width of the *water* areas across the mouth must not exceed twenty-four miles; thus in the case described here, the bay could be inland water, subject to the usual calculations. Another possibility is presented in the bay that is more

---

[1]The Monaco Conference was a hydrographic conference where problems of hydrography and marine geology were discussed and definitions formulated. The conference at The Hague dealt with politicogeographical and legal matters. See S. W. Boggs, "Delimitation of the Territorial Sea," *Amer. J. Internat. Law,* 24, 3 (July 1930), 541.

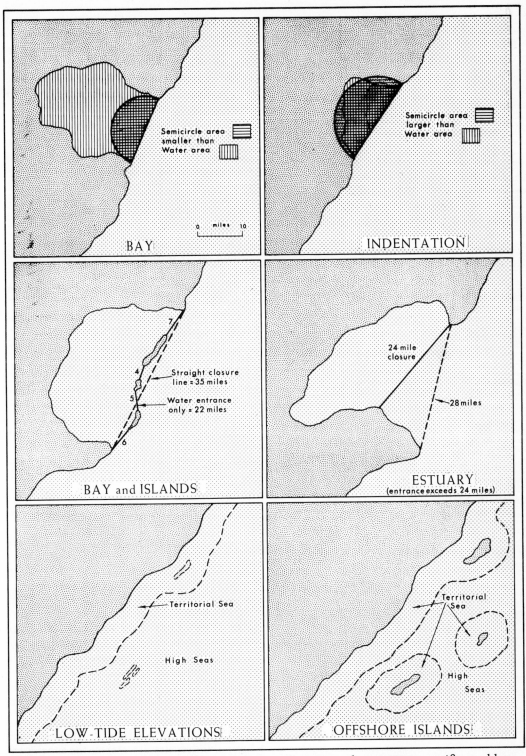

BAY

Semicircle area smaller than Water area

INDENTATION

Semicircle area larger than Water area

0   miles   10

BAY and ISLANDS

Straight closure line = 35 miles

Water entrance only = 22 miles

ESTUARY
(entrance exceeds 24 miles)

24 mile closure

28 miles

LOW-TIDE ELEVATIONS

Territorial Sea

High Seas

OFFSHORE ISLANDS

Territorial Sea

High Seas

than twenty-four miles wide at its mouth, but which tapers inland. Can the state draw a closure line where the width becomes twenty-four miles? It can, according to the 1958 Geneva Convention.

Estuaries also present specific problems. According to the 1958 Geneva Conference, they should be treated as bays in the application of the line of closure. This is so because the term "estuary" is not sufficiently clearly defined geographically (and therefore legally). Although the question of estuaries was discussed at the 1958 Geneva Conference, no agreement could be reached on the matter, and the Convention does not specifically refer to estuaries. Thus the associated problems are left without solution. Estuaries are the drowned valleys of rivers; often they mark the mouths of major rivers such as the St. Lawrence and De la Plata. Major ports may be located along their banks; the rivers themselves may constitute the state's most important waterway. Understandably, the states may be reluctant to apply the twenty-four mile rule to these water bodies. They may be so elongated that the semicircle across the mouth is larger than the enclosed water; on the other hand, they may be more than twenty-four miles wide at their mouth. In both cases the high seas would invade them.

State faced with this problem have one recourse. They can claim these estuaries and bays as *historic waters*. Three types of historic waters can be recognized: first, bays and estuaries; second, waters lying between the mainland and offshore islands; and third, waters lying between the islands of a fragmented, archipelago state. Once again, the Geneva Conference could not agree on the exact nature of historic waters, and the question is still under legal discussion. A number of states have, for many years, laid claim to bays on this basis: Norway has drawn baselines across its fiords, in excess of twenty-four miles in length; Iceland has done the same. The Netherlands has claimed the Wadden Sea between its northern string of islands and the Friesland-Groningen mainland. Indonesia, as mentioned in Chapter 9, has claimed all waters separating its islands.

Although not legally recognized, another type of internal waters exist. These might be called *strategic waters*, water bodies closed off on the basis of only one argument—power. The Soviet Union has closed off Vladivostok Bay to all foreign shipping, and it is reported to be testing naval equipment there. Other states have temporarily or permanently sealed off waters that, under the rule of law, would form part of the high seas.

PROCEDURES AND METHODS

The determination of the baseline, thus, is a complicated matter. Now the question is how

the actual measurement of the offshore boundary is best carried out. Once again there are several possibilities, each possessing advantages as well as disadvantages. These methods were outlined at the 1930 Hague Conference, where decisions were made regarding their applicability.

1. *The Replica Method.* By this method, an exact replica of the sinuosities of the coastline is delimited a given distance from the coast, the distance depending upon the extent of territorial waters claimed by the state. This method, especially in the case of heavily indented, fiorded coastlines, presents insurmountable problems. Such a boundary would have to be demarcated everywhere, for it would result in the creation of inlets of high seas between "peninsulas" of territorial water. Any coastline reproduced and shifted several miles outward would result in a belt of territorial waters of unequal width, and it does not require a great deal of imagination to envisage a whole series of problems. The best way to view some of these problems is to make an actual attempt at drawing a replica offshore boundary. The crossing of a zigzag replica boundary through a heavily trawled fishing ground could lead to an incredibly complicated set of legal claims and counterclaims of violations and infringements.

2. *The Straight Baseline (Conventional) Method.* Here, straight baselines are drawn from point to point along the coast. These baselines are confined to the closure of bays and estuaries, but run along the entire coast. Again, the boundary is then measured from these baselines, and the resulting maritime boundary is a reproduction of the coastal baselines (though not a replica), the distance between the coastal baselines and the offshore boundary being determined by the state's claims. As we have seen, baselines should not cut off mere indentations in the coastline, nor should they exceed twenty-four miles in length. The practice of bounding an entire coastline with baselines is clearly in contravention of that rule. But where baselines are legally justified, they are employed.

3. *The Envelope Method.* "The seaward limit of the territorial waters is the envelope of all arcs and circles drawn from all points on the coast . . . or from the seaward limit of those interior (internal) waters which are contiguous with the territorial waters." So reads the proposal defining this method at the

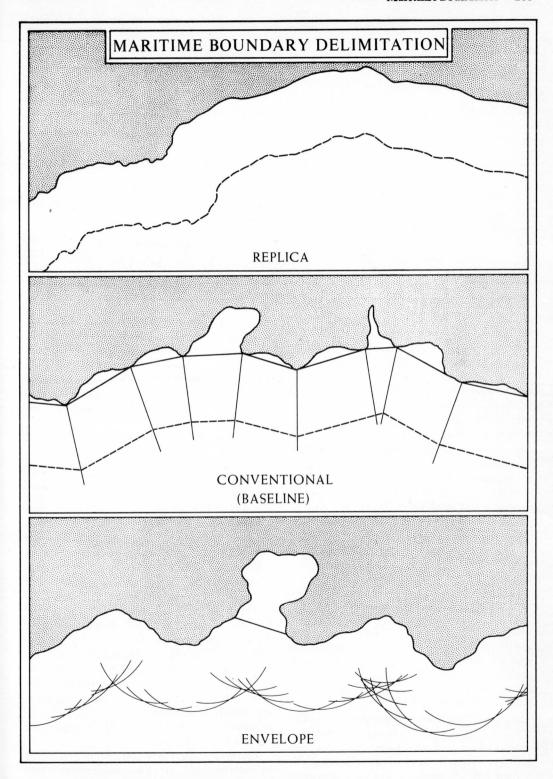

MARITIME BOUNDARY DELIMITATION

REPLICA

CONVENTIONAL
(BASELINE)

ENVELOPE

1930 Conference at The Hague.[2] This method has the advantage of relative simplicity. In fact, a combination of this method and the baseline method is actually in use. Where baselines are employed, the use of arcs from baselines produces a line parallel to the baseline, a fixed distance away. Where the sinuosities of the coastline are employed, a series of arcs results, and the exactness of the boundary finally delimited depends upon the

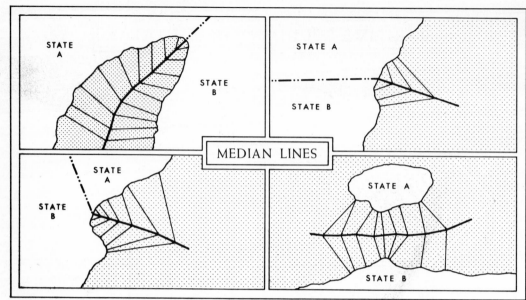

precision with which the cartographic work was carried out. Thus it is possible to calculate from any point at sea, when land is in sight, whether a vessel is within the radius of the arc, or whether it is still on the high seas. All that is required is a simple application of the method of triangulation. Except in those areas where the territorial sea borders internal waters, therefore, it may be unnecessary to delimit the exact maritime boundaries of all states on navigational charts. When the extent of the coastal state's claim to the territorial sea (3 miles, 4 miles, or 12 miles) is known, no fishing vessel need be in doubt regarding its position with reference to that state's sovereign maritime territory. Neither the replica nor the baseline method has this advantage of utility.

THE MEDIAN-LINE BOUNDARY

The problems discussed thus far all refer to the maritime boundaries of states—that is, the seaward limit of the coastal state. One question remains, and it refers to the manner in which two neighboring coastal states establish their mutual boundary on the seas. The outer limit of the territorial sea, it will be recalled, defines the boundary between a coastal state and the high seas. But two adjacent coastal states, both claiming the same width of territorial waters, still require an offshore border to connect their land boundary to their high-seas boundary. A

variety of cases exist. Two states might share an estuary, or a wide bay. Two states might lie along a relatively straight coast, with their boundary reaching that coastline at right angles. In other cases that boundary might be oblique. The adjacent states may be interested in the territorial waters as well as the continental shelf beyond. A glance at the world map will indicate the many examples that apply. The Swedish-Finnish boundary at the head of the Gulf of Bothnia, the Israel-Jordan border on the Gulf of Aqaba, and the Uruguay-Argentina boundary in the estuary of the Rio de la Plata are but three of nearly two hundred cases. Sometimes the islands of states lie so close together that the delimitation of their territorial waters shows an overlap; at other times states face each other across a narrow channel. The Caribbean Sea is full of actual and potential situations of this kind.

The most generally acceptable (and, in the few places where required, adopted) solution for these problems is that of the median-line boundary.[3] The median line is defined as a line (or boundary) every point of which is equidistant from the nearest points on the baselines from which the breadth of the territorial sea is measured. In practice, this produces a boundary about which there can be no argument: there is only one median line.

The median line is not, of course, prescribed by international law. Two neighboring states may rather enter into bilateral agreement

[3]For a complete and detailed analysis of this problem see G. Etzel Pearcy, "Geographical Aspects of the Law of the Sea," *Ann. A.A.G.*, 49, 1 (March, 1959), 16–20.

regarding the position of the boundary separating their territorial waters. Often median-line delimitation is complicated by the presence of smaller and larger islands. Bays and estuaries are frequently subject to historical claims. In areas where the territorial waters constitute a major resource, however, or where the continental shelf contains resources about to be exploited, the median-line solution can ward off a long series of discussions and negotiations.

One alternative to the median line, sometimes used in estuaries and bays which form more or less heavily traveled waterways, is the rule of the *thalweg*. This resembles the navigable-channel method of determining river boundaries, and has similar advantages and disadvantages. One contrast lies in the width of the *thalweg* as opposed to a river's navigable channel: while the navigable channel may be so narrow that traffic must always cross the international boundary, the *thalweg* may be sufficiently wide so that each state can accommodate within its own section both incoming and outgoing ocean traffic.

CLAIMS TO TERRITORIAL WATERS

Quite apart from the problems and alternatives associated with the actual measurement of the state's territorial sea, there is a growing question that has to do with the very survival of the high seas concept. That question, simply, is whether the states will continue to claim more and more of the seas until the right of free passage is a thing of the past, or whether it will be possible to find some maximum distance to which all states will adhere. Until now, such a maximum outward limit has not been determined. And what would have seemed to be outrageous aggrandizement a few decades ago is now quite commonplace on the international maritime scene. Some states are claiming privileges in "territorial" waters some 200 miles wide!

The trend began after World War II. In 1950, the three-mile limit was claimed by more than 40 states. Just four states claimed four miles; 11 demanded that their rights be observed in six miles of territorial waters. Among the states claiming just three miles were the major maritime powers of the world, including most of the colonial powers. This meant that these powers themselves *and* their dependencies claimed this minimal belt of territorial sea. But colonial empires began to break up during

the 1950's, and a large number of coastal territories became independent. Those newly independent states were no longer bound to adhere to their former colonial powers' rules, and several of them decided to enlarge their territorial seas. In response, some of the 40-odd states that had originally claimed only three miles also announced that their territorial waters would henceforth be wider. Thus in 1960, only 22 states still claimed three miles, while no less than 13 states now claimed 12 miles. By 1970, another set of former dependencies had become sovereign states, and 25 states claimed three miles. And an astounding 44 states now claimed 12 miles.

But this was not the worst of it. In 1952, several South American states issued the Declaration of Santiago, in which they claimed exclusive fishing rights to a line some 200 miles from their coasts. The Declaration was signed by Chile, Peru, and Ecuador, and when they issued it these countries pointed out that their claim was not so very different from the Truman Declaration of 1945, by which the United States had claimed exclusive rights to the wealth of the continental shelf. Chile, Peru, and Ecuador, on the west coast of South America, do not possess a potentially rich continental shelf, so these countries felt justified in claiming sole rights in some of the world's richest fishing waters—the waters of the Humboldt Current. Later, Peru and Ecuador actually claimed the entire 200-mile belt not just as a contiguous zone, but as territorial waters.

It was only the beginning. By 1971 there were nearly a dozen Latin American states claiming the 200-mile limit, either as territorial sea or for exclusive fishing, including Argentina, Uruguay, Brazil, Panama, Nicaragua, and El Salvador. In Africa, Guinea and Senegal (once French dependencies) claimed 130 miles and Sierra Leone (a former British colony and protectorate) announced a claim of 200 miles. India claimed a 100 mile fishing zone. And a number of the states still clinging to the concept of the three-mile limit were nevertheless extending their privileged fishing zones to the 12-mile limit, including the United States.

This is not to suggest that the decolonization process alone led to the enormous expansion of territorial seas, or that Latin American countries have been solely responsible for the mushrooming of wide-belt claims. The ideological conflicts of the post-1950 era

also have had much to do with these developments. There were states that had little to lose
by a widening of the territorial seas and much
to gain from the resulting impediments to
worldwide traffic, not to mention the disputes
that arose between the parties involved. Very
often these disputes involved comparatively
wealthy, seafaring nations and much poorer
countries; the seafaring states wished to
maintain the narrowest of territorial seas
while the poorer (often newly independent)
states could flex their political muscles by
pushing their maritime boundaries far outward. Mainland China was among the first
states to promote the 12-mile limit; Japan has
held to the three-mile zone. The Netherlands
has long supported the three-mile principle;
Algeria has pushed its maritime boundary 12
miles out into the Mediterranean.

The "scramble for the oceans" was soon
recognized as a serious threat by the maritime
powers of the world, and in 1958 the United
States, along with a number of other states,
sought a compromise by proposing that the
six-mile limit be universally adopted, with
another six-mile zone in which the coastal
state would have exclusive fishing rights. That
proposal was defeated, but a 1960 conference
held at Geneva, Switzerland, seemed to hold
greater hope for compromise. There, the
United States made its proposal again, but the
Soviet Union countered by suggesting that a
"rule of flexibility" be adopted. By this rule,
each state would be permitted to determine its
territorial sea as extending from three to 12
miles out; beyond that, a 12-mile fishing zone
would belong exclusively to the coastal state.
In retrospect, the Soviet proposal was not so
unreasonable, but the United States held out
for its 1958 proposal. With the votes divided,
neither the United States nor the Soviet Union
proposal gained the required majority.

By the early 1970's the 200-mile claim was
becoming more common, and the prospect of a
partitioning of much of the oceans seemed an
ever greater reality. In the event that the
200-mile limit was to be generally adopted,
about one-third of all the earth's waters would
cease to be high seas; all passages and channels
between islands and between continents and
islands would fall under national jurisdictions.
Now the Soviet Union and the United States
could at last agree: things had gone too far. In
1971, delegates were called together at a
preparatory meeting in Geneva to lay the
groundwork for a full-scale conference to be
held in 1973. Both the United States and the
Soviet Union argued in opposition to the
200-mile limit; the United States gave up its
earlier position and called for the universal
adoption of the 12-mile zone. This would be a
compromise, and not a very agreeable one to
many states still holding out for the three-mile
limit. As a glance at the world map shows,
even the 12-mile limit, by closing off all
maritime passages less than 24 miles wide,
would pose actual and potential problems.
One of the world's busiest channels, the
English Channel, would be among those
ceasing to be free and open waters, since the
distance from Dover to Calais is only some 22
miles. Thus the 12-mile limit would require a
host of international guarantees of passage.

The prospect for general international agreement in the early 1970's appears as dim as it
was at Geneva on earlier occasions. To the
states now claiming 200 miles, a retreat to the
12-mile limit would constitute an unacceptable defeat; in any case, Ecuador has already
given evidence that the claim can be upheld by
its series of arrests of United States fishing
vessels. And ideological factors again are part
of the picture; China has given vigorous
support to the states claiming the 200-mile
zone. The scramble is far from over.

Claims: Distribution

The historical development of the concept of a
territorial sea is to some extent still reflected
by the geographic distribution of offshore
claims today. The *three-mile* limit is still
claimed by many of the states in the region
where the concept had its modern origins; the
United Kingdom, the Netherlands, Belgium,
France, and Ireland are among these. Some
former colonies and states spawned by Europe
also adhere to the three-mile limit, including
Kenya, Ivory Coast, Australia, and New
Zealand. The *four-mile* limit is now claimed
only by Finland, Norway, and Sweden, although in 1971 there were signs that the
Norwegians were having second thoughts
about their maritime boundary. The *five-mile*
limit in 1971 was claimed only by Cambodia,
and several of the states of the Mediterranean
region presently claim the *six-mile* limit.
These include Greece, Israel, Italy, Lebanon,
Tunisia, and Turkey. But a very long list of
widely distributed states now claim the
12-mile limit, in the Americas (Mexico,
Colombia, Venezuela), Africa (Ghana, Nigeria,

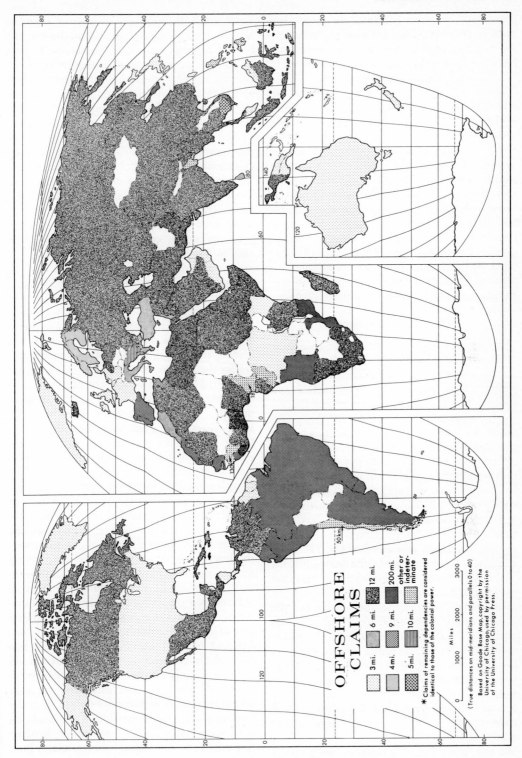

OFFSHORE
CLAIMS

3 mi.		12 mi.
4 mi.		200 mi.
5 mi.		other or indeterminate

10 mi.
6 mi.
9 mi.

* Claims of remaining dependencies are considered identical to those of the colonial power.

Miles
0   1000   2000   3000
(True distances on mid-meridians and parallels 0 to 40)

Based on Goode Base Map, copyright by the University of Chicago, used by permission of the University of Chicago Press.

Tanzania), Europe (Poland, Bulgaria, Romania), and Asia (China, Thailand, Pakistan). As the map shows, there are still states that have not formally declared their intentions in connection with their territorial seas.

Many of the states whose claims are recorded on the accompanying map claim exclusive fishing rights in a zone beyond that claimed as territorial waters. For example, by the European Fisheries Convention several Western European states claim the right to exclusive fishing in a zone three miles beyond their territorial seas; another six-mile zone is reserved for exploitation only by the signatories (Belgium, Denmark, France, Ireland, and the Netherlands). In effect this means control over a 12-mile zone; in 1971, another 17 states officially claiming less than 12 miles of territorial seas nevertheless insisted upon sole fishing rights up to 12 miles from their coasts.

The Continental Shelf

The complicating factor introduced by claims to the continental shelf has further clouded the picture. On land, boundaries are vertical planes which intersect the land surface and apply in the air as well as underground. Claims to the continental shelf, however, have produced an unprecedented situation, whereby the boundaries of states, represented by planes, do not run vertically, but nearly horizontal and parallel to the surface of a landform. Thus the maritime boundary consists of three planes: one vertical cutting the territorial sea off from the high seas; one nearly horizontal lying, in fact, on top of the continental shelf; and another vertical plane continues downward from the seaward limit of this. Apart from the obvious difficulties that may arise (and already have arisen) over the relationship between the shelf-plane and the actual surface of the shelf (the "seabed"), this creates a situation on the surface of the high seas that is bound to require modification. As the importance of the continental shelf and subsoil increases in terms of resource production, the overlying waters will more and more become effectively occupied territory of the coastal state. Installations of a permanent and semipermanent nature will grow in number and size, and when this happens, we have the situation which Van Bynkershoek discussed in theory without realizing that the practical situation could develop—"continuous and intended occupation." Thus the possibility exists that the states that adjoin extensive continental shelves will ultimately demand that their entire boundary will be constituted by the margin of the continental shelf. This could have at least three consequences. First, the concept of a standard-width territorial sea would be abandoned; second, there would be conflicts over the allocation of "shared" continental shelves, such as that constituted by the North Sea; and third, states without continental shelves might seek redress by claims to vast reaches of the oceans. In effect, we have already arrived at the beginning of all three of these circumstances. Several states, including Ghana and Ceylon, have already announced that they might establish what they identify as "conservation zones" as far as 100 miles from their coasts. Pakistan has proclaimed its intention of controlling all exploitative activity on the continental shelf adjoining its land areas. And, of course, we ought to mention the Truman Declaration in this context. It, too, may eventually come to be recognized as the first of a series of steps leading to a continental shelf-margin boundary for the United States. As for the allocation of "shared" continental shelves, discussions to divide Western Europe's continental shelf in just this fashion have been in progress for some years, and maps proposing allocations based on various grounds (chiefly the land areas and populations of the coastal states) have been appearing for nearly two decades. A sample from 1957 is reproduced here.[4] But the Western European case is not unique. A similar situation may be in the offing for Southeast Asia, whose coastal, peninsular, and insular states lie in a region of comparatively shallow water whose subsoil is just coming within man's technological reach. The Southeast Asian shelf may become a region of competition involving not only the adjoining states, but also the states that have the ability to explore and exploit the subsoil. It was reported in 1971 that South Viet Nam had granted United States oil companies certain rights to search for petroleum in the continental shelf; the question immediately arose whether South Viet Nam did indeed have the right to grant such permission. And already we have seen states without potentially productive adjoining continental shelves claim hundreds of miles of territorial waters. More are

[4]See map entitled "Sharing Out the Continental Shelf of Northwestern Europe," in W. G. East and A. E. Moodie, *The Changing World*, New York, World Book Company, 1957, p. 951.

likely to follow. They ask this relevant question: Should a state be allowed to claim for itself all resources found below a depth of zero to 600 feet of water—just because the water ends there—for hundreds of miles from its coast, while another state cannot claim more than 12 miles of water or subsoil because that subsoil drops away precipitously? Why can the United States claim continental shelf resources 100 miles from its coastline, while Ecuador cannot claim marine resources a similar distance away? Ecuador and several of its neighbors in South America say they should be able to make such claims, they have done so, they have sustained them, and they are not likely to abandon them.

MARITIME BOUNDARIES AND FISHING DISPUTES

The fishing industries of some states are but a small and relatively insignificant part of the total economic complex. In other states, however, fishing is a major—perhaps *the* major—economic activity. And in certain additional states, the importance of the fishing industry is rapidly growing as the food possibilities of the seas are recognized. Japan and the U.S.S.R. have expanded their fishing activities manyfold during the past decades; the Japanese fleets are plying all oceans. The concept of the territorial sea, as we have seen, arose in large measure out of the early disputes over the fishing grounds of the North Sea. The function of the maritime boundary as a part of the state complex is to protect the rights and resources of nationals of a coastal state in the face of encroachment by other states. The pressure upon these boundaries has been increasing for many years.

There are several important differences between land resources and sea resources. A mineral resource, once secured by land boundary, is a permanent (if expendable) part of the inventory of the controlling state. But maritime resources, the fish fauna of the oceans in particular, are mobile and renewable, unless harvested carelessly. A maritime state may protect the rights of its fishermen within its maritime borders, but it has a vital interest in the size of the catch made outside the borders, for overfishing outside those borders leads to destruction. Thus a Norwegian or Icelandic government will be very sensitive to large fishing fleets from Japan that come to make major hauls just outside their territorial

waters. In order to reduce the likelihood of damage to the fish resources of the oceans, states have entered into agreements limiting their catches. But quotas have been exceeded and friction has been frequent.[5]

One of those states that possess large fishing fleets capable of fishing in distant waters is Great Britain. In the total economic picture of that state, fishing does not loom very large. Iceland, on the other hand, depends to a great extent upon returns from fishing—and some of the world's best fishing grounds are located within a dozen miles of the Icelandic coast. Iceland has claimed some extensive bays as historic waters, thereby cutting off major fishing grounds; in addition the Icelanders have claimed twelve miles as the seaward limit of sovereignty—twelve miles, that is, beyond the baselines which already ring most of the island state.

Iceland may properly be described as an emergent state; it was long part of the Danish Empire and has been acknowledged as a sovereign state since 1918. Formal ties with Denmark existed until near the end of the second World War. Denmark and Britain in 1901 had agreed that Icelandic fishing waters extended but three miles from the coast, and that bays should be closed off only if their mouths were ten miles wide or less. After independence, the Icelanders began to expand their territorial sea, claiming exclusive fishing rights first (1952) in a four-mile belt extending from newly drawn baselines, and later (1958) in a twelve-mile zone measured from these baselines. British fishing vessels, which had been very active within those waters now closed off, thus were required to withdraw. The British government, which might have agreed to accept the four-mile limit, now decided to support its fishermen and sent warships to protect British trawlers working within the Icelandic twelve-mile zone. Some minor friction did occur, and when British importers severely curtailed the quantity of fish bought from Icelandic sellers, Iceland turned to the Soviet Union as its best market.

Unlike a number of other cases of this sort, the Britain-Iceland fishing dispute never reached the International Court of Justice. Britain and Iceland eventually reached an

[5]Specific cases involve the annual whale catch and salmon catches. For an excellent study of the latter, see J. V. Minghi, "The Conflict of Salmon Fishing Policies in the North Pacific," *Pacific Viewpoint*, 2 (March, 1961), 59–84.

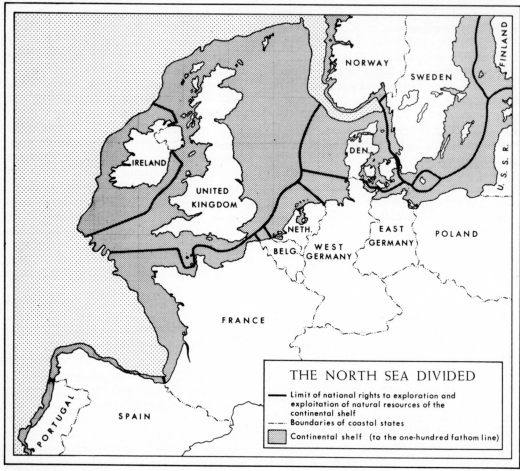

THE NORTH SEA DIVIDED

— Limit of national rights to exploration and
exploitation of natural resources of the
continental shelf
---- Boundaries of coastal states
▓ Continental shelf (to the one-hundred fathom line)

agreement whereby the British secured a postponement and the Icelanders achieved recognition of their claims. These claims were based upon two major premises: the great reliance of the country upon its fishing industry, and the need for conservation, which overfishing might endanger. Both factors seemed likely to form grounds for subsequent, even broader Icelandic claims, and in 1970 Iceland appropriated sole rights as far as the edge of the continental shelf.

While the British quarrel with Iceland concerned the width of the territorial sea and to a lesser extent the length and position of the baselines, the question of baselines was the focal issue of another dispute involving the British, this time with Norway. Several Norwegian baselines, delimited in 1935, were much longer than ten miles, and the 1935 claim to a four-mile belt of territorial waters from these new baselines pushed Norwegian sovereignty far into fishing grounds trawled by British vessels. In 1951 the British submitted the matter to the International Court of

Justice, arguing that the Norwegian practice with regard to baselines contravened international law, that these baselines were in several cases excessively long, and that the baselines did not conform with the configuration of the Norwegian coast. The Court found in favor of Norway, and again, as in the case of Iceland, the coastal state prevailed.

These examples of international conflict illustrate in regional terms what is rapidly becoming a worldwide issue: the rights of fishing nations in territorial as well as international waters and the responsibility of the large "technocracies" to conserve the oceans' resources for all. The vast majority of disputes involving a coastal state and a distant fishing nation have been resolved or adjudicated in favor of the coastal state, even those involving apparently exorbitant claims by the coastal state. South American states claiming 200 miles, for example, have defied strong and wealthy "invaders," and have, in effect, made their claims stand up. An especially significant event occurred in August, 1971, when the states of Trinidad and Tobago agreed to buy fishing licences from Brazil, to permit 50 of its shrimp boats to fish within Brazil's 200-mile limit. This decision not only had the effect of recognizing Brazil's right to claim exclusive rights in its wide territorial sea; it also made unauthorized fishing raids by the richer fishing nations look like clear violations of the rights of coastal states. In the absence of international law or agreement to standardize all coastal maritime rights, it has been generally true that the coastal state's claims have been upheld, whether 3, 12, or 200 miles.

But whose responsibility is the resource content of the diminishing high seas? The oceans' fish move into, through, and out of territorial waters; if their numbers are severely depleted by high-seas fishing, even coastal states with 200 miles of territorial sea will not reap much from their waters. The fact is that conservation of these resources remains in a primitive condition. One state may act alone or in combination with several associates to restrict catches or to prohibit the importing of certain items (whale products, for example), but such action is piecemeal, often violated by competitors, and ineffective. Again there is no generally applicable international law; for some species of marine fauna it may already be too late.

THE STATE AND AIRSPACE

It is an unhappy fact that the United States and the Soviet Union have collectively impeded the establishment of general rules for territorial waters. The United States, which in 1970 finally abandoned its three-mile preference and indicated that it would agree to the 12-mile limit, has played this role in part because of a related concern: the question of the airspace *over* territorial seas. The 1958 Geneva Conference stipulated that the airspace over the continental shelf cannot be appropriated by the coastal state laying claim to it, but the airspace over actual territorial waters does become part of the coastal state. Thus the expansion of maritime claims involves a contraction of the open skies, to the detriment of states with a great deal of air transportation. The 200 mile limit, if generally adopted, would require the renegotiation of innumerable air transit guarantees, and it would potentially increase the cost of such rights to national and private air line companies.

Because of the high speed with which aircraft travel, and the altitudes at which they operate, states have established air corridors to and through their territories. The aircraft of other states have the right of innocent passage over these corridors, but not over other parts of the national territory. Such corridors lie over the territorial sea as well, and aircraft must approach coastal airports via established routes. In addition, the United States, among other countries, has created zones of air defense (Air Defense Identification Zones), which are areas within the nation's approach routes within which airplanes are expected to identify themselves.

A Roof?

There is also the question of the vertical limit of state sovereignty. Does a state's authority extend indefinitely skyward or is there a vertical limit beyond which there are "open skies," just as there is a maritime boundary, beyond which there is a high seas? In other words, does the state have a "roof"?

It is still an unanswered question. Air and space technology are changing so rapidly that any solution would have to be viewed as temporary, in any case. Several theories have emerged with regard to the air lying upon the territory and territorial waters of the state. One theory views the air above in the same manner as the high seas: open and free for use by all states. Another theory considers the airspace (and all space beyond) an integral part of the sovereign realm of the state. This position holds that any state wishing to orbit satellites would have to ask permission to do so from all states over whose territory the satellite would pass. The third theory forms a compromise between these extremes; airspace is indeed part of the state, but free and innocent passage is guaranteed to all craft, as in the contiguous zone. But these are merely abstract considerations; the entire question is even farther from any solution than the offshore boundary problem. Again, conferences have been held to consider the issue (in 1919, 1928, 1944, and 1947), but the only real result of these was the recognition of the concept of "national airspace," without exact specifications and without determination relating to the rights of other states in such airspace.

Space

The development of space technology and the orbiting of artificial satellites and quasipermanent manned laboratories have further complicated the matter. While all craft were air-supported, it was possible for a state to claim full sovereign rights over all air that could be used by airplanes, however high they might fly. But spacecraft travel beyond the Earth's air layer, and thus beyond this jurisdiction. Nevertheless, they pass over the national territory of states. Among their missions are ground reconnaissance; the term "spy satellite" has already made its appearance. And orbiting spacecraft might carry weapons that could be activated at given times—a formidable threat. It would not be surprising if a majority of states moved to obtain some form of control by law over the space beyond their atmosphere.

At present, there still is the distinction between spacecraft and aircraft, and it is possible to argue that the "roof" of the state, effectively, is the upper limit of earth-based flying craft. But the distinction between aircraft and spacecraft is rapidly disappearing; work is in progress on aircraft that will be able to leave and enter the atmosphere at will. When that is achieved, a new issue will have arisen, for then it becomes impossible to distinguish immediately between an orbiting satellite and an hovering air/space craft. The problem of the air and space is only in its infancy.

The Regional Sea:
A Theoretical Division of the Gulf of Mexico and the Caribbean Sea

Donald L. Capone

Alan F. Ryan

In view of the rapid progress in the development of new techniques by technologically advanced countries, it is feared that . . . the seabed and ocean floor . . . will become progressively and competitively subject to national appropriation and use . . . .

Arvid Pardo, 1967

The world community is undertaking a fundamental review of international law of the sea. Since 1967, when Ambassador Pardo of Malta introduced the problem of maintaining the deep seabed beyond national jurisdiction for the peaceful uses of mankind, the United Nations (through the Seabed Committee of the General Assembly) has grappled with several major problems. What kind of international regime or mechanism can be employed to utilize the resources of the deep seabed while preserving the peace? What actions can be taken to prevent pollution of the world ocean? And what can a revision of existing law of the sea accomplish to reconcile the diverse and competing interests of those states who favor maximum freedom of the seas versus those who claim exclusive sovereign rights over great expanses of sea space?[1]

The gulf between developed and developing countries on the many issues of marine use—resource extraction, military activity, pollution control—is wide. The alternatives to effective action to reconcile competing interests are friction, increased hostility, perhaps open conflict. But worldwide agreement on these issues is difficult to accomplish when the world community is unable to agree on

substantive issues for discussion. Alternatives to a worldwide regime to control marine resource exploitation might take the form of interim, regional seabed regimes designed to regulate marine activity on a regional scale.

The trend toward sovereign claims to ever-wider areas of ocean space has been well documented. Should claims to 200-mile territorial seas continue to spread, as they have in parts of Latin America, overlapping jurisdictions will increase the potential for conflict. Political geographers can help to minimize this conflict potential through research designed to illuminate problems in the marine environment before they surface.

The Gulf of Mexico and the Caribbean Sea are an excellent example of a marine region fraught with conflict potential. As the pressures of fishing by distant-water fleets increase (such as by the highly efficient fleet of the Soviet Union) and problems of passage through international straits enclosed by extensive territorial sea claims arise, the need for consistent, viable rules is obvious. Large expanses of the seabed of the region are the shallow waters of the continental shelf, at depths which are capable of being exploited in the near future. Major shelf areas are located off the Gulf coast of the United States, throughout the Bahama Islands, north of the Yucatan Peninsula, in the vicinity of the east

[1] United Nations, *Report of the Committee on the Peaceful Uses of the Sea-Bed and the Ocean Floor Beyond the Limits of National Jurisdiction,* (New York, 1971).

Donald L. Capone and Alan F. Ryan, "The Regional Sea: A Theoretical Division of the Gulf of Mexico and the Caribbean Sea," *Transactions of the Miami Geographical Society,* Vol. III, No. 1, March, 1973, pp. 1–9.

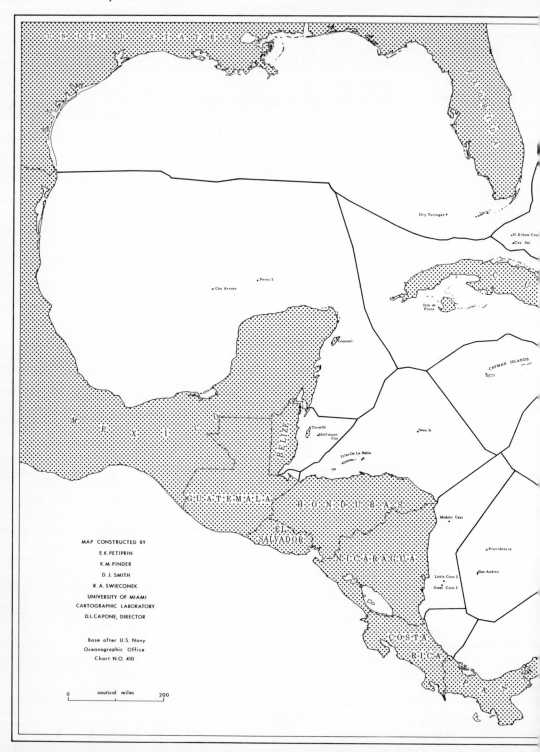

MAP CONSTRUCTED BY
E.K. PETIPRIN
K.M. PINDER
D. J. SMITH
R. A. SWIECONEK
UNIVERSITY OF MIAMI
CARTOGRAPHIC LABORATORY
D.L.CAPONE, DIRECTOR

Base after U.S. Navy
Oceanographic Office
Chart N.O. 410

0   nautical miles   200

coasts of Honduras and Nicaragua, through some of the islands of the Lesser Antilles, and off the northeast coast of Venezuela in the vicinity of Trinidad and Tobago. Which states have jurisdiction in these crowded waters? And how can disagreements be averted? Panama has already claimed a 200-mile terri- torial sea, and its northern neighbors, Costa Rica and Nicaragua, have laid claim to all resources out to that distance.[2] A proliferation

[2]F.V. Garcia Amador, "Latin America and the Law of the Sea," in *Proceedings of the Sixth Annual Conference*, edited by Lewis M. Alexander, Law of the Sea Institute (Kingston, R. I.: 1971), pp. 104–105.

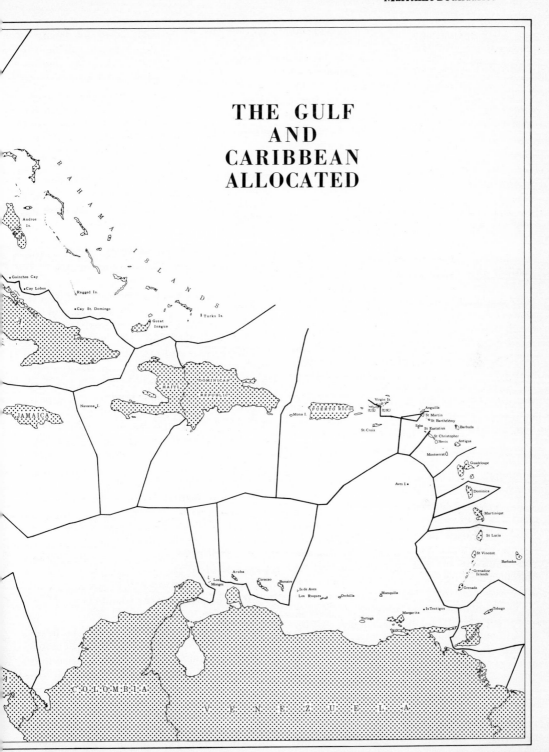

THE GULF
AND
CARIBBEAN
ALLOCATED

of 200-mile claims in the region would result in overlapping jurisdiction, and the Gulf of Mexico and the Caribbean Sea would become closed seas.

The map presented here is a theoretical division of these closed seas, with boundaries constructed using median, or equidistant lines (as recommended in Article 6 of the Geneva Convention on the Continental Shelf). Median lines and lateral boundaries (the boundaries between adjacent states in the territorial sea), were constructed at two different scales which were then combined to produce the final map. The inshore portion of all lateral boundaries and median lines between nearby opposing shorelines were plotted at 1:1,000,000 using the U.S. Army Map Service World Series 1301 (Edition 1). These were then transferred to U.S. Naval Oceanographic Office Chart N.O. 410, "Gulf of Mexico and Caribbean Sea" at a scale of 1:3.322,500. The farther offshore portions of the lateral boundaries and distant median lines were then plotted at this scale. The resulting map shows the extent of territorial sea that would be allocated to each of the states of the region under application of existing procedures for the determination of lateral boundaries and median lines.[3]

The allocation of territorial seas in the Gulf of Mexico and the Caribbean Sea illustrates many of the problems and areas of potential conflict that emanate from any attempt to create equitable marine boundaries in a politically complex region. Some states receive vast areas of sea space while others are limited to much smaller areas of territorial sea by the intervening claims of neighboring states or by offshore islands which effectively block off the seaward extension of the mainland state's territory. The Caribbean Sea in particular abounds with examples of states that are shelf-locked in this way.

Shelf-locking by neighboring states is common along concave coastlines, such as that of Central America in the western Caribbean. Guatemala presents an extreme example of this situation, the territorial sea of the state being sharply limited by the converging territorial waters of its neighbors, Honduras and Belize. Costa Rica's position is similiar to that of Guatemala, although less pronounced. The concavity of this part of the Central American coastline results in the restriction of Costa Rican territorial waters as the claims of Panama and Nicaragua intervene, blocking Costa Rica from further extension of its seaward claim. The territorial waters of Belize are likewise restricted by the converging claims of Mexico and Honduras.

Elsewhere in the Caribbean, other states find themselves shelf-locked by offshore islands. The coast of Venezuela presents two examples of the impact of offshore islands on the territorial sea of the mainland state. At the eastern end of the Caribbean, the island of Trinidad, lying just off the coast, blocks the Venezuelan claim to an area of the shallow waters of the continental shelf. Further to the west, the Dutch islands of Aruba, Curaçao, and Bonaire, restrict the extent of Venezuela's territorial sea in the shallow shelf areas and preempt the mainland state's claim to a large area of the central Caribbean. Along the Central American coastline, Nicaragua is partially shelf-locked by the Colombian islands of Providencia and San Andres. Cuba's territorial sea is sharply restricted by offshore islands along much of its extensive coastline; on the north by the Florida Keys and the tiny islands fringing the Bahama Bank, and on the south by the Cayman Islands and Jamaica.

There are other circumstances where islands, by their fortuitous location, contribute to the expansion of the territorial waters of the mainland state. Swan Island, in the western Caribbean, lies almost 100 miles off the Honduran coast and extends the state's territorial sea far to the north. In the Gulf of Mexico, Perez Island and Cay Arenas, north of the Yucatan Peninsula, extend Mexico's territorial waters almost 50 miles further into the central Gulf. The location of the Colombian islands of Providencia and San Andres, 100 miles off the Nicaraguan coast and over 300 miles west of the mainland of Colombia, produces a dramatic westward expansion of the state's territorial sea. Aves Island, in the eastern Caribbean, also produces a dramatic expansion of the mainland state's territorial sea. This Venezuelan island, situated almost 300 miles north of the mainland, extends the state's territorial waters substantially northward and truncates those of Puerto Rico and the Virgin Islands, and the island states of the Lesser Antilles.

This theoretical division of the Gulf of Mexico and the Caribbean Sea clearly demonstrates the problems that are likely to arise and the difficulties inherent in any attempt to reach agreement on territorial boundaries in the regional sea. Final resolution of these problems can only be achieved through negotiation between the states of the Gulf and Caribbean region. Through politico-geographic analysis of the type presented here all interests are made aware of the potential sea space available to them in order that the negotiating process may produce a peaceful, viable regime for the common good of the region.

---

[3]A.L. Shalowitz, *Shore and Sea Boundaries*, Vol. I, U. S. Department of Commerce (Washington, D. C.: U.S. Government Printing Office, 1962) pp. 230–235 outlines procedures for constructing boundaries in the territorial sea.

REFERENCES

Alexander, Lewis M., *A Comparative Study of Offshore Claims in Northwestern Europe.* Washington, Office of Naval Research, 1960.

———, "Offshore Claims and Fisheries in North-West Europe," *Yearbook of World Affairs, 14* (1960), 236–260.

———, *Offshore Geography of Northwestern Europe: The Political and Economic Problems of Delimitation and Control.* Chicago, Rand McNally, 1963.

Becker, Loftus, "The Breadth of the Territorial Sea and Fisheries Jurisdiction," *U.S. Dept. of State Bull., 40,* 1029 (March 16, 1959), 369–375.

Bloomfield, L. M., and Gerald F. Fitzgerald, *Boundary Waters Problems of Canada and the United States.* Toronto, Carswell Co., 1958.

Boggs, S. Whittemore, "Delimitation of Seaward Areas Under National Jurisdiction," *Amer. J. Internat. Law, 45,* 2 (April, 1951), 240–266.

———, "Delimitation of the Territorial Sea," *Amer. J. Internat. Law, 24* (1930), 541–555.

———, "National Claims in Adjacent Seas," *Geog. Rev., 41,* 2 (April, 1951), 185–209.

———, "Problems of Water Boundary Definition," *Geog. Rev., 27,* 3 (July, 1937), 445–456.

Cagle, Malcolm W., "The Gulf of Aqaba—Trigger for Conflict," *U.S. Naval Inst. Proc., 85,* 1 (January, 1959), 75–81.

———, "The Neglected Ocean," *U.S. Naval Inst. Proc., 84,* 11 (November, 1958), 54–61.

Clement, Donald B., "Locating Our Coastal Boundaries," *Our Public Lands, 8,* 1 (July, 1958), 8 ff.

Cohen, Saul B., "The Oblique Plane Air Boundary," *Prof. Geog., 10,* 6 (November, 1958), 11–15.

Dean, Arthur H., "The Geneva Conference on the Law of the Sea: What Was Accomplished," *Amer. J. Internat. Law, 52,* 4 (October, 1958), 607–628.

———, "The Law of the Sea," *U.S. Dept. of State Bull., 38,* 980 (April 7, 1958), 541–581.

———, "The Second Geneva Conference on the Law of the Sea: the Fight for Freedom of the Seas," *Amer. J. Internat. Law, 54,* 4 (October, 1960), 751–790.

Denz, Ernest J., "Regulation of Lake Ontario," *Military Engineer, 54,* 357 (January–February, 1962), 22–25.

Evensen, J., "The Anglo-Norwegian Fisheries Case and Its Legal Consequences," *Amer. J. Internat. Law, 46,* 4 (October, 1952), 609–630.

Goodwin, H. L., *Space: Frontier Unlimited.* Princeton, N.J., Van Nostrand, 1962.

Gross, Leo, "The Geneva Conference on the Law of the Sea and the Right of Innocent Passage through the Gulf of Aqaba," *Amer. J. Internat. Law, 53,* 3 (July, 1959), 564–594.

Guill, James H., "The Regimen of the Seas," *U.S. Naval Inst. Proc., 83,* 12 (December, 1957), 1308–1319.

Jessup, Philip C., and Howard J. Taubenfeld, "Outer Space, Antarctica, and the United Nations," *Internat. Organization, 13,* 3 (Summer, 1959), 363–379.

Joesten, Joachim, "The Second U.N. Conference on the Law of the Sea," *World Today, 16,* 6 (June, 1960), 249–257.

Keyser, C. Frank, *Tidelands; Selected References on the Question of Ownership and Development of Resources Thereof.* Washington, Library of Congress Legal Reference Service, 1957.

Kumar, C. K., "International Waterways: Strategic International Straits," *India Quart., 14,* 1 (January–March, 1958), 87–94.

Leistikow, Gunner, "The Fisheries Dispute in the North Atlantic," *Amer.-Scandinav. Rev., 47,* 1 (March, 1959), 15–24.

Melamid, Alexander, "Legal Status of the Gulf of Aqaba," *Amer. J. Internat. Law, 53,* 2 (April, 1959), 412–413.

———, "The Political Geography of the Gulf of Aqaba," *Ann. A.A.G., 47,* 3 (September, 1957), 231–240.

Moodie, A. E., "Martimime Boundaries," in *The Changing World,* W. Gordon East and A. E. Moodie (eds.). New York, World Book Company, 1957.

———, "Some Territorial Problems Associated with the Continental Shelf," *Advance. Sci., 11,* 41 (June, 1954), 42–48.

Noel, H. S., "The Law of the Sea? No! The Law of Survival," *World Fishing, 7,* 7 (July, 1958), 30–38.

Padwa, David J., "Submarine Boundaries," *Int. and Comp. Law Quart., 9,* 4 (October, 1960), 628–653.

Pearcy, G. Etzel, "Geographical Aspects of the Law of the Sea," *Ann. A.A.G., 49,* 1 (March, 1959), 1–23.

———, "Hawaii's Territorial Sea," *Prof. Geog., 11,* 6 (November, 1959), 2–6.

Renner, George T., "Arizona's Lost Seaport," *J. Geog., 61,* 2 (February, 1962), 57–59.

Selak, Charles B., "A Consideration of the Legal Status of the Gulf of Aqaba," *Amer. J. Internat. Law, 52,* 4 (October, 1958), 660–698.

Shalowitz, A. L., "The Concept of a Bay as Inland Waters," *Surveying and Mapping, 13,* 4 (October–December, 1953), 432–440.

———, "Where are Our Seaward Boundaries?" *U.S. Naval Inst. Proc., 83,* 6 (June, 1957), 616–627.

Smith, Richard Austin, "Troubled Oil on Troubled Waters," *Fortune, 54,* 6 (December, 1956), 115 ff.

Somogyi, Joseph de, "The Question of the Turkish Straits," *J. Central European Affairs, 11,* 3 (October, 1951), 279–290.

Sorensen, Max, "Law of the Sea," *Internat. Conciliation,* No. 520 (November, 1958), 195–255.

Strøyberg, Ole, "A City on the Sound," *Danish Foreign Office Journal,* No. 42 (July, 1962), 13–16.

Sundstrom, Harold W., "Exploring Korea's Seashores," *Korean Rep., 1,* 3–4 (August, 1961), 2–20.

Tuori, Heikki, "On the Technical Delimitation of Territorial Waters," *Soumen Geodeettisen Laitoksen Julkaisuja,* No. 46 (1955), 157–170.

Whiteman, Marjorie M., "Conference on the Law of the Sea: Convention on the Continental Shelf," *Amer. J. Internat. Law, 54,* 4 (October, 1958), 629–659.

CHAPTER
11
LANDLOCKED STATES:
THE PROBLEM OF ACCESS

Some two dozen states (not including a number of microstates) possess no seacoasts, and are therefore landlocked (Table 1). Almost all of these states possess more than one neighbor, and it is upon these neighbors that they depend for the transit of their overseas trade. All states require the oceans to carry a part of their external commerce, and the jealousy with which coastal states guard their rights on the high seas as well as in territorial waters indicates the importance they attach to these avenues. The landlocked state, thus, is in a disadvantageous position, unless it is guaranteed the right to use the high seas as do coastal states, the right of innocent passage in other states' territorial waters, a share of port facilities along suitable coasts, and a means of transit from that port to the state territory. That is a long list of guarantees, and in view of the international political situation, it is not surprising that landlocked states have faced crises of isolation. Indeed, a number of land boundary disputes, to which reference was made in a previous chapter, arose directly out of landlocked states' efforts to secure a permanent and free access to the open ocean.

The oceans, which at one time isolated peoples whose technology was not advanced sufficiently far to traverse them, ultimately became the routes to power and eminence for many modern states. Thus the ocean route became a major part of the state system. It carried technological skills to colonial areas and brought needed resources back to the coastal state. Bulky raw materials were unloaded at ports, where industries turning them into finished products were often located to avoid the need for another transport haul inland. A stream of goods and ideas passed constantly through the growing port cities, and the very heart of a number of states is located around such thriving centers of activity.

The landlocked state can never have such a seaboard window to the world. It can never escape the expense of hauling seaborne goods from the foreign coastal port to its own territory. Its only hope is to be permitted to carry its overseas trade to and from the nearest and cheapest port without interference and harassment. Everything may, therefore, depend upon the landlocked state's relations with its neighbor or neighbors, for the coastal state may be able to choke off these avenues in bringing political pressure to bear.

The question of maritime access became an urgent one during the nineteenth-century expansion of maritime trade, although it had been the subject of individual disputes even earlier. A state need not be absolutely landlocked to require the use of a neighboring state's facilities: its coast may be short and rocky or otherwise unsuitable for port development. That state may then develop a port along a river whose lower reaches traverse the territory of another state. If the state possessing the river mouth closes off that entry, the port upstream is left without egress. This, basically, is what occurred when the Dutch closed off the lower Schelde (Scheldt) River, in the middle of the seventeenth century. The port city of Antwerp was isolated and stagnated until almost a century and a half later. With the consolidation of colonial empires during the nineteenth century and the rapid increase in the volume of overseas trade, the search began for permanent solutions to prevent similar situations from developing.

Recent years have added another liability to the list of landlocked states' disadvantages: the partitioning and allocation of the world's continental shelves. Note that Europe's landlocked states do not get a share of the European continental shelf as shown divided by the map on page 212, it is the coastal states that lay automatic claim to these areas. Certainly a case can be made for landlocked states' rights to a measure of the continental shelves' resources, but are coastal states likely to accept such a position? In the light of

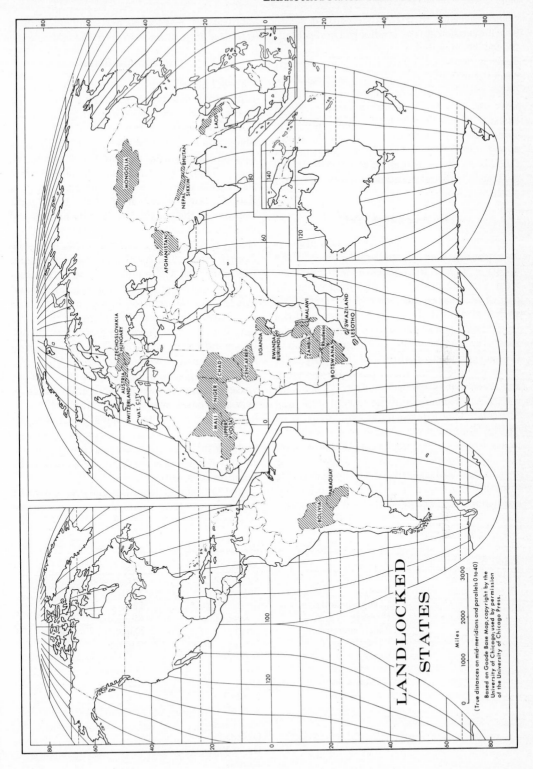

LANDLOCKED
STATES

Miles
0   1000   2000   3000

(True distances on mid-meridians and parallels 0 to 40)

Based on Goode Base Map, copyright by the
University of Chicago, used by permission
of the University of Chicago Press.

several decades of aggrandizement, it seems not. Nevertheless, the landlocked states *could* indeed be awarded a share if a system were devised whereby continental shelves were parceled into blocs of equal size (say square or hexagonal in shape) and clusters of these blocs were awarded to all states on some equitable basis. Unfortunately, landlocked states are comparatively few in number, none is a major power, and several, far from questing for sections of the continental shelf, still do not possess secure and permanent overland routes of access and egress.

THE ALTERNATIVES

Access to the coast and the high seas, then, is an essential part of the state system. The question is how such access is best provided, with a minimum loss of sovereignty on the part of the coastal state providing transit, and with a minimum degree of dependence of the landlocked state upon the whims of the coastal state. Depending to a large extent upon the geographical realities of the particular situation, there are three possibilities. First, any river that is navigable and traverses both the landlocked state and the coastal state may be declared by international agreement to be an international river, similar to the high seas in its freedom. Second, the landlocked state may be provided with an actual corridor or strip of land leading either to the open ocean or to an international river. Third, the landlocked state may be guaranteed the use of adequate facilities at a specified port, and freedom of transit along a connecting railroad and/or road.

International Rivers

Chronologically, the concept of the international river developed first. The world's major rivers served as means of penetration when the European expansion into colonial realms took place, and a number of these rivers, declared of international status at that time, remain so today. The idea of the international river had its origins in eighteenth-century concepts of natural law, which held that rivers form avenues to the oceans provided by nature, and thus cannot be closed off by man's actions. Hence the Amazon and the Rio de la Plata, the Congo, Niger, and Zambezi, as well as the St. Lawrence and Colorado, all became international rivers according to various international agreements and treaties, as did the Rhine and the Danube. But some other, minor rivers did not, and they later came to present problems. In several cases, rivers became the subject of treaties signed between interested states only, and were reserved exclusively for use by vessels flying the flags of the riparian states. In very few cases where a river forms the sole natural outlet for the landlocked state has the coastal neighbor ever obstructed its use. Perhaps international commerce was restricted, but not the use made of the waterway by the interior country.

Use is made of international rivers also by states that do have their own coasts but desire

Table 1 LANDLOCKED STATES

America	Europe	Africa	Asia
Bolivia	(Andorra)[a]	Botswana	Afghanistan
Paraguay	Austria	Burundi	Bhutan
	Czechoslovakia	Central African	Laos
	Hungary	Republic	Mongolia
	(Liechtenstein)	Chad	Nepal
	Luxembourg	Lesotho	Sikkim
	Switzerland	Malawi	
	(San Marino)	Mali	
	(Vatican City)	Niger	
		Rhodesia[b]	
		Rwanda	
		Swaziland	
		Uganda	
		Upper Volta	
		Zambia	

[a] Microstates are in parentheses.
[b] Officially still a British dependency.

supplementary exits. Thus the Schelde remains a major exit route for Belgium, which has its own North Sea coast, and the Parana system serves southern Brazil. The United States is served by the St. Lawrence Seaway, which is a supplementary outlet for the Midwest. West Germany has its own northern ports, but sends and receives a great deal of trade on rivers and canals traversing the Netherlands. Again, this may be regulated by separate treaty or sanctioned by general international agreement.

Corridors

Before the pattern of world boundaries attained its present condition of relative permanency and stability, and disputes, shifts, and land exchanges were still being carried on, the idea of the land corridor as a solution to the plight of landlocked states was popular. Today, few would propose such a solution for Uganda, Zambia, or Bolivia. Even in Africa, where internal colonial borders have only recently become international political boundaries, the rearrangement of boundaries is not contemplated, despite the obvious liabilities many African boundaries constitute. But in the Europe of a half century ago, the aftermath of war and the search for permanent peace produced several suggestions of corridors for landlocked states.

The most famous example of the type is the Polish Corridor, established after the end of the first World War. Without a Baltic outlet, Poland would have been landlocked, and, worse, its transit exits would have been under the control of peoples who had a history of enmity with the Poles. Hence the establishment of a corridor was deemed essential, but in all probability no suitable site could have been found without the fortuitous location, near the coast, of a body of people possessing ethnic and historic ties with the Poles. This combination—the need for a physical outlet and the existence in the coastal zone of an ethnic group justifiably incorporated with Poland—led to the creation of the Polish Corridor. Poland obtained the use of the port at Gdynia, but in turn the Germans were granted free transit on railroads crossing Poland between Germany and East Prussia.[1]

[1]For a detailed discussion of the Polish (primary) case see R. Hartshorne, "The Polish Corridor," *The Journal of Geography,* XXXVI, 5 (May, 1937) 161–176. A secondary case is described by R. A. Helin, "Finland Regains an Outlet to the Sea: The Saimaa Canal," *The Geographical Review,* 58, 2 (April, 1968), 167–194.

When a state obtains a corridor, its territory is actually expanded, its shape may become prorupt (in view of the functions of the corridor, it may be argued that the shape characteristic of such a state is *always* prorupt), and sovereignty extended over the corridor zone. Obviously this is a more desirable solution for any state than either a river route through another state or the use of a neighbor's port facilities and railroads. The power of the state applies in the corridor also; it never applies in the international river and may not be of much use where transit rights are violated. This principle has also been recognized by states that already possessed coasts, but which desired supplementary outlets for various reasons. Thus it is possible to recognize several types of corridors: those resembling the Polish case, which may be referred to as primary, those extending from coastal states and territories toward international rivers, perhaps best described as secondary, and those established for reasons other than trade and commerce.

Another example of the Polish case, though with certain important differences, is that of Finland and its Arctic Corridor. The similarity lies in the fact that an actual land transfer took place here, and the differences lie in the usefulness of the corridor and the cultural landscape through which it was laid. Finland's Arctic Corridor was, in a way, a birthday present, for it was granted sovereignty over the corridor at the time the state emerged as a sovereign political entity, 1920. Unlike the Polish Corridor, the belt of land involved was barely populated, but it was expected to give the young state a winter outlet, which the icebound southern ports did not provide. Indeed, Finland in winter is a practically landlocked state. The port of Petsamo was established in the hope that its development would justify the creation of the corridor itself. But while the Polish Corridor lies relatively near the heart of that country, Finland's Arctic Corridor was about as far from the core of the country as it could possibly be. The ocean journey to Petsamo, despite the ice-free aspect of the port, remained a considerable undertaking. Then goods were to be shipped hundreds of miles southward, and vice versa. Petsamo never developed, the corridor never justified itself, and at the end of the second World War the territory was taken over by the U.S.S.R.

Elsewhere in Europe, corridors were temporarily established through boundary nego-

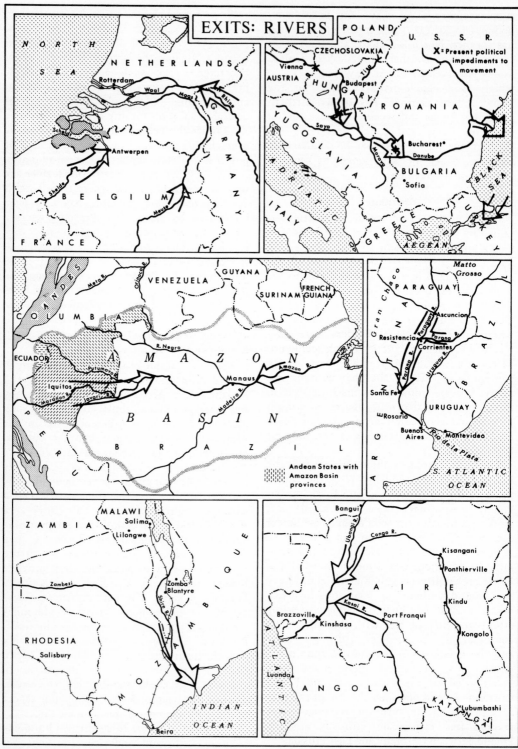

tiation or actual armed hostilities. The Kingdom of Hungary once possessed a corridor to
the Adriatic. Bulgaria fought for and gained
access to the Aegean Sea, but lost its corridor
less than a decade after gaining it. The

Kingdom of Serbia, one of the components of
the present state of Yugoslavia, attempted to
reach the Adriatic Sea through territory now
part of the state of Albania. The Hungarian
corridor was a primary one; the Bulgarian push

to the Aegean Sea took place despite the fact that this country possessed a Black Sea coast (and frontage on the Danube River) at the same time.

In Africa and the Middle East, a number of corridors of both a primary and secondary nature have developed. Corridors for Iraq to the Persian Gulf and Jordan to the Gulf of Aqaba constitute the only coastal exists for these states. Except for the final definition of Israeli territory, the Middle East boundary framework was mainly consolidated during the interwar period. Iraq, for example, acquired its corridor in 1922. Israel's share of the Gulf of Aqaba is properly a secondary corridor, for that state also possesses a Mediterranean coast. However, the denial of rights in the Suez Canal prior to the 1967 June War rendered the Gulf of Aqaba a potentially important avenue for the Israeli state, despite the fact that the United Arab Republic also sought to block this waterway to Israeli shipping. These attempts provided the motive for the 1967 conflict. The most obviously prorupt territories in Africa are the Congo Republic (Zaïre) and South West Africa. The Zaïre corridor to the ocean is a primary one; South West Africa possesses an extensive coastline. The Belgian government exchanged land with the Portuguese as late as 1927 in order to render the Congo corridor an effective one. The Belgians acquired a small area of just over one square mile for the development of the ocean port of Matadi; they yielded 480 square miles to the Portuguese elsewhere. South West Africa's proruption (the Caprivi Strip) was established in response to German demands at the 1885 Berlin Conference, where Germany stated a desire to link its South West African realm to the international Zambezi River. The Strip was established between mostly geometric boundaries, and constitutes one of the major politicogeographical liabilities in Southern Africa. Its original purpose has never been fulfilled, and its major function at present is to extend the South African sphere of influence deeply into the northern sector of Southern Africa.

In South America, secondary corridors have been the subject of a number of boundary disputes. Ecuador, though possessing Pacific Ocean ports, has attempted to establish a corridor along the Rio Marañon, to include the (Peruvian) river port of Iquitos. The object of this eastward extension, of course, is to provide its eastern interior an outlet to the Atlantic via the great international waterway of the Amazon River.[2] Peru, however, has retained control over Iquitos, and in 1922 yielded to Colombia the Leticia corridor, thus connecting that country to the Marañon River. Leticia is Colombia's Amazon port, and the corridor is defined, as in the case of South West Africa, by geometric boundaries.[3]

Study of the world map will reveal a number of other primary and secondary corridors, such as that acquired by the Portuguese, extending up the Zambezi River to Zumbo, another claimed by the Bolivians, extending into present-day Paraguay and toward the Parana River system, and so forth. Some corridors have disappeared, while others still survive on the world map. Afghanistan's Wakhan Province (or Wakhan Strip, as it is often called) no longer performs the function of separator, as it did during the last century when Russian and English realms were kept apart by a buffer zone of which Afghanistan formed a part. Despite the formidable barrier created by the Hindu Kush, that corridor was viewed as extremely important in the maintenance of a delicate peace in Asia; today the politicogeographical situation is quite different. Nevertheless, the corridor exists as an apparently permanent part of the Asian boundary framework, and like some other corridors, it may come to play a role of importance once again.[4]

Transit

The third and last solution to the problem of the landlocked state is that of free transit. This is the means of access upon which most of the landlocked states of the world depend. In 1921, a Freedom of Transit Conference was held at Barcelona, and some forty coastal states signed

[2]For a useful discussion of the origins and development of the Ecuador-Peru territorial conflict see L. A. Wright, "A Study of the Conflict between the Republics of Peru and Ecuador," Geog. J., 98 (1941), 253–272.

[3]For a summary of the whole question involving the Upper Amazon territories see R. S. Platt, "Conflicting Territorial Claims in the Upper Amazon," in Geographical Aspects of International Relations, Chicago, University of Chicago Press, 1938, p. 243.

[4]The Caprivi Strip, for example, long a relatively useless (to the South African government) area of Bantu occupance, in 1965 attained sudden strategic significance with the emergence of an independent Zambia (formerly Northern Rhodesia). Exposed to a black African state along the Zambezi River, South Africa immediately began construction of a major military base in the Strip. See Sunday Times, Johannesburg, June 20, 1965.

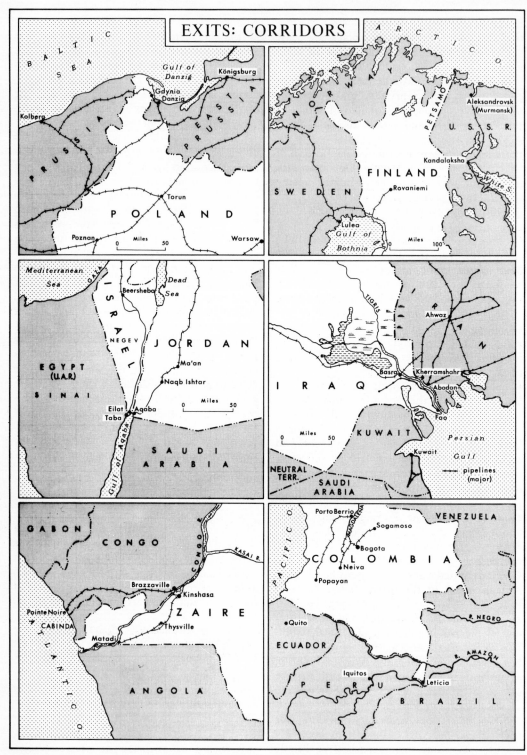

EXITS: CORRIDORS

a Convention which was later ratified by more than three quarters of them. This Convention holds that such states as are signatories shall assist the movement of goods across their territory from landlocked states to the nearest seaport, levying no discriminatory toll, tax, or freight charges. A number of bilateral treaties were also signed, especially by those states that did not finally ratify the Convention of 1921, binding the signatories to similar cooperation.

In 1957, the United Nations took up the

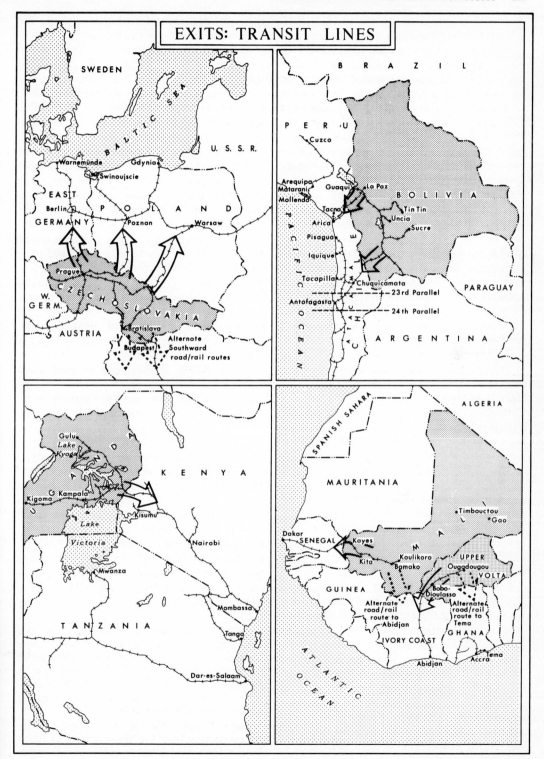

EXITS: TRANSIT LINES

question of landlocked states once again, in an effort to codify general practice in a new, internationally observed treaty. Since the 1958 Law of the Sea Conference at Geneva did not specifically address itself to this matter, a brief conference was held prior to this meeting, to which about a dozen landlocked states' representatives were invited. Several draft proposals were prepared, and when the Geneva Conference formally convened, the rights of landlocked states were recognized when the rights of states on the high seas and in territorial waters were redefined. However, the representation at this conference indicates to what extent the situation has changed in the past few years. In 1958, no African landlocked state was represented; today there are 14 landlocked African states. This almost doubles the number of interested states as of 1958, and it brings with it a whole new set of actual and potential problems. Already, African states such as Mali and Upper Volta have had occasion to divert their trade from primary ports (in this case Dakar) to other outlets, because of political friction. The internal political situation in independent Malawi is closely related to that state's dependence upon neighboring, Portuguese-administered Mozambique. Zambia needs an outlet through Portuguese Angola or through Tanzania. In order to avoid the uncertainly of dependence upon a white-controlled territory, Zambia now awaits the completion of the *Tanzam* Railroad, which will provide a link to the sea via Tanzania and its port, Dar es Salaam.

Uganda's only usable exit is the port of Mombasa, Kenya, but there are deep-seated problems in East Africa which could cause Uganda to search for other outlets. Chad and Cameroun depend heavily upon the Nigerian transport system, while Upper Volta is sending the bulk of its external trade through the Ivory Coast port of Abidjan. But if the lessons of the Balkans, the Middle East, and South America are any guide, trouble must be expected to arise in some of these instances. The Barcelona Conference was the result of decades of adjustment and readjustment, violent and nonviolent. The African situation is quite new, and adjustment here has only begun.

This is not to suggest that the principles of free transit do not apply in Africa, or that African states are likely to be less willing than other states to adhere to the general practice as stated at Barcelona. But in Southern Africa, the adjacent location of Sovereign African and white-ruled territories, and the great ideological barrier between them, creates political tensions which are bound to have economic consequences. Elsewhere on the great continent political associations and alignments are just taking shape. The ill-fated Mali Federation is an example: the state of Senegal and the former Republic of Soudan joined in a federal state. Soudan lay in the hinterland of Dakar, and had always exported and imported through that port. When a political crisis rent the federation apart, Soudan (which retained

the name Mali) found itself having to use the far less suitably positioned port of Abidjan.

Although it is generally true that coastal states honor their obligation to permit the transit of landlocked states' trade, there are exceptions. These exceptions, as in the case of Southern Africa quoted above, usually involve serious ideological disputes, and the interruptive boundaries across which such trade cannot move are often of the superimposed variety. Arab states refuse to permit the transit of Israeli goods. South Africa has refused to permit certain individuals and some goods to enter Lesotho. Recent interference with traffic between West Germany and West Berlin illustrates this point also, and yet goods bound for Czechoslovakia have long been handled at Hamburg and have crossed the Iron Curtain without difficulty. But where the boundary between the landlocked state and the coastal state upon which it would normally depend is an ideological boundary of great contrast, problems tend to arise, despite temporary adherence to the principle of free transit.

The question of the rights of landlocked states was again taken up in 1964 and 1965 by a committee of twenty-four delegations representing landlocked, transit, and other interested states.[5] The draft convention considered by this committee had been prepared by Afro-Asian landlocked countries, so that the interests of the new landlocked states were represented. Important among the twenty articles in the draft convention were those relating to the expediting of transit trade, limitations on dues and expenses incurred by the landlocked state's traffic, customs exemptions, free storage, and the provision of free zones at ports of entry. Still, there remain clauses that inevitably put the coastal state in a favored position:

No Contracting State shall be bound by this Convention to afford transit to persons whose admission into its territories is forbidden, or for goods of a kind of which the importation is prohibited, either on grounds of public morals, public health or security, or as a precaution against diseases of animals or plants.[6]

[5]United Nations, *Report of the Committee on the Preparation of a Draft Convention relating to Transit Trade of Land-locked Countries,* March, 1965. Participating were delegations from Afghanistan, Argentina, Austria, Bolivia, Chile, Czechoslovakia, India, Ivory Coast, Japan, Liberia, Mali, Nepal, Netherlands, Niger, Nigeria, Pakistan, Paraguay, Senegal, Switzerland, U.S.S.R., United Kingdom, U.S.A., Upper Volta, Yugoslavia. Only ten of these states are landlocked.

[6]Ibid., p. 41.

In many ways the most recent Convention, signed in mid-1965, resembles that of Barcelona.[7] The inescapable fact is that even the present Convention still does not guarantee the landlocked state the freedom of access it desires. We have seen how difficult it is for any state to give up any degree of sovereignty, however small. Real freedom of transit, obviously, demands this. As soon as the coastal state can decide that the goods purchased by, and in transit to, a landlocked neighbor are injurious to its "security," the principle of free transit comes to depend upon the good relations between the two states. When relations deteriorate, the question is likely to become one of power. And here, the coastal state has a great initial advantage.

A few states that enjoy a guaranteed access route to the sea fought for a corridor, and lost. In Europe, Hungary may be cited as an example, and it once did have a coast on the Adriatic Sea—unlike the Kingdom of Serbia, which was to be amalgamated before it achieved its goal. The most telling case, from many points of view, is that of Bolivia, a state that also once possessed a corridor to the Pacific Ocean, and which lost that corridor through mismanagement and misfortune.

THE PACIFIC (TRIANGULAR) WAR

The misfortunes of landlocked states are probably nowhere more dramatically illustrated than by the historical geography of Bolivia. As recently as the 1930's Bolivia was at war with its neighbors, an objective being the improvement of the country's routes to the outside world. After their 1932–1935 war with Paraguay, the Bolivians hoped to be able to establish a port on the Rio Paraguay, thus creating an eastward transit to complement the tenuous routes to the Pacific coast of Chile. That the attempt failed was only a confirmation of a century of frustration.

The wind of change came to Latin America a century and a half ago. During the first quarter of the nineteenth century, a number of Latin American territories rebelled against Spanish overlordship, and with success. Bolivia became an independent state in 1825, after a war of independence that lasted several years. In fact Bolivia (named after the great Latin American, Simon Bolivar) then was part of

Peru, and known as Upper Peru; at the time of independence its separation from Peru became effective and its new name was adopted. But independence did not bring stability, and uprisings in Bolivia and Peru kept sapping the state's energies. In those days of ill-defined and undemarcated boundaries, Bolivia had a sphere of influence along what is today the north Chilean coast. When, in the early 1860's, rich deposits of nitrate and guano were discovered in the coastal areas of the Atacama Desert, there was a threat of war over these resources between Bolivia and Chile. But the Treaty of 1866 prevented an open outbreak of hostilities and at the same time defined the Chile-Bolivia boundary as lying along the 24th parallel of latitude. This meant that such towns as Antofagasta, Cobija, and Tocopilla were within Bolivian territory—certainly an ample outlet for that state. Bolivia, however, did have to make some concessions. It was determined by the same treaty that Chile should have a half share of all the customs, and free use of all facilities for trading, along that part of the coast lying between 23 degrees and 24 degrees south latitude. In addition, Chile was to be allowed to mine and export such resources as this area contained, without being liable to Bolivian taxation or any interference whatsoever.

Following the signing of the treaty there was another series of revolutions and takeovers in Bolivia, and when A. Ballivan was president, in 1873, Bolivia signed a secret agreement with Peru. This agreement was due, in large part, to the increasing amount of Chilean activity in the area north of the 24th parallel and the strength of Chilean capital in the wealthier parts of the region. Ostensibly it was a collective security agreement, but the main cause of it obviously was a joint fear of Chilean expansionism. Bolivia also continued to seek adjustments with Chile itself, and by a new treaty drawn up in 1875 Chile agreed to give up its half of the customs collected at Bolivian ports, while being granted a twenty-five-year tax-free period for its enterprises in Bolivian territory. But this treaty was never actually signed, and subsequently Bolivia demanded a nitrate tax and threatened seizure of Chilean exports from territory north of the 24th parallel. The Chilean reply was swift: it sent the fleet to blockade the Bolivian ports, and in 1879 the Chileans occupied Antofagasta. The *Guerra del Pacifico* had begun.

Now the secret treaty with Peru came to play its role. Peru offered to mediate in the

[7]Additional signatories to the Convention, represented in 1965, were Chad, Malawi, Mongolia, and Zambia. Nepal, Niger, and Nigeria, which did not previously sign, also did so in 1965.

Chilean-Bolivian war, but Chile realized that the treaty existed and that this rendered the Peruvian offer of dubious validity. Chile demanded the abrogation of the treaty, and Peru refused. The result was the involvement of Peru in the hostilities, and Arica, Iquique, and Pisagua were soon taken by the Chileans. In fact Chile came close to taking all of Peru, for by 1881 Lima and Callao had fallen and only the interior of Peru remained free. In 1883 the inevitable capitulation agreements were signed—Bolivia ceding all of its coastal area to Chile, and Peru losing Arica and several other ports in the south. Thus Bolivia lost doubly, not only its own seaport of Cobija, but also the use of its ally's ports.

By 1895, Chile had returned to a conciliatory attitude, and in a treaty signed that year Chile promised to furnish Bolivia with one or more outlets, "in accord with the . . . necessity that the future development and commercial prosperity of Bolivia require her free access to the sea." But again a secret agreement had grave consequences for the Bolivians. This time their partner was powerful Argentina (involved in a lengthy boundary dispute with Chile along the Andes). The Argentinians and Chileans eventually settled their dispute, and Chile, upon hearing of the secret treaty with Bolivia, changed its positive attitude concerning any return of land and ports to Bolivia. It was another decade until, in 1904, the two countries finally settled their postwar negotiations. In some ways Bolivia was fortunate, although the country did become permanently landlocked by the 1904 treaty. The Chileans, however, agreed to build a railroad to connect the Bolivian capital of La Paz to the coastal port of Arica, and undertook to guarantee Bolivia free transit through Chilean territory to certain ports including Arica. But, as C. F. Jones has said, in effect "Bolivia . . . lost 30,000 square miles of territory in the province of Antofagasta, its valuable nitrate and copper deposits, and the outlet to the Pacific, from which the country can never recover completely."[8]

Thus did one of the two dozen landlocked states of the world come to find itself in this situation. There can be no question that Bolivia would have progressed to a far greater extent had it retained exits of its own. Still, it may be argued that Bolivia's present position, in view of its political activities, is more

[8]C. F. Jones, *South America*, New York, Holt. 1942, p. 227.

fortunate than it might have been. Chile does guarantee free transit and has fulfilled its promises. Nevertheless, the threat of a political disagreement with Chile and the possible consequences hangs constantly over the Bolivian government.

THE FUTURE

"During the interwar years," wrote Pounds in 1959, "there was a tendency, politically motivated in part, to deprecate the need for corridors and to stress the adequacy of guaranteed rights of transit. Since the end of the second World War, along with a weakening of the rule of law, the tendency has been in the opposite direction."[9] The proliferation of landlocked states in Africa, the deepening of world and regional ideological conflicts, and the intensification of politicomilitary activity along the inner tier of states in south and southeast Asia all support this assertion. As we have seen previously, states' own interests, in the absence of a world policing force, still can and do transcend the restraints theoretically imposed by international law. Adherence to international law still is largely voluntary, and landlocked states depend upon the conscience of their neighbors. In the present-day world, that is a precarious position.

REFERENCES

Barton, Thomas Frank, "Outlets to the Sea for Landlocked Laos," *J. Geog.*, 59, 5 (May, 1960), 206–220.

Berber, F. J., *Rivers in International Law*. London, Stevens and Sons, 1959.

Bindoff, S. T., *The Scheldt Question*. London, George Allen & Unwin, Ltd., 1945.

Brunskill, G. S., "Navigable Waterways of Africa; Urgent Need for a Co-ordinated International System," *Dock and Harbour Authority*, 30, 345 (July, 1949), 75–76.

Campbell, John C., "Diplomacy on the Danube," *Foreign Affairs*, 27, 2 (January, 1949), 315–327.

Crary, Douglas D., "Geography and Politics in the Nile Valley," *Middle East J.*, 3, 3 (July, 1949), 260–276.

Donald, Sir Robert, *The Polish Corridor and the Consequences*. London, Thornton Butterworth, Ltd., 1929.

East, W. Gordon, "The Geography of Land-locked States," *Trans. and Papers, Ins. Brit. Geographers*, Publ. No. 28, 1960, pp. 1–20.

[9]The quotation is from the conclusion of an excellent summary of the major problems associated with landlocked states. See N. J. G. Pounds, "A Free and Secure Access to the Sea," *Ann. A.A.G.*, 49, 3 (September, 1959), 256–268.

Fifer, J. V., *Bolivia: Land, Location, and Politics Since 1825,* Cambridge University Press, 1972.

Freeman, T. W., and Mary M. Macdonald, "The Arctic Corridor of Finland," *Scot. Geog. Mag.,* 54, 4 (July, 1938), 219–230.

Gerson, L.L., *Woodrow Wilson and the Rebirth of Poland.* New Haven, Conn., Yale University Press, 1953.

Hamel, J.A. van, *Danzig and the Polish Problem.* New York, Carnegie Endowment for International Peace, 1933.

Helin, R. A., "Finland Regains an Outlet to the Sea: the Saimaa Canal," *Geog. Rev.,* 58, 2 (April, 1968), 167–194.

Hill, N., *Claims to Territory in International Law and Relations.* New York, Oxford University Press, 1945.

Hirsch, Abraham M., "Utilization of International Rivers in the Middle East; a Study of Conventional International Law," *Amer. J. Internat. Law,* 50, 1 (January, 1956), 81–100.

Huang, Thomas T. F., "Some International and Legal Aspects of the Suez Canal Question," *Amer. J. Internat. Law,* 51, 2 (April, 1957), 277–307.

Kain, Ronald Stuart, "Bolivia's Claustrophobia," *Foreign Affairs,* 16, 4 (July, 1938), 704–713.

Kerner, R. J., *The Urge to the Sea: the Course of Russian History.* Berkeley, University of California Press, 1942.

Kuehnelt–Leddihn, Erik R. V., "The Petsamo Region," *Geog. Rev.,* 34, 3 (July, 1944), 405–417.

Langlands, B. W., "Concepts of the Nile," *Uganda J.,* 26, 1 (March, 1962), 1–22.

Laylin, John G., and Rinaldo L. Bianchi, "The Rôle of Adjudication in International River Disputes," *Amer. J. Internat. Law,* 53, 1 (January, 1959), 30–49.

Mance, Sir O., *International River and Canal Transport.* London, Oxford University Press, 1945.

Morris, Kenton W., "The St. Lawrence Seaway—Its Development and Economic Significance," *J. Geog.,* 55, 9 (December, 1956), 447–452.

Munger, Edwin S., *Geography of Ocean Outlets for the Belgian Congo.* Elizabethville, Congo, Institute of Current World Affairs, 1952.

Newbigin, Marion I., *Geographical Aspects of the Balkan Problems in Their Relation to the Great European War.* New York, G. P. Putnam & Sons, 1915.

Pendle, George, *Paraguay, a Riverside Nation.* London and New York, Royal Institute of International Affairs, 1954.

Platt, Robert S., "Conflicting Territorial Claims in the Upper Amazon," in *Geographical Aspects of International Relations,* Charles C. Colby (ed.). Chicago, University of Chicago Press, 1938.

Pounds, Norman J. G., "A Free and Secure Access to the Sea," *Ann. A.A.G.,* 49, 3 (September, 1959), 256–268.

Smith, H. A., "The Waters of the Jordan; a Problem of International Water Control," *Internat. Affairs,* 25, 4 (October, 1949), 415–425.

Smogorzewski, Casimir, *Poland, Germany and the Corridor.* London, Williams and Norgate, 1930.

Van Cleef, Eugene, "Finland—Bridge to the Atlantic," *J. Geog.,* 48, 3 (March, 1949), 99–105.

Wright, L. A., "A Study of the Conflict between the Republics of Peru and Ecuador," *Geog. J.,* 98, 5–6 (November-December, 1941), 253–272.

Part
III
Theories and Models

CHAPTER
12
LINEAGES AND KINSHIPS

It is probably true that the majority of all the research and writing done in political geography was produced in the past 25 years or so. It is also true that political geography, among the various fields within the discipline of geography, was relatively late in developing fully. But this does not mean that political geography is without an ancient heritage. On the contrary; in the Aztec state, in the Mali empire, in ancient Egypt, and in pre-Han China there were philosophers who sought answers to questions about the political behavior of man in his relationships with the environment. Conjecture about politics never has been the monopoly of societies that have left a written history; preliterate societies, too, had their scholars. All too often we can only guess at their thoughts and opinions, or we have to use the reports of outsiders to piece things together. The Spanish invaders wrote about the Aztec and Inca states they conquered. Arab writers such as Ibn Battuta described what they saw in the cities of indigenous West Africa. Undoubtedly, there were geographers among those ancient philosophers—and some of them were political geographers.

Although it would be unreasonable to claim that Aristotle was a political geographer, the fact is that some of his writings are among the oldest known pieces of politicogeographical description and speculation. Aristotle spent most of his lifetime (384 to 322 B.C.) in Athens, and he wrote about the Greek city-states in the context of their populations and resources. Long before the concept of environmental determinism became fashionable, Aristotle speculated about the effect of the environment on the qualities of people. Thus, he suggested, peoples living in the cold climate of Europe were "full of spirit," but of inadequate intelligence and skill; they would be free, but poorly organized politically and incapable of ruling others. And the people of Asia (as known to Aristotle) were "intelligent and inventive," but without the spirit of the Europeans; they were destined to live in subjugation. Between the Europeans and the Asians lived the Greeks, who had it all—intelligence, skill, freedom, and good government.

Aristotle also wrote about the idea of national self-sufficiency (many centuries before the doctrine of mercantilism emerged), about the role of the capital city, about boundaries, aspects of relative location, urban planning, and even conservation. Certainly he had the spatial orientation of a geographer, and many of the specific interests of a political geographer.

To Strabo (63 B.C. to 24 A.D.), geography was no mere sideline. Strabo, also a Greek scholar, must have been one of the world's first professional geographers. He studied in Rome and lived for a time in Alexandria, and he traveled widely through the world as it was known by his contemporaries. He, too, took a determinist view of man-environment relationships, and in the work for which he principally remains known, his *Geography*, he searches for a definition of the "ideal" environment.[1] Strabo's work was not strictly a political geography, of course, but through its references to earlier works and its enormous detail it constitutes an invaluable window on ancient geography in general.

Strabo's massive works apparently did not encourage his successors to follow in his footsteps, for nothing even remotely approaching them was done for more than 1000 years. Strabo's *Geography* soon became a classic, but the rebirth of geography did not come until the sixteenth- and seventeenth-century map makers began to produce their work. And the seventeenth century also witnessed the research of a man who has been called the pioneer of political geography, William Petty. Dr. Petty was trained in medicine, and in 1650

[1]The *Geography* may have been an appendix to his *History*, a 47-volume work, which, except for a few small parts, has been lost. The *Geography* consists of two introductory volumes, followed by eight on Europe, six on Asia, and one on Africa.

taught anatomy at Oxford, apparently setting out on a career in that field. But in 1654 he began an enormous project, involving the creation of an atlas of Ireland at a scale of 1:10,000. The work was eventually completed and published two years before his death; it was so accurate that it remained the standard reference for more than a century.

William Petty was more than a diligent compiler and cartographer, however. His training was in medicine, and he knew the usefulness of field observation and experimentation. In a work published in 1662, he discussed the evolution of urban centers and the territorial and demographic elements in the power of states. In his *Political Anatomy of Ireland* and in another volume entitled *Political Arithmetic*, he identifies and discusses a host of politicogeographical issues, such as the concept of the sphere of influence, the factor of distance in human activity, the role of capital cities, natural defenses, agglomeration and dispersal as factors in the strength of states, and more.

Petty never identified himself as a geographer, and later biographers have described him as a political scientist and as an economist. But his appreciation of the spatial element in his assessments of states, cities, and so many other relevant phenomena was clearly that of a geographer. Petty recognized problems that still confront political geographers today. In many instances he was the first to state those problems, and his search for solutions pointed the way quite clearly for other practitioners of the discipline.[2]

Somehow, Petty's ideas were allowed to lie dormant for more than a century, until Karl Ritter (1779 to 1859) and Alexander von Humboldt (1769 to 1859) brought new life to geography in general and, notably in Ritter's case, to political geography. Ritter's *Allgemeine Vergleichende Erdkunde (General Comparative Geography)*, in a sense, was the first real attempt to develop theory in relation to the growth of states and the evolution of cultures. Ritter thought that these processes had cyclic characteristics, and this gave him an opportunity to write predictively, to forecast the rise and decline of states. It was an important step, an initial try at the creation of *models* in political geography.

[2]Notwithstanding Petty's pioneering work, he is often omitted entirely from discussions of the rise of political geography. For a detailed report on his contributions see Y.M. Goblet, *Political Geography and the World Map*, London, Philip & Son, 1955, p. 5 ff.

FRIEDRICH RATZEL

Often called the father of modern political geography, Friedrich Ratzel (1844 to 1904) deserves special attention in any discussion of the emergence of this field. What Ritter had written about the growth of states was not lost on Ratzel, but Ratzel carried the idea of cyclic state growth much farther. He proposed that states, like biological organisms, experience life cycles. Thus Ratzel's *organic theory* of state evolution has been interpreted to suggest that states, as organisms, go through stages of growth and decay. Just as an organism requires food, so the state needs space. Any state, to retain its vigor and to continue to thrive, must have space in increasing quantity. Space, or territory, is therefore the state's life-giving force. Hence boundaries are obstructive, static phenomena, negative factors in the state-organism's life cycle, for they inhibit growth. Frontiers, on the other hand, are desirable and necessary, for they afford opportunities for expansion and assimilation.

Ratzel's comparison of the state to a biological organism was rooted in his early training in zoology, chemistry, and journalism. He was a keen observer and a powerful writer, and an immensely prolific one. The best known among his 24 books are his *Anthropogeography* (published in several parts between 1882 and 1912) and *Political Geography*, published in 1897. But much of what Ratzel wrote has never been translated into English; one of his most important articles, *The Laws of the Spatial Growth of States*, was published for the first time in an English translation in 1969.[3] In this article, Ratzel identifies seven laws governing the territorial growth of states:

1. The size of the state grows with its culture.

2. The growth of states follows other manifestations of the growth of peoples which must necessarily precede the growth of the state.

3. The growth of the state proceeds by the annexation of smaller members into the agglomerate. At the same time the relationship of the population to the earth becomes continuously closer.

4. The boundary is the peripheral organ of

[3]This article, *Die Gesetze des Raumlichen Wachstums der Staaten*, was published in *Petermanns Mitteilungen*, XLII, in 1896. It was published, translated by Ronald L. Bolin, in R.E. Kasperson and J.V. Minghi, *The Structure of Political Geography*, Chicago, Aldine, 1969, pp. 17–28.

the state, the bearer of its growth as well as its fortifications, and takes part in all the transformations of the organism of the state.

5. In its growth the state strives toward the envelopment of politically valuable positions.

6. The first stimuli to the spatial growth of states come to them from the outside.

7. The general tendency toward territorial annexation and amalgamation is transmitted from state to state and continually increases in intensity.[4]

What is clear from these "laws" is that Ratzel was trying to do what Petty had done before him, apply the methods of the natural sciences to problems of geography. But Ratzel was aware of the problems involved; several times in his books and essays he stresses the point that the "laws" do not derive from exact statistical measures but instead from accumulated probabilities.

Ratzel's prodigious output of geographical writing had an enormous impact upon the field's development in Europe, and not just on political geography. Like his predecessors, Ratzel took a determinist view of the relationships between man and his environment. An American geographer, Ellen Churchill Semple, studied with Ratzel at the University of Leipzig in the early 1890's, and in her book, *Influences of Geographic Environment*, she brought the salient features of Ratzel's views to the English-speaking audience.[5] Here the determinist philosophy was espoused by Ellsworth Huntington, and it became a dominant refrain in American geography for several decades. And Ratzel's organic theory seemed to be a direct parallel to contemporary viewpoints in physical geography. In the early part of the twentieth century, the American physical geographer William Morris Davis (1850 to 1934) propounded a cyclic theory of landscape evolution, in which he suggested that the several stages involved might be termed those of youth, maturity, and old age.[6] What would be more natural than to attach these terms to the life cycle of the state?

This was done in the United States by S. van Valkenburg, who in the 1930's—borrowing from Ritter, Ratzel, and Davis—proposed a cycle theory of the development of states.

Although this is no longer an important or popular theme in political geography, Van Valkenburg's statement of the idea gives insight into the essentials of this concept in a clear and concise manner. He describes it as

. . . based on a cycle in the political development of nations, recognizing four stages, namely *youth, adolescence, maturity,* and *old age.* After completion the cycle may renew itself, possibly with a change in political extension, while the cycle can also be interrupted at any time and brought back to a former stage. The time element (the length of a stage) differs greatly from nation to nation and depends on the character of the State; correspondingly no forecast can be made on the time shift to a next stage.[7]

According to the theory, states in these various stages will exhibit certain characteristics which will be reflected in their external relationships. The stages and characteristics of the states are identified as follows:

1. *Youth.* An emergent state, immediately after its creation or attainment of sovereignty, is characterized by the need for internal organization, and that is where the nation's attention will be focused. The consolidation of its internal structure will take up practically all its energies, so that it exhibits no tendency toward territorial expansion. Thus such a state is stable as far as its boundaries are concerned.

According to Van Valkenburg, the youthful period of the United States dates from 1776 (although some might date it earlier) to 1803 when the Louisiana Purchase took place and terminated the period of internal consolidation. He adds that some observers would extend the youthful period to 1815 when it was brought to a close by the peace treaty with England. Today, however, there are some youthful states that would belie his criteria. Certainly some of the emergent states, youthful as they are, have not confined their activities to internal consolidation. Indonesian action toward West Irian (New Guinea) and Malaysia is a case in point, as is the conflict between the Somali Republic and its neighbors of Ethiopia and Kenya over the incorporation of Somali-occupied territories of those two countries in the Somali Republic. If the Cuban revolution was a rejuvenation of the cycle, it cannot be claimed that the Cuban have confined their activities to their own country. Of course, it must be remembered

---

[4]R.E. Kasperson and J.V. Minghi, op. cit., p. 7.

[5]Ellen Churchill Semple, *Influences of Geographic Environment*, New York, Holt, 1911.

[6]W.M. Davis, "The Geographical Cycle," *Geographical Journal*, XIV (1899), 481–504.

[7]S. van Valkenburg, *Elements of Political Geography*, New York, Prentice-Hall, 1939, p. 5.

that some of the emergent states have experienced a lengthy period of internal organization in preparation for complete independence, so that they may not actually experience the youthful stage as defined by Van Valkenburg.

2. *Adolescence.* The stage of adolescence is one of territorial expansion after internal organization and consolidation have been accomplished. The state now possesses great dynamic qualities, and is able to turn its resources toward aggressive activities. As a result of the hostilities in which the state may become engaged, the nation-building process is strengthened. Many states in later stages of their evolution owe the unity of their nations to the adolescent period, which was one of great drive and patriotism, when the importance of national prestige was supreme.

In the United States, this period began in 1803 and ended more than a century later in 1918 with the purchase of the Danish West Indies. During those 115 years, the United States fought wars with Britain, Mexico, and Spain, and penetrated the Caribbean and Pacific, there to occupy vital territory. Other states expanded their colonial empires during their adolescent period: Italy's invasion of Ethiopia, British-Dutch struggles over hegemony on the sea, and German expansionism all are evidence of adolescence. Today, it may perhaps be asserted that mainland China, after its rejuvenation beginning with the Communist takeover, has now begun to enter its adolescent stage after two decades of youth and internal organization. Its territorial designs on Indian lands and its expansionist tendencies north and northwestward suggest that Chinese expansionism, which was predicted by several political geographers, may only be beginning.

3. *Maturity.* The mature state has ceased to expand, and in fact is prepared to abandon certain overseas possessions if they no longer serve a purpose in defense or trade. Armed forces now become defensive in nature rather than aggressive, and new equipment for these forces is largely designed to perform defensive functions. Commonly mature states favor international cooperation in such organizations as the United Nations, and they also display tendencies of supranationalism, seeking union with other states in the interest of economic development and collective security. Stability is at a maximum.

The United States may be said to be in this stage of its evolution, having given some evidence of willingness to give up territorial possessions in the interest of good relations with other states. In 1964 such an agreement was made with Mexico concerning a small area of El Paso, Texas, which had been changed in location as a result of the changing course of the Rio Grande River. What was hailed in Mexico as the "greatest triumph ever of Mexican diplomacy" was at least partly the result of American forbearance and a desire to retain good relations with this Latin American neighbor. The granting of independence to the Philippines fits the picture of a mature United States, although the adventure in Viet Nam does not.

Several Western European States, also, are in this group. Among the best examples are Britain and France, both of which have willingly granted independence to vast former colonial realms which were taken during the period of adolescence. Both are also involved in projects aimed at a Greater Europe—France in the Common Market (the Inner Six) and Britain in the European Free Trade Association (the Outer Seven). Many of the other states of Western Europe—Sweden, Norway, Denmark, the Netherlands, Belgium, and Italy—are examples of the type.

4. *Old Age.* This stage, according to Van Valkenburg, is one of declining power, by which we must assume is meant a failing internal organization. Internal disintegration occurs, and parts of the state may separate from the main body or may be absorbed by its neighbors. Some states have been on the verge of such decline but proved themselves able to adjust to new circumstances, which means that by changing their organizational frameworks they were able to make new use of economic and other opportunities—a sign of maturity. Several of the Western European states appeared headed for old age when they lost their colonial realms (such as the Netherlands and Belgium), but their prosperity continued within the new European economic framework. These two countries participated in the forerunner of European economic cooperation—Benelux. Others, however, seem destined to break down: Portugal continues to rely economically upon "overseas provinces" (such as Angola and Mozambique) which are not to be granted independence in the British and French manner but will be defended against internal rebellion and outside attack.

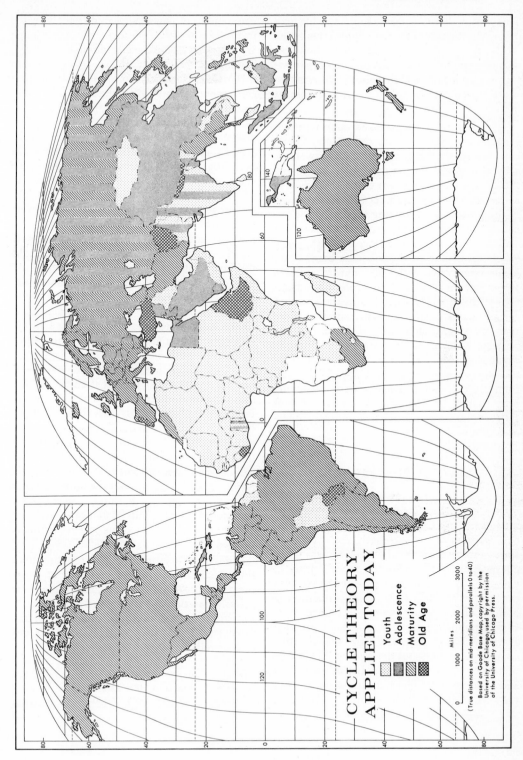

CYCLE THEORY
APPLIED TODAY

Youth
Adolescence
Maturity
Old Age

Miles
0   1000   2000   3000
(True distances on mid-meridians and parallels 0 to 40)

Based on Goode Base Map, copyright by the
University of Chicago, used by permission
of the University of Chicago Press.

This means that Portugal is not preparing for a day when the colonies are no longer available, while the cost of the seemingly hopeless defense will heavily tax the military organization of the state—which requires an army to shore up its shaky political organization at home.

The cycle theory was based upon politico-geographical research into the nineteen thirties. Today, we might prefer to classify states according to type rather than stage, still using the behavior pattern as our guide. It is possible to recognize a large number of states that are in the process of organizing themselves internally. This *organizing* type corresponds to Van Valkenburg's state in the stage of youth. Some other states may be described as being of an *expanding* type, while the mature state is perhaps better identified as *stable*. The advantage of this nomenclature lies in the fact that certain states exhibit characteristics of more than one stage (Indonesia is youthful in some respects, adolescent in others; organizing-expanding seems a clearer description). Furthermore, certain states have apparently gone from stage 1 or 2 to stage 4 without having been mature, so that the "cyclic" nature of state evolution is not always brought out by case studies.

ALTERNATIVE APPROACHES

Strabo had described the nations of the world as known to the Greeks; William Petty had made an historical analysis of Ireland; Ratzel had written of the strength and power of states—but still political geography was without clear direction. In Europe, as we will see in Chapter 13, some of Ratzel's successors used his ideas to evaluate and even to influence the policies of competing powers. In France, Y.M. Goblet published an important book entitled *Political Geography and the World Map,* completed in 1939 but delayed by World War II, which seeks to define political geography and to identify its methods and scope. But in the United States it was not until 1950 that a true landmark paper[8] appeared that addressed itself specifically to these questions (although Whittlesey's *Impress* paper, published in 1935, had dealt effectively with aspects of scope). In this article, Hartshorne proposes that political geographers should view the state (and other politically organized areas) in terms of structure and functions. The state is a politically organized space that functions effectively. How does it succeed? By overcoming the *centrifugal* forces—forces that tend to break a state apart—with the cohesion provided by prevalent *centripetal* forces, which bind the state together. Centrifugal forces exist in every state; in some states they are so powerful that they disrupt the state system completely. In Nigeria, the Biafran secession movement of the late 1960's was barely overcome; in the early 1970's the fate of a united Pakistan was sealed and the state broke up. These are highly publicized instances, but even older, more tightly knit states are not without centrifugal elements. Regional differences, ethnic pluralism, religious divisions, and other factors can afflict the state in this way. The centripetal, binding forces must prevail if the state is to have a raison d'être, a reason for existing. Professor Hartshorne suggests that "the greatest single weakness in our thinking in political geography" has been our preoccupation with the disruptive, divisive forces affecting politically organized areas, without considering the forces that manage to hold the state together. This set of centripetal forces, then, is the *functioning* state, and, Hartshorne argued a quarter of a century ago, this process should be studied.

Hartshorne's lengthy paper touches upon several additional topics, including the concepts of nation and core area, the internal and external relations of states, and all within the context of the functioning of the political unit involved. The paper still bears a careful reading today.

[8]R. Hartshorne, "The Functional Approach in Political Geography," *Annals of the Association of American Geographers, XL,* 2 (June, 1950), 95–130.

The Functional Approach in Political Geography*

Richard Hartshorne

University of Wisconsin

The subject of this paper and that of President Russell's address of last year reveal in striking fashion the wide scope of the field in which geographers work. Comparison of the treatment in the two papers will, I hope, demonstrate the justification for assuming that the same body of readers may find common interest in the two extremes. This is possible in all our work only if each of us, in developing our special area of interest, will follow Russell's example in striving to maintain its geographic quality.[1]

We can do this if we keep in the forefront of our thinking, that the core of geography is "the study of places,"[2] that is, the analysis of the significant differences that distinguish the various areas of the world from each other. Among the differences that are significant to this areal differentiation, one of the more obvious are differences in landforms; one of the least obvious to the eye, but nonetheless important in molding the character of areas, are the differences in their political organiza-

tion. In pursuing these and other separate topics, geographers "radiate out in diverse directions" "and for various distances, toward the cores of other disciplines." As long as they remain "ever conscious of where they are" in reference to the central core, they may hope to understand each other's purposes. "Questions of boundaries always seem pedantic in comparison with questions concerning the cores of disciplines."

SURVEY OF PROGRESS

From this common viewpoint, let us cast a critical eye over the progress of political geography in the twenty years since it was described as "the wayward child of the geographic family"—the field that was "least scientific," in which "method and material are free to the choice of the student," and whose relationship to the field as a whole was difficult to determine.[3] I wish that we could justify a very different description; that we could claim to have developed a sound structural evolution of political geography, clearly integrated into geography as a whole, with established methods of scientific analysis.[4]

It would be easy to point to many outward signs of success. The threat that political geography would be driven off the reservation has subsided. Whereas formerly but one or two departments of geography gave courses under this name, today political geography is found in many college curricula.

---

[1] Richard Joel Russell, "Geographical Geomorphology," *Annals of the Association of American Geographers,* XXXIX (1949): 1–11; Presidential address of the 1948 meetings delivered under the title "Towards a More Geographical Geomorphology." My title, in presenting the present paper at the April 1950 meetings was an intentional imitation: "Towards a More Geographical Political Geography."

[2] As a demonstration of the similarity of viewpoints, the phrases in this paragraph in quotation marks are taken alternately from Russell's address, *op. cit.*, p. 11, and from my own article on "On the Mores of Methodological Discussion in American Geography," *Annals of the Association of American Geographers,* XXXVIII (1948): 122. The first phrase, quoted from Russell, geography as "the study of places," stems from Vidal de la Blache and no doubt from many writers centuries before him. Any concerned with more full discussion of the function of geography are referred to my *Nature of Geography,* published by this association, 1939, 1949 particularly to Chapters II, IV, and VIII.

[3] Carl Sauer, "Recent Developments in Cultural Geography," in *Recent Developments in the Social Sciences,* E.D. Hayes, editor, Philadelphia, 1927, p. 207.

[4] On the status of political geography fifteen years ago, with extensive bibliography, see Richard Hartshorne, "Recent Developments in Political Geography," *American Political Science Review,* XXIX (1935): 785–804, 943–966.

---

*Presidential address delivered before the Association at its Forty-sixth Annual Meeting in Worcester, Mass., April 7, 1950.

One cannot but be amazed by the temerity of American geographers who feel ready to teach this subject without previous training, with but a minimum of study of the literature of the field, and with the barest amount of materials available to put in the hands of students.

True, we have more such materials than we had twenty years ago. Whereas then we had hardly more than a single volume in the English language entitled political geography, today there are many and more are promised. Unfortunately these are mostly textbooks. Better textbooks are essential for better teaching, but the publication of more textbooks can do little to give standing to a field unless we can produce a really good text. To seek that result by simply writing more and better texts is an attempt to pull ourselves up by our bootstraps. A really good textbook can be produced only from the digest of sound scholarly studies. Whether to provide the basis for a first class text, or to establish scholarly standing for the field of political geography, our need is for an organized structure of scholarly knowledge—one in which students can build upon what has been written before.

I do not wish to belittle the scholarly work that has been accomplished in this field. In one or two directions, I think we might claim to have laid down a few fundamental concepts and principles, to have established a few technical terms. Perhaps "established" is too strong a word, since some textbook writers continue to confuse students with terms, such as "natural boundaries," although long since discredited by scholars in the field.

In an effort to appraise our situation, a graduate seminar joined me a year ago in an examination of a wide range of studies in political geography. We sought to determine what methods geographers use and what materials they employ in studies in this field. We found the greatest variety of methods, and the use of almost every kind of material conceivable. We found no indication of common purpose or objective. In fact, in most cases we could not find that the authors had any clear purpose or objective in mind, other than the rather general idea that geography somehow has a lot to do with international affairs, and the political geographer should endeavor to find all the ways in which that was the case. I do not think you could find a comparable situation in other branches of geography. If you take a half dozen studies in

economic geography you will no doubt find different systems in the same text. It has been a long time since one could accuse economic geography of being nothing more than a collection of geographic aspects of economics. In that field we have developed specific objectives and methods, and have even arrived at some degree of agreement as to the materials to be studied.

What are the writers in political geography trying to do? Using the device of the census, let me throw together into several groups the works of a large number of students, in order not to reveal the operations of any specific author.[5]

In one of these groups, we find that each state is studied in terms of a series of "aspects"—physical, human, and economic—with subheads like landforms, climate . . . agriculture, industry, cities, etc. In this treatment, differing little from that of a conventional geographic study, political flavoring is added by a section on historical aspects and a discussion of boundaries and conflicts with other states.

The thought behind this appears to be simply that in order to study the state, one must know a lot about its geography. We may all agree to that, but to supply a collection of information, some of which may be pertinent, some not, is not a technique of analysis and will not build a field of political geography.

More distinctive is what I may term the "historical" approach. This at least starts with a definite problem—namely to explain how a state has come to occupy the particular area included within its present limits. One way of doing this—the easiest and quickest way—is to start with what exists, point out apparent correspondence of physical and political features and then conclude that history somehow or other has resulted in what was more or less bound to develop. In short, as Vidal de la Blache observed, another form of geographic determinism.

German students, indoctrinated with Ratzel's misleading concept of the state as an

[5]On the other hand the occasion of this paper, as well as its substantive purpose as a progress report may permit specific indication of the relation of my own work during the past twenty years to the theme developed herein. I have therefore referred, at appropriate points, to all my previous publications in this field. At the same time I should express my indebtedness to the other members of the Centennial Committee on Political Geography for their criticisms and suggestions on the first outline drafted for that committee and utilized freely in this paper.

organism, have attempted by comparative studies of a handful of examples, to develop principles of state territorial development. We are all too familiar with the dangerous consequences of this form of pseudo-scientific thinking on political action.

To decipher the processes of state territorial development from present facts—as the geomorphologist is forced to do in attempting to recapitulate the evolution of landforms—may be intellectual sport, but hardly intelligent science. For the processes of state development are recorded, in great detail and commonly with contemporaneous explanation, in historical records. The student who undertakes to study this topic, whether he be historian or geographer by profession, must therefore master a very large amount of historical material. To attain a definitive analysis of a single change in a relatively small area may require examination of a vast amount of both historical and geographic material. To comprehend fully what that means, a student might check through the references in my recent study of the boundary in Lorraine,[6] or observe the scholarship that underlies Whittlesey's study of Andorra[7] and the voluminous historical research needed for his study of the territorial evolution of France.[8]

Before concluding that all who wish to work in political geography must do likewise, we must first ask: Is this approach necessary? How significant are the findings of such studies for an understanding of the present political geography of a state? If I use again the study of Lorraine as an example, its author will not be provoked. Even if Alsace-Lorraine were still part of Germany, would it matter to the geography of Germany whether the reason for the inclusion of the Côtes de Moselle was because of its strategic importance in the military technology of 1871 or because of the iron ores imbedded in its strata? The fact is that Germany got both.

Or consider the story of how the Garonne Basin came to be part of the present state of France. This would, I think, involve examination of such factors as the langue d'oc branch of Romance languages, the relative productive resources of the Aquitaine lowland and the Paris Basin, the theoretical significance of the Kingdom of the West Franks as a unit division of Charlemagne's empire, the centuries of success of French Queens in producing male offspring, and the long period of conflict with the alien kings of England. But how much of all this is needed for an understanding of the political geography of France today?

Isn't it enough to say that these regions have shared in common social, economic, and political life of the French kingdom and republic for many generations, so that in spite of linguistic differences they are now integral parts of the French nation, and therefore will choose to adhere to the French state?

It is not clear to me therefore that such historical studies of genesis are essential for every study in political geography. This is not to say that the geographer does not have a distinct contribution to make to the study of the evolution of a state. But has he not contributed perhaps more to history and to our knowledge of political processes than to political geography?

In short, if we accept the analogy that Maull and East[9] have suggested between studies of the evolution of state-areas and those of the evolution of landforms, we may still be uncertain, in both cases, as to whether such studies form a necessary and integral part of the study of the present geography of areas.

I want to make certain that I cannot be misunderstood in saying that I am uncertain concerning the place of genetic studies.[10] In thus straddling the fence—on the grounds that the attempt to determine boundaries in science is pedantic—I am not saying that I wish to push such studies beyond the fence, or that I recognize the existence of an actual fence. On the contrary, so far as individual geographers are interested in making such studies of states, I personally shall be more than interested in their results. I shall no doubt wish to make more of such studies myself. And if historians or political scientists should wish to claim this part of the field, like my predecessor, I would feel happy to agree on

[6]Richard Hartshorne, "The Franco-German Boundary of 1871," World Politics, II (Jan. 1950): 209–250.

[7]Derwent Whittlesey, "Andorra's Autonomy," Journal of Modern History (June 1934): 147–155.

[8]Derwent Whittlesey, The Earth and the State: A Study in Political Geography. New York, 1939, pp. 129–165.

[9]Otto Maull, "Politische Geographie und Geopolitik," Geographischer Anzeiger, 1926:251; William G. East, "The Nature of Political Geography," Politica II (1937): 270.

[10]Similar statements of uncertainty regarding the place of geomorphology in geography, though expressed as a definite refusal to pass judgment (in The Nature of Geography: 423–424) have led some readers to suppose that I would exclude that subject.

joint exploration; and be somewhat dejected if either side attempted to pass the topic over to the other.[11]

The only negative conclusion I am suggesting that is significant to our present theme is that I am not convinced that such studies form an essential part, or a necessary preliminary section, in the study of the political geography of any state. But neither do I assert the opposite; rather I conclude that only in the course of his study of the present political geography of a state can a student determine how far he need dip back into its historical development.

Let us turn to a third approach, which I may describe as the "morphological approach." This is represented in substantive works primarily in the German literature. It was presented in outline form to American geographers in an article I published some fifteen years ago.[12] Its chief claim to consideration, I think, is that it focusses attention at the start on the major subject of study in nearly all political geography—the present state-area as a geographic phenomenon.

This approach calls for a descriptive and interpretive analysis of the external and internal structure of the state-area , considered as a geographic object. The items are familiar: externally—size, shape, location, and boundaries; internally, the regional breakdown in natural regions, cultural regions, regions of different kinds of people, and the location of the capital.

This is almost pure morphology, and therefore static and dull. I am not surprised that no other student, so far as I know, has seen fit to use this outline. It does represent a method or system, but not one that seems likely to produce significant results.

Just what is it that is wrong with this morphological approach? Similar approach led I suppose to successful results in geomorphology, possibly in some other branches of geography. In certain fields, however, I think we would find it did not. As long as agricultural geography was tied down to the measurement of crops and fields, ignoring the functioning of farms as organized units of production, we were prevented from making significant advances. Likewise in manufactural geography, or in the geography of cities, the morphological approach often led to results far

less significant than the study of functions.

Whether or not you agree with me on that, I think you will agree that the significance of state-areas in geography is to be sought far more in their functioning than in the morphology in itself. A school child may be interested, or amused, by the peculiar elongated shape of Chile on the map or the fact that it adds up to a larger size than France, but this interest is not on the same level as our direct interest in the form and size of Mount Shasta, say, in contrast with the Sierra Nevadas.

In a review of certain works in German political geography, Bowman once poured ridicule on the elaborate detail of morphological analysis, the detailed classification of state-areas by size and shape leading, sofar as he could find, to no significant conclusions.[13]

In other words, there is a certain fallacy in the comparison of a state-area with a landform. As a definitely organized section of land, a state-area is a real phenomenon, but it is not an object as a mountain is an object. It is not of "direct importance to areal differentiation," rather its place in a geographic study is due to "its indirect importance through its causal relation to other phenomena."[14]

The morphology of a state-area, I conclude, is significant primarily as it effects the functions of the state. If that is true, aren't we putting the cart before the horse in starting with the details of morphology in order in each case to look for significant relations to functions? I suggest that this is another example of our inheritance in geography in general, which leads us to look first at the physical environment and then attempt to draw conclusions about its significance for human relations.

So I suggest that we start with the functions of politically organized areas, and that we maintain this procedure throughout.

LIMITATION IN SCOPE OF THIS PAPER

In confining our attention to politically organized areas, I do not mean to assert by implication that there are not other political phenomena of concern to the geographer. Wright's classic study of the areal differentiation in voting habits of the American people is a highly significant contribution to a full understanding of the geography of this

[11]Russell, op. cit., p. 11.
[12]Richard Hartshorne, "Recent Developments in Political Geography," op. cit., pp. 943ff.

[13]In Geographical Review, XVII (1927): 511–512.
[14]Nature of Geography, p. 464.

country.[15] Wigmore and Whittlesey have examined the areal distribution of different legal codes over the world.[16] If such studies are valuable contributions to geography, as I think they are, it would be pedantic, at this stage of our development at least, to discuss whether they form a part of an integrated field of political geography or are to be classified in some other branch, such as social geography. Suffice it to say that a distinct type of problem is presented us in the study of the geography of politically organized areas and I will therefore confine myself to that type of problem.

There are of course many varieties and different levels of politically-organized areas. If one were studying certain areas of Africa or Asia at an earlier period of history, one would be primarily concerned with the very loose form of territorial organization effected by tribal units. In a future, we trust better, world, the geographer may be concerned with the political organization of large international territories—ultimately, one hopes, of the whole world. In the present world, however, there are but two types of politically-organized territories, which together cover theoretically the entire inhabited world and are of transcendent importance—namely, the areas of the independent, sovereign states and those of dependent countries, whether called colonies, protectorates, or possessions, which are organized in greater or less degree by members of the first group, the imperial states. (This statement intentionally overlooks the problem of defining the actual status of countries at present disorganized, like China, or those whose independence from outside control is debatable.) The uninhabited oceans, together with Antarctica, do not constitute units for study under our major heading because they are not politically organized. Their use and control however will present us with problems in considering the relations among the politically organized areas.

There is of course a place for the geographic study of politically organized areas of lower levels—the subdivisions of states. The relationship between the units at different levels is not however comparable to that in non-political regional geography. A sub-region of the Corn Belt may include all the functions

found in the Corn Belt, and its validity as a region is independent of the larger region. In contrast, the subdivisions of states—whether provinces, departments, counties, or townships—are generally created by the state and are specifically excluded from certain political functions performed for them by the state of which they are a part. This statement must be qualified in significant, but on the whole minor, degree in respect to the autonomous units of federal states—the States of the United States, or Australia, or the Provinces of Canada.

Units of political organization at a higher level than the sovereign states include the empires that have been organized individually by certain of those states. Organizations of territory including more than one sovereign state have hitherto been represented only by the British Commonwealth, but both France and the Netherlands are now attempting to construct similar organizations. Finally students are not limited to what exists; we are free to use our imagination to study the potential basis for other larger units—whether an Arab union, a Western European Federation, a North Atlantic Union, or a world union.

For the purposes of this paper, I wish to focus attention solely on one type of political area—the sovereign state, even though that ignores the large part of the world that is organized in units dependent on outside sovereign states.

My method of procedure may give the impression of a second major limitation—that I am concerned only with the regional approach in political geography—the study of the individual states—that I ignore the systematic approach. Other students have urged that we should start with the systematic approach, that we must first establish generic concepts, precise terminology, and general principles which then can be applied to specific, regional, cases. I submit that the history of development of geography in general demonstrates that we must do both simultaneously and that, like both Ritter and Humboldt, we must start with specific and actual cases.[17] It is only in the attempt to make analyses of specific regions that we can determine what are the specific topics that need to be examined systematically for all states in order to yield generic concepts and definitive terminology.

---

[15]John K. Wright, "Voting Habits in the United States," *Geographical Review*, XXII (1932): 666–672.

[16]John H. Wigmore, "Present Day Legal Systems of the World," *Geographical Review*, XIX (1929):120; Whittlesey, *The Earth and The State*, pp. 557–565.

[17]Cf. *Nature of Geography*: 54–57, 72–74, 79–80.

Failure to follow this procedure in the past has led, by deductive reasoning to *a priori* principles that have not stood the test of comparison with reality.

Even when we have established the significant generic concepts, we should not be over-sanguine of the possibilities of establishing general principles in political geography. In other branches of geography we deal with units—whether landforms, farms, factories, or cities—of which there are thousands or even millions, many of them very much like each other in character and purpose. The state units of political geography number less than one hundred in the world, and each of them is notably different from all the others. By dipping back into past history we may add a few score more cases, but in doing so we run the danger of carrying back assumptions of motivations and processes that may be valid today but not in the earlier historical framework. More than in any other branch of geography therefore we are handicapped in developing scientific principles, are restricted to the consideration of unique cases.[18]

PRACTICAL VALUE?

One final statement on the purpose of this paper. Will it provide a method by which geographers may undertake studies directed to the solution of the great critical problems facing the world today? Most certainly geographers should be urged to apply their training and knowledge to the solution of these problems in all cases in which that training and knowledge is adequate to aid more than it hinders. But let us not deceive ourselves, for we will deceive few others. The major problems that face the world today are not problems in political geography; and fortunately so. For our training and knowledge in this field are still far from adequate to prepare us to tackle with assurance any of its major practical problems.

At the end of the First World War a major problem facing the world did fall right in our field—the problem of reorganizing the territorial division of Europe on a basis that would make it possible for the many nationalities of that continent to live in productive harmony. The geographers who were called upon to

assist at that time,[19] however much they could contribute of factual knowledge, were drastically handicapped by immaturity of thinking in political geography.

If today we must leave to others the solution of the problem of the atomic bomb and the problem of Communist Russia, we must also anticipate other crises ahead. When the need comes for a soundly developed science of political geography, we should be prepared to offer it.

I do not mean to say that political geography has at present no value in public affairs. We all have the constant opportunity, in teaching students and adults, to contribute to a wider understanding among thinking people concerning the nature of the world we live in and its international problems.

Further, those of us who have attained specialized knowledge and understanding of particular foreign areas of concern to this country may be called upon to offer both information and advice to our government. We are rightly proud of the fact that during and since the war many of us have been called upon for such service. It will be a great misfortune, not only for us, but for our country if geographers are prevented from contributing to students, the public, and the government the maximum of objective knowledge and of sincere and loyal counsel on foreign countries. But insofar as we geographers are able to contribute to the problems of American foreign policy, we find ourselves—like our colleagues in other social science fields—exposed to the danger of attack from political demagogues who find in any divergence of opinion from their own a sign of disloyalty to the state. We cannot foresee where the blind lightning of ignorance will strike, but must recognize that such attack on any one of us is attack on the freedom and integrity of all our profession.[20]

At the same time, the freedom we require as scientists carries special obligations, greater

---

[18]For discussion of this problem in general see *The Nature of Geography*: 378–386, 431–434, 446–451.

[19]See "War Services of Members of the Association of American Geographers," *Annals of the Association of American Geographers*, IX (1919): 53–70. A list, probably incomplete, of European geographers brought to Paris is given in Richard Hartshorne, "Recent Developments in Political Geography," *op. cit.*, p. 791.

[20]If to any future readers the pertinence of this paragraph is not clear, they may count themselves fortunate for living in a better era. Any who are historically minded may find the pertinent connection by looking to the front pages of almost any American newspaper for any day during the month of March, 1950.

than those of ordinary citizens. Amateurish ideas or foolish proposals from men of no standing may do little harm. But when we write as professors and as geographers, the public presumes that we speak with some authority and they cannot know how little that authority may be in the field of political geography. We must recognize that, as long as our knowledge is as unorganized as it is in this field, and commonly without discipline, some of us may contribute only misunderstanding. In particular, the publication in critical times of misinformation, or of irresponsible recommendations purporting to represent more than the personal views of the author, or of such a character as to arouse animosity in foreign countries can do serious damage to this country—as we learned during the last war.[21]

We may have produced no atom bombs in political geography, but the field is nonetheless strewn with dynamite—it is no place for sophomores to play with matches. Fortunately, we appear to have escaped the danger of repeating, in American terms, the crime of those of our colleagues in Germany who were responsible for the dangerous doctrines of geopolitics.[22] But we will be exposed to similar dangers until the foundations of our knowledge in this field are on a much firmer basis than appears now to be the case.

Only then will our contributions to public thinking be more than additional small voices entering the general argument. The function of scientific learning is to establish knowledge on such firm foundations that argument disappears, and acceptance becomes relatively enduring. This we can accomplish only the long, hard way. We must get at the fundamentals; lay the groundwork for a solid structure of knowledge, on the basis of which we may hope one day to arrive at applications of sound value in the solution of actual problems.

[21]The evidence demonstrating that an article in "political geography" published in a popular American magazine caused serious repercussions in several foreign countries, both allied and neutral, is still classified material in state department documents or in confidential statements of one of our ambassadors.

[22]It should be added that the men primarily responsible for the development of Geopolitik were for the most part not men of high standing in German geography, see Carl Troll, "Geographic Science in Germany, 1933–1945," *Annals of the Association of American Geographers*, XXXIX (1949): 128–135. Of the dangerous tendencies of geopolitics, American students were warned—in what appears now as much too cautious a manner—in Richard Hartshorne, "Recent Developments in Political Geography," *op. cit.*, pp. 960–965.

ANALYSIS OF THE POLITICAL GEOGRAPHY OF A STATE: INTERNAL

I propose, as stated earlier, to consider the central problems of political geography in terms of the functions of state-areas. What comes first? The fundamental purpose of any state, as an organization of a section of land and a section of people, as Ratzel first put it, is to bring all the varied territorial parts, the diverse regions of the state-area, into a single organized unit.

What does the state attempt to organize, in all regions of the state-area?

In all cases, it attempts to establish complete and exclusive control over internal political relations—in simplest terms, the creation and maintenance of law and order. Local political institutions must conform with the concepts and institutions of the central, overall, political organization.

In many social aspects—class structure, family organization, religion, and education—a state may tolerate considerable variation in its different regions. But because of the significance of these factors to political life, there is a tendency—in some states a very marked effort—to exert unifying control even over these institutions.

In the economic field, every modern state tends to develop some degree of unity of economic organization. At the minimum, it establishes uniform currency, some uniformity in economic institutions, and some degree of control over external economic relations. Beyond that, states of course vary greatly in the degree to which all aspects of production and trade—price and wages levels, etc.—are placed under uniform control.

Finally, and most importantly, because we live in a world in which the continued existence of every state-unit is subject to the threat of destruction by other states, every state must strive to secure the supreme loyalty of the people in all its regions, in competition with any local or provincial loyalties, and in definite opposition to loyalty to any outside state-unit.

Throughout this statement of the organization of the state-area as a unit, the geographer is primarily concerned with emphasis on *regional* differences. The state of course is no less concerned to establish unity of control over all classes of population at a single place. In political geography, our interest is in the problem of unification of diverse regions into a single whole; the degree of vertical unification within any horizontal segment concerns us only as a factor aiding or handicapping regional unification.

Parenthetically, we may also note the ways in which this primary function of the state affects the general field of geography. Land-use, industrial development, trade, and a countless list of social aspects of human geography in any region will differ in greater or less degree as a result of the efforts of the state in which it is included to control its development as part of a single whole. Only the peculiarity of geographic study in such a large country as the United States, where we are usually forced to do most of our work within the territory of our single state, has permitted us to study geography as though we could ignore political geography.

Our analysis of the primary function of any state leads directly to the primary problem of political geography. For no state-area constitutes by the nature of its land and people, a natural unit for a state, in which one merely needs to create a government which shall proceed to operate it as a unit. The primary and continuing problem of every state is how to bind together more or less separate and diverse areas into an effective whole.

For the political geographer, this presents a wide range of specific problems for analysis. In every state area, larger than such anomalies as Andorra or Liechtenstein, the geographer finds: (1) regions that are more or less separated from each other by physical or human barriers; (2) regions that in greater or lesser degree diverge in their relations with outside states; and (3) regions that differ among themselves in character of population, economic interests, and political attitudes. Let us look briefly at each of these types of problems.*

Centrifugal Forces

Geographers are familiar with the effect of particular types of physical features in handicapping communication between regions. Semple and others have described for our own early history the political consequences of the forested Appalachians and later of the mountain and desert barrier of the west. Whittlesey's study of the Val d'Aran depicts in detail the problem in that bit of Spain north of the Pyrenees.[23] In most modern states, however, these problems have largely been overcome by the development of the telegraph and the railroad. They continue of importance however in parts of the Balkans, in the highland states of Latin America, and in China.

Since state-organization requires communication not only from one region to the next, but from a central point to each peripheral region, distance itself is a centrifugal factor. Obviously distance within a state depends on its size and shape. Size and shape are significant to the state in other, quite different respects, but I suggest we wait until we have determined that in our analysis, rather than attempt to proceed deductively from size and shape to consequences.

Of human barriers, the most common is the absence of humans. Uninhabited or sparsely inhabited areas were, until recently, difficult and dangerous to cross. It was primarily on this account that relatively low mountains, in central Europe or the Appalachians, long functioned as dividing zones. Even in the Alps, the problem of surmounting high elevations was less serious, in the Middle Ages, than the difficulty of securing supplies along the way and the ever-present danger of attack from "robber barons."

Further, the presence of such relatively empty areas created, and still creates, a feeling of separation in the regions on either side. Both on this account and because of distance, oceans continue to function as the strongest separating factors, other than the Arctic ice, even though they have long been crossed with relative ease.

France has first inaugurated the interesting experiment of incorporating trans-oceanic areas into the organization of its state. Its West Indian islands and the island of Reunion in the Indian Ocean are now departments of metropolitan France, sending delegates to its national assembly. We may be about to do the same with Hawaii.

Perhaps the most difficult barrier to overcome is separation by a zone populated by a different people, especially an unfriendly people. The Germans have apparently convinced the world that the separation of East Prussia by the Polish Corridor was an experiment that is never to be repeated. (They overlooked the

---

*Throughout this discussion the term "region" is used to indicate merely an area in some way distinct or different from neighboring areas, with no implication that a region is a unit. See The Nature of Geography, op. cit., Chap. IX.

[23]Derwent Whittlesey, "Trans-Pyrenean Spain: The Val d'Aran," Scottish Geographical Magazine, 1933: 217–228.

fact that there were not one but two alternatives to that device.)[24]

Serious difficulties may arise for a state if any of its regions have closer relations with regions of outside states than with those within the state. This is commonly the case where a boundary has been changed so that it now cuts across an area formerly within a single state. The partition of Upper Silesia, in 1922, presented a particularly intense case.[25] But there are many cases, not dependent on boundary changes, in which a region has closer connections, particularly economic connections, with regions of other countries than with other regions of its own state. We are familiar with the political importance of this factor in each of the major regions of Canada, each more closely related in certain respects with the adjacent areas of the United States than with the other regions within the Dominion. In some cases mutual interdependence among the regions of the state-area is less than the dependence of individual regions on remote, overseas countries. This is a major problem of the Australian Commonwealth, in which each state unit is primarily dependent on separate trade with Great Britain. In Western Australia, this factor, together with notable physical and human separation has led at times to demand for secession from the Commonwealth. Northeastern Brazil offers a somewhat similar problem for study.

The geographer however must beware of drawing conclusions from the physical map, or, on the other hand, of assuming that an economic situation to which we are accustomed represents a "normal" development in economic geography independent of a particular political framework. Consider southern California, separated by thousands of miles of desert and mountain from the main body of the United States, facing the Pacific highway to densely populated lands of the Orient. And yet which region of the United States is more completely bound into the economy of the country as a whole?

All the previous examples are relatively extreme cases. In most instances the potentialities are highly flexible. The plain of Alsace, separated from the rest of France by the rugged heights of the Vosges, facing southern Germany across the narrow band of the Rhine flood-plain and easily connected with northern Germany by that navigable river—with which state does it fit in terms of economic geography? Surely the answer must be that in terms of modern technology all these features are of minor importance and in terms of the economic potentialities of the area it can be associated almost equally well in either the French or the German economic unit.

Separation of regions by barriers or by divergence of outside connections are commonly less important than the centrifugal forces that result from diversity of character of the population. To secure voluntary acceptance of a single common organization requires some degree of mutual understanding; obviously this is easier in a population homogeneous in character. Further, where regions differ in social character, the tendency of the state to force some degree of uniformity of social life meets with resistance. Thus the very attempt to produce unity may intensify disunity. Hungary, before 1918, was the classic example; since then Yugoslavia has been perhaps the leading, among several, successors.

What particular social characteristics may be important depends on the particular state. Everyone thinks of language and religion. I suggest, also, education and standards of living, types of economic attitudes and institutions, attitudes toward class and racial distinctions, and, especially, political philosophy.

For materials on these topics we look to that branch of geography that has been least developed—social geography. In most cases what materials we have provide only the raw data, the facts about the distribution of, say, religions or races, rather than the regional differences in social attitudes towards these facts; it is the latter that we need.

Thus, the fact that Alsace was predominantly Roman Catholic, like France but unlike most of Germany, was less important than the fact that its attitude toward the relation of church and state was similar to that in the German Empire of 1871–1918, and was in conflict with the anti-clerical attitude of the French Republic.

Racial differences, in the terms studied by the physical anthropologist, may be of no relevance to our problem. The distribution, percentage-wise, in the different countries of Europe, of blondes and brunettes, dolichocephalic versus brachycephalic—what does it

[24]Richard Hartshorne, "The Polish Corridor," *Journal of Geography*, XXXVI (1937): 161–176.

[25]Richard Hartshorne, "Geographic and Political Boundaries in Upper Silesia," *Annals of the Association of American Geographers*, XXIII (1933): 195–228.

matter? These facts have no reflection in social or political attitudes in those countries. Though standard material in most geographies of Europe, I submit that they have no significance to political geography, or for that matter, to geography in general.

In contrast, the United States is a country in which regional differences in attitudes of people toward the racial components of the regional group—as indicated by skin color—are of tremendous importance in social, economic, and political life. We have mapped and studied the underlying differences in racial composition,[26] but we have not studied the phenomenon itself—namely the differences in attitudes. We need a map, a series of maps, portraying different kinds and degrees of Jim Crowism in the United States. These I would rate as a first requirement for an understanding of the internal political geography of the United States, for in no other factor do we find such marked regional cleavages, such disruption to the national unity of our state. For geography in general, in one quarter of our country, these attitudes are fundamental factors in every aspect of the human geography, and are significantly related to its physical geography.

Geographers are more familiar with differences in economic interests, since these are more closely bound to the land. But these are seldom seriously disrupting to national unity. It is true that almost every modern state has experienced marked political tension between the divergent interests of highly industrial regions and those of still primarily agricultural areas. But these very differences tend to lead to interlocking, rather than competing, interests. Even when competing, economic differences, Marx to the contrary notwithstanding, are easier to compromise than differences in social and political attitudes.

Furthermore, the state is only in partial degree an economic unit. Since it is basically a political unit, the state necessarily imposes the greatest degree of uniformity in political life. Political attitudes are peculiarly inflexible. If a region is accustomed to one set of political concepts, ideals and institutions—most especially if its people feel that they have fought in the past to establish those political values—it may be extremely difficult to bring them under the common cloak of a quite different system. Even where regions

[26]Richard Hartshorne, "Racial Maps of the United States," Geographical Review, XXVIII (1938): 276–288.

formerly in separate states have voluntarily joined together to form a state, on the basis of common ethnic character—for example the three Polish areas in 1918, or the Czech and Slovak areas—the marked difference in past political education led to difficult problems.

In times and areas of relatively primitive political development such factors were no doubt of minor importance. In long-settled areas of relatively mature political development they may be of first importance. The classic example is, again, Alsace. Thanks particularly to the French Revolution, the people of that province had become strong supporters of political concepts, ideals, and institutions that could not be harmonized within the semi-feudal, authoritarian monarchy of Hohenzollern Germany.

Conversely, one may understand, on this basis, the negative reaction of the Swiss in 1919, to the proposal that the adjacent Austrian province of Vorarlberg should be added to their state.[27]

Centripetal Forces

The preceding discussion of political attitudes points to an essential ingredient that has been lacking in the discussion up to this point. We have been considering a variety of centrifugal factors in the regional geography of a state-area which make it difficult to bind those regions together into an effective unit. In considering how such difficulties may be overcome, we have not asked whether there was any force working to overcome the difficulties, anything tending to pull these regions together into a state.

This omission, I suggest, has been the single greatest weakness in our thinking in political geography. If we see an area marked clearly on both physical and ethnic maps as suitable for a state, but which for many centuries was not integrated as a state—as in the Spanish peninsula, the Italian peninsula, or the German area—we cudgel our heads to find factors in its internal geography that will explain the failure. We forget that before we speak of failure, we must ask what was attempted.

The Italian peninsula, together with the northern plain attached to the mainland but isolated by the Alps, with a settled population

[27]As reported to me years later by two geographers: Lawrence Martin, who had been sent to Switzerland by President Wilson to sound out the Swiss reaction, and Peter H. Schmidt, of St. Gallen, with whom he had discussed the proposal.

speaking approximately a common tongue since the Middle Ages, has offered one of the most obvious geographic units of Europe for the development of a state. Yet Italy, as an Austrian minister jeered, was only a geographic expression; there was nothing that could be called even the beginnings of a state of Italy. For no one of importance had any idea of producing an Italian state and had anyone tried, his purpose would have shattered in conflict with two opposing ideas: one, the concept of the Papal States, the secular control of mid-Italy by the Pope in order to secure his undivided domination of Rome as the spiritual capital of Western Christendom; the other, the concept of a single great empire in the heart of Europe, extending from northern Germany to northern Italy. Only after the power of these centuries-old ideas had been irrevocably destroyed by the ferment of the French Revolution was it possible for any Italian leader to consider seriously the unification of Italy.

One of the concepts that prevented integration in Italy is likewise the key to the failure of medieval Germany to develop a unified state, at the time when the kingdoms of France and England were being effectively established. For centuries the persons holding the title of King of Germany, and whatever opportunity that might give, were far more affected by the higher title of Emperor. Inspired by the grander idea of reincarnating the empire of Rome, they fought to build a state straddling the Alps, uniting many different peoples. The sacrifices made in the vain attempt to accomplish the greater idea destroyed the possibility of achieving the lesser when later emperors finally were reduced to considering German unity.

The fact that a country has a name and a government, that an international treaty recognizes its existence as a state and defines its territorial limits—all that does not produce a state. To accomplish that, it is necessary to establish centripetal forces that will bind together the regions of that state, in spite of centrifugal forces that are always present.

The State-Idea

The basic centripetal force must be some concept or idea justifying the existence of this particular state incorporating these particular regions; the state must have a *raison d'être* —reason for existing.

Although ignored in much of the literature of political geography, this is not a new thought. Ratzel defined the state as a section of land and a section of humanity organized as a single unit in terms of a particular, distinctive idea.[28] Maull, among other German geographers, has discussed the concept at some length.[29] It was presented to this Association a decade ago.[30]

At the primitive level, Ratzel explained, this idea may be no more than the will of a ruler to which, for whatever reasons, all the regional parts through their local leaders grant their loyalty. In such a case, as in the empire of Charlemagne or that of Ghengis Khan, the state may endure hardly longer than the lifetime of the individual ruler. In the attempt to perpetuate the binding idea of loyalty to a personal ruler, there evolved the concept of hereditary monarchy. Where that succeeded, however, we find there was always something more—politically-minded people in the various parts of the kingdom came to regard the state, for reasons independent of the monarch, as representing something of value to them. Today the monarchical institution is safe only in those states in which the monarch has exchanged the active power to rule for the passive role of personification of the national heritage.

To be sure, a state in which the original idea has lost its validity will not fall apart at once. The forces of inertia, vested interests, and fear of the consequences of change may keep it going more or less effectively for some time. But inevitably a structure that has lost its original *raison d'être*, without evolving a new one, cannot hope to stand the storms of external strife or internal revolt that sooner or later will attack it. For when that day comes, the state, to survive, must be able to count upon the loyalty, even to the death, of the population of all its regions.

It is not mere coincidence that the terms I have been using came to me from a Viennese geographer, in his analysis of the failure of the Habsburg monarchy. Unless Austria-Hungary, Hassinger wrote after the First World War, had been able to discover and establish a *raison d'être*, a justification for existence, even

[28]Friedrich Ratzel, *Politische Geographie*, 3rd ed., Munich and Berlin 1923, pp. 2–6.

[29]Otto Maull, *Politische Geographie*, Berlin 1925, pp. 112–115.

[30]Richard Hartshorne, "The Concepts of 'Raison d'Etre' and 'Maturity of States'," (abstract), *Annals of the Association of American Geographers*, XXX (1940): 59.

without the calamity of the war, it could not long have continued to exist.[31]

Those states are strongest, Ratzel had concluded, "in which the political idea of the state fills the entire body of the state, extends to all its parts."[32]

What does this mean for our study of the political geography of a state? It means, I am convinced, that before we can begin to study the problems presented by the centrifugal forces I have previously outlined, we must first discover the motivating centripetal force, the basic political idea of the state. Under what concept, for what purposes, are these particular regions to be bound together into one political unit, absolutely separated from every other political territory?

Does this seem too remote from geography? Too much like political science? The student of geography of climates must understand the nature of air-masses, as analyzed by the meteorologist. We cannot intelligently study the geography of soils until we have grasped the soil scientist's analysis of soil types. In agricultural geography it is not sufficient, we now know, to study crops and animals; we are concerned with the farm unit of organization of crops from fields, livestock in barns and pasture, all directed toward ultimate production of food for the farmer and products to be sold from his farms. We are not ready to begin the study of farm geography until we have analyzed the farmer's purpose—the idea under which his piece of land is organized.

Geographers usually know quite a bit about farming, so they may know beforehand what is in the farmer's mind, or perhaps they can infer that from observation of the visible facts—the fields, silo, corncrib, or cow-barn. But to know for certain, you must ask the farmer.

Whom shall we ask concerning the idea of the particular state? Obviously one must go to those who actually operate the state in question. This is not so easy as in the case of the farm or factory. A modern state is an organization operated, in greater or less degree, by all of the politically-minded people included in it—ideally its entire adult population.

One might logically suppose that geographers should be able to find the answer to this question in studies in political science. Unfortunately, from our point of view, political

scientists seem to have concerned themselves solely with the idea and purpose of the generic state—the purposes, that is, that are common to all states. This ignores the very thing that is of direct concern to the geographer—namely the idea that is distinct for the particular state in contrast with that of other states, that which makes for significant differences from country to country. Perhaps that means that it is logically a problem for the geographer.

In any case, unless we can find the answer to this fundamental question in the works of other students—perhaps of the historians if not the political scientists—we are apparently forced to work it out for ourselves. We must discover and establish the unique distinctive idea under which a particular section of area and of humanity is organized into a unit state.

I realize that the problem is remote from the geographer's training and knowledge. But years of stumbling effort have convinced me that there is no circumventing it. Until we can determine for any particular state the idea under which it is organized, we shall have no basis on which to analyze its political geography; we shall not have started on the significant contribution that geography can make to the study of states.

Perhaps we exaggerate the difficulty of the problem because it is unfamiliar. To pin down precisely the particular idea on which any state is based is certainly very difficult, but study of the essential historical documents may enable one to come fairly quickly to a rough statement sufficiently close to the mark to be usable.

Let me give you a case in which one of my advanced graduate students[33] had particular difficulty—the state of Iraq. He finally arrived at something like this: The idea of an Iraqi state sprang from two factors: (1) the recognition by the Great Powers of the special strategic and economic significance of the Mesopotamian region, and (2) the need to provide a *pied à terre* for Arab nationalism banished from Syria. On the basis of these two considerations there was established a territory embracing the settled Arab region of the Tigris-Euphrates plain, together with adjacent but dissimiliar regions of mountain and desert tribes, the whole to be developed as a separate Arab state.

You note that the idea of this state was a compound of purposes and those, external:

[31]Hugo Hassinger, in R. Kjellen and K. Haushofer, *Die Grossmächte vor und nach dem Weltkriege*, Berlin and Leipzig, 1930, p. 34.
[32]Ratzel, *op. cit.*, p. 6.

[33]Mr. John Paterson in an unpublished manuscript.

foreign diplomacy and transported nationalist fire. That was the case in 1919. One would need to determine whether the Iraqi have since evolved a truly native concept.

In much older states, we may expect to find that an indigenous *raison d'etre* has evolved that may have little or no relation to the original genesis. To determine the distinctive idea of such a state, therefore we must study the current situation, rather than the remote past. In the well-developed modern state politically-minded people in all regions of the state-area are conscious of their loyalty to the state and have some common understanding, even though not clearly phrased, of what that state means to them. In such a case, we may recognize, I think, the existence of a *nation*—as something distinct from the state itself.

The Concept of Nation

At what I choose to call the more primitive level, the concept of nation represents simply a feeling of kinship, of belonging together, an extension of the concept of family, more properly an extension of the concept of the in-group versus outsiders. While usually expressed in terms derived from the language of the family—terms like "blood," "breed," "race," etc.,—it is in reality less of *kin* and more of *kind*—similarity of cultural, rather than of biological characteristics.

The direct significance of this elementary concept of nationality to the state lies first in the fact that all peoples tend to prefer government by those of their own kind, even if inefficient or unjust, rather than any government over them by foreigners, however beneficient. The second reason is that the individual seeks to identify himself with his state; nationality, someone said, is "pooled self-esteem." Indeed the state is sure of the loyalty of the people only if there is such identification. Each citizen must feel that the state is "his" state, its leaders, "his" leaders. For this to be possible he must feel that those who operate his state, who govern him, are people like himself.

The main purpose of a state however is not the furtherance of a particular language or culture. Its main purposes are political. The values over which it has complete control are political values. As the people in a state mature in positive political experience, their feeling of belonging together becomes less dependent on such obvious similarities as common language, and more dependent on common adherence to particular political concepts, ideals, and institutions. It is for the sake of these that they are ready to devote their ultimate loyalty to their state.

It is in terms of these concepts, more specifically defined to fit the particular case, that we can explain the evolution of a Swiss nation out of a collection of many small regions, using four different languages, separated by imposing physical barriers, with sharply diverging outside connections, and originally brought together by a series of historical accidents, including force of arms.

In sharp contrast to Switzerland, and the other small states of long historic evolution in Western Europe, is the situation in most of the small states of Eastern Europe. These owe their existence primarily to the opposition of individual nationalities, based on cultural kinship, to alien rule, but the geographic distribution of the nationalities made impossible a system of states each confined to the single nationality. In the relatively short period of their independent existence as states, none has been able to evolve political values and institutions commanding national loyalty on a higher level than that of cultural kinship—i.e., they have not been able to bring the national minorities, present in almost every case, into membership in the nation.

It is difficult to summarize the analysis of the concept of nation into a single statement, but, for those readers who wish a definition, I would suggest that a "nation" may be defined as a group of people occupying a particular area who feel themselves held together in terms of common acceptance of particular values that are of such prime importance to them that they demand that their area and people should be organized in a distinct state, as the political agency by which those values may be preserved and furthered.[34]

The relations between the state and the nation are mutual and manifold. In the older national states of western Europe, the nation, as Vidal de la Blache has pointed out, was in no small part the product of the state. William of Normandy, as successor to the Anglo-Saxon kings, established a relatively effective state, the kingdom of England, later expanded to include Wales. In the process, however, what-

[34]This statement is a product of exchange of views with Professor Hardy Dillard, Dean of the Law School, University of Virginia.

ever degree of Anglo-Saxon nation had developed was destroyed in the conflict with the Norman French conquerors. But in the course of centuries the state created a new nation, the English. Although most of the kingdom came to have a common tongue, the concept of the nation was accepted in areas of the state beyond the limits of the English language—notably in the Celtic highlands of Wales. The subsequent union of two states, England and Scotland, each of which had evolved a distinct national character, led in time to the development of a larger, single, British nation. On the other hand, the greater part of the island of Ireland, though included in the English kingdom for centuries and largely converted to English tongue, never became part of the British nation.

Likewise there was no French nation—nor even a common language of what we think of as the single French people—until centuries after the kings of France had established more or less effective unity over the state area we call by that name. Or, to take a different kind of example, the French-speaking cantons of Lausanne, Geneva, and the Valais were included in the Swiss state long before their populations came to regard themselves as part of the Swiss nation, and the process of becoming part of that nation involved no lessening in their adherence to the language of France rather than the Germanic language of the greater part of Switzerland.

In Norway and Eire the relation of state and nation was reversed: the nation antedated and demanded the state. In the case of Poland we see a nation, originally produced in part by the long history of a state, which survived the total destruction of that state and more than a century later demanded the restoration of the state.

The story of Austria-Hungary is particularly illuminating. The Habsburg monarchy did not disintegrate directly because of the large number of different ethnic regions of which it was formed, but rather because that state never evolved political concepts or institutions that could gain acceptance, not to say enthusiasm, in its diverse regions.[35]

For an example in current process, consider Yugoslavia. Ignoring for the moment the German, Magyar, and Albanian districts, three

regional groups—Serbs, Croats, and Slovenes—voluntarily joined to form a state. Though based on close relationship of South Slavic language, the main motivating impulse was opposition to foreign rule by German Austria and Magyar Hungary. In the hope of creating a nation they invented a new national word —Yugoslav. But finding no positive political concept for their state—or failing to make real the concept of a federation of related but different groups—the state became increasingly an imperial expansion of the dominant Serbian group. In consequence, under the force of outside attack by Germany, it broke internally. Again, however, the common suffering under foreign tyranny brought increased unity of feeling among the three Slavic groups. This rise of Yugoslav nationalism however was split by the socio-political conflict of communist revolution, dividing the country by classes, rather than by regions. If communism had the capacity to win over the adherence of all the people of an area to its faith, the country might attain national unity on that basis—but no doubt only to be merged in the larger unity of a Communist Eastern Europe. Today, dictatorial orders from outside have again awakened Yugoslav nationalism. In the struggle against alien rule from Moscow, the regional nationalities may conceivably be merged into a genuine Yugoslav nation—unless the class conflict inherent in communism destroys the possibility of unity of the people of even the smallest area.

The United States, one of the most striking and intense of national states, presents still a different type. The nation antedated the state, but was itself originally only a part of an older British nation that had been developed by the United Kingdom. Separated from its then larger part by the Atlantic Ocean, the American sector became a new nation, brought to high temper in the revolutionary fires of the War for Independence. But this new nation found itself then not organized in one state but in thirteen. The Constitutional Convention of 1787 was brought together to create a single state organization to serve a nation recognized as already in existence.

One further ramification may be briefly suggested. Once the concept of a nation has been well established within an area, its spread outward is not necessarily limited by the frontier of the state-area. Thus, when the French national army in 1792 entered the French-speaking regions of Savoy, a region

[35]Richard Hartshorne, "The Tragedy of Austria-Hungary: A Post-Mortem in Political Geography," (abstract) *Annals of the Association of American Geographers*, XXVIII (1938): 49.

that had never been a part of the French kingdom, they found that the national concepts of revolutionary France had preceded them. The Savoyards, who had never belonged to a nation, but had merely been subject to a feudal state lacking in political ideals, were prepared to regard themselves as part of the nation of France. It would be interesting to compare their attitude with that of the French-speaking areas of Switzerland and Belgium which were likewise conquered at that time by the French armies.

The Concept of the "Core Area"

These considerations should enable us to look more critically than has hitherto been done, I believe, at the concept of the core area of a state. Commonly we look at France, England, Scotland, or Sweden—the classic cases in which the core area appears so important, whether in the history of development of the state-area or that of the evolution of national unity. Or we contrast the situation in those countries with that in Spain, where the central area, the Meseta, is relatively weak. But consider the territory of the old kingdom of Hungary, where the core-area of Magyar population in the rich plain of the Mid-Danube would appear to provide the natural focus for surrounding smaller lowlands and mountain highlands. While this situation no doubt facilitated conquest and organization of the large area included in the kingdom, national unity was never achieved.

In contrast the many scattered nuclei of the Norwegian people, connected only by sea, provided the basis for national unity and a modern state. In the United States, no one area ever functioned as a single core, but rather the association of a large number of regions, closely interrelated in an ever-shifting balance, forms the basis for effective unity.

Clearly we must draw negative as well as positive conclusions. A core area is neither sufficient nor essential to the evolution of a nation or state. What is essential is a common idea that convinces the people in all the regions that they belong together. Historically in certain states a core area *may* have played a major role in spreading that idea to other regions and it *may* continue today as in France, Argentina, or Mexico, to focus the interest of the regions on itself as the center of what has become a functioning unit; but the common idea for a state may develop where no core area exists.

The Application of the State-Idea in Political Geography

Whatever is found to be the *raison d'etre*, the underlying idea of the state, it is with this concept, I submit, that the geographer should start in his analysis of the state-area. What use is he then to make of it?

His first concern is to determine the area to which the idea applies, then, the degree to which it operates in the different regions, and finally the extent of correspondence of those regions to the territory actually included within the state.

On this basis we may approach the most elementary problem in political geography—namely that of distinguishing within the legal confines of its territory, those regions that form integral parts of the state-area in terms of its basic idea, and those parts that must be recognized as held under control in the face of either indifference or of opposition on the part of the regional population.

The vast areas of the subarctic lands, whether in Alaska, Canada, Sweden, or the Soviet Union, sparsely populated by primitive tribes, with a few scattered settlements of civilized peoples, are organized politically as though they were colonies of an outside state, even where there is no break in the extent of territory under the same flag. The same is true of tropical lowland areas, in almost all the Latin American countries. In most of the latter, these essentially unorganized territories constitute over half the total area officially credited to the country.[36]

A more difficult question for definition is raised in examining the areas of long-settled Indian population in the highlands of tropical America—both in Central American states and in the Andes. Are these areas of native language and culture to be considered as integral parts of states or are they not still colonial areas subject to outside control, even though the center of control is not in Spain but in the neighboring districts of Spanish-American culture?

A similar situation may be found in more highly developed countries. Thus during the centuries in which all of Ireland was recognized in international law as part of the United Kingdom, its greater part was certainly operat-

[36]For more complete discussion, with an attempt to map these areas see Richard Hartshorne, "The Politico-Geographic Pattern of the World," *Annals of the American Academy of Political and Social Science*, CCXVIII (Nov. 1941): 45 ff.

ed in fact as a subject area, distinct from the controlling state. Much the same may be true today of certain portions of the Soviet Union, notably the so-called republics of Central Asia—but the difficulty of determining the actual operations of the Soviet government makes definite statement impossible. On the other hand, we have in the United States clear-cut though tiny relics of internal colonialism in the Indian reservations.

If the idea of the state is based on the recognition of the existence of a nation, then the major geographic question to consider is whether there is close correspondence between the area of the nation and that of the state. Are there regions within the state whose populations do not feel themselves part of the nation? Are there regions of the nation that are not included within the state—the issue of irridentism?

It is not easy to measure the area to be included in a particular national group. In many cases we must approach the question indirectly. If we can determine the essential factors involved in the particular nationality, we may be able to measure the area over which each of these factors exists. On this basis we may establish certain areas that are clearly included in the given nation, and other areas that adhere in terms of some factors, but not in terms of others.

The entire area over which the nation extends, but in varying degrees of intensity, may then be compared with the area presently included in the state. We have thus determined not only the areal correspondence of state and nation, but also the regions in which the national character is partial rather than complete. We shall thereby have presented, in part in map form, the basic factors and relationships involved in the primary problem of political geography—the analysis of the degree to which the diverse regions of the state constitute a unity.

Internal Organization

At this point we reach one other problem for analysis—the relation of the internal territorial organization of the state-area to the regional diversities we have analyzed. Though all the regions of a state are clearly included under the state-idea, have complete loyalty to the overall concepts of the national unit, regional differences inevitably cause some differences in interpretation and implementation of those concepts.

If these differences are relatively minor, as in most of France or, I presume, in Uruguay, the regions may accept unitary government from a single central authority. If the differences are great, the attempt to impose such a uniform system may provoke opposition endangering the national unity. Since such regional differences are important in most countries, but most states attempt to operate under a uniform, centralized government, the number of examples of this type of problem is very large. Spain, at the moment, provides one of the most striking.

Certain states recognize openly the need to permit diverging interpretations of the overall concepts of that state and hence significant differences in the institutions and laws thereunder. This is the system of the federal state, of which Switzerland provides the oldest example, the United States the largest. In both cases, a notable degree of regional heterogeneity is guaranteed by the constitutional division of powers.

In this country we are at the moment engaged in one of our periodic crises in determining just how much social and political autonomy is to be permitted the regions that are crudely represented by our so-called States. This crisis, incidentally, causes the Congress of the United States to work for the social and political geographer, producing raw material useful to us in measuring differences in intensity of regional attitudes towards the facts of racial composition.

The possible ways of organizing the state-area are not limited to the unitary and the federal systems. The United Kingdom, for example, has evolved in the course of its long history a most complicated system under which Wales, Scotland, Northern Ireland, the Isle of Man, and the Channel Islands—each has a different degree of autonomy adjusted to its particular linguistic, religious, economic, and political geography.

In determining the method of state-organization of a country, the student must study the actual method of government, not merely the words written into a constitution. He will recognize that while the constitution of the Soviet Union grants on paper more independence to its member republics than is true of the individual States of this country, and even though it encourages and exploits a great variety of languages and folk cultures, in every other aspect of economic and political life it operates its vast area of radically different regions as a highly centralized, monolithic state.

ANALYSIS OF EXTERNAL FUNCTIONS

In a functional approach to the analysis of the political geography of a state, our first half was concerned with the internal problems of the state-area. The second half is concerned with the external relations of the state-area to the other areas of the world, whether those are also organized as states, controlled by outside states, or unorganized. For convenience we may group these relations as territorial, economic, political, and strategic.

Territorial Relations

Under territorial relations we are of course concerned in the first instance with the degree to which adjacent states are in agreement concerning the extent of territory which each includes. Whether the area in question is large or small, agreement ultimately requires the determination of a precise boundary.

Of all the problems of international relations, these concerning the allocation of territories and hence the determination of boundaries are the most obviously geographic. It is no doubt for that reason that they have been the most common object of study by geographers. In the last two decades American geographers can point to notable progress in the development of generic concepts and useful generalizations, if not definite principles, concerning international boundaries.[37]

In much of this work however, we still tend to start on the wrong foot. In the initial classification of internal boundaries we have, as geographers, looked first at the physical character of the zones in which the boundary lines are drawn. This is not a classification of international boundaries, but rather of the features with which such boundaries are associated.

If we start with what we are studying—the state-areas—we can recognize the essential function of the boundary from its name: it is that line which is to be accepted by all concerned as *bounding* the area in which everything is under the jurisdiction of one state as against areas under different jurisdiction. In well-developed regions of the world it must be determined to the exact foot. (Consideration of the functions of a boundary zone, as an element of military defense, for example, is a separate question to be considered elsewhere.)

The first thing to know about an international boundary therefore is the degree to which it is accepted by all the parties concerned—i.e., the adjacent states and the population whose statehood is determined by the location of the boundary.[38]

Consider the following cases of international boundaries; the boundary between Great Britain and France (including the Channel Islands with Great Britain); that between France and Spain; that between Switzerland and Italy (including the Ticino boundary that reaches far down the Alpine slopes almost to the Po Plain); and, finally, the boundary between the United States and Mexico both east and west of El Paso. These run through radically different types of physical zones. Some correspond closely with ethnic divisions, others do not. But from the point of view of the primary function of an international boundary, all are in the same category, namely that of boundaries completely accepted as final by the states themselves and the people of the border areas.

In a different category is the Franco-German boundary (considered as of 1930). Though this was fully accepted by France and officially so by Germany in the Treaty of Locarno, one could not assume that the German leaders intended that acceptance to be final and by imprisoning certain of the local leaders in Alsace the French government demonstrated its lack of faith in the complete acceptance by the Alsatian people of their inclusion in the French state.

Still different is the case of the German-Pol-

---

[37]The following series is unusual in American political geography in that each derives much from the preceding studies and from earlier studies by European geographers: Richard Hartshorne, "Geographic and Political Boundaries in Upper Silesia," *Annals of the Association of American Geographers*, XXIII (1933): 194–228; idem, "Suggestion on the Terminology of Political Boundaries," *Mitteilungen des Vereins der Geographen an der Universität Leipzig*, Heft 14/15 (1936): 180–192; abstract in *Annals of the Association of American Geographers*, XXVI (1936): 56 f.; S. Whittemore Boggs, *International Boundaries*, New York, 1940; Stephen B. Jones, *Boundary-Making: A Handbook for Statesmen, Treaty Editors and Boundary Commissioners*, Columbia University Press, 1945.

[38]A consideration of a large number of international boundaries from this approach is given in Richard Hartshorne, "A Survey of the Boundary Problems of Europe," in *Geographic Aspects of International Relations*, C.C. Colby, editor, University of Chicago Press, 1938, pp. 163–213.

ish boundary of the inter-war period, which neither state accepted as more than a temporary division of teritory claimed by both sides.

Where boundaries run through primitive, essentially colonial, regions which at present have very slight productive value but offer possibilities for future importance, we may need to recognize a different set of categories. Thus we may find cases in which for a time the states concerned, while not committing themselves to an ultimate boundary, raise no question concerning the line lost in the wilderness, but may at any moment challenge, with the force of arms, the line that had apparently been accepted.[39]

If we first establish such a system of classification, based on the primary function of boundaries, and only then seek to determine to what extent those of particular categories are based on different types of features—e.g., on natural divides of population, on ethnic divisions, or on boundaries antecedent to state development—we may hope to avoid one of our more common forms of geographic determinism.

The second question concerning any international boundary (whether or not it is fully accepted) is the degree to which its bounding function is maintained by the bordering states, the degree, that is, to which all movements of goods and persons across the line are effectively controlled by the boundary officials. In examining that, the geographer will of course observe the ways in which the control is made easier or more difficult by the character of the zone through which the boundary line is drawn.

A special aspect of boundary problems emerges where the territory of a state reaches to the sea. Though open to use by all, the seas are in fact little used by anyone. Hence, it is sufficient for most purposes to define the boundary simply as following the coast, as most treaties do. But for certain purposes, notably fishing, border control, and naval warfare, the exact determination of the line in the waters may be critical. There is no overall agreement in international law either as to the width of territorial waters—the zone of sea included as part of the possession of the bordering state—or as to the manner in which the off-shore line bounding those waters follows the indentations of the coast. The

literature on this problem is voluminous, but among geographers, Boggs, so far as I know, is the only one who has made special study of the problem.[40]

The use of territorial waters by merchant ships of a foreign state, commonly for the purpose of entering the ports of the country concerned, represents the most common occurrence of use of territory of one state for the purposes of another state. In this case the purpose is mutual. In other, more special cases, problems arise from the desire or need of the people of one state to utilize the territory of a foreign country in order to have access to still other countries, or in some cases to a different part of their own state. Both Canada and the United States have permitted the construction of railroads across portions of their territories whose major purpose was to connect regions of the other country—e.g., the Michigan Central across Ontario from Detroit to Buffalo, or the Canadian Pacific across the State of Maine from Montreal to St. John, New Brunswick. European countries commonly will not tolerate foreign railraods across their territories, but the Polish railroads in the inter-war period operated, for Germany, through trains between East Prussia and the main part of Germany.

Nearly all states recognize the need of providing transit service for trade across their territories between states on either side, though this involves a multiplicity of minor problems of control. Most important are provisions for transit from an inland state to the seacoast in order to have access to the countries of the world accessible by sea routes. The Grand Trunk Railroad of Canada, now a part of the Canadian National Railways, not only crosses New Hampshire and Maine to reach the sea, but, when the winter ice closes the St. Lawrence, uses the harbor of Portland, Maine as its port of shipment for foreign trade of interior Canada, which constitutes most of the total traffic of that American port. In certain European cases more specific arrangements seem necessary: a section of a port, as at Trieste or Hamburg, may be allocated exclusively to handle the transit trade of a foreign country.*

Economic Relations

Trade in commodities among states is an

---

[39]Cf. Robert S. Platt, "Conflicting Territorial Claims in the Upper Amazon," in *Geographic Aspects of International Problems*, C.C. Colby, editor, University of Chicago Press, 1938, pp. 243–278.

[40]Boggs, *op. cit.*, pp. 184–192.

*Air Transport has of course added a new variety of transit problems.

essential part of the field of economic geography, treated usually as simply a form of interregional trade for which definite statistics happen to be available. Other forms of international economic relations, as in services, investments, etc., might no less logically be studied in economic geography, but as yet few geographers have attempted to do this. While it is obvious that these economic relations between individuals or corporations in one state and those in others are somehow significant to the states concerned, it is by no means easy to determine what that significance is. In consequence many writers in political geography see no alternative but to throw in a section treating the international trade of the country in standard economic-geographic fashion.

In the analysis of a state-area the need to consider its economic relations with outside areas arises from the fact that in many respects a state operates, must operate, as a unit economy in relation with other unit economies in the world. The difficulties arise because, while it must operate completely as a political unit, a state-area operates only partially as an economic unit.

The first problem is to determine to what extent the economy of one state-area is dependent on that of others, though the mere analysis of self-sufficiency is only a beginning. If one says that the United States produces a surplus of coal and iron, but is dependent on foreign countries for much of its supply of tin, nickel, and manganese, of sugar and rubber —such a statement, even in precise percentage figures, tell us directly little of importance. If a country has plenty of coal and iron it can normally secure the other metals mentioned from wherever in the world they are produced. Under abnormal conditions of war, or threat of war, it is essential to know that the manganese normally comes from the Transcaucusus in the Soviet Union, the tin from British Malaya (but can be obtained in Bolivia), whereas the nickel comes from adjacent Canada. Natural rubber supplies are available in adequate amounts only in one remote region—Malaya-East Indies—but nearby Cuba can supply most of our sugar needs.

In general, the geographer will analyze the economic dependence of one state-area on others in terms of the specific countries concerned and their location and political association in relation to the state he is studying.

Since all sound trading is of mutual advantage to both parties, to say that one state is economically dependent on any other necessarily implies also the converse. But the degree to which any particular commodity trade, shipping service, or investment is critically important varies in terms of the total economy of each of the two states concerned. It is only in this sense that the common question "Is a particular state economically viable?" has any validity, since every state above the most primitive level is in some respects critically dependent on others.

The problem is far from simple, but perhaps we can suggest two generalizations. As between two countries that differ greatly in the size of their total national economy, the economic relationships between them are more critically important for the lesser country (though this might not be true under war conditions). This is true because these economic relationships, which may be taken as equalized through international balance of payments, will form a larger proportion of the total national economy of the lesser state. An obvious example is found in the relation of Eire to Great Britain, of Cuba to the United States.

The second generalization rests on the fact that the critical significance of the trade depends on the possibility of alternatives, of finding other sources for needed supplies or other markets for products which must be sold to maintain the national economy. Most popular discussions tend to think only of the former, whereas under the capitalist profit-system under which most international trade operates, it is the latter that is more significant. The reason is that for most commodities of world production there are alternative sources of supply at moderate increase in cost; there may not be alternative markets even at greatly reduced selling prices.

Finally we may note that relatively few areas of the world now produce a surplus of manufactured goods requiring a high degree of technological development and these constitute therefore a relatively limited market for the surplus of primary products of farm, forest, and mine which can be produced widely over the world. Consequently the countries producing primary products, even the very necessities of life, may find it more difficult to find alternative markets for their products than the industrial countries producing articles less essential to life. With wider spread of industrialization over the world, this situation would of course be altered, conceivably reversed.

It should not be assumed however that these rough generalizations will provide the answer in any given case. Consider the problem posed by the independence of Austria after the dissolution of the Habsburg empire—a problem which Austria still faces. To survive as a viable economic unit, Austria needed to maintain with the adjacent regions, re-organized as independent states, a high degree of economic relationship. Its position in competition with otherwise more favored regions of industrial Europe, made it peculiarly dependent on markets immediately to the east. For these eastern neighbors such relationships were also necessary for the maximum economic progress, but were not vitally necessary to economic life. If, for political reasons, and to develop their own industries at greater cost, they preferred not to trade freely with Austria, they had the choice of the less profitable plan, whereas for Austria the alternative was economic collapse.

In the nineteenth century, international economic relations, though both supported and retarded by state action, were generally operated as the private business of individuals and corporations. With the depression of the 1930's, the rise of totalitarian states, and the last war, there has been an increasing tendency for the state itself to direct the operations of international trade and investment. In these respects states function increasingly as economic units so that the economic relations among them become increasingly important in the politico-geographic analysis of the state.

Political Relations

The most obvious form of political relation of a state to any outside territory is that of effective political control—as a colony, possession, dependency, or "protectorate." Commonly we recognize only a small number of states as colonial, or imperial, powers: eight or nine in western Europe together with the United States, Japan, Australia, and New Zealand (the two latter functioning in islands of the Southwest Pacific). Germany was eliminated from the list by the First World War, Japan by the Second. If, however, we recognize the colonial reality of areas adjacent to a state and legally included in its territory but actually not forming an integral part of that state (as discussed earlier in this paper), the list is far longer—including Canada, Norway, Sweden, the Soviet Union, China,

the Union of South Africa, and most of the Latin American states. A new comer to this list is the Indonesian Republic, with large territories subject to it in the primitive areas of Borneo, Celebes, etc.

The legal forms of colonial relationship vary widely—even within a single empire, such as that of Great Britain. Further, these legal forms may or may not express the reality of the relationship, the degree to which political organization is imposed and operated by the outside state. It is the latter, I presume, that is our concern in political geography.

One characteristic of colonial areas that is of particular concern from our present point of view is the degree to which the governmental system of the home state is extended over the colonial territory. France is in the process of fully incorporating certain formerly colonial areas into metropolitan France, but others only partially. Many imperial powers have always extended their legal systems into colonial areas so far as citizens from the home country are concerned, so that within any colonial area there may be an overlapping of two authorities—one having jurisdiction over citizens of the home state, the other over native people.

Many countries recognized by treaty as independent states, and functioning in large degree as such, are nonetheless under some particular degree of political control by an outside power. This may be limited to utilization of small fractions of the territory of one state by the government, usually the armed services, of the other—e.g., Great Britain in military control of the Canal Zone of Egypt, the United States Navy at Guantanamo Bay. The most important, relatively, is the American control for essentially an indefinite period, of the Panama Canal Zone, across the most populous part of the Republic of Panama. In other cases, the outside country may control directly no part of the territory, but rather exercise limited control, as through an adviser, over major aspects of government, especially foreign relations, customs, or the national budget. The United States has in the past exercised such control for limited periods over small states in the Caribbean area; a group of outside powers for years operated the tariff customs of China to raise money to pay the Chinese foreign debts. The clearest case of political domination of supposedly independent states by an outside state today is found in the obvious control by the Soviet Union over the internal policies as well as foreign policy of the "satellite" states on its west, from Poland to Bulgaria, even though this relationship is expressed in no formal treaties.

Generally speaking, recognition of independent sovereignty of a state by the other states of the world presumes that the state will maintain similar political relations with all friendly states, will not be bound by special political associations with any particular states. Numerous exceptions however are widely recognized. Thus the dominions of the British Commonwealth are recognized as having emerged from colonial to independent status, even though they continue to be held together in continuously voluntary confederation with the United Kingdom, extending to each other numerous political and economic privileges not extended to other states. Likewise outside states have long recognized the special political concern of the United States for the Latin American republics, a concern now finally expressed in treaty as a mutual policy of association. Likewise they have recognized the longstanding political interest of the United States in the negro state of Liberia. The recent North Atlantic Pact, though intended primarily for military purposes, contains political clauses which, if implemented, would tend to create a special political association of the United States, Canada and the states of western Europe.

Finally, of course, nearly all the states of the world have accepted certain political commitments in joining the United Nations; insofar as this applies to all states, such commitments are universal, rather than geographically distinctive.

Strategic Relations

In no phase of political geography does the geographer experience such difficulty in maintaining his geographic point of view or in keeping his eye focussed on problems he is competent to study as in the field of strategic relations. Strategy obviously depends on national power and this is a subject on which the geographer feels ready to contribute his share, in "geographic foundations of national power." But in so doing he is migrating into a field whose core and purpose is not geography, but military and political strategy. Further, to answer the questions raised in that field—e.g., "How strong is a state?"—one must analyze not only the geographic conditions, but a wide

host of other factors including the effect of party systems on the conduct of foreign policy, morale of fighting troops, effectiveness of personal leadership, size of standing armies, and number of fighting planes.

It is therefore not merely an intellectual exercise to attempt to distinguish between political geography and the study of the power of states (to which geography has much to contribute); it is a problem of practical importance for the individual geographer concerned to outline a unitary field of political geography in which he may competently work.

The literature of political geography provides no clear answer, so far as I can find, to this problem. Certainly the development of Geopolitik greatly confused the problem for the German geographers, and those of our own colleagues who have hoped to establish a purified field of geopolitics have inherited that confusion. Some writers evidently solve the problem by simply omitting any consideration of strategic relations. But surely this produces an incomplete study. In the analysis of the external relations with other state-areas, we must certainly recognize that the state-area, as a unit, has vitally important strategic relations with the other areas of the world.

I therefore approach this problem with no assurance that we have a satisfactory answer.[41] But in this progress report, it may be appropriate to present as current thinking even very tentative conclusions.

Every state-area in the world lives in a strategic situation with other states, a situation that may be in part created by its own actions and policies, but in major part is determined for it by those other states.

Thus Switzerland in modern times has been a unit area of relatively small offensive power, though not inconsiderable defensive power, situated in the midst of a group of larger neighbors, each fearful of expansion of power by the others. In this situation Switzerland has found its best hope for security in a policy of armed neutrality because such a neutralized area was in the mutual interest, defensively, of

[41]As examples of attempts to handle this problem in specific cases, reference may be made to two studies, by the writer, one written early during the last war (though published somewhat later), the other just after the end of that war: "The United States and the 'Shatter Zone' of Europe," in Hans W. Weigert and V. Stefansson, *Compass of the World*, New York, 1944, pp. 203–214; and "The Geopolitical Position of the United States and the Soviet Union," *Education*, (October 1946): 95–100.

the neighboring powers. In a much earlier period, in the sixteenth and seventeenth centuries, when Austria was the only major power bordering Switzerland, and many of its neighbors were small states, the Swiss Confederation followed a very different policy of strategic relations, frequently allying itself with any of various neighbors in conflict with the others.

The strategic relations of a state, in other words, must be adjusted to the particular strategic situation in which it finds itself at any time. With the unification of Germany in 1871, the strategic map of Europe was changed no less than the political map. Because that new unit increased in economic production, population, and power faster than any of its neighbors, and was able to establish close strategic relations with Austria-Hungary, forming a solid block of power across Central Europe, all the other states of Europe including Great Britain, were forced to change their strategic relations with each other.

Within the last five years the United States has found itself forced to abandon one of its most time-honored principles of international relations—that of having no strategic relations in peacetime with any states outside of the Americas. The new relationships entered into under the North Atlantic Pact followed an appraisal of the new pattern of space-relationships of power as created by the changed system of states in Europe. It might be significant, though now too late, to ask whether an equally realistic appraisal of that situation in 1938 or 1939 would not have shown the need for a similar strategic association at that time.

Whatever reaction the reader may have to that idea, our concern in this theoretical discussion is merely to illustrate the type of problem that seems appropriate for inclusion in the analysis of the political geography of a state-area. In studying the relations which such an area, operating as a unit, enters into with other areas, we are concerned with engagements which it has, or has not, made with other units, whether for defensive or offensive purposes. Interpretation of these associations necessarily involves an appraisal of the space relationships of all the strategic areas involved, whether as power units or as territories of passage. The problem is logically inherent in the political geography of states and its geographic quality seems clear.

It is equally clear from our examples

however that in making such a study, one must assume as given quantities certain factors the determination of which forms a main part of the study of national power, the field we are attempting here to separate from political geography. But is this difficulty not inherent in most, if not all, branches of geography? We are constantly dependent on other fields to provide us, as result of lengthy research, with conclusions which we accept and use as established.

Ideally, the student in political geography would have at his command conclusions already arrived at in studies of the potential military power of states, upon which he would base his interpretation of the strategic relations of the state he has under study. If such studies have not been made, the political geographer may find it desirable to make them himself; as a geographer he has command of much of the basic material necessary and with the help of colleagues from other fields may be able to reach reasonably reliable conclusions. But if our distinction between the two fields is valid, the general requirement that a student should not lose his orientation in reference to the core of his field is of particular importance in this case; for otherwise the attractiveness of studying questions of such great moment as national power may result in his never returning to the field in which by training and experience he is fully competent.

Relation of Territorial, Economic, Political, and Strategic Relations

For purposes of organization, we have considered separately four different types of associations which the state-area has with other areas of the world. It is also necessary to see them together in their interrelationships. If one were to suppose that there would generally be a high degree of correspondence among them, the examination of concrete cases would reveal many discrepancies. Thus, popular thought assumes that Great Britain's most important economic associations are with the countries of the Commonwealth and Empire, but actually her largest and most critical economic trade is with the United States. Argentina is more important economically to Great Britain than any of her African possessions. Throughout our history, the dominant economic and strategic concern of the United States was with European states and our major territorial problems were settled with those states. And yet until 1949, the United States carefully abstained from any continuous political association with any European states. But it was primarily our strategic concern toward European states that led us into our special relationship with Latin America under the Monroe Doctrine. On the other hand our political guardianship of Liberia was unrelated to any territorial, economic, or strategic concern until the Firestone Tire Company utilized that political relationship for economic purposes, in its project for rubber production in the 1920's, and in the last war we discovered at least a temporary strategic value in the need for airports in West Africa.

SUMMARY AND CONCLUSION

Political geography, as a distinct unit branch of geography, is to be justified neither in terms of political aspects of geography nor in terms of geographic foundations of politics, since each of those constitutes but a collection of partial solutions separated from the problems involved. The core of political geography is the study of one distinctive phenomenon in the total differentiation of areas, namely the sections of area organized as political units. Areal differentiation is both most marked and most important in respect to units of land at the level of state-areas.

The state-area, like a farm or an industrial plant, but unlike these sections of area that we ordinarily study as "regions," is an organized unit of land and people, organized by man according to a particular idea or purpose. Though in no proper sense an organism, the state-area is an organization that has genesis, structure, and function. Logically, therefore, the analysis of a state-area may be approached from any or all of these three viewpoints. In contrast to genuine organisms, there is no close mutual relationship between genesis on the one hand and structure and function on the other; on the contrary, states have tended to add pieces of territory whenever it was possible to do so, regardless of need, and then to adapt function to the automatically resulting structure. Hence the study of the genesis of state areas tends to be largely historical in interest, throwing little light on structure and function.

Likewise, in contrast with such areal units as farms or industrial plants, the state is not able to plan or evolve its regional structure, but must simply operate in whatever structure its history and geography have happened to produce. Since these vary for every state, not in minor degree, but fundamentally, the attempt to find a general principle of regional structure of state-areas is futile. Further, the state-area, though a genuine geographic phenomenon, is not a concrete object exciting direct interest in its morphology for its own sake. Hence the morphological approach to the study of the state-area is either a dull and lifeless description of something that appears real only on a map, or, if used as a method of approach to the understanding of function, tempts the student to naive forms of geographic determinism.

State-areas are important, both in the practical and in the academic sense, primarily in terms of their functions: namely what the state-area as a whole means to its parts and its relations as a whole with outside areas. These functions, determined by the human forces that operate the state-area as a unit, are greatly affected by the structure of the state-area, which of course is the current product of its past development. In a sequence of cause-and-effect relationships, science can safely proceed from cause to effect only in those situations in which the relatively small number of factors and a multiplicity of similar cases makes possible the establishment of reliable scientific laws or general principles. These requirements are lacking in political geography.

Consequently we conclude that the rational, scientifically reliable, and realistic approach to the study of state-areas is to start with the phenomena with which we are most concerned—the functions of the state-area—to determine how these have been affected by the character of the area itself, its structure and contents, and to utilize historic facts of genesis insofar as those aid us in understanding structural features previously determined to be significant.

There is however a practical situation in which we may be forced to reverse this procedure. If plans are being made for the construction of an entirely new state-area, or for major territorial alterations in an existing one, one is forced to attempt some prediction of the capacity of such a projected organization to function effectively as a unit. Political geographers will be able to claim superior competence in attempting predictions in such cases only if they have established a high degree of understanding of the reasons why present or past state-areas have or have not functioned effectively.

The fundamental internal function of the state-area is to establish itself as an effective unit in fact, rather than merely in international law. This requires the conception and establishment of an idea of the state, a purpose or set of purposes, sufficiently strong to overcome the centrifugal tendencies resulting inevitably from the separate and divergent interests of the diverse regions that are included, in a particular geographic pattern, in the structure of the state-area.

Externally, the state-area functions as a unit area in friendly or unfriendly relations with other state-areas and other outside areas, relations that may be classified as territorial, economic, political, or strategic. Its specific relations with any one outside area may involve a complex of all these and further they are interrelated to its similar relations with all other outside areas in a world system which forms a single whole. The study of these interrelations among state-areas is primarily a study in space relationships among unit-areas differing in internal character, production, and power.

I trust that the categorical manner in which these conclusions are stated will mislead no one to suppose that this paper is intended as a blue-print which future studies in political geography should follow. We are not ready for that, if indeed we ever should be. Rather the attempt has been to suggest how we may construct a system for the study of state-areas, a system that must be sufficiently flexible to be bent to the differences that distinguish each state-area from all others, but which may enable students to work cumulatively, to build upon what has been produced by previous students.

Because the theme of my paper is limited to one branch of geography it might appear to be addressed to only a limited number of our members. I hope that will prove to be a large number, since we need the combined efforts of many to work out more effective methods of study. But this is not a call to all geographers to leave whatever they are studying to work in this particular field.

In another sense however the paper is addressed to all geographers, certainly to all geographers who specialize in any foreign areas. In your regional studies you inevitably come face to face with problems in political geography. As specialists for your particular region you know more about the underlying factors in its political geography than does the student of political geography in general who is not at home in your region. In order that such knowledge may be analyzed and organized into studies useful to other students, lasting contributions both to regional geography and to political geography, we need to develop effective methods for study that will give political geography an organized structure of knowledge, clearly integrated into the field of geography as a whole. This paper is a progress report of efforts to achieve that goal.

ADDITIONAL THEMES

Several years after "The Functional Approach" appeared, Hartshorne restated his view of political geography.[9] In 1954, he discussed four distinct approaches within the field, including the functional studies described in the preceding paper. The other three themes are the morphological approach, the historical approach, and power analysis. In previous chapters we have considered data relevant to each of these themes in political geography.

The *morphological* approach focuses upon the shape, structural features, and patterns of political phenomena. All states have boundaries; practically all states have core areas. Capital cities, provincial divisions, overpopulated and underpopulated areas, all form part of the shape and structure of the state, and they are capable of comparative analysis. In this discussion of political geography, Hartshorne produces a definition of the field: political geography is "the study of areal differences and similarities in political character as an interrelated part of the total complex of areal differences and similarities."[10]

By "total complex" is meant the full range of world phenomena: physiographic, biotic, cultural. Thus we can detect a trace of the Moodie definition quoted previously, in which political geography is seen as the study of the relationships between community and environment. Hartshorne's definition suggests that this is only one part of the whole.

The morphological approach in many ways is less involved and complex than the other approaches enumerated by Hartshorne. Often it is a process of identification, for example, of the location, shape, and extent of the core area

[9]R. Hartshorne, "Political Geography," in Preston E. James and Clarence F. Jones (eds.), *American Geography: Inventory and Prospect*, Syracuse University Press, 1954, pp. 174 ff.

[10]Ibid., p. 178.

of a state, or the description of boundary features in a certain section. This does not mean that valuable results cannot be obtained. The emerging states of Africa, for example, have core areas whose limits are sometimes difficult to determine. Such criteria as might be employed in the Western world are not always relevant, and the choice of other criteria is a matter for much deliberation. When we say that Ghana is a highly centralized unitary state focusing upon a single-core area and Nigeria is a federal state possessing three distinct core areas, we have an immediate insight into one reason for the choice of politicoterritorial organization these states have made. But when it comes to identifying those core areas in any but the most general way, we lack precise data. Here the morphological approach will be employed.

Historical political geography, also recognized by Hartshorne as a major theme in the field, focuses upon time as the main element and upon the changes in earth-state relations time has brought. The growth of states around early core areas, the invasion of a frontier, the effects of colonial expansion—all these require the historical approach. One result of this approach is the cartographic representation of the sequence of events that led to the establishment of a state's current boundaries, showing how expansion and incorporation led to the present heterogeneous internal situation. The evolution of the state of France has been described in detail by Whittlesey in *The Earth and the State.* Historical political geography may involve the painstaking investigation of treaties and agreements, requires a detailed understanding of the technological realities of the past, and always demands full knowledge of the methodology of history.

The *power analysis* approach, involving the assessment of the actual or potential power of states, is a field in which nongeographers have also been active. F.C. German's article, reproduced in Chapter 4, exemplifies this approach. A geographer, S.B. Cohen, has suggested that we recognize five inventory categories of political applicability:[11]

1. The physical environment (landforms, climate, soils, vegetation, water bodies, etc.)

2. Movement (the directional flow of transportation and communication of goods, men, and ideas)

3. Raw materials, semi-finished and finished goods (employed and potential, in both time and space terms)

[11]S.B. Cohen, op. cit., p. 8.

4. Population (in its various characteristics, particularly qualitative and ideological)

5. The body politic (its various administrative forms, ideals, and goals in their areal expression, such as county, state, national and international bloc frameworks)

A sixth and distinct category is recognized: location, shape, and boundaries of the state, as well as the "impact of space upon the internal character and external relations of such political entities." But like other geographers and non-geographers as well, Cohen ultimately faces the problem common to all: the selection of relevant data and their weighing. Cohen points out that it is as great an error to include unnecessary or irrelevant data as it is to omit vital material. Obviously, the power analysis approach involves many pitfalls—but it does marshall for this specific purpose a wide range of data, yields valuable insights, and stimulates interdisciplinary debate with favorable results.

Whatever work is done in political geography, however, the functional approach appears to be most commonly employed. This is not surprising, considering our view of the state as a system of many functioning parts. Most questions appear immediately or ultimately to lead to the matter of functions. When, in discussing the morphological approach, we indicated that it is possible to compare capital cities or core areas or boundaries, would it not seem more meaningful to ask how the *functions* of these state elements compare? Is the binding function of the capital of Ghana similar to that of Thailand? Is the function of the boundary between the Soviet Union and Poland identical to that between France and the Federal Republic of Germany? What, in fact, can we say in terms of a generalization about boundaries as functioning parts of the state system? Or capital cities? Or core areas? These are questions that will be of concern in the following chapters and articles.

REFERENCES

Alexander, Lewis M., "Major Trends in the World Political Patterns," *Institute of Indian Geography,* Bihar, Publ. No. 1, 1954, pp. 6–12.

——, *World Political Patterns.* Chicago, Rand McNally, 1963.

Bowman, Isaiah, *The New World.* Yonkers, N.Y., World Book Co., 1921.

——, *The Pioneer Fringe.* New York, American Geographical Society, 1931.

Campbell, Robert D., *Pakistan: Emerging Democracy.* Princeton, N.J., Van Nostrand, 1963.

Carlson, Lucile, *Geography and World Politics.* Englewood Cliffs, N.J., Prentice-Hall, 1958.

Cohen, Saul B., *Geography and Politics in a World Divided.* New York, Random House, 1963.

Cole, J.P., *Geography of World Affairs.* Harmondsworth, Eng., Penguin Books, 1959.

East, W. Gordon, and A.E. Moodie (eds.), *The Changing World; Studies in Political Geography.* Yonkers, N.Y., World Book Co., 1956.

Fairgrieve, J., *Geography and World Power.* New York, E.P. Dutton & Co., Inc., 1941.

Fisher, Charles A., "South-east Asia: The Balkans of the Orient?" *Geography,* 47 (1962), 347–367.

Fryer, D.W., "Economic Aspects of Indonesian Disunity," *Pacific Affairs,* 30, 3 (September, 1957), 195–208.

Goblet, Y.M., *Political Geography and the World Map.* New York, F.A. Praeger, 1955.

Gottmann, Jean, "The Political Partitioning of Our World; an Attempt at Analysis," *World Politics,* 4, 4 (July, 1952), 512–519.

Hartshorne, Richard, "Political Geography," in *American Geography: Inventory and Prospect,* C.F. Jones and Preston James (eds.). New York, Syracuse University Press, 1954, 167–225.

———, **"The Politico-Geographic Pattern of the World,"** *Ann. Amer. Ac. of Pol. & Soc. Sci.,* No. 218 (1941), 45–57.

Hoffman, George W., "East Europe: A Study in Political Geography," *Texas Quart.,* 2, 3 (Autumn, 1959), 57–88.

Iwata, Kozo, "The Recent Trend of Political Geography," *The Human Gography, The Jimbun-chiri,* 8, 3 (1956), 165–175.

Jackson, W.A. Douglas, *Politics and Geographic Relationships.* Englewood Cliffs, N.J., Prentice-Hall, Inc., 1964.

———, **"Whither Political Geography?"** *Ann. A.A.G.,* 48, 2 (June, 1958), 178–183.

Kalijarvi, T.V., *Modern World Politics.* New York, Crowell, 1942.

Kriesel, K.M., "Montesquieu: Possibilistic Political Geographer," *Annals, A.A.G.,* 58, 3 (September, 1968), 557–574.

Kristof, L.K.D., "The Origins and Evolution of Geopolitics," *Jour. Conflict Resolution,* IV, 1 (March, 1960), 15–51.

McNee, R.B., "Centrifugal-Centripetal Forces in International Petroleum Company Regions," *Ann. A.A.G.,* 51, 1 (March, 1961), 124–138.

Moodie, A.E., *Geography Behind Politics.* London, Hutchinson's University Library, 1949.

Mookerjee, Sitanshu, "A Review of Political Geography," *Geog. Rev. India,* 18, 1 (March, 1956), 34–46.

Nicholson, Norman L., "Some Aspects of the Political Geography of the District of Keewatin," *Canadian Geographer,* No. 3 (1953), 73–83.

Pearcy, George Etzel, and others, *World Political Geography,* 2nd ed. New York, T.Y. Crowell Co., 1957.

Pounds, Norman J.G., *Political Geography.* New York, McGraw-Hill, 1963.

Prescott, J.R.V., "The Function and Methods of Electoral Geography," *Ann. A.A.G.,* 49, 3 (September, 1959), 269–304.

Roucek, Joseph S. (ed.), *Contemporary Political Ideologies.* New York, Philosophical Library, 1961.

Sauer, C.O., "The Formative Years of Ratzel in the United States," *Annals, A.A.G.,* 61, 2 (June, 1971), 245–254.

Schuman, F.L., *International Politics.* New York, McGraw-Hill, 1948.

Sharp, W.R., and Grayson Kirk, *Contemporary International Politics.* New York, Farrar & Rinehart, Inc., 1940.

Shreevastava, M.P., "Political Problems of India; A Functional Approach," *The Indian Geog. J.,* 37, 2 (April-June, 1962), 35–44.

Simonds, F.H., and Brooks Emeny, *The Great Powers in World Politics.* New York, American Book Company, 1939.

Sprout, Harold and Margaret, *Foundations of International Politics.* Princeton, N.J., Van Nostrand, 1962.

Tarlton, C.D., "The Styles of American International Thought: Mahan, Bryan, and Lippman," *World Politics,* XVII, 4 (July, 1965), 584–614.

Van Valkenburg, Samuel, "A Political Geographer Looks at the World," *Prof. Geog.,* 12, 4 (July, 1960), 6–8.

———, **and Carl L. Stotz,** *Elements of Political Geography.* New York, Prentice-Hall, 1954.

Weigert, Hans W., and others, *Principles of Political Geography.* New York, Appleton-Century-Crofts, Inc., 1957.

Whittlesey, Derwent, *The Earth and the State.* New York, H. Holt, 1939.

CHAPTER
13
EXHORTATIONS AND PRESCRIPTIONS

The impetus and direction given to political geography by Friedrich Ratzel were altered in the United States by the work of Whittlesey and Hartshorne, among others. But in Europe, Ratzel's forceful and persuasive writings led to something very different. There, it generated a school of *geopolitics*, a deviant direction of the field that was "doomed" to extinction because the followers of geopolitik departed from scholarly methods."[1] This harsh judgment has been rendered in large measure as a result of the work and activities of geopolitical practitioners in Germany of the 1920's and 1930's, who contributed importantly to the philosophical foundations of Naziism.

Was Ratzel the chief villain in this context? He has often been accused of combining an inflexible determinism with a view of the state that, through the organic analogue, had all the elements of inevitability. It was tempting to use these ideas in evaluating then-current and prospective power relationships among states, and, in the process, to propose policies states might follow to reap the benefits involved. Thus geopolitics became geostrategy, and frequently rather unscholarly geostrategy at that. But Ratzel was a scholar, and he himself warned repeatedly against excessive extrapolation from his organic model; at the same time he methodically trod a path of true scientific enquiry. If his determinist position was in error, he shared that viewpoint with many contemporaries (and successors) who did not fall into the trap of wild geostrategic speculation. And it is well to remember that the rise of Nazi Germany came nearly two generations after Ratzel published his most significant writings.

Nor were Ratzel and his successors alone in their contribution to the "school" of geopolitics. As we will note in the following pages, the whole idea was given a boost by the work of a British political geographer named Halford

Mackinder, who in the year of Ratzel's death produced an assessment of the power potential of the Eurasian continent that is still worth reading today.[2]

If there is one man whose name is associated with geopolitics even more closely than Ratzel, it is the Swedish political scientist Rudolf Kjellen (1864 to 1922). Indeed, Kjellen apparently was the first to apply the term *geopolitik* to this variety of political geography. He elaborated on Ratzel's organic theme by introducing aspects of the quality of the population, the nation whose aggregate constitutes the body of the state. In addition to moral capacities, there was, in Kjellen's view, the *will*, the cumulative psychological force of the state. In assessing power, Kjellen reasoned that "the great power *(Grossmacht)* is a concept which is not mathematical but dynamic, not ethnic or cultural but psychological. . . . The great power is, above all, a will richly endowed with power means."[3] Kjellen saw the state in a condition of constant competition with other states; larger states would extend their power over smaller ones, and ultimately the world would have only a few very large and extremely powerful states. As Professor Kristof remarks, "he sanctioned as natural the instinct of men and nations to satisfy their desires at another's expense. Kjellen's followers concluded that this instinct, being natural, must also be good."[4]

Such a viewpoint quite naturally fell on fertile ground in Germany after World War I. Germany, a unified state for less than 50 years, had been defeated by its European adversaries, and its colonial empire had been carved up by the victors. But Germany still had great potential, a substantial domestic resource

[2]H.J. Mackinder, "The Geographical Pivot of History," *Geographical Journal, XXIII,* (1904), 421–444.

[3]Quoted from a superb article entitled "The Origin and Evolution of Geopolitics," *Conflict Resolution, IV,* 1 (March, 1960). The quotation is from footnote 20; the paper provides a richly detailed and annotated review of the rise of and contributors to geopolitical thought.

[4]Ibid., p. 26.

[1]"Studies in Political Geography," in *The Science of Geography,* Washington, National Academy of Sciences—National Research Council, 1965, p. 34.

base, and a large population. The prescriptions of geopolitics would be just the stimulant to recreate the will about which Kjellen had written. And so a group of German geopoliticians, chief among whom was Karl Haushofer (1869 to 1946), began to write the final, fateful chapter in the sequence of *geopolitik.*

The German geopoliticians of the interwar period used Ratzel's concepts of the territorial growth of states by annexation and amalgamation and the growing state's increasing need for life space *(Lebensraum)* to counter the effects of defeat and containment, imposed after World War I. The allied powers had imposed territorial, political, and economic restraints upon Germany; Kjellen's geopolitics could be invoked to "prove" that these restrictions were "unnatural" and therefore unacceptable. Moreover, Mackinder had written that any power that could make itself the master of interior Eurasia would be in a position to rule the world. Small wonder that Haushofer proposed that "*geopolitik* shall and must become the geographic conscience of the state."[5] The geopolitics he and his colleagues were speaking of was not the political geography of Ratzel or even Kjellen, but a prescriptive form of geostrategy for a German state bent on the undoing of the ignominy of defeat and determined to resurrect an even greater *Reich.* Schools of geopolitics emerged in a number of German universities, but the atmosphere was clearly not good for objective analysis. *Geopolitik* was to serve and indeed to guide the territorial policies of a Germany resurgent under National Socialism and Naziism. That Ratzel had carefully qualified many of his "laws" mattered little. Whatever served the ends of *geopolitik* was used; whatever did not was ignored.

Such practices naturally signaled the end of political geography as a legitimate pursuit, and the Ratzel-Kjellen lineage was submerged in this morass of exhortation. But the geopoliticians did make one contribution, at least, that remains worth considering. German geography has always been known for its high-quality cartography, and the geopoliticians used the map with great effectiveness to promote their objectives. One example of this was the boundary between eastern Germany and Czechoslovakia. As any atlas map still shows, Czechoslovakia pushes eastern Germany's boundary far to the west. How did the geopoliticians represent this situation? They drew the map of Germany as though a Czech knife was being thrust into the corpus of the German state. Maps such as this appeared in newspapers, on election platforms, in schoolbooks. They seemed to cry out for action to provide the threatened German state with elbowroom. (There were other ways of looking at this German-Czech boundary situation. A British cartographer replied with a map showing Czechoslovakia caught, like a fish, in the giant jaws of an aggressive German state.) Cartographic geopolitics is still practiced in Germany today—and elsewhere, too. When the South Africans decided on racial segregation or *apartheid,* the candidates supporting this idea went around the country with large maps showing where "white" and "nonwhite" South Africa were to lie. *Apartheid* certainly is a manifestation of geopolitics.

To what extent the German geopoliticians managed to influence Nazi policies and strategies is open to doubt. Haushofer was close to the Nazi elite, but it was probably the aura of academic legitimacy given to practices of territorial aggrandizement that contributed to public support and enthusiasm—the *will* about which Kjellen wrote so effectively.

GEOPOLITICS ELSEWHERE

What has just been said should not lead to the conclusion that the Germans had a monopoly on geopolitical thinking, or that geopolitics as such died out after the demise of the Third Reich in 1945. Geopolitical analyses of a more moderate sort are still being made today by geographers and nongeographers alike, and Mackinder was by no means the only non-German to engage in quasiprescriptive geopolitical assessments. Before the turn of the twentieth century the question of sea power versus land-based power occupied the minds of several strategists. In the United States, a prominent contributor was Captain A.T. Mahan, who was an ardent proponent of sea power as the key to world domination and who sought to determine just what it was that produced such power. As early as 1890 Mahan published a book in which he listed six factors affecting the development and maintenance of sea power among states.[6] These were:

[5]K. Haushofer et. al., *Bausteine zur Geopolitik,* Berlin, Vowinckel, 1928, p. 27.

[6]A.T. Mahan, *The Influence of Sea Power upon History, 1660–1783,* Boston, 1890, Chapter 1.

1. *Geographical position* (location). Whether a state possesses coasts on a sea or ocean (or perhaps more than one), whether these waters are interconnected; whether it also has vulnerable, exposed land boundaries; whether it can maintain overseas strategic bases and command important trade routes.

2. *Physical "conformation" of the state* (the nature of its coasts). Whether the coastline of a state possesses natural harbors, estuaries, inlets and outlets; an absence of harbors will prevent a people from having its own sea trade, shipping, or navy; the importance of navigable rivers to internal trade but their danger as avenues of penetration by enemies.

3. *Extent of territory* (length of the coastline). The ease with which a coast can be defended.

4. *Population numbers.* A state with a large population will be more capable of building and maintaining a merchant marine and navy than will a state with a small population.

5. *National character.* Aptitude for commercial pursuits; sea power is "really based upon a peaceful and extensive commerce."

6. *Governmental character.* Whether government policy is taking advantage of the opportunities afforded by the environment and population in order to promote sea power.

Mahan, too, refers (in items 5 and 6) to the question of the national "will," in terms reminiscent of Kjellen's. Indeed, Mahan's writing in places is quite similar to that of the German geopoliticians; he "was characteristically disposed to view politics in terms of force, whose efficacy was qualified only by inexorable natural and moral laws . . . only the fittest nations could successfully sustain themselves in the constant grappling. Fitness was measured in terms of national strength. This national strength was characteristically viewed, by Mahan, in military terms. It depended, in turn, on the moral and martial fiber of the population."[7]

And Mahan was a practical man. Like the German geopoliticians, he had prescriptions for United States foreign policy, and his advice did not go unheeded. He advocated that the United States should occupy the Hawaiian Islands, take control of the Caribbean, and build a canal to link the Atlantic and Pacific Oceans. President Theodore Roosevelt's administration used several of Mahan's suggestions as the basis of its foreign policy.

Of even more interest to the political geographer are the glimpses of Mahan's world view from his later book, *The Problem of Asia.*[8] In this work, Mahan recognizes a core area in Asia and Russia's domination of it; he anticipates a struggle between Russian land power and British sea power. Not surprisingly, he presumed that British sea power would be able to contain Russian expansionism. He also predicted that the containment of Russia and the control of China would become the joint concern of the United States, Great Britain, Germany, and Japan (it is well to remember that he was writing *before* the turn of the present century). Thus he proposed that Russia should be provided warm-water ports in China by guaranteeing it the use of those exits. By this means, he argued, the Russian push toward the sea, felt in Europe and the Near East, might be alleviated. It almost seems that Mahan forgot where the Russian concentration of population and productive capacity were located—the factor of distance alone negated his idea.[9]

H.J. MACKINDER

The name of Sir Halford Mackinder is closely tied to questions of geopolitics, power analysis, and global strategy. A Scottish geographer, Mackinder too pondered the "problem of Asia" and the balance of land and sea power. In many respects, Mackinder disagreed with Mahan's conclusions, and for some very fundamental reasons. As Jones has put it, "It is not surprising that the United States, painfully land-minded since the opening of the West and the decline of sailing ships, should have produced (the naval isolationist) Mahan, while Britain, most maritime of the great powers, should have produced Mackinder."[10] It was Mackinder's view that land-based power would increase as a result of improved surface communication systems, and that no sea power would be able to dislodge the ultimate land power from its natural fortress. Mahan, on the other hand, saw the key to world

[7]Charles D. Tarlton, "The Styles of American International Thought: Mahan, Bryan, and Lippmann", *World Politics,* XVII, 4 (July, 1965), 585, 586.

[8]A.T. Mahan, *The Problem of Asia,* Boston, 1900, pp. 24 ff.

[9]For an evaluation of Mahan as a historian see K.L. Moll, "A.T. Mahan: American Historian," *Military Affairs,* 27, (1963), 131–140.

[10]S.B. Jones, "Global Strategic Views", *Geog. Rev.,* 45, 4 (1955), 492 ff.

domination as sea power. In 1904, Mackinder read a paper at the Royal Geographical Society in London entitled "The Geographical Pivot of History." This was a true milestone in the geopolitical debate of that period; in fact, the contents of that article (afterward published in the *Geographical Journal*) are still a subject of discussion and evaluation today, three generations later.

It is easy to regard Mackinder's paper as sophisticated speculation and to suggest that it has little value as a contribution to political geography (other than as a manifestation of "proper" geopolitical analysis). That Mackinder was closer to the truth than he himself may have realized is sometimes dismissed as accident. But it is worth remembering the main elements of the world situation when he produced his remarkable piece. Russia was losing a disastrous war with Japan, Germany was still a youthful, organizing state. Yet Mackinder in 1904 expressed the view that there was a Eurasian core area that, protected by inaccessibility from naval power, could shelter a land power that might come to dominate the world from its continental fortress. This Eurasian core area Mackinder called the Pivot Area in his original paper, but later he renamed it the Heartland. As Mackinder suggested, the Heartland's rivers drain into the Arctic, distances to warm-water oceans are huge, and only the Baltic and Black Seas could form avenues for sea power penetration, but these are easily defended.

Mackinder reasoned that this Eurasian Pivot Area would become the source of a great power, which would dominate the Far East, southern Asia, and Europe—most of what he called the "World-Island," which he conceptualized as consisting of Eurasia and Africa. He presumed that the Pivot Area contained a substantial resource base, capable of sustaining a power of world significance. The key, he argued, lay in Eastern Europe, the "open door" to the pivotal Heartland. Thus he formulated his famous hypothesis:

Who rules East Europe commands the Heartland
Who rules the Heartland commands the World-Island
Who rules the World-Island commands the World

Because Germany occupied the west of Mackinder's hypothetical Heartland, and Russia the east, he thought that effective control of this region for the purposes he had identified could be achieved only by the alliance of two or more states. It is hardly necessary to emphasize how well a modified version of the Heartland hypothesis fit into the extrapolations of the German geopoliticians: there, eastward, it lay, the key to world domination. Rather than an alliance, the Germans had quite another idea in mind for the disposition of the Heartland. Before we turn to Mackinder's paper, let us remind ourselves of the present situation and take the advantage of hindsight. The Heartland is now under the control of a single power; the power that also controls East Europe—and East Germany as well. As yet, the Soviet Union does not command the world, but compare its world position today with that of the Russia of 1904!

The Geographical Pivot of History.

H.J. Mackinder, M.A.

Reader in Geography in the University of Oxford; Director of the London School of Economics and Political Science.

When historians in the remote future come to look back on the group of centuries through which we are now passing, and see them fore-shortened, as we to-day see the Egyptian dynasties, it may well be that they will describe the last 400 years as the Columbian epoch, and will say that it ended soon after the year 1900. Of late it has been a common-place to speak of geographical exploration as nearly over, and it is recognized that geography must be diverted to the purpose of intensive survey and philosophic synthesis. In 400 years the outline of the map of the world has been completed with approximate accuracy, and even in the polar regions the voyages of Nansen and Scott have very narrowly reduced the last possibility of dramatic discoveries. But the opening of the twentieth century is appropriate as the end of a great historic epoch, not merely on account of this achievement, great though it be. The missionary, the conqueror, the farmer, the miner, and, of late, the engineer, have followed so closely in the traveller's footsteps that the world, in its remoter borders, has hardly been revealed before we must chronicle its virtually complete political appropriation. In Europe, North America, South America, Africa, and Australasia there is scarcely a region left for the pegging out of a claim of ownership, unless as the result of a war between civilized or half-civilized powers. Even in Asia we are probably witnessing the last moves of the game first played by the horsemen of Yermak the Cossack and the shipmen of Vasco da Gama. Broadly speaking, we may contrast the Columbian epoch with the age which preceded it, by describing its essential characteristic as the expansion of Europe against almost negligible resistances, whereas mediaeval Christendom was pent into a narrow region and threatened by external barbarism. From the present time forth, in the post-Columbian age, we shall again have to deal with a closed political system, and none the less that it will be one of world-wide scope. Every explosion of social forces, instead of being dissipated in a surrounding circuit of unknown space and barbaric chaos, will be sharply re-echoed from the far side of the globe, and weak elements in the political and economic organism of the world will be shattered in consequence. There is a vast difference of effect in the fall of a shell into an earthwork and its fall amid the closed spaces and rigid structures of a great building or ship. Probably some half-consciousness of this fact is at last diverting much of the attention of statesmen in all parts of the world from territorial expansion to the struggle for relative efficiency.

It appears to me, therefore, that in the present decade we are for the first time in a position to attempt, with some degree of completeness, a correlation between the larger geographical and the larger historical generalizations. For the first time we can perceive something of the real proportion of features and events on the stage of the whole world, and may seek a formula which shall express certain aspects, at any rate, of geographical causation in universal history. If we are fortunate, that formula should have a practical value as setting into perspective some of the competing forces in current international politics. The familiar phrase about the westward march of empire is an empirical and fragmentary attempt of the kind. I propose this evening describing those physical features of the world which I believe to have been most coercive of human action, and presenting

H.J. Mackinder, "The Geographical Pivot of History," *Geographical Journal*, Vol. XXIII (1904), 421–444. Read at the Royal Geographical Society, January 25, 1904.

some of the chief phases of history as organically connected with them, even in the ages when they were unknown to geography. My aim will not be to discuss the influence of this or that kind of feature, or yet to make a study in regional geography, but rather to exhibit human history as part of the life of the world organism. I recognize that I can only arrive at one aspect of the truth, and I have no wish to stray into excessive materialism. Man and not nature initiates, but nature in large measure controls. My concern is with the general physical control, rather than the causes of universal history. It is obvious that only a first approximation to truth can be hoped for. I shall be humble to my critics.

The late Prof. Freeman held that the only history which counts is that of the Mediterranean and European races. In a sense, of course, this is true, for it is among these races that have originated the ideas which have rendered the inheritors of Greece and Rome dominant throughout the world. In another and very important sense, however, such a limitation has a cramping effect upon thought.

The ideas which go to form a nation, as opposed to a mere crowd of human animals, have usually been accepted under the pressure of a common tribulation, and under a common necessity of resistance to external force. The idea of England was beaten into the Heptarchy by Danish and Norman conquerors; the idea of France was forced upon competing Franks, Goths, and Romans by the Huns at Chalons, and in the Hundred Years' War with England; the idea of Christendom was born of the Roman persecutions, and matured by the Crusades; the idea of the United States was accepted, and local colonial patriotism sunk, only in the long War of Independence; the idea of the German Empire was reluctantly adopted in South Germany only after a struggle against France in comradeship with North Germany. What I may describe as the literary conception of history, by concentrating attention upon ideas and upon the civilization which is their outcome, is apt to lose sight of the more elemental movements whose pressure is commonly the exciting cause of the efforts in which great ideas are nourished. A repellent

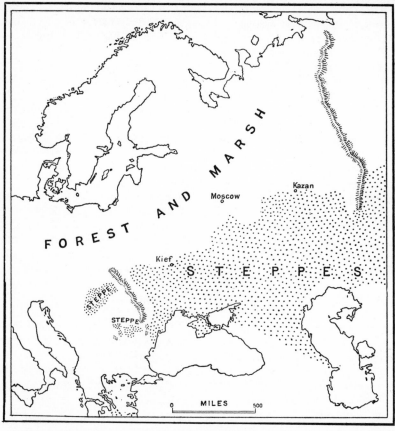

Eastern Europe before the 19th century, (after Drude in Berghaus' Physical Atlas).

personality performs a valuable social function in uniting his enemies, and it was under the pressure of external barbarism that Europe achieved her civilization. I ask you, therefore, for a moment to look upon Europe and European history as subordinate to Asia and Asiatic history, for European civilization is, in a very real sense, the outcome of the secular struggle against Asiatic invasion.

The most remarkable contrast in the political map of modern Europe is that presented by the vast area of Russia occupying half the Continent and the group of smaller territories tenanted by the Western Powers. From a physical point of view, there is, of course, a like contrast between the unbroken lowland of the east and the rich complex of mountains and valleys, islands and peninsulas, which together form the remainder of this part of the world. At first sight it would appear that in these familiar facts we have a correlation between natural environment and political organization so obvious as hardly to be worthy of description, especially when we note that throughout the Russian plain a cold winter is

opposed to a hot summer, and the conditions of human existence thus rendered additionally uniform. Yet a series of historical maps, such as that contained in the Oxford Atlas, will reveal the fact that not merely is the rough coincidence of European Russia with the Eastern Plain of Europe a matter of the last hundred years or so, but that in all earlier time there was persistent re-assertion of quite another tendency in the political grouping. Two groups of states usually divided the country into northern and southern political systems. The fact is that the orographical map does not express the particular physical contrast which has until very lately controlled human movement and settlement in Russia. When the screen of winter snow fades northward off the vast face of the plain, it is followed by rains whose maximum occurs in May and June beside the Black sea, but near the Baltic and White seas is deferred to July and August. In the south the later summer is a period of drought. As a consequence of this climatic *régime*, the north and north-west were forest broken only by marshes, whereas

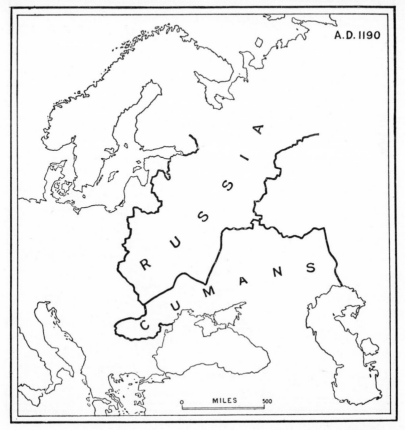

Political divisions of Eastern Europe at the time of the 3rd Crusade. (after The Oxford Historical Atlas).

the south and south-east were a boundless grassy steppe, with trees only along the rivers. The line separating the two regions ran diagonally north-eastward from the northern end of the Carpathians to a point in the Ural range nearer to its southern than to its northern extremity. Moscow lies a little to north of this line, or, in other words, on the forest side of it. Outside Russia the boundary of the great forest ran westward almost exactly through the centre of the European isthmus, which is 800 miles across between the Baltic and the Black seas. Beyond this, in Peninsular Europe, the woods spread on through the plains of Germany in the north, while the steppe lands in the south turned the great Transylvanian bastion of the Carpathians, and extended up the Danube, through what are now the cornfields of Roumania, to the Iron Gates. A detached area of steppes, known locally as Pusstas, now largely cultivated, occupied the plain of Hungary, ingirt by the forested rim of Carpathian and Alpine mountains. In all the west of Russia, save in the far north, the clearing of the forests, the drainage of the marshes, and the tillage of the steppes have recently averaged the character of the landscape, and in large measure obliterated a distinction which was formerly very coercive of humanity.

The earlier Russia and Poland were established wholly in the glades of the forest. Through the steppe on the other hand there came from the unknown recesses of Asia, by the gateway between the Ural mountains and the Caspian sea, in all the centuries from the fifth to the sixteenth, a remarkable succession of Turanian nomadic peoples—Huns, Avars, Bulgarians, Magyars, Khazars, Patzinaks, Cumans, Mongols, Kalmuks. Under Attila the Huns established themselves in the midst of the Pusstas, in the uttermost Danubian outlier of the steppes, and thence dealt blows northward, westward, and southward against the settled peoples of Europe. A large part of modern history might be written as a commentary upon the changes directly or indirectly ensuing from these raids. The Angles and

Political divisions of Eastern Europe at the accession of Charles V. (after The Oxford Historical Atlas).

Saxons, it is quite possible, were then driven to cross the seas to found England in Britain. The Franks, the Goths, and the Roman provincials were compelled, for the first time, to stand shoulder to shoulder on the battlefield of Chalons, making common cause against the Asiatics, who were unconsciously welding together modern France. Venice was founded from the destruction of Aquileia and Padua; and even the Papacy owed a decisive prestige to the successful mediation of Pope Leo with Attila at Milan. Such was the harvest of results produced by a cloud of ruthless and idealess horsemen sweeping over the unimpeded plain—a blow, as it were, from the great Asiatic hammer striking freely through the vacant space. The Huns were followed by the Avars. It was for a marchland against these that Austria was founded, and Vienna fortified, as the result of the campaigns of Charlemagne. The Magyar came next, and by incessant raiding from his steppe base in Hungary increased the significance of the Austrian outpost, so drawing the political focus of Germany eastward to the margin of the realm. The Bulgarian established a ruling caste south of the Danube, and has left his name upon the map, although his language has yielded to that of his Slavonic subjects. Perhaps the longest and most effective occupation of the Russian steppe proper was that of the Khazars, who were contemporaries of the great Saracen movement: the Arab geographers knew the Caspian as the Khazar sea. In the end, however, new hordes arrived from Mongolia, and for two centuries Russia in the northern forest was held tributary to the Mongol Khans of Kipchak, or "the Steppe," and Russian development was thus delayed and biassed at a time when the remainder of Europe was rapidly advancing.

It should be noted that the rivers running from the Forest to the Black and Caspian seas cross the whole breadth of the steppe-land path of the nomads, and that from time to time there were transient movements along their courses at right angles to the movement of the horsemen. Thus the missionaries of Greek Christianity ascended the Dnieper to Kief, just as beforehand the Norse Varangians had descended the same river on their way to Constantinople. Still earlier, the Teutonic Goths appear for a moment upon the Dniester, having crossed Europe from the shores of the Baltic in the same south-eastward direction. But these are passing episodes which do not invalidate the broader generalization. For a thousand years a series of horse-riding peoples emerged from Asia through the broad interval between the Ural mountains and the Caspian sea, rode through the open spaces of southern Russia, and struck home into Hungary in the very heart of the European peninsula, shaping by the necessity of opposing them the history of each of the great peoples around—the Russians, the Germans, the French, the Italians, and the Byzantine Greeks. That they stimulated healthy and powerful reaction, instead of crushing opposition under a widespread despotism, was due to the fact that the mobility of their power was conditioned by the steppes, and necessarily ceased in the surrounding forests and mountains.

A rival mobility of power was that of the Vikings in their boats. Descending from Scandinavia both upon the northern and the southern shores of Europe, they penetrated inland by the river ways. But the scope of their action was limited, for, broadly speaking, their power was effective only in the neighbourhood of the water. Thus the settled peoples of Europe lay gripped between two pressures——that of the Asiatic nomads from the east, and on the other three sides that of the pirates from the sea. From its very nature neither pressure was overwhelming, and both therefore were stimulative. It is noteworthy that the formative influence of the Scandinavians was second only in significance to that of the nomads, for under their attack both England and France made long moves towards unity, while the unity of Italy was broken by them. In earlier times, Rome had mobilized the power of her settled peoples by means of her roads, but the Roman roads had fallen into decay, and were not replaced until the eighteenth century.

It is likely that even the Hunnish invasion was by no means the first of the Asiatic series. The Soythians of the Homeric and Herodotian accounts, drinking the milk of mares, obviously practised the same arts of life, and were probably of the same race as the later inhabitants of the steppe. The Celtic element in the river-names *Don, Donetz, Dneiper, Dneister,* and *Danube* may possibly betoken the passage of peoples of similar habits, though not of identical race, but it is not unlikely that the Celts came merely from the northern forests, like the Goths and Varangians of a later time. The great wedge of population, however, which the anthropolo-

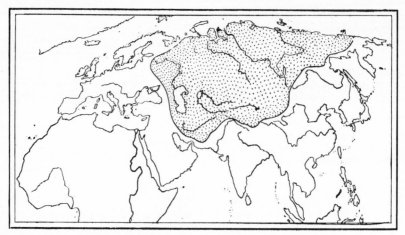

Continental and arctic drainage Equal area projection.

gists characterize as Brachy-Cephalic, driven westward from Brachy-Cephalic Asia through Central Europe into France, is apparently intrusive between the northern, western, and southern Dolico-Cephalic populations, and may very probably have been derived from Asia.[*]

The full meaning of Asiatic influence upon Europe is not, however, discernible until we come to the Mongol invasions of the fifteenth century; but before we analyze the essential facts concerning these, it is desirable to shift our geographical view-point from Europe, so that we may consider the Old World in its entirety. It is obvious that, since the rainfall is derived from the sea, the heart of the greatest land-mass is likely to be relatively dry. We are not, therefore, surprised to find that two-thirds of all the world's population is concentrated in relatively small areas along the margins of the great continent—in Europe, beside the Atlantic ocean; in the Indies and China, beside the Indian and Pacific oceans. A vast belt of almost uninhabited, because practically rainless, land extends as the Sahara completely across Northern Africa into Arabia. Central and Southern Africa were almost as completely severed from Europe and Asia throughout the greater part of history as were the Americas and Australia. In fact, the southern boundary of Europe was and is the Sahara rather than the Mediterranean, for it is the desert which divides the black man from the white. The continuous land-mass of Euro-Asia thus included between the ocean and the

desert measures 21,000,000 square miles, or half of all the land on the globe, if we exclude from reckoning the deserts of Sahara and Arabia. There are many detached deserts scattered through Asia, from Syria and Persia north-eastward to Manchuria, but no such continuous vacancy as to be comparable with the Sahara. On the other hand, Euro-Asia is characterized by a very remarkable distribution of river drainage. Throughout an immense portion of the centre and north, the rivers have been practically useless for purposes of human communication with the outer world. The Volga, the Oxus, and the Jaxartes drain into salt lakes; the Obi, the Yenesei, and the Lena into the frozen ocean of the north. These are six of the greatest rivers in the world. There are many smaller but still considerable streams in the same area, such as the Tarim and the Helmund, which similarly fail to reach the ocean. Thus the core of Euro-Asia, although mottled with desert patches, is on the whole a steppe-land supplying a wide-spread if often scanty pasture, and there are not a few river-fed oases in it, but it is wholly unpenetrated by waterways from the ocean. In other words, we have in this immense area all the conditions for the maintenance of a sparse, but in the aggregate considerable, population of horse-riding and camel-riding nomads. Their realm is limited northward by a broad belt of sub-artic forest and marsh, wherein the climate is too rigorous, except at the eastern and western extremities, for the development of agricultural settlements. In the east the forests extend southward to the Pacific coast in the Amur land and Manchuria. Similarly in the west, in

[*] See 'The Races of Europe,' by Prof. W.Z. Ripley (Kegan Paul, 1900).

prehistoric Europe, forest was the predominant vegetation. Thus framed in to the north-east, north, and north-west, the steppes spread continuously for 4000 miles from the Pusstas of Hungary to the Little Gobi of Manchuria, and, except in their westernmost extremity, they are untraversed by rivers draining to an accessible ocean, for we may neglect the very recent efforts to trade to the mouths of the Obi and Yenisei. In Europe, Western Siberia, and Western Turkestan the steppe lands lie low, in some places below the level of the sea. Further to east, in Mongolia, they extend over plateaux; but the passage from the one level to the other, over the naked, unscarped lower ranges of the arid heart-land, presents little difficulty.

The hordes which ultimately fell upon Europe in the middle of the fourteenth century gathered their first force 3000 miles away on the high steppes of Mongolia. The havoc wrought for a few years in Poland, Silesia, Moravia, Hungary, Croatia, and Servia was, however, but the remotest and the most transient result of the great stirring of the nomads of the East associated with the name of Ghenghiz Khan. While the Golden Horde occupied the steppe of Kipchak, from the Sea of Aral, through the interval between the Ural range and the Caspian, to the foot of the Carpathians, another horde, descending south-westward between the Caspian sea and the Hindu Kush into Persia, Mesopotamia, and even into Syria, founded the domain of the Ilkhan. A third subsequently struck into Northern China, conquering Cathay. India and Mangi, or Southern China, were for a time sheltered by the incomparable barrier of Tibet, to whose efficacy there is, perhaps, nothing similar in the world, unless it be the Sahara desert and the polar ice. But at a later time, in the days of Marco Polo in the case of Mangi, in those of Tamerlane in the case of India, the obstacle was circumvented. Thus it happened that in this typical and well-recorded instance, all the settled margins of the Old World sooner or later felt the expansive force of mobile power originating in the steppe. Russia, Persia, India, and China were either made tributary, or received Mongol dynasties. Even the incipient power of the Turks in Asia Minor was struck down for half a century.

As in the case of Europe, so in other marginal lands of Euro-Asia there are records of earlier invasions. China had more than once to submit to conquest from the north; India

several times to conquest from the north-west. In the case of Persia, however, at least one of the earlier descents has a special significance in the history of Western civilization. Three or four centuries before the Mongols, the Seljuk Turks, emerging from Central Asia, overran by this path an immense area of the land, which we may describe as of the five seas—Caspian, Black, Mediterranean, Red, and Persian. They established themselves at Kerman, at Hamadan, and in Asia Minor, and they overthrew the Saracen dominion of Bagdad and Damascus. It was ostensibly to punish their treatment of the Christian pilgrims at Jerusalem that Christendom undertook the great series of campaigns known collectively as the Crusades. Although these failed in their immediate objects, they so stirred and united Europe that we may count them as the beginning of modern history—another striking instance of European advance stimulated by the necessity of reacting against pressure from the heart of Asia.

The conception of Euro-Asia to which we thus attain is that of a continuous land, ice-girt in the north, water-girt elsewhere, measuring 21 million square miles, or more than three times the area of North America, whose centre and north, measuring some 9 million square miles, or more than twice the area of Europe, have no available water-ways to the ocean, but, on the other hand, except in the subarctic forest, are very generally favourable to the mobility of horsemen and camelmen. To east, south, and west of this heart-land are marginal regions, ranged in a vast crescent, accessible to shipmen. According to physical conformation, these regions are four in number, and it is not a little remarkable that in a general way they respectively coincide with the spheres of the four great religions—Buddhism, Brahminism, Mahometanism, and Christianity. The first two are the monsoon lands, turned the one towards the Pacific, and the other towards the Indian ocean. The fourth is Europe, watered by the Atlantic rains from the west. These three together, measuring less than 7 million square miles, have more than 1000 million people, or two-thirds of the world population. The third, coinciding with the land of the Five Seas, or, as it is more often described, the Nearer East, is in large measure deprived of moisture by the proximity of Africa, and, except in the oases, is therefore thinly peopled. In some degree it partakes of the characteristics both of the marginal belt and of the central area of Euro-Asia. It is mainly devoid of forest, is patched with desert, and is therefore suitable for the operations of the nomad. Dominantly, however, it is marginal, for sea-gulfs and oceanic rivers lay it open to sea-power, and permit of the exercise of such power from it. As a consequence, periodically throughout history, we have here had empires belonging essentially to the marginal series, based on the agricultural populations of the great oases of Babylonia and Egypt, and in free water-communication with the civilized worlds of the Mediterranean and the Indies. But, as we should expect, these empires have been subject to an unparalleled series of revolutions, some due to Scythian, Turkish, and Mongol raids from Central Asia, others to the effort of the Mediterranean peoples to conquer the overland ways from the western to the eastern ocean. Here is the weakest spot in the girdle of early civilizations, for the isthmus of Suez divided seapower into Eastern and Western, and the arid wastes of Persia advancing from Central Asia to the Persian gulf gave constant opportunity for nomad-power to strike home to the ocean edge, dividing India and China, on the one hand, from the Mediterranean world on the other. Whenever the Babylonian, the Syrian, and the Egyptian oases were weakly held, the steppe-peoples could treat the open tablelands of Iran and Asia Minor as forward posts whence to strike through the Punjab into India, through Syria into Egypt, and over the broken bridge of the Bosphorus and Dardanelles into Hungary. Vienna stood in the gateway of Inner Europe, withstanding the nomadic raids, both those which came by the direct road through the Russian steppe, and those which came by the loop way to south of the Black and Caspian seas.

Here we have illustrated the essential difference between the Saracen and the Turkish controls of the Nearer East. The Saracens were a branch of the Semitic race, essentially peoples of the Euphrates and Nile and of the smaller cases of Lower Asia. They created a great empire by availing themselves of the two mobilities permitted by their land—that of the horse and camel on the one hand, that of the ship on the other. At different times their fleets controlled both the Mediterranean as far as Spain, and the Indian ocean to the Malay islands. From their strategically central position between the eastern and western oceans, they attempted the conquest of all the marginal lands of the Old World, imitating Alexander and anticipating Napoleon. They could even threaten the steppe land. Wholly distinct from Arabia as from Europe, India, and China were the Turanian pagans from the closed heart of Asia, the Turks who destroyed the Saracen civilization.

Mobility upon the ocean is the natural rival of horse and camel mobility in the heart of the continent. It was upon navigation of oceanic rivers that was based the Potamic stage of civilization, that of China on the Yangtse, that of India on the Ganges, that of Babylonia on the Euphrates, that of Egypt on the Nile. It was essentially upon the navigation of the Mediterranean that was based what has been described as the Thalassic stage of civilization, that of the Greeks and Romans. The Saracens and the Vikings held sway by navigation of the oceanic coasts.

The all-important result of the discovery of the Cape road to the Indies was to connect the western and eastern coastal navigations of Euro-Asia, even though by a circuitous route, and thus in some measure to neutralize the strategical advantage of the central position of the steppe-nomads by pressing upon them in rear. The revolution commenced by the great mariners of the Columbian generation endowed Christendom with the widest possible mobility of power, short of a winged mobility. The one and continuous ocean enveloping the divided and insular lands is, of course, the geographical condition of ultimate unity in the command of the sea, and of the whole theory of modern naval strategy and policy as expounded by such writers as Captain Mahan and Mr. Spencer Wilkinson. The broad political effect was to reverse the relations of Europe and Asia, for whereas in the Middle Ages Europe was caged between an impassable desert to south, an unknown ocean to west, and icy or forested wastes to north and north-east, and in the east and south-east was constantly threatened by the superior mobility of the horsemen and camelmen, she now emerged upon the world, multiplying more than thirty-fold the sea surface and coastal lands to which she had access, and wrapping her influence round the Euro-Asiatic landpower which had hitherto threatened her very existence. New Europes were created in the vacant lands discovered in the midst of the waters, and what Britain and Scandinavia were to Europe in the earlier time, that have America and Australia, and in some measure even Trans-Saharan Africa, now become to Euro-Asia. Britain, Canada, the United States, South Africa, Australia, and Japan are now a ring of outer and insular bases for sea-power and commerce, inaccessible to the land-power of Euro-Asia.

But the land power still remains, and recent events have again increased its significance. While the maritime peoples of Western Europe have covered the ocean with their fleets, settled the outer continents, and in varying degree made tributary the oceanic margins of Asia, Russia has organized the Cossacks, and, emerging from her northern forests, has policed the steppe by setting her own nomads to meet the Tartar nomads. The Tudor century, which saw the expansion of Western Europe over the sea, also saw Russian power carried from Moscow through Siberia. The eastward swoop of the horsemen across Asia was an event almost as pregnant with political consequences as was the rounding of the Cape, although the two movements long remained apart.

It is probably one of the most striking coincidences of history that the seaward and the landward expansion of Europe should, in a sense, continue the ancient opposition between Roman and Greek. Few great failures have had more far-reaching consequences than the failure of Rome to Latinize the Greek. The Teuton was civilized and Christianized by the Roman, the Slav in the main by the Greek. It is the Romano-Teuton who in later times embarked upon the ocean; it was the Graeco-Slav who rode over the steppes, conquering the Turanian. Thus the modern land-power differs from the sea-power no less in the source of its ideals than in the material conditions of its mobility.*

In the wake of the Cossack, Russia has safely emerged from her former seclusion in the northern forests. Perhaps the change of greatest intrinsic importance which took place in Europe in the last century was the southward migration of the Russian peasants, so that, whereas agricultural settlements formerly ended at the forest boundary, the centre of the population of all European Russia

*This statement was criticized in the discussion which followed the reading of the paper. On reconsidering the paragraph, I still think it substantially correct. Even the Byzantine Greek would have been other than he was had Rome completed the subjugation of the ancient Greek. No doubt the ideals spoken of were Byzantine rather than Hellenic, but they were not Roman, which is the point.

now lies to south of that boundary, in the midst of the wheat-fields which have replaced the more western steppes. Odessa has here risen to importance with the rapidity of an American city.

A generation ago steam and the Suez canal appeared to have increased the mobility of sea-power relatively to land-power. Railways acted chiefly as feeders to ocean-going commerce. But trans-continental railways are now transmuting the conditions of land-power, and nowhere can they have such effect as in the closed heart-land of Euro-Asia, in vast areas of which neither timber nor accessible stone was available for road-making. Railways work the greater wonders in the steppe, because they directly replace horse and camel mobility, the road stage of development having here been omitted.

In the matter of commerce it must not be forgotten that ocean-going traffic, however relatively cheap, usually involves the fourfold handling of goods—at the factory of origin, at the export wharf, at the import wharf, and at the inland warehouse for retail distribution; whereas the continental railway truck may run direct from the exporting factory into the importing warehouse. Thus marginal ocean-fed commerce tends, other things being equal, to form a zone of penetration round the continents, whose inner limit is roughly marked by the line along which the cost of four handlings, the oceanic freight, and the railway freight from the neighbouring coast, is equivalent to the cost of two handlings and the continental railway freight. English and German coals are said to compete on such terms midway through Lombardy.

The Russian railways have a clear run of 6000 miles from Wirballen in the west to Vladivostok in the east. The Russian army in Manchuria is as significant evidence of mobile land-power as the British army in South Africa was of sea-power. True, that the Trans-Siberian railway is still a single and precarious line of communication, but the century will not be old before all Asia is covered with railways. The spaces within the Russian Empire and Mongolia are so vast, and their potentialities in population, wheat, cotton, fuel, and metals so incalculably great, that it is inevitable that a vast economic world, more or less apart, will there develop inaccessible to oceanic commerce.

As we consider this rapid review of the broader currents of history, does not a certain persistence of geographical relationship become evident? Is not the pivot region of the world's politics that vast area of Euro-Asia which is inaccessible to ships, but in antiquity lay open to the horse-riding nomads, and is to-day about to be covered with a network of railways? There have been and are here the conditions of a mobility of military and economic power of a far-reaching and yet limited character. Russia replaces the Mongol Empire. Her pressure on Finland, on Scandinavia, on Poland, on Turkey, on Persia, on India, and on China, replaces the centrifugal raids of the steppemen. In the world at large she occupies the central strategical position held by Germany in Europe. She can strike on all sides and be struck from all sides, save the north. The full development of her modern railway mobility is merely a matter of time. Nor is it likely that any possible social revolution will alter her essential relations to the great geographical limits of her existence. Wisely recognizing the fundamental limits of her power, her rulers have parted with Alaska; for it is as much a law of policy for Russia to own nothing over seas as for Britain to be supreme on the ocean.

Outside the pivot area, in a great inner crescent, are Germany, Austria, Turkey, India, and China, and in an outer crescent, Britain, South Africa, Australia, the United States, Canada, and Japan. In the present condition of the balance of power, the pivot state, Russia, is not equivalent to the peripheral states, and there is room for an equipoise in France. The United States has recently become an eastern power, affecting the European balance not directly, but through Russia, and she will construct the Panama canal to make her Mississippi and Atlantic resources available in the Pacific. From this point of view the real divide between east and west is to be found in the Atlantic ocean.

The oversetting of the balance of power in favour of the pivot state, resulting in its expansion over the marginal lands of Euro-Asia, would permit of the use of vast continental resources for fleet-building, and the empire of the world would then be in sight. This might happen if Germany were to ally herself with Russia. The threat of such an event should, therefore, throw France into alliance with the over-sea powers, and France, Italy, Egypt, India, and Corea would become so many bridge heads where the outside navies would support armies to compel the pivot

allies to deploy land forces and prevent them from concentrating their whole strength on fleets. On a smaller scale that was what Wellington accomplished from his sea-base at Torres Vedras in the Peninsular War. May not this in the end prove to be the strategical function of India in the British Imperial system? Is not this the idea underlying Mr. Amery's conception that the British military front stretches from the Cape through India to Japan?

The development of the vast potentialities of South America might have a decisive influence upon the system. They might strengthen the United States, or, on the other hand, if Germany were to challenge the Monroe doctrine successfully, they might detach Berlin from what I may perhaps describe as a pivot policy. The particular combinations of power brought into balance are not material; my contention is that from a geographical point of view they are likely to rotate round the pivot state, which is always likely to be great, but with limited mobility as compared with the surrounding marginal and insular powers.

I have spoken as a geographer. The actual balance of political power at any given time is, of course, the product, on the one hand, of geographical conditions, both economic and strategic, and, on the other hand, of the relative number, virility, equipment, and organization of the competing peoples. In proportion as these quantities are accurately estimated are we likely to adjust differences without the crude resort to arms. And the geographical quantities in the calculation are more measurable and more nearly constant than the human. Hence we should expect to find our formula apply equally to past history and to present politics. The social movements of all times have played around essentially the same physical features, for I doubt whether the progressive desiccation of Asia and Africa, even if proved, has in historical times vitally altered the human environment. The westward march of empire appears to me to have been a short rotation of marginal power round the south-western and western edge of the pivotal area. The Nearer, Middle, and Far Eastern questions relate to the unstable equilibrium of inner and outer powers in those parts of the marginal crescent where local power is, at present, more or less negligible.

In conclusion, it may be well expressly to point out that the substitution of some new

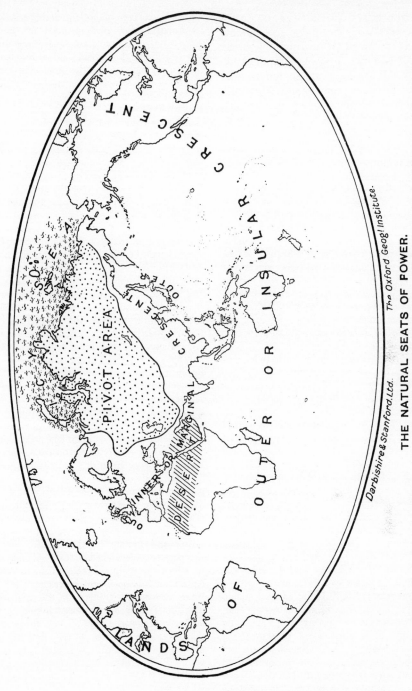

THE NATURAL SEATS OF POWER.

Pivot area—wholly continental.   Outer crescent—wholly oceanic.   Inner crescent—partly continental, partly oceanic.

control of the inland area for that of Russia would not tend to reduce the geographical significance of the pivot position. Were the Chinese, for instance, organized by the Japanese, to overthrow the Russian Empire and conquer its territory, they might constitute the yellow peril to the world's freedom just because they would add an oceanic frontage to the resources of the great continent, an advantage as yet denied to the Russian tenant of the pivot region.

Before the reading of the paper, the President said: We are always very glad when we can induce our friend Mr. Mackinder to address us on any subject, because all he says to us is sure to be interesting and original and valuable. There is no necessity for me to introduce so old a friend of the Society to the meeting, and I will therefore at once ask him to read his paper.

After the reading of the paper, the President said: We hope that Mr. Spencer Wilkinson will offer some criticism on Mr. Mackinder's paper. Of course, it will not be possible to avoid geographical politics to a certain extent.

Mr. Spencer Wilkinson: It would occur to me that the most natural thing and the most sincere thing to say at the beginning is to endeavour to express the great gratitude which, I am sure, every one here feels for one of the most stimulating papers that has been read for a long time. As I was listening to the paper, I looked with regret on some of the space that is unoccupied here, and I much regret that a portion of it was not occupied by the members of the Cabinet, for I gathered that in Mr. Mackinder's paper we have two main doctrines laid down: the first, which is not altogether new—I think it was foreseen some years back in the last century—that since the modern improvements of steam navigation the whole of the world has become one, and has become one political system. I forget the exact expression that Mr. Mackinder used; I think he said that the difference was something like that of a shell falling into an enclosed structure and falling into space. I should wish to express the same thing by saying that, whereas only half a century ago statesmen played on a few squares of a chess-board of which the remainder was vacant, in the present day the world is an enclosed chess-board, and every movement of the statesman must take account of all the squares in it. I myself can only wish that we had ministers who would give more time to studying their policy from the point of view that you cannot move any one piece without considering all the squares on the board. We are very much too apt to look at our policy as though it were cut up into water-tight compartments, each of which had no connection with the rest of the world, whereas it seems to me the great fact of to-day is that any movement which is made in one part of the world affects the whole of the international relations of the world—a fact

which, it seems to me, is lamentably neglected both in British policy and in most of the popular discussions of it, and I am exceedingly grateful to Mr. Mackinder for having laid so much stress on that in his paper. Then the other point—the main point, I take it, which he has brought out is really as to the enormous importance to the world of the modern expansion of Russia. I cannot say that I am thoroughly convinced of some of Mr. Mackinder's historical analogies or precedents, unless, indeed, we are to take his paper as carrying us a very long way ahead. Mr. Mackinder takes us back over four hundred years, and talks of the Columbian epoch. Well, I cannot pretend to be able to go four hundred years forward; if one can go a generation forward, it is quite as much as some of us can manage. Now, these great movements of Central Asian tribes on to Europe and on to the different marginal countries may, I think, be over-estimated in their importance. They have left occasional survivals of the past, but they have not left the world much richer in ideas, and very seldom represented any permanent alterations in the conditions of mankind; and they have been possible because the expanding forces of Central Asia hit upon a very much divided margin. For instance, the movement of the Ottoman Turks, and before that the Turkish movements upon the Byzantine Empire and upon the region that had been the Byzantine Empire, invariably struck upon regions in which government was in decay or obsolescent, and most of the movements which struck upon Central Europe, the movements north of the Black sea, struck upon Europe at a time when government was very little organized, and when the states had very little of solidarity between them. Therefore, I hold they do not afford very much parallel for the future; and I should be disposed to dwell on the counterbalancing phenomenon, which is that you have had in the west of Europe a small island, which, having attained to its own political unity, and having in the conflict for its own independence developed its sea-power, has been able to affect the marginal regions and to acquire the enormous influence which was revealed to us, a little exaggerated, perhaps, on the map which Mr. Mackinder showed—the British Empire—exaggerated because it was a map on Mercator's projection, which exaggerated the British Empire, with the exception of India. My own belief is that an island state like our own can, if it maintains its naval power, hold the balance between the divided forces which work on the continental area, and I believe that has been the historical function of Great Britain since Great Britain was a United Kingdom. Now we find a smaller island state rising on the opposite side of the Euro-Asian continent, and I see no reason at all to suppose that that state should not be able to exercise on the eastern fringe of the Asiatic continent a power as decisive and as influential as that which the British Isles, with a smaller population, have exercised upon Europe.

Sir Thomas Holdrich: When one hears a lecture

such as Mr. Mackinder has just given us, so full of thought and so thoroughly well worked out, with such an amount of food for reflection contained in it, it takes a great deal of moral digestion to assimilate it, and more assurance than I possess either to criticize it, or even to discuss it. But there is just one question I should like to ask Mr. Mackinder, and in co-relating the facts of geographical conditions with the history of the human race, it seems to me a not unimportant one. Mr. Mackinder has told us that in the beginning of things the Mongol races all started from a centre in high Asia, spreading outwards, westwards, southwards, and eastwards, finding, however, Tibet an impossible barrier in their way, and never exactly occupying India. But we must remember that before the Mongolians spread, there were other Central Asian tribes who spread equally from districts which were not so very far removed from the position which the Mongolians themselves first occupied—the Scyths and the Aryans—and that they did find their way into India. That, however, is a matter of detail. What I should like to know from Mr. Mackinder is, what he considers to be the original reason of that extraordinary overflow from the country which we are disposed to consider to be the cradle of the human race, to all the different parts of the world. Was it simply the nomadic instincts of the people, a sort of hereditary compulsion which obliged them to flow outwards; or was it an actual alteration in the physical characteristics of the country in which they dwelt? We know that the physical conditions of the world alter very much from time to time, and it seems to me impossible to reconcile the idea of a great inland country, which must once have been full of a teeming population, and have supported that population, as you may say, with an abundant power of agricultural wealth——that under such conditions a people should have had a desire to spread out and to wander forth into other parts of the world, seeking for they knew not what. I fancy, myself, that one of the great reasons, one of the great compelling reasons, for all these migrations really has been a distinct alteration in the physical condition of the country. That is a point which seems to me to be rather important when we are discussing a subject like the present one, which brings the conditions of geography to bear on the facts of history. There is just one other little matter which was referred to somewhat doubtfully by Mr. Mackinder to which I might refer. He pointed to South America as a possible factor in that outer belt of power which was to bring coercion to bear on the inner power pivoting about the south of Russia. Now, from what I have seen lately, I have not the least doubt that that will be the case. The potentiality of South America as a naval power I look upon as very great. I believe that in the course, say, of the next half-century, in spite of the fact that just now Argentina has sold two ships to Japan, and Chili has sold a couple of ships to us—in spite of that fact, there will be an increase of naval strength in South America, resulting from purely natural

causes, for the defence of her own coast and the protection of her own traffic, which will be only comparable to the extraordinary development which we have seen during the last half-century in Japan. This seems to me certainly to be one of the factors, if we are to look forward, with which, in the future naval politics of the world, we shall have to reckon.

Mr. Amery: I think it is always enormously interesting if we can occasionally get away from the details of everyday politics and try to see things as a whole, and this is what Mr. Mackinder's most stimulating lecture has done for us to-night. He has given us the whole of history and the whole of ordinary politics under one big comprehensive idea. I remember when I did Herodotus at the university, he made the whole of history base itself upon the great struggle between the east and the west. Mr. Mackinder makes the whole of history and politics base themselves on the great economical struggle between the great inside core of the Euro-Asiatic continent and the smaller marginal regions and islands outside. I am not sure myself that these two struggles are not one and the same, because now we have discovered that the world is a sphere, east and west have only become relative terms. I would criticize one thing Mr. Mackinder said when he described Russia as the heir of Greece. It was not the ancient heir of Hellenic Greece, but of Byzantium, and Byzantium was the heir of the old Oriental monarchies with the Greek language and a tinge of Roman civilization thrown over it. I should like to go back, if I might, for a moment to this geographical economic foundation on which Mr. Mackinder built the framework of his lecture. I think I would conceive the thing somewhat differently. There are, to my mind, not two, but three economico-military forces. If we begin with the ancient world, you have the broad geographical division into the "steppes" of the interior, the rich marginal land suitable for agriculture, and the coast, and you have corresponding with these, three economical and three military systems. There is the economical and military system of the agricultural country, the system of the coast and sea-faring people, and the system of the steppes; each had its peculiar weaknesses and its peculiar sources of strength. The strongest in many ways was the marginal and agricultural state. There you got the great solid military Empires, your Egyptian, your Babylonian, your Roman Empire, your large armies and citizen infantry, your great development of wealth. But these contained certain elements of weakness. Their own prosperity or the defects of their form of government would lead ultimately to slothfulness and weakness. Now, outside those you had two other systems. You had the steppe system, whose military strength lay, firstly, in its mobility, and, secondly, in its inaccessibility from the slower-moving agricultural powers. As regards the supposed "hordes" of invaders which came from the interior, I do not myself believe there ever were those very large hordes and large populations in the interior. The fact is this, the steppe populations were small then as now, but from the fact of their mobility the heavier and slower military armies could not successfully attack them. In ordinary times, when the agricultural states were strong, the people of the steppes simply ran away from them, and the others found it too much trouble to conquer them. You remember the difficulty the Roman legions had with the Parthians; and I think we can find a very much more recent example of the difficulty a civilized state finds in conquering a steppe-power. Only a short time ago, the whole of the British army was occupied in trying to coerce some 40,000 or 50,000 farmers who lived on a dry steppe-land. That photograph Mr. Mackinder was showing reminded me exactly of what you could have seen not so many months ago in South Africa—I mean, that picture of waggons crossing the river was, except for the shape of the roof over the waggon, exactly like a picture of a Boer commando crossing a drift. We had the same difficulty in coercing them that all civilized powers have had with steppe people. Now, whenever the civilized powers on the marginal countries have grown weak and have allowed small hired armies to do their work, they have got into difficulties, and that is where, it seems to me, the strength of the steppes has always come in. There is no great economic strength at bottom, but the fact that they could retire into their inaccessible wilderness, and come upon the others in times of their weakness, gave the steppe peoples their power. Then there is the third system, that of the maritime coast peoples: they had even less pure military strength, but they had the greatest mobility—the mobility, I mean, of the Vikings or the Saracens when they ruled the Mediterranean, and the Elizabethan Englishmen when they harried the Spanish Main. Coming to more modern times, there has been a certain further change in the agricultural conditions, and the development, out of the old agricultural states, of the modern industrial state. Then I would also notice that many countries which were steppe became agricultural and industrial. You have that, and you have also the fact that very rarely in history do you get any state rising to great power by one system alone. The Turks began by being the people of the steppes, and came down and swept over Asia Minor; they then formed a regular military power, and conquered the great Turkish Empire; lastly, for a period they became the leading naval power in the Mediterranean. In the same way, you find the Romans, in order to beat the Carthaginians, became a sea-power as well as a land-power; and, in fact, for a power to be great it must have both these elements of strength. The Romans were a great military power with the marginal region as their base and with sea-power behind them. We ourselves have always had as a base the industrial wealth of England. The Russian Empire, which covers the great steppe region, but is no longer in the hands of the old steppe people, is really a portion of the agricultural world, economically, which has conquered the steppe and

is turning it into a great agricultural industrial power, and therefore giving a power which the pure steppe people never possessed. Mr. Mackinder referred to the fact that it is only within the last century that the agricultural races have occupied and populated the southern steppe of Russia proper. They are doing the same thing in Central Asia; in fact, the old steppe people are being squeezed out altogether, and you get, coming closer and closer together, two leading industrial-military powers, the one radiating out from a continental centre, and the other beginning from the sea, but gradually going further into the continent in order to have the big industrial base which it requires, because sea-power alone, if it is not based on great industry, and has a great population behind it, is too weak for offence to really maintain itself in the world struggle. I do not intend to make many more remarks, but there is just one point—a word of Mr. Mackinder's suggested it to me. Horse and camel mobility has largely passed away; and it is now a question of railway-mobility as against sea-mobility. I should like to say that sea-mobility has gained enormously in military strength to what it was in ancient times, especially in the number of men that can be carried. In the old days the ships were mobile enough, but they carried few men, and the raids of the sea-people were comparatively feeble. I am not suggesting anything political at the present time; I am merely stating a fact when I say that the sea is far better for conveying troops than anything, except fifteen or twenty parallel lines of railway. What I was coming to is this: that both the sea and the railway are going in the future—it may be near, or it may be somewhat remote—to be supplemented by the air as a means of locomotion, and when we come to that (as we are talking in broad Columbian epochs, I think I may be allowed to look forward a bit)—when we come to that, a great deal of this geographical distribution must lose its importance, and the successful powers will be those who have the greatest industrial basis. It will not matter whether they are in the centre of a continent or on an island; those people who have the industrial power and the power of invention and of science will be able to defeat all others. I will leave that as a parting suggestion.

Mr. Hogarth: As the hour is rather late and the temperature rather low, I will not take up your time with any very lengthy remarks. We certainly have had a wonderfully suggestive paper, and I think it is neither necessary to advise the reader of the paper nor any one who has listened to it to try and think imperially. I would only ask Mr. Mackinder, when he replies, to make me certain about one point. Does he really mean to imply—I think it is an interesting fact if he meant to establish it—that the state of things which is coming to pass in this inner pivot land will be entirely different to anything that has been seen there before? That is to say, something like a stationary state of things has been brought about, and the country is being developed, till it will even be able to export its own products to the rest of the world; and therefore we are never to see again the state of things that has existed all through ancient history in that a great central region which has continually sent its populations down into the marginal countries, while the marginal countries have sent back to it their influences of civilization, each operating in turn upon the other. The only other observation I would like to make is to reinforce Mr. Amery's objection to Mr. Mackinder's Graeco-Slav. I am afraid I cannot accept that division of civilization between the Greek and the Roman. So far as Russia can be called a civilized country at this moment, it has, I think, not been civilized by the Orthodox Church; in fact, I have yet to learn of any civilizing influence exerted by the Orthodox Church on a great scale. Its civilization is far more due to the social culture which was introduced by Peter the Great, and that was more Roman than Greek. But it is to my first question I should like Mr. Mackinder to give a clear answer. I should like to know what he seriously anticipates is going to be the effect on the world of this new distinction between the marginal and the central pivot lands.

Mr. Mackinder: I have to thank all the speakers for dotting my *i*'s and crossing my *t*'s. I am delighted to find my formula work so well. I do mean exactly what Mr. Hogarth says; I mean that for the first time within recorded history—and this is in reply to Sir Thomas Holdich as well—you have a great stationary population being developed in the steppe lands. This is a revolution in the world that we have to face and reckon with. I doubt very much, and there I agree with Mr. Amery, whether the numbers who came from the heart of Asia were very great. It seems to me quite as he puts it, and that their mobility was of the very essence of the whole thing. A small number of people coming from the steppe lands could do many things, given relative mobility as compared with the agricultural population. With regard to Sir Thomas Holdich's inquiry as to what should send them forth, Sir Clements Markham has pointed out that the nomads did not pour forth once only. I dealt with the fact that for a thousand years the nomadic peoples came through Russia. I fail to see that, when you have this constant succession of descents upon the marginal lands, you are called upon to ask for any special physical change to explain it. All the accounts we have from the time of the earliest Greeks describe the drinkers of mares' milk, and picture for us the nomadic mode of life; therefore I start with the fact that these peoples were nomadic and remained nomadic through two thousand years, and I do not see any evidence that we need either to call in any great physical change or yet to assume any great settled population. As far as I can see, Sven Hedin refuses the idea that you must necessarily ask for a great change of climate in order to explain the existence of the remains in Central Asia. You have powerful winds and much sand, and from time to time the sand is swept over hundreds of

miles across the desert. The sand determines the flow of the rivers and the position of the lakes, and some great strom diverting a river into another course would no doubt suffice to ruin a town abandoned by the water. The mere fact that there were nomads, and that there were rich countries to be plundered, seems to me to be almost sufficient for my theory. In the future, I think, you are bound to have different economic provinces, one based mainly on the sea, and the other on the heart of the continent and on railways. I do not think Mr. Amery has allowed sufficiently for the fact that the very largest armies cannot be moved by means of a navy. The Germans marched nearly a million men into France; they marched, and used the railways for supplies. Russia, by her tariff system and in other ways, is steadily hastening the accomplishment of what I may call the non-oceanic economic system. Her whole policy, by her tariff system, by her break of gauge on her railways, is to separate herself from external oceanic competition.* With regard to the basis of sea-power in industrial wealth, I absolutely agree. What I suggest is that great industrial wealth in Siberia and European Russia and a conquest of some of the marginal regions would give the basis for a fleet necessary to found the world empire. Mr. Amery's way of putting the three groups of powers is slightly different from mine, but it is essentially the same. I ask for an inner land mobility, for a margin densely populated, and for external sea forces. It is true the camel-men and the horse-men are going; but my suggestion is that railways will take their place, and then you will be able to fling power from side to side of this area. My aim is not to predict a great future for this or that country, but to make a geographical formula into which you could fit any political balance.

There was a point with regard to the Graeco-Slav: in the sense in which Mr. Hogarth and Mr. Amery have taken me, I agree with them, but after all I cannot help feeling that Christianity fell on two very different soils—the Greek philosophic and the Roman legal, and that it has in consequence differently influenced the Slav and the Teuton. However, that is, a mere incident, and if I qualify my statement by speaking of the Byzantine, I shall then get near to what Mr. Amery asks, and I think I shall do away with the necessity of introducing the example of Rome which Mr. Hogarth brought forward. As regards the potentialities of the land and of the people, I would point out that in Europe there are now more than 40,000,000 people in the steppe land of Russia, and it is by no means yet densely occupied, and that the Russian population is probably increasing faster than any other great civilized or half-civilized population in the world. With a decreasing French population, and a British not increasing as fast as it was, and the native-born

*The Russian customs ring is, of course, so placed as to add to the pivotal area for economic purposes considerable sections of the marginal lands, although not of the oceanic coasts.—H.J.M.

populations of the United States and Australia coming nearly to a standstill, you have to face the fact that in a hundred years 40,000,000 people have occupied but a mere corner of the steppe. I think you are on the way to a population which will be numbered by the hundred million; and this is a tendency which you must take into account in assigning values to the variable quantities in the equation of power for which I was seeking a geographical formula. The point with regard to Korea and the Persian gulf which was put by Mr. Spencer Wilkinson exactly illustrates my correlation of the Far Eastern, Middle Eastern, and Near Eastern questions. I represent these as being the present temporary form of the collision between the external and internal forces acting through the intermediate zone, which is itself the seat of independent forces. I quite agree that the function of Britain and of Japan is to act upon the marginal region, maintaining the balance of power there as against the expansive internal forces. I believe that the future of the world depends on the maintenance of this balance of power. It appears to me that our formula makes it clear that we must see to it that we are not driven out of the marginal region. We must maintain our position there, and then, whatever happens, we are fairly secure. The increase of population in the inner regions and the stoppage of increase in the outer regions may be rather serious; but perhaps South America will come in to help us.

The President: I confess I have been entranced by Mr. Mackinder's paper, and I could see by the close attention with which it was listened to by the audience that you all shared my feeling in that respect. Mr. Mackinder has dealt with the old, old story from the very dawn of history, the struggle between Ormerzd and Ahriman, and he has shown us how that struggle has continued on from the very dawn of history to the present day. He has explained all this to us with a brilliancy of description and of illustration, with a close grasp of the subject, and with a clearness of argument which we have seldom had equalled in this room. I am sure you will all with me give a unanimous vote of thanks to Mr. Mackinder for his most interesting paper this evening.

THE HEARTLAND DEBATE

Mackinder's hypothesis immediately became one of the most intensively debated geographical ideas of all time. He himself joined in the discussion, modifying the concept in some minor areas, but arguing, as late as 1943, that it "is more valid and useful today than it was either twenty or forty years ago."[11] Upon and beneath the Heartland, Mackinder asserted, lies a store of rich soil for cultivation and of ores and fuels for extraction, "the equal—or thereabouts—of all that lies upon and beneath the United States and the Canadian Dominion."[12]

Among those geographers who disagreed was N.J. Spykman, whose criticism was directed at two weak points in the Heartland concept, both of which are reflected by the quotations in the previous paragraph. In the first place, Spykman felt, Mackinder had overemphasized the potentialities of the Heartland. In many respects, the real power potential of Eurasia lay in what Mackinder had called the "Inner or Marginal Crescent." This region Spykman called the "Rimland," and he countered with his own theory:

Who controls the Rimland rules Eurasia;
Who rules Eurasia controls the destinies of the world.[13]

Although this answer came some decades after Mackinder had stated his final hypothesis and thus had the benefit of a longer period of history, Spykman's basic objections were as true in 1904 and 1919 as they were in 1944. Furthermore, Spykman pointed out relevantly that history involving the Heartland never really was a simple landpower-seapower opposition; some of the states in the Rimland were at one time or another allied with Russia; at other times Russia and Great Britain had been allied in opposition to a Rimland power.

Mahan, Mackinder, and Spykman all discussed the Heartland concept in terms of land and sea power. But air power has gained to such an extent in the world strategic picture that their theories may be completely invalid today. Mackinder in 1943 was not convinced that this could happen:

Some persons today seem to dream of global air power which will "liquidate" both fleets and armies. I am impressed, however, by the broad implications of a recent utterance of a practical airman: "Air power depends absolutely on the efficiency of its ground organization." . . . It can only be said that no adequate proof has yet been presented that air fighting will not follow the long history of all kinds of warfare by presenting alternations of offensive and defensive tactical superiority, meanwhile effecting few permanent changes in strategical conditions.[14]

[11]H.J. Mackinder, "The Round World and the Winning of the Peace," *Foreign Affairs*, 21 (July, 1943), 595–605.
[12]Ibid., p. 603.
[13]N.J. Spykman, *The Geography of the Peace*, New York, Harcourt, Brace and Company, 1944, p. 43.
[14]H.J. Mackinder, op. cit., 1943, p. 600.

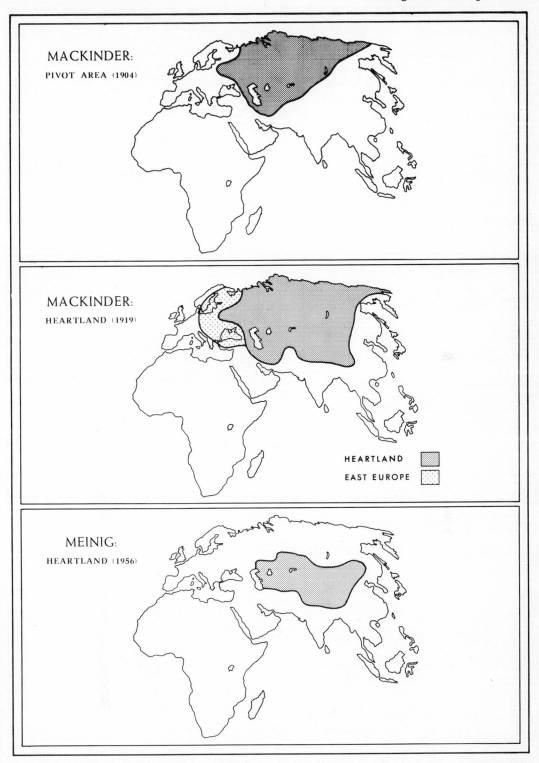

MACKINDER:
PIVOT AREA (1904)

MACKINDER:
HEARTLAND (1919)

HEARTLAND
EAST EUROPE

MEINIG:
HEARTLAND (1956)

One strategist who was indeed convinced was A.P. de Seversky, who in 1950 published the view that the land and sea forces of the world have been subordinated to the greater power of the air.[15] De Seversky advocated the development of massive air superiority as the

[15]A.P. de Seversky, *Air Power: Key to Survival*, New York, Simon and Schuster, 1950.

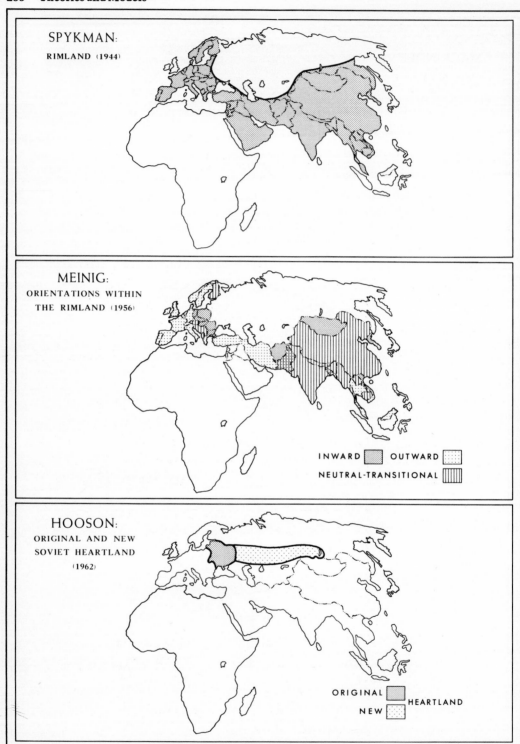

prime goal for American policy makers. Small wars (such as that in Viet Nam) are a useless sapping of United States energies (while costing the adversaries almost nothing); overseas bases are costly luxuries that should be abandoned. United States superiority should be so complete that it would be possible to contain any enemy by stating exactly the line across which he may not step; any such aggression will result in the total annihilation of the enemy by the massive retaliatory forces of superiority that air power has brought the United States. De Seversky looks at the world map in a different way—not conventionally as did Mackinder and Spykman, but on the azimuthal equidistant projection centered on the North Pole, showing quickly the areas of air dominance of the United States and the U.S.S.R.

De Seversky's map leads us to another major criticism of Mackinder's Heartland concept, and to a most comprehensive statement of the assets and shortcomings of the idea. In 1955, A.R. Hall pointed out that Mackinder had overlooked, in his world scheme, the existence of another heartland in Anglo-America which was and remains capable of occupying as important a place in planetary affairs as the one in Eurasia.[16] Peculiarly Mackinder mentions this heartland in his 1943 paper quoted above, but he fails to follow up the apparently obvious consequences. De Seversky emphasizes this weakness, and Hall views it as one of the major faults in the thesis.

Another weakness in the Heartland concept relates to its date of publication, 1904. Although time was to substantiate Mackinder's assumptions regarding the Heartland to a degree even he himself could probably not have imagined, it must not be forgotten that the original statement of the thesis was based upon data available prior to 1904. If, indeed, Mackinder's hypothesis constituted a "geographical formula into which you could fit any political balance," as Mackinder himself asserted, and if the Pivot Area gave so much power to the possessor, why was Russia in 1904 not more of a world power than it was?

Perhaps the most frequently leveled charge against the Heartland concept is that it constitutes an oversimplification of history and a dangerous determinist prediction.[17] Mackinder's greatest fault, revealed especially in his 1943 statement, seems to have been his inability to recognize the role of changing technology in the present-day political world. In 1956, D.W. Meinig published an article that sought to tighten the definitions involved in

Mackinder's original thesis and in subsequent discussions of it.[18]

Meinig stressed that Mackinder as well as his most important critic (Spykman) had focused their attention upon the particular geopolitical context of their time. This, he argued, resulted in an inflexibility in their concepts, so that their relevance would become increasingly historical and less and less applicable to the dynamic changes of the present-day world. If such terms as Heartland and Rimland are to have maximum utility, "applicable beyond any momentary context of strategic patterns, those definitions must become specific in concept yet felxible in historical-spatial use. . . . Our definitions of heartland and rimland must . . . be rooted in cultural, or, I should like to term them, functional criteria."[19] Thus Meinig retraces the criteria on the basis of which Mackinder established his Heartland, pointing out that hydrographic considerations were paramount: he then defines a new heartland, calling it more stable, yet functional. The qualities of this heartland include broadly similar physical conditions and basically similar cultures, an indisputable interior location (i.e., nodal position), and the nexus of all the historic land routes interconnecting the several rimland areas of China, India, the Levant, and Europe.

More significant and useful, perhaps, is Meinig's reevaluation of the Rimland. He points out that both Mackinder and Spykman, though they gave different names to this region, viewed this area as the natural realm mainly of the sea powers of the world. But what of the states forming part of the Rimland? Their own orientation is of paramount importance and changes with time. Some rimland states have been closely tied to the Heartland power in terms of ideology and trade during one period of recent or distant world history; at other times the orientation may have been outward and maritime. Within the past two decades Yugoslavia's orientation as a rimland state has changed very much from "inner" (toward the Heartland power) to "outer." On a functional basis, thus Meinig suggests that a *continental* rimland and a *maritime* rimland should be recognized. In this scheme, certain states might perhaps be considered to be transitional or neutral. There are signs that Pakistan, for example, is moving

[16]A.R. Hall, "Mackinder and the Course of Events," *Ann. A.A.G.*, 45, 2 (June, 1955), 109–126.

[17]See, for example, W.G. East, "How Strong is the Heartland?" *Foreign Affairs*, 29 (1950), 80 ff., D.R. Mills, "The U.S.S.R.: A Re-Appraisal of Mackinder's Heartland Concept," *Scot. Geog. Mag.*, 72 (December, 1956), 144–152; and W.G. East, "The Soviet Union and the 'Heartland,'" in W.G. East and A.E. Moodie (eds.), *The Changing World*, New York, World Book Co., 1957, 432–449.

[18]D.W. Meinig, "Heartland and Rimland in Eurasian History," *Western Political Quart.*, 9 (1956), 553–569.
[19]Ibid., 555, 556.

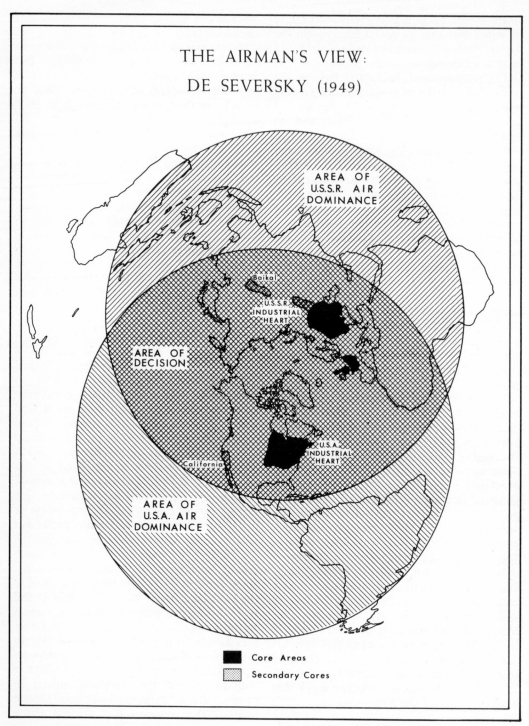

THE AIRMAN'S VIEW:
DE SEVERSKY (1949)

AREA OF
U.S.S.R. AIR
DOMINANCE

Baikal

U.S.S.R.
INDUSTRIAL
HEART

AREA OF
DECISION

U.S.A.
INDUSTRIAL
HEART

California

AREA OF
U.S.A. AIR
DOMINANCE

■ Core Areas
▦ Secondary Cores

from an "outer" orientation toward an "inner" one: like Yugoslavia, it may go through a neutral phase.

A very recent contribution to our thinking regarding the Heartland is that of D.J.M. Hooson.[20] In attempting to define the core of

[20]D.J.M. Hooson, A New Soviet Heartland?, Princeton, Van Nostrand, 1964.

the Soviet Union, and to identify the real heart of that state, Hooson examines a number of regions which form part of the whole Heartland identified by Mackinder. He uses a set of most relevant criteria: the Soviet Union, as today's Heartland power, is sustained to a greater degree by certain parts of the Heartland than by others. In Mackinder's day the focus

Top: Ideological unity in the Heartland: Red Square, Moscow. Seemingly endless lines of visitors from all parts of the Soviet Union (and indeed from all parts of the world) wait countless hours outside the walls of the Kremlin to be permitted to walk past the final resting place of V. I. Lenin. Only a small number of the waiting thousands are shown here, many of whom have made the journey for this specific purpose. As the architect of the modern Soviet State, the person of Lenin continues to pervade Soviet daily life to an astonishing degree. Bottom: Stalin, on the other hand, who at one time shared the Lenin Mausoleum, now has a grave outside the Kremlin walls (foreground). Unlike the graves of other prominent Soviet leaders, Stalin's grave is currently unadorned (Harm J. de Blij).

was well to the west—where is it today? What is the scale of contribution to the national economy as a whole of certain parts of the Heartland? What is the rate of population growth, and the rate of urbanization and urban development? Where are the bulk of the *accessible* resources? In which areas is there that critical economic specialization involving both agriculture and industry? Is there historical association and cohesiveness? What are the ethnic conditions? What emerges from Hooson's examination is a recognition of the established "European" core around Moscow and to the Black Sea—the center of Russian and Soviet power for many decades—and a significant eastern zone, the Volga-Baikal Region. It is this eastern zone which Hooson views as critical: ". . . what happens to and in this zone, between the Volga and Lake Baykal, might well have a decisive effect on the fortunes of the Soviet Union as a world power . . ."[21]

If, indeed, this region becomes the focus of the Soviet state—it is presently outstripping the established Moscow core in terms of rate of development—the point of gravity of the Heartland will be nearer to that suggested by Meinig. Just as Meinig has pointed out that the term Rimland constitutes an oversimplification, so Hooson indicates that the Heartland really consists of a long-established core, an expanding and vital eastern triangle, and a marginal zone whose contribution to the Heartland power's strength is yet relatively insignificant. In any view of the role of the Heartland in world politics, this must be understood.

A CONTINUING THEME

Have speculative discussions of this kind ceased, and have modern times eliminated this lineage in political geography altogether? Far from it. Political geographers are still tempted, in the tradition of Fairgrieve's *Geography and World Power* and Newbigin's *New Regional Geography of the World*, to debate the course of the world, the essential underlying forces guiding that course, and their views of a better, more logical political world.

A recent contribution that proves the point is S.B. Cohen's *Geography and Politics in a World Divided*, a book of extraordinary insight and interest.[22] In an absorbing chapter

entitled "Geostrategic and Geopolitical Regions: Alignments for Our Age," Cohen engages in some geopolitics ("At present, the keys to our Middle Eastern position are Turkey, Iran, and Israel. . . ."),[23] and in a chapter on "Maritime Europe: The Emergence of a New Type of Superstate," he argues that "European-North African geopolitical unity must now be achieved by subtle economic and political persuasion—not naked force; by appeal to the self-interest of each side—not one-way economic exploitation."[24] His map of the world's geostrategic regions and their geopolitical subdivisions still suggests the traditional view of maritime-continental geopolitics, but with Southeast and Southwest Asia as shatter belts. He envisages a Europe bound, across the Mediterranean, to western North Africa as one of the world's major power cores. And he still recognizes a heartland in central Eurasia. First published some 10 years ago, the volume states some truths that have been confirmed; other points would look different in the perspective of the 1970's. Happily, there are still political geographers willing on occasion to take a holistic view.

REFERENCES

Adams, D.K., "A Note: Geopolitics and Political Geography in the United States between the Wars," *Australian J. Politics and History*, 6, 1 (May, 1960), 77–82.

Andrews, John, "Antarctic Geopolitics," *Australian Outlook*, 11, 3 (September, 1951), 3–9.

Armstrong, Hamilton Fish, "The World is Round," *Foreign Affairs*, 31, 2 (January, 1953), 175–199.

Augelli, John P., "The Rimland-Mainland Concept of Culture Areas in Middle America," *Ann. A.A.G.*, 52, 2 (June, 1962), 119–129.

Boggs, S. Whittemore, "Geographic and Other Scientific Techniques for Political Science," *Amer. Political Sci. Rev.*, 42, 2 (April, 1948), 223–238.

Bowman, Isaiah, "The Geographical Situation of the United States in Relation to World Policies," *Geog. J.*, 112, 4–6 (1948), 129–145.

———, "Geography Versus Geopolitics," *Geog. Rev.*, 32, 4 (October, 1942), 646–658.

———, *The New World; Problems in Political Geography*. Yonkers-on-Hudson, N.Y., World Book Company, 1921.

Bywater, H.C., *Navies and Nations*. Boston, Houghton Mifflin, 1927.

Chaudhuri, Manoranjan, "Evolution of Ideas in Political Geography," *Calcutta Geog. Rev.*, 9, 1–4 (1947) (pub. 1949), 23–31.

[21]Ibid., p. 18.

[22]S.B. Cohen, *Geography and Politics in a World Divided*, Random House, New York, 1963.

[23]Ibid., p. 60.

[24]Ibid., p. 141.

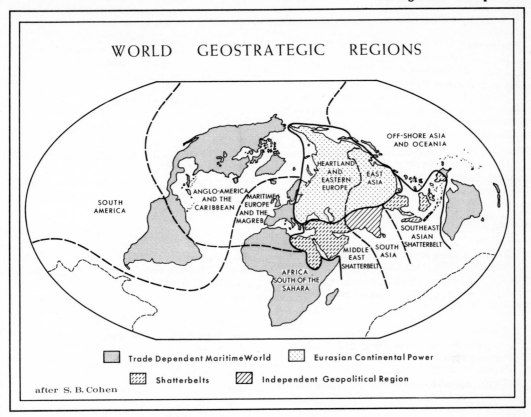

WORLD   GEOSTRATEGIC   REGIONS

OFF-SHORE ASIA
AND OCEANIA

HEARTLAND
AND
EASTERN
EUROPE

EAST
ASIA

ANGLO-AMERICA
AND THE
CARIBBEAN

MARITIME
EUROPE
AND THE
MAGREB

SOUTH
AMERICA

SOUTHEAST
ASIAN
SHATTERBELT

MIDDLE
EAST
SHATTERBELT

SOUTH
ASIA

AFRICA
SOUTH OF THE
SAHARA

▨ Trade Dependent Maritime World   ▦ Eurasian Continental Power

▨ Shatterbelts   ▨ Independent Geopolitical Region

after S. B. Cohen

——, "Geo-political Aspects of World Population," *Calcutta Geog. Rev.*, 11, 3–4 (September-December, 1949), 48–54.

Chubb, Basil, "Geopolitics," *Irish Geographer*, 5, 1 (1954), 15–25.

De Seversky, A., *Air Power: Key to Survival.* New York, Simon and Schuster, 1950.

Dikshit, R.D., "Toward a Generic Approach in Political Geography," *Tijdschrift Economische Sociale Geografie*, LXI, 4 (July/August, 1970), 242–245.

Dorpalen, A., *The World of General Hanshofer.* New York, Farrar & Rinehart, Inc., 1942.

East, W. Gordon, "How Strong is the Heartland?" *Foreign Affairs*, 29, 1 (October, 1950), 78–93.

——, "The Mediterranean: Pivot of Peace and War," *Foreign Affairs*, 31, 4 (July, 1953), 619–633.

Fairgrieve, James, *Geography and World Power*, 8th ed. New York, E.P. Dutton & Co., Inc., 1941.

Falls, Cyril, "Geography and War Strategy," *Geog. J.*, 112, 1–3 (January-March, 1948), 4–18.

Fisher, C.A., "The Expansion of Japan: A Study in Oriental Geopolitics," *Geog. J.*, 115, 1–3 (January-March, 1950), 1–19; and No. 4–6 (April-June, 1950), 179–193.

Goblet, Y.M., *Political Geography and the World Map.* New York, F.A. Praeger, 1955.

Gottmann, Jean, "Geography and International Relations," *World Politics*, 3, 2 (January, 1951), 153–173.

——, "The Political Partitioning of Our World: An Attempt at Analysis," *World Politics*, 4, 4 (July, 1952), 512–519.

Gyoygy, A., *Geopolitics: The New German Science.* Berkeley, Calif., University of California Press, 1944.

Hall, A.R., "Mackinder and the Course of Events," *Ann. A.A.G.*, 45, 2 (June, 1955), 109–126.

Hartshorne, Richard, "Political Geography in the Modern World," *J. Conflict Resolution*, 4, 1 (March, 1960), 52–66.

Hennig, Richard, *Geopolitik.* Leipzig, Teubner, 1931.

Hooson, D.J.M., "The Middle Volga—An Emerging Focal Region in the Soviet Union," *Geog. J.*, 126, Pt. 2 (June, 1960), 180–190.

——, "A New Soviet Heartland?" *Geog. J.*, 128, Pt. 1 (March, 1962), 19–29.

Jackson, W.A. Douglas, "Mackinder and the Communist Orbit," *Canadian Geographer*, 6, 1 (Spring, 1962), 12–21.

Jones, Stephen B., *The Arctic: Problems and Possibilities.* New Haven, Conn., Yale Institute of International Studies, Memorandum No. 29, 1948.

——, "Global Strategic Views," *Geog. Rev.*, 45, 4 (October, 1955), 492–508.

——, "Views of the Political World," *Geog. Rev.*, 45, 3 (July, 1955), 309–326.

——, and Marion Fisher Murphy. *Geography and*

World Affairs, 2nd ed. New York, Rand McNally, 1962.

Kantorowicz, H.U., *The Spirit of British Policy and the Myth of the Encirclement of Germany.* New York, Oxford University Press, 1932.

Karan, Pradyumna P., "India's Role in Geopolitics," *India Quart.,* 9, 2 (April-June, 1953), 160–169.

Kish, George, "Political Geography into Geopolitics: Recent Trends in Germany," *Geog. Rev.,* 32, 4 (October, 1942), 632–645.

Krishan, Radha, "Geopolitics of Petroleum," *Indian Geographer,* 6, 1 (August, 1961), 90–110.

Kristof, Ladis D., "The Origins and Evolution of Geopolitics," *J. Conflict Resolution,* 4, 1 (March, 1960), 15–51.

Kruszewski, C., "The Pivot of History," *Foreign Affairs,* 32, 3 (April, 1954), 388–401.

Mackinder, Halford J., *Democratic Ideals and Reality; A Study in the Politics of Reconstruction.* New York, H. Holt and Co., 1919.

———, "The Physical Basis of Political Geography," *Scot. Geog. Mag.,* 6, 2 (February, 1890), 78–84.

Martin, Geoffrey J., "Political Geography and Geopolitics," *J. Geog.,* 58, 9 (December, 1959), 441–444.

Meinig, Donald W., "Heartland and Rimland in Eurasian History," *Western Political Quart.,* 9, 3 (September, 1956), 553–569.

Melamid, Alexander, "The Political Geography of the Gulf of Aqaba," *Ann. A.A.G.,* 47, 3 (September, 1957), 231–240.

Mills, D.R., "The U.S.S.R.: A Re-Appraisal of Mackinder's Heartland Concept," *Scot. Geog. Mag.,* 72, 3 (December, 1956), 144–152.

Moll, Kenneth L., "A.T. Mahan, American Historian," *Military Affairs,* 27 (1963), 131–140.

Moodie, A.E., *Geography Behind Politics.* London, New York, Hutchinson's University Library, 1949.

Panda, B.P., "Geopolitical Problems of Middle East," *J. Geog.* (University of Jabalpur), 1, 1 (November, 1959), 27–36.

Pearcy, G. Etzel, and others, *World Political Geography,* 2nd ed. New York, Crowell, 1957.

Polisk, A.N., "Geopolitics of the Middle East," *Middle Eastern Affairs,* 4, 8–9 (August-September, 1953), 271–277.

Pounds, N.J.G., *Political Geography,* 2nd ed., New York, McGraw-Hill, 1972.

———, "The Political Geography of the Straits of Gibralter," *J. Geog.,* 51, 4 (April, 1952), 165–170.

Prescott, J.R.V., *Political Geography,* New York, St. Martin's Press, 1972.

Price, A. Grenfell, *The Geopolitical Transformation of the Pacific and Its Present Significance,* reprint from Royal Geographical Society, South Australian Branch, Session 1950–51, vol. 52, 1951.

Rose, A.J., "Strategic Geography and the Northern Approaches," *Australian Outlook,* 13, 4 (December, 1959), 304–314.

Roucek, Joseph S., "The Geopolitics of Congo," *United Asia,* 14, 1 (January, 1962), 81–85.

———, "The Geopolitics of Greenland," *J. Geog.,* 50, 6 (September, 1951), 239–246.

———, "The Geopolitics of Pakistan," *Social Studies,* 44, 7 (November, 1953), 254–258.

———, "The Geopolitics of Spain," *Social Studies,* 46, 3 (March, 1955), 89–93.

———, "Geopolitics of Thailand," *Social Studies,* 45, 2 (February, 1954), 57–63.

———, "The Geopolitics of the Adriatic," *Amer. J. Econ. Sociol.,* 11, 2 (January, 1952), 171–178.

———, "The Geopolitics of the Aleutians," *J. Geog.,* 50, 1 (January, 1951), 24–29.

———, "The Geopolitics of the Baltic States," *Amer. J. Econ. Sociol.,* 8, 2 (January, 1949), 171–175.

———, "The Geopolitics of the Mediterranean," *Amer. J. Econ. Sociol.,* 12, 4 (July, 1953), 346–354; 13, 1 (October, 1953), 71–86.

———, "Geopolitics of the U.S.S.R.," *Amer. J. Econ. Sociol.,* 10, 1 (October, 1950), 17–26; and No. 2 (January, 1951), 153–159.

———, "The Geopolitics of the United States," *Amer. J. Econ. Sociol.,* 14, 2 (January, 1955), 185–192; No. 3 (April, 1955), 287–303.

———, "Geopolitics of Yugoslavia," *Social Studies,* 47, 1 (January, 1956), 26–29.

———, "Nigerian Geo-Politics," *United Asia,* 14, 3 (March, 1962), 182–185.

Semmell, Bernard, "Sir Halford Mackinder: Theorist of Imperialism," *Canadian J. Econ. & Political Sci.,* 24, 4 (November, 1958), 554–561.

Sombart, Werner (ed.), *Volk und Raum.* Hamburg, Hanseatische Verlagsanstalt, 1928.

Sprout, Harold, "Geopolitical Hypotheses in Technological Perspective," *World Politics,* 15, 2 (January, 1963), 187–212.

———, "Political Geography as a Political Science Field," *Amer. Political Sci. Rev.,* 25, 2 (May, 1931), 439–442.

Spykman, N.J., *America's Strategy in World Politics.* New York, Harcourt, Brace & Co., Inc., 1942.

———, *The Geography of the Peace.* New York, Harcourt, Brace & Co., Inc., 1944.

Strausz-Hupe, R., *Geopolitics.* New York, Putnam, 1942.

Taylor, Griffith, "Geopolitics and Geopacifics," in *Geography in the Twentieth Century,* Griffith Taylor (ed.). New York, Philosophical Library, 1951, 587–608.

Troll, C., "Geographical Science in Germany during the Period 1933–1945," *Ann. A.A.G.,* 39, 2 (June, 1949), 99–137.

Van Valkenburg, Samuel, *Elements of Political Geography.* New York, Prentice-Hall, Inc., 1939.

Weigert, H., *Generals and Geographers.* New York, Oxford University Press, 1942.

———, and others, *Principles of Political Geography.* New York, Appleton-Century-Crofts, 1957.

———, and Vilhjalmur Stefansson (eds.), *Compass of the World: A Symposium on Political Geography.* New York, Macmillan, 1945.

————, and Richard E. Harrison (eds.), *New Compass of the World: A Symposium on Political Geography.* New York, Macmillan, 1949.

Whittlesey, Derwent, *The Earth and the State.* Madison, Wisc., publ. for the United States Armed Forces Institute by H. Holt, 1944.

————, *German Strategy of World Conquest.* New York, Farrar & Rinehart, Inc., 1942.

Wiens, Herold J., *Pacific Island Bastions of the United States.* Princeton, N.J., Van Nostrand, 1962.

Wright, J.K., "Training for Research in Political Geography," *Ann. A.A.G., 34,* 4 (December, 1944), 190–201).

CHAPTER
14
DEFINITIONS AND MODELS

Practically every political geographer has tried, in one or more of his or her publications, to find a satisfactory definition of the field. This, of course, is in part what Hartshorne was doing when he wrote his paper on the functional approach in political geography. It is useful to have a look at what other prominent political geographers have written in this context. Some of the definitions we run across are so complex and involved they seem almost meaningless, whereas others are so broad and general that they seem to encompass almost everything even remotely related to politics. Professor Pounds focuses his definition on the nation state: "Political geography is concerned with politically organized areas, their resources and extent, and the reasons for the particular geographical forms which they assume . . . in particular, it is concerned with that most significant of all such areas, the State."[1]

Compare this definition to that of L.M. Alexander, who simply says that "political geography is the study of political regions as features of the earth's surface."[2] But what kind of study? Do we simply try to determine how large they are, how they are related to each other by trade and alliance, or is there a specific approach that belongs to political geography? Some political geographers feel that there is such an approach, or at least, a specific area of concern. To the British geographer A.E. Moodie, political geography is fundamentally the analysis of the relationships between community and environment.[3] To S.B. Cohen, it is the spatial approach to international affairs.[4] To W.A. Douglas Jackson, it is "the study of political phenomena in their areal context, whether that involves an analysis of boundaries, the geographical patterns resulting from the application of governmental authority, or the political viability of new State units."[5]

APPROACHES

Reading the definitions just quoted, it becomes clear that political geographers generally agree on *what* they should study, but the question now arises *how* they should carry out those studies. And this is a question that has kept political geographers debating for many decades; indeed, it is the very question that led Hartshorne to express his views in the paper to be presented. "Much of the methodology of political geography is . . . of an empirical nature," writes Moodie;[6] it "can never become an exact science and it would be a mistake to suppose that its problems are as susceptible to solution as those of the 'pure' sciences."[7] But does this necessarily apply to *all* problems in political geography? J.V. Minghi, among others, has suggested that the answer to certain research problems in political geography—for example, the study of exclaves—may well lie in quantitative analysis, in this case of the processes of interaction between the exclave, its contiguous state, and the state of which it is politically a part.[8] Of course, there are many problems in political geography that are not capable of solution through such detailed work. But political geography, no less than other areas of geography, can and does lend itself to quantitative approaches.

There are other ways of coming to grips with the problem of delimitation. One of these is to define by example rather than by prescription. If a search for meaning and relevance leads to

[1] N.J.G. Pounds, *Political Geography*, New York, McGraw-Hill, 1963, p. 1.

[2] L.M. Alexander, *World Political Patterns*, Chicago, Rand McNally, 1963, p. 1.

[3] A.E. Moodie, *Geography Behind Politics*, London, Hutchinson, 1957, pp. 7–18.

[4] S.B. Cohen, *Geography and Politics in a World Divided*, New York, Random House, 1963, pp. 1–23.

[5] W.A. Douglas Jackson, "The Nature of the Political Geographical Problem," in *Politics and Geographic Relationships*, Englewood Cliffs, Prentice-Hall, 1964, p. 1.

[6] A.E. Moodie, op. cit., p. 165.

[7] Ibid., p. 14.

[8] J.V. Minghi, "Point Roberts, Washington: The Problem of an American Exclave," *Yearbook of the Association of Pacific Coast Geographers*, Vol. 24, 1962.

results that excite other political geographers and causes them to pursue the issue farther, then a contribution to political geography has obviously been made—whether the search took place in accordance with a "definition" of the field or not. One well-known political geographer who led by example is J. Gottmann. Like many of his colleagues, Gottmann long had an interest in the processes whereby space is organized politically. In 1951, he published an article dealing with the organization of differentiated space, pointing out that the *spirit* of each nation is commonly very different from the spirit of other nations: ". . . boundaries exist because each country *feels* it is different from the other . . . this spirit is always made of many components: historical background . . . local environment . . . in the Old World stubborn regionalisms have evolved toward nationalism in modern times, partitioning lands more and more."[9] What, then, distinguishes the political region? It requires, Gottmann asserts, a strong belief based upon some religious creed, a certain social viewpoint, or a "pattern of political memories"; often, he argues, it is in fact a combination of all three. Thus regionalism in this sense has some *iconography* as its basis (*icon*: an image or representation, portrait; the holy picture or emblem regarded as sacred in the Greek and Russian Churches). Each political region cherishes some symbol, certain values. In no two of the many political compartments of the earth are these symbols and values exactly the same, and everywhere they are complex in nature, made of many interwoven patterns. It is the political geographer's task to identify as many of the strands and patterns as possible.

What, Gottmann asked himself in a subsequent paper, brought about this recognizable partitioning?[10] One key, obviously, is accessibility. Areas to which man has no access do not have political standing or problems. But certain areas are more accessible that others. The degree of accessibility can be determined by an analysis of traffic and communication links, trade and transportation. This is *circula-*

tion—encompassing "all the variety, the complexity, and the fluidity of the exchanges developing throughout the world."[11]

This idea—that circulation in a wide variety of forms has much relevance in political-spatial processes—was no minor development. In fact, while Gottmann was writing his statement, another political geographer, S.B. Jones, also was contemplating this phenomenon. Jones gave the process a different name (he referred to it as *movement*) and he placed it in a wider context. In 1954, he published an important paper entitled "A Unified Field Theory of Political Geography," in which he viewed movement as a process involving the flow of ideas as well as goods and other tangibles, and in which movement becomes linked with several other processes.[12] The unified field theory holds that there are, in the process of spatial-political organization, at least five clearly recognizable "hubs" of activity, each related to and connected to the other. The first of these is the generation of an *idea*. A political idea—say an ideology—may well have spatial ramifications. Colonialism is such an idea, so was geopolitics in interwar Germany, and Zionism today. Ideas may lead to *decisions* to occupy territory, to announce claims, to make promises. All this can generate *movement*, of people, goods, ideas, money, and more. While the process proceeds, the "links" in the chain interact with each other. Movement can influence the decision and alter it; the original idea can be changed, too. The whole development takes place in a *field* that, like the movement phase of the model, has tangible (spatial) as well as intangible characteristics. And at the end of the "chain" lies the politically organized *area*.

The unified field theory came to be known as the idea-area chain, suggesting a one-way sequence of development from political idea to politically organized area. But Jones himself cautioned against misinterpretation by emphasizing the underlying principle of two-way interaction; the links in the chain have reverse as well as forward effect. Before proceeding to some illustrative cases, let us consider the full statement of the theory as it first appeared.

[9]J. Gottmann, "Geography and International Relations," *World Politics, 3,* 2 (1951), 153–173.

[10]J. Gottmann, "The Political Partitioning of Our World: an Attempt at Analysis," *World Politics, 40,* 4 (1952), 512–519.

[11]Ibid., p. 514.

[12]S.B. Jones, "A Unified Field Theory of Political Geography," *Annals of the Association of Political Geographers, 44,* 2, June, 1954, 111–123.

A Unified Field Theory
of Political Geography*

Stephen B. Jones

Yale University

The current urge for theory in geography reminds me of an earlier period when a scientific nomenclature was thought necessary for the maturity of our subject. From this word-seeking only a few terms have survived, yet, looking back, I do not feel that the search for words, even though it turned up some mouthfuls like "nemoriculture," was wasted effort. Many of the words disappeared, but ideas were clarified in the process of word-coining. So the current search for theory may not revolutionize geography or make it any more scientific, but a valid theory, however minor, is at least three things: a compact description, a clue to explanation, and a tool for better work. Theory in this sense is immanent in the facts of the humblest termpaper. No young geographer should feel that theory is reserved for balding professors. Anyone can contribute to theory if he sees the least bit of meaning in his work. If he lacks the wit to see meaning in facts, there is not much that a body of theory, handed down to him by his professors, can do to make him a creative scientist.

Meaning of some sort is latent in any set of related facts, and geographical facts are nothing if not related. Incubated by thought, meaning may be borne as theory. A vital theory may fertilize new masses of facts. The uniqueness of the geographer's material, the uniqueness of the regional complex he studies or of the regional context within which his study is made, is not the barrier to theory that has sometimes been claimed, for a theory is not necessarily a statistical generalization. One of the most vital of modern theories, the

*This article is derived in part from a study of national power being made under a grant from the Office of Naval Research. All opinions expressed are the responsibility of the author.

anthropological theory of culture, is based on the study of human cultures, which are unique when considered as wholes. Born of the study of primitive peoples in far away lands, this theory has proved a magnificent working tool throughout the world.

The most magnificent thing about the present theory is its name. You are likely to be disappointed in the content. I am not sure the theory is able to stand on its own feet in a critical world. It may, however, have its uses and the way to find out is to push it out before the public. The beginnings of this unified field theory of political geography go back about ten years, when I was thrown among political scientists and had to teach political science students. Out of the attempt to make political geography intelligible and useful to political scientists grew the conviction that some sort of theoretical union of the fields must exist. It makes no sense to use the adjective "political" unless we mean by it something more fundamental than the mere geography of political units. The adjective, it seems to me, is just as important as the noun in defining a border field. I have been unable to split the hair that separates political geography from what might be called geographical politics. There must be a continuum from geography to politics, as, indeed, there must be a continuum connecting all the sciences that study man.

That there must be a continuum between geography and political science does not mean that there is no difference between a political geographer and a political scientist. It does, I hope, mean that in the future the attitude of geographers towards political science and of political scientists toward geography may be less naive than it has been in the past. We geographers, I fear, get most of our political science from the newspapers. To many politi-

S.B. Jones, "A Unified Field Theory of Political Geography," *Annals of the Association of American Geographers*, Vol. 44 (1954), 111–123.

cal scientists, I know, geography means physical geography, and political geography means the influence of the physical environment on politics.

Ten years ago, in the heyday of American geopolitics, I thought that political scientists would advance into and perhaps take over political geography. But interest in geopolitics has dropped. Currently, what may be called psychopolitics is a focus of interest. Studies of political behavior, of the processes of decision-making, of the images that one group forms of another are holding the attention of many political scientists. There is thus an opportunity for political geographers to expand their efforts. Unfortunately we are few in number, weighted with teaching, tapped for committees. Perhaps even more serious is the lack of a methodology that carries us surely and rapidly through the early stages of research.[1] Each of us has had to hammer out his own methodology, the hard way. If the theory I am about to present has no other utility than to provide a feeble guiding light in the wilderness, it will have served a purpose.

RELATION TO PRIOR WORK

Although its name is a vainglorious imitation of theoretical physics, the unified field theory is not based on a physical analogy. Its intellectual base includes substantial borrowings from three eminent political geographers—Derwent Whittlesey, Richard Hartshorne, and Jean Gottmann. In fact, the adjective "unified" in the title stems from the belief that the concept of "field" unifies the ideas of these three men, as well as unites them with political science.

In a paper published in 1935 which bears the now somewhat quaint title of "Recent Developments in Political Geography,"[2] Richard Hartshorne stated that any definition of political geography must be based on a definition of the field of human geography. He adopted the definition of geography as the science of earth-areas. Thus political geography was defined as "the science of political areas, or more specifically, the study of the state as a characteristic of areas in relation to

the other characteristics of areas."[3] As if anticipating Korzybski's general semantics, Hartshorne followed this Aristotelean definition with an operational definition. The second half of his paper opened with an outline for the study of a single state-area. The three main headings of this outline are Descriptive Analysis, Interpretation, and Appraisal, but all three parts are essentially chorological and morphological. Such items as political events, political power, and political processes are touched on very gingerly and only to the extent that they serve to explain the development of the state-area.

The logic of "Recent Developments" seemed unimpeachable to the present writer, who is a chorologist at heart, and it was a blow to find that it aroused no enthusiasm among his political science students. From their point of view, all the channels of event, power, and process that might have connected political chorology with their own problems seemed dammed or dried up. Moreover, as we all know, Hartshorne himself became dissatisfied with the morphological approach, castigating it, in his presidential address, far more severely than the present writer thinks it deserves.[4] He calls it "static and dull," "putting the cart before the horse." Such self-criticism hardly seems necessary, for morphology can be fascinating and, in science, a cart can become a horse, and vice versa, as knowledge develops. Let us say, rather, that the error of "Recent Developments" lay in enthroning morphology and in reducing to humble servitude those concepts that might have united it with political functioning.

Hartshorne's famous presidential address of course added function to his theory of political geography. The departure from the path of "Recent Developments" was not however a complete change of direction. The emphasis of "The Functional Approach" was still on the state-area and, for convenience, the discussion was limited to organized states of the national variety. For the present purpose, the pertinent part of "The Functional Approach" is the discussion of centrifugal and centripetal forces operating in the state-area.

The centrifugal forces that tend to pull a state-area apart include physical barriers (which, Hartshorne points out, have largely been overcome in most modern states by the

---

[1]cf. Richard Hartshorne, "The Functional Approach in Political Geography," *Annals of the Association of American Geographers*, XL (June 1950): 96–97.

[2]Richard Hartshorne, "Recent Developments in Political Geography," *The American Political Science Review*, XXIX (Oct. and Dec. 1935): 785–804, 943–966.

[3]Hartshorne, "Recent Developments . . .": 804. (Italics in original omitted.)

[4]Hartshorne, "The Functional Approach . . .": 99–100.

telegraph and railroad, not to mention newer forms of circulation), human barriers, differences in regional relations with outside states, different regional characteristics of populations, economic interests, and political attitudes. The miracle of state formation requires centripetal forces to overcome the centrifugal forces. The basic centripetal force, according to Hartshorne, is "the idea of the state." The state-idea need not be identical with nationalism, though it has been increasingly congruent with it. Not all ideas for states are viable state-ideas. The Holy Roman and the Austro-Hungarian emperors had ideas for forming states for which they could create no mass acceptance. Hartshorne points out that political science has been more concerned with generic concepts such as nationalism and federalism than with the state-ideas of particular states, so the political geographer must pursue politics and history far enough to nail down the raison d'etre of his particular object of study.

"The Functional Approach" was only two years off the press when Jean Gottmann presented related thoughts upon the political partitioning of the world.[5] Like Hartshorne, he speaks of two sets of forces, which are called circulation and iconography. Circulation is used in the sense familiar to geographers, to cover communication and movement of many kinds. Iconography describes "the whole system of symbols in which a people believes." "Symbol" is used broadly enough to include memories of past history and principles of religion, so we may think of iconography as a system of beliefs from which symbols, material and non-material, arise. Circulation is a system of movement, iconography of resistance to movement. Circulation, according to Gottmann, makes for change, iconography is a factor of political stabilization. Circulation permits space to be organized, and technical improvements in circulation make theoretically possible the widening of organized space. Iconography lags behind technology and expands its areas with difficulty. Circulation and iconography are not always in spatial conflict. Both focus at crossroads, though it would

seem that circulation usually comes first, creating the crossroads, and that iconography fixes itself at the point so established.

There are similarities and differences between the ideas of Hartshorne and Gottmann. Hartshorne recognized that circulation was a means of overcoming the physical barriers to state integration, but he did not list it as a centripetal force nor discuss its possible role in the development of a state-idea. He appears to consider circulation an expression of economic and political forces, rather than a primary force. Certainly an established state-area conditions the pattern of circulation to an astonishing degree, even though circulation originally helped shape the state-area. Iconography also can be recognized in Hartshorne's theory, both as the third of his centrifugal forces—"regions that differ among themselves in character of population, economic interests, and political attitudes"—and as the master centripetal force itself, the state-idea. Circulation, according to Hartshorne, does not necessarily make for instability and change. It may help stabilize a state, as railroads have done for Canada. Iconography does not always make for stability. There can be conflicts of lesser and greater iconographies, of sectionalism and nationalism, of national and international iconographies. Another of Hartshorne's ideas, that of the maturity of states, expresses a state-area co-extensive with the national iconography.[6]

THE IDEA-AREA CHAIN

Let us proceed to our unified field theory of political geography. The theory simply states that "idea" and "state" are two ends of a chain. The hyphen with which Hartshorne connects them represents the three other links of the chain. One of the links is Gottmann's circulation, which I shall call movement.[7]

The chain is as follows: Political Idea—Decision—Movement—Field—Political Area. This "chain" should be visualized as a chain of lakes or basins, not an iron chain of separate links. The basins interconnect at one level, so that whatever enters one will spread to all the others.

[5]Jean Gottmann, La politique des etats et leur geographie. Paris, 1952. Especially Chapter 8. Summaries of Gottmann's ideas appear in two articles by him: "Geography and International Relations," World Politics, III (Jan. 1951): 153–73, and "The Political Partitioning of Our World: An Attempt at Analysis," World Politics, IV (July 1952): 512–519.

[6]Richard Hartshorne, "The Concepts of 'Raison d'Etre' and 'Maturity of States'," (abstract), Annals of the Association of American Geographers, XXX (March 1940): 59.

[7]Gottmann himself thinks "movement" an inadequate translation and suggests "movement factor" ("The Political Partitioning of Our World": 515). The present writer has adopted "movement" as more compact and commonplace than either "movement factor" or "circulation."

Political idea, in this sequence, means more than just the state-idea. It means any political idea. It might be the idea of the state or it might be the idea of a speed limit on a country road. It might merely be a gregarious instinct, not consciously expressed. "War begins in the minds of men" and so does all other politics. But there are many political ideas that never reach the stage of action. They die aborning, remain in the realm of pure thought, or are rejected by the powers-that-be. A favorable decision is a necessary prerequisite to action. A formal, parliamentary decision is not necessarily meant. Much current research in political science is focussed on the informal or unconscious aspects of the idea-decision end of the chain, through studies of political behavior. Though most of the fishermen in the basins of idea and decision are political scientists, Gottmann and Hartshorne, both geographers, enter them when they speak of iconography and the idea of state.

Both political scientists and geographers have studied the phenomena at the other end of the chain—political areas. This term is used very inclusively to mean any politically organized area, whether a national state, a dependent area, a subdivision of a state, or an administrative region or district. It includes all three categories of areas listed by Fesler[8]: general governmental areas, special or limited-purpose governmental areas, and field service areas. The one common characteristic of all political areas is that they have recognized limits, though not necessarily linear or permanent. An administrative center within the area is common, but not universal.

Movement, I have said, is essentially Gottmann's circulation. What new twist it is given comes from placing it in a chain of concepts relating it to decisions. Every political decision involves movement in one way or another. There may be exceptions, but I have been unable to think of any. Some decisions create movement, some change it, some restrict it. Some create a new kind of movement to replace or to control the old. The movement may not involve great numbers of men or great quantities of matter—it may consist only of radio waves—but usually persons and things move as a result of political decisions. These politically-induced movements may be thought of as "circulation fields." The movements of state highway

[8]James W. Fesler, *Area and Administration*. University, Alabama, 1949. p. 6

patrolmen produce a field, shipments of military-aid materials produce a field, the despatch and delivery of farm-subsidy checks produce a field.[9]

A concrete example may clarify the thought behind this chain of terms. National prohibition had a long history as an idea. The Eighteenth Amendment and the Volstead Act were the final decisions that took national prohibition from the realm of ideas to that of action, though, to be sure, many smaller decisions had preceded these or were necessary later to implement them. The prompt effect of the Volstead Act was to inaugurate sweeping changes in movement. Legal shipment of liquor ceased, raw materials no longer flowed to distilleries, illicit movements were organized along new lines, enforcement officers went patrolling and prowling. The fields of these movements were not of uniform density nor did they exactly coincide with the boundaries of the United States. City slums and Appalachian valleys became centers of activity. Zones near the international frontiers were heavily policed. Enforcement reached twelve miles to sea. The effect on movement was felt overseas. No change in national territory resulted, but new administrative areas were set up. Had the law remained and been rigidly enforced, it is conceivable that our concept of the marginal sea might have changed, as later it was changed by the expanding field of activity of oil exploration. An earlier and more successful attempt at compulsory reform—the suppression of the slave trade—produced a field of enforcement on the high seas and led to the establishment of colonial areas in West Africa. Similarly, the idea-to-area chain is beautifully illustrated by the founding of Liberia.

In the case of prohibition, the existence of the political area of the United States gave general shape to the major fields produced by the Volstead Act, for obvious reasons. A political area in being is a condition of political ideas, decisions, and movements. Our linked basins, I have said, lie at one level. Add something to one, and it spreads to others. There is a general distinction, however,

[9]The general outlines of this theory were presented to a small audience at the University of Toronto in the spring of 1952. At that time, Dr. Ali Tayyeb suggested that, since political science tends to focus on ideas and decisions and political geography on political areas, the links of movement and field might be called geopolitics. My feeling is one of regret that "geopolitics" has been used in so many ways that this interesting suggestion may be impractical.

between flow from idea towards area and in the reverse direction. The former is essentially a process of controlling or creating. The prohibition law controlled some movements and created others. The idea of colonizing free negroes created a migration to Liberia. The reverse spread is more correctly described as conditioning. The existence of a political area, field, movement, or decision conditions what may take place in the basins lying idea-ward. Eric Fischer's paper, "On Boundaries," is full of good examples of such conditioning.[10] Benjamin Thomas has shown how the political area of Idaho, created upon a flimsy and essentially negative idea in the first place, conditioned further political thoughts and decisions until the present Idaho-idea is as firm as any.[11]

The essential characteristic of a field, in physics, is not movement, but spatial variation in force. The gravitational field exists even when no apples fall. Since we are not bound to a physical analogy, this distinction need not greatly concern us. However, it may sometimes be important to keep in mind that movements and fields are not necessarily identical. A higher percentage of Democrats goes to the polls where the party is neck-and-neck with the Republicans than where the party is overwhelmingly strong. Movement to polls creates a field, but it is not identical with the field of party power.

In a recent publication,[12] Karl Deutsch has suggested a "field" approach to the study of political community. "According to this view, every individual is conceived as a point in a field consisting of his communications or other interactions with all other individuals." Deutsch suggests that this concept may be applied to both small and large "clusters," including families, villages, towns, countries, regions, peoples, nations, and federations. Some clusters are political areas, some are geographical but not political areas, others, like families and peoples, are not necessarily found in definable areas. Thus Deutsch's "interaction field" may be the general case of which the present writer's concept may be the politico-geographical sub-type. On later pages of the same publication,[13] Deutsch gives fourteen tests of integration and a check-list of thirty-two possible indicators of social or political community, which should prove of value to the geographer as well as the political scientist.

A field exists in time as well as in space. Applying the ideas of Whittlesey,[14] we may say it has a time dimension as well as space dimensions and that the time dimension has three derivatives: velocity, pace, and timing. Highway patrols produce a field, as was mentioned above, but obviously it is important for both law-breaker and law-enforcer to know when the patrolmen operate as well as where. The effective scheduling of their patrols is a problem in timing. The whole of traffic and of traffic regulation can be considered a space-time field. Warfare and traffic are alike in this respect as in some others.

APPLICATION TO POLITICAL AREAS

Application of this theory to a case of one new national state is fairly simple: Zionism is the idea, the Balfour Declaration the conspicuous decision, permitting migration and other movements. A field of settlement, governmental activity, and war leads to the state of Israel. Such telegraphic brevity oversimplifies history, but the theory seems to fit. For a state with a longer and more complicated evolution, history could not be so readily compressed. The theory provides a path between geographical and political study, but not necessarily a short-cut. It does not reduce political geography to five easy steps. It does not permit world politics to be shown on a chart in five columns headed "idea," "decision," and so forth. It may, however, provide some intellectual clarification and it may prove a handy way of working back and forth among historical, political, and geographical ideas and data.

Karl Deutsch has recognized eight uniformities in the growth of nations from other political forms of organization.[15] Five of these

[10]Eric Fischer, "On Boundaries," World Politics, I (Jan. 1949): 196–222. The final paragraph on page 197 is a good description of the conditioning process.

[11]Benjamin E. Thomas, "Boundaries and Internal Problems of Idaho," The Geographical Review, XXXIX (Jan. 1949): 99–109.

[12]Karl W. Deutsch, Political Community at the International Level: Problems of Definition and Measurement. Organizational Behavior Section, Foreign Policy Analysis Project, Foreign Policy Analysis Series No. 2, Princeton University, September 1953. 30–31.

[13]Deutsch, op. cit., 37–62 and 70–71.

[14]Derwent Whittlesey, "The Horizon of Geography," Annals of the Association of American Geographers, XXXV (March 1945): 1–36.

[15]Karl W. Deutsch, "The Growth of Nations: Some Recurrent Patterns of Political and Social Integration," World Politics, V (Jan. 1953): 168–195.

are clearly "field" phenomena: the change from subsistence to exchange economy, the growth of core areas, towns, and communication grids, and the concentration of capital and its effect on other areas. The seventh and eighth are "iconographical," but have "field" connotations: the growth of ethnic awareness and its relation to national symbols and to political compulsion. The sixth item, the rise of individual self-awareness, is more difficult to relate directly to a field though decisions made in a framework of an increasingly individualistic philosophy would lead to changes in established fields. In short, the process of national integration, whether looked at by geographers, like Hartshorne or Gottmann, or by a political scientist, like Deutsch, can be interpreted as a process of changing fields. Conceivably the outlines of the political area may not change. The former colony of Burma is perhaps en route to becoming a true national state without change of boundaries or capital, but a study of the political fields would show changes.

One virtue of the field theory is that it is not confined to politically organized areas. It is applicable without difficulty to an unorganized area like the Mediterranean, which is undoubtedly a political field. As William Reitzel showed, decisions may affect the Mediterranean as a whole and may create or control movement over the entire sea.[16] The ideas may vary: Mussolini's dream of a new Roman empire, Britain's concern with sea command, the American strategy of the containment of communism. Reitzel showed how American policy in the Mediterranean evolved as the cumulative result of small decisions taken first with the idea of winning specific military campaigns. These decisions, and the successful military movements that resulted, involved the United States in political and economic administration. The Soviet Union replaced the Axis as the rival Mediterranean power, Britain slumped down the power scale, and the United States found itself deeply embedded in Mediterranean politics. The Truman Doctrine of support to Greece and Turkey was an outcome, indicating the unity of the Mediterranean sea-power field. The accumulation of decisions created a field, the sea conditioned it.

In the case of administrative areas, a political area may arise from a decision with little or possibly no intervening movement. A new governmental agency may lay out its field service areas before it actually engages in any actions. In some cases, analysis will show that these field service areas reflect pre-existing fields, such as the areas used by other branches of government or known fields of economic activity, and in many cases existing boundaries will be followed. It is possible, however, that an administrative area might spring directly from a decision and reflect no existing field. T.V.A. may be an example, unless we say a field had been created by river boatmen, hillside farmers, hydrographic surveyors, and so forth. This seems far-fetched; rather it seems that the Tennessee Valley was proclaimed a political area and that a field of activity resulted. It should be noted, however, that the field spread beyond the limits of the drainage basin, once electricity began to circulate.

There is nothing deterministic about the idea-area chain. A given idea might lead to a variety of areas, a given area might condition a variety of ideas. Pelzer's study of Micronesia under four rulers demonstrates this point.[17] Although the area ruled was not identical in all four eras, it was basically the same. The number of possible uses for these small islands was limited. Nevertheless, the four rulers—Spain, Germany, Japan, and the United States—made different choices. Their fields were different in kind and intensity. If one insists (which the dictionary does not) that a theory must be able to predict specific behavior, then the field theory may not deserve its name.[18] With no theory whatsoever, a well-informed person with some map-sense could have predicted many American problems and decisions in Micronesia. As a guide to study, however, the field theory is applicable to such cases.

STUDIES OF NATIONAL POWER

Studies of national power may also be fitted into the field theory. Lasswell and Kaplan define power as "participation in the making of decisions."[19] If power is participation in the

---

[16]William Reitzel, *The Mediterranean: Its Role in America's Foreign Policy.* New York, 1948.

[17]Karl J. Pelzer, "Micronesia—A Changing Frontier," *World Politics, II* (Jan. 1950): 251–266.

[18]The definition of "theory" most appropriate to the present paper is: "The analysis of a set of facts in their ideal relations to one another." Webster's Collegiate Dictionary, fifth edition, 1947.

[19]Harold D. Lasswell and Abraham Kaplan, *Power and Society: A Framework for Political Inquiry.* New Haven, 1950. p. 75.

304 Theories and Models

making of decisions, if power is necessary before an idea can produce movement, then we can easily fit power into our theory. Hartshorne distinguished between political geography and the study of power.[20] He felt a geographer might sometimes tackle the question of "how strong is a state?" if no one else had done so, but that in so doing he was "migrating into a field whose core and purpose is not geography, but military and political strategy." That power is linked with decision supports Hartshorne, to the extent that geography has been more closely associated with the other end of the chain, but our aim is to pull political science and geography together, not to separate them. If power is more concentrated in the basin of decision, it is by no means absent in the others.

BOUNDARIES, CAPITALS, CITIES

The unified field theory fits boundary studies into the general pattern of political geography. A boundary is of course a line between two political areas, but it is also a line in a region, as was emphasized in Hartshorne's Upper Silesia study and in the present writer's book.[21] The boundary region is truly a field in which the line between the political areas conditions much of the circulation.[22] A boundary field may even be or become a political area as in the case of buffer states and frontier provinces.

Studies of capital cities also may be expressed in field-theory terms. Cornish listed the crossways, the stronghold, the storehouse, and the forward headquarters as characteristic situations for capital cities.[23] To these Spate added the cultural head-link.[24] There are other possibilities, such as compromise sites and geometric centrality. All of these words have meaning in terms of movement and field either explicitly (as in the case of crossways,

forward headquarters, and cultural headlink) or implicitly (as in the case of storehouse). The idea of, or need for, central administration leads to a decision on the site of the capital. The choice is conditioned by the field and in turn distorts or recreates the field. Once the capital is chosen and the field about it established, many further decisions and movements are conditioned, leading in most cases to the creation of a primate city much larger than any other in the country.[25]

Not only capitals, but other cities, may be brought into the scope of the theory. In Gottmann's terminology, many of the problems of a growing city arise from the fact that its circulation expands faster than its iconography. The metropolitan district outgrows the political limits, and vested local interests and loyalties make political expansion difficult. A sort of "metropolitan-idea" may develop, leading usually to functional authorities rather than to political integration. In a few words, the urban problem is to make the political area fit the field.[26] There are a number of choices possible such as annexation of suburbs, city-county consolidation, metropolitan districts, functional authorities, state assumption of local functions.

KINETIC AND DYNAMIC FIELDS

Since politics consists of conflicts and the resolution of conflicts (though neither conflict nor resolution need be accompanied by violence), these fundamental activities must be expressible in field terms. There are conflicts of ideas, but they do not amount to much until they are embodied in decisions that create or obstruct movement. (It may be wise to re-emphasize that "movement" includes such things of little bulk as messages and money. A restriction on foreign exchange is a restriction on movement.) Fields may be in contact, but not in conflict, may indeed overlap but not conflict, if the movement is merely kinetic. But if there is a dynamic aspect, conflict often will arise. For example, New York City's growing need for water forces its activity in this respect to be dynamic, bringing conflict with other claimants to Delaware River supplies. The international oil industry is inherently dynamic, since new sources must

[20]"The Functional Approach . . .": 125–127.

[21]Richard Hartshorne, "Geographic and Political Boundaries in Upper Silesia," *Annals of the Association of American Geographers*, XXIII (1933): 195–228. Stephen B. Jones, *Boundary-Making: A Handbook for Statesmen, Treaty Editors and Boundary Commissioners.* Washington, 1945. Especially Part I.

[22]The pertinence of Eric Fischer's work on historical boundaries has already been mentioned.

[23]Vaughan Cornish, *The Great Capitals, an Historical Geography.* London, 1923.

[24]O.H.K. Spate, "Factors in the Development of Capital Cities," *The Geographical Review*, XXXII (Oct. 1942): 622–631.

[25]Mark Jefferson, "The Law of Primate Cities," *The Geographical Review*, XXIX (April 1939): 226–232.

[26]A.E. Smailes, *The Geography of Towns.* London, 1953. pp. 153–156.

be discovered. The result is potential conflict, sometimes anticipated and resolved at least pro tempore. The relations of political dynamics to such fundamentals as resource needs and population pressures have of course been repeatedly studied,[27] and the present theory does little more than incorporate them into the concept of the field.

The general attitude of Americans toward world politics is that dynamic problems should if possible be reduced to kinetic situations by agreement, or in other words that dynamic fields should be converted to kinetic fields. The philosophy of communism, however, is in many respects the opposite, except for temporary tactical purposes. In its grand strategy, communism would like to convert kinetic fields to dynamic fields, with the pressure from the communist side, of course. (The Nazis held a similar philosophy.) The failure of the United States to understand this difference accounts for a number of American blunders in diplomacy. The notion of peaceful co-existence of capitalism and communism, sincerely held by millions outside the Iron Curtain and occasionally uttered, with what sincerity is not known, by major figures within the Curtain, expresses the belief that the fields of the two ideologies can be merely kinetic in their relations, a belief that so far has little to support it.

There are no upper or lower limits on the magnitude of an idea. Man thinks easily of world government and can dream of spaceships and planetary empires. There are upper limits on decisions, movements, fields, and political areas, though these limits change with events (often, but not necessarily, upwards). Such ideas as the great religions, nationalism, liberalism, and communism have, in so far as they could produce decisions and movements, created fields. Whittlesey has shown how man's ideas of space have changed through primal and regional to worldwide conceptions, and how the third and fourth dimensions of the human habitat have been explored and put to use.[28] Ideas, fields of exploration, in some cases political areas have expanded, reached above and below the earth's surface, and made better use of time. The idea of a Columbus, the decision of an Isabella, a voyage of discovery, a new field, a new empire—this progression might figuratively be compared to the idea of a chemist, the decision of an entrepreneur, an experiment, a new field of production, an economic domain.

Many of the most influential of ideas have been composite, or "culture-ideas." Western culture, for example, is more than just capitalism or democracy or Christianity—it is a composite of these and other factors. Toynbee holds that every culture tends to evolve its "universal state," a domain roughly co-extensive with the culture.[29] If this is true, then we have another example of the chain from idea through a vast number of decisions (not necessarily consciously derived from the general culture-idea) and movements, creating a field and tending towards a political area which would be the universal state of that culture.

UTILITY OF THE THEORY

It is time to get back down to earth from the heights and ask that rude question, "So what?" Here is a theory; what can it *do*? Is it just word mongering? Of course, mere words have uses. A word of general meaning may replace phrases, sentences, even whole paragraphs. Whether "field" is such a word remains for time to tell. Or, as we said at the start, the word may die, but the clarification of thought that went into its coinage or adoption may be a useful accomplishment. Here, again, only time can tell whether thought has been clarified or made more murky by this paper.

On an earlier page it was said that a valid theory, however minor, is at least three things:

a compact description, a clue to explanation, and a tool for better work. It this theory merely provides nomenclature it satisfies the first requirement. Perhaps it goes farther than merely supplying words. It may reduce the apparent diversity of aims and methods in political geography, found by Hartshorne and his students.[30] It may help to unify not only the theories of political geography, but political theories in general. It may help complete the tie between morphology and function, between region and process. It may show a relationship between "grand ideas" and the earth's surface.

This unified field theory can provide no more than a clue to explanation, if it even

---

[27]For examples, by Frederick S. Dunn, in his *Peaceful Change*. New York, 1937 and by Brooks Emeny, in *The Strategy of Raw Materials*. New York, 1934.

[28]"The Horizon of Geography."

[29]Arnold Toynbee, *A Study of History*. London, 1939. Vol. 4, pp. 2–3.

[30]"The Functional Approach . . .": 96–97.

attains that success. It can hardly provide an ultimate answer to any question. But to relate several disciplines, to show connections, may give hints. The user of this theory is at least sure to be warned against single-factor explanations and be led to seek contributions from sister sciences.

It is as a tool for better work that I have the most hopes for this mental gadget. The chain of words in which the theory is expressed constitutes a sort of check-list ("check-system" might be better), by means of which one can orient oneself and tell where one should explore further. To return to the analogy of a chain of basins, one knows through which basin one has entered and where one can travel back and forth. If one begins with the study of a political area, ideas lie at the other end. If a study begins with movement, the scholar knows he should explore in both directions. For some of the basins one may need pilots from other disciplines, but at least one has a map of the chain. The theory tells students of geography and politics what (in very general terms) they need to learn from each other, what each has to add, but not how each fences himself off.

Another possible effect of this theory upon geographical work is that it may inspire the making of new types of studies and the compiling of new kinds of maps. Many maps either show or imply a field, but with the idea-area chain in mind, new sources of data suggest themselves: public-opinion polls, content analysis of publications, shipments of significant materials, movements of governmental officers, monetary transactions and so forth. The theory is "geographical" in that it makes mappable, through the concept of the field, the results of ideas and decisions that are themselves not mappable.

Conceivably the general plan of this theory can be extended to other than political studies. In fact, recent work in economic geography suggests a similar theory for that branch of our science. The idea-area chain may unite in one concept two main parts of geographical theory, the possibilist and regionalist views. Possibilism focusses on man's choices among environ-

mental possibilities. Choices are decisions. They imply ideas and must lead to movements. The regional or chorological approach, beginning with the study of areas, can lead through movement to decisions and ideas.

Finally, the unified field theory may have utility outside academic circles. It seems possible that the concept can be used as an aid in evaluating diplomatic and strategic ideas and plans. This is an ambitious thought and may prove illusory. However, diplomacy and strategy begin with ideas, lead to decisions, result in movement, and therefore produce fields. In reverse, diplomacy and strategy are conditioned by the political areas and fields of the earth, which limit the possible decisions and practical ideas. No doubt such thinking goes on in high places unaided by our theory, but perhaps this bit of intellectual guidance will clarify some cases.

Does the unified field theory have practical utility? It is tempting to apply the idea in relatively simple ways. For example, the state of Israel could be viewed according to the Jones model in terms of the concept of Zionism (the original idea); the Balfour Declaration of 1917 (the crucial decision); the modern exodus of Jewish people from many parts of the world to Palestine (major movement); the Eastern Mediterranean, conflicts with Arab states, connectivity of Israel to Western states (aspects of the field) and the modern state of Israel (political area). Similarly, it would be possible to place the idea of the abolition of slavery at one end of the "chain" and the state of Liberia at the other. Recently an attempt was made to apply the model to an emergent state, a territory long under British hegemony but with surviving local historical traditions. At the two ends of the chain are the idea of African nationalism and the state of Uganda.[13] Still more recently, the model was used in an analysis of wildlife conservation areas in East Africa, principally Kenya.

[13]H.J. de Blij, "Uganda and the Problem of Politics," in A Geography of Subsaharan Africa, Chicago, Rand McNally, 1964, pp. 264–278.

Wildlife Conservation Areas in East Africa: An Application of Field Theory in Political Geography

Harm J. de Blij and Donald L. Capone

Like many other countries in Africa and the remainder of the developing world, the young states of East Africa are presently reorganizing their political structures and, in so far as possible, reorienting their economies to reflect new goals and aspirations. In the political arena, the familiar trend toward the one-party state prevails: the conditions under which independence was achieved have already been greatly modified. Tanzania has attained one-party status; in Kenya the organized opposition to the government (K.A.N.U.) party is losing on all fronts under heavy pressure; and in Uganda the power and influence of the traditionalist Buganda Kingdom, which extracted federal guarantees at independence, were submerged in a nationalist revolution that came after sovereignty had been acquired.[1] In the economic sphere, the three republics also have chosen individual directions. The central concern, of course, is land and the policies relating to its ownership. The British left Uganda, Tanzania, and Kenya with laws and attitudes which reflected alien as well as African objectives. Tanzania has undertaken a communalization program for which freehold tenure was replaced by leasehold tenure; land in effect became the property of the state, and farmers were organized into multi-tribal cooperative villages under the control of party and government.[2] Heterogeneous Uganda has decided on a policy of tribal autonomy so far as land ownership is concerned, which in principle means that different sorts of individual land tenure prevail. And Kenya, whose land issue helped provoke the Mau Mau revolt of the 1950's, has seen the end of racial restrictions in the fertile and productive Highlands, where vacated European estates became available for African use. Even before independence, a successful program of land consolidation was in progress, and now the country's hopes are pinned—in contrast to Tanzania—upon a large and productive base of African smallholders.

Whether owned by the state, by national groups, or by individuals, land is the chief concern for the overwhelming majority of East Africans. All East African states depend for their external trade as well as local subsistence upon the products of the soil; mineral resources have but minor importance in the economic picture. Land drew the European settlers to the region, and land became the central political issue during the colonial period. East Africa certainly had its share of ill-considered inter-territorial boundary delimitation as well as ill-advised intra-territorial boundary shifting, especially in the case of Kenya's 'native reserves'. Not surprisingly, land was a major theme of African politicians when the colonial period drew to a close, and hopes were sometimes falsely raised that the end of British rule would constitute a solution to existing land problems. Unsympathetic outsiders saw indications that the commercially productive Kenya Highlands would revert to non-remunerative subsistence, and that East Africa's great wildlife heritage would fall to the encroachment of tribal peoples and

[1]Young, M. Crawford, "The Obote Revolution," Africa Report, Vol. 11, 1966, pp. 8–14.

[2]Burke, F., "Tanzania's Search for a Viable Rural Settlement Policy," Proceedings, 1967 Annual Meeting of the African Studies Association of the United Kingdom, London, 1967.

[3]Segal, Aaron, "The Politics of Land in East Africa," Africa Report, Vol. 12, 1967, pp. 46–50.

H.J. de Blij and D.L. Capone, "Wildlife Conservation Areas in East Africa: an Application of Field Theory in Political Geography," The Southeastern Geographer, IX, 2 (Fall, 1969) 93–107.

their livestock. Wildlife conservation, after all, had been a totally foreign innovation in black Africa; African peoples had within living memory been deprived of their land for this purpose.

PURPOSE

Although the pressures on the wildlife conservation areas of East Africa, since independence, have been severe and in some instances damaging, the fact is that the Africans have strengthened prevailing conservation policies. Moreover, they have come to grips with issues which the colonial government, by virtue of its imposed, non-consent administration, could conveniently submerge. In recent years, tourism, almost all of it attracted by the region's wildlife, has grown rapidly: Kenya's foreign exchange earnings from this industry, estimated at $20 million in 1964, had more than doubled by 1967.[4] Far from abandoning their wildlife heritage, the governments of East Africa have recognized both its value and the responsibilities involved in its protection. Large financial investments are being made to prepare for future growth; lodges are under construction, roads are being built and improved, park fences are being erected, and the administration and operation of the wildlife sanctuaries are undergoing an overhaul. And some political and social investments also have had to be made: encroachments on wildlife reserves have been resisted by force, squatters have been evicted, notably from Serengeti, and laws against poaching and illegal hunting have been tightened beyond what was the rule even under British administration. This is a sensitive matter, for an African tribesman who sees a licenced American hunter kill an elephant and is then jailed for killing a buck for its meat, and on his own traditional hunting ground, thinks little of the rewards of independence.

Demands for farm land, the activities of hunters and poachers, and pastoralism are some of the pressures on wildlife in East Africa, and in 1967 the authors, in collaboration with A.A. Nazzaro and S.S. Edison, prepared a research proposal designed to investigate these and other dangers, as well as the responses at local and national levels.[5] The

present paper constitutes a first report on one phase of this research, which encompasses (a) an impact study in a secondary urban center directly affected by the existence of a major game park in its hinterland, Malindi, (b) a case study of a park-border people whose economy has been transformed, the Taita, and (c) an attempt to arrive at indices of stress —isothreat lines—on the boundaries of the wildlife conservation areas themselves. All three of these objectives have practical value for Kenya, and policy discussions based on our preliminary findings have already taken place.

In the present paper, however, we focus on a politico-geographical aspect of our work. The emergence of Kenya as an independent state, with nearly 10 per cent of its territory set aside as wildlife conservation areas, endowed the country with not just one but two sets of boundary and territorial problems—international and internal. As we traced the complex origins of Kenya's national parks, the decisions that defined and delimited them, their frequent revision, the interference with established migration patterns and the creation of new ones, and the continuing spatial adjustments arising out of these circumstances, we recognized that the prominent hubs of activity we were recording related directly to the main elements of S.B. Jones' unified field theory model.[6] Although this model's most direct application is to the evolution of a *total* political area, its utility in the context of an *internal*, lower order or organized space can, we believe, be proved.[7]

FIELD THEORY

The unified field theory model is also known as the idea-area chain because these are the first and last of its five stages; decision, movement, and field intervene. The first question is whether the idea of wildlife conservation, in its African setting, really has political relevance. Of course, it was entirely alien to the region where it was introduced. Not only was the concept itself unknown; the practice of single-purpose allocation of land was foreign to the cultures upon which it was imposed. But let there be no mistake: wildlife conservation was more than a humanitarian principle when, in the late 19th century, the

[4]Republic of Kenya, *Economic Survey*, 1968, The Government Printer, Nairobi, 1968, p. 96.

[5]De Blij, H.J., Capone, D.L., Nazzaro, A.A., and Edison, S.S., "Spatial Transformation in Southeastern Kenya: Changing Perceptions of a Regional Resource Base," *Proposal for a Research Project and Training Program*, Michigan State University African Studies Center (mimeographed), East Lansing, 1967, 23 pp.

[6]Jones, S.B., "A Unified Field Theory of Political Geography," *Annals*, Association of American Geographers, Vol. 44, 1954, pp. 111–123.

[7]For an example of the former, see De Blij, H.J., "Uganda and the Problem of Politics," in *A Geography of Subsaharan Africa*, Rand McNally, Chicago, 1964, pp. 264–277.

idea was being debated. The British East Africa Company was impoverished, and needed support at home and revenue in the field. Politically the promise of a great heritage preserved for all mankind was a magnet for public opinion in England; economically the income potential from controlled hunting was quickly recognized. The Europeans themselves, furthermore, produced the threat that made conservation necessary. They found the African peoples, their farms and herds, and the wildlife in an ecological balance, a balance they disturbed by stimulating the poaching business.

The first concrete expression fo the conservation idea is contained in the British East Africa Company's "Sporting Licences Regulation of the 5th September, 1894," which proposes hunting restrictions and a limit on the number of kills that may be made per licence. Much of the hunting country lay in African tribal land (Fig. 1), and the Regulation stipulates that its application to African hunters should be relaxed.[8] But it was not in Kenya, but in what is today Tanzania where East Africa's first real sanctuaries were created. This was the work in large measure of Von Wissman, who apparently made the earliest appeals for such a move; his recommendations were reported in 1896 by Gosselin, the British representative in Berlin, to Foreign Secretary Salisbury.[9] Mainly through Von Wissman's proposals, there were two large wildlife conservation areas in German East Africa by late 1896: a Northern Reserve extending from the Masai Steppe south of Mount Kilimanjaro to present-day Serengeti, and a Southern Reserve coinciding largely with the modern Selous National Park (Fig. 2). For British East Africa, Sir John Kirk proposed that "large wild game preserve areas" be created, while F.C. Selous in a statement to the Foreign Office in 1897 advocated the introduction of closed seasons on every species and additional reserve areas where no hunting of any kind should be permitted.[10] What is remarkable about these early expressions of the conservation idea is the lack of knowledge relating to basic questions, for example the space requirements of a truly viable ecological unit, and, more importantly, the apparent lack of concern for the African peoples whose lands were being

considered as desirable sanctuary areas. The seeds of political trouble were sown early.

FROM IDEA TO DECISION: THE CONVENTION OF 1900

This situation is reflected also by the outcome of a conference, convened in London in 1900 and attended by representatives of the colonial powers with African dependencies and who shared an interest in the large-scale implementation of the conservation idea. Two articles of the resulting Convention reads as follows:[11]

II. (The signatories favor the) establishment, as far as it is possible, of reserves within which it shall be unlawful to hunt, capture, or kill any bird or other wild animal except those which shall be specially exempted from protection by the local authorities.

By the term "reserves" are to be understood sufficiently large tracts of land which have all the qualifications necessary as regards food, water, and, if possible, salt, for preserving birds or other wild animals and for affording them the necessary quiet during the breeding time.

III. The contracting parties undertake to . . . communicate . . . within 18 months (giving) information as to areas which may be established as reserves.

In British East Africa, this Convention led directly to the consolidation of one game reserve and the definition and delimitation of several others. The reserve that was consolidated was the "whole of the Kenia District of Ukamba Province, except the area within 10 miles around the Government Station at Kikuyu,"[12] and a comparison of Figures 1 and 2 shows that this incorporated a large part of the land of the Kamba and the Masai. Newly delimited sanctuaries included an expanded version of the Sugota Reserve, which had been proclaimed unofficially and without sanction by Sir H. Johnston in 1900,[13] and the Aberdare and Mount Kenya areas north of Nairobi.[14] In Britain, there were pressures for still greater expansion of East Africa's wildlife conservation areas as influential organizations took up the cause. In 1905 the Society for the Preservation of the Fauna of the Empire sent a deputation to Colonial Secretary Lyttleton calling for additional reserves,[15] and on March

[8]Parliamentary Papers, 1898, *Africa*, No. 7, LX, Command 8683, p. 641.
[9]Parliamentary Papers, 1906, *Africa*, No. 58, LXXIX, Command 3189, Correspondence Relating to the Preservation of Wild Animals in Africa (November 1906), pp. 2–3.
[10]*Ibid.*, pp. 42–44.
[11]*Ibid.*, pp. 86–91.
[12]*Ibid.*, p. 59.
[13]Parliamentary Papers, 1906, *op. cit.*, No. 67, pp. 113–114.
[14]Parliamentary Papers, 1906, *op. cit.*, No. 116, p. 173.
[15]Parliamentary Papers, 1906, *op. cit.*, No. 181, pp. 249–257.

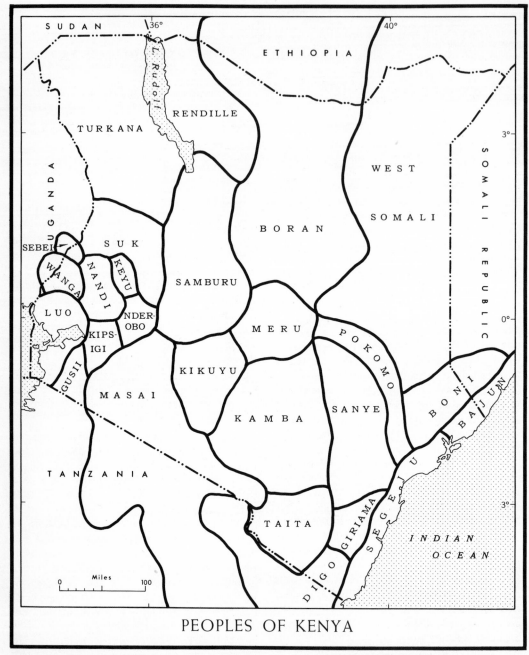

FIG. 1. Modified after Murdock, G. P., Africa—Its Peoples and Their Culture History, McGraw-Hill, New York, 1959. Map in rear pocket.

23, 1906 the Zoological Society of London in a communication to the Colonial Office demanded restrictions on human settlement in areas where wildlife was protected—the first time that this important issue was raised.[16]

As Jones stated, the idea-area chain's links are not separate, rather, they "interconnect at one level, so that whatever enters one will spread to all the others."[17] The decisions underlying the proclamation of British East Africa's wildlife sanctuaries were not always made with adequate knowledge of the local situation; the advice of Britishers in Kenya

[16]Parliamentary Papers, 1906, *op. cit.*, No. 216, pp. 335–336.

[17]Jones, S.B., *op. cit.*, p. 115.

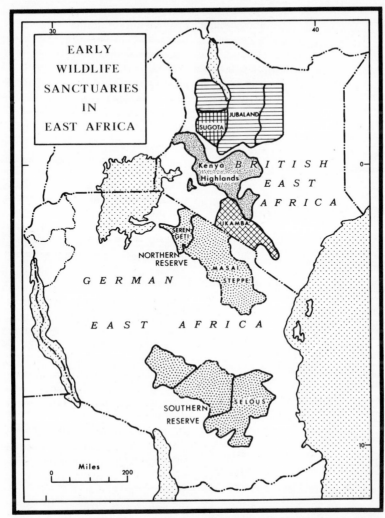

EARLY
WILDLIFE
SANCTUARIES
IN
EAST AFRICA

JUBALAND

SUGOTA

Kenya
Highlands

B R I T I S H

E A S T

A F R I C A

UKAMBA

SEREN
GETI

NORTHERN
RESERVE

MASA
STEPPE

G E R M A N

E A S T   A F R I C A

SOUTHERN
RESERVE

SELOUS

Miles
0   200

FIG. 2. Sources: For British East Africa: Parliamentary Papers, 1906, Africa, No. 58, LXXIX, Command 3189, p. 39. For German East Africa: Ibid., pp. 2-3 and 34-36. The modern boundary framework is superimposed for reference.

was not always followed. The consequent interference with local hunting rights on traditional hunting grounds, the interruption of ancient nomadic migration routes, the restriction of settlement to one side of a line demarcated on the ground—all these policies produced problems that demanded a revision of the whole conservation idea. It became clear, for example, that while total protection could be afforded to wildlife in certain areas there were other reserves in which humans and animals would have to share the land. Thus the concept of a hierarchy of conservation areas emerged, and this was a central theme of the 1933 Convention Relative to the Preservation of Fauna and Flora in their Natural State, the product of an international

conference on the question held, once again, in London.[18]

The 1933 Convention recognized no less than 6 levels of protection and control in wildlife areas, ranging from "national parks" to "controlled areas."[19] Naturally this had an impact on the disposition of land considered suitable for conservation purposes: There were alternatives other than complete protection or total abandonment. Where pastoralists drove

[18]The Convention was amended by the Third International Conference on the Protection of the Fauna and Flora of the Empire (Africa), Bukavu, 1933 (White Paper, Command 5230, 1936); the proceedings are summarized in the Final Act, H.M.S.O., London, 1938.

[19]Colony and Protectorate of Kenya, Report of the 1956 Game Policy Committee, Sessional Paper No. 7 of 1957/58, The Government Printer, Nairobi, 1958, pp. 62–64.

their cattle, the objective now became the maintenance of an ecological balance; where hunting was the chief mode of life, control to ensure the survival of adequate numbers became conservation's goal. As time went on, the six levels of protection defined in London proved too complex for satisfactory administrative operation, but the concept of a hierarchy of areas did become a cornerstone of wildlife conservation in East Africa. Today, Kenya still has three categories of wildlife reserves: the national park, the game reserve, and the game-controlled area.[20]

DECISION AND MOVEMENT

The majority of Kenya's 10 million people inhabit the southwestern quarter of the country, whose core area extends from the vicinity of Nairobi north and northwestward to Lake Victoria.[21] When the Europeans first saw Kenya, the Kikuyu dominated the Highlands (although they had temporarily vacated this area in the late 1890s); the Masai were grazing their cattle widely across southern Kenya and what is today northern Tanzania. The Kikuyu and the Masai were longtime rivals, but the British in 1904 forcibly restricted the Masai to two reserves, a northern one in the Laikipia area and a southern reservation of 4,350 square miles, south of Nairobi along the boundary with German East Africa. This was an unfortunate fragmentation of the Masai domain, and violations of the reserve boundaries were frequent. In 1911 a land exchange occurred whereby the Masai abandoned their northern reservation in exchange for nearly 6,000 square miles of territory westward along the border from their southern reserve; in the following year they were allotted a further 3,700 square miles to bring their total to about 15,000. This, of course, was a far cry from their former range (Fig. 1), and the Masai certainly were not among the beneficiaries of the colonial advent. Worse: when wildlife conservation decisions were applied in Kenya, the Masai found themselves in an area of great interest for this purpose. The Masai were not hunters (other than for ceremonial purposes and to protect their livestock); their cattle competed for the wildlife's range, but they

were never directly responsible for large-scale destruction of fauna. Now the decision to establish 'national reserves' (in the terms of the 1933 Convention) in their territory was seen as a further encroachment upon their already shrunken domain. The situation was mitigated, however, by the involvement of the Masai themselves in the conservation effort. Instead of creating national parks in Masailand, so-called game reserves were introduced in Amboseli and Mara (Fig. 3). Here the rewards of conservation are made directly visible through the collection of revenues from visitors, and the Masai's own District Council is responsible for control and supervision. In return, the Masai contracted to leave small sections of both Amboseli and Mara for the exclusive use of wildlife.

Mara and Amboseli today are examples of the best and the worst in this sort of cooperative venture between the Nairobi government and the local people. The Masai-Mara Game Reserve is stable and productive of revenues, and the range is in no danger. At Amboseli, however, excessive numbers of cattle (Fig. 4) are destroying the pastures and causing severe erosion, and in March 1969 the situation seemed practically irreversible (Fig. 5). In the words of a recent Kenya Game Department Annual Report, ". . . it is to be regretted that no progress was made to secure even an inadequate area for the sole use of wildlife. The (District) Council did not enforce the agreement to exclude domestic stock from the inner sanctuary of 30 square miles and further considerable damage was done to the vegetation."[22]

The political overtones of the conservation issue, then, are as strong today in an independent Kenya as they were under colonial rule. In a country of many ethnic groups, the government cannot impose its decisions on one tribal people without thereby arousing the fears of others as well, propaganda about the 'national interest' notwithstanding. And although the Masai have been intensely criticized for their failures in Amboseli, they have not been alone in their opposition:

The Samburu felt it was unfair that the Government should maintain game on their land and yet not share with them the benefits of its exploitation. Should a national park be created this feeling was

[20]Colony and Protectorate of Kenya, *A Game Policy for Kenya,* Sessional Paper No. 1 of 1959/60, The Government Printer, Nairobi, 1959, p. 1.

[21]Fair, T.J.D., "A Regional Approach to Economic Development in Kenya," *South African Geographical Journal,* Vol. 45, 1963, pp. 55–77.

[22]Government of Kenya, *Game Department Annual Reports 1964 and 1965,* The Government Printer, Nairobi, 1967, p. 27.

SUDAN

ETHIOPIA

36°

40°

3°

MARSABIT
NATIONAL
RESERVE

UGANDA

0°

S O M A L I   R E P U B L I C

MOUNT ELGON
NATURE RESERVE

SAMBURU
G.R.

ISIOLO BUFFALO
SPRINGS G.R.

MERU
NATIONAL
PARK

MT. KENYA
NATIONAL PARK

L. NAKURU N.P.
S.W. MAU
NATURE RESERVE

ABERDARE NATIONAL PARK

LAMBWE G.R.

MASAI
MARA
G.R.

NAIROBI
NATIONAL
PARK

KENYA

CONSERVATION AREAS

MASAI
AMBOSELI
G.R.

TSAVO

NATIONAL

PARK

INDIAN OCEAN

3°

NATIONAL PARKS

GAME RESERVES & NATIONAL RESERVES

CONTROLLED AREA BLOCKS & NATURE RESERVES

SHIMBA HILLS
NATIONAL RESERVE

Miles

0   100

FIG. 4. *Masai cattle herd within sight of Ol Tukai, Masai-Amboseli District Council Game Reserve. The general denudation evident here is symptomatic of much of Amboseli today.*

likely to be exacerbated. Exploitation would still be by an alien body in the shape of the (National Parks Board of) Trustees and as soon as the exclusion of livestock was enforced, as it would have to be, a friction line would develop round the park boundaries and reprisals might well be taken when game "trepassed" onto surrounding land in the course of its seasonal movement . . . the resulting ill-feeling would prejudice all other conservation measures in Samburu District.[23]

Through the cooperative principle of the District Council Game Reserve, the Samburu now participate in a conservation area that consists of both a Reserve and a game-controlled area (where licenced hunting is permitted), and the success of this particular program evinces Nairobi's determination to strengthen wildlife protection in Kenya (Fig. 3).

Movement, in the Jones model, may be created, changed, or restricted by the politically motivated decision. Decisions with political implications produce so-called "circulation fields." The Kenya case produces so many examples that only a few can be alluded to here. A clear instance relates to the policing of the conservation areas. Except in District Council Game Reserves, the officers of the Kenya Game Department are frequently drawn from distant ethnic areas, so that a Kikuyu officer may be in charge of patrolling a sanctuary located in Kamba country. It has been purposeful policy to recruit rangers for the large anti-poaching Field Force from the

north—the Rendille, Turkana, Samburu, and Orma. This kind of movement is somewhat analogous to the British use of Ganda administrators in non-Ganda sections of Uganda.[24] More broadly, the distribution of Kenya's wildlife refuges (Fig. 3) has produced fields of administrative contact between the central government and peoples whose involvement with Nairobi would otherwise be less direct. In another context, the location of Kenya's game sanctuaries has had an impact upon the development of the road system; certain parts of Kenya which might otherwise not be considered for road construction are on the priority list of the 1966—1970 Development Plan.[25] One such road is between Voi and Malindi along the Sabaki River, another connects Masai-Amboseli to Tsavo and the Voi-Taveta road, and a third improvement will link Meru Game Reserve to the network of the core area.

In the field of restrictive movement, it would be difficult to find a better example than the interference of park and reserve boundaries with the nomadic, rain-pursuing migrations of men and animals. A special case involves the Aberdares National Park, whose animal herds migrate back and forth across farmland to the slopes of Mount Kenya (Fig. 6). Fences and moats have been constructed to channel this flow through as narrow a corridor

[23]Government of Kenya, *Game Department Annual Report 1962*, The Government Printer, Nairobi, n.d., p. 5.

[24]De Blij, H.J., *op. cit.*, 1964, p. 272.
[25]Republic of Kenya, *Development Plan 1966–1970*, The Government Printer, Nairobi, 1966, pp. 214–215. See also Chapter 9.

FIG. 5. *Cattle-induced erosion, Masai-Amboseli District Council Game Reserve. Dust-bowl conditions are spreading in Amboseli, which is in danger of destruction.*

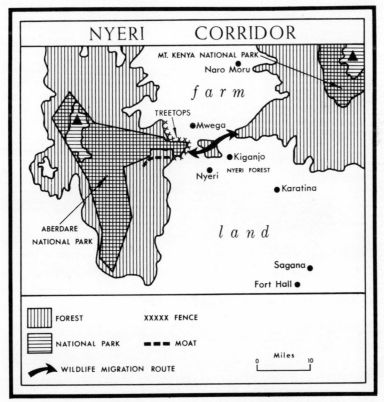

FIG. 6. *Source: Woodley, F. W., "Game Defence Barriers," East African Wildlife Journal, Vol. III, 1965, p. 89. There are reports that fences and moats are being planned also on the margins of Mount Kenya National Park.*

FIG. 7. *Masai encroachment on Amboseli's maximum game protection area: a boma built illegally near the swamp. This boma was photographed in late December 1968 shortly after it had been discovered by the authorities. Its residents have been forced to leave.*

FIG. 8. *To ensure that the Masai do not return to their village, it is burned to the ground. This photograph was taken in early March 1969.*

as possible, but the National Parks Board has heard some angry complaints from farmers in the area.[26] Still another aspect of restrictive movement is the removal of squatters from conservation areas. In Amboseli, Masai *bomas* (villages) have been built even in the vicinity of the exclusive game area of Ol Tukai (Fig. 7). When these settlements are found, their inhabitants are sent away and the dwellings are burned to the ground (Fig. 8).[27]

Other forms of field-creating movement, all with direct or indirect political implications,

[26]Woodley, F.W., "Game Defence Barriers," *East African Wildlife Journal*, Vol. 3, 1965, pp. 89–94.

[27]Silver, L., *Politics and Game in East Africa*, Mimeographed, n.d. (prob. 1966), 23 pp. See p. 16.

involve the tourist industry itself. More than 90 per cent of Kenya's hotels and other tourist-oriented establishments are still owned by non-Africans; members of the Kenya Peoples' Union, the opposition party, argue that the tourist trade and the government's land policies in general have combined to make for status-quo politics. The economic impact of the tourist industry is reflected dramatically in the luxurious hotels and travel and safari offices of high-rise central Nairobi, and more subtly almost everywhere else in the country. Diminutive (44 square miles) Nairobi National Park is one of Africa's great tourist attractions: it annually draws well over a hundred thousand visitors. With their money and their demand for luxury, the tourists are bringing change to distant corners of Kenya—as the German-speaking African labor force of Malindi's beachfront hotels will attest.

FIELD AND POLITICAL AREA: CONCLUSION

The apparently apolitical idea of wildlife conservation in a colonial dependency has led, in Kenya, to a fragmented national territory whose conservation areas in fact constitute and represent much more than that. In this paper, we have used the conservation idea in the context of the unified field theory to verify (1) the forward-and-reverse interaction among the five elements of the idea-area chain, (2) the political implications of an initially non-political idea, which is appropriate especially in view of Jones' own reference to the Tennessee Valley Authority in this connection, (3) the inherent political nature of any idea that has spatial expression, (4) the existence of all three types of movement also identified by Jones as emanating from the model, and (5) the manifestation of several "circulation fields" arising from the increasing complexity and multiple functions of the conservation idea.

The politically organized area of Kenya, like all such areas, is the outgrowth of many ideas and decisions. But Kenya's wildlife conservation areas are sufficiently large, involve sufficient numbers of people, and have resulted over a long time period from so concentrated a set of decisions that they are themselves a political area within the state. Represented in Nairobi by their own administrative officers and policed by a separate government department, they generate their own circulation fields, pressures, and modifications of the underlying idea. Their boundaries are more than simply administrative. Their resources represent one thing to the state, and another to the people living on the site. In multi-ethnic Africa, the effects of the conservation idea underscore the utility of the field theory model in the search for relevance.

A SYSTEMS ANALYSIS MODEL

Early in 1971 an article appeared whose authors, Professors S.B. Cohen and L.D. Rosenthal, sought to build further on the methodological heritage of Whittlesey, Hartshorne, Gottmann, and Jones.[14] "What is needed," say the authors, "is a methodology to link effectively political process and its spatial attributes—a methodology that, having identified a specific political process, can pinpoint spatially significant phenomena which relate to this process, can observe the impact of these phenomena within some control context, and can connect one process or parts thereof to another."[15] Thus they argue here that political geographers should focus on political processes in their research, and to the spatial expression of these processes. In this call they follow directly the direction established by Jones. And, like so many other political geographers, they cannot resist an attempt at definition of the field. It does not rank among the simpler ones:

". . . political geography is concerned with the spatial attributes of *political process*.[1] Process unites two elements intrinsic to the institutional act of governing: *transactions*,[2] legal, quasi-legal, or informal, which provide the operational tools for the structural act; and the existence of overriding *societal forces*,[3] including assemblages of past or

[14]S.B. Cohen and L.D. Rosenthal, "A Geographical Model for Political Systems Analysis," *Geographical Review*, 61, 1 (January, 1971), 5–31.
[15]Ibid., p. 5.

[1]*Political process* refers (within the setting of political-ideological forces) to the succession of events, actions, or operations that man employs to establish, to maintain, or to change a political system. These events are dependent on characteristic energizing agents (for example, elections and other methods of succession; land and other resource transfers).
[2]*Transactions* are the specific arrangements and agreements that give political sanction to the events, actions, practices, or operations of a political system.
[3]*Societal forces* are the ideological influences that concern the organization and goals of the social lives of large aggregations of persons.

contemporaneous transactions, which provide meaning and direction for political man. Transactions are viewed as episodes in the political group behavior that are the operational expressions of structure. Spatial attributes encompass four elements: *distributional patterns and spatial relationships*,[4] *political area formation and interaction*,[5] *territoriality*,[6] and *landscape*.[7]

Here is how the authors themselves dissect their prescription:

POLITICAL PROCESS

A major point of departure for analysis of political process is the *political system*[8] within which process operates.[9] Indeed, the concepts of process and system are inseparable. The bases for political systems are the societal forces that shape political institutions and the transactions through which the institutions operate, together with the pertinent environment. In such a context, the political system can be viewed as the end product of the processes by which man

[4]*Distributional patterns and spatial relationships* refers to existing pathways that the distribution of a phenomenon takes from place to place(s), and to the linkages in space that the distributed phenomenon has with pertinently related phenomena.

[5]*Political area formation and interaction* refers to the areal limit of a political unit and to the areal interaction of political units, or to the spatial limit of a political unit and to the interaction in space of political units.

[6]*Territoriality* is used as a group's sense of attachment to land or, more broadly, to geographical area.

[7]*Landscape* refers to the differentiated visible surface of the earth (including cultural alterations thereof) that constitutes geographical area.

[8]*Political system* is a set of related political objects (parts) and their attributes (properties) in an environment. In our usage here, political system refers to a functional entity composed of interacting, interdependent parts. Such a system has three dimensions: (a) its purpose or function; (b) its state of maturity or development; (c) its geographical or spatial base. (This is an adaptation of the definitions of systems and environment offered by Hall and Fagen [see text footnote 3].)

[9]This definition includes environment as *part* of the system, in distinction to the following views. Harry S. Hall and Richard R. Fagen define system as "a set of objects together with relationships between the objects and between their attributes" ("Definition of System," in General Systems Yearbook of the Society for the Advancement of General Systems Theory, Vol. 1 [edited by Ludwig von Bertalanffy and Anatol Rapoport; Ann Arbor, Mich., 1956], p. 18). Their view of environment is "for a given system . . . the set of all objects a change in whose attributes affect the system and also those objects whose attributes are changed by the behavior of the system" (ibid., p. 20). David Easton states that "a political system can be designated as those interactions through which values are authoritatively allocated for a society" (David Easton: A Systems Analysis of Political Life [New York, 1965], p. 21), and distinguishes a political system from other systems in its environment.

organizes himself politically in his particular social and physical environment and in response to outside political systems with their unique environments.

Other elements of the framework of analysis are the *locational perspective*[10] and the *open/closed political system*.[11] The locational perspectives in which the political system is viewed by those both within and outside it is essential to the understanding and the analysis of political process. Where the system is assumed to be (on the local, regional, or global scale) has a great deal to do with the strategy for shaping the system, both by those who guide it and by those who would try to change or otherwise affect it.

A France on the western extremity of the European continent and on the fringe of the Mediterranean and Atlantic worlds could, in the eyes of a Schuman or of a Monnet, be a partner to Britain as the core of maritime European unity and a focus for NATO. This is not the France of De Gaulle, which is located in a Europe that extends from the Atlantic to the Urals and which, as the leader of a unified Western Europe, could emerge as a partner with the Soviet Union in European unity. Locational perspective may become an important part of political myth. Without acceptance of the De Gaulle perspective, acquiescence by the French people to De Gaulle's rejection of NATO in favor of the goal of political unification of the Old World would scarcely have been possible.

Locational perspective is related to perceived needs for external links, or connectivity—that is, the degree to which the system is open or closed.[12] Although no system, be it physical, economic, or political, ever achieves a completely open or a completely closed

[10]*Locational perspective* refers to a mental view of the locational relationships or connections from a focal point or focal area to other points or areas. The focus (local position) may be treated at varying scales, national, subnational, or supranational, as may the connected parts that are viewed from this local position.

[11]*Open political system* has a maximum degree of external connectivity to other, parallel systems in the hierarchy. Connectivity is measured through the politically regulated movement of men, goods, and ideas and is reflected in specialized, intensive, and cosmopolitan use of geographical spaces. *Closed political system* seeks to cut itself off from other, parallel systems. Its political and economic isolation is reflected in generalized extensive use of geographical space.

[12]This definition differs from other usages, such as that of Hall and Fagen (op. cit. [see footnote 3 above], p. 23), which states that "Whether a given system is open or closed depends on how much of the universe is included in the system and how much in the environment."

state, political systems can be classified according to their position along a spectrum, ranging from most nearly open to most nearly closed.

The relationship of the political system to the landscape is direct and far-reaching. We may hypothesize that the open system molds landscapes that are the products of interdependence. Patterns of agglomeration, features of specialized resource use (intensivity and fast rates of change), port-of-entry buildups, internationally diffused features and symbols—these are some of the landscape consequences of the open system. The closed system molds landscapes that are the products of self-containment. Patterns of uniform spread, features of diversified resource use (extensivity and slower, more even, rates of change), larger numbers of interior central-place facilities, nationally diffused features and symbols—these are consequences of the closed system. Viewing a system within its open or closed context, then, provides a bench-mark from which to interpret and forecast landscape change.

The early nineteenth-century Japan that Perry found, the Soviet Union of Stalin's Second Five-Year Plan (1933–1937), or the Chinese People's Republic of Mao Tse-tung following the break with the Soviet Union cannot be classified as completely closed systems, but they do lie at the closed end of the spectrum. The United States just before World War I or modern Switzerland, though never completely open, lie at the open end. Political systems can be compared and broadly classified during one time period, that is, synchronically. They can also be analyzed diachronically, as they shift their positions along the spectrum through time (for example, Japan of the sixteenth century, of the early Meiji period, and of today provide open-system examples, in contrast with the closed systems of early nineteenth-century Japan and the Japan of the 1930's). Since open/closed systems are produced by the movement of men, goods, and ideas, the system can be measured through indexes such as visa and immigration policies, diplomatic and other political ties, tariff and trade practices, and the use of communications media.

Time scale is implicit in any discussion of process, not just with reference to the open/closed system and locational perspective.[13] In considering relationships between process and spatial attributes, there are several different time dimensions. The introduction of the transaction and its diffusion from place to place may be short term. The resulting area formation and area interaction, and the attendant changes in basic political structure, take considerably longer. Finally, the relationship of changing political structure, as a process in effecting change within societal forces, and attendant fundamental landscape change, would take still longer.

If we were to view political process in its restricted sense as the act of governing through formal political institutions, or even more narrowly through transactions, analysis might be simpler. However, political processes are inseparable from the overriding societal forces by which man orders his political life. Formal political institutions and social structures such as kinship, class, status, authority, communications, elitism, and bureaucracy are mechanisms (aided by symbols and myths) by which man makes operational such forces as nationalism, internationalism, feudalism, capitalism, socialism, democracy, totalitarianism, imperialism, colonialism, tribalism, religion, and racism. These are examples of societal forces that are inspired by combinations of individual and group drives such as security, authority, love, hate, repression, frustration, self-preservation, hunger, and territorial affinity. When such forces, or the ideas and beliefs behind them, relate directly to the political system they become appropriately defined as ideology.[14] The same forces are involved in many, if not all, of the identifiable facets of human existence; it would be impossible to try to limit them to political ideology and to political concepts. Although some of the forces are primarily political (nationalism, democracy, totalitarianism), others that are commonly thought of as economic or cultural are implemented through the political structures of a society and are therefore included.

By casting political process within the context of societal forces, it becomes operationally feasible to view individual transactions as interconnected episodes. Thus transactions dealing with the prevention of land fragmentation may be viewed within the principal forces of feudalism and democracy. Legal systems of primogeniture and land consolidation are intertwined with kinship and class structure, reflecting such human

[13]Derwent Whittlesey: The Horizon of Geography, *Annals Assn. of Amer. Geogrs.*, Vol. 35, 1945, pp. 1–36.

[14]Edgar Litt, edit.: The Political Imagination (Glenview, Ill., 1966), pp. 93–95.

drives as self-preservation, authority, security, and territorial affinity, and are instruments that have preserved or changed the social order. In the case of primogeniture, this law of undivided inheritance by one principal heir maintained class structure in feudalism by warding off dilution of wealth and power. The same law, when applied to small farmers and peasants, fulfilled a secondary function of guarding against uneconomical farm plots.

Primogeniture law, abolished in England only in 1926, maintained intact the great estates that were the source of wealth and power, not just for the landed nobility but for their familial offshoots who were impelled, encouraged, and assisted to apply their energies to the church, the military, or the colonial service. Because land was so scarce and, with the introduction of enclosures perhaps as early as the fourteenth century, so limited in its capacity to support a farm population (the enclosure system brought with it a shift from cereals to sheep, thus increasing the farm-labor surplus), subdivision for the small farmer would have led to excessive fragmentation almost immediately. Without primogeniture in England, more farmers would have remained on the land but in less affluent conditions, and the early enclosure laws could not have been used to transform agriculture from row crops to livestock.[15] The link between English manorial landscape and the focuses for English surplus farm population—whether the settlements in North America of the seventeenth and eighteenth centuries or the towns and industrial centers of Britain of the eighteenth and nineteenth centuries—is direct.

Land consolidation laws, such as those promulgated in northwestern Europe since the mid-eighteenth century, helped to change kinship and class structure by altering relationships of individuals to the village and to the family. Most consolidation laws served to change the social order, encouraging democracy directly by aiding the emergence of an independent farm class, or indirectly by encouraging economic progress in the hope of maintaining political stability.

Knowledge of the spatial setting for consolidation laws is crucial to an understanding of their impact. For instance, in Ireland implementation of the consolidation acts of the past century was facilitated by the availability of land on the western part of the island for planned migration (a supplement to the urban employment opportunities in the United States and England). In Denmark, between the mid-eighteenth century and the mid-nineteenth, the quality of the soil and the availability of water facilitated an intensification of agriculture that permitted consolidation to take place without creating rural overpopulation. After the mid-1800's industrialization was able to absorb the surplus farm population.[16]

Legal systems that militate against alienation of land (for example, Anglo-Saxon law) are a sharp contrast to those systems that permit transfer and alienation of land (for example, Roman law and its derivative, the Code Napoleon). Studies of both types of legal systems in their landscape contexts are useful starting points for analysis of the broader relationship between political process and spatial attributes.

Concern with overriding societal forces, then, can find a focus in the sutdy of acts of governing that flow from these forces. In turn, the act of governing, whereby man applies power, usually through law, to shape the institutions by which the governing process operates, is the key to law-landscape analysis. Significant subsets of governance are elections and other forms of leadership legitimation and succession, the degree of compliance with rules of law and tradition, and the perpetuation of military, social-class, and trade-union elites. These acts are made operational by specific political transactions, legal, quasi-legal, and extra-legal, the spatial characteristics of which form the analysis thread.

SPATIAL ATTRIBUTES

A basic objective of analyzing process in a spatial context is to examine man's behavior in space. The law-landscape thread is viewed,

[15]For a general discussion of primogeniture, see "Inheritance," in Encyclopaedia Britannica (14th edit.; Chicago, 1970), Vol. 12, pp. 253–254. For reference to the part played by primogeniture in stimulating landless aristocracy to take up leading roles in the early drive for empire in the Western Henisphere and India (as adventurers, administrators, or privateers), and in the nineteenth-century colonization of Australia and New Zealand, see J. Holland Rose, A.P. Newton, and E.A. Benians, edits.: The Cambridge History of the British Empire (8 vols.; Cambridge, England, 1929–1963), Vol. 1, p. 98; Vol. 2, pp. 448–449.

[16]For Ireland and Denmark, see Bernard O. Binns: The Consolidation of Fragmented Agricultural Holdings, FAO Agricultural Studies No. 11, Washington, 1950, pp. 41–54 and 64–76.

therefore, as a reflection of the broader political process-spatial attributes theme. We may be concerned with man's activity in space, expressed in distinctive patterns that emerge in terms of scale, distance, direction, mass, diffusion rate, and nearest neighbor; with man's perception of, and his psychological affinity to, space; or with man's impact on space, which eventually may lead to landscapes with changed or different characteristics, whose aggregation will shape or reshape political areas. In all of these contexts, place and landscape may play an active role in influencing man's action in space as well as a neutral role in reflecting his actions.

As has been said, "spatial" is defined as the distributional patterns of political processes and the spatial relations of these patterns with pertinently related phenomena, using space in its sense as a boundless medium. Such patterns and relations form unique *political action areas*[17] or fields of action.[18] In the political context such action may or may not be synonymous with *political area*.[19] Indeed, though the action area may not often be identical with the political area at the outset, the interaction of political process and landscape impact comes to a close when action field and political area *are* identical. In the usual sequence, it is a major objective for the central authority to establish eventually a state of conformity between political action area and the original political area, if for no other reason than that lack of conformity is commonly accepted as a challenge to the effectiveness and legitimacy of the government.

Jones made no specific reference to the issue of area interaction in his unified field theory, but at a later date he did consider area interaction, or repercussion, as an element worthy of treatment.[20] In the present discus-

[17]*Political action area* refers to the specific area on which political transactions make their impact. The effect of the impact is variable (with peaks of intensity at the point of origin and at tension areas, such as political boundaries), so that impact can be measured in hypsometric terms. Reaction by a competing political body through counter-transactions establishes a *counteraction area*.

[18]Jones, *op. cit.*, 1954. Jones uses "field" as part of a unified chain through which political ideas operate to affect political areas.

[19]*Political area* refers to a part of the earth's surface that has location and content and is legally organized and bounded (after Norton Ginsburg: Area, in International Encyclopedia of the Social Sciences [edited by David L. Sills; New York, 1968], Vol. 1, pp. 398–401).

[20]Stephen B. Jones, personal communication, February, 1965.

sion, area interaction arising out of the spatial impact of political decisions is a major element in the analysis—an output of area change. The dialectic in the process of action and reaction (either internally or externally) applies both to a political action area and to a political area. Thus, in connection with the development of a political action area, one can anticipate the development of a counteraction area. A *counteraction area* reflects the political efforts of any counterforce—individual or group, formal or informal, centralized or dispersed—to limit the extent of an emergent political action area or to counter it.

The force and extent of political action areas and counteraction areas are expressed, in the short run, by various measures of political socialization—that is, attitudes toward, and participation in, political institutions and other expressions of the political system. What creates an action area is the acceptance of political policy by groups that count politically and the attendant social and economic consequences. In the medium run specific landscape amendment, and in the long run general landscape change, become the output of the political process input. One can hope to forecast the landscape changes attendant on specific political transactions, given either a deductive theory or an empirical-inductive base. The accumulation of a number of landscape changes, stemming from one or a series of reinforcing processes, may even create the basis for converting a political action area into a new political area, by becoming a part of political myth and, eventually, by influencing ideology to include territorial annexation (for example, "Germanization" of the Sudetenland, which, after annexation in 1938, became a Reich District, Sudetengau).

THE MODEL

Figures 1 and 2 attempt to show man in his political role in society and the relation of that role (as expressed in political ideology, political structure, and political transaction) to the land (places, areas, and the general landscape), and to indicate the consequences of that relation in the formation of the political system.

Figure 1 illustrates the interactions between the several facets of man's political role and the multidimensional aspects of the land. For example, the interaction between political

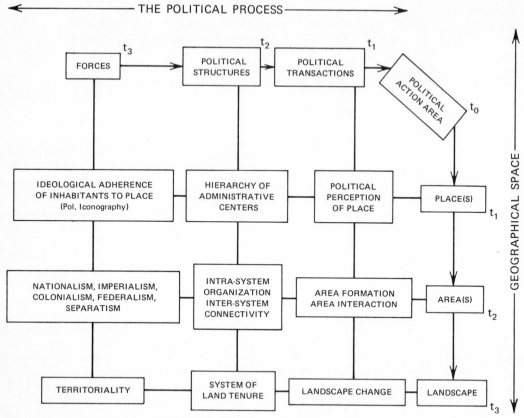

FIG. 1. *The political system with time scale.*

transaction and place (defined as a locational attribute) is a building block in the formation of political area, and the relationship between political structure and political area (defined as having content and organization) is expressed through area formation or area interaction or both. The results can be traced back to the interaction of transaction and places that forms hierarchies of centers and forge the area's internal organization and external relations.

Figure 2 is a simplified version of Figure 1 and emphasizes the interactions between political man and the land where the spatial aspects of man's political role are first encountered. These interactions are also the major points of tension between political man and the land, and they are unique to that relation. The interactions that precede these (hierarchy, ideologies) are less spatially concerned; those that follow (land-tenure systems, area dynamics, landscape change), though directly spatially concerned, are not unique to the political process. For man in his other roles, economic and cultural, will also generate landscape

change, area formation, and interaction, in addition to a system of land possession. In territoriality, internal organization and its external impact, and political perception of place, we have the three interactions that contribute most to an analysis of the political action area. The issues with which we are concerned (spatial attributes of political processes) are forged by the sense of territoriality and by places politically perceived whether within or outside the area's system (relating in turn to the open/closed nature of the system). The political action area is often a mosaic of the conflict between territoriality and political place perception, and the action area may be confined to, or may go beyond, the original political area and the system or systems under which that area is organized.

Dissolution of the political action area or resolution of the conflict occurs when the area (or counteraction area) coincides with the original political area—that is, when territoriality, political perception of place, and functional organization are coincident with the legally defined area. Figure 1 includes the

MAN

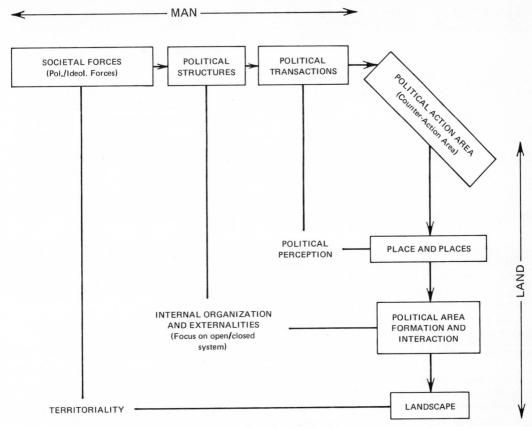

FIG. 2. *The political system.*

time-scale within which the system operates in its entirety and in its parts. The impact of political action area is, successively, on place, on political area, and on landscape. Overriding societal forces precede in time the political processes that issue forth from the structure. As we move to the left of, and down on, the matrix, the time-scale lengthens. Thus we would expect societal forces to change more slowly than political structures, which in turn change more slowly than political transactions.[21] Similarly, the impact on place, area, and landscape will differ according to the time-scale used; place evinces change sooner than area and both sooner than landscape (in the sense of fundamental modification of the

[21]This presupposes that institutions serve societal forces and can be quickly changed to suit ideological needs. Where political institutions become frozen or ossified, in part because ideology functions to preserve the structure and in part because ideology becomes the capitve of structure, then of course structural change may take longer than changes in societal forces. An example of the first condition is the establishment of a new pattern of economic regions in France; an example of the second is the maintenance of the county system in the United States.

landscape). The totality—political process and geographical space—constitutes the political system.

Although it is true that each aspect of the total system, or matrix, interacts with every other so that political transactions amend political structures, and that these in turn alter the value system of a society, our concern here is man or society perceiving and acting on the land that he or it occupies or covets. Figure 2 emphasizes the concern with the political action area and its components; the long-term impact of man on the land is subordinated to a short-term analysis—the transitional relation between man and the land.

A major problem in measuring interaction between process and geographical space in the context of political systems is that within a political system landscape and area change may take place as a result of population growth, economies of scale, and so on, regardless of political inputs. The political input that we trace must, then, affect the *rate* of change in landscape, whether this rate formerly was zero (a static equilibrium state) or a steady rate of growth or decline (a dynamic equilibrium state).[22]

The authors conclude their paper with a case study of Venezuela, where two dominant forces—nationalism and social democracy—provide vantage points for the study of the impact of process on geographical space. In the context of laws relating to petroleum exploitation and immigration, aspects of Venezuela's spatial organization are examined. The conclusion is that the Venezuelan case confirms the law-landscape thread as the key to the analysis of the political system. For example, "the hierarchical role of administrative centers and the political significance of place are essential characteristics in the understanding of place. Political conflict, as expressed through rivalry between state capitals (Ciudad Boliver) and new development centers (Ciudad Guayana) over where to build bridges, to locate factories, or to build up the strength of local political parties, exemplifies the operation of the political process in space."

The Cohen-Rosenthal study connects with Whittlesey's "Impress" statement, with Hartshorne's call for functionalism, and with Jones' interaction chain. Its political systems model suggests that the law-landscape association remains to be added as the focus for the analysis of the effect of political process on the organization of territorial space.

REFERENCES

Apter, David E., *The Gold Coast in Transition*. Princeton, N.J., Princeton University Press, 1955.

Ashford, Douglas E., *Political Change in Morocco*. Princeton, N.J., Princeton University Press, 1961.

Bailey, Sydney D., "The Path to Self-Government in Ceylon," *World Affairs*, n.s., *3*, 2 (April, 1949), 196–206.

Baldoria, Pedro L., "Political Geography of the Philippines," *Philippine Geog. J., 1*, 1 (January, 1953), 15–23.

Beard, C.A., and George Radin, *The Balkan Pivot: Jugoslavia*. New York, Macmillan, 1929.

Bentwich, Norman, *Israel Resurgent*. New York, F.A. Praeger, 1960.

Cervin, Vladimir, "Problems in the Integration of the Afghan Nation," *Middle East J., 6*, 4 (Autumn, 1952), 400–416.

Cohen, S.B., and L.D. Rosenthal, "A Geographical Model for Political Systems Analysis," *Geog. Rev., 61*, 1 (January, 1971), 5–31.

Dearden, Ann, *Jordan*. London, R. Hale, 1958.

Easterlin, Richard A., "Israel's Development: Past Accomplishments and Future Problems," *Quart. J. Economics*, 75, 1 (February, 1961), 63–86.

Fisher, Charles A., "The Malaysia Federation, Indonesia and the Philippines: A Study in Political Geography," *Geog. J., 129*, Pt. 3 (September, 1963), 311–328.

Gottmann, Jean, "The Political Partitioning of Our World: An Attempt at Analysis," *World Politics*, 4, 4 (July, 1952), 512–519.

Hadawi, Sami (ed.), *Palestine Partitioned 1947–58*. New York, Arab Information Center, Document Collections No. 3, 1959.

Hoffman, George W., "The Political Geography of a Neutral Austria," *Geog. Studies*, 3 (1956), 12–32.

Howe, Marvine, "The Birth of the Moroccan Nation," *Middle East J., 10*, 1 (1956), 1–16.

Ingrams, Harold, *Uganda; A Crisis of Nationhood*. London, H.M. Stationery Office, 1960.

Jackson, W.A. Douglas, "The Nature of the Political Geographical Problem," in *Politics and Geographic Relationships*, W.A. Douglas Jackson (ed.). Englewood Cliffs, N.J., Prentice-Hall, 1964, pp. 1–5.

Karan, Pradyumna P., and William Jenkins, Jr., *The Himalayan Kingdoms: Bhutan, Sikkim, and Nepal*. Princeton, N.J., Van Nostrand, 1963.

Khadduri, Majid, *Modern Libya: A Study in Political Development*. Baltimore, The Johns Hopkins Press, 1963.

McKee, J.O., "An Application of the Jones Field Theory to Rhodesia and the Concept of the Historical Time Period," *Virginia Geographer*, VI, 1 (Spring-Summer, 1971), 11–14.

Melamid, Alexander, "Political Geography of Trucial 'Oman and Qatar,'" *Geog. Rev., 43*, 2 (April, 1953), 194–206.

Pillai, R.V., and Mahendra Kumar, "The Political and Legal Status of Kuwait," *Int. and Comp. Law Quar., 11*, 1 (January, 1962), 108–130.

Randall, Richard R., "Political Geography of the Klagenfurt Basin," *Geog. Rev., 47*, 3 (July, 1957), 406–419.

Smith, Joseph B., "The Koreans and their Living Space: An Attempted Analysis in Terms of Political Geography," *Korean Rev.*, 2, 1 (September, 1949), 45–52.

Sprout, Harold and Margaret, *Man-Milieu Relationship Hypotheses in the Context of International Politics*. Princeton, N.J., Center of International Studies, Princeton University, 1956.

Taylor, Alan R., and Eugene P. Dvorin, "Political Development in British Central Africa (1890–1956)," *Race*, 1, 1 (November, 1959), 61–78.

Voss, Carl Hermann, *The Palestine Problem Today: Israel and Its Neighbors*. Boston, Beacon Press, 1953.

[22]Kurt Lewin treats all behavior as a change of some state of a field in a given unit of time (Kurt Lewin: Field Theory in Social Science: Selected Theoretical Papers [edited by Dorwin Cartright; New York, 1964], p. xi), and Robert A. Dahl, in discussing ways of comparing influence, suggests, "Why not measure A's influence by the extent of the amount of the change in B's behavior from what it would have been?" (Robert A. Dahl: Modern Political Analysis [Englewood Cliffs, N.J., 1963], p. 41).

CHAPTER
15
NEW DIRECTIONS

Political geographers for several decades have been interested in topics such as those discussed in the preceding chapters. They have done case studies relating to the elements of the state; they have speculated about the power relationships between states; they have theorized about the development and the life of states. But in recent years, other areas of study have come to the fore. These areas can be grouped together under the term *behavioralism*—the way people behave, individually and collectively, under certain circumstances. In what manner is political behavior expressed in political geography? How are decisions made? Is it possible to predict political responses, given certain stimuli? How does a person living in the suburbs of a major city perceive the threat of, say, a low-income housing project to be constructed near his home? What leads people to vote as they do—and can lessons be learned in political geography from the study of voting patterns?

Although the study of behavioralism in political geography has taken numerous directions, and research in other fields of geography (economic geography, for example) has proved relevant to political geography, it is possible to discern some distinct areas of focus. These include the study of voting behavior (or *electoral geography*), decision making, spatial perception as it relates to political geography, and territoriality.

VOTING BEHAVIOR

In 1959, J.R.V. Prescott published an article about electoral geography in which he remarked that while the study of election statistics has value for political geography, few studies of that kind had been done.[1] Actually, there had been some research in this area, beginning with a paper that appeared as long

ago as 1916 by E. Krebheil, dealing with British parliamentary elections.[2] But certainly the output was far smaller than that, say, relating to boundary studies. In the United States, the next really significant article on electoral geography did not appear until 1932, when J.K. Wright published maps to illustrate the results of presidential elections over the period 1876 to 1928. He briefly analyzed these maps in terms of large-scale regional contrasts (the Republican North and Democratic South) and more specific factors, such as farming areas and ethnic minorities.[3]

After World War II, interest in electoral geography grew somewhat stronger. In 1949, V.K. Dean's article on the geographical aspects of an important vote in Newfoundland was published. This referendum was held to decide what kind of government Newfoundland should have—confederal or "responsible." Involved here were several factors, including strong religious opposites and industrial-rural conflicts of interest.[4] Not long after this article appeared, R.M. Crisler briefly discussed voting habits in the United States in an article in the *Geographical Review*, and H.R. Smith and J.F. Hart made a contribution in a different direction by looking in detail at regional differentiation in the American tariff map.[5] Thus there was some slight increase in the attention given to electoral geography, but not a great deal. Prescott in 1959 could point to just a few studies in the United States, a somewhat stronger interest in Europe, especially in France, and a substantial literature in political science rather than geography.

[2]E. Krebheil, "Geographic Influences in British Elections," *The Geographical Review*, 2, 2 (March, 1916), 419–432.

[3]J.K. Wright, "Voting Habits in the United States," *The Geographical Review*, 22, 3 (October, 1932), 666–672.

[4]V.K. Dean, "Geographic Aspects of the Newfoundland Referendum," *Annals of the Association of American Geographers*, 29, 2 (March, 1949), 70–77.

[5]R.M. Crisler, "Voting Habits in the United States," *The Geographical Review*, 62, 2 (April, 1952), 300–301; H.R. Smith and J.F. Hart, "The American Tariff Map," *The Geographical Review*, 65, 3 (July, 1955), 327–346.

[1]J.R.V. Prescott, "The Function and Methods of Electoral Geography," *Annals of the Association of American Geographers*, 49, 3 (September, 1959), 296–304.

Since 1960, the picture has changed. A number of significant articles appeared during the 1960's, and in the process, methodologies were refined and distinct directions within electoral geography could be identified. An example of classical analysis was A.F. Burghardt's 1964 article on political parties in Burgenland, a province of Austria. In this paper, Burghardt examines spatial patterns of voting behavior and seeks to determine the underlying factors that influenced the voting. He carefully analyzes the demographic and economic qualities of the population and argues that locational and religious characteristics were the major factors affecting the vote.[6] The use of one of several techniques of quantitative analysis of voting tallies was illustrated in a paper by M.C. Roberts and K.W. Rumage, dealing with leftist voting in urban areas of England and Wales. Here, use is made of multiple regression analysis, and maps show regression residuals rather than straight data.[7] In another example of the modernization of electoral geography, K.R. Cox studied the spatial contrasts in voting behavior in the city of London, comparing the suburbs and the central city in terms of voter turnout and party preference. In this article, Cox uses methods of factor analysis and correlation techniques.[8] An especially interesting article, employing some qute different techniques, appeared in 1965. Here, P.F. Lewis used methods of cartographic representation and analysis to study the impact of immigration by blacks on the electoral geography of Flint, Michigan. In his introduction, Lewis stresses these methodological points:

(1) That maps, heretofore largely neglected as tools in the study of urban elections, are economical and accurate devices for measuring the voting behavior of urban minority groups, providing that certain preconditions are satisfied.

(2) That detailed electoral maps can provide the geographer with a considerable fund of demographic information which cannot easily be obtained by other methods.[9]

He then proceeds to demonstrate the use of map overlays to produce useful information about the voting behavior of minority groups in U.S. cities, and the potential usefulness of precinct-by-precinct electoral maps as research tools for the political geographer as well as the social geographer. For the latter, these maps provide information about the changing boundaries of black neighborhoods in intercensal periods, when such information might not otherwise be available at all.

The growth of interest in electoral geography and the increased use of voting data in analysis is reflected by a recent issue of the *Southeastern Geographer*, which was devoted exclusively to political geography. Of eight articles, four deal directly or indirectly with statistics derived from the ballot box.[10] One of these focuses upon the spatial pattern of electoral support for third-party candidate George Wallace in the 1968 Presidental election. It is an excellent illustration of research in electoral geography.

[6]A.F. Burghardt, "The Bases of Support for Political Parties in Burgenland," *Annals of the Association of American Geographers, 54*, 3 (September, 1964), 372–390.

[7]M.C. Roberts and K.W. Rumage, "Spatial Variations in Urban Left-Wing Voting in England and Wales in 1951," *Annals of the Association of American Geographers, 55*, 2 (March, 1965), 161–178.

[8]K.R. Cox, "Suburbia and Voting Behavior in the London Metropolitan Area," *Annals* of the Association of American Geographers, *58*, 2 (March, 1968), 111–127.

[9]P.F. Lewis, "Impact of Negro Migration on the Electoral Geography of Flint, Michigan, 1932–1962," *Annals* of the Association of American Geographers, Vol. 55, No. 1, (March, 1965), 1–25.

[10]R.E. Kasperson, "Ward Systems and Urban Politics;" D.M. Orr, Jr. "The Persistence of the Gerrymander in North Carolina Congressional Redistricting;" S.S. Birdsall, "Preliminary Analysis of the 1968 Wallace Vote in the Southeast;" S.D. Brunn, W.L. Hoffman, and G.H. Romsa, "The Defeat of a Youngstown School Levy: a Study in Urban-Political Geography," *The Southeastern Geographer, IX*, 2 (November, 1969), 17–25, 39–79.

Preliminary Analysis
of the 1968 Wallace Vote
in the Southeast

Stephen S. Birdsall

During the past century, national elections in the United States have rarely included a significant showing by a third party. Political parties other than the Republican and the Democratic have usually suffered from limited constituencies, either regionally or in terms of issues. An extremely interesting phenomenon, therefore, was the presence of a "third" party in 1968. Before the Fall elections, it was believed to have had considerable appeal across the country. George Wallace's American Independent Party (or occasionally, American Party or Independent Party) was frequently discussed as having the best opportunity since Theodore Roosevelt's efforts in 1912 of upsetting the political plans of the two larger parties.

The general results of the 1968 Presidential Election are known. Although receiving the electoral support of nearly 10 million voters, Wallace polled over half of this total in eleven Southern states. Furthermore, the American Independent Party carried only five states, all in the Southeast: Arkansas, Louisiana, Mississippi, Alabama, and Georgia. The 1968 Wallace-for-President effort, therefore, has some appearances of the limited regional appeal typical of third-party activities in Presidential politics.[1]

Less clear than the general results are the characteristics and spatial pattern of elector support. This paper reports briefly upon preliminary research which deals with voter characteristics and the distribution of voter support for George Wallace in 1968. Data have been analyzed by statistical methods for eight

states in the Southeast: North and South Carolina, Tennessee, Georgia, Florida, Alabama, Mississippi, and Louisiana. Although Wallace received many votes in Arkansas, Virginia, Texas, and Kentucky, among other states, data for one of the variables considered important to the analysis were not available for these states.[2] Visual examination of the election results is extended to include Virginia and Arkansas.

ORGANIZATION AND LIMITATIONS

The analyses presented here have been divided into three sections. First, the county-to-county distribution of Wallace vote is examined. This pattern is the per cent of votes received by Wallace from the total number cast in each county. Second, an attempt is made to identify some of the significant characteristics of Wallace supporters. This attempt is made through statistical analysis of county population characteristics for the eight-state region. Third, the relationship between degree of support and the population providing this support is studied. As location is taken to be a significant aspect of this relationship, the purpose of this last set of analyses is to determine whether or not there is significant regional variation in the relationship between support for Wallace and characteristics of the population giving it. More loosely, is the appeal of the American Independent Party interpreted differently by voters in one portion of the Southeast than by voters elsewhere in the region? Or again, is the Southeast homo-

[1]Some might argue that the five million voters who cast their ballots for Wallace outside of the Southeast indicate a significant non-regional basis of support. This issue is not of immediate concern here.

[2]These data, the number of Negro registered voters, by county, were also unavailable for Tennessee. This state was included in the analysis, however, for reasons demonstrated in the paper.

S.S. Birdsall, "Preliminary Analysis of the 1968 Wallace Vote in the Southeast," *Southeastern Geographer*, Vol. IX (1969), 55–66.

geneous in the interpretation of the appeal from a largely regional candidate? The third portion of this paper, therefore, is a combination of the analyses of the first two sections.

There are numerous difficulties attending the analyses. As with any study using general population characteristics and voting returns, it is impossible to determine the character of the non-voting population. It should also be made clear that the use of grouped (in this case, county) data precludes the assignment of motive or detailed characteristics to any member of the group. Therefore, although conclusions can be stated in terms of specific bases for voter support, individuals cannot be characterized with these results.[3] Additional problems are raised by the use of voter registration records. For example, some counties have more registered voters than eligible voters; deceased and departed registrants might not have been purged from the rolls. More rigor is lost by the necessity of examining 1968 election returns in light of 1960 population characteristics. In spite of these and other problems, the conclusions reached are believed valid as indicators of the general relation between the phenomena studied as well as the direction for further research.

THE PATTERN OF SUPPORT

The spatial pattern of voter support for George Wallace contains several items of interest (Fig. 1).[4] As had been expected, the highest proportion of county support was given Wallace in Alabama and much of eastern Mississippi. As distance from Alabama increases, there appears to be a gradual, mixed decline in the level of support. Louisiana, northern Florida, and Georgia provided strong support (mostly over 40 per cent of the county vote), but this is still somewhat below the large areas of over 60 per cent received in the Alabama and Mississippi "core" region. At greater distance from Alabama, in southern Florida, the Carolinas, Virginia, Tennessee, and Arkansas, the propor-

tion of votes received by Wallace drops to under 40 per cent, and in many counties to under 20 per cent. At the same time, there are significant sections of this "peripheral" Southeast which gave between 40 per cent and 60 per cent of their votes to the American Independent Party.

Perhaps of greater interest than the rather broad "friends-and-neighbors" pattern of support for Wallace[5] is 1) the importance of state boundaries upon this level of support, and 2) the striking similarity between the distribution of votes received by Wallace and the patterns of other phenomena.

By far the most impressive state boundary effect visible on Figure 1 is that between Tennessee and the states to its south. Whether passing from Mississippi, Alabama, or Georgia into Tennessee, there is a drop of about 20 per cent in the level of voter support for Wallace. This difference is remarkably consistent along Tennessee's southern boundary. The decline could be a function of information level or type (with Tennessee voters subjected to different quantities and sources of campaign propaganda), a function of home-state allegiance (leading voters in usually-Republican northern Alabama to cast their ballots for Wallace), or a function of a very different set of attitudes among the Tennessee population.

Several other state boundaries appear to have had the effect of dividing varying levels of support for Wallace. Although less clear than the Alabama-Tennessee boundary, the state line between Alabama and much of Georgia also separates distinct levels of Wallace vote. Georgia has some appearance of being a transition state with respect to 1968 Wallace strength because its boundary with South Carolina is also rather distinct. It is possible that the level of support for the American Independent Party was low in South Carolina (generally under 40 per cent) and distinct from that in Georgia because of the strong pro-Nix-

---

[3]Although this limitation of probability-based techniques of analysis should be well-known, it is repeated here because of the potentially controversial nature of the subject matter. For a good discussion of the limits on "proving" hypotheses by statistical methods, see Hubert M. Blalock, Jr., Social Statistics, McGraw-Hill, New York, 1960, chapter 8.

[4]The percentages for this map were calculated by the author from official election returns. The returns were obtained from the several Secretaries of State.

[5]Strictly speaking, the pattern shown may be too broad to be called a "friends-and-neighbors" pattern. There are, however, sufficient similarities to justify the qualified use of the term. For a more detailed discussion of this factor in electoral geography, see V.O. Key, Jr., Southern Politics, Alfred A. Knopf, New York, 1949; Harold H. McCarty, "McCarty on McCarthy: The Spatial Distribution of the McCarthy Vote, 1952," (unpublished manuscript), State University of Iowa, Department of Geography; and, David R. Reynolds, "A 'Friends-and-Neighbors' Voting Model as a Spatial Interactional Model for Electoral Geography," (unpublished manuscript), read at the annual meetings, The Association of American Geographers, Washington, D.C., August 1968.

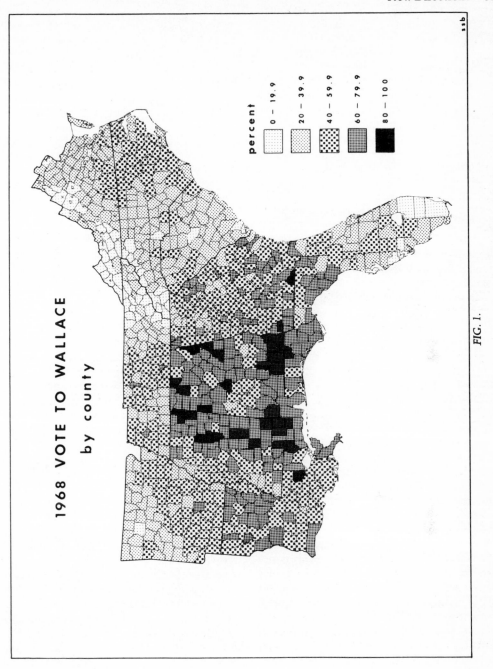

FIG. 1.

on arguments put forth during the campaign by South Carolina Senator Strom Thurmond. It is equally possible that the steep rise in Wallace strength across the Georgia boundary with South Carolina is an indication of the decline in the Senator's influence outside his own state, at least relative to Wallace's influence with the voters. It should be mentioned that these state boundary effects, if indeed they are the effect of something, are not cartographic illusions. The apparent drop in percentage of votes to Wallace across the Louisiana-Arkansas boundary is such an "illusion" in that it is partly a function of the classes used in the construction of Figure 1. There is a decline in Wallace strength southeast-to-northwest in Arkansas, but it is not coincidental with the state line as are those discussed above.

The recognition of non-political patterns on Figure 1 provides some insight into the second task of this paper, i.e., the identification of phenomena correlated with variations in the Wallace vote. One of the more easily recognized patterns is the lower level of Wallace vote given by many of the counties with large cities. Arlington and Richmond are visible in Virginia, Charlotte can be picked out in North Carolina, and Columbia can be identified as a low Wallace vote area in central South Carolina. Although they do not stand out as clearly, the counties containing Atlanta, Montgomery, Tallahassee, and Jacksonville also provided somewhat lower support for Wallace than their surrounding counties might suggest.

It is clear, however, that a high level of urbanization is not the only explanatory variable for lower proportions of county returns gained by the American Independent Party. Several exceptions to the general "friends-and-neighbors" pattern described above are also visible. Those counties in south-central Alabama which granted their home-state candidate less than 40 per cent of the local vote are counties possessing the highest proportion of the population Negro. Several of these counties were over 75 per cent black in 1960. The large Negro percentages in the Delta region of western Mississippi are also visible in the somewhat lower voter support given to Wallace in 1968. Conversely, in those portions of the Southeast which have never had a large Negro population (i.e., the Appalachian portions of North Carolina and Tennessee), the populations also gave most of their votes to either Nixon or Humphrey.

Southern Florida, similarly, has proportionately fewer Negroes than northern Florida, and it was the northern part of the state that voted overwhelmingly for Wallace. It can be proposed, then, that within those portions of the Southeast where Wallace's electorate strength was greatest, the presence of a high proportion of Negroes resulted in a low Wallace vote. And where Wallace generally received a lower level of voter support in the Southeast, the presence of Negroes in above average numbers resulted in higher-than-expected voting for Wallace (e.g., see eastern North Carolina on Figure 1). This will be pursued more carefully in the next section.

EXPLANATORY CHARACTERISTICS

The identification of significant explanatory variables for patterns as complex as that of the Wallace vote is often difficult. The variables used in this preliminary analysis were chosen in light of the observed pattern of support for the American Independent Party and also with some consideration given to existing stereotypes of the strong Wallace supporter. Although these characteristics were based on diverse subjective impressions, there was sufficient consistency to provide assistance in the choice of variables to be used. It was expected, therefore, that Wallace would receive a smaller proportion of the total vote in those counties containing a large Negro population, in counties with highly urban populations, with populations possessing high median annual incomes and also higher levels of education. In other words, the supporters of George Wallace, especially in the Southeast, were frequently stereotyped as low-income (but not poor), rural or small-town whites who had earned less than a high school education.

It was also believed that the proportion of registered voters who are black would be a better measure of Negro, i.e., assumed anti-Wallace, political strength than would be the proportion of population black. Obviously, much of the Negro population in the region has been placed on voter registration rolls only recently,[6] with many counties still having a wide discrepancy between the percentage of population black and the percentage of registered voters black. In spite of the difficulties of using such data, as discussed above, the

[6]References to this are numerous. For a brief discussion of some of the less well-known results, see Marvin Rich, "Civil Rights Progress Out of the Spotlight," *The Reporter*, Vol. 38, March 7, 1968, pp. 25–27.

Table 1

State	Independent Variables in Order Chosen X_i	Simple Correlation Coefficients r	Multiple Correlation Coefficients R	Coefficient of Multiple Determination R^2
N.C.	X_2	.7790		
	X_4	-.2439	.7811	.6101
TENN.	X_2	.4744		
	X_5	.0374		
	X_3	.1075	.5309	.2819
S.C.	X_1	-.5924		
	X_3	-.2043	.7415	.5498
GA.	X_4	-.3039		
	X_1	-.2673	.4795	.2299
FLA.	X_3	-.7305		
	X_5	-.6804		
	X_2	.1178		
	X_4	-.5937	.7980	.6368
ALA.	X_1	-.7130		
	X_3	.1045	.7358	.5414
MISS.	X_1	-.8364		
	X_4	.2219		
	X_3	.4472	.8566	.7338
LA.	X_1	-.5431		
	X_5	-.4603		
	X_4	-.2693	.7919	.6271

N.B. All coefficients of multiple correlation are significant at the .01 level.

proportion of registered voters who are Negro was considered the best available measure of black political strength.[7]

A series of stepwise multivariate correlation and regression analyses were conducted to determine the strength and form of the explanatory relationships hypothesized. The following five independent variables and one dependent variable were used:[8]

Y=percentage of the total vote received by Wallace, 1968, by county

X_1=percentage of all registered voters who are Negro, 1968, by county

X_2=percentage of the total county population which was Negro, 1960

X_3=median number of school years completed by the adult county population, 1960

X_4=median annual family income, 1960, by county

X_5=percentage of the county population classified "urban" by the United States Census, 1960.

[7]These percentages were calculated by the author from data in "Voter Registration in the South, Summer, 1968," Voter Education Project, Southern Regional Council, Atlanta.

[8]Data for X_2, X_3, X_4, and X_5 were obtained from the *County and City Data Book, 1967*, U.S. Department of Commerce, Government Printing Office, Washington, D.C.

Two of the independent variables, X_1 and X_2, are specifically racial in nature, and the remaining three are not. X_1 and X_2 are also not independent, i.e., there could be some interaction in their joint explanation of the dependent variable. Therefore, they were not used together in the same analysis.

The results of the analyses are shown in Table 1. Because of indications from Figure 1 that there were marked differences in Wallace support from state to state, eight analyses were performed, one for each state. Six of the eight analyses had coefficients of multiple correlation greater than 0.73. The proportion of the variation in Y which is "explained" by the independent variables, therefore, exceeds fifty per cent in each of these states. Only for Tennessee and Georgia were R^2-values below 0.50. Indeed, in both states, less than 30 per cent of the variation in Wallace vote was explained by significant variables.[9]

Before proceeding to the final section of analysis, it should be pointed out here that of

[9]For a readily available discussion of the difference between the statistical significance of the multiple correlation coefficient and that of the partial correlation coefficients, see Leslie J. King, *Statistical Analysis in Geography*, Prentice-Hall, Englewood Cliffs, 1969, pp. 142-48.

Table 2

Region	Indep. Var. in Order Chosen X_i	Simple Corr. Coef. r	Multiple Corr. Coef. R	Multiple Coef. of Deter. R^2	Regression Coef. b_i	Regression Constant a
A	X_2	.8004			0.501	
	X_4	.0031			0.003	
	X_3	-.0053	.8149	.6641**	-2.281	29.706
B	X_2	.8107			0.368	
	X_3	-.2000			2.420	
	X_4	-.6720	.8967	.8041**	-0.003	22.061
C	X_2	.3848			0.483	
	X_5	-.0336			-0.271	
	X_4	.1319	.5691	.3239**	0.007	25.693
D	X_1	-.5924			-0.592	
	X_3	-.2043	.7415	.5498**	-5.005	91.993
E	X_3	-.2924			-3.947	
	X_1	-.2616	.4180	.1747	-0.254	
F	X_3	-.8229			-9.351	
	X_5	-.7469			-0.185	
	X_4	-.6065	.8649	.7481**	0.006	114.678
G	X_1	-.6237			-0.720	
	X_4	-.1171			-0.005	
	X_5	-.3696			-0.125	
	X_3	.0204	.8562	.7331**	2.072	74.276
H	X_1	-.6576			-0.687	
	X_4	-.1743			-0.005	
	X_3	-.0062			1.805	
	X_5	-.3398	.7801	.6086**	-0.067	83.474
I	X_1	-.4747			-0.677	
	X_4	-.3184	.7183	.5160**	-0.005	84.156
H+I	X_1	-.6298			-0.735	
	X_4	-.1523			-0.007	
	X_3	.0558	.7475	.5588**	2.617	78.468

**Significant at the .01 level

the six states with reasonably high coefficients of multiple correlation (over 0.70), only in Florida was one or the other of the racial variables of less than primary significance. That is, one of the racial variables provided the greatest single source of explanation for the Wallace vote in most of the states studied. In three states, Mississippi, Alabama, and North Carolina, this was by far the most important explanatory factor. (Note that the relationship in North Carolina is positive while it is negative in the other two states. This will be discussed later.)

SUPPORT REGIONS

It would be unusual for state boundaries to be totally effective dividing lines between types of support for national political candidates, even those with strong regional alliances. That differences exist between states is clear from the preceding analyses. Education is a significant variable in explaining the pattern of support for Wallace in Florida and Mississippi, but it is not as important in North Carolina and Louisiana. Furthermore, even Florida and Mississippi are different in this regard. The relation between these variables is negative in Florida (i.e., the higher the median school years completed, the lower the percentage of county vote to Wallace), but it is positive in Mississippi. It was expected that differences such as these often extended across state boundaries.

In an attempt to identify distinct regions of support for Wallace which differ in the form of the relationship described by the significant variables, each state was grouped with adja-

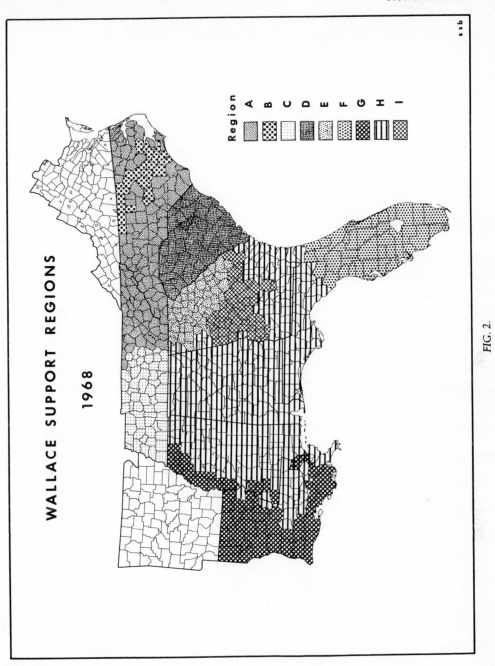

FIG. 2.

cent states and stepwise analysis was performed independently for each group. Residuals from the obtained regression equations were then obtained and plotted. In this way, it was possible to identify support regions which were not limited by state boundaries.[10] These regions were then gradually grouped, a procedure subjected to three self-imposed constraints. First, it was necessary that the coefficient of multiple determination for each group of counties be greater than those for the states of which they are a part. Second, in no case was the R^2 permitted to drop below an arbitrarily chosen level of 0.50. Third, each region was composed of conterminous counties. It was necessary to make one exception to this last constraint, however, in North Carolina.

The regions derived and the form and strength of the relationships between the variables for each are shown in Figure 2 and Table 2. Tennessee, it was found, should be divided into at least two parts when discussing the relation between Wallace support and population characteristics. The form of this relationship in eastern Tennessee was seen to be very similar to that in most of North Carolina. The R^2 for this group indicates that nearly two-thirds of the variation in Y across this region (Region A) can be explained by the linear equation, $Y = 29.706 + 0.501X_1 = 2.281X_2 + 0.003X_4$. Western Tennessee remains less well explained; this *might* be changed with knowledge of X_1 values for the state. (Note, for example, the similarity in the eastern margin of Region H and the eastern margin of Region C.)

It was found that by separating Region B from the remainder of North Carolina, thus violating the conterminous constraint, the explanations of both Regions A and B were improved. The very high R^2 for Region B, largely due to a high *positive* correlation between Y and X_2, gives rise to some speculation. The relation indicates that the larger the percentage of black population in a county, the greater the proportional voter support given to Wallace. Before concluding that he had the support of the Negro population here and in Region A, the relation between population and political strength must be examined again. Within Region B, no county has more than 35

[10]For a discussion of this use of residuals from regression, see Edwin N. Thomas, "Maps of Residuals from Regression," in *Spatial Analysis*, Brian J.L. Berry and Duane F. Marble, eds., Prentice-Hall, Englewood Cliffs, 1968, pp. 326–52.

per cent of the registered voters Negro (most are about 25 per cent), while the populations in these counties are in most cases over 35 per cent Negro. Furthermore, the non-contiguous portion of Region A, in northeastern North Carolina, is the area of primary concentration for Negroes in the state. In other words, those areas with a low proportion of the population Negro and those with a high proportion Negro are more alike with regard to the Wallace vote in the state than either is to a group of counties intermediate in the level of Negro population. In light of the other relationships indicated in Table 2, it is posible to postulate that where the conditions of Region B hold, i.e., a large but not majority portion of the population Negro, income and education are more important explanatory variables than elsewhere.

Several other states were divided in the process of regionalizing by form of Wallace support. Southern Florida stands out in sharp distinction to northern Florida. In this respect, at least, Florida is two separate states. Southern Florida, Region F, is also atypical in the Southeast. Of the three independent variables providing significant improvement in the explanation of the pattern of Wallace voting, none is racial. That is, neither racial variable was statistically important enough for inclusion in the analysis. Even without the racial element, nearly three-quarters of the variation in Y was explained. It was also meaningful to separate much of Louisiana and portions of the Mississippi Delta from the remainder of the Southeast. Except for Baton Rouge (which suffers here from the contiguity requirement), none of the larger Louisiana cities and towns are placed in Region H.

Region H is "Wallace Country." This portion of the Southeast, and to a lesser extent Region I, not only gave the American Independent Party candidate an overwhelming proportion of its available votes (see Fig. 1), it also gave these votes from a rather consistent social environment. This is not to say that the region is homogeneous in either social characteristics or support for the former Governor of Alabama. If, however, it is possible to assume that political perceptions and actions are in large part a function of, or better, reflected by, socio-economic characteristics, then it is possible to say that Region H, or the joint region of H and I, is somewhat homogenous in the relation between Negro registration, income, and education and the pattern of Wallace vote. It is most interesting to note that in both Regions G and H+I, there is a strong inverse relation between the vote for Wallace and the proportion of registered voters Negro. If in fact, "the southern Negro vote is 'issue-oriented,' and race is the issue,"[11] then it is clear that the voting black population in this portion of the Southeast views George Wallace's posture on racial issues with considerable disfavor.

Two final comments are in order with respect to Figure 2. South Carolina remains distinct from the rest of the Southeast. An increase in explanation of the pattern of Y does not follow from grouping with either Regions A, E, I, or H. This appears to be further confirmation of a specifically statewide, and probably state-oriented, influence; Senator Thurmond, again, may be the best explanation. Northeastern Georgia remains a region which is not well-explained. Although the relationship described in Table 2 for this region, Region E, is statistically significant at the .01 level, the coefficients of correlation and determination are low. The low degree of explanation for Region E may be a function of factors not included in the analysis, purely local issues, or some combination of these. Indeed, it may well be related to Senator Thurmond's influence. If this region were to go less for Wallace than "expected" from state-wide characteristics (as was the case in fact), then the relation described by the variables could be consistent with neither South Carolina's nor the rest of Georgia's patterns. Whatever the solution to this problem, Georgia contains some of the character of the Wallace South and some of the character of South Carolina.

CONCLUDING REMARKS

The pattern of voter support for George Wallace in 1968 has been analysed. Visual examination of the pattern indicates that Alabama, Mississippi, and Louisiana voters gave Wallace a very large proportion of their ballots. Southern Georgia and northern Florida can also be included with these states. In general, there appeared to be some relation between distance from the candidate's home state and his influence with the voters. Significant exceptions to this pattern were seen in the lower voter support given Wallace in urban counties and those containing very large percentages of Negro population. In several cases, state boundaries coincided with clear changes in the level of Wallace's voter support. Using multivariate correlation and regression analysis, it was possible to identify several regions distinctly different in their basis of support for Wallace and also the characteristics of the population giving this support. Except for southern Florida, one or the other of the two racial variables used was of primary importance in each region. The relationship was clearly negative in the regions of greatest Wallace electoral strength but more speculative in North Carolina and Tennessee.

The analyses reported in this paper are essentially preliminary ones. Problems such as northern Georgia and western Tennessee remain unsettled. Additional aspects of the relation between Negro political strength and support for the American Independent Party must be examined. Other areas of the border Southeast, Virginia, Kentucky, Arkansas, and eastern Texas, have not been touched. They should be included in a more thorough treatment of the subject.

DECISION MAKING

Political geographers have also tried to gain deeper insight into the processes whereby decision making takes place. What were the elements that went into Malawi's decision to relocate its capital at Lilongwe? What leads to the voters' decision, in a particular area, to select one candidate over another? How does a government choose an irredentist course of action toward a neighboring state?

For answers to such questions, it is necessary to turn to the work of psychologists and other social scientists who have researched

[11]Donald R. Matthews and James W. Prothro, *Negroes and the New Southern Politics*, Harcourt, Brace & World, New York, 1966, p. 159.

the behavior of decision making. Decisions emanate from a complex set of processes. They are made because the person or group of persons making them desires a state of affairs different from the one that prevails. They are based on information, but in order to assess the process of decision making in a given context we must know the amount of information the decision makers had and the degree of accuracy of that information. And that is not all. There are different *kinds* of decisions; they are made as a matter of habit, or they may be made subconsciously, or they are controlled—that is, they are made in response to a perceived choice of alternatives.

Fortunately, geographers other than political geographers have also been interested in research on decision making, and political geography has benefited from this work. R. Kates studies the decision-making behavior of people living in river flood plains, people who faced the dangers of breaking levees and repeated inundation.[11] Economic geographers have focused on the element of rationality as part of a decision-making model. This is the concept of the "intendedly rational man," who may have an incomplete and imperfect information set, but who makes rational decisions when confronted with alternative courses of action. J. Wolpert incorporated this factor into his search for the behavioral elements involved in people's decision to move elsewhere—the decision to migrate. In this and several other articles of great relevance to political geography, Wolpert stresses a number of dimensions of decision making.[12] *Place utility* has to do with a decision maker's relationship with the locale where the decision is being made. Is he satisfied, adjusted? Or the opposite? The *decision environment* is constituted by the decision maker's perceptions of alternatives, information, cues, and stresses. This brings forward another, related item: *threat*. Not infrequently, decisions must be made in haste, in a crisis atmosphere. This tends to reduce not only the time involved, but also the range of choices that might have been considered. This has obvious relevance to strategic decision making. In the face of armed hostilities, or under actual conflict, decisions often must be made rapidly. Again, this leads us into another dimension of decision making: *risk* and *uncertainty*. When President Nixon, in May, 1972, announced his decision to mine the entrances to North Viet Namese ports, he did so with considerable risk and uncertainty. Voters, too, face uncertainty when they select among presidential candidates; they cannot be sure that platform promises will be kept.

The literature on decision making in political geography is still limited. Noteworthy are two articles by R. Kasperson, one dealing with the interplay of geography and politics in the city of Chicago (but with important implications of a wider nature) and another focusing on political decision making under crisis conditions, involving the allocation of water resources.[13] Another valuable article, dealing with a wholly different aspect of decision making, was discussed in some detail in our chapter on capital cities (Chapter 6). Here, D. Lowenthal analyzes the tangible as well as intangible inputs that led toward the decision to select Trinidad as the capital of the short-lived West Indies Federation.[14]

SPATIAL PERCEPTION

Over the past decade, geographers have evinced a strong interest in an elusive subject: perception. The subject is elusive because it is often difficult for individuals to express their feelings, attitudes, or ideas as they relate to their perception of the world around them—and it is still more difficult to measure these uncertainties. But few would question the value of research in this direction. In one way or another, we have all had occasion to notice expressions of this phenomenon. Who has not seen the postcards sold in Texas, California, and elsewhere, showing those states hugely oversized, crowding all the other states along a narrow edge of the United States like tiny pieces of a jigsaw? Those postcards are intended to be funny, but none of us has a precise image of the layout of our town, state, country, or world. And when we are asked to draw our "mental map" of our country, we will distort it in a way that may significantly reflect our misconceptions. In other words, we hold a "model" of the spatial environment involving notions of distance, direction, shape, accessibility, and so forth—and on the basis of this model, which is at variance with reality, we operate.

So, too, do politicians. Complicated issues are simplified and thus distorted, and then decisions are made (and opinions swayed) accordingly. Out of distorted perceptions of the situation in Southeast Asia came policies that, had their consequences been known

[11]R.W. Kates, *Hazard and Choice Perception in Flood Plain Management*, University of Chicago, Department of Geography Research Paper No. 78, Chicago, 1962.

[12]J. Wolpert, "Behavioral Aspects of the Decision to Migrate," *Papers*, Regional Science Association, 15, (1965); J. Wolpert, "The Decision Process in Spatial Context," *Annals of the Association of American Geographers*, 54, 4 (October, 1964), 537–558; J. Wolpert, "Departures from the Usual Environment in Locational Analysis," *Annals of the Association of American Geographers*, 60, 2 (April, 1970), 220–229.

[13]R.E. Kasperson, "Toward a Geography of Urban Politics: Chicago, a Case Study," *Economic Geography*, 41, 2 (April, 1965), 95–107; R.E. Kasperson, "Political Behavior and the Decision-Making Process in the Allocation of Water Resources Between Recreational and Municipal Use," *Natural Resources Journal*, No. 2, 1969.

[14]D. Lowenthal, "The West Indies Chooses a Capital," *The Geographical Review*, 68, 3 (July, 1958), 336–364.

beforehand, would not have been followed. Ask the next colleague who raises the "Domino Theory" to draw you a map, by heart, to show you how it will work.

Spatial perception, of course, is only one dimension of a complex of images we hold of the world around us (including ourselves), a totality that has been called the *perceptual field*. This perceptual field is affected by numerous conditions: our cultural conditioning and the values attached thereto, our attitudes, motivations. In the spatial context, at least within cultures, it may be possible to discover broad patterns of common behavior. J. Sonnenfeld addresses himself to these matters in a recent paper. He recognizes geographical, *operational*, perceptual, and behavioral environments.[15]

Again, the relevance to political geography of the study of perception is very great indeed. It is hardly necessary to stress the changed perceptions minority voters hold of the power of the ballot; campaigns to register voters, greater accessibility of polling places, and the elimination of obstacles to minority voting have had an enormous impact upon public life. The busing of schoolchildren, official insistence upon equal job opportunities for minority peoples, and other efforts to reduce racial discrimination have, in turn, resulted in changed perceptual fields among millions of white voters—who gave evidence of their attitudinal change during the 1972 presidential primaries.

TERRITORIALITY

Actually, the subject of territoriality belongs under the heading of perception. But ever since R. Ardrey published his now-famous work entitled *The Territorial Imperative*, the topic of territoriality has had a discrete place in the social sciences.[16] There were people who had researched this topic previously, of course. But Ardrey's work forcefully brought it to general attention.

On the very first page of his first chapter, Ardrey makes some statements political geographers could hardly ignore. "A territory," he writes, "is an area of space, whether of water or earth or air, which an animal or group of animals defends as an exclusive preserve. The word is also used to describe the inward compulsion in animate beings to possess and defend such a space. A territorial species of animals, therefore, is one in which all males, and sometimes females too, bear an inherent drive to gain and defend an exclusive property . . . we may be permitted to wonder if in all territorial species there does not exist, more profound than simple learning, some universal recognition of territorial rights."[17] And then Ardrey asks himself whether *man* is such a territorial species. His conclusion: "Man . . . is as much a territorial animal as is a mockingbird singing in the clear California night."[18]

The implications of such a statement, obviously, are enormously far-reaching. If it is essentially correct, then man's sense of territoriality as an instinctive drive is a greater determinant of his politicoterritorial adjustment and organization than what he has learned through social and cultural evolution. Ardrey's argument is spun out in detail throughout *The Territorial Imperative*—but not everyone was convinced. And so there developed a debate about this subject that is still going on today.

If we define the concept of territoriality as a pattern of behavior whereby living space is fragmented into more or less well-defined territories whose limits are viewed as inviolable by their occupants, it becomes clear that political geographers have for some time recognized this phenomenon. Any such territories, after all, will acquire certain particular characteristics—Gottmann called it *iconography* and we discussed this idea in Chapter 14. The Ratzel-Kjellen-Haushofer school of geopoliticians were in the process of defining a form of territoriality when they conceptualized the state as an organic being. R. Hartshorne and S.B. Jones urged that the state be viewed as an entity whose characteristics could be linked, ultimately, to the behavior of the individuals constituting it.

And therein lies one of the problems with the concept of territoriality. Much of what is known about territorial behavior comes from research in two areas, ethology (the study of behavior in animals) and psychology. Critics of the concept of human territoriality as Ardrey defined it doubt that it is appropriate to make inferences about aggregate or group

---

[15]J. Sonnenfeld, "Geography, Perception, and the Behavioral Environment," in P.W. English and R.C. Mayfield, *Man, Space, and Environment*, New York, Oxford University Press, 1972, pp. 244–251.

[16]R. Ardrey, *The Territorial Imperative*, New York, Atheneum Press, 1966.

[17]Ibid., p. 3.
[18]Ibid., p. 5.

behavior from research dealing mainly with the behavior of individuals; they also wonder to what extent it is safe to equate human behavior with animal behavior. These critics do not suggest that Ardrey was entirely wrong, but they urge caution when it comes to sweeping generalizations. They feel that much more research needs to be done before the nature of human territoriality can be defined with any confidence.

One promising area of research ought to be familiar to all of us. It relates to the way we spread ourselves out in classrooms and theaters, restaurants and libraries. If we do not *have* to be crowded, we like to put a little distance between ourselves and the next person. This is *personal space*—a sort of envelope of territory we carry about with us, as an extension of ourselves. Apparently humans as well as animals carry such envelopes around, but the shape and the size of the envelope varies in humans, from culture to culture. In terms of shape, we can tolerate greater proximity in front of us than beside us, and less behind us. Thus our "portable territory" is not symmetrical around our body. And, as R. Sommer remarks, Englishmen keep farther apart than Frenchmen or South Americans.[19] This whole subject was first touched upon by E.T. Hall in a book called *The Silent Language* and later more fully developed in *The Hidden Dimension*.[20] In the latter work he introduced the term proxemics for the study of the way people perceive space and use it in various cultures.

How can we interpret the territorial behavior of societies and cultures from what we know about personal space and small-group proxemics? It is still a cloudy problem, but some things are becoming clear. Psychologists and geographers have had occasion to refer to ranking and hierarchies in human society. W. Christaller made this a central issue in his work on urban centers; in A.K. Philbrick's book, *This Human World*, it is a dominant theme. In R. Sommer's 1969 book, *Personal Space: the Behavioral Basis of Design*, the idea that human territorial organization relates to rank and hierarchy is explored in some detail. Perhaps an example from Africa will be useful. In a recent study of the city of Mombasa,

where more than a dozen of Kenya's tribal peoples are represented by substantial numbers in the population of some 200,000, it was noted that the people of the "stronger" tribal groups generally possessed better residential locations than those of "weaker" tribal groups. The strengths of several of the major tribal peoples in Kenya may be a matter for debate, but their influence in the government is a good indicator. In any case, few would argue that the Kikuyu and the Luo hold positions of power compared to, say, the Nandi and the Gyriama. Now, this indefinite power hierarchy is somehow reflected by the urban residential pattern in Mombasa—the spatial adjustment those peoples have come to within the confines of that city. This is an example of *dominance behavior*—and it may apply not just to tribal peoples living in urban centers, but to nation-states and even power blocs, as well.

Combining the concepts of territoriality and dominance behavior, perhaps we may extrapolate to the superimposed boundaries that evolved from truce lines or colonial imposition, to the racial compartmentalization of South Africa (surely an especially good example of dominance behavior), to the ghettoization of U.S. cities, and to the competition for Northern Ireland (where the social order that arose out of dominance behavior is being challenged). In so doing we assume that territoriality in man does exist more or less as Ardrey proposed, and that dominance behavior prevails—a sort of generally accepted superior-inferior, dominant-subordinate hierarchy that operates vertically and is expressed spatially. To repeat—these are still assumptions of whose details we cannot yet be sure.

One area about which there is still much uncertainty lies in the roots of territoriality. If, indeed, territoriality is a phenomenon of human behavior, is it instinctive or has it been acquired and modified by learning—through cultural evolution? In other words, is it less an "imperative" than Ardrey suggested? And the concomitant, human aggression—is it similarly universal and is it genetic in its origins or is it neither?[21] There are social scientists who think that the answers given by Ardrey and Lorenz, among others, are inaccurate. E.W. Soja writes:

Only when human society began to increase significantly in scale and complexity did territorial-

---

[19]R. Sommer, *Personal Space: the Behavioral Basis of Design*, Englewood Cliffs, Prentice-Hall, 1969, p. 27.

[20]E.T. Hall, *The Silent Language*, Doubleday, Garden City, 1959, and E.T. Hall, *The Hidden Dimension*, Garden City, Doubleday, 1966.

[21]For a discussion of this position see K. Lorenz, *On Aggression*, New York, Harcourt, Brace and World, 1966.

ity reassert itself as a powerful behavioral and organizational phenomenon. But this was a cultural and symbolic territoriality, not the primitive territoriality of the primates and other animals-
. . . Thus, although "cultural" territoriality fundamentally begins with the origins of the cultured primate, man, it achieves a central prominence in society only with the emergence of the state. And it probably attains its fullest flowering as an organizational basis for society in the formally structured, rigidly compartmentalized, and fiercely defended nation-state of the present day.[22]

What Soja is saying, of course, is that territoriality as it is expressed by our complex societies is not the same phenomenon as that which commanded out distant ancestors—or our animal contemporaries. Nor, according to some anthropologists, is man the "naked ape," driven by savagery and killer instincts. A. Alland argues forcefully that aggressiveness and territoriality are not universal human "imperatives" at all; in fact, he goes so far as to say that territoriality is born with and nurtured by culture.[23] Viewing some "primitive" peoples like those still living a hunting-and-gathering existence, Alland notes that these have the weakest of territorial imperatives; supposedly they are the ones that should have the strongest instinct of this sort, if territoriality is indeed a biological urge. And Alland is not so convinced either about the vigor with which nation-states are inevitably defended; he views draft laws, anthem-singing, pledge-reciting, and flag-waving as evidence that states do not find defenders so easy to come by.

The subject of territoriality and its many ramifications is obviously of crucial interest to political geographers. They are among those new dimensions that revitalize the field.

REFERENCES

Alford, R.R., "The Role of Social Class in American Voting Behavior," Western Political Quarterly, 16, 1 (March, 1963), 80–86.

Alland, A., The Human Imperative, New York, Columbia University Press, 1972.

Ardrey, R., The Territorial Imperative, New York, Atheneum Press, 1966.

Barnett, J.R., "Scale, Process, and the Diffusion of a Political Movement," Proc. A.A.G., 4 (1972), 9–14.

Birdsall, S.S., "Preliminary Analysis of the 1968 Wallace Vote in the Southeast," Southeastern Geographer, IX, 2 (November, 1969), 55–66.

Boulding, K.E., "National Images and International Systems," Journal of Conflict Resolution, III, 2 (June, 1959), 120–131.

Brunn, S.D. et al., "Some Spatial Considerations of the Flint Open Housing Referendum," Proc. A.A.G. 1 (1969), 26–32.

———, "The Defeat of a Youngstown School Levy: a Study in Urban-Political Geography," Southeastern Geographer, IX, 2 (November, 1969), 67–79.

Burghardt, A.F., "The Bases of Support for Political Parties in Burgenland," Ann. A.A.G., 54, 3 (September, 1964), 372–390.

Bushman, D.O., and W.R. Stanley, "State Senate Reapportionment in the Southeast," Ann. A.A.G., 61, 4 (December, 1971), 654–670.

Cox, K.R., "Suburbia and Voting Behavior in the London Metropolitan Area," Ann. A.A.G., 58, 2 (March, 1968), 111–127.

———, "The Voting Decision in Intra-Urban Space," Proc. A.A.G., 1 (1969), 43–47.

Crisler, R.M., "Voting Habits in the United States," Geog. Rev. 62, 2 (April, 1952), 300–301.

Dean, V.K. "Geographical Aspects of the Newfoundland Referendum," Ann. A.A.G., 29, 2 (March, 1949), 70–77.

Getis, A., and B.N. Boots, "Spatial Behavior: Rats and Man," Prof. Geog., XXIII, 1 (January, 1971), 11–14.

Gould, P.R., On Mental Maps, Ann Arbor, University of Michigan Department of Geography, 1966.

Hall, E.T., "Proxemics," Current Anthropology, 9 (1968), 83–108.

———, The Hidden Dimension, Garden City, N.Y., Doubleday, 1966.

———, The Silent Language, Garden City, N.Y., Doubleday, 1959.

Herman, T., "Group Values Toward the National Space: the Case of China," Geog. Rev., 49, 1 (January, 1959), 164–182.

Horton, F.E., and D.R. Reynolds, "An Investigation of Individual Action Spaces: a Progress Report," Proc. A.A.G., 1 (1969), 43–47.

Johnston, R.J., "Activity Spaces and Residential Preferences: Some Tests of the Hypothesis of Sectoral Mental Maps," Econ. Geog., 48, 2 (April, 1972), 199–211.

Kasperson, R.E., "Political Behavior and the Decision-Making Process in the Allocation of Water Resources Between Recreational and Municipal Use," Natural Resources Journal, VIII, 2 (April, 1969), 7–18.

———, "Toward a Geography of Urban Politics: Chicago, a Case Study," Econ. Geog., 41, 2 (April, 1965), 97–107.

———, "Ward Systems and Urban Politics," Southeastern Geographer, IX, 2 (November, 1969), 17–25.

Kates, R.W., Hazard and Choice Perception in Flood Plain Analysis, Chicago, University of Chicago Department of Geography Research Paper No. 78, 1962.

[22]E.W. Soja, The Political Organization of Space, Association of American Geographers, Resource Paper No. 8, 1971, p. 30.

[23]A. Alland, The Human Imperative, New York, Columbia University Press, 1972.

Kelman, H.C. (ed.), *International Behavior: a Social-Psychological Analysis*, New York, Holt, Rinehart & Winston, 1965.

Klineberg, O., *The Human Dimension in International Relations*, New York, Holt, Rinehart & Winston, 1964.

Krebheil, E., "Geographic Influences in British Elections," *Geog. Rev.*, 2, 2 (March, 1916), 419–432.

Lewis, P.F., "Impact of Negro Migration on the Electoral Geography of Flint, Michigan, 1932–1962," *Ann. A.A.G.*, 55, 1 (March, 1965), 1–25.

Lorenz, K. *On Aggression*, New York, Harcourt, Brace & World, 1966.

Lowenthal, D. (ed.), *Environmental Perception and Behavior*, Chicago, University of Chicago Department of Geography Research Paper No. 109, 1967.

———, "The West Indies Chooses a Capital," *Geog. Rev.*, 68, 3 (July, 1958), 336–364.

Montagu, M.F.A., *Man and Aggression*, New York, Oxford University Press, 1968.

Morris, D., *The Naked Ape*, New York, McGraw-Hill, 1968.

Orr, Jr., D.M. "The Persistence of the Gerrymander in North Carolina Congressional Redistricting," *Southeastern Geographer*, IX, 2 (November, 1969), 39–54.

Philbrick, A.K., "Principles of Areal Functional Organization in Regional Human Geography," *Econ. Geog.*, 33, 4 (October, 1957), 299–336.

Prescott, J.R.V., "The Function and Methods of Electoral Geography," *Ann. A.A.G.*, 49, 3 (September, 1959), 296–304.

Reynolds, D.R., and J.C. Archer, "An Inquiry into the Spatial Basis of Electoral Geography," *Discussion Paper Series*, No. 11, Iowa City, University of Iowa Department of Geography, n.d.

Roberts, M.C., and K.W. Rumage, "Spatial Variations in Urban Left-Wing Voting in the London Metropolitan Area," *Ann. A.A.G.*, 55, 2 (March, 1965), 161–178.

Rowley, G., "Electoral Behavior and Electoral Behaviour: a Note on Certain Recent Developments in Electoral Geography," *Prof. Geog.*, XXI, 6 (November, 1969), 398–400.

Rushton, G., "Analysis of Spatial Behavior by Revealed Space Preference," *Ann. A.A.G.*, 59, 2 (June, 1969), 391–400.

Salter, P.S., and R.C. Mings, "A Geographic Aspect of the 1968 Miami Racial Disturbance: a Preliminary Investigation," *Prof. Geog.*, XXI, 2 (March, 1969), pp. 79–86.

Smith, H.R., and J.F. Hart, "The American Tariff Map," *Geog. Rev.*, 65, 3 (July, 1955), 327–346.

Smyth, W.J., "Social Space in an Irish Rural Community," (Abstract), *Proc. A.A.G.*, 3 (1971), 195.

Soja, E.W., *The Geography of Modernization in Kenya*, Syracuse, Syracuse University Press, 1968.

———, *The Political Organization of Space*, Washington, A.A.G. Resource Paper No. 8, 1971.

Sommer, R., *Personal Space: the Behavioral Basis of Design*, Englewood Cliffs, Prentice Hall, 1969.

Sonnenfeld, J., "Geography, Perception, and the Behavioral Environment," in P.W. English and R.C. Mayfield, *Man, Space, and Environment*, New York, Oxford University Press, 1972, pp. 244–251.

Stea, D., "Space, Territoriality, and Human Movements," *Landscape*, 15 (1965), 13–16.

Tuan, Yi-Fu, "Environmental Psychology: a Review," *Geog. Rev.*, 62, 2 (April, 1972), 245–256.

Wirt, F., "The Political Sociology of American Suburbia: a Reinterpretation," *American Sociological Review*, 25 (1960), 514–526.

Wolpert, J., "Behavioral Aspects of the Decision to Migrate," *Papers*, Regional Science Association, 15 (1965), 17–29.

———, "Departures from the Usual Environment in Locational Analysis," *Ann. A.A.G.*, 60, 2 (April, 1970), 220–229.

———, "The Decision Process in Spatial Context," *Ann. A.A.G.*, 54, 4 (October, 1964), 537–558.

Wright, J.K. "Voting Habits in the United States," *Geog. Rev.*, 22, 3 (October, 1932), 666–672.

Part
IV
Policies and Practices

CHAPTER
16
UNITARY AND FEDERAL STATES

Political geographers are naturally interested in the ways in which states are organized in spatial-political terms. Such organization is the result of lengthy processes of experimentation and modification—processes that have not ceased. State systems are continuously being altered, sometimes through deliberation and consultation and at other times because the system cannot withstand certain centrifugal pressures or forces. We are all aware that the federal state that is the United States of America is not the United States of 100 or even 25 years ago. For the France of today, Napoleon laid certain foundations, but the France inherited by Charles de Gaulle was something very different. In recent years Nigeria, Pakistan, Malaysia, and the United Kingdom, among other states, have been confronted by the kinds of circumstances that dictate change. The political system—and the politicoterritorial framework—of these states had in some manner failed, and a new order was necessary. This new order can in part be read off the map. Nigeria established an entirely new federal framework following the Biafra secession movement, Malaysia lost Singapore, its leading city, the United Kingdom was forced to reassess its position in Northern Ireland, and Pakistan lost its eastern flank.

THE UNITARY STATE

In the broadest terms, we recognize *unitary* states and *federal* states. The word "unitary" derives from the Latin *unitas* (unity), which in turn comes from *unus* (one). It thus emphasizes the oneness of the state and implies a high degree of internal homogeneity and cohesiveness. The term "federal," on the other hand, has its origins in the Latin *foederis*, meaning league. Its implication is one of alliance, contract, and coexistence of the state's internal, diverse regions and peoples. The unitary state, therefore, theoretically has but one strong focus, and its internal differ-

ences are few; the federal state may have a number of separate foci, and its component areas may have quite different characteristics.

In practice the two terms refer to the functions of the central authority of the state. All states, as we have seen, are divided for political purposes into administrative units. Each of these units has a local government to deal with local matters. In the case of the unitary state, the central authority controls these local governments and determines how much power they shall have. The central authority may, under certain circumstances, take over temporarily the functions of a local government. It can impose its decisions upon all local governments, irrespective of their unpopularity in certain parts of the country. In a national emergency the central authority can assume greater powers to meet the crisis, while in times of stability it may grant increased responsibilities to local governments.

Under the federal system, as we shall see in detail later, the rights and responsibilities of local governments are protected by constitutional stipulations. Here the central authority cannot simply assume the functions of local governments temporarily, to relinquish them only when its demands have been met. The individual regions of the state possess a certain degree of autonomy which is protected, and there is a constant watch against overcentralization. This is what permits diverse peoples and even cultures to join in a single state. Their first allegiance may be to their own region, but their ultimate loyalty is to the state. Centrifugal forces which might rent a unitary state apart can be accommodated in a federal state.

From the foregoing statements, it should not be difficult to formulate a model unitary state. In the first place, such a state should not be in the "large" or "very large" categories of state territory. The larger a state, the more likely it is to straddle more than one cultural region, and the more varied will be the historical mainstreams to have touched its peoples. The larger a state, the greater may be the physiographic impediments to effective communications and transportation. Effective control by the central government of all parts of the state is a prime requirement of the smooth-functioning unitary state, and anything that would intensify the centrifugal forces present in any state reduces the efficacy of a single, central authority.

Secondly, the ideal unitary state is compact in shape. A fragmented or prorupt territory may present obstacles to unity and cohesion, and require a measure of autonomy for various individual regions. When a state is fragmented and the separate sections lie hundreds of miles apart, it is unlikely that the population is homogeneous. Racial, religious, and linguistic diversity are likely in a fragmented state, and only a federal political framework may function to the satisfaction of the majority of the people.

Thirdly, the unitary state should be relatively densely populated and effectively inhabited. There should be no vast territory with separate concentrations of population, interspersed with empty and unproductive areas. This leads to isolation and regionalism.

Finally, the unitary state should have only one core area. Multicore states reflect strong regionalism, an undesirable condition in unitary states. Theoretically the most suitable location for the single core area of the unitary state is central to its compact territory. This brings all peripheral areas within the shortest distance of the capital city and makes the presence of the core area and capital strongly felt in all parts of the state. With reference to the capital city, it is clear that Jefferson's Law of the Primate City is especially applicable to the model unitary state. A single urban center which is disproportionately large and influential in the affairs of the state, where the central authority resides, and where national feeling is strongest, obviously constitutes a binding agent and a focus not only for the core area but for the state as a whole.

EVOLUTION AND PRESENT DISTRIBUTION

Many of the unitary states in existence today do not conform to the requirements of the model just described. Several examples that show a close approximation to the ideal occur in Western Europe. The old European states

fostered a strong central authority, and it is here that the unitary state as it is known today emerged. But this system of politicoterritorial organization has been copied in many other parts of the world—and the copies are often far removed from the original. Nevertheless, states that must be described as unitary outnumber the federal states of the world by about five to one. In 1972 there were less than two dozen federal states and over a hundred unitary states on the world map.

Even in Europe, comparatively few unitary states feature the conditions embodied in the model described. Denmark, for example, is a smoothly functioning unitary state, but it has a fragmented territory. Belgium is indeed a compact state, but its core area is indistinct and its internal cultural division (between Fleming and Walloon) is regionally expressed and constitutes a major centrifugal force. This division obstructs the functioning of government and frequently leads to internal dissension. Italy, another European unitary state, has an elongated territory which is also fragmented. A brief examination of the socioeconomic geography of Italy will indicate to what extent the north and south are opposites in this state.

The state that is often described as the best example of the type is France. Though large by European standards (213,000 square miles), this country, apart from insignificant Corsica, is compact in shape, has a core area with a lengthy history and at its heart a capital city of undoubted eminence, as well as a large politically very conscious population with much historical momentum and strong traditions. Modern France was forged, in effect, by Napoleon, who swept away the old system of loosely tied divisions (Artois, Piccardy, etc.) and replaced them with ninety separate districts, "departments," based upon rough equality of size. Each of these departments possessed the same relationship to the central political authority as did the next, and each sent representatives to Paris. Napoleon also developed an entirely new system of communications, focusing very strongly on Paris, to act as a unifying agent. Until the days of Napoleon, allegiances in France had been to individual divisions rather than to France, despite the forces of revolution and the overthrow of the monarchy. Today, the French nation-state is close to reality.

Many of the formerly colonial territories of the world have adopted a unitary form of organization, especially those in which the indigenous population has taken control. In those areas where Europeans remain dominant (Australia, Canada, Brazil) the federal arrangement has sometimes been employed. In Latin America, all of the Central American republics are unitary states. In South America, Colombia, Ecuador, Peru, Chile, Bolivia, and Paraguay function as unitary states. In Africa and the Middle East, all Arab countries are unitary states, while the majority of the emergent black African states also have chosen this form of organization. Subsaharan Africa affords some excellent examples of recent experimentation with European concepts of government. The former French territories with only one exception have become unitary states, but some of the former British dependencies have adopted a federal form of territorial organization. British-influenced unitary states in Africa include Kenya, Tanzania, Sierra Leone, and Ghana. The case of Ghana is especially interesting, for there are several bases of comparison with Nigeria, which has become a federal state.[1]

In Asia, China is the largest unitary state in terms of both area and population. The Southeast Asian states, with the exception of Malaysia, are also unitary states, as are Afghanistan and Ceylon. Again, the European contribution can be recognized: the fragments of the former French Indo-Chinese realm have become unitary states, as have Indonesia (the former Netherlands East Indies) and the Philippines.

Viewing these unitary states in relation to the model described previously, it is clear that comparatively few approach the stated ideal. A number are territorially fragmented, including Japan, the Philippines, Indonesia, and New Zealand. Several are in size categories that would appear to contradict the required internal homogeneity and unity, such as China and Sudan. The case of Sudan is especially revealing, for its huge territory extends into the Arab world as well as black Africa:

During the entire colonial period, the focus of activity, political as well as economic, was in the region north of 12 degrees North Latitude. The southern part of the Sudan, while under British administration, remained almost completely separated and isolated from such progress as took place

elsewhere, and was little involved in the continuing administrative struggle among the Egyptians, northern Sudanese, and British. To the linguistic, ethnic, physiographic, and religious individuality of the south was added a form of administrative separation which had the character of a protectorate in all but name. Thus, rather than submerging the large-scale regional differences of the Sudan, British administration actually helped foster them, leaving the problem of actual integration and adjustment to the independent State. . . . When independence came, and even before the actual date of its achievement, violence accompanied the withdrawal of British government and military personnel from the south and their replacement by Sudanese (of course, northern Moslems). . . . Refugees streamed over the Uganda and Congo borders . . . in northern Uganda there was talk of uniting the southern extreme of the Sudan with Uganda. . . . these suggestions . . . were undeniably popular with a segment of the population of the southern Sudan [because] people in the south consider themselves occupied by the north. . . .

. . . The heart of the Sudan lies at the confluence of the two major arteries, the Blue and White Nile Rivers; there is the largest irrigated region of cash cropping, the capital, Khartum, with its sister city of Omdurman (with a combined population of 500,000), the focus of the railroad system, and the northern limit of uninterrupted navigation on both Nile Rivers. This is also the most densely populated area of the country, producing by far the bulk of the exported products. It has long been the focus of administrative, religious, and educational activity, and was the core area of the Fung Empire of old. It lies 490 miles by rail from Port Sudan (50,000), to which exports are funneled, and forms the major domestic market for the country. . . .

The development of the Sudan has been concentrated in this (northern) region to such an extent that in 1964 the main (southern) town, Juba, possessed better connections with the Congo and Uganda than it did with the rest of the Sudan. . . . Democratic government, predictably, has faltered, and military leadership has replaced it. Efforts to develop the south, to educate and integrate the (southern) peoples in the framework of the country are under way, but the process will be a slow and laborious one.[2]

Another group of unitary states possess more than one core area, although it may be argued that the core areas of several of these states are yet too indistinct and undeveloped to be so labeled. Nevertheless, Ecuador and Colombia in South America, and Tanzania and Chad in Africa, display multicore characteristics which reflect centrifugal forces with-

---

[1]For a study of the Ghanaian example see D.S. Rotchild, "On the Application of the Westminster Model to Ghana," *The Centennial Review*, IV (Fall, 1960), 465.

[2]H.J. de Blij, "Sudan: Bridge Between African and Arab?" in *A Geography of Subsaharan Africa*, Chicago, Rand McNally, 1964, pp. 312, 313, 318, 319.

in these unitary states. This phenomenon is not confined to areas outside Europe. The United Kingdom, Spain, and Sweden likewise possess more than one core area, while functioning as unitary states.

TYPES

Although unitary states are based upon the premise of national unity and considerable homogeneity, their high degree of political centralization often belies their internal cultural variety. The imposition of the will of a minority upon the majority of the people within a state may produce a unitary state which might function better as a federal state. In certain former colonies, indigenous, Europeanized elites have taken control and have administered the country in much the same way as did the colonists themselves. Latin America has shown that such political arrangements can be very durable. In such unitary states, the response to heterogeneity and regional problems often is an even greater degree of concentration of power in the central government. The flexibility of the federal arrangement would, theoretically at least, result in just the opposite action.

Whatever the mode of government in the unitary state—whether a monarchy, a dictatorship, or a democracy—certain adjustments are made over time in the politicoterritorial system which reflect the internal conditions of the state. As was pointed out earlier, some unitary states have emerged simply because of the almost total assent and satisfaction on the part of the population with regard to the existing authority. On the other hand, certain other unitary states have seen an increase in the power vested in the central authority, whether a person, a group of persons, or the representatives of a minority ethnic group. As we shall see, such changes—whether in the direction of greater centralization of power or the reverse—often reflect geographical conditions within the state. In the emergent states, tribalism remains a force that obstructs the evolution of real nations; in many of those states the governing authority has taken over more and more of the powers of the local chiefs. In some older unitary states, on the other hand, local governments are given an increasing number of functions, indicating that regionalism, while not completely eliminated, no longer forms a threat to the state system as a whole. Indeed, it is possible to identify unitary states in which government is less centralized than it is in some states which are, on paper, federal states. The following types may be recognized.

1. Centralized

This is the "average" unitary state, true to the basic rule of centralization of governmental authority, but without excesses either in the direction of totalitarianism or in the direction of devolution of power. Normally in such a state, stability has been achieved by virtue of the homogeneity of the population and the binding elements of culture and traditions—a general approval of the state on the part of the nation.

States in this category usually possess only one core area. They are generally older states, in the mature stage of the Van Valkenburg classification. Most of the examples are in fact found in Europe, such as Denmark, Sweden, and the Netherlands. These three monarchies, by their very retention of this form of government, reflect the satisfaction of the majority of the population with the status quo. In centralized unitary states, the population participates in the government through the democratic election of representatives. No single ethnic minority or political party has sole claim to leadership. This is not to suggest that there is no ethnic diversity within centralized unitary states, and no regionalism. Despite its small size, the Netherlands has at times been mildly aware of regionalism in Friesland, with Frisians demanding that their language be taught in Holland's schools if Frisians must learn Dutch. The overriding factors of proximity, interdigitation, interdependence, and historical association produce the centripetal forces that bind the state together.

Other centralized unitary states are Italy, Ireland, Finland, and France. The case of France once again provides useful insights, for the shift toward greater power for the central authority (specifically, the chief of state) which accompanied the demise of the Fourth and the ascent of the Fifth Republic was related to problems in the Empire, first in Indo-China, then in Algeria, and barely warded off in black Africa. Elsewhere, Japan and New Zealand, and perhaps Uruguay, fit this category.

2. Highly Centralized

In this type of unitary state, internal diversity or dissension, ethnic heterogeneity, tribalism, and/or regionalism, threatening to disrupt the state system, are countered by tight and omnipotent control. This authority may be in the hands of an individual or a parliament. The leader or leaders often are the representatives of a minority group within the country, or of the only political party that may operate within the state. Three major groups of states may be recognized within this category: unitary states within the Communist sphere, one-party emergent states in Africa and other parts of the decolonized world, and dictatorships elsewhere.

Although the Soviet Union and Yugoslavia are both federal states, the majority of the Communist-bloc states are unitary states and highly centralized. Here, the geographical bases for unitary politicoterritorial organization are reinforced by the character of Communist control. Single-core, relatively densely populated, compact states such as Poland, Hungary, Rumania, and Bulgaria would appear suited to the unitary system under any circumstances, but the nature of Communist control over practically every aspect of state organization—the means of production, communications, education, etc.—differentiates this group from those described as centralized (above). Despite recent evidence of amelioration in some Communist states, virtual dictatorships still prevail in others, for example, in Albania. The largest unitary state functioning today, China, fits this category.

States displaying these characteristics are, however, not confined to the Communist world. Portugal and Spain in Europe, Paraguay and Guatemala in Latin America, Ethiopia and Ghana in Africa, and Iran and Indonesia in Asia are some of the non-Communist, highly centralized unitary states of today, and it is not difficult to list others. Some of these states have recently emerged from several generations of colonial rule, and although some were endowed with a multiparty system, many have become what is described as "one-party democracies."

The case of Ghana illustrates well this shift toward increasing centralization. Ghana attained independence in 1957, and was left with a constitution and governmental apparatus that was based upon the Westminster model. There were regional and tribal problems (in parts of northern Ghana the majority of the people favored a delay in the granting of independence), and the Opposition Party in the Ghana Parliament was essentially a regional phenomenon. As government plans and projects were thwarted, and the power of tribal chiefs continued to influence Ghanaian politics, the government party began to seek ways to diminish the effectiveness of the Opposition. The main object was to gain more control over the recalcitrant north and to silence the chiefs. This eventually led to the elimination of the Opposition, the proclamation of a republic, the establishment of a one-party state, and the assumption of virtually dictatorial powers by former President Nkrumah. In one way or another this pattern has been and will be repeated in other emergent states, and it is perhaps reasonable to describe it as inevitable in most cases.

In certain other emergent states the shift toward highly centralized control on the part of a single party, small group of individuals, or single individual has simply involved the transfer of power from the European colonists to a local, acculturated, and privileged elite. This has occurred in some of the French-influenced states in Africa and Asia, and the example of South Viet Nam requires no elaboration.

3. Adjusted

The unitary system is capable of adjustment in the direction of decentralization as well as greater centralization. Multicore unitary states may show such adjustment, as do unitary states in which regional identities are strong. In this case, the state is likely to have functioned for a very long time, with several results. First, stability and permanency have been achieved, and the state system is satisfactory to the population. Second, the concentration of the many functions of government in one place is beginning to obstruct the efficiency of the administration. Third, the congested government departments begin to place a part of their burden upon local authorities. This, of course, means the execution of government directives rather than decision making on the part of these local authorities, but the direction of change is opposite to that, for instance, of Ghana.

Not many adjusted unitary states can be identified. The prime example is that of the United Kingdom, which has more than one core (London region and Edinburgh-Glasgow region), several distinct and individual regions (Wales, Scotland, Ulster), and a tremendous bureaucratic complex in London. Decentralization has long been in progress, and although Welsh and Scottish nationalists have decried the state system as favoring England, the fact is that their scope for regional expression and individualism is probably greater here than it is for any other region forming part of a unitary state.

In Northern Ireland, it has not been enough, however. The partition of Ireland into the republic and Ulster always had been a source of friction and even some intermittent violence, but in 1970 the tension erupted into near-civil war. Charges of discrimination by the minority catholic population against the Ulster protestants were underscored by bombings, street fighting, and other forms of violence. The Catholics allegedly received assistance from the Irish Republican Army; the Protestants argued that they possessed insufficient power to end the civil strife. British troops were able in some measure to restore order, but they were incapable of anticipating the random acts of terrorism that marked the early 1970's. Britain's system could accommodate the ephemeral nationalisms of Wales and Scotland, but it proved vulnerable in the face of the deep divisions within Ulster and the pressures inherent in the proximity of an irredentist Ireland.

THE FEDERAL STATE

Would the problems faced by the United Kingdom in Northern Ireland have been less intense if the United Kingdom had a different form of politicoterritorial organization? Would a greater (or lesser) degree of autonomy for Northern Ireland have constituted a better formula than the existing one? These are unanswerable questions, but they are ponderable indeed. Whenever a unitary state faces regionally expressed difficulties, one is given to speculate whether a *federal* system might have accommodated the forces involved more effectively.

In the unitary state, the central government exercises its power equally over all parts of the state. The federal framework, on the other hand, is one that permits a central government to represent the various entities within the state where they happen to have common interests—defense, foreign affairs, communications, etc.—while allowing these various entities to retain their own identities and to have their own laws, policies, and customs in certain fields. Thus each entity (such as a

state, province, or region) has its own capital city, its own governor or premier, and its own internal budget. And each entity is in turn represented in the federal capital, to have a say in matters concerning the entire federation.

History has shown that federal states, like unitary states, evolve and change over time. In North America, when the thirteen states found themselves with more common interests to unite them than conflicting ideas to divide them, a federation emerged which is, in many ways, a far cry from the United States of today. The number of functions of government has grown tremendously, and the federal government must involve itself more and more in the affairs of the states—affairs that at one time would have been considered domestic to these states. Thus, just as some unitary states show signs of adjustment in the direction of decentralization, many federations are shifting toward greater centralization of authority. In fact, some federal states are so highly centralized as to function, in effect, as unitary states.

Theoretically, the federal framework is especially suitable for states in the large and very large size categories. Poor communications and ineffective occupation of large areas within the state still affect, for example, Brazil and Zaïre. Such impediments to contact and control might disrupt a unitary state, while a federal framework can withstand these centrifugal forces. In terms of shape, it is obvious that fragmented states and states with pronounced and important proruptions may be best served by a federal system. An elongated state possessing more than one core area also might turn to a federal arrangement.

Federal states can adjust to the presence of more than one core area (or a number of subsidiary cores) more easily than unitary states. A number of the federal states in existence today are multicore states, and in the case of Canada, Nigeria, Pakistan, and Australia it is probable that only a federal constitution could have bound the diverse regions together—in the case of Pakistan, even temporarily. Thus the federal state often has a number of individual population agglomerations, separated by large areas which are sparsely populated and relatively unproductive. These population clusters and their urban foci exist in some degree of isolation from each other. Canada and Australia, two of the largest federations in terms of area and two of the smallest in terms of population, illustrate this principle.

Ideally, the government of the federal state functions in a capital city which is located in an area of federal territory, cut off from the state for the specific purpose of administration. This forestalls any friction over the choice of an existent major city as the capital and prevents regional favoritism from occurring, as it has in some federal states. In Nigeria, an existing city was separated from the Western Region (one of the political divisions of the state) and made the capital, for two reasons: first, it was a long-term colonial capital and housed most government records and existing facilities, and second, it happens to be the leading port of the country, guaranteeing the landlocked north an exit through a federal rather than a regional port.

The federal arrangement, also, is a political solution for those territories occupied by peoples of widely different ethnic origins, languages, religions, or cultures. This is especially true in those cases where these differences have regional expression, in that various peoples see individual parts of their country as a homeland. The promise of an autonomous Macedonian Republic, part of a Balkan Federation, rallied Macedonians around Tito's war effort. Although the Macedonian Republic (which was to include parts of Greece and Bulgaria as well as Yugoslavia) did not materialize, Macedonians today have a small, national territory within the Yugoslav Federal State. For them, it has been the only alternative to absorption, and it constitutes a closer approximation to their original goal than they have enjoyed in centuries. In a unitary Bulgaria, such status would have been impossible.

Federal frameworks, by their flexibility, have been able to accommodate expanding territories. Provisions were made for areas that were not yet incorporated; the status of incorporated territories was changed subsequently. Both the United States and the Union of Soviet Socialist Republics have within the past few years altered the political status of certain territories. The Soviet Union has elevated the status of Tannu Tuva, and the United States has added Alaska and Hawaii to its membership. This process is carried out more easily in the federal state than it is in the unitary state. A number of the younger federations of the emergent world are contemplating revision of their internal boundaries and, hence, their federal parliaments. Their constitutions provide for such alterations.

Another advantage offered by the federal arrangement is its encouragement of individual and local enterprise. Economic development in the United States took place as fast as it did largely for this reason; the westward push of Brazil, as exemplified by the relocation of the capital, is an effort to stimulate a similar chain of events in its hinterlands. Of course, this accommodation of individualism has not prevented the emergence of conflicts of interest. Some, like the Civil War in the United States, helped bring about revisions in the federal framework; others resulted in the collapse of the state itself. The French-British conflict in Canada is testing the Canadian federal system today. Clashes also have occurred between state and federal interests, and as in the case of the unitary state, the key to an effectively functioning government lies in efficient communication systems, which increase intrastate and interregional circulation, help diminish differences, and tend to bind the various regions closer to the federal government.

In a few instances in recent history, the principle of federation has been employed by a minority group to gain control over adjacent territory. We have seen that minority groups may rule in unitary states; an equivalent exists here. The prime example is the now-defunct Central African Federation, which survived a decade, having been created in 1953. In effect, the white minority of Southern Rhodesia sought to extend its influence into Northern Rhodesia and Nyasaland by "federating" the three territories and placing them under a federal government seated in Salisbury. Black African opposition to federation was almost universal, and the federation survived until Nyasaland became the independent state of Malawi. The absorption of some of the "republics" of the Soviet Union reflect aims that are not altogether dissimilar. Georgians and Armenians are encouraged to retain their culture and identity, but by educational and other means their allegiance is slowly diverted from their region to the central authority of a Russian state.

When, therefore, we examine a list of federal states of the world, we find that several are in the very large or large size category, that populations tend to be sparse and widely dispersed, that multicore development has frequently taken place, and that several large cities form prominent and distinct foci. For comparative purposes, a number of unitary states also is included in Table 1.

another way, the centripetal forces must outweigh the centrifugal forces present in any federal state. Some federal constitutions, indeed, provide for the possibility of secession on the part of any participating territory,

Table I—FEDERAL AND UNITARY STATES: POPULATION DENSITYa

Federal State	Size Square Miles	Population Density	Unitary State	Size Square Miles	Population Density
Australia	2,967,909	4.1	United Kingdom	94,216	589
Canada	3,851,809	5.5	Netherlands	41,140	916
Brazil	3,286,470	27.6	Belgium	11,784	820
United States	3,615,210	56.6	France	210,038	241
Russia	8,600,350	28.1	Denmark	17,169	269
Argentina	1,072,157	22.7	Poland	120,756	271
Venezuela	352,143	29.5	Austria	32,374	228
Switzerland	15,945	388	Tanzania	364,900	36.4
Yugoslavia	98,766	208	Colombia	439,735	46.5
Nigeria	356,669	186	Chad	495,750	7.1

aFigures are derived from Britannica Book of the Year 1971, Chicago, Encyclopaedia Britannica, 1971, p. 604.

TYPES

"A federation," wrote Professor K.W. Robinson in an article about Australian federalism, "is the most geographically expressive of all political systems. It is based on the existence of regional differences, and recognizes the claims of the component areas to perpetuate their individual characters . . . Federation does not create unity out of diversity; rather, it enables the two to coexist."[1] In the creation of the state system, internal variety and diversity can be treated in two ways. One way, as we noted earlier in this chapter, is to render the state the great equalizer, the eliminator of internal differences, even to the point of making certain expressions of regional individuality illegal. The other way seeks to permit the perpetuation of internal contrasts and to provide the possibility of coexistence within one state of peoples with varied backgrounds and interests. Thus the advantages of participation in the state must, for all these peoples, outweigh the liabilities that inevitably are involved as well. To put it

should the people of that territory be dissatisfied with their lot within the framework of the state.

Such an agreement may have been made at the time the federal state was forged—but could it become operational today? There is a clause in the Soviet federal framework that allows for secession, but who seriously believes that such secession, say by Armenia or Latvia, would really be tolerated? As we enter the final quarter of the twentieth century, we observe that federal states born of one set of circumstances are now sustained by conditions that are quite different. Thus we ought to look at the fundamental stimuli that led to the early federations as well as the functioning federal systems that have grown from those beginnings.

Most of the federal states of the world were established specifically to solve politicogeographical problems existing in these states as they consolidated. The great majority of the world's federations are in the "new" world—in the Americas and Australia—and in the "emergent" world, in recently decolonized areas. Canada, the United States, and Mexico are federal states, as are Venezuela, Brazil, and

[1]K.W. Robinson, "Sixty Years of Federation in Australia," Geog. Rev. 50, 1 (January, 1961), 2.

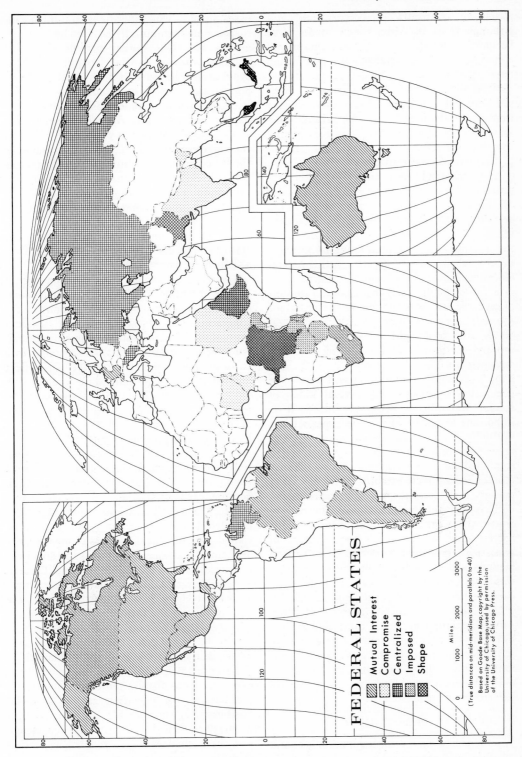

FEDERAL STATES

Mutual Interest
Compromise
Centralized
Imposed
Shape

(True distances on mid-meridians and parallels 0 to 40)

Based on Goode Base Map, copyright by the
University of Chicago, used by permission
of the University of Chicago Press.

Miles
0   1000   2000   3000

Argentina. Australia is a federation, and although most of Africa's new states have become unitary states, some have chosen and achieved a federal arrangement (and some have had federalism thrust upon them!). Among other decolonized territories, both India and Pakistan emerged as federations. It is from the study of these new federations and a view of how the older ones are functioning that we can learn much about this form of politicoterritorial organization.

Any such study soon proves that there are different *types* of federal states. In some present-day federal states, such as Australia and Argentina, internal variety and diversity seem so insignificant (compared to that existing in other countries) that a unitary arrangement might be just as effective. Other federal states, including Canada and Nigeria, incorporate the sort of diversity that a certain amount of give and take was and remains essential for the well-being of the state. In still other federal states, the geographical obstacles to any unitary system were such as to render a federal arrangement imperative. On the basis of these factors (as well as others that will emerge in the following discussion), several kinds of federal states have been recognized. It is important to realize that these types are not mutually exclusive, for the elements of two or more kinds of federalism may be recognized in some federal states existing today. Furthermore, a federal state established for one set of reasons may continue to exist today for an entirely different set of reasons. The case of South Africa exemplifies both instances: this federal state was originally the result of an armistice agreement between two warring factions, and the major element in its creation was *compromise*. But today, the erstwhile enemies have grown together, and they face a totally new threat in the advance of black African nationalism. Hence *mutual interest* is by far the stronger centripetal force in the state at the present time. In the classification that follows, the causes underlying the formation of the state take precedence over those that are paramount at the present time.

1. Mutual Interest

In some federal states, the population is bound together by common ethnic origins, a single language, a joint economic effort, and shared political objectives. This, thus, is the federal state that might well function as a unitary state without fragmenting. In certain other

cases, peoples who differ in several important respects may temporarily be faced by the same enemy, and their mutual interest may lie in warding off that danger. Examples of both types exist. The federal state of Australia has a population marked by a common (English) language, a fear of imperialist activity in the Pacific, and economic vigor. Professor Robinson's case study quoted previously indicates the degree of mutual interest of the peoples of the six colonies. The United States of America constitutes another mutual interest federation, and while the joint concern of the original thirteen states no longer faces the United States today, the strength and eminence of the country are based upon the contributions made by all; thus every state has a stake in its perpetuation.

The case of Canada illustrates change in another direction. Canada is a bilingual federal state, and its present political geography might suggest to the observer that this is not a mutual interest federation. French regionalism, even separatism, in Quebec points to a cultural division which hardly seems to reflect mutual interest.[2] But the state undoubtedly has its origins in the mutual interests of the residents of British North America, a certain degree of compromise with and on the part of French-speaking residents notwithstanding.

A comparison between Canada and Australia provides some insights into the nature of federalism and its flexibility. Australia, which became a federal state in 1901, did so with a territory and political framework that have changed but little in the ensuing decades. Canada, on the other hand, has changed a great deal since it attained this status in 1867. Four territorial units joined in the original Canadian federal state: Ontario, Quebec, New Brunswick, and Nova Scotia. These comprise the eastern littoral and major core area of Canada, but the larger portion of Canadian territory was to be joined with the federation at later dates: British Columbia in 1871, Mackenzie District in 1895, Alberta and Saskatchewan in 1905; Newfoundland attained provincial status within the federation as late as 1949. Furthermore, considerable boundary change occurred within the country after federation, and these changes were attended by serious disputes among the member provinces. The boundaries of Ontario, Quebec, and Manitoba

[2]For an impassioned statement of the separatists' view see M. Chaput, *Why I Am a Separatist*, Toronto, The Ryerson Press, 1962.

today are not those of the days when federation was established.

Unlike Australia, also, Canada has seen major changes in its population distribution. The development of the wheat belt in the interior plains led to a westward migration which completely altered the balance of population among the member provinces. Such did not occur in Australia, where the population grew, but where the proportions remained far closer to those prevailing at the time of federation.

Australian population concentrations—indeed, the Australian core areas—lie along the coasts of that country. Canada's greatest population agglomerations, on the other hand, lie along the boundary shared with one of the great world powers of today. In Australia peripheral settlement is mainly related to the water problem; in Canada, to the limitations of the growing season. For Canada there are several important consequences. First, there are a number of effectively landlocked provinces which play a crucial role in the economy of the federation (in Australia, each participating state has its own outlet to the open ocean). Canada's landlocked provinces partake of the country's major core area, they need outlets, and those outlets lie in other provinces. Hence interprovincial communication patterns in Canada look very different from those of Australia, and the federal link here is obviously one involving mutual interest. Second, the history of Canada has been very much affected by a joint concern of the various population groups in the original colonies and territories over the role of the United States. In the nineteenth century the United States was expanding, and despite the definition of the northern boundaries of the United States, the War of 1812 was not forgotten in 1867. Jointly, a challenge from the south could obviously be met more effectively than individually.[3] As Lower has put it: ". . . the American wolf must be kept as far from the British North American door as possible: in fact, but for the loud howling of the American wolf in 1864 and the following years, it is probable that the different provinces would not have come together. . . . This fear of the great, heaving neighbor was reflected in a hundred ways . . ."[4]

But if the United States posed a threat, it also provided an example. The American experiment in federalism was under constant scrutiny by those who eventually erected the Canadian federal state, and many of the lessons learned in the U.S.A. were heeded in Canada.

If Canadian federalism involved mutual interests, it also required a certain degree of compromise. In Australia, as in Canada, the indigenous population was too small and insignificant to produce major problems, and in both countries the vast majority of the population is white. But whereas Australian origins lay virtually solely in one culture, those of Canada were in two—British and French. At the time of federation in Canada, guarantees were written into the constitution to permit those of French origin to perpetuate their heritage. However, in Canada geography has at times seemed to conspire to divide and regionalize: French Canadians were and remain concentrated largely in one province, Quebec. They were not absorbed and assimilated; neither is there the cultural interdigitation of white South Africa. To safeguard French rights, the provinces in Canada were granted powers in areas such as civil law and education; French gained equal status in Quebec, the federal parliament, and the country's courts. But the strength of the Canadian union has been tested, most severely of late, by the dissatisfaction of perhaps a minority of French Canadians with their status as nationals. Quebec nationalism has expressed itself in a variety of ways, including calls for secession and independence. Many French Canadians see the history of Quebec as one of conquest and compromise, and to them, the interests favoring continued participation in the union are decidedly one-sided.

Two other federal states that belong in the present category are the United States of Brazil and Switzerland. The Swiss Confederation began its lengthy evolution as early as 1291, when four cantons found themselves in a position to control trade through the St. Gotthard Pass. The merchants who shipped their goods across the Alps required the help of the local people, and in turn goods and ideas reached these formerly isolated mountain dwellers. They profited immensely from the trade, and one by one adjacent and surrounding cantons joined the original group, which developed into Switzerland's first core area. That core area ultimately shifted to the Swiss

[3]For several views of federal Canada see A.R.M. Lower, F.R. Scott, et. al., *Evolving Canadian Federalism*, Durham, N.C., Duke University Press, 1958.

[4]Lower, *ibid.*, pp. 9, 10. A strong pro-annexation movement existed, for example, in British Columbia.

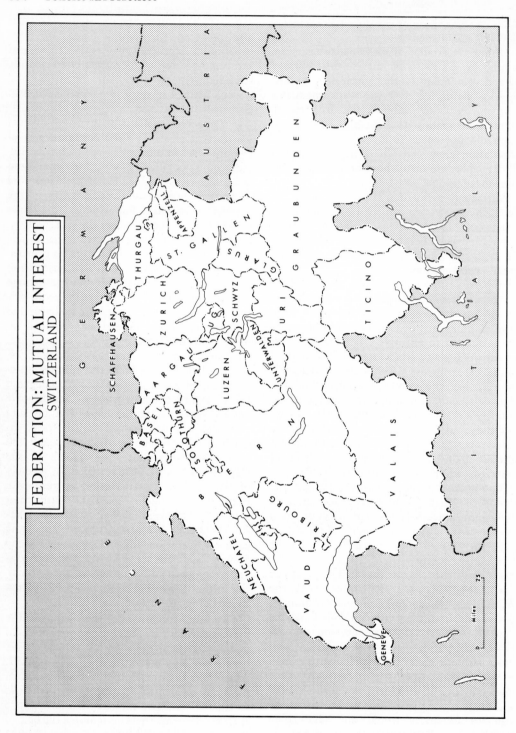

FEDERATION: MUTUAL INTEREST
SWITZERLAND

Plateau, but the Swiss state retained some of the attributes which rendered the first four cantons the heart of the original political entity: the Alps provided a natural defense and lasting security; the peoples have been isolated from the mainstreams of European political conflict for centuries; even with today's modern transport systems, the territory remains of importance in north-south and east-west communications across Europe. Switzerland is a federal state of great internal diversity, and yet its stability is unequaled. Alone in Europe it retains, virtually unchanged, boundaries of a century and a half ago. Alone in Europe it has been neutral through decades of violent conflict. Nevertheless, its six million people are culturally divided as in few other states. Those living in the west, near the French border, speak mainly French. The north and central section of the country is German-speaking. In the southeast, Italian is spoken, as well as an old derivative, Romansh. Neither is the country unified in religious terms. Still, the course of the ship of state itself has become a major rallying point for this divided population. Switzerland's historic neutrality, its nonparticipation in international or regional organizations, and the momentum produced by its seven centuries of independence and national pride have produced the binding forces that hold the state together.

The United States of Brazil is a relatively young state, and its federal system was established quite recently. After its independence in 1822, the country experienced imperial government until 1889, a republican period from 1891 until 1945, and in 1946 adopted its current federal constitution. Although the constitution adopted at the start of the republican period (1891) was modeled to a considerable extent on the American federal experiment, centralization of power and dictatorial rule prevailed until the end of the second World War. Brazil, large and internally diverse, with a peripherally located core area and great contrasts between regions in terms of wealth and development, was divided into twenty-one states and five federal territories, as well as a federal district containing the capital, then Rio de Janeiro. The new capital, Brasilia, lies in a more recently delimited federal district. The terms of the federal system include a stipulation that tax revenues must be distributed on a proportional basis to state and local treasuries. Another goal is the opening up for development of the hitherto Amazon Valley (the states of Amazonas and Para), while the recurrent drought problem of the northeastern *sertao* also received attention.

Brazil contains over ninety million people, which is half the population of South America; its area is only slightly less than half that of the entire continent. In a Latin America that almost everywhere else is Spanish-influenced, Brazil is the legacy of Portuguese colonialism. Mixture of racial groups has taken place here perhaps more completely than in any other country. What has been achieved has often been attained through intense struggles: independence, the abolition of slavery, the termination of the period of dictatorial rule. To Brazil, geography and economics permit no other form of politicoterritorial organization than federalism.

2. Compromise

Some federal states have been established as a result of the willingness of the participating peoples to give up some of their individual advantages in the interests of a greater state. The alternative to federation, in parts of Asia and Africa, is a large number of unitary tribal states, only a few of which might be viable. Thus tribal peoples have been bound together by federal systems, and in return for comparative economic well-being they have had to make sacrifices in such areas as language, education, tariffs, and the like. The case of the former Union (now Republic) of South Africa was mentioned previously, and here is a somewhat different situation. In such formerly colonial federal states as Brazil and Australia, the white, European element in the population has been the controlling influence, and no numerically superior indigenous peoples have been present to threaten white domination. But in South Africa, while the white element still rules, it is confronted today by the ascent of African nationalism to the north. The two major European elements in the population, the Afrikaners and the English, were locked in combat during the Boer War at the turn of the present century. It was a struggle for independence and hegemony on the part of the Boers, and one primarily for economic gain on the part of the British. The War was the end product of a century of friction between these two groups, which had been struggling intermittently ever since the British takeover at the Cape of Good Hope

FEDERATION: MUTUAL INTEREST
BRAZIL

VENEZUELA

GUYANA

COLOMBIA

SURINAM

FRENCH
GUIANA

RIO
BRANCO
(T.F.)

AMAPÁ
(T.F.)

A T L A N T I C

O C E A N

A M A Z O N A S

P A R Á

MARANHAO

CEARÁ

RIO GRANDE
DO NORTE

PARAÍBA

PERNAMBUCO

PIAUI

ALAGOAS

A C R E
(T.F.)

PERU

RONDONIA
(T.F.)

SERGIPE

GOIÁS

BAHIA

MATO
GROSSO

BOLIVIA

D.F.

MINAS
GERAIS

ESPÍRITO SANTO

SAO PAULO

RIO DE
JANEIRO

GUANABARA

CHILE

PARAGUAY

PARANA

SANTA CATARINA

RIO GRANDE
DO SUL

T.F. = FEDERAL TERRITORY

D.F. = FEDERAL DISTRICT

ARGENTINA

URUGUAY

P A C I F I C   O C E A N

0   Miles   500

(1806). At the time of the Boer War, two
political entities in South Africa were British:
the Cape Colony and Natal; two were Boer
republics: the Orange Free State and the South
African Republic (Transvaal). Finally the British, using their coastal territories to advantage, defeated the landlocked Boers, and by
1902 the British took total control. There was
a Boer element which favored carrying on the
war to the finish, and there was a British
viewpoint which held that the Boers should be
kept in serfdom as were the Africans of the

country. But British nineteenth-century liberalism, through the efforts especially of Campbell-Bannerman, prevailed. It was felt that no white people should be kept in the bonds of another white people in the colonies, and so the Boers (Afrikaners) were approached with the aim to establish a federal Union. In 1910, that union—of victorious British and vanquished Boers, in equal partnership—became reality. Extremist elements on both sides bitterly opposed the move, and even the majority had reservations regarding the scheme. But it was agreed that a federal scheme was superior to the status quo. South Africa's federal framework actually functions practically as a unitary state, and centralization has increased since 1948, when the nationalist Afrikaner element took over the reigns from a more moderate British-Afrikaner coalition. At present, though issues occasion-

Ideological focus for a highly centralized federal state born of compromise: the Voortrekker Monument to the early frontiersmen, in the capital city of South Africa, Pretoria. Commemorating the victory at Blood River in 1838, when Boer trekkers defeated an overwhelming force of Zulu warriors, this monument was not dedicated until after the second World War. Indeed, only during the past two decades has the spirit of nationalism reached unprecedented peaks in this troubled country, most powerful on the African continent. Reflecting this nationalist fervor, the whites' determination to resist African encroachment, as well as a fierce allegiance to Christianity, the monument in many ways personifies the rulers of the South African state (Harm J. de Blij).

ally arise over language use and freedom of cultural expression, the major problem of both white groups in the country is the rise of African nationalism, within South Africa as well as elsewhere on the continent. One of the advantages of the unitary state, we have seen, is its capacity to marshal all resources immediately in a critical national effort. Not surprisingly, in the face of the coming storm, South Africa's whites have pulled ever closer together, and the state is becoming increasingly centralized in crucial areas.

The Indian federation has required a great deal of compromise and adjustment on the part of many people. With partition of the Indian subcontinent and the independence of India and Pakistan in 1947, the Indian state consisted of a patchwork of more than two dozen provinces and some 562 "princely states," the largest of which was nearly the size of France, and the smallest no larger than a large American city. These traditional states had survived the British period of rule, but in a modern federation they clearly had no place. Thus the internal boundaries of India's provinces were altered to include these principalities, while some "unions" were created out of a large number of these political entities. One of the greater subdivisions thus created, Saurashtra, included more than two hundred of these small states. The process of consolidation did not take place without friction, and there were riots in which thousands were killed. Finally, the Union of India emerged with twenty-seven states and a number of federal territories covering the capital city, several islands, recently acquired colonial enclaves, and some of the northern frontier areas.

Almost as soon as this framework was established, pressures arose on the government from several of the states for a revision of boundaries according to language divisions. More than two hundred languages are spoken in India, of which some of the chief are Hindi, Urdu, Gujarati, and Bengali. Thus the state of Bombay was divided into a Gujarati-speaking north and a Marathi-speaking south (Gujarat and Maharashtra respectively), a move that led to street demonstrations and violence in Bombay. Ultimately the Union of India was reorganized into fourteen states and nine federal "territories."

The degree of compromise required to render the Indian state a permanent and stable entity is quickly recognized when it is remembered that millions of Moslems remain

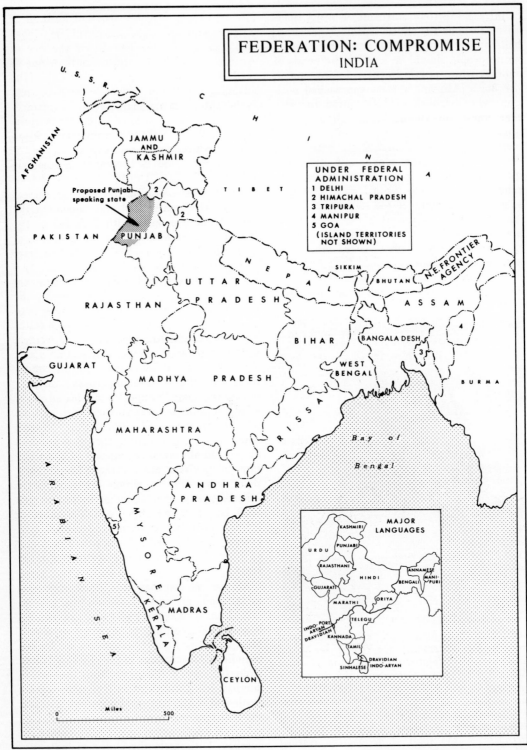

FEDERATION: COMPROMISE
INDIA

Proposed Punjabi speaking state

UNDER FEDERAL
ADMINISTRATION
1 DELHI
2 HIMACHAL PRADESH
3 TRIPURA
4 MANIPUR
5 GOA
(ISLAND TERRITORIES
NOT SHOWN)

MAJOR
LANGUAGES

in this Hindu-dominated country, that peoples of very diverse race, religion, and language have been thrown together not only within the confines of India as a whole, but within the individual states of India as well. In 1964 the government-proclaimed goal of making Hindi the official language of the state led to further friction and loss of life, especially in the south. In Kerala, Communist strength has been countered by stern federal action. The follow-

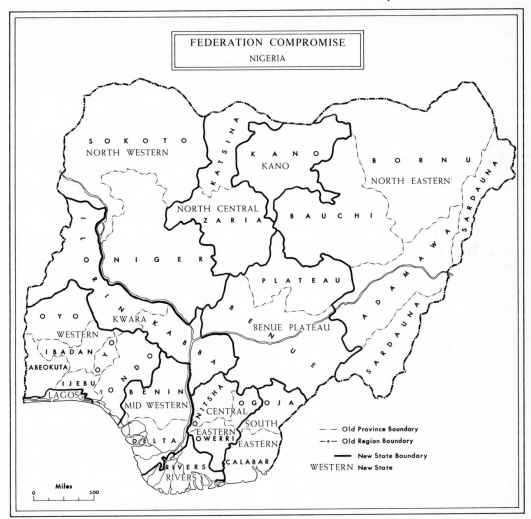

FEDERATION COMPROMISE
NIGERIA

ing quotation could be repeated many times, with different provincial and place names:

The growth of provincialism . . . is indeed most disturbing. In 1960 it led in Assam to widespread anti-Bengali riots, the underlying cause of which was the bitter rivalry between Assamese and Bengalis for employment. More recently the introduction of Assamese as the official language of the state has given rise to serious troubles in Cachar, many of the inhabitants of which have a dialect of Bengali as their mother tongue. The Assam government has been censured in some quarters on the ground that they made no real effort to control the Assamese rioters, but took swift action against the Bengali trouble makers in Cachar.[5]

[5]For a study of the Indian Federation see P. Griffiths, *Modern India*, New York, Praeger, 1962. The quotation is from p. 129.

Nigeria constitutes another compromise federation. Its initial federal framework was developed during discussions between the (British) colonial rulers and Nigerian political leaders, and was put into effect before independence, in 1954. Nigeria has a population approximating sixty million, and possesses three distinct and separate core areas. These core areas form the foci for three of the dominant peoples in the country: the Yoruba in the southwest, the Ibo in the southeast, and the Hausa in the north. When the state achieved independence in 1960, it consisted of three major federal regions, each focusing upon its own capital, and a federal district at Lagos, the federal capital. In view of the fact that Nigeria contains literally hundreds of tribal peoples and more than two hundred languages are spoken today, the measure of compromise can be understood. Some Nigerian politicians immediately warned against the inadequacies of the system, insisting that the state would not survive unless a greater number of regions were established to satisfy the demands of minority peoples. In 1963 the decision was reached to establish a Midwest Region, carved out of territory of the Western Region and populated dominantly by the Edo people. If the Nigerian Federation were to survive, Azikiwe cautioned, other subdivisions would follow:

In order to evolve a near perfect union, the whole of Nigeria should be divided and so demarcated geographically and demographically that no one region would be in position to dominate the rest. . . . Irrespective of the number of regions suggested and in the light of the present situation, the idea of dividing Nigeria into many regions is basically sound because the aim is to consolidate national unity. [There is] wisdom in further splitting this country according to the main *nationalities* or *linguistic groups* [not ethnic groups] which form the bulk of the population.[6]

Azikiwe and numerous other African leaders had foresight. The Nigerian federation had been so divided that the Northern Region, by far the most populous unit within the state, was in a position to dominate the state. Counterbalancing this was the north's landlocked situation, which rendered it dependent upon southern ports for its external trade; but exacerbating the situation was the vast chasm of contrast between Nigeria's northern and southern regions. Indeed, the north is a world apart from the south, the strength of its Islamic traditions deriving in large measure from British methods of indirect colonial rule (see Chapter 17). When independence was under discussion, there were appeals from the north that sovereignty be delayed—views that appeared treasonable to the independence-oriented south. Northern fears were aggravated by the prevalence of southerners (especially Ibo) in key positions and jobs in the north.

Following independence, there were outbreaks of violence against Ibo people living in the north, and an exodus of survivors to the south was the result. Eventually the southeastern section of the federation (the original Eastern Region) declared its secession from Nigeria and pronounced itself the sovereign state of Biafra. The state was plunged in a

[6]N. Azikiwe, "Essentials for Nigerian Survival," *Foreign Affairs*, 43, 3 (April, 1965), 457.

costly and bitter civil war, and the failure of the federal framework was a fact. In early 1968, while the war still raged, the Nigerian government decided to redivide the country into 12 regions, in the hope that such an arrangement would preclude any future Biafra-type conflicts. At the same time a military administration took control over the country, and Nigeria had gone from compromise to centralization.

3. Centralized

In this category are the federal states that today function as centralized or highly centralized unitary states, their federal constitutions notwithstanding. Indeed, the origins of such federations may lie in compromise or mutual interest, but the overriding feature of their existence is the degree of centralization prevailing today. Again, the South African case is relevant here, but other examples exist in the Communist world (the Soviet Union and Yugoslavia) and, intermittently, in Latin America, where several states possessing federal constitutions have experienced periods of intense centralization of power. Thus Brazil, in 1972 still under a military government, has the characteristics of a centralized federation, as do Argentina and Venezuela.

The Union of Soviet Socialist Republics is the world's largest federal state. It was the tsars who originally expanded Russia into eastern and southern Eurasia, but they did little to bring Russian culture to the peoples they ruled: the Georgians, Armenians, Tatars, the Islamic Khanates of middle Asia, and numerous other cultural, linguistic, and religious groups. When, in 1917 the tsarist era was terminated by the revolution that brought Communism to the vast empire, the Russians themselves constituted only about one-half of the country's total population. The architects of the new Russia had to face some urgent and serious problems of national integration, for the state was one of not a single, but several nationalities.

This question of the nationalities became a major issue in the Soviet state after 1917. Lenin, we know, brought the philosophies of Marx to Russia; in his earliest proclamations he talked about the "right of self-determination for the nationalities." The first response on the part of a number of Russia's subject peoples was to proclaim independent republics, as was done in the Ukraine, in Georgia and Armenia, in Azerbaydzhan, and even in

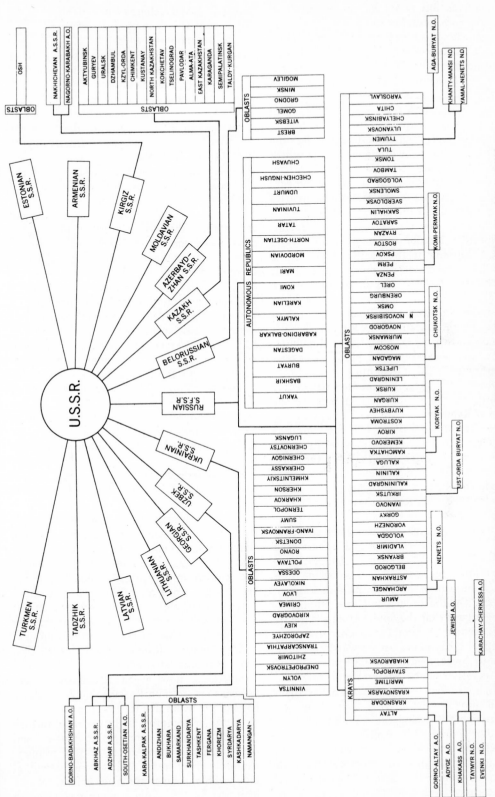

Political subdivisions of the U.S.S.R. as of October, 1968. Reprinted by permission from Paul E. Lydolph, Geography of the U.S.S.R. (Second Edition), New York, John Wiley & Sons, p. 25.)

middle Asia. But Lenin had no intention of permitting the actual breakup of the state, and in 1923, when his blueprint for the new Soviet Union went into effect, the last of these briefly independent units was absorbed into the sphere of Moscow. Nevertheless, the whole framework of the Soviet Union remains essentially based on the cultural identities of the peoples it incorporates. Since the days of Lenin there has been modification, but the major elements of the original system are still there. The country is divided into 15 Soviet Socialist Republics each of which broadly corresponds to one of the major nationalities in the state. By far the largest of these S.S.R.'s is the Russian one, the Russian Soviet Federated Socialist Republic, which extends from west of Moscow to the Pacific Ocean in the east. The remaining 14 republics lie in a belt which extends from the Baltic Sea (where Estonia, Latvia, and Lithuania retain their identity as S.S.R.'s) to the Black Sea (north of which lies the Ukrainian S.S.R.), and through Georgia and Armenia, both Union Republics, to the Caspian Sea, beyond which lie several Asian Soviet Socialist Republics.

Theoretically these 15 republics have equal standing in the Union, but in practice the Russian Republic has the leadership and the others look upward. With half the country's population, the capital and most of its major cities, and over three-quarters of its territory, Russia remains the nucleus of the Soviet Union. The Russian language is taught in the schools of the other republics; the languages of these other areas are not taught compulsorily in Russia. Although the country's constitution, again theoretically, would permit each republic to carry on its own foreign policy, to issue its own money, and even to secede from the Union, none of this has occurred in practice. On the other hand, even though it can be argued that the Soviet Union is highly centralized and a federal state only in theory, no republic has made use of wartime conditions to break away. The Germans, during their invasion of the Soviet Union in World War II, hoped that an anti-Russian nationalism would provide them with support in the Belorussian S.S.R. and the Ukrainian S.S.R., but they found only isolated instances of cooperation and no attempts were made to proclaim sovereign states outside Moscow's sphere. Undoubtedly there is a great deal of acquiescence to the status quo among Soviet peoples, and, in view of the racial, cultural,

linguistic, and religious complexity of the population, this is no small achievement.

The 15 republics identified above do not themselves constitute homogeneous entities either. Most of them include smaller groups of people with some cultural identity; once again, the subdivisions of the republic are largely based on the recognition of these identities. In decreasing rank, there are the so-called Autonomous Soviet Socialist Republics (thus, a republic within a republic) or A.S.S.R., the Autonomous Oblast, and the National Okrug. The Autonomous Oblast (A.O.), as opposed to an Oblast, has within its borders a nationality group of some size and importance; the Oblast is simply an administrative creation without such considerations. The National Okrug or N.O. is usually very large, and exists for the administration of large, sparsely-populated areas such as northern Siberia. Sometimes the A.O. and the N.O. are combined into a kray. This political system is quite complicated, needless to say, but it has served the state well, in two important areas: (1) the integration of all peoples into a framework that would provide them with avenues for effective representation in and contact with Moscow and (2) the organization of territory and population in such a manner that state control over the resource base and economic production would be effective.

The Soviet political framework, then, serves the interests primarily of Russia; it is federal in name only, and the centralization and, indeed, totalitarianism it has promoted in many ways is reminiscent of the period of the tsars. Stalin, heir to Lenin's position of leadership, was as ruthless a ruler as Russia had known in the pre-1917 era. But if the system developed after 1917 proved to have some of the liabilities of the pre-1917 era, it also had some hitherto unknown assets. For the first time the entire country was brought under effective national control. For the first time the Russians, recipients of European innovations, now began to transmit these innovations to non-Russian and non-Slavic parts of the realm. For the first time there were elements of compromise in the relationships between Russians, other Slavic peoples, and the non-Slavic population of the country. Certainly there were conflicts, and individual groups at various time have held separatist feelings. But in general there has been an awareness of progress brought by the Soviet

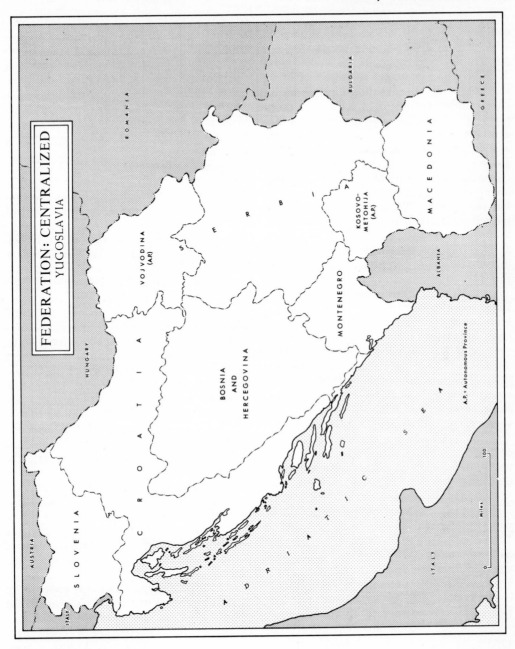

FEDERATION: CENTRALIZED
YUGOSLAVIA

SLOVENIA

CROATIA

VOJVODINA
(A.P.)

S E R B I A

BOSNIA
AND
HERCEGOVINA

MONTENEGRO

KOSOVO-
METOHIJA
(A.P.)

MACEDONIA

A D R I A T I C   S E A

A.P. = Autonomous Province

AUSTRIA
ITALY
HUNGARY
ROMANIA
BULGARIA
GREECE
ALBANIA
ITALY

MILES
0   100

administration; after the terror of the Russian conquest itself the Soviet contributions in such areas as Armenia and Georgia are proof positive that membership in the Soviet Union does have its advantages. Standards of living have been raised, educational opportunities have improved, housing projects have taken place of city slums, and the economy has accelerated—all this without any enforced abandonment of local culture, including language. The Soviets, of course, like to claim that their half century of control has brought unanimous approval of their system throughout the country. While this is not so, their treatment of minority nationalities does appear to have achieved greater domestic approval than that of some colonial powers and, indeed, of some governments of sovereign states.[7]

Yugoslavia, another Communist federal state, and also centralized, nevertheless presents quite a different picture. The 1919 constitution was a unitary one, and it failed because it was not adjusted for Yugoslavia's most obvious characteristic: its immense internal cultural diversity. In 1939 a federal constitution was drawn up, in which Croats, Serbs, Slovenes, and minority groups obtained some regional autonomy. In 1953 the system was again refined by the creation of six autonomous republics (Serbia, Croatia, Slovenia, Macedonia, Montenegro, Bosnia-Hercegovinia) and two "autonomous areas." Although the system today operates in a centralized manner, it appears to possess the essentials for survival in this difficult part of Europe, especially with the aid of the feeling of national unity with which Yugoslavia emerged from the second World War. There are signs that some decentralization of authority will take place in Yugoslavia, and that federalism will succeed in an area that has long presented insurmountable political problems.

4. Imposed

Some federations have been established against the wishes or without the consent of the majority of the peoples involved. These have been created by a powerful minority within the country, or by a colonial power, or through some other outside agency. History has taught us that most imposed federations are short-lived. Witness the list of federations which have arisen and collapsed after the end of the second World War: the Mali Federation, the Central African Federation, the West Indies Federation, Pakistan. Internal as well as external forces are today threatening the Malaysian Federation and the Federation of Ethiopia and Eritrea, as well as other federal unions.

Imposed federations usually have their origins in the desire of an interest group to perpetuate its privileged status or position. Thus federalism becomes a political football, and the consequences to the countries involved have often been very negative. The best example is that of the Central African Federation of Southern and Northern Rhodesia and Nyasaland. Economically, federation of these three territories was warranted and indeed desirable: Nyasaland is mainly dependent upon agriculture, Northern Rhodesia upon mining, while Southern Rhodesia had a better balanced economy. Participation within a greater framework can be shown to be economically sound. The federal framework, however, was imposed upon the region by the European minority (of 350,000 whites as opposed to 10 million Africans); and the economic benefits, promised as a political lure, never did materialize. Dissolution of the federation became the rallying cry of Africans everywhere, and the federal state lasted just a decade, from 1953. The fact remains that federation is a sound objective in this part of Central Africa, and the tragedy is that the word and the concept are now associated with white supremacy, colonialism, and imperialism.[8]

Very often, European colonial concepts of federalism do not fit the real situation in the colonial areas, so that even well-intentioned efforts in the direction of a cooperative venture may fail. This was Azikiwe's argument with reference to Nigeria: he applauded the concept but called for sweeping changes in its execution. So it has been in the West Indies Federation, partially launched in 1958 and foundered by inter-island fears, jealousies, and rivalries. Any glance at the area of the Malaysian Federation must produce fears for its future. The federal constitution of Uganda

[7]Part of the preceding section was adapted from H.J. de Blij, "The Soviet Union: Region and Realm," in *Geography: Regions and Concepts*, John Wiley & Sons, New York, 1971, pp. 149, 150.

[8]For more complete support of this position see H.J. de Blij, "Forced Wedding: Federation in the Rhodesias and Nyasaland," in *Africa South*, Evanston, Northwestern University Press, 1962, pp. 292–350.

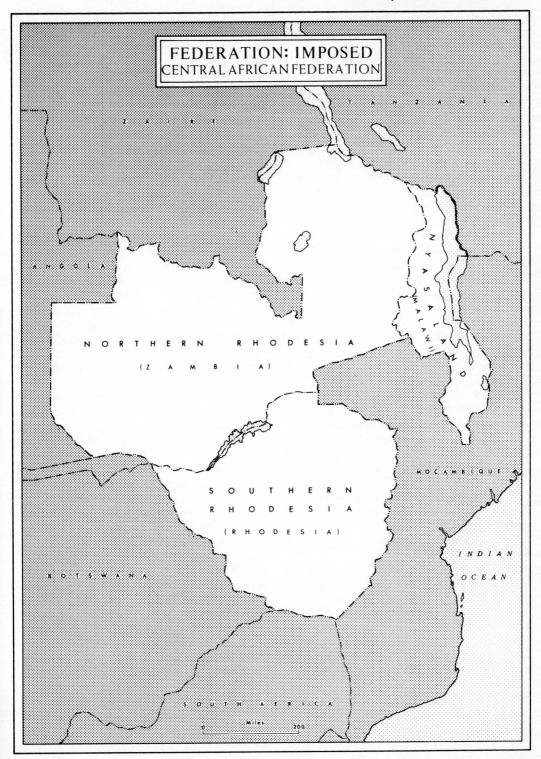

FEDERATION: IMPOSED
CENTRAL AFRICAN FEDERATION

is extremely complex, and while it has served that state so far, there are latent problems which have not been solved. To some extent Uganda's federal arrangement was imposed by the British; there appeared no alternative in the face of the breakup of the political entity of Uganda. In the case of Ethiopia-Eritrea, the United Nations effected the merger of the former Italian dependency and the old African state, a move that did not fail to arouse resentment in Eritrea.

The Factor of Territorial Morphology

The territorial layout of states—their shape —often has much to do with their choice of politicoterritorial organization. When Pakistan began its quarter-century of existence as a federal state, it was an anomaly; other Islamic states are unitary and highly centralized. Undoubtedly the fragmentation of the territory of the two-flank state played a major role in influencing the decision-making processes that brought the federation about. Of course, there were other, weighty factors; the Islamic faith united Pakistan, but there was always much to divide West from East. Not only was Pakistan fragmented, it also lay in two culture realms. In terms of language, ethnicity, and means of existence, West Pakistan always was quite unlike the East. To Easterners it seemed anomalous that their more populous flank should be in a secondary position to the West. While West Pakistan was six times larger territorially than East Pakistan, its population was only two-thirds of the East. But while the center of gravity, in this context, appeared to lie in the East, the capital city of the country always remained in the West and the crucial government decisions were made in the West as well—most of them by Westerners. Furthermore, Urdu is the official language of West Pakistan, while the East was Bengali-speaking; it took seven years after independence (1947) for the Pakistani government to recognize Bengali as an official language.

With its lower living standards, its extreme crowding and grindingly poor subsistence levels, Pakistan's economic and political actions often seemed inappropriate to the East. Economically, there arose a chorus of objections to the dependent position of the East —which was frequently described as no more than a colony of the West. There seemed to be little "partnership" in West Pakistan's treatment of the East. Politically, there was never much enthusiasm in the East for Pakistan's conflict with India in Kashmir or its intermittent quarrels over the Rann of Kutch. These appeared rather pointless luxuries to an East whose relationships with adjoining India were never as poor as those of the West.

In the late 1960's, all these issues led to serious civil unrest in East Pakistan. In 1970 there was rioting and widespread violence aimed directly at the West Pakistani presence, and a new name appeared in the news, that of Bangladesh, the nationalist identification of an independent East. In 1971 a combination of Indian intervention and partisan resistance destroyed the Pakistani forces in the East and Bangladesh was proclaimed a sovereign state.

To what extent did Pakistan's territorial qualities affect this course of events? Such a question cannot be answered with any precision, of course, but there can be no doubt that the 1000 miles of India separating Pakistan's flanks exacerbated a potentially difficult situation considerably. The 1000 miles constituted more than an obstacle to communications and, in the end, an insurmountable strategic disadvantage. It created a *psychological* division that could not be overcome, by federalism, by appropriate responses to demands for autonomy, or by the imposition of near-military rule. There was simply no further commitment to a Pakistani state-idea, federal or otherwise, in what was East Pakistan, and there was no way to weld the opposites into any sort of whole.

If East Pakistan had been positioned nearer to the West, would the federation have survived? Again, it would be impossible to prove anything of the sort. Nigeria was a compact, four-region federal state when the Biafran secession movement broke out; its compactness and the proximity of Biafra to the rest of the country did not forestall the conflict. But it did give Nigeria an opportunity to solve the problem by itself, an advantage Pakistan did not have. The vulnerability of East Pakistan and the obvious problems of logistics faced by the West in a preventive war emboldened the Bangladesh partisans to carry their campaign forward; the probability of Indian intervention had much to do with their persistence. Still more relevant to the entire situation, however, was the character of the federal *system* and its manipulation. If the West seemed remote and indifferent from Eastern viewpoints, so the East seemed backward, distant, and inferior in Western perceptions. The West had been the hearth of Islam from early times; the great cultural heritage embodied in its large cities, and its leadership in the original struggle with India rendered this region the natural choice for continued preeminence in a unified state—in Western eyes. East Pakistan, less purely Islamic, much less urbanized, less productive of revenues,

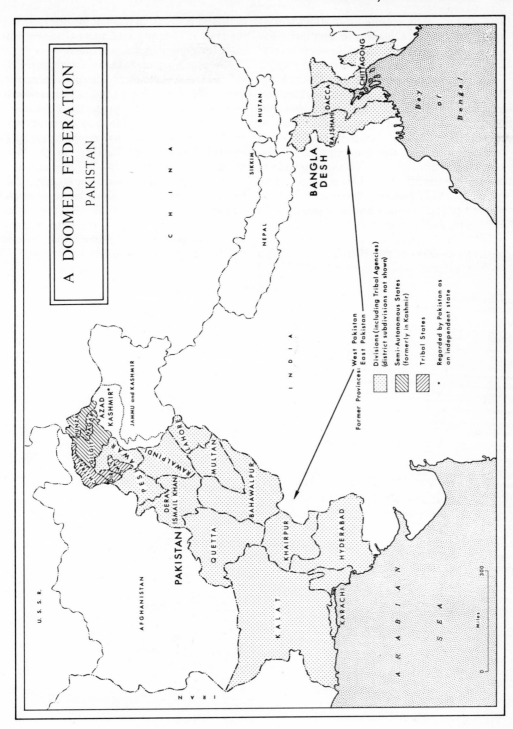

A DOOMED FEDERATION
PAKISTAN

BANGLA DESH

CHITTAGONG
DACCA
RAJSHAHI

Bay of Bengal

CHINA

SIKKIM
BHUTAN
NEPAL

INDIA

U.S.S.R.

AFGHANISTAN

HUNZA
GILGIT
JAMMU and KASHMIR
AZAD KASHMIR*
PESH
LAHORE
RAWALPINDI
DERA ISMAIL KHAN
MULTAN
BAHAWALPUR
PAKISTAN
QUETTA
KHAIRPUR
HYDERABAD
KALAT
KARACHI

IRAN

ARABIAN SEA

Miles
0   300

Former Provinces: West Pakistan
                  East Pakistan

Divisions (including Tribal Agencies)
(district subdivisions not shown)

Semi-Autonomous States
(formerly in Kashmir)

Tribal States

*   Regarded by Pakistan as
    an independent state

was all too easily counted out when federal appointments were made and appropriations handed out. East Pakistan could never mount a threat to the West, any more than Nigeria could ever have threatened the United Kingdom during the colonial era. So the East was forgotten, underrepresented, taxed but not fairly rewarded. There was a strong Western presence in the East, but never much of an Eastern presence in the West, until it was too late. Here is one reflection on that question of greater proximity and what it might have meant; it would probably have contributed to a much greater flow of job seekers from East to West and, hence, a greater interdigitation of population. Certainly the East could not have been in a weaker position than it found itself, a thousand miles from most of the machinery of the state (and in practice, more than that: the route lay *around*, not across India).

The problems of Pakistan are repeated, in different ways, in the Malaysian Federation and in the ill-fated West Indies Federation. In both of these entities, the factor of territorial fragmentation weighed heavily in the effort to create state systems that could function to overcome this major liability. In the West Indies, the experiment has hitherto failed; in Malaysia, the system could not accommodate the force of Singapore, which broke away as a city-state. Still, peninsular Malaysia dominates the insular sectors of the state; will this federation survive the stresses that doomed the Pakistani experiment?

Sixty Years of
Federation in Australia

K.W. Robinson

Mr. Robinson is senior lecturer in geography at Newcastle University College, The University of New South Wales.

Constitutions," said Bryce, "are expressions of national character, as they in turn mould the character of those who use them. Forms of government are causes as well as effects."[1] However difficult political influence is to measure, and however subordinate to the physical environment it may appear, we cannot afford to ignore it.[2]

In the interpretation of regional geography the political character and institutions of the inhabitants should always be considered. But, so far, the link between geography and political forces has not been generally acknowledged by Australian geographers, though it has been appreciated by workers in other fields. Yet there is reason to believe that, because of the growing significance of political influence, strengthened by the conflict between state and federal governments, political forces now deserve a place along with "environment" in the interpretation of the regional geography of Australia. Nowhere else has a whole continent been under single political control for almost two centuries. If the basis of this control has changed from an expansive colonialism to more localized pressure and big business, the arena has remained the same. The turning point, from colonies to nation, came with the turn of the century, when the Act of Federation instituted a new order. It is therefore appropriate, in this discussion of Australian federalism, to consider first the idea of federation, both as a political medium and as a geographical expression.

THE IDEA OF FEDERATION

A federation is the most geographically expressive of all political systems. It is based on the existence of regional differences, and recognizes the claims of the component areas to perpetuate their individual characters. At the same time, it also recognizes their limitations as completely functioning units; it stresses the necessity for linking them with a common thread that draws them toward a common goal. This goal is national cohesion within the larger political framework. Federation does not create unity out of diversity; rather, it enables the two to coexist.

Countries of large area and small population, or even of rather large population concentrated in widely scattered areas, are obviously suitable for this kind of system. New Zealand, which possessed neither of these qualifications, nevertheless had the beginnings of such a system in its earlier provincial governments; but the total area was too small, and the central government too strong from the outset, to make federation workable. Regional strength and pride are prerequisites, but no single section of the community should be more powerful than the rest.[3]

[1] James Bryce: The American Commonwealth (2 vols., new edit., New York, 1918), quoted in "Report of the Royal Commission on the Constitution, 1929" (Canberra, 1929), p. 282.

[2] Professor Griffith Taylor has remarked that, in the past, Providence, priests, potentates, and politicians were given more attention than environment. "The best economic programme for a country to follow," he writes, "has in large part been decided by Nature, and it is the geographer's duty to interpret this programme. Man is able to accelerate, slow or stop the progress of a country's development. But he should not, if he is wise, depart from the directions as indicated by the natural environment" (Australia [London and New York, 1947], pp. 444 and 445).

[3] See J.D.B. Miller: Australian Government and Politics (2nd edit., London, 1959). "The vital point [of a federal system] is the sense of *locality*, the belief that the area in which one lives is different from other areas, even though contiguity with them may provide many interests in common" (p. 138). However, it is recognized that, for political purposes, the "needs" of the various areas within a state cannot always be satisfied by state authority; hence dissident groups make claims either for increasing the authority of the central government or for creating new states.

In the older federations, including Australia, the system is regarded as one of practically watertight compartments, allotted with a varying degree of balance between the central government and the states. Experience has shown that a greater concurrence of powers than the constitution prescribes is necessary; that the working of the constitution and rapid advances in technology create new situations to which a rigid constitution is ill suited. In practice these situations have been met by *ad hoc* devices such as administrative cooperation and the acquisition of federal monopolies over the taxation of income and profits.

It is worth noting that the idea of concurrence is written into newer federal constitutions such as those of India and The West Indies. The things are lacking that in Australia exacerbate State–Commonwealth disputes and stimulate the autonomous and individual feeling in the states. Under this new phase of cooperative federalism, the central government is empowered to levy income tax, and states may *confer* powers on the central government. States, as entities, are weak from the beginning; in Australia they strive to be strong.[4] Federalism, then, is both a mirror of the present and a molding influence for the future, and the primary aim of this discussion of federalism in Australia is to suggest some avenues of investigation and research that should be more fully explored.

THE AUSTRALIAN FEDERAL CONSTITUTION AS A GEOGRAPHICAL EXPRESSION

The Australian Constitution, which received the Royal assent in 1900 and became operative in 1901, is a reflection of the attitudes and conditions of sixty years ago. Attitudes were based on a combination of colonial patriotism, Australian nationalism, and economic expediency. Then, as now, they were the opinions of voluble minorities rather than of the mass of the people. These minorities, which have been identified with economic pressure groups

rather than with colonies,[5] were the driving force behind the drafting of the Constitution. Economic development was best served by retaining local governments; it was also assisted by the fact that unimpeded transport was possible from one state to another. The federal, as distinct from the unificationist, idea was the only one acceptable to the most influential groups, and in any case the only one defensible on most other grounds as well.

The conditions mirrored in the Constitution were the result of a century of colonial impact on a varied and frequently harsh environment. The study of Australia's historical geography clearly reveals the profound influence that the physical environment has exerted on the political framework of the Commonwealth. Economic potential and habitability were matters of prime consideration in the selection of sites and the growth of settlements, and consequently in the definition of political units. Thus for decades before federation the colonies that were to become states possessed clearly separated nuclear areas, enclosed by distinctly arbitrary boundary lines. It is contended that this pattern demonstrates one facet of the influence of physical geography on politics, and that in Australia this influence reached its peak before federation. Federation consolidated an existing pattern and gave scope for subsequent development within an already well-defined framework.

Two features in the Australian geography of 1900 most pertinent to this discussion are related to boundaries and to the process of centralization. The geographical significance of the boundaries (Fig. 1) lies in the fact that they had already been stable for almost forty years or more. The oldest line—aside from the naturally defined boundaries of Tasmania, recognized since 1825—was the eastern boundary of Western Australia (1829); the youngest was the boundary separating Queensland from the Northern Territory (1862). The Act of Federation, in ratifying these lines, made them more nearly permanent because it made them more difficult to change. Today they have at least a century of history behind them, divided between the colonial period of formulation and the Commonwealth period of crystallization.

The description "six seaports with in-

[4]Cf. A.H. Birch: Federalism, Finance and Social Legislation in Canada, Australia and the United States (Oxford University Press, 1955). Birch defines the new cooperative federalism as follows: "A federal system of government is one in which there is a division of political powers between one general and several regional authorities, each of which, in its own sphere, is co-ordinate with the others, and each of which acts directly through its own administrative agencies" (p. 306).

[5]R.S. Parker: Australian Federation: The Influence of Economic Interests and Political Pressures, *Historical Studies in Australia and New Zealand*, Vol. 4, No. 13, 1949, pp. 1–24.

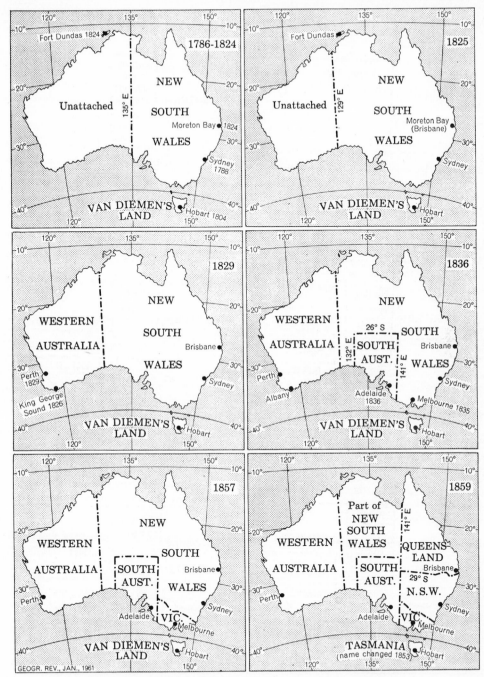

FIG. 1. Historical development of political entities in Australia.

dependent legislatures devoted to their special interests"[6] aptly fits the centralization pattern. This pattern, common in countries of advanced technology, was intensified in Australia by a number of additional features. (1) Economic resources, particularly water (including potential hydroelectric power) and coal, were unequally distributed. Each new discovery weighted the balance in favor of the east and southeast, aiding seaboard locations. (2) The small-farming program met with early failure, and landed power became concentrated in the hands of a few influential people. The power was backed by the capital (often British

[6] Arthur Jose: Australia, Human & Economic (London, Bombay, Sydney, 1932), p. 73.

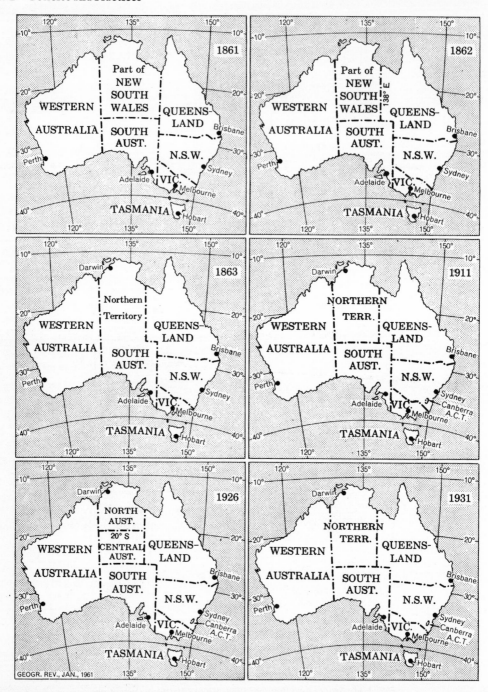

GEOGR. REV., JAN., 1961

capital) of banks and large stock and station agencies[7] requiring centralized head offices. This was the *sine qua non* of much of Melbourne's big business, extending from sheep to cattle and greatly strengthened by the boom following the gold rushes. (3) Primary products were exported that required han-

[7]Brian Fitzpatrick: The British Empire in Australia (2nd edit., Melbourne, 1949), p. 143.

dling, transport, warehousing, collecting, distributive, disposal, and administrative facilities at the ports, which were also the administrative capitals. Docks, bulk storages, silos, offices—all added to the city's stature and to the general stake in congestion. (4) The enormous expansion of railways from 1880 to 1900 boosted centralization by creating a tentacular pattern focused on the great ports and centralized in its administration—necessarily so because of the vast distances and small population concerned.

Thus by 1900 the stage was set for the intensification of a process already well under way.

CHANGES THROUGH SIXTY YEARS

It is impossible to discuss here all the significant trends in the Australia of 1900 that were to be suspended or redirected by the new machinery. The problems of isolation, distance, lack of development funds, and absence of a common voice on "national" affairs were all apparent. Before federation there were probably few matters in which the idea of Australia as a whole was grasped;[8] for the most part colonial rivalries were strong, as in the free trade versus protection battle between New South Wales and Victoria.

We may, however, examine the changes that have occurred since federation in attitudes, in conditions, and in the Constitution itself. Changed attitudes are reflected in such facts as the growth of Labour as a political and industrial force, the hardening of the White Australia policy, and resentment at the increasing centralization of government. Changed conditions can be seen in the concurrent growth of urbanism and manufacturing, increased mobility, the recognition of Australia as a nation-state in world councils, and, in some cases at least, the crystallization of political boundaries into true geographical boundaries. The Constitution has been changed to some extent by amendment, but more especially by the kind of interpretation that has given power to the central government (and, incidentally, the strength of adversity to individual states).

We are concerned here with the evaluation of such changes geographically, particularly with reference to four factors: the growth and development of individual character in the states themselves; the relationship between the states; the relationships between the states collectively and the Commonwealth; and the growth and development of individual character in the Commonwealth.

[8]One of them was international cricket. "It may safely be said that, to many men now in middle age, the occasion of a test match was the only time during their boyhood when they realized Australia as a whole, apart from their own particular colonies" (G.V. Portus: Australia: An Economic Interpretation [Sydney, 1933], p. 64).

THE STATES

Growth within the states has been largely conditioned by the federal Constitution, which reserves to them most developmental functions. Thus the trend in such matters as labor and industry, forestry, water conservation, and railways has to a considerable extent been influenced by internal policy within the states. Victoria affords the best illustration of this internal hegemony. The early concentration of public and private capital in that state, together with the selection of Melbourne as a temporary site for the federal capital, had some influence on general progress. This was assisted by the combination of substantial soil-water resources and relatively small area, and by the independence of other states in power-material supply. The result has been a spectacular increase in irrigation, dairying, brown-coal power supply, and manufacturing. Urbanization, immigration, and industrialization have been special features of the postwar years. The port of Melbourne has been extended to keep pace with a volume of shipping not inferior to Sydney's. Not only have the patterns of colonial Victoria remained, but the whole trend has been toward a rural intensification and industrial concentration that have had to be evolved within a given political framework.

In Queensland, politico-economic elements have worked in a different way. With an area seven times that of Victoria, Queensland has been hampered in its development by the great extent of its tropical lands and of its semiarid belt, poverty of soils, and remoteness from early points of settlement. Weaker centralization and industrialization, stronger regional consciousness and provincial-town development, and a marked coastal grouping of the population are features of the emergent pattern. Yet in Queensland perhaps more than in any other state is found a deep-seated belief in the future and in a vast economic potential that is, as yet, scarcely realized. Changes since 1900 have been in degree rather than in kind. Pride in the all-white sugar industry (made possible by federal ratification of colonial anti-Kanaka laws) is at once an expression of faith in the state's ability to solve its own problems (with the help of the Colonial Sugar Refining Company, whose head office is in Sydney) and of fear lest the immigration laws be relaxed.

Between these two states, with divergent

interests and disparate areas, New South Wales has advanced solidly on its coal, its sheep, and its historical momentum. Coal has without question wrought the greatest change, both by attracting the iron and steel industry and by serving as a basis for power and transport. Assisted by this abundant and easily accessible resource, tariff-protected manufactures progressed more swiftly here in the early years of the century than in any other part of the Commonwealth. At the same time, the evolution of wheat-sheep rotation techniques and the expansion of refrigerated dairy products were favoring the intensification of interior lowland and coastal plain alike. Progress in New South Wales was therefore steady and confident on many fronts, up to the point where confidence was shaken by labor unrest (itself born of industrialization) and steadiness degenerated into complacency, with the result that leadership in development during recent years has been in danger of slipping from the shoulders of New South Wales onto those of Victoria.

In each of the outer, or "mendicant," states there is also evidence of internally stimulated development—in this case, however, assisted by Commonwealth grants to help offset natural disadvantages. The superiority of Western Australia and South Australia in techniques of grassland management, the industrialization of Tasmania on the basis of hydroelectric power, and, especially, the diversification and rapid expansion of South Australia's manufacturing industries are cases in point. All these things suggest that the opportunities for independent expansion within each state are theoretically as strong as, and perhaps stronger than, they were in colonial days,[9] even if in practice they are limited by finance.

[9]Cf. W.K. Hancock: Australia (New York [1930]), pp. 75–76: "Australia frequently impresses the outside observer as being the most uniformly monotonous of continents, and the Australians impress him as being the most monotonously uniform of peoples. . . . The housewife, whether her iron-roofed kitchen is situated on the 'polar front' of Southern Victoria or in the steaming coastal plains of Queensland, observes the same hours of labour, cooks the same stews and puddings, and goes shopping in the same fashion of hat. Despite all this, provincial sentiment is still strong in Australia. The colonies . . . still hold obstinately to the 'sovereignty' proper to them as States." To what extent industrial development in any shape is assisted by public finance, and to what extent the subsequent drain on state funds affects the progress of the state in other ways, are matters requiring more investigation.

INTERSTATE RELATIONSHIPS

The relationships between the states have had visible expression in matters such as the New South Wales—Queensland Border Rivers Agreement. But it is in the other kind of relationship—whether tacit or explicit—that we are more interested. In their day-to-day life, and in their dealings with one another, the people are as much concerned with the virtues, advantages, and disadvantages of their own states as they were in the days of colonial government. These feelings find expression in the tourist and publicity devices of the governments, in the distinctiveness of the state education systems, in the state railway systems, geared to distribute goods in economic regions largely conterminous with the states themselves, and in the relatively small amount of interstate trade.

Over the past sixty years, as an increasingly larger proportion of the state populations has accrued in the capital cities, the viewpoint of the state has come more and more to be identified with that of its capital city. But this has not weakened the feeling of statehood; rather, the metropolis has become the nerve center of an organized and individual community. The authority that state governments possess to legislate on matters touching the people most closely—transport, education, factory conditions, gambling, and so on—ensures that a certain amount of division must remain. Thus the state civil-service traditions, educational background, industrial-training regulations, and similar matters may act as brakes to interstate movement. Where this does occur, the reasons are to be found more usually in greater economic opportunity than in such basic "geographical" differences as climate.

Recent population statistics do, in fact, show some interesting developments in movement between the states. The most striking changes have occurred during the postwar period; figures for absolute population increase by migration (Table I) show increases in Victoria for the period 1953–1957 greater than those in New South Wales. In each of the years 1953–1956, and again in 1958–1959, Victoria's total numbers increased by more than those of New South Wales; although the rates of natural increase were slightly higher in Victoria than in New South Wales, the special force was migration inflow (or net migration). Table I shows how important migration has been, though it does not distinguish between oversea and interstate movements. It is impossible to measure interstate migration precisely, but investigation of census figures suggests that states receiving most oversea migrants do not necessarily gain by interstate migration.[10] Both Victoria and South Australia stand out as significant migrant states; the position of Queensland and Tasmania, relative to their total numbers, is poor.

change marked by the increasing centralization of power. For Australia as a whole this change has been far more significant than the progress within individual states. Geographically, its influence has been to override state identity in order to produce uniformity in the economic, political, and administrative fields. It has not destroyed state identity, but it has succeeded in relegating the states to a secondary role; and, as a corollary, it has strength-

Table I—ABSOLUTE INCREASE IN NUMBERS BY NET OVERSEA AND INTERSTATE MIGRATION (IN THOUSANDS)

Period	N.S.W.	Vic.	QLD.	S.A.	W.A.	TAS.	N.T.	A.C.T.	Australia
1946–50	137.9	88.4	25.2	31.9	40.8	20.8	3.4	4.2	353.0
1951–55	101.3	156.9	39.6	46.6	46.6	13.5	1.4	7.4	413.8
1953	4.5	16.3	5.4	2.7	8.2	2.8	0.7	1.8	42.8
1954	15.9	31.7	3.5	9.9	7.2	1.4	0.2	1.1	68.2
1955	21.7	40.3	6.8	15.4	10.0	0.7	0.5	1.9	97.2
1956	20.7	43.0	8.0	15.9	2.7	1.4	0.4	1.9	93.9
1957	26.0	31.6	0.4	12.3	3.7	2.2	0.1	1.3	78.7
Total by migration 1953–57	88.8	162.9	24.1	56.2	31.8	5.7	1.9	8.0	380.8
Absolute total 1953–57	292.4	333.8	130.0	117.2	87.0	31.1	3.7	11.1	1007.7

Source: Commonwealth of Australia Official Year Book No. 44, 1958, pp. 578–580. (Figures in the column for Australia do not add up to totals, owing to rounding.)

THE STATES AND THE COMMONWEALTH

In the relationships between the states collectively and the Commonwealth, and in the emergence of an Australian "nation," we meet the core of the problem. The two are bound up in a process of constitutional and political

[10]In the intercensal period 1947–1954, New South Wales (50,500), Victoria (12,100), and Tasmania (800) had a net outward movement of the Australian-born. "Even if this loss [of 35,000] overseas were excluded, it seems clear that N.S.W. and Victoria, the states which gained most from overseas migration, suffered a loss of population as a result of migration to other states. Queensland, which in terms of proportion gained least from overseas migration, appears to have benefited more than any other state from the immigration of the Australian-born" (Ruth Dedman: The Growth and Distribution of Australia's Population, 1947–1954 [paper read to Section P (Geography), Thirty-Third Congress, Australian and New Zealand Association for the Advancement of Science, Adelaide, 1958]).

ened the centralist tendencies within each state.

We must admit that this trend toward unification has proceeded within the legal framework of the Constitution. But it has gone further than would appear to have been intended. By interpretation of the Constitution as in the Engineers' Case of 1920,[11] which overruled doctrines of implied restrictions on Commonwealth power to override state powers, and in the Uniform Tax Case of 1942,[12] which made it virtually impossible (though not illegal) for the states to impose tax, the Commonwealth has extended its functions and greatly increased its power. Dominance held through the power of the purse is well known and has led to bitter conflict between the states as developmental agencies and the

[11]28 C.L.R. 129
[12]65 C.L.R. 373.

Commonwealth as a disbursing authority. The extent to which "national" institutions such as the defense system, immigration policy, and departmental votes encroach on total revenue is a measure of the restrictions placed on state progress.

Viewed in this context, the states no longer matter; they have become virtually "pensioners of the Commonwealth." We are looking, not at an organized collection of distinctive entities, but at groups among which, over the past sixty years, many of the divergences on which federation was based have disappeared. The transport revolution has enormously reduced the problems of isolation and distance; tariff policy has introduced a degree of economic uniformity hardly dreamed of in colonial days. In this sense, there is but one Australia, brought into maturity through the machinery of federation itself. An advocate of unification[13] has put the case as follows:

Industrialisation and continued urbanisation have created an Australia radically different from that of 1900 . . . the Grants Commission, after detailed analysis of conditions in the various states, came to just this conclusion—that Australian economic life was closely integrated, that industry was organised on a national and not on a local basis, that the economic structure of the states revealed a marked similarity . . . the key problems of the day in the economic sphere, production, marketing, employment, industrial relations are national problems, and can best be dealt with by the national parliament, or the agents which it creates.

Yet to agree with the implications of this statement is not to deny the fact that the strength of the Commonwealth does not negate the existence of its various parts. It was asserted earlier that federation enabled unity and diversity to coexist; because the unity is *national* in scope, and directed toward the outside world, it operates in many ways on a different plane from the local interests of the individual states. If, through its uniform tax policy and its liberal interpretation of excise as set out in Section 90 of the Constitution, the Commonwealth has reduced the financial flexibility of the states,[14] it has not thereby

destroyed them. Resistance to central authority has the effect of strengthening state sentiment as it weakens state power.

Urbanization and industrialization are distinctive national characteristics, to which attention has already been drawn; although federalism has created neither, it has certainly encouraged both. Not only have the early administrative and economic advantages of seaboard capitals been continued, but the expansion of manufacturing behind a tariff wall and assisted by two world wars has been an inseparable part of the urbanization process. Protection is the federal policy that, since 1908,[15] has given scope for manufacturing to increase in diversity, absorb a larger and larger proportion of the work force (to its present 30 per cent), and overtake and far exceed agriculture in net value of production. The extreme view regards this as an avoidable process that has been engineered by an unholy alliance of Liberal and Labour politicians to depopulate the rural areas and enhance the superiority of metropolitan life:

Had Australia remained Free Trade, she would still have remained a largely rural country. . . . But the policy of protecting manufactures was avowedly for the purpose of bringing population and wealth into the capital cities. . . . The predominance of the capital cities in manufacture . . . was greatly assisted by . . . railway freight policy.[16]

One can accept the truth of such views as partial explanations, but not as serious interpretations, of Australian urbanization. The course of history had already allied with the facts of physical geography to ensure this pattern before manufacturing expanded or Labour won its first seat in any state house. The great increase in volume of manufacturing has accelerated the process, but in spite of free trade, and allowing for reversals in railway freight fares, it is probable that manufacturing would have grown precisely in the places where it has in fact appeared. What the constitutional provisions for tariffs and free interstate trade *have* done is to create an

[13]Gordon Greenwood: The Case for Extended Commonwealth Powers, *in* Federalism in Australia: Papers Read at the Fifteenth Summer School, Australian Institute of Political Science, 1949 (Melbourne, 1949), pp. 37–63; reference on p. 44.

[14]Alan Davies and Geoffrey Serle, edits.: Policies for Progress: Essays in Australian Politics (Melbourne, 1954), especially Chapter 2, "Constitutional Issues," by Geoffrey Sawer, pp. 13–34, reference on pp. 23–24.

[15]The Commonwealth Tariff was introduced in 1901, with federation, but its effectiveness as an instrument of protection for Australian manufactures dates from 1908, when tariff rates were radically revised with this end in view; until that time it had been purely revenue-producing. The Tariff Board, set up in 1921 to advise the government on questions relating to trade and customs, has subsequently become the central organ of the protective system.

[16]Colin Clark: Australian Hopes and Fears (London, 1958), pp. 276–279.

integrated industrial structure, based on the free movement of raw materials and manufactured goods throughout all parts of the Commonwealth. The iron and steel industry is located in New South Wales, but it draws on widely scattered areas for raw materials; motor vehicles begun in Adelaide and Melbourne are finished in Brisbane; refrigerators from a Sydney factory sell under different names in a competitive market in various states.

Whether top-heavy or not, the flourishing manufacturing industry of modern Australia, "full of energy, zest and sweat,"[17] is a symbol of the emergent nationalism that is something more than the sum of the various states. At the same time, it has been stimulated by state rivalry, and the states have themselves gained in productive strength and in population because of it. This can also be said for the immigration policy, which, in the postwar years, has added a million "New Australians." Most of them have shown preference for the cities, and recently for the state of Victoria in particular.

It is in trends of this kind that we can clearly see the cause and effect significance of the form of government. But the relationship must not be pushed too far; in most things the Constitution has been a stimulus rather than a cause—especially of centralization. Conversely, it has, except in times of national emergency, acted against decentralization and "regional balance." However strong the need for regional devolution may be,[18] the trend has been otherwise; and this trend, it is contended, is a natural one, aided and abetted by tariffs, transport systems, and administrators, but not caused by them.

The propensity of the people to select urban habitats, to contribute more and more to secondary and tertiary industries, to move freely and rapidly by air from one capital city to another, and to share a belief in the rightness of White Australia is among the

important facts of political geography that have grown to maturity under the aegis of the federal Constitution.

THE STATES AS GEOGRAPHICAL REGIONS

The enduring position of the states[19] is neither generally recognized nor universally accepted. There are those who believe that the ultimate objective is unification, and there are those who think that greater fragmentation, either through the creation of new states or through regional reorganization, is a desideratum. However, careful appraisal of developments over the past sixty years supports the contention that the states are, in some respects, more geographically distinct than they were at the time of federation. It may be true, as Partridge[20] has suggested, that "it is the existence of the six separate governments which chiefly produces the sentiments, attitudes and interests which in turn support those governments." But precisely because this process has been operating for two generations under federalism, and before that for almost another two under colonialism, local sentiments have become firm, real, and permanent.[21] In other words, we now have political units the boundaries of which have remained largely unaltered for a century or more, and within each of which autonomous developmental policy has been applied at an increasing tempo. Surely this, in itself, connotes geographical individuality.

The creation of a dichotomy of state governments and federal Parliament was far more than a recognition of existing patterns of development and current problems at the turn of the century. It provided scope for concen-

[17]C.L. Sulzberger, writing in the New York Times, and quoted in the Newcastle Morning Herald, Nov. 10, 1959, p. 15: "Australia has accepted a twentieth-century role that may bring with it distortion and ugliness, but nevertheless rushes forward full of energy, zest and sweat."
[18]"Geographical circumstances and a hundred and fifty years of human effort have demonstrated the need for the continuous process of decentralization, and this becomes paralleled in the local regions themselves by the growing development of a regional consciousness" (J.M. Holmes: The Geographical Basis of Government, Specially Applied to New South Wales [Sydney and London, 1944], p. 10).

[19]"Even with the scales heavily weighted in favour of the Commonwealth, the States retain an enduring position in the federal structure" (Sir Douglas Copland: The Impact of Federalism on Public Administration, in Federalism: An Australian Jubilee Study [edited by Geoffrey Sawer; Melbourne, 1952], pp. 135–173; reference on p. 153).
[20]P.H. Partridge: The Politics of Federalism, in Federalism: An Australian Jubilee Study (op. cit.), pp. 174–210; reference on p. 195.
[21]To draw a parallel from New Zealand again, provincial feeling is still apparent there, particularly in the South Island, though the provincial governments were abolished eighty-four years ago. It is fair to add, however, that such feeling has weakened, or been subdivided, in the North Island, where population expansion during the twentieth century has been much more rapid than in the South Island.

Table II—AGGREGATE POPULATION OF CITIES AND TOWNS, 1954*

State	Cities and Towns Outside the Metropolitan Area with a Population of						% In Largest City (B)	% "Urban" (A+B) (2,000 +)
	3,000 and over			2,000 and over				
	No.	Population	% of Total	No.	Population	% of Total (A)		
N.S.W.	67	806,373	23.55	98	881,391	25.75	54.42	80.17
Vic.	40	376,347	15.35	56	415,690	16.95	62.15	79.10
Qld.	29	374,328	28.40	41	404,520	30.69	38.10	68.79
S.A.	9	62,008	7.78	14	74,502	9.35	60.66	70.01
W.A.	7	67,440	10.54	13	82,139	12.84	54.50	67.34
Tas.	6	83,412	27.31	8	89,003	28.83	30.84	59.67
N.T.	1	8,071	49.01	2	10,856	65.92	—	—
A.C.T.	—	—	—	—	—	—	93.28	93.28

Source: *Commonwealth of Australia Official Year Book No. 44*, 1958, pp. 570–571 and 573.

*Exclusive of fullblood aboriginals. "In reckoning the numbers of the people of the Commonwealth, or of a State or other part of the Commonwealth, *aboriginal natives shall not be counted*" (Section 127 of the Constitution; italics are the present author's).

trated effort within formerly arbitrary boundaries—effort directed at the progress and welfare of each of the states as a political entity in competition with the others. Although we may not wish to assert that differences between the states have crystallized to the point of making them individual geographical regions (this is something that needs to be argued exhaustively), there are some aspects at least in which they may be so regarded. A few illustrations must suffice to support this view.

PATTERNS OF URBAN SETTLEMENT

States show notable differences in the pattern of urban settlement, not only in the degree of urbanization, but in the distribution and number of towns of various size groups.

The reasons for the weakness of provincial towns in Victoria, Western Australia, and, particularly, South Australia are probably different, but they distinguish these states from New South Wales, Queensland, and Tasmania, where provincial-town life is definitely more vigorous. However, the "% urban" column in Table II links New South Wales with Victoria, Queensland with Western Australia and South Australia, and sets Tasmania apart as the most rural of the states. Similarly, in number of towns in various size groups (Table III), no two states show the same

pattern.[22] Although the national lack of medium-sized cities (50,000–200,000) is apparent, state disparities are perhaps even more remarkable. The provincial-town strength of Queensland and Tasmania is a well-known feature that corresponds to greater rural regional strength and a degree of decentralization not found elsewhere. The paucity of substantial country towns in South Australia is most marked, especially if the industrial character of the largest (Port Pirie) is borne in mind. In this respect, Victoria shows a pattern midway between South Australia and New South Wales, but different from both; wheat-belt towns in Victoria have not reached anywhere near the prominence that they have in New South Wales and have developed even less in Western Australia, where the larger provincial towns are either mining towns or ports.

Patterns of urgan settlement thus form one of the clearest examples of state individualism.

STATE SPECIALISMS

States have continued to specialize in various

[22]The dangers of drawing too many conclusions from sets of figures as presented here are realized. It is possible that alternative groupings of towns would show a somewhat different pattern, but this would not alter the fact that significant differences do exist between the states. The term "urban" is here used with reservation and caution—in an arbitrary rather than a functional sense.

Table III—NUMBER OF TOWNS IN VARIOUS SIZE GROUPS, 1954

State	Million	500,000–Million	100,000–500,000	50,000–100,000	20,000–50,000	10,000–20,000	5,000–10,000
N.S.W.	1	—	2	—	7	10	24
Vic.	1	—	—	2	1	5	15
Qld.	—	1	—	—	7	4	4
S.A.	—	1	—	—	—	2	4
W.A.	—	—	1	—	1	1	4
Tas.	—	—	1	1	—	2	1
N.T.	—	—	—	—	—	—	1
A.C.T.	—	—	—	—	1	—	—
Total	2	2	4	3	17	24	53

Based on table, p. 572, *Commonwealth of Australia Official Year Book No. 44, 1958*, and on 1954 Census Reports.

ways, partly because of the differing environments, but also partly because they are distinct political units.

New South Wales, leader in population numbers, owes this position to its diversity of resources and its greater area as compared with Victoria. Black coal, steel, wool, and meat are of special significance in the economy. It has more factories and a greater factory production than any other state, but in proportional numbers engaged in manufacturing it is less industrialized than Victoria. The southern state, more compact and densely populated than any other, has through its concentration of capital and financial and political power become a cornerstone of Australian development. Victoria has a reputation for dairying, irrigation farming, dual-purpose sheep, and the methodical development of brown coal. Its road and rail networks are the most comprehensive of all the states in relation to total area.

Queensland has always been important for its output of tropical products; the influence of its sugar production needs no emphasis here. It has been argued that the success of sugar settlement was hindered, not helped, by the southern states, which were concerned more with the cheapness of sugar than with the problems of the growers. Other notable "Queensland" characteristics are the pastoral occupation of the interior, largely by leasehold tenure (the Labour influence, it is asserted), for wool and beef export, and the coastal decentralization of population, expressed in railway and port development and in "New State" movements of the north.

South Australia and Western Australia are "outer areas," alleged to be at a disadvantage through their remoteness from the more populous east. In each, a core of fertility in a vast area of waste has produced a compactness of settlement and a consciousness of environment that have stimulated agricultural research. Subterranean clover and top-dressing have distinguished the agriculture; fruit and vine products have long been associated with wheat in the rural economy. A considerable output of diversified manufactures and the absorption of migrants have been special features in South Australia; Western Australia still remains distinctive for its output of gold and karri timber, its "separateness" intensified by distance from the other centers of population.

Tasmania requires little comment. Its obvious and natural distinctiveness has been enhanced by the impressive agricultural traditions of apples, potatoes, and berry fruits; by the hydroelectric power that supports a number of large industries; and by a united front against all those who think of the island as culturally, as well as physically, separate from the continent.

OCCUPATIONAL STRUCTURE

There is no question that our concepts of state individuality have expanded and deepened with the years. The very *national* process of industrialization has stimulated state rivalry, and the statistical breakdown of the work force into primary, secondary, and tertiary industries shows a disparity that does not

Table IV—OCCUPATIONAL DIVISIONS OF THE WORK FORCE, 1954
(In percentages)

State	Primary	Secondary	Tertiary
New South Wales	13.4	29.1	57.5
Victoria	11.6	32.7	55.7
Queensland	22.1	20.6	57.3
South Australia	15.5	24.9	59.6
Western Australia	19.3	19.0	61.7
Tasmania	19.5	22.0	58.5

Calculated from 1954 Census Reports.

entirely reflect the differences in the natural environment (Table IV).

The strong contrast between Victoria and Queensland is particularly noteworthy—in fact, the significance of the figures in Table IV is that no two states are alike. With respect to balance, Victoria appears to be further than New South Wales from Colin Clark's ideal of a more rural community,[23] while Queensland presumably comes nearest to it.

BOUNDARIES

Boundaries are, on the whole, less significant than core areas, especially for the larger and less populous states, where the boundary runs through practically uninhabited country. But in the southeast they have become important. Rose[24] has written of significant differences between the two sides of the New South Wales–Queensland border and has indicated elsewhere[25] the transition in building materi-

als between South Australia and Victoria. Again, the unifying influence of the Murray River has been largely offset by the Victorian railway system, which attracts custom and interest across the state border; in the same way, Broken Hill has become economically linked with South Australia and has indeed contributed much to that state's industrial progress. Because these boundaries are politically weak, they are best thought of as "frames of reference" within which state developmental programs occur. It is questionable whether they will ever develop into clear-cut regional lines, but they do act as limits within which distinctive policies can be recognized.

CONCLUSIONS

What conclusions can be drawn? The major lesson to be taken from this survey is that politics—the regulation of human conduct within a defined political area—can be geographically significant.

First, for many Australians the workings of the federal Constitution are part of their genre de vie. This statement applies particularly to those petitioning for new states in various parts of the country, but for most people the federal government impinges to some extent on their daily lives—through taxation, through interstate-transport regulations, through the application of federal industrial awards alongside state ones, through the regulation of the basic wage, and in many other ways. It is not to government alone but to the dichotomy of governmental institutions that we must turn for a complete explanation of Australia's human geography.

Second, the actions of politicians have, to an

[23]Clare, op. cit. [see footnote 16 above], p. 264: "What stands out as a quite ineluctable conclusion is that Australia needs more agriculture. Quite apart from any political or cultural considerations, an increased production and export of agricultural products is an urgent economic necessity." And on p. 266: "The root of the trouble is that Australian agriculture has been starved of labour, by making the Australian exporter accept prices much below world market level . . . but predominantly by the policy of protection and undue encouragement to manufacture. This policy has been carried to extraordinary lengths."

[24]A.J. Rose: The Border between Queensland and New South Wales, Australian Geographer, Vol. 6, No. 4, 1955, pp. 1–18.

[25]A.J. Rose: Regional Variations in the Use of Building Materials in Australia (paper read to Section P [Geography], Thirty-Third Congress, Australian and New Zealand Association for the Advancement of Science, Adelaide, 1958).

undetermined extent, contributed to existing geographical patterns; although the environment has provided the potential, political action has often decided how this potential should be turned to account. The Snowy Mountains Hydroelectric Authority at the national level and the town of Kwinana[26] at the state level are cases in point. The accumulation of greater power by the Commonwealth is also a result of political action, though its effects on geographical patterns may be more subtle. Just as significant as these overt manifestations are the operations of powerful pressure groups—economic, political, and religious. The motives of such groups may be outside the scope of geographical study, but the results of their actions are not; this would appear to be one of the most fruitful and necessary fields for research in the future.

Third, the states have acquired sufficiently distinctive character, or "personality," for them to be treated as geographical units. Behind the original idea of federation lay the belief in separate identities with common objectives. Despite unifying tendencies such as fast transport and national industrialization, these identities have not been weakened by federation. A strengthening process, operating through the constant fluctuations in the balance of power between the states, has, if anything, given them greater relative stature

in 1961 than they had in 1900. They are just as conscious of their individuality as before, and because they are more populous and more highly developed, the feeling is more justified. The proof of this does not rest in the ability to establish "community of interest" boundaries so much as in the idea of how we should study the geography of the Commonwealth. If we are to give due weight to political forces as geographical agents, then there is a strong argument for using the states as primary regional divisions.

Finally, the concept of Australia as a nation has matured with federation, particularly since the Second World War. This country is no longer an outpost of empire but a responsible Pacific nation, economically tied to remote regions but with vital interests in neighboring Southeast Asia. Clearly, it is in the larger geographical setting of the Western Pacific that Australia's major national role is to be played. Its obligations under SEATO and ANZUS, the Colombo Plan, and the trusteeship system of the United Nations are indicative of this. The cultural and economic implications of these affiliations must be viewed against a background of awakening nationalism abroad and persistent adherence to "White Australia" at home. In the reconciliation of these conflicting ideals lies Australia's greatest problem and greatest hope for the future.

REFERENCES

Abuetan, Barid, "Eritrea: United Nations Problem and Solution," *Middle Eastern Affairs*, 2, 2 (February, 1951), 35–53.

Archibald, Charles H., "The Failure of the West Indies Federation," *World Today*, 18, 6 (June, 1962), 233–242.

Arnade, Charles W., *The Emergence of the Republic of Bolivia*. Gainesville, University of Florida Press, 1957.

Arora, Satish Kumar, "The Reorganization of Indian States," *Far Eastern Survey*, 25, 2 (February, 1956), 27–30.

Awa, Eme O., *Federal Government in Nigeria*. Berkeley, University of California Press, 1964.

Ayearst, Morley, *The British West Indies: The Search for Self-government*. New York, New York University Press, 1960.

Azikiwe, N., "Essentials for Nigerian Survival,"

Foreign Affairs, 43, 3 (April, 1965), 447–461.

Baldoria, Pedro L., "Political Geography of the Philippines," *Philippine Geog. J.*, 1, 1 (1953), 15–23.

Baratz, Morton S., "The Crisis in Brazil," *Social Res.*, 22, 3 (1955), 347–361.

Barbour, Nevill, "Aden and the Arab South," *World Today*, 15, 8 (August, 1959), 302–310.

Best, Harry, *The Soviet State and Its Inception*. New York, Philosophical Library, 1950.

Blood, Sir Hilary, "Federation in the Caribbean," *Corona*, 8, 5 (May, 1956), 166–1969.

———, "The West Indian Federation," *J. Roy. Soc. and Arts*, 105, 5009 (August 2, 1957), 746–757.

Bose, N.K., "Bengal Partition and After," *Calcutta Geog. Rev.*, 9, 1–4, 1947 (1949), 14–22.

Bradford, S., *Spain in the World*. Princeton, N.J., Van Nostrand, 1962.

Brown, W. Norman, *The United States and India and Pakistan*. Cambridge, Harvard University Press, 1953.

Buchanan, K., "Northern Region of Nigeria: The Geographical Background of its Political Duality," *Geog. Rev.*, 43, 4 (October, 1953), 451–473.

Burns, Sir Allan, "Toward a Caribbean Federation," *Foreign Affairs*, 34, 1 (October, 1955), 128–140.

[26]Kwinana is a new town and port in Western Australia, 17 miles south of Fremantle, created for the express purpose of establishing a petroleum refinery (completed in 1955) and later a steel-rolling mill and a cement factory. The site had no specific advantages other than its strategic position in Western Australia, an "outer state" that provides the eastern steel industry with some of its iron ore.

Campbell, R.D., *Pakistan: Emerging Democracy.* Princeton, N.J., Van Nostrand, 1963.

Canaway, A.P., *The Failure of Federalism in Australia.* London, Oxford University Press, 1930.

Chandrasekhar, S., "The New Map of India," *Population Rev.,* 1, 1 (January, 1957), 32–36.

Chapin, Miriam, *Contemporary Canada.* New York, Oxford University Press, 1959.

Chatterjee, S.P., "The Changing Map of India," *Geog. Rev. India,* 19, 2 (June, 1957), 1–5.

Church, R.J. Harrison, "The Islamic Republic of Mauritania," *Focus,* 12, 3 (November, 1961).

Cowan, L. Gray, "Federation for Nigeria," *Internat. J.,* 10, 1 (1954–1955), 51–60.

Crowder, Michael, "Two Cameroons or One?" *Geog. Mag.,* 32, 6 (November, 1959), 303–314.

Cumming, Duncan Cameron, "The Disposal of Eritrea," *Middle East J.,* 7, 1 (Winter, 1953), 18–32.

Cunningham, J.K., "A Politico-Geographical Appreciation of New Zealand Foreign Policy," *New Zealand Geographer,* 14, 2 (October, 1958), 147–160.

Currie, David P. (ed.), *Federalism in the New Nations.* Chicago, University of Chicago Press, 1964.

Dale, Edmund H., "The State-Idea: Missing Prop of the West Indies Federation," *Scot. Geog. Mag.,* 78, 3 (December, 1962), 166–176.

Das, Taraknath, "The Status of Hyderabad During and After British Rule in India," *Amer. J. Internat. Law,* 43, 1 (January, 1949), 57–72.

Das, Gupta, Sivaprasad, "The Changing Map of India," *Geog. Rev. India,* 22, 3 (September, 1960), 23–33; and 4 (December, 1960), 13–32.

Dean, Vera Micheles, "Yugoslavia: A New Form of Communism?" *Foreign Policy Rep.,* 27, 4 (May, 1951), 38–47.

Dening, B.H., "Greater Syria; A Study in Political Geography," *Geography,* 35, Pt. 2, 168 (June, 1950), 110–123.

Deshpande, C.D., "India Reorganized; A Geographical Evaluation," *Indian Geography,* 2, 1 (August, 1957), 164–169.

Dikshit, R.D., "Geography and Federalism," *Annals, A.A.G.,* 61, 1 (March, 1971), 97–115.

——, "The Failure of Federalism in Central Africa; a Politico-Geographical Postmortem," *Prof. Geog.* 23, 3 (July, 1971), 224–228.

Dobby, E.H.G., "Malayan Prospect," *Pacific Affairs,* 23, 4 (December, 1950), 392–401.

Dugdale, John, "Can Federation Work in Rhodesia?" *New Commonwealth,* 33, 2 (January 21, 1957), 61–62.

Dunlop, Eric W., and Walter Pike, *Australia . . . Colony to Nation.* London, Longmans, 1960.

Finkelstein, Lawrence S., "The Indonesian Federal Problem," *Pacific Affairs,* 24, 3 (September, 1951), 284–295.

Fisher, Charles A., "The Changing Political Geography of British Malaya," *Prof. Geog.,* 7, 2 (March, 1955), 6–9.

——, "The Problem of Malayan Unity in its Geographical Setting," in *Geographical Essays on British Tropical Lands,* Robert Walter Steel and Charles A. Fisher (eds.). London, G. Philip, 1956, pp. 271–344.

Franklin, H., *Unholy Wedlock: The Failure of the Central African Federation.* London, George Allen & Unwin, 1964.

Furber, Holden, "The Unification of India, 1947–1951," *Pacific Affairs,* 24, 4 (December, 1951), 352–371.

Furnivall, J.S., "Twilight in Burma: Independence and After," *Pacific Affairs,* 22, 2 (June, 1949), 155–172.

Gangal, S.C., "An Approach to Indian Federalism," *Political Sci. Quart.,* 77, 2 (June, 1962), 248–253.

Gathorne-Hardy, G.M., and others, *The Scandinavian States and Finland; A Political and Economic Survey.* London, Royal Institute of International Affairs, 1951.

Gerbrandy, P.S., *Indonesia.* London, Hutchinson, 1950.

Gilbert, E.W., "Practical Regionalism in England and Wales," *Geog. J.,* 94, 1 (July, 1939), 29–44.

Gillin, John, and K.H. Silvert, "Ambiguities in Guatemala," *Foreign Affairs,* 34, 3 (April, 1956), 469–482.

Ginsburg, Norton S., "China's Changing Political Geography," *Geog. Rev.,* 42, 1 (January, 1952), 102–117.

Golay, J.F., *The Founding of the Federal Republic of Germany.* Chicago, University of Chicago Press, 1958.

Gorbold, R., "Tanganyika: the Path to Independence," *Geog. Mag.,* 35, 7 (November, 1962), 371–384.

Greenidge, C.W.W., "The British Caribbean Federation," *World Affairs,* 4, 5 (July, 1950), 321–334.

Hance, William A., "Economic Potentialities of the Central African Federation," *Political Sci. Quart.,* 69, 1 (March, 1954), 29–44.

Hardy, W.G., *From Sea Unto Sea: Canada—1850 to 1910; the Road to Nationhood.* Garden City, N.Y., Doubleday, 1960.

Herman, Theodore, "Group Values Toward the National Space: the Case of China," *Geog. Rev.,* 49, 2 (April, 1959), 164–182.

Hoffman, George W., "The Political Geography of a Neutral Austria," *Geog. Studies,* 3, 1 (1956) 12–32.

Huke, Robert E., "Republic of the Philippines," *Focus,* 11, 8 (April, 1961).

Jefferson, Mark, "The Problem of the Ecumene: the Case of Canada," *Geografiska Annaler,* 16 (1934), 146–158.

Jesman, C., *The Ethiopian Paradox.* London, Oxford University Press, 1963.

Johnson, James H., "The Political Distinctiveness of Northern Ireland," *Geog. Rev.,* 52, 1 (January, 1962), 78–91.

Karnes, Thomas L., *The Failure of Union: Central Americas, 1824–1960.* Chapel Hill, University of North Carolina Press, 1961.

Kimble, George H.T., "The Federation of Rhodesia and Nyasaland," *Focus,* 6, 7 (March, 1956).

King, Frank H.H., *The New Malayan Nation; A Study of Communalism and Nationalism.* New York, Institute of Pacific Relations, 1957.

Kinnane, D., *The Kurds and Kurdistan.* London, Oxford University Press, 1964.

Kirchheimer, Otto, "The Decline of Intra-State Federalism in Western Europe," *World Politics, 3,* 3 (April, 1951), 281–298.

Krehbiel, E., "Geographic Influences in British Elections," *Geog. Rev., 2,* 6 (December, 1916), 419–432.

Linke, Lilo, *Ecuador, Country of Contrasts.* London, Oxford University Press, 1960.

Little, Tom, *Egypt.* New York, F.A. Praeger, 1958.

Livingstone, William S., "A Note on the Nature of Federalism," *Political Sci. Quart., 67,* 1 (March, 1952). 81–95.

Lowenthal, David (ed.), *The West Indies Federation; Perspective on a New Nation.* New York, Columbia University Press, 1961.

Lydolph, Paul E., "The New Map of the Soviet Union," *Prof. Geog., 10,* 4 (July, 1958), 13–17.

MacKintosh, John P., "Federalism in Nigeria," *Political Studies, 10,* 3 (October, 1962), 223–247.

MacKirdy, K.A., "Conflict of Loyalties: The Problem of Assimilating the Far Wests into the Canadian and Australian Federations," *Canadian Historical Rev., 32,* 4 (December, 1951), 337–355.

———, "Geography and Federalism in Australia and Canada," *Australian Geographer, 6,* 2 (March, 1953), 38–47.

Macmahon, A. (ed.), *Federalism Mature and Emergent.* New York, Doubleday, 1955.

Maddick, Henry, "Decentralization in the Sudan, Part II; a Critical Appraisal," *J. Local Admin. Overseas, 1,* 2 (April, 1962), 75–83.

Malcolm, George A., *First Malayan Republic: The Story of the Philippines.* Boston, Christopher Publishing House, 1951.

Mansergh, Nicholas, "Ireland: the Republic Outside the Commonwealth," *Internat. Affairs, 28,* 3 (July, 1952), 277–291.

McWhinney, Edward. *Comparative Federalism. States' Rights and National Power.* Toronto, University of Toronto Press; London, Oxford University Press, 1962.

Mason, Philip, "Partnership in Central Africa," *Internat. Affairs, 33,* 2 (April, 1957), 154–164; and 3 (July, 1957), 310–318.

Merrill, Gordon, "The West Indies—The Newest Federation of Commonwealth," *Canadian Geog. Journal, 56,* 2 (February, 1958), 60–69.

Oduho, J., and William Deng, *The Problem of the Southern Sudan.* London, Oxford University Press, 1963.

O'Reilly Sternberg, H., "Brazil: Complex Giant," *Foreign Affairs, 43,* 2 (January, 1965), 297–311.

Panikar, K.M., "Indian States Reorganization," *Asian Rev.,* n.s., *52,* 192 (October, 1956), 247–258.

Pankhurst, E. Sylvia, and Richard K.P. Pankhurst. *Ethiopia and Eritrea; the Last Phase of the Reunion Struggle, 1941–1952.* Woodford Green, Essex, Lalibela House, 1953.

Park, Richard L., "East Bengal: Pakistan's Troubled Province," *Far Eastern Survey, 23,* 5 (May, 1954), 70–74.

Patten, George P., "Gabon," *Focus, 12,* 2 (October, 1961).

Perham, Margery, "The Sudan Emerges into Nationhood," *Foreign Affairs, 27,* 4 (July, 1949), 665–677.

Perlmann, M., "The Republic of Lebanon," *Palestine Affairs, 2,* 11 (November, 1947), 109–114.

Porter, Philip W., "Liberia," *Focus, 12,* 1 (September, 1961).

Pratt, R.C., "The Future of Federalism in British Africa," *Queens Quart, 67* (1960), 188–200.

Prescott, J.R.V., "The Geographical Basis of Nigerian Federation," *Nigerian Geog. J., 2,* 1 (June, 1958), 1–15.

———, "Nigeria's Regional Boundary Problems," *Geog. Rev., 49,* 4 (October, 1959), 485–505.

Proctor, Jesse Harris, "Britain's Pro-Federation Policy in the Caribbean; An Inquiry into Motivation," *Canadian J. Econ. and Political Sci., 22,* 3 (August, 1956), 319–331.

———, "The Effort to Federate East Africa: A Post-Mortem," *Political Quarterly, 37,* 1 (January–March, 1966), 46–69.

Ravenholt, Albert, "Formosa Today," *Foreign Affairs, 30,* 4, (July, 1952), 612–624.

Roberts, Margaret, "Political Prospects for the Cameroun," *World Today, 16,* 7 (July, 1960), 305–315.

Robertson, Sir James, "The Sudan in Transition," *African Affairs, 52,* 209 (October, 1953), 317–327.

Robinson, K.W., "The Political Influence in Australian Geography," *Pacific Viewpoint, 3,* 2 (July, 1962), 21–24.

———, "Sixty Years of Federation in Australia," *Geog. Rev., 51,* 1 (January, 1961), 1–20.

Rodman, Selden, *Haiti: The Black Republic.* New York, Devin-Adair Co., 1954.

Rose, A.J., "The Border between Queensland and New South Wales; A Study of Political Geography in a Federal Union," *Australian Geographer, 6,* 4 (January, 1955), 3–18.

Ryan, C., "The French-Canadian Dilemma," *Foreign Affairs, 43,* 3 (April, 1965), 462–474.

Sage, Walter N., "British Columbia and Confederation," *Brit. Columbia Quart., 15,* 1–2 (January–April, 1951), 71–84.

Schiller, A. Arthur, *The Formation of Federal Indonesia, 1945–1949.* The Hague, W. Van Hoeve, 1955.

Shabad, Theodore, *China's Changing Map; A Political and Economic Geography of the Chinese People's Republic.* New York, F.A. Praeger, 1956.

Shaudys, Vincent K., "Geographic Consequences of Establishing Sovereign Political Units," *Prof. Geog., 14,* 2 (March, 1962), 16–20.

Sheean, Vincent, "The People of Ceylon and Their Politics," *Foreign Affairs, 28,* 1 (October, 1949), 68–74.

Silberman, Leon, "Ethiopia: Power of Moderation," *Middle East J., 14,* 2 (1960), 141–152.

Solly, Marion B., "Yugoslavia; A Case Study in

Political Geography," *New Zealand Geographical Society. Proceedings* of the first geographical conference, Auckland, 1955 (1956), pp. 61–66.

Somerville, J.J.B., "The Central African Federation," *Internat. Affairs, 39*, 3 (July, 1963), 386–402.

Stanislawski, Dan, *The Individuality of Portugal; A Study in Historical-Political Geography*. Austin, University of Texas Press, 1959.

Stauffer, Robert B., "The Political Importance of China's Northeast," *Minister of Hawaii*, Occasional Paper No. 59, May, 1953, pp. 112–130.

Stokes, William S., *Honduras; An Area Study in Government*. Madison, University of Wisconsin Press, 1950.

Sukhwal, B.L., *India: a Political Geography*, New Delhi, Allied Publishers, 1971.

Sweet-Escott, Brickham, *Greece; a Political and Economic Survey, 1939–1953*, London, New York, Royal Institute of International Affairs, 1954.

Symonds, Richard, *The Making of Pakistan*. London, Faber, and Faber, 1950.

Taylor, Alice, *Egypt and Syria*. Garden City, N.Y., Doubleday, 1960.

Valkenier, Elizabeth K., "Eastern European Federation; A Study in the Conflicting National Aims and Plans of the Exile Groups," *J. Central European Affairs, 14*, 4 (January, 1955), 354–370.

Varma, S.N., "National Unity and Political Stability in Nigeria," *Internat. Studies, 4*, 3 (January, 1963), 265–280.

Villard, Henry Serrano, *Libya: the New Arab Kingdom of North Africa*. Ithaca, N.Y., Cornell University Press, 1956.

Wahl, N., *The Fifth Republic*. New York, Random House, 1959.

Walker, R.G., "Brazil : Political and Economic Evolution," *World Affairs*, n.s., *3*, 3 (July, 1949), 300–309.

Walker, Richard L., "Taiwan's Development as Free China," *Ann. Amer. Ac. Pol. & Soc. Sci., 321* (January, 1959), 122–135.

Welensky, Roy, "Toward Federation in Central Africa," *Foreign Affairs, 31*, 1 (October, 1952), 142–149.

Wheare, K.C., *Federal Government*. New York and London, Oxford University Press, 1947.

Wheeler, G., *Racial Problems in Soviet Muslim Asia*. London, Oxford University Press, 1962.

Whetten, Nathan L., *Guatemala; the Land and the People*. New Haven, Conn., Yale University Press, 1961.

Whittlesey, Derwent, "The Impress of Effective Central Authority upon the Landscape," *Ann. A.A.G., 25*, 2 (June, 1935), 85–97.

Wilson, Thomas (ed.), *Ulster under Home Rule; A Study of the Political and Economic Problems of Northern Ireland*. London, Oxford University Press, 1955.

Windmiller, Marshall, "The Politics of States Reorganization in India: the Case of Bombay," *Far Eastern Survey, 25*, 9 (September, 1956), 131–143.

Wriggins, W. Howard, *Ceylon: Dilemmas of a New Nation*. Princeton, N.J., Princeton University Press, 1960.

Wright, J.K., "Sections and National Growth," *Geog. Rev., 22*, (1932), 353–360.

Young, Richard, "The State of Syria: Old or New?" *Amer. J. Internat. Law, 56*, 2 (April, 1962), 482–488.

Zaidi, I.H., "Toward a Measure of the Functional Effectiveness of a State: the Case of West Pakistan," *Annals, A.A.G. 56*, 1 (March, 1966), 52–67.

Zarur, J., "The New Brazilian Territories," *Geog. Rev., 34*, 1 (January, 1944), 142–144.

CHAPTER
17
COLONIALISM AND
RESURGENT NATIONALISM *

Colonialism has been the vehicle upon which the ideas and skills of Europe were carried to many parts of the world. The massive emigration of people from European countries to the colonies began as a trickle in the fifteenth century and, after reaching a peak during the nineteenth and early twentieth centuries, subsided only during the past two generations. The various colonized areas received vastly different numbers of European immigrants, and at different times: the Americas were occupied and settled over a period of several centuries, while the major influx in Africa began, in most parts of that continent, less than a hundred years ago. When the United States had reached the crisis period of the Civil War, neither the diamonds of Kimberley nor the gold of Johannesburg had been discovered in Africa. Australia, one fourth the size of Africa, received several times as many European immigrants as did the black continent. Certain spheres of influence, like Argentina and New Zealand, became European states, with a dominant or almost exclusively European population and social order. Elsewhere the Europeans, though a minority, took control and ultimately asserted their independence from their European homelands. In the remainder of the colonial world, European states ruled their wards through governors and other representatives.

Having been colonized at different times, the various colonial realms freed themselves of foreign rule at different times. The wind of change came to South America early in the nineteenth century: Argentina in 1816, Chile in 1818, Peru in 1824, and Bolivia in 1825. It came to the Arab world in the interwar period, when Syria, Iraq, and Jordan threw off the colonial yoke. To most of Africa and Asia it

came after the end of the second World War, as it did in Indonesia, India and Pakistan, Algeria, and in Ghana, Nigeria, and Zambia, to name but a few of the recently established sovereign states.

In political geography, a number of questions concerning colonialism and its consequences are relevant. In the first place, its impact, in spatial terms, upon both the colonial power and its colonized territories is significant. Different colonial powers have organized and administered their colonial territories in different ways. Are these ways reflected by the politicoterritorial organization of the emergent states of today? Secondly, the various colonial powers obtained spheres of influence of greatly varying wealth and productiveness. Some of these colonial powers benefited economically from their new possessions, but others, in the final analysis, made a greater contribution to their dependencies than the colonies returned in profit and wealth. What has been the impact of this upon the colonial power? Thirdly, some states have sought to extend colonial control over areas that were known to be of little real value; nevertheless the effort was made, sometimes at great cost. What, then, are the motives of colonial powers, and do all states pass through a period during which colonial acquisitions are sought? and finally, the question of colonialism leads into that of resurgent nationalism. Is the nationalism of the present-day African, Arab, and Asian world comparable to the European nationalism of the seventeenth and eighteenth centuries, and can similar results be expected?

COLONIALISM AND GEOPOLITICS

The study of colonialism is the study of power and geopolitics. Expansionism has been a characteristic of many states, and it has always been made possible by superior power and organization. Such expansionist tenden-

---

*In this chapter, the names of colonies and states are used as they apply temporally. Thus the Congo will be referred to as the Congo during the period of Belgian Administration, and as Zaïre thereafter; when Malawi is called Nyasaland, the commentary relates to its colonial past.

cies were exhibited by states long before the most recent wave of colonialism: the Inca Empire grew by colonial acquisitions and the subjugation of outlying areas and peoples, as did the Roman Empire. Many European states in recent centuries sought to control parts of the non-European world because their populations and technology permitted them to do so, and the scale of European colonialism was unprecedented. We are here concerned with colonialism as a phenomenon related to the emergence of the modern nation-state, so that our interest is in the European drive for colonial possessions. However, it should be remembered that territorial acquisitiveness is not unique to European states, nor to the states that have existed only during the past two or three centuries.

We have seen that some terms in political geography are not well defined, and few of these present as many difficulties as does colonialism. If a "colonized" territory is contiguous to the colonial power, is it proper to speak of a colony in this case, or must a colony always be physically separated from the colonial power? And is an empty, occupied, and settled area colonized in the same terms as is one that was inhabited by an organized local population? Cohen has defined colonialism as separate from imperialism: "Colonialism, as a process, involves the settlement from a mother country, generally into empty lands and bringing into these lands the previous culture and organization of the parent society. Imperialism, as distinct from colonialism, refers to rule over indigenous people, transforming their ideas, institutions, and goods."[1] Frankel has attempted to bring greater clarity to the term colonization by recognizing *primary* colonization as the occupation of the lands and the domination of indigenous peoples, while *secondary* colonization is the acquisition by a colonial power of virtually empty territory.[2]

The very names of some of the dependencies of recent decades indicate how difficult it is to establish a definition for colonialism. Kenya Colony, for example, was a territory where empty-land "colonization" did take place in a few areas, but mostly the processes of occupation and control were those of imperialism. So it was with Rhodesia, another colony, and

Gold Coast. Thus we should perhaps speak of imperial colonization as involving the superimposition of foreign values upon traditional indigenous societies. Again, this does not solve the problem of "contiguous colonies"—whether it is proper to speak of, say, Tibet as a colony of China, or the Islam republics within the U.S.S.R. as Soviet colonies, or South Africa's Bantustans as colonial territories. It is worth recalling that colonialism, within the framework of the organic theory, is considered a necessity for any state that finds itself hemmed in by permanent political boundaries. Carrying the organic theory to its logical conclusion, and keeping in mind the thesis that the state requires territorial expansion as a constant life-giving force, it is obvious that the state that is without frontiers must seek alternate avenues for territorial growth. If contiguous territories can provide the life-giving elements needed, then noncontiguous territories can clearly do so as well. Hence it may be argued that China's occupation of Tibet, however justified on ethnic grounds and nonrewarding in economic terms, is as much an act of colonization as was Portugal's acquisition of Angola.

The geopolitical aspects of colonialism are self-evident. Taking the term at its narrowest meaning (i.e., referring to the German school of several decades ago), the relationships between German fears of "encirclement" and British imperialist activity are clear. Haushofer had personally visited the Eurasian perimeter, ringed by British bases; his doctrines constituted a direct reaction to that situation. Comparisons between land and sea powers such as those of Mahan and Mackinder served to emphasize the value of colonial possessions: Britain possessed a worldwide network of bases which more often than not were located within larger colonial entities, and Mahan advocated the acquisition of similar facilities by the United States. When, later, the subject of motivation is discussed, the geostrategic factor will be seen to be of great importance.

The subject of colonialism cannot be discussed without reference to its cyclic aspects. Van Valkenburg, as we have seen, has argued that the "adolescent" state goes through a stage of aggressiveness and territorial acquisition. Whether or not that is true, it cannot be denied that European states became capable of colonialist activities after a history of political evolution which, as Stoessinger has put it, "is

[1]S.B. Cohen, *Geography and Politics in a World Divided*, New York, Random House, 1963, p. 204.

[2]S.H. Frankel, *The Concept of Colonization*, Oxford, Clarendon Press, 1949.

the story of white men dominating other white men."[3] The French Revolution, a nationalist movement, produced imperialism. European imperial colonization on the part of the Napoleonic Empire produced a new rise of nationalism. French nationalism was a major factor in French participation in the colonial scramble of the past century and a half, and here in turn arose the nationalist movements which threw off the colonial yoke and achieved the sovereign state. And now, "the germs of imperialism are already in evidence in the nationalism of some of the new countries."[4] Imperial colonialism, then, appears to be a recurring phenomenon. It is less a matter of geographical location than it is one of state direction. It is and has been practiced by Asian, African, as well as European States, and is exhibited even by those countries that have recently suffered its negative consequences.

MOTIVES AND REWARDS

Geostrategic considerations, as indicated, have been prominent among the motives for colonial expansionism. The acquisition of overseas realms was a power struggle, sustained by the nationalist zeal of European states. The power of a state could, especially during the nineteenth century, be measured by the extent of its overseas possessions. States that were in competition with each other in Europe also vied with one another in the overseas scramble for territory. Britain and France were the major rivals, with Germany making a later entry; these states represent the major power cores of nineteenth-century Europe. While the British achieved success on all continents, to establish the greatest colonial empire ever to exist, the French attained a vast contiguous colonial territory in Africa and another in Southeast Asia. German colonial activity, which was confined to Africa, was in large part an attempt to thwart the designs of Britain and France. In West Africa the Germans succeeded in establishing themselves in Togo, thereby canceling any British plans to link their Gold Coast and Nigerian dependencies. In Kamerun, the Germans pushed far northward and came close to fragmenting the extensive French West African realm. In East

Africa, Germany obtained the mainland part of what is today the Republic of Tanzania, thereby dealing a final blow to British intentions regarding a Cape-to-Cairo axis. In South West Africa, Germany made use of a lapse in British attentiveness to gain a foothold adjacent to the richest part of the continent.

Geostrategic planning in colonial acquisition is reflected by the starting points of colonizing activity. The major avenues into the interior areas of colonized continents lay along the river valleys, so that much competition took place over river mouths and estuaries. The French and British negotiated in West Africa, the British recognizing French influence at the mouth of the Senegal River, while obtaining sovereignty over the Gambia River. The British also claimed the Volta and Niger mouths, but the French were successful at the Ogowe and Congo Rivers. In Asia, the British gained the vast Indian subcontinent, while the French established themselves at the Mekong. Today, the French still hold the natural outlet of Ethiopia (in the Territory of the Afars and Issas), but the British have yielded sovereignty at the mouth of the Mazaruni-Essequibo system, the pivotal geographic feature of Guyana. Elsewhere, British strategic planning led to the occupation and control of such vital points as Gibraltar, Suez, Aden, Singapore, Hong Kong, Cape Town, and many others. It was part of a worldwide imperial scheme, and it was indeed true that the sun never set over the British Empire.

Britain and France were neither the first nor the last European states to embark upon colonial expansion. Spain and Portugal vied for hegemony in the Americas as early as the final decade of the fifteenth century, and the Dutch, Danes, and Brandenburgers at the same time competed for colonial beachheads on the West African coast. The Treaty of Tordesillas may have greatly influenced the course of colonial history, for it appeared to divide between Spain and Portugal not only the Americas but all newly discovered and undiscovered lands. It has been postulated that this may be why Portugal, which for decades had almost unobstructed opportunity to extend its sphere of influence in Africa, actually established only a few centers needed to facilitate and protect the Cape route to the Indies. Subsequently, when Britain, France, Germany, and Belgium entered the scene, Portugal could only claim historical rights over areas which by the realities of power fell to other states. Even in

[3]J.G. Stoessinger, *The Might of Nations*, New York, Random House, 1961, p. 79.
[4]*Ibid.*

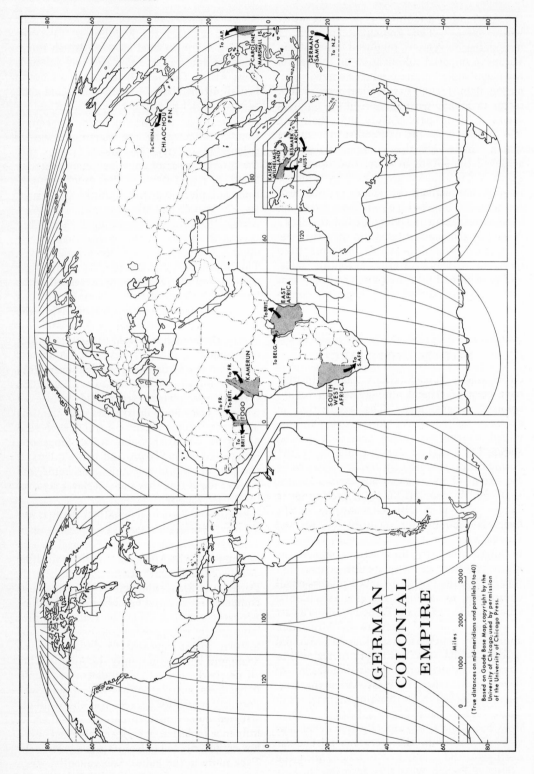

GERMAN COLONIAL EMPIRE

Miles
0   1000   2000   3000

(True distances on mid-meridians and parallels 0 to 40)

Based on Goode Base Map, copyright by the
University of Chicago, used by permission
of the University of Chicago Press.

South America the treaty did not ward off other invaders: the British, French, and Dutch established colonial domains in the area where, according to the treaty, Portuguese and Spanish colonial realms should have met.

The last European power to engage in a deliberate program of colonization in noncontiguous territories was Italy. Its invasion of Ethiopia, shortly before the second World War, was a demonstration of power and a quest for prestige; it would be difficult to justify the act by any other means. The region involved is not a rich one and presents severe problems of organization and administration, and the Italian contribution in terms of road building and other programs (not to mention the military campaign) exceeded any returns that were realized.

Coupled with the geostrategic motives for colonization were a number of other inducements. "God, greed, and gold" sustained the Spanish in their penetration of the Americas, implying that they were there not only to gain wealth but also to make a contribution to the spiritual well-being of their wards. This missionary zeal was not unique to the Spanish in America. The calling to bring the benefits of what Europeans saw as their more advanced civilization and their "true" religion to the backward colonial world constituted another driving force. Indeed, the first penetration was often made by actual missionaries, who established stations which sometimes became the centers from which colonial control was extended. One of the more illustrative cases in point is that of South West Africa, which made its first permanent contacts with Europe through several German missionaries. It was the small German missionary population that found itself in trouble during an ensuing intra-African war, appealed for help—and brought German occupation to this area.

Missionary zeal was not confined to missionaries. A relatively small number of European explorers and adventurers, wishing to make a contribution to their fatherland, had an enormous impact upon the process of colonization. Cecil Rhodes was possessed of this spirit, and he almost singlehandedly penetrated the region of the Zambezi River on behalf of the British Crown. He strongly influenced the course of events in South Africa, and the map of Africa eventually carried his name in Northern and Southern Rhodesia. Luderitz, a wealthy German mer-

chant, similarly helped initiate and sustain the German drive in South West Africa, while Karl Peters did the same in East Africa. De Brazza represented France in the area of the lower Congo River. In nineteenth-century Europe, such activities carried the highest honor and approval.

At times the governments of the states of Europe, as a result of the colonial scramble in which they were involved, found themselves confronted with requests for "protection" by peoples facing the threat of penetration by colonists. Such protection, if granted by the government, would prevent the colonists from conquering the indigenous people by force and taking their land. Such "protectorates" were occasionally granted, especially if the government of one state received such a request from a people facing colonization by colonists from another state. We might term this type of colonization as resulting from a particular kind of moral obligation, as distinct from that exhibited by the individual missionaries and explorers.

In many parts of the colonized world, the major motive that drove the colonial power to control was the economic one. For three centuries the Netherlands East Indies "were one vast coffee plantation yielding enormous revenues for the Dutch government . . . the indigenous population was forced to give up its land, volunteer its labor, and generally devote itself to the improvement of the economy of the Netherlands."[5] Some other colonies, too, sustained the home economy for many decades. King Leopold, in his acquisition of the Congo, foresaw great profits to be derived from ivory and rubber. Portugal introduced a system of compulsory cropping in its African domain to support the metropolitan economy. But very often, the vast wealth of the colonial world turned out to be more imagined than real, and some colonies became liabilities rather than assets. Until the ascent to power of the Salazar regime, Portugal was barely able to administer Angola and Mozambique; Salazar's acceptance of the leadership of Portugal was made under condition that he should be empowered to initiate economic reform programs in the colonies aimed at their contributing to Portuguese finances. Mauritania, Chad, Somalia, Surinam, New Guinea, Laos—their economic contribution to the

[5]*Ibid.*, p. 84.

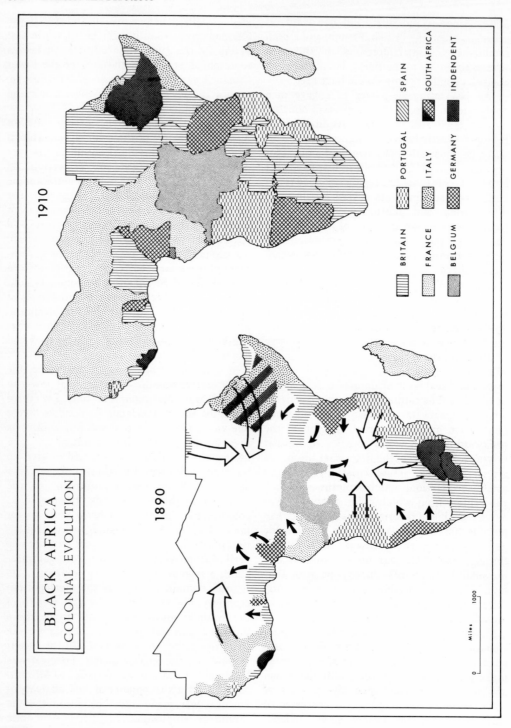

BLACK AFRICA
COLONIAL EVOLUTION

1890

1910

Miles
0   1000

BRITAIN

FRANCE

BELGIUM

PORTUGAL

ITALY

GERMANY

SPAIN

SOUTH AFRICA

INDENDENT

colonial power was mainly negative. Then, some colonized territories produced richly for a few decades, but soon were exhausted. The quest for gold in the Americas initially met with staggering success, but the sources were rapidly expended.

Many colonial territories benefited from the introduction of crops by the European colonizers, and the European homeland in turn benefited from the successful introduction of these crops. Sudan, Uganda, and other countries find their economies sustained today by crops introduced on farms in some cases laid out by European colonizers. Portugal pays below-world prices for Mozambique cotton, but British Commonwealth and French Community countries receive preferential rates for certain crops introduced during the colonial period. In Tanzania, Cameroun, Ghana, and Nigeria the ways of life of hundreds of thousands of people were changed by the introduction of cash cropping. The local people often objected to the methods of its introduction, and doubtlessly the European power benefited from the availability of the agricultural produce. But ultimately the advantages seem to lie with the colonial territory, which needs sources of revenue to achieve viability at independence.

It is difficult to draw up a balance sheet showing the credits and debits of every association between a European power and each of its dependencies. Whatever the motives of the colonial power in each case, the returns probably failed to reach expected levels in more cases than not. Katanga proved to be a great asset to the Belgian economy, but ultimately the Congo put a severe strain upon the Belgian state. The vastness of the British Empire brought a wide variety of riches into Crown coffers, but the Empire included (and still includes) a long list of territories whose organization and administration have been costly and difficult. It is indeed unwise to generalize colonialism as an exploitative system wholly in favor of the colonial power. In the first place, the benefits have on occasion been on the side of the dependency, and in the second, there have been as many different types of colonialism as there have been colonial powers. Some, as we shall see, have been blatantly exploitative in their colonial administration, but others have seen their colonial task as one involving major responsibilities for the welfare of the colonized population.

METHODS AND RESULTS

The methods employed by European powers to organize and administer the territories and peoples in their dependencies have varied widely. As a result, the indigenous peoples' responses have differed greatly. Among the very few aspects all imperial colonial systems have had in common is that they have all fostered nationalism—but they have treated this phenomenon in their individual ways. Some have managed to turn local nationalism into constructive directions. Others fought it bitterly as an evil force, only to render it more extreme and, in many cases, destructive of progress and unity even among the colonized peoples themselves.

Political geographers are especially interested in the spatial features of colonial administrative policies, although many other aspects are obviously relevant as well. Colonial powers have had to subdivide their dependencies in order to govern them; they have had to choose capital cities and establish boundaries. Some have experimented with political philosophies that are successful in Europe. Others have not even attempted to apply the political ideas of the metropolitan homeland in the colonies. And some, like the Netherlands, have shifted their mode of operation considerably as a consequence of experience.

The total range of colonial policies is displayed by the activities in this sphere of Britain, France, Belgium, and Portugal. Although, among these four, Belgium is no longer a colonial power, its colonial practices exemplified one type of approach which requires discussion. Other states—namely, the Netherlands, Spain, and Denmark—still retain overseas possessions, but not on the same scale.

Portugal alone still clings to the philosophy that its distant possessions are in fact "provinces" of the metropolitan Portuguese state, whose residents can aspire to Portuguese citizenship and to representation in the Portuguese government. Such major changes as have come to overseas Portugal during the past five centuries have come during the last few years, when the pressure of the wind of change was beginning to affect Portugal's major empire in Africa. Portugal's colonial policies have often been compared to those of the Netherlands in the East Indies, but the comparison is not altogether appropriate. The Indies produced more readily than could

Angola and Mozambique, and the role of the Dutch East Indies in the Netherlands economy was much more significant than that of overseas Portugal was to the Portuguese economy. Only during the Salazar regime have Angola and Mozambique begun to approach a similar role.

Although Portugal still controls various non-African territories, including Macao and Eastern Timor, Portuguese colonial policies are most clearly displayed in its vast African domain. Here, an economic framework of organization was long superimposed upon a political framework. Politically, the two "provinces" are administered through the governor general in the capital city (Lourenco Marques in Mozambique, Luanda in Angola). For purposes of administrative control each territory is subdivided into subprovinces, where decisions made in Lisbon and transmitted through the governor general are implemented. Economically, however, there is a system of producing regions that affects the population much more directly than the internal political subdivisions. These economic units, in many ways, are the *de facto* political subdivisions of the provinces, where the European's control over the daily lives of the indigenous population is most strongly felt. The system has recently been modified, in the face of international objections, but its impact continues to be felt, for it existed in full force when Portuguese Africa reached the crucial period of the 1950's:

The system whereby Mocambique has been administered is that of the circumscription, an idea that originated with Antonio Enes in the 1890s . . . but . . . the economic possibilities have been most fully exploited by Salazar's *Estado Novo*.

The circumscription is perhaps best defined as a geographical area inhabited by a dominantly rural African population, controlled by a single administrator assisted by one or more "chiefs-of-post." In 1958, the median population under the control of a single administrator in Mocambique was 63,000, and 15 of the more than 80 such districts had populations numbering over 100,000. The circumscriptions were arbitrarily defined, incorporating a certain number of villages and surrounding lands. Boundaries were almost never demarcated, but the African headmen and chiefs were informed under whose jurisdiction they fell.

. . . The administrators of the circumscription were given extraordinary powers. No African may leave or enter a circumscription without the chief-of-post's permission . . . for the majority . . . the circumscription is the enforced place of residence for life. According to labor laws long in operation, the men must be in gainful employ or, between the ages of 18 and 55, must serve the State six months every year . . . [and] they are liable for conscription to work, for very low wages and under severe conditions. . . .

The activities of the African inhabitants within the circumscription are closely controlled by the administrator's staff. He (the administrator) has jurisdiction over the amount of land to be placed under crops, the types of crops to be grown, and all transactions involving cattle must carry his approval.

. . . [Elsewhere, away from the cities, as in the north of Mocambique] the enforced contribution until very recently was the growing of a prescribed acreage of crops (cotton in northern Mocambique) . . . in a sense, the people under the forced-crop system were worse off even than those working for the State on public projects, for the system reduced the acreage upon which subsistence crops could be grown, and at times had disastrous effects upon the food situation. . . .

A number of consequences are of significance to the political geography of the provinces. First, the circumscription arrangement has divided even further an already tribally heterogeneous population. . . . Second, the hopelessness of life in the circumscriptions and the recurring prospect of low-wage work for the State has driven many men from the territories. . . . Third, the system has practically prevented, especially in interior Mocambique, the mental association of the people with their whole homeland, the whole province. Not only has it prevented circulation, it has also eliminated communication, to an extent not repeated anywhere else in Subsaharan Africa. . . . Fourth, the black populations of Mocambique and Angola are probably farther removed from nationhood than any others in Subsaharan Africa.[6]

The price paid by these Portuguese dependencies for their new role in the state has indeed been high. Even the Netherlands, after its loss of the Indies, altered its colonial policies in the direction of "association" with what remained of its colonial empire. Today, only Portugal persists in an imperial colonial policy which is reminiscent of another century.

[6]H.J. de Blij, *A Geography of Subsaharan Africa*, Chicago, Rand McNally, 1964, pp. 180–181. For a detailed description of the circumscription see M. Harris, *Portugal's African Wards*, New York, American Committee on Africa, 1958. Also see J. Duffy, *Portuguese Africa*, Cambridge, Harvard University Press, 1959. A later volume by Dr. Duffy is *Portugal in Africa*, New York, Penguin Books, 1962.

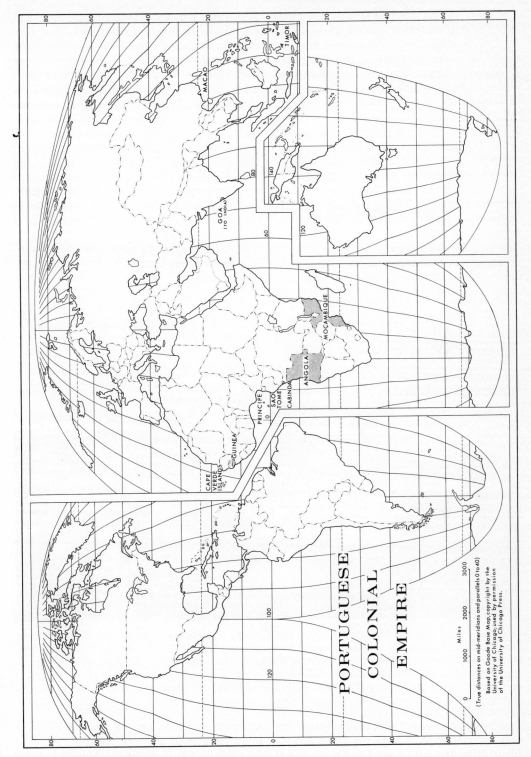

PORTUGUESE COLONIAL EMPIRE

MACAO

GOA
(TO INDIA)

TIMOR

MOÇAMBIQUE

ANGOLA

CABINDA

SAO TOME

PRINCIPE

GUINEA

CAPE VERDE ISLANDS

Miles
0   1000   2000   3000

(True distances on mid-meridians and parallels 0 to 40)

Based on Goode Base Map, copyright by the
University of Chicago, used by permission
of the University of Chicago Press.

Belgium saw its colonial task as a paternal one. The Belgians never viewed the Congo as an "overseas Belgium," and neither did they intend to make Belgians of the Congolese population. Apart from the mandate and trusteeship over Ruanda-Urundi, the Belgians possessed only one dependency: the Congo. Once the personal possession of King Leopold II, the Congo administration was taken over by the Belgian state as recently as 1907, after the reputation of the country had suffered through the exposure of the "Congo atrocities" which took place during the King's administration. The Belgian colonial administration thus lasted for only a half century, during which the infrastructure of the present Zaïre Republic was created.

The shape characteristics of Zaïre were discussed in Chapter 3 and its multicore administration, and was connected by rail to the port of Matadi. But Kinshasa (as Leopoldville is now called) lies on the periphery of the vast Congo basin, and its communications with outlying parts of the country have never been good. The Belgians thus established six major provinces, each with a capital, and each extending over a section of the highland rim of the Congo as well as over a part of the interior basin. The capital cities became the headquarters of lieutenant governors, whose tasks included the implementation of Brussels policy as conveyed by the governor general from his Leopoldville office. Each province was in turn divided into a number of districts, where lesser officials were in charge.

A glance at even the most general geographic patterns in the Congo reveals the shortcomings, from the Zaïrian viewpoint, of this

One of few remaining colonial capitals: Lourenco Marques, a Portuguese colonial city. While reflecting, through its spacious avenues, its recent development, Lourenco Marques retains a strong Portuguese flavor. Inlaid sidewalks, monuments commemorating Portuguese national heroes, clustered suburban homes with walled grounds, and the dominant architectural style all contribute to this atmosphere. The major source of income is the well-appointed port facility, used by vessels whose cargo is destined for a foreign country, the Republic of South Africa (Harm J. de Blij).

aspects in Chapter 5. These realities faced the Belgian colonist as they do the Zaïre government today. It was necessary to have a capital city relatively near the ocean, but the narrow proruption leading to the Atlantic Ocean did not provide space for one. Hence Leopoldville became the permanent headquarters of the arrangement. Each province was so positioned as to lie astride a major transport route to Leopoldville, but provincial boundaries cut through tribal and linguistic units while fragmenting others. Some (such as the Kivu-Katanga boundary) were geometric: the system obviously was created for administrative convenience rather than the integration of the whole country. The capital cities became the places of power, the embryo core areas for each province, and the provinces in some ways became separate colonies, with Leopoldville a distant and foreign center. This was reflected by the events immediately after independence, when the cities of Stanleyville, Luluabourg, and Elizabethville—all provincial capitals —became centers of control for secessionist leaders who took over from the Europeans and failed to heed Leopoldville's dictates. Thus Belgium, unwittingly, prepared the country for near-feudal conditions by imposing the administrative framework of the six provinces.

Belgian colonial policies were such that decisions regarding the Congo were made only in Brussels. In the Congo, neither the European representatives of the Belgian government, the settlers, nor any other European group possessed any political rights or any voice in the fate of the territory. Neither, until a matter of months before independence, did the indigenous inhabitants. Furthermore, the paternalist approach to colonial administration had its effects in economic, educational, and social spheres: much progress was made at elementary but very little at higher levels. While the Portuguese have opened a narrow avenue for Africans to attain *assimilado* status, theoretically implying full Portuguese citizenship, the Belgian *evolués* could not aspire to Belgian nationality and equality. Even the "evolved" indigenous population was viewed as in need of paternal restrictions.

The areas of productive capacity of Zaïre, as we have seen, are concentrated in several rather clearly defined regions. The Belgians did not need to bring the Congo into the European economy in the Portuguese manner, for the Katanga and other, less important productive areas constituted major sources of income. But it was Belgium, not the Congo, that benefited principally from the Congo's productivity. While Belgian financial interest groups in the Congo thrived, the colonial administration struggled to overcome the internal diversity of the country, usually with inadequate resources. In the three-headed power structure in the Congo, consisting of the colonial government, the church, and the economic concerns, each had its own goals, and the common denominator was the paternalist approach, which suited the aims of all three. Such progress as was made served first of all to further these aims. The transport system permitted the coastward transit of interior products. The churches and missions, while doing sterling work in the fields of education and medicine, strengthened the role of the white man as the father of the African masses. Under the colonial administration, "very little was done to draw the various regions and peoples together under the flag of a single and unified State."[7] The object was control, not organization in the sense that applies to the functioning state system.

Among the questions relating to colonialism of interest in political geography is the extent to which the colonial framework of administration survives in the emergent independent state. The Congo, as we know, became a federal state, an apparently logical move in view of its multi-core character and the nature of the provincial arrangement. But the internal diversity of the country, especially its ethnic diversity, soon brought about a complete change in the political framework. In 1963 the country established twenty-one provinces, based largely upon tribal realities.[8] This attempt to do away with the major units that served colonial purposes is mirrored by similar plans proposed repeatedly in another African federation, Nigeria. The hope is that a larger number of units, with roughly equal populations, will render it vastly more difficult, if not impossible, for any one unit to secede from the state, or to dominate or obstruct the course of progress as determined by the majority. While the colonial administration ruled the country, such secession or obstruction was out of the question. But the colonial administration only submerged and delayed the emergence of the centrifugal forces which the geography of the Congo contains. In the years just prior to independence, the colonial power itself was the centripetal force in the territory, and tribalism was buried in the wave of nationalist fervor. But after independence, the situation changed, and the country required outside help to prevent its disintegration.

France once adhered to the concept of a *France d'Outre Mer*, an Overseas France, but that idea was largely abandoned with the demise of the Fourth Republic. If the best one-word definition for Belgian colonial policy is paternalism, the most appropriate term for

[7]A.P. Merriam, *Congo, Background of Conflict*, Evanston, Northwestern University Press, 1961, p. 28.

[8]M. Crawford Young, "The Congo's Six Provinces Become 21," *Africa Report, 8*, 9 (October, 1963) 12.

French colonialism is assimilation. Like the Portuguese, but with more to offer and more success, the French have brought French culture to their overseas domain, where it remains very much in evidence despite the fact that French control has ceased. Unlike the Belgians, the French desired the quick development of an educated, acculturated elite, which would have French interests at heart and French culture to boast. This elite, it was reasoned, would support the French presence in the empire as a matter of self-protection, for by accepting and adopting French values and ways of life, these people often separated themselves from their own countrymen, most of whom remained mired in the stagnant pool of tribalism. In Southeast Asia as well as Africa, many of the modern leaders of the independent "French" emergent states are products of this elite and the system that helped erect it. The late President Diem of South Viet Nam was such a representative, as are a number of the present-day African leaders: Houphouet-Boigny, Senghor, and others.

French colonial subjects, then, were to be assimilated in the greater French Empire, and they could obtain a voice in the politics of the French realm through representation in Paris. A number of overseas territories of France had such representation, and French dependencies were placed in a hierarchy, their position in terms of closeness to France determined by their historical associations with the motherland.

The French Empire, in its fullest development, consisted of two major, contiguous areas (one in Africa, the other In Asia), and a number of smaller settlements scattered in many parts of the world, including Caribbean America. The politicoterritorial aspects of French colonialism are perhaps most clearly revealed in Africa, where the bulk of French territory was located. In Africa, Algeria always occupied a special position, because of its large settled French population and its proximity and effective communications with European France. The remainder of French Africa was divided into two major "federations"—the term "federation" was here used to imply "grouping" or "association" rather than its technical meaning—French West Africa and French Equatorial Africa. These territories were not, however, administered as undivided units. A number of separate political entities were established, often defined in West Africa

by geometric boundaries, each focusing upon a single core area and capital. French Equatorial Africa consisted of Moyen Congo, Gabon, Ubangi-Shari, and Chad, with their respective capitals of Brazzaville, Libreville, Bangui, and Fort Lamy. The administrative headquarters of French Equatorial Africa, however, were in Brazzaville, so that this city attained a greater importance than the others and grew to greater size. But although French Equatorial Africa shares many of the characteristics of Zaïre, the French never attempted to unify their entire equatorial realm into one political unit. The four states of French Equatorial Africa (now Congo, Gabon, the Central African Republic, and Chad) are in the same size category as the provinces of the Belgian colony, but the French always saw them as individual and separate entities, despite their association for administrative convenience in a "federation." Major colonial policies were transmitted through Brazzaville, but decisions regarding each individual country were implemented directly through the local capitals.

French West Africa, including such important territories as Senegal, the Ivory Coast, Guinea, Mali, and Upper Volta, also had its administrative headquarters: Dakar, today the capital of the Republic of Senegal. Again, each individual country had its own focus, and some of these core areas are of considerable significance today. Southeastern Ivory Coast, with its impressive capital, Abidjan, is a core area of the first order in West Africa. Dakar remains French-influenced Africa's most important port, but Conakry and Porto Novo-Cotonou serve Guinea and Dahomey respectively. Only in landlocked Upper Volta can two embryo cores be recognized: the capital, Ouagadougou, and the second city, Bobo Dioulasso, form separate foci for individual population sectors of that state.

Although these various territories enjoyed a measure of individuality even during the period of French control, they never functioned as self-contained units. Those which were, and are, landlocked, including Mali, Niger, and Upper Volta, had secure outlets through other French-controlled territories. With independence, boundaries that long had functioned as administrative conveniences suddenly acquire international significance, capitals that had required only a minimum of facilities needed immediate expansion, and core areas of productivity that had only partially paid the territories' way became the

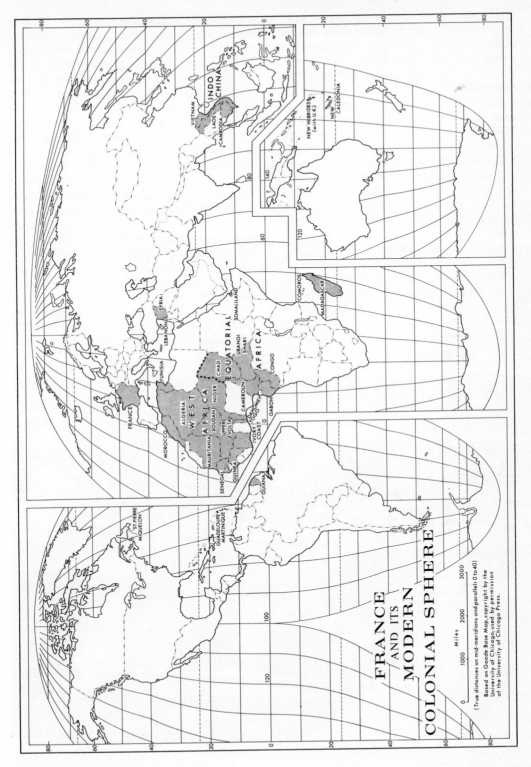

FRANCE
AND ITS
MODERN
COLONIAL SPHERE

Miles
0   1000   2000   3000

(True distances on mid-meridians and parallels 0 to 40)

Based on Goode Base Map, copyright by the
University of Chicago, used by permission
of the University of Chicago Press.

vital resources of states struggling for viability. Not surprisingly, a number of the emergent states tried to establish new associations aimed at the reduction of unnecessary duplication of facilities. This feature of former French Africa is discussed in the next chapter.

Britain possessed an empire that was larger than any other colonial realm, and was confronted by a wider variety of indigenous cultures and peoples than any other European colonial power. British colonial policies were often adapted to the requirements of individual dependencies, but British policy, like that of Belgium and France, had a basic premise: indirect rule, British colonial policy, then, always was the least centralized among the European colonial powers.

The principle of indirect rule was intended to prevent the destruction of indigenous culture and organization. In such fields as tribal authority, law, and education, the British often recognized local customs and permitted their perpetuation, initially outlaw-

ing only those practices that constituted, in British eyes, serious transgressions. Then the people were slowly introduced to the changes British rule inevitably brought. Prior to the second World War, the emphasis was especially upon slowness; haste in bringing about reforms was seen as an evil and danger. Despite this attitude, however, the British from very early on professed that their ultimate goal was the independence and self-determination of the peoples under their colonial flag. In this, British colonial policy differed from that of other European powers, which either planned to convert their overseas realms into integral parts of the European state, or indicated that they did not foresee any time, within the next several generations, when colonial areas could become self-governing. After the second World War, the pace of change became faster than anyone, including the British, had expected. The British response, in general, was to help dependencies destined for independence develop parliamen-

The French colonial presence in black Africa. Dakar, largest French-developed city in Subsaharan Africa, was the headquarters for the vast "federation" of French West Africa, and its largest port. The modern central city continues to reflect the colonial period, with its skyscraper offices and apartment buildings, sidewalk restaurants, and architectural imitations of French structures. Now the capital of the state of Senegal, Dakar remains the focus for a country in which the French influence, cultural as well as political, can still be felt (Harm J. de Blij).

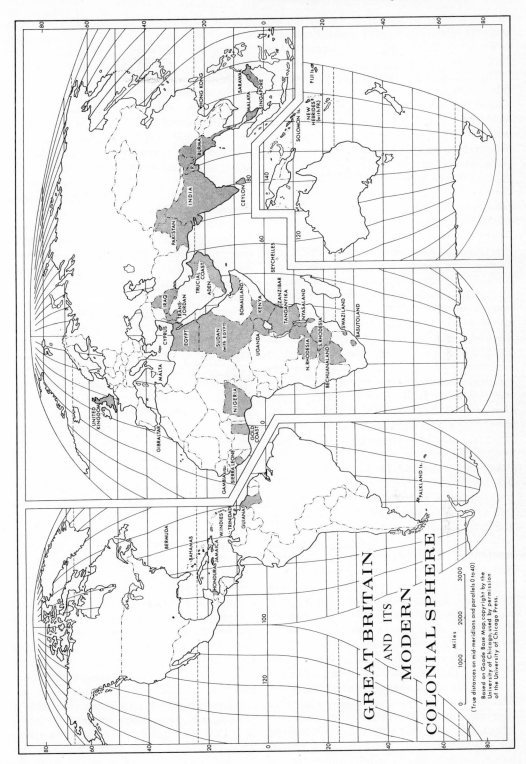

GREAT BRITAIN
AND ITS
MODERN
COLONIAL SPHERE

Miles
0   1000   2000   3000

(True distances on mid-meridians and parallels 0 to 40)

Based on Goode Base Map, copyright by the
University of Chicago; used by permission
of the University of Chicago Press.

tary systems of government. Less attention was paid to the principle of indirect rule, and more to the development of elected local African government.

The variety of British approaches to colonial rule in their numerous colonies also was related to the size and character of the European "settler" population in these dependencies. What was said in the previous paragraphs concerning indirect rule was especially true in territories with a small immigrant European population, little land alienation, and a history of peaceful penetration rather than violence and conquest. In territories where the settler population was large and powerful, the desires of London were often overridden by those of the local whites. Cases in point are a former colony, Kenya, and a territory on the verge of crisis, Rhodesia. Kenya saw a major rebellion before the white population relinquished its political and other privileges to the majority African peoples, and Rhodesian whites declared their colony an independent state in response to the British government attempts to interfere in the political situation there, which has always been heavily in favor of the European population sector. But elsewhere, as in Sudan, Ghana, Sierra Leone, and Uganda, the white colonists presented far fewer obstacles in the path toward independence.

Britain's intent to award independence to its dependent territories was initially evinced by the creation of the dominions. Canada, Australia, New Zealand, and South Africa all attained sovereignty within the Commonwealth long before the beginning of the second World War. But among these four, only South Africa possessed a white minority population. The indigenous peoples of the other three countries had long been insignificantly small sectors of the total population. In these states the Europeans performed the tasks of state formation and organization, and with their European heritage the results were to be expected. The real problems arose first in the Middle East during the interwar period, when Arab nationalism waged a struggle for national liberation against the British administration which had taken over after the destruction of the Ottoman Empire. The announced British policy had been one of self-determination for the indigenous population, but bringing it about was a difficult matter. Then, after the second World War, the drive toward independence intensified greatly, and the pace of

change accelerated immeasurably. In Asia, Africa, and America, Britain found itself having to hasten a process which, by the very nature of British colonial policy, was to be successful only if ample time were available.

The variety to be found within the British Empire (i.e., the British dependencies) just after the second World War was immense. In terms of political geography, Britain was administering territories in all size ranges and in all shape categories. British India included more than one and a half million square miles; Swaziland less than seven thousand. Some dependencies, like Uganda, Basutoland, and Nyasaland, were landlocked; others, like Malta, Jamaica, and Fiji, were island territories. In certain territories the population was to be counted in the thousands, in others, in the hundreds of millions. Some colonies were single-core political units, as were the Gold Coast, Sierra Leone, and British Guiana; others were multicore territories, like Nigeria, Tanganyika, and Northern Rhodesia. The capital cities of the colonies were in some cases indigenous cities, and in others they were founded and developed. In one case, Bechuanaland, the capital, Mafeking, actually was located *outside* the boundaries of the political entity! The variety was practically endless, and it is not surprising that different means of control and administration had to be applied.

Apart from the white settler element playing a role in the Crown's colonial administration, the historical factor also influenced the status of the territory within the framework of the empire. Any territory invaded, conquered, and settled by a white immigrant population became a *colony*, implying a considerable amount of self-determination for the settler population. However, those territories whose indigenous leaders had requested and been granted Crown "protection" became *protectorates*. While the principle of indirect rule, in the white-controlled colonies, was mainly replaced by local European control, the principle was adhered to quite strictly in any territory that had been granted the status of protectorate. Sometimes adjacent territories possessed a different status: Northern Rhodesia was a protectorate, but Southern Rhodesia, by virtue of conquest from the south, became a colony. Uganda, in East Africa, became a protectorate, while Kenya was a colony. Sometimes different parts of the same political entity came under different

The British colonial impact in Southern Africa. Salisbury, capital of Rhodesia, was the headquarters of the illfated Central African Federation (see Chapter 16). The modern urban plan, with its wide avenues and thoroughfares, sprawling suburbs, and considerable vertical development reflect the brevity of British overlordship in this area—Salisbury's growth began only shortly before the turn of the present century. Unlike the congestion and narrow streets of British cities, Salisbury's downtown rectangularity is reminiscent of many smaller American cities (Harm J. de Blij).

kinds of administrative control: southern Nigeria, in contact with Britain much more effectively than the north, became a colony, while northern Nigeria remained under indirect rule.

Britain also administered a number of territories in cooperation with other colonial and noncolonial powers. This joint administration produced the *condominium,* and the Anglo-Egyptian Sudan is the prime example, ruled as it was by the British and the Egyptians. It was never a smooth-working administration, for the Sudan is a vast and divided country with a history of fear and enmity toward Egypt in the north and uneasiness toward black Africa in the south. A less significant condominium, the New Hebrides, is the product of administrative cooperation between Britain and France.

Britain, like other European powers after the first World War, was made responsible for a number of territories which were dependencies of the defeated powers in that war. In the Middle East and Africa, the breakdown of the Ottoman Empire and the German colonies required new administrations in these territories. Britain obtained mandates in the Middle East as well as Africa, the largest of these being

that of Tanganyika. Britain still administered this territory at the time of the outbreak of the second World War and placed it under United Nations Trusteeship Commission auspices afterward. Thus the *trust territory* constitutes another type of British dependency.

Finally, Britain held several territories that cannot be grouped with any of the preceding categories. The Suez Canal Zone was among these, as were the sheikdoms of Kuwait, Qatar, Muscat, and Oman, as well as the Ellice and Gilbert Islands. For various strategic or economic reasons, Britain either directly or indirectly controlled these and a number of other areas. Several have since attained a different status, but others still form parts of the remnant British Empire of today.

THE RESPONSE TO NATIONALISM

We have characterized Portuguese colonial policy as integration with the homeland, Belgian policy as paternalism, French policy as assimilation, and British policy as varied, with indirect rule the major principle. During the past two decades, each of these colonial powers has had to deal with the rise of

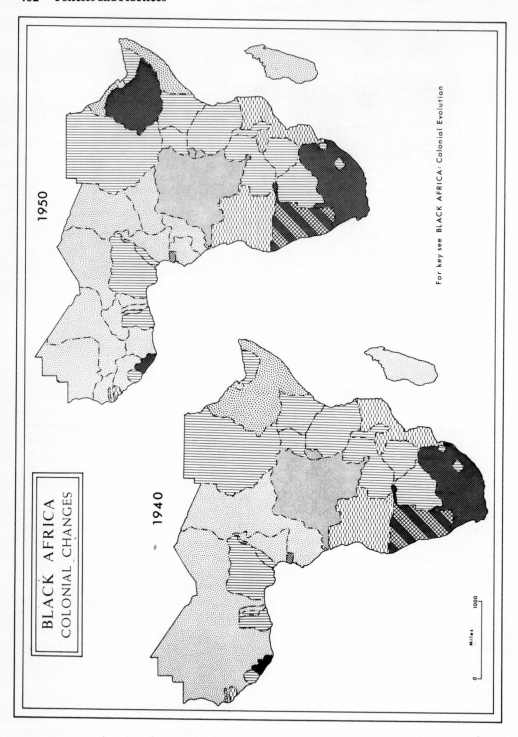

BLACK AFRICA
COLONIAL CHANGES

1940

1950

Miles

0   1000

For key see BLACK AFRICA: Colonial Evolution

nationalism within their colonial realms. In general that wave of nationalism came earlier and more intensely than had been anticipated, and the rapidity with which colonial territories became independent states was quite unexpected. In the beginning of this chapter we asked ourselves whether this resurgent nationalism is comparable to the nationalism of the Europe of several centuries ago, and whether the results can be expected to be the same. Kautsky says the following with regard to European nationalism:

With the revolutions of the seventeenth century in Britain and the late eighteenth century in France, broader strata of the population (notably the middle classes) came into a position to influence the government. It became the government of "the people," and the people were defined in terms of their language. Thus, the Bourbon kings had been kings of France, of a territory once inhabited by people speaking various languages or dialects, but Napoleon was emperor of the French, of a people speaking a single language. There now arose the entirely novel identification of the "State," i.e., the government and the territory under its control, and of the "nationality," i.e., the language and culture group, as the "nation." People with a common language regarding a government composed of individuals speaking the same language as "their own" government, or the desire of such people to have such a government, would seem to be an essential element of nationalism as it appeared in Europe.
. . . Nationalism may be defined from this European experience as an ideology and a movement striving to unite all people who speak a single language, and who share the various cultural characteristics transmitted by that language, in a single independent State and in loyalty to a single government conducted in the people's language.[9]

But nationalism in the former colonial world is a very different matter. In Europe, language and nationality factors were key elements in the growth of nationalism. A considerable amount of economic and political integration and circulation existed in Europe, and single languages were used over large areas and by many people. Even prior to the evolution of the modern nation-state, people had experience in certain forms of

participation in politics and had representation in a government that was theirs, not that of some outside power. On the other hand, the colonial territories incorporated many languages and distinct tribal peoples, and practically every colony's population spoke several (if not dozens or hundreds) of mutually unintelligible dialects. This (quite apart from restrictive colonial policies) greatly impeded communication among these peoples. Furthermore, while religious homogeneity existed in some colonies (and religion has played its role in the recent reemergence of nationalism), ethnic heterogeneity and cultural variety mark the indigenous populations of almost all recent colonial areas. The role of religion in the rise of Arab nationalism is obviously significant, and the added factor of linguistic unity over much of the Arab world would indicate that Arab nationalism might be comparable to European nationalism. And yet the Arab world is internally divided, and local "nationalisms" confront each other in hostility.

The nationalism of the colonial world has not sought to reunite peoples speaking the same or similar languages who were divided from one another by colonial boundaries. The imposition of one language as a unifier has sometimes come after the period of most intense nationalist activity had come to an end, as in the case of India in recent years. Resurgent nationalism has respected colonial boundaries and has in many instances carefully guarded them. Indeed, the main element common to the nationalisms in the various recently colonial areas appears to be anticolonialism. It is, thus, a negative force in that its greatest strength lies in a receding object, for which a replacement must be found. A number of replacements have already been devised, some imagined and some real. Indonesian nationalism has been fanned, after the ouster of the Dutch, by a campaign against West Irian's continuing Dutch administration, and subsequently against the Federal State of Malaysia. Still in store for the Indonesians, on this basis, would be an anti-Portuguese campaign in Timor and a policy of expansionism toward Mindanao, southern major island of the Philippines. Elsewhere, neocolonialism serves similar purposes, as does "economic imperialism." In Subsaharan Africa, the common enmity toward Portugal's colonial policies and South Africa's segregationist practices has done much to strengthen an African

---

[9]For an excellent summary, including many useful references, of the role of nationalism in the underdeveloped world see J.H. Kautsky, *Political Change in Underdeveloped Countries*, New York, Wiley, 1962. The quotations are from the essay entitled "Nationalism," pp. 31 and 32.

solidarity which, without these, might well be very much less real.

If anticolonialism is perhaps the major common factor in the nationalisms that arose in the colonial world, it may well be a mistake to describe such anticolonialism as nationalism. Among the many peoples thrown together within a colony, the joint goal of decolonization may have been pursued for different purposes. Certain groups of people found themselves in a position to succeed the colonial power in its control of the territory involved; their joint efforts to oust the foreign ruler were followed by a breakdown in cooperation and a struggle for supremacy. The Ganda of Uganda, seeing their intent to dominate an independent state of Uganda thwarted by a British-designed constitution, threatened to secede from the country even before sovereignty was achieved. The apparent centripetal nature of nationalism becomes real only when anticolonialism ceases to have a function in the emergent state.

How have the colonial powers reacted to the rising tide of nationalism in their empires? The responses have been as varied as the colonial policies themselves. Portugal has mainly taken a stance that negates the existence of any local nationalisms within its domain; such anticolonial movements as are recognized to exist are generally attributed to outside agitation and propaganda. The only nationalism that is possible and natural is Portuguese nationalism, expressed as a profound pride in the achievements of Portuguese culture. Since all African citizens can aspire to Portuguese citizenship, and since Portuguese culture is self-evidently far advanced compared to any indigenous culture, any non-Portuguese nationalism is in effect a form of willful rebellion. African nationalist organizations are not tolerated, and Portuguese African nationalism is considered a contradiction in terms.

The coming of nationalist activity to the Belgians' Congo was a shock to most Belgian colonial officials and administrators. While no arrangements had been made to cope with any such eventuality, the Belgians, unlike the Portuguese, gave some scope to political-cultural organizations which were, in effect, nationalist movements. The pace of change and the intensity of the nationalism that developed in the 1950's were such that whatever scope was granted was insufficient. Nationalist activity was centered in the larger towns and cities of the Congo, and while there was a major *Mouvement National Congolais* (Lumumba's organization) favoring a strong central government and a unitary state, a number of regionalist-federalist factions also arose. One of these was Tshombe's *CONAKAT*; another, Kasavubu's *ABAKO*. Other movements were provincial-tribal in nature, such as *BALUBAKAT*.[10] The regionalism of Congo "nationalism" was intensified by the Belgian system of colonial control, described previously; the urban centers became foci for the forces of disruption rather than unification, especially after the removal of Lumumba. In the Congo's struggle for survival, the latent centrifugal forces within the territory, kept dormant by Belgian control and submerged by the nationalist anticolonial drive, have taken their inevitable toll after the colonialists' withdrawal.

French reaction to the emergence of nationalism has varied, not only in time, but also in space. France faced this test during the Fourth Republic, and before the Belgians or the Portuguese were confronted by it. In Southeast Asia as well as Algeria, the initial response to anti-colonial movements, which were political as well as revolutionary in nature, was one of armed force. The war in Southeast Asia was lost with finality at Dien Bien Phu, and that in Algeria appeared a matter of time when the person of De Gaulle entered the scene and reversed France's colonial policies dramatically. The Fifth Republic saw an attempt to replace the concept of assimilation with a spirit of voluntary association in a French-flavored community. Algeria was awarded its independence, and before serious nationalist problems arose in subsaharan Africa (there had, previously, been brief, warning uprisings in such territories as Madagascar and Ubangi-Shari) De Gaulle proposed his Community concept as a road toward independence for France's African domain. Given the choice, all but one of France's African territories (Guinea) chose independence within a French Community. Guinea chose independence outside the Community, which was one alternative, and no territory wished to continue its dependent status, the second alternative.

France's Community clearly has its origins in the British idea of a Commonwealth, and the benefits for France, despite its colonial

[10]CONAKAT: *Confederation des Associations du Katanga;* ABAKO: *Alliance des Bakongo;* BALUBAKAT: *Association des Baluba du Katanga.*

abdication, are considerable. In return for aid projects of various kinds, France retains a considerable amount of political influence in its former colonial realm, which has at times been reflected impressively by the United Nations voting behavior of certain "French African" states. Nevertheless, the French reaction to the inevitable wind of change in Africa was swift and effective, and the transition to independence has generally been calmer than that which occurred in the Congo and that which looms in Portuguese dependencies.

The British response to indigenous nationalism in its colonial realm also has varied. While the stated aim of British colonialism long was the eventual emancipation of the colonized peoples, the principle of slowness in bringing about change was carefully adhered to. Hence the acceleration of the pace of change, the mushrooming demands by nationalist leaders, and the intensity of anticolonial pressure still caught the British by surprise. The Crown had yielded a considerable amount of its power to European settler communities in such colonies as Kenya and Southern Rhodesia. In certain other territories it had ruled partly directly, and partly by indirect rule, and while those peoples under direct colonial rule agitated for independence, those who had remained under indirect rule often had a different view, and wished a delay in any award of sovereignty. They feared that they might be dominated by their more educated, politically sophisticated countrymen. Elsewhere again, the British were in effect preventing the outbreak of hostilities between rival population sectors, as in the Sudan between Arab and African, in Guiana between Indian and Negro, and in Cyprus between Greek and Turk. Their departure might lead to a civil war and thus endanger peace, and yet their colonial role must come to an end.

In some of its dependencies, cooperation between representatives of the colonized peoples and British administrators led to the establishment of governmental and administrative frameworks which prepared these territories for independence, and in a remarkably short time. Independence for the Sudan, Ghana, and Nigeria came without a struggle, though not without much negotiation and the safeguarding of the rights of minority peoples for whom the British felt responsible. After independence, these states have all changed their internal organization: the Sudan has seen

Arab–African strife, Ghana has abandoned its two-party system, and in 1972 the army took control. Nigeria completely reconstructed its regional divisions. But the British legacy of a sound civil service and many other attributes, vital to the operation of the state system, survives in all.

The effects of contrasting modes of colonial rule are felt everywhere. Ghana's now-defunct Opposition Party was, in effect, a regional movement representing the north, which had opposed the rapid transfer of sovereignty to a south-dominated government. The Northern Region of Nigeria, though numerically dominant in terms of population and representation in Nigeria's federal parliament, was nonetheless the most backward from the point of view of literacy, urbanization, and modernization in general. It was in the north where indirect rule prevailed, while the south experienced strong and effective contact with the colonial power. In Uganda, on the other hand, southern Buganda was most exposed to colonial contact, and the north remained distant and backward. With independence, these differences have become strong centrifugal forces in the states involved.

Former protectorates of Britain, such as Sierra Leone, became independent without a great deal of difficulty because of the premises upon which their administration was carried on. This statement must be qualified in view of events in former Nyasaland and Northern Rhodesia, which were joined with white-dominated Southern Rhodesia in the ill-fated Central African Federation. However, the absence of a sizable white landowning population, and the continuous involvement of Africans in the administration of such territories, rendered the task of accommodating emerging nationalist forces somewhat less difficult than it was in European-settled colonies. In Kenya, the land issue, in addition to other factors, produced the Mau Mau rebellion, and in Rhodesia the white population threatened to declare itself independent from Britain when confronted with British demands for greater political rights for the African population sector. In these colonies the problems of British colonialism have been most serious, and the solutions least satisfactory. The Mau Mau rebellion was eventually crushed, but not without massive armed counteraction and much loss of life. The Rhodesian situation of 1965 led to UDI—Unilateral Declaration of Independence. Not until

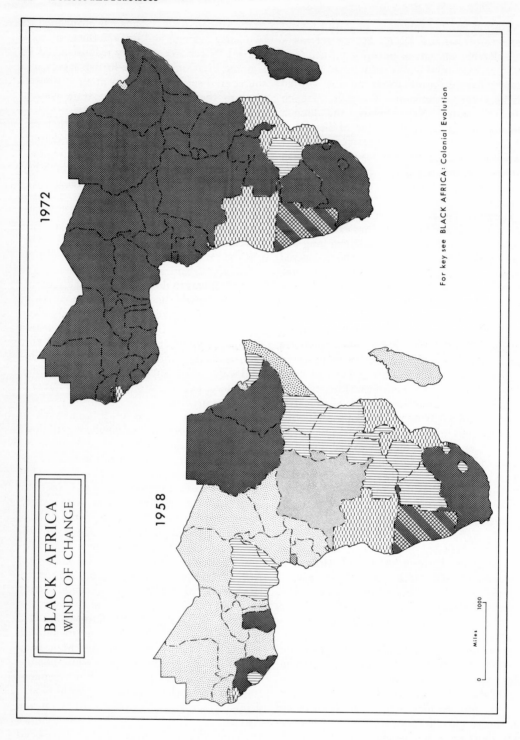

BLACK AFRICA
WIND OF CHANGE

1958

1972

For key see BLACK AFRICA: Colonial Evolution

Miles   0   1000

late 1971 were there signs of a settlement, which in 1972 faded away again.

In general, however, British colonial policy has successfully accommodated the nationalism of recent decades. The transfer of power to the leadership of India and Pakistan constituted a major success; in view of the many divisive forces in former British India, and the initial emergence of only three states (rather than several dozen) is a credit to British efforts. British contributions to the planning of the politicoterritorial systems of many states have been of paramount importance. Some federal states have failed to take shape, as did the West Indies Federation, but others, including Nigeria, India, and Malaysia, have been successfully launched. Time has taken its toll; Pakistan, at first a success, has broken down. But the overall record remains favorable.

NATIONALISM AND IRREDENTISM

Although the unification of people speaking a single language has not been a characteristic of anticolonial nationalism, and such nationalism has generally respected existing boundaries, border tension has nevertheless developed in certain parts of the former colonial world. Colonial boundaries were mainly superimposed upon existing cultural patterns, and they still divide, in many parts of the world, peoples who have historic, linguistic, and ethnic ties. Indeed, this situation exists in Europe as well as the colonial world: there are Italian-speaking people in France, French-speaking people in Belgium, German-speaking people in Switzerland. In most cases the boundary has functioned for a long time, and is accepted by the governments and the peoples in the border areas alike.

On occasion, however, circumstances such as these lead to political problems. Sometimes it is felt, in a state, that people who really form part of its nation, but who live across a boundary in another state, are ill-treated as a minority. The state shows its support for its "nationals across the border" through propaganda, and pressure is put on the neighboring government to improve its treatment of these people. Those may be only initial steps. Ultimately the state may show its dissatisfaction by openly claiming that the land and people involved are historically and culturally a part of its domain, and begin a compaign for unification and a boundary shift. Such a policy

At the outbreak of the first World War, Italy bargained with both sides for a reward in return for participation in the hostilities. The Allies promised that Italy, upon an Allied victory, would be given territory as far north as the Brenner Pass—including, therefore, a large part of the Austrian province of Tyrol. By the Treaty of St. Germain (1919), Italy thus obtained an area in which the latest census indicated over 200,000 German-speaking people against less than 20,000 Italians. In Austria, the matter has not been accepted without protest, and the irredentist sentiments find their expression not only in occasional acts of violence and sabotage, but in officially sanctioned road signs, such as that shown in the photograph, designed to remind Austrians (and others as well) that Tyrol was fragmented artificially and unjustly. The sign stands near the entrance to the Brenner Pass (Robert Janke).

toward a neighboring country is an *irredentist* policy.

Irredentism (the name comes from *Terra Irredenta*, an area once claimed in this fashion by Italy) poses serious problems wherever it arises. The case described above, of course, has many variations; even if the neighboring state does not mistreat its ethnic minority, irredentist policies can be justified in all sorts of ways. Both Greece and Turkey have shown irredentist tendencies in their reactions to the Cyprus dispute. Turkey has threatened war to protect the Turks on the island, and Greece has openly favored *enosis*—the merger of Cyprus with the Greek "motherland." China's

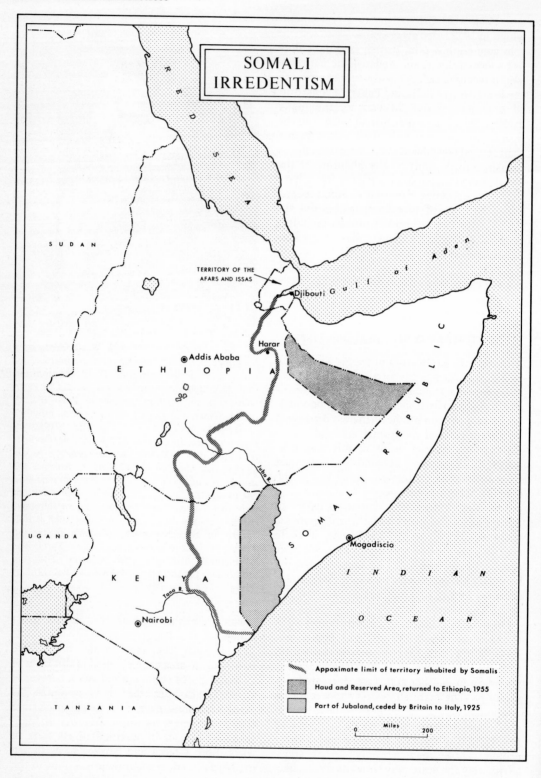

SOMALI
IRREDENTISM

RED SEA

SUDAN

TERRITORY OF THE
AFARS AND ISSAS

Djibouti Gulf of Aden

Harar

Addis Ababa

ETHIOPIA

SOMALI REPUBLIC

Juba R.

UGANDA

Mogadiscio

KENYA

INDIAN

Tana R.

Nairobi

OCEAN

TANZANIA

Appoximate limit of territory inhabited by Somalis

Haud and Reserved Area, returned to Ethiopia, 1955

Part of Jubaland, ceded by Britain to Italy, 1925

Miles
0   200

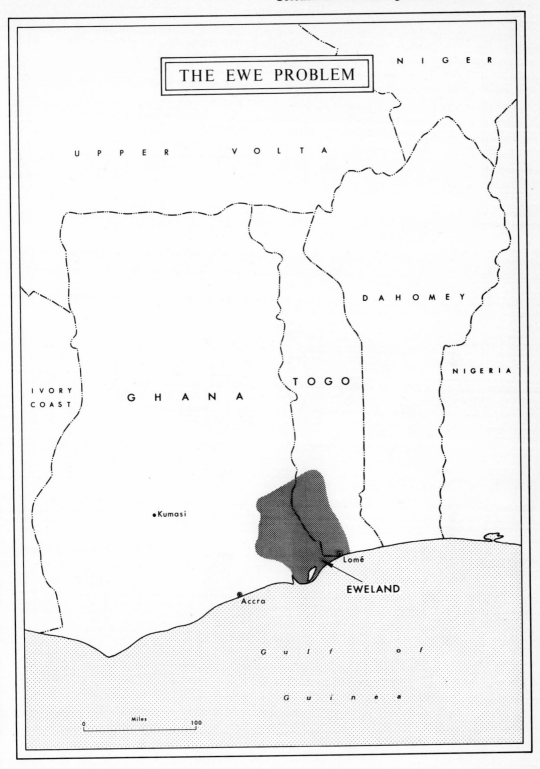

THE EWE PROBLEM

N I G E R

U P P E R   V O L T A

D A H O M E Y

I V O R Y
COAST

G H A N A

T O G O

NIGERIA

•Kumasi

Lomé

EWELAND

⊚Accra

G u l f   o f

G u i n e a

Miles
0   100

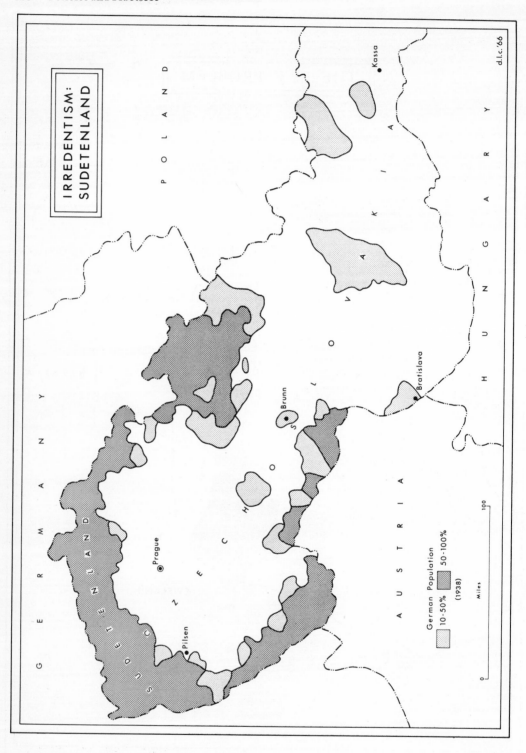

IRREDENTISM:
SUDETENLAND

POLAND

GERMANY

SUDETENLAND

●Pilsen

◉Prague

CZECHO

S

SLOVAKIA

●Brunn

Bratislava
●

AUSTRIA

HUNGARY

●Kassa

German Population
(1938)

50-100%

10-50%

Miles

0   100

d.l.c. '66

"South Tyrol Wants to Be No Colony" proclaims this crudely painted sign in Austria. Feelings over the the Italo-Austrian boundary, and German-speaking residents in South Tyrol have described their status in the Italian state as one of second-class citizenship. Would it be difficult to imagine, in place of South Tyrol, the words "Quebec," or "East Pakistan," or "Eweland"? (Robert Janke).

boundary disputes with India have irredentist overtones, and any Indonesian expansionism toward Mindanao would no doubt be based in large part upon claims of ethnohistorical and cultural ties with that region.

The most clear-cut case today is probably that involving the peoples of the "Horn" of Africa, the Somali. Somali are Arabic-speaking Moslems, and their homeland is the Somali Republic, the result of the merger of Italian and British Somaliland. Many Somali, however, live in eastern Ethiopia, divided from the Somali Republic by geometric boundaries. These boundaries are the result of a settlement between the Ethiopian emperor, Menelik, and the colonial powers—and Menelik was with justification described as an imperialist, for he pushed the boundaries of his empire far beyond their former positions. The Somali in Ethiopia, thus (as well as those outside of that country), consider themselves the victims of an Ethiopian colonialism-imperialism, and they want to "reunite" in a "Greater Somalia."[11]

Somali irrendentism toward Ethiopia has involved the active support of uprisings among Ethiopian Somali, the distribution of literature containing "academic" justifications of the Somali claims, and calls for boundary studies with a view to relocation. At the same time relations between independent Kenya and the

Somali Republic have deteriorated as a result of similar policies in that direction. Thousands of Somali live within Kenya, and the Somali government has indicated that it wished a reconsideration of the geometric Somali–Kenya border. A "Greater Somalia" would include not only part of Kenya and Ethiopia, but also a section of French Somaliland.

The Ewe problem, involving Ghana with its neighbor, Togo, has similar overtones, although the area affected here is smaller and less significant than the Horn of Africa. German Togoland, the erstwhile colony, was divided, for purposes of League of Nations Mandate Administration into two sections: French Togoland and British Togoland. This meant that the Ewe people, who occupy the south of this part of West Africa, found themselves divided into three political units: the Gold Coast Colony, the British Mandate, and the French Mandate. In 1950 the number of Ewe people in Ghana was about 376,000, in British Togoland, 137,000 and in French Togoland, 174,000.[12] When the wind of change struck this part of Africa, the people of British Togoland were asked to vote whether they wished to join with French Togoland or with the new state of Ghana. The majority of the Ewe people wished to unite with French Togoland, but the majority of the total

[11]For a discussion of the background to this entire problem see J. Drysdale, *The Somali Dispute*, New York, Praeger, 1964.

[12]J.S. Coleman, "Togoland," *International Conciliation*, No. 509 (September, 1956), 13.

population of British Togoland wanted to join Ghana. Thus, against their will, the Ewe of British Togoland were forced to join Ghana. Irrendentist problems have arisen since the implementation of the merger, and relations between the neighbors (Ghana and the Togo Republic) have not been good.

Again, irredentist problems are not confined to tribal areas or to the developing world. Many actual and latent cases remain, such as those of the BaKongo people in the fragmented region of the Angola–Zaïre border, the Ovambo people on the Angola–South West Africa border, as well as the Italo–Yugoslav and German–Polish contact zones. The infamous case involving German claims to Czechoslovakia's Sudentenland during the 1930's, and that of Tyrol (see map and photograph) underscore the universality of the issue. With its regional expression and inevitable boundary significance, irredentism is indeed a fertile field for politicogeographical study.

Cultural Pluralism
and The Political Geography
of Decolonization:
The Case of Surinam[1]

Harm J. de Blij

University of Miami
Coral Gables, Florida

The problems involved in the process of decolonization are nowhere more strongly felt than in those present and former dependencies which are inhabited by plural societies. Colonial rule had the effect of submerging or controlling latent internal conflicts; alien subjugation even constituted a temporary centripetal force in that it provided a common adversary for otherwise disparate peoples. Perhaps more often than not, however, the colonial administration fostered circumstances which, upon independence, left the newly independent state with serious difficulties. It was not enough that peoples of vastly different qualities had been thrown together during the colonial scramble: colonial practices often favored one indigenous people over another, arousing fears and jealousies which were stored up during the colonial period and exploded after independence. In Rwanda, the Watusi were confirmed in their minority hegemony over the Bahutu during Belgian control, but after independence the Bahutu rose in a wave of retribution that cost thousands of Watusi their lives. In Uganda, British administration gave the traditionalist Buganda Kingdom a place of privilege and power, but after independence the monarchy was destroyed and the king exiled by the forces of nationalism. In Nigeria, the Ibo of the East had long been the favored entrepreneurs, and in search of jobs they entered the Moslem North in large numbers. There they served the British well, but shortly after independence Northern resentment burst into widespread violence in which perhaps as many as a

hundred thousand Ibo were killed. Subsequently the apparently ill-fated Biafran secession movement became the final chapter in the Ibo tragedy.

Elsewhere it was not favoritism, but negligence and a lack of foresight that formed the basis for post-independence crises. In the Sudan, where Moslem Arab and animist black African were confined within the same political boundary, the British proceeded to intensify regional contrasts and potential Arab–African conflicts by permitting Christian missionaries to proselytize in the black African part of the country; since independence the southern Sudan has been ravaged by a war which, by some reports, has already cost a half million lives. The breakup of the British Indian subcontinent, the secession of Singapore from Malaysia, and the failure of the Federation of the West Indies add further to the evidence that colonial powers were more successful exploiters of the present than builders for the future. But the colonial rulers had the power to delay the often inevitable outbreak of open hostilities until after they had terminated their tenure—and then the new indigenous governments were unable to cope with the release of pent-up tensions. And so, today, the cry frequently is that the decolonized peoples cannot govern themselves. They hardly deserve all the blame.

Still another aspect of colonial administration lies in the mass migration—much of it forced—of millions of people from their homelands. Apart from the slave trade from Africa to the Americas, many other migrations were induced. The Dutch carried Malays to the Cape of Good Hope, and Javanese to South America; the British indentured tens of thou-

[1]This article is based on data gathered during a pilot study in the Netherlands in September and October, 1969.

sands of Asians for labor in East and South Africa. Thus colonial plural societies were made still more complex, endowing the emerging states with even greater potential problems. Displaced peoples all over the world, from Brazil's Negroes to Kenya's Asians, attest to the colonialists' power over men as well as land.

THE NETHERLANDS IN THE NEW WORLD

Although the chief theater of Dutch colonialism lay in what is today Indonesia, the Netherlands also acquired several territories in the Americas. Unlike the Netherlands East Indies, which achieved full independence as early as 1950, the Dutch possessions in Caribbean America, though nominally autonomous, still remain parts of the Kingdom of the Netherlands today. The Netherlands sphere in Middle America includes the "A.B.C." islands off the coast of Venezuela (Aruba, Bonaire, and the important petroleum refining center of Curacao), three Windward islands (Saba, Saint Eustatius, and southern

Saint Maarten, the last shared with France), as well as the South American mainland territory of Surinam (Fig. 1). The Netherlands Antilles, as the islands are collectively identified, are territorially small, although Curacao and Aruba are comparatively populous and reflect the benefits of their location near one of the world's major oil-producing areas. Surinam, on the other hand, is a medium-sized territory with a 1970 population estimated to be just under 400,000 (Table 1).

Thus the Netherlands finds itself in the anomalous position of having been among the first colonial powers after the end of the Second World War to be forced to yield a major overseas empire—and today being among the last still to have substantial overseas responsibilities. In this context, several questions arise. Does the cultural pluralism of Surinam (the largest part of the empire) have indigenous roots or is it largely the result of Netherlands-induced immigration? Is Surinam's pluralism reflected in an ethnic regionalism? Has the decolonization process begun to transform spatial patterns of organization in Surinam as

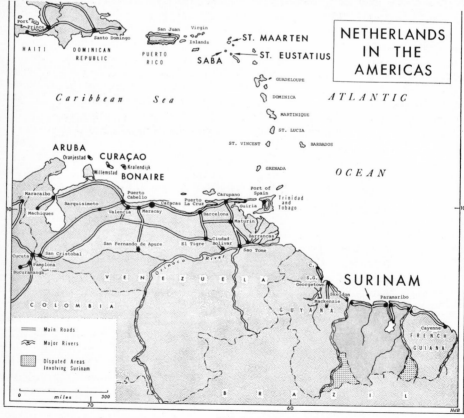

FIG. 1.

Table 1—CARIBBEAN UNITS OF THE KINGDOM OF THE NETHERLANDS

Territory		Area (Sq. Mi.)	Population	Principal Urban Center
	Aruba	73.3	60,000	Oranjestad
	Bonaire	108.5	6,000	Kralendijk
Netherlands	Curacao	182.2	130,000	Willemstad
Antilles	Saba	5.0	1,100	The Bottom
	Saint Eustatius	8.1	1,100	Oranjestad
	Saint Maarten	13.1	3,300	Philipsburg
Surinam		63,251[2]	380,000	Paramaribo
		55,143		

[2]The dual figure for Surinam's area reflects unresolved boundary disputes with Guyana, its western neighbor, and French Guiana to the east.

it has in Africa? Have the lessons of Indonesia been applied in Surinam and the Antilles? It is the purpose of this paper to report on some preliminary findings relative to these issues.

CULTURAL PLURALISM IN SURINAM

When the first Europeans came to Surinam, this part of South America was peopled by Amerindians, chiefly Caribs and Arawaks. Today, fewer than ten thousand Amerindians remain in the country and, unlike several other South and Middle American states, the Indian component in the population is quite insignificant. The surviving Amerindians subsist much as they did when the 16th century saw the first white men arrive: they mix hunting and fishing with some patch farming. In Surinam, they are divided into two groupings, the so-called Lowland (Benedenlandse) Amerindians, concentrated near the middle and lower courses of the rivers that flow northward across the coastal plain into the Atlantic Ocean, and the Upland (Bovenlandse) Amerindians, who live in comparative isolation in the forested mountainland of the interior.[3]

[3]For incidental information as well as hard data the author is indebted to several persons who assisted him in the Netherlands. At the Royal Institute for the Tropics in Amsterdam, Mrs. A. Everse provided invaluable assistance, and Mr. P.E. van Nierkerk gave freely of his time in discussions. Also in Amsterdam, the STICUSA society made cartographic as well as bibliographic materials available. In The Hague, aid was extended by the office of the Kabinet van de Vice-Minister President, the offices of the Stichting tot Bevordering van Investeringen in Suriname, and the office of the Kabinet van de Gevolmachtigde Minister van Surinam. Special thanks are due to Mrs. L. Pengel-Ruskamp and Mr. H. Telgt.

The first European settlement of consequence was established in the middle of the 17th century by British colonists, after a hundred years of visits and brief footholds by parties of various nationalities, including Spanish and French. The Amerindians, who had repelled several earlier attempts at colonization, entered into an agreement with the British, and by the early 1660s thriving sugar plantations lay in the coastal zone of Surinam. The British were the first to bring forced labor to the country—in the form of both slaves from black Africa and convicts from England. Willoughbyland (as the settlement was known) was a penal colony as well as a source of profit for the man who financed the operation and who obtained a royal charter there, Lord Willoughby. But British influence was to be shortlived. In 1667 a Dutch fleet took the colony from the British, and ever since the flag of the Netherlands has prevailed in Surinam.[4]

Dutch practice confirmed British directions: plantation agriculture was greatly expanded, polders were diked, and black slave labor was brought to the colony now named after one of its major rivers. Most of this slave labor came from West Africa, but it was drawn from many different West African peoples and as a result it was quite heterogeneous. Nevertheless, in the plantation region of Surinam the black people began to forge a kind of union with its own distinct language and culture. This was

[4]A wealth of detail on this period is included in J. Wolbers, Geschiedenis van Suriname, Amsterdam, De Hoogh, 1868. A useful summary is H.J. Wolff, Historisch Overzicht over Suriname, The Hague, Van Scherpenzeel, 1934.

the beginning of the *Creole* sector of Surinam's population, the sector which has its roots in Africa, speaks its own, vibrant language, and is today one of the two numerically dominant groups in the country. Thus, scarcely a hundred years after white men first set foot in Surinam, there already were three population sectors: the Amerindians, who were being forced into the interior, the Europeans, and the Creoles.

The harsh life of slavery, and the beckoning, protective forests of the interior, from very early on led numerous . African slaves to escape, and to seek a new life away from the European sphere of influence. Before the middle of the 18th century, sizeable settlements of escaped African slaves had been formed in the interior, and by their growing numbers and their need for foodstuffs and farming tools they came to form a threat to the white men's plantations, which they raided in desperation and retaliation. The plantation owners, in turn, established a series of armed stations in an east-west line across the country, connected by a road. This constituted an early attempt at *apartheid* in Surinam, but the threat to the farms continued. Eventually the colonists in the early 1760s formally agreed to recognize the rights of escaped slaves and promised to provide them with certain essential supplies, in return for which the raids would cease. Thus fully a century before slavery was abolished in Surinam (1863) there already was a regional division in the black population, namely between the Creoles of the coastal areas ,and the escaped, free blacks of the interior. These latter came to be called *Bosnegers*—Negroes of the forest—and they are still identified as a separate population sector today. Like the Amerindians, they cluster along the rivers in the midsection of the country, especially the Saramacca, Suriname, and Marrowijne Rivers (Fig. 2).[5]

The traffic in African slaves was prohibited and terminated in 1808, and although illegal and indirect forced black immigration continued for another decade, Surinam soon began to feel the impact of an increasingly serious labor shortage. With the approach of the abolition of slavery, the planters feared that this shortage would become critical as newly freed slaves would leave the plantations for

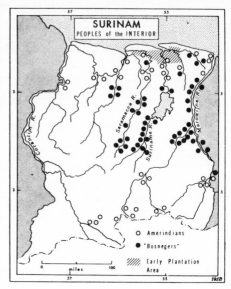

FIG. 2. Sources: C. Nachtegaal, Suriname, Amsterdam, Koninklijk Nederlands Instituut voor de Tropen, 1964, p. 17, and Schakels, Vol. S. 68, 1968, p. 14.

the forests to the south, or seek small holdings elsewhere. Now the Dutch administration turned to British India for indentured labor, and in 1873 the vanguard of still another population sector arrived. Until as late as 1916, thousands of East Indians—Hindustani, as they are called by the Dutch—arrived at Paramaribo, and today this East Indian population sector vies with the Creole sector for numerical supremacy in Surinam.[6] As they did in East and South Africa, the East Indians brought to Surinam their strong cultural imprint, which is reflected in the architecture of the towns, in the temples and shrines of their faiths, in their mode of dress, the language, in ceremonial feasts and festivals, and in many other ways. In less than a century the East Indians have challenged the numerical dominance of the Creoles in the demographic makeup of Surinam, for they have the highest annual rate of increase among the major population sectors.

Yet another major population group remained to be added to Surinam's mosaic at the behest of the Dutch. In their East Asian possessions, the Hollanders had a ready source of labor, and beginning in 1890 they transport-

[5]One of the earliest and most authoritative discussions of the life of Surinam's African descendants is M.J. and F.S. Herskovits, Surinam Folklore, New York, Columbia University Press, 1936.

[6]In this paper the term *East Indians* is used to identify the Asian Indian component of Surinam's population, whereas the term *Amerindian* denotes the original, indigenous population—the "American Indian" sector.

ed thousands of indentured Indonesian workers to Surinam. Today this Indonesian population sector, still often identified as *Javanese* by the Dutch, is the third largest in the territory (Table 2).

Thus Dutch colonialism transformed a sparsely peopled, subsistence-Amerindian area on South America's north coast into one of the most heterogeneous societies to be found anywhere. In the cultural makeup of the modern territory, the indigenous inhabitants play a minor role, and in the political context their influence is minimized still further by their tribal isolation and fragmentation. Modern Surinam, therefore, is almost entirely the creation of Dutch colonialism and, more specifically, the product of the influence of profiteering plantation owners over successive colonial administrations. While similar to some Caribbean American territories in this respect, Surinam differs markedly from the model of former colonies in Africa and Asia, where such population movements as were induced by colonial administrations normally were superimposed upon large and numerically dominant indigenous bases.

ETHNIC REGIONALISM IN SURINAM

Among many causes of conflict between different population groups in newly or nearly independent countries, two stand out strongly: (1) a master-serf relationship of long standing, such as that of the Watusi and

Bahutu in Rwanda; and (2) actually or potentially competing regional foci or tribal core areas within a single state, as in the case of Nigeria. In Surinam, it is certainly possible to recognize a social stratification that correlates with race, though the relationships are not nearly as well defined as they were, for example, in Belgian-administered Ruanda–Urundi. Thus the East Indians have been much more successful in the economic life of Surinam than the Indonesians; they also have displaced the Creoles from many of the most profitable jobs in Paramaribo, the country's only city, and in the rural areas they have done better in the acquisition of small holdings. Javanese as well as Creoles have become the servants of the East Indians, though not their serfs. If there is resentment among the Javanese it arises more out of disillusionment with their entire *milieu* than out of their lack of success in the economic pursuits of Surinam. The East Indians also have been able to capitalize to a greater extent than the Creoles on the urbanization of the Paramaribo area; although they make up a much smaller proportion of the urban population, they have come to dominate not only the market gardens in the city's environs, but also the jobs in transportation, marketing, and retailing. They prevail in Paramaribo's economic life much as they have done in the towns of East Africa, and they play a larger role in the farming areas. Here, then, is a crucial difference: in Paramaribo the East Indians are in a minority as they have been in each of the East African states as

Table 2—COMPOSITION OF SURINAM POPULATION[7]

Group	1964 Census	1970 Estimate	Paramaribo 1959
Creoles	114,961	136,000	77,721
Indians	112,633	136,000	22,585
Indonesians	48,463	54,000	5,529
Bosnegers	27,698	31,000	
Amerindians	7,287	8,000	
Chinese	5,339	6,000	3,285
Whites	4,322	5,500	2,835

[7]The 1964 figures are from the official census, reported in *Surinaams Nieuws*, Vol. 19, No. 48, December 1969, p. 9. The 1970 estimate is based on extrapolations from the 1964 figures according to known and estimated growth rates; Surinam has one of the world's highest overall rates of population increase (between 3 and 4 per cent annually). The population clustered in Paramaribo in 1959 is derived from information listed in C. Nachtegaal, *Suriname*, Amsterdam, Tropenmuseum, 1964, p. 2. The 1964 figure for the Amerindians includes 2,979 persons in the money economy and 4,308 persons in the subsistence interior.

a whole, but in Surinam as a whole their numbers are now at least equal—and growing faster—than those of the Creoles.[8]

Ethnic regionalism has been a part of Surinam's existence for a very long time. European occupation pushed the indigenous Amerindian population deeper into the forests of the interior; the desperation of slavery drove black Africans into the same hinterland almost from the beginning. The old demarcation road and its armed posts epitomize the coastal development of Surinam and the isolation of its interior; the Amerindians and Bosnegers in their present distribution continue to reflect this episode.

The majority of modern Surinam's inhabitants, however, remain clustered in the northern coastal and near-coastal zones of the country. Nearly 40 per cent live in Paramaribo and its immediate environs. After the termination of slavery, the Creoles who wanted to leave the plantations and estates had a choice: to move south and join their co-descendants, or to move into the city. They overwhelmingly chose the latter course, precipitating a problem of urban crowding that still bedevils Paramaribo today. The capital is still nearly 70 per cent Creole, but, as has been noted, the minority East Indian sector has succeeded in capturing many of the available jobs. The East Indians arrived later than the Creoles and their purpose was to replace Creole labor in the farmlands, and their distribution still reflects this, not only in their minority position in Paramaribo, but also in their strength in the rural areas—notably in the Districts of Suriname and Para (south of the city) and also in Nickerie in the northwest. Like the Creoles, however, the East Indians have been attracted to the city, and their comparative strength in Paramaribo is growing.

Thus Surinam's early drift toward ethnic regionalism has been checked by the interdigitation of the two majority population sectors. Paramaribo is not a monopoly of the Creoles, nor are the rural areas the monopoly of the East Indians. With the Indonesian sector functioning in a sense as a buffer (it is substantially represented in all but one of the northern districts), Surinam has escaped the ethnic clustering and consequent politicoterritorial polarization that afflicts so many other multiracial countries that have recently emerged from a colonial era.

THE DECOLONIZATION PROCESS

The withdrawal of the Netherlands from the affairs of Surinam is still not complete, but the process has been going on for nearly twenty years. As early as 1954 the colonial relationship of Surinam with the Kingdom of the Netherlands was altered by the proclamation of a new *Charter*, whose preamble states that

The Netherlands, Surinam, and the Netherlands Antilles, considering that they have expressed freely their will to establish a new constitutional order in the Kingdom of the Netherlands, in which they will conduct their internal interests autonomously and their common interests on a basis of equality, and in which they will accord each other reciprocal assistance, have resolved by mutual consent to establish the Charter for the Kingdom . . .[9]

Although this Charter brought a measure of internal autonomy to Surinam, it stops far short of granting the territory full sovereignty. Where external affairs and mutual defense are concerned, for example, the decisions involved rest with the Council of Ministers, in which the Netherlands has a majority. The ultimate authority in Surinam as well as the Antilles remains with the representative of the King (or Queen), the Governor. Thus the 1954 step in the decolonization process was a significant one, but it also opened the door to demands for greater independence, demands which have since been heard in the political arena of Surinam.

When the former Belgian administration in the Congo saw itself threatened, it asked for "just a decade more, to get the country more ready for independence." But the impatient Congolese were unwilling to grant any delay in the decolonization of their country. The hurried Belgian development plans of the 1950s were abrogated. The Belgian story in Africa is not unique. In the postwar period, colonial powers often made hasty and belated efforts to modernize their longtime dependencies and to prepare them for what was not infrequently seen as a premature independence. Surinam has now had the luxury of more than two decades of such preparation, and indeed a considerable amount of progress has been achieved in both the economic and the political sphere.

---

[8]Although this is technically true, the Creoles have direct ethnic ties with the Bosnegers, now numbering over 30,000. There is a small but growing flow of Bosnegers to Paramaribo and environs. See G.J. Kruijer, *Terra Suriname*, Meppel, Boom en Zoon, 1966, pp. 44–93.

[9]*Charter for the Kingdom of the Netherlands*, The Hague, Vice Prime Minister's Cabinet Department, n.d., p. 1.

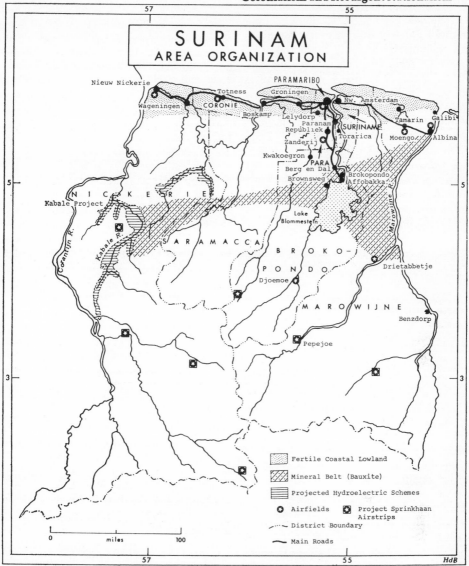

FIG. 3. Data compiled from various sources.

The economic progress of Surinam can to a considerable extent be read off the map. Development of the "bauxite belt" across north-central Surinam has taken the modern sphere southward, beyond the coast-confined farming areas. Completion of the enormous Brokopondo hydroelectric scheme on the Suriname River has produced a large man-made lake; a modern road extends from Paramaribo to this site (Fig. 3).[10] Expansion of

[10]A second scheme, the Torarica Project, is intended to dam the Suriname River downstream from Brokopondo, near Torarica, in order to provide additional electric power but also to irrigate extensive areas in Suriname and Commewijne Districts. A third scheme is the Kabale Project, planned to provide electricity for the refining of bauxite in western Surinam. This project will be built on the Kabale tributary of the Corantijn River.

rice production around Wageningen in the Nickerie District is the result of a large research operation. Operation *Sprinkhaan* (Grasshopper) has resulted in the construction of seven small airfields in central and southern Surinam and the beginning of regular contact with the outside world for these areas. Operation *Schildpad* (Tortoise) is designed to improve surface communications, initially through a road from Brokopondo southward along the west side of the lake and through the middle of the country, first to Djoemoe and subsequently beyond. An east-west connector already links Nieuw Nickerie in the west to Albina in the east. The growth of Paramaribo is itself evidence of the increasing number of functions the city performs. First a landfall, then a tenuous colonial settlement, and eventually a colonial headquarters, Paramaribo will undoubtedly become the capital of an independent state—thereby following the model sequence of so many African towns which began as European bases of operation and rose to become primate cities for sovereign states. Certainly developments in Surinam, especially under the Ten-Year Plan, mirror similar progress made by other dependencies prior to their separation from their European colonial powers. Actually, the Surinam achievement is quite substantial when it is seen in the context of the country's limited resources and comparatively small population. In terms of territory, Surinam is considerably larger than Liberia or Cuba; it is nearly as large as Senegal (or, for more familiar reference, England and Wales). But its population is approximately the same as that of Gambia. In this frame of comparison, Surinam's growth is quite remarkable.

POLITICAL MODERNIZATION

It now remains to answer the fourth of the questions posed in the introduction to this paper: have the lessons of Indonesia been applied in Surinam? Certainly the contents of the 1954 Charter do not suggest that they were, for just such an attempt was earlier made to involve Indonesia as an "equal partner" in a greater Kingdom of the Netherlands, a proposal that was rejected outright by the Indonesians. But the big difference has been time—time which was not available in the swift current of events that swept the East Indies to a precipitous independence. In Surinam this time was probably better spent than it would have been without the experiences gained in the events surrounding Indonesia's emergence. As Kruijer put it, ". . . in the Netherlands, too, the concept became current that many countries, especially colonies, had in the past been retarded and neglected, and that something should be done about that. Quick action was required, and the best chance for success appeared to lie in the planned intervention of the Netherlands government (in Surinam)."[11]

The resulting achievements in the economic sphere were accompanied by an equally important political apprenticeship. Political parties emerged, and their leaders were thrown

[11]G.J. Kruijer, Op. Cit., 1968, p. 228, in translation.

into national prominence. Apart from the management of and responsibilities for home affairs, the political parties in Surinam's government faced the issue of total independence, and could weigh the consequences of a demand for final separation from the Kingdom of the Netherlands. Although some political parties did indeed stand on a platform of early independence (notably the small but vocal Partij Nationale Republiek), others have viewed such a drive as undesirable in view of the economic gains being made. In the 1969 elections, one party—the powerful Verenigde Hitkarie Partij (United Hitkari Party, formerly the United Hindustani Party) even carried as its chief motto the assertion that "Independence Now is Fatal for Our Country." Relevant here is the association, established in 1962, between Surinam and the European Economic Community (the Common Market). The P.N.R. was always opposed to this association, since it represented, in its view, a neocolonialism that would replace the old form of dependency.[12] To the V.H.P., on the other hand, this association constituted a national asset whose advantages should be made use of and not endangered by premature talk of total independence. What is interesting in this context is that both the P.N.R. and the V.H.P. represent predominantly East Indian voters in Surinam. The P.N.R., then, represents the left—its kinship is with Jagan's leftist party in neighboring Guyana. But the majority of Surinam's East Indian voters have chosen a moderate course on independence, and support the V.H.P.

As in Nigeria, Kenya, Guyana, and so many other multi-racial states whose independence is of recent vintage, the political parties of Surinam have developed mainly along ethnic lines, but there is intra-group division and some inter-group coalition. Thus the two most powerful parties are the V.H.P. and the Creole-based Nationale Partij Suriname, representing as they do the majority segments of Surinam's two dominant population sectors. In the 1967 election campaign, the large N.P.S. at first ran on a platform demanding "Independence Now," but eventually this stand was modified into something called "Independence New Style," whereby a drive for greater self-determination was deemed not to

[12]For a detailed analysis of this relationship see P.H.J.M. Houten, De Associatie van Suriname en de Nederlandse Antillen met de Europese Economische Gemeenschap, Leiden, A.W. Sijthoff, 1965.

require the total severance of all ties with the Royal House of the Netherlands. Again, the visible economic progress of Surinam was cited in this shift of emphasis.

Undoubtedly the balance of power in Surinam is shifting toward the Indian sector. In the 1967 election, the three dominantly Indian-supported parties received a total of 33,735 votes (36.4 per cent of the total), but in 1969 they combined to receive 40,843 votes, or 44 per cent of the total. Meanwhile the Creole-supported parties attained exactly 53.6 per cent of the total vote both in 1967 and in 1969, but significantly the 1969 total was achieved because the Javanese-supported K.T.P.I. threw its support to the P.N.P. (Table 3).

Indian opposition to early independence, then, is certainly related to Indian recognition that such independence would be likely to lead to a confirmation of Creole supremacy. Indian progress in the elections suggests that any delay favors the Indian population sector, but the Creoles do have two remaining advantages. These are (1) the apparent consolidation of a Creole–Indonesian alliance and (2) the potential involvement of a Creole-oriented population sector that hardly shares yet in the national political life of the country—the Bosnegers. Thus the Indians must press for the deferment of independence and the Creoles can afford to wait; meanwhile the Netherlands has the time to support Surinam's economic development.

In this connection it is worth pointing out that the non-regional character of Surinam's ethno-political groupings constitutes a vital asset to the country, and one of the great fortunes to emerge from its colonial era. In Africa, too there were instances where one major population sector desired a delay in the acquisition of full sovereignty, for fear that another sector would, in that event, come to dominate the new state. So it was in Ghana, where the dominantly Moslem northerners feared a southern-dominated independence, and in Nigeria, where the Hausa of the north appealed through official channels to the British for a moratorium on independence. In Uganda the BaGanda feared that their traditionalist kingdom would be swept away in a nationalist republic; in the Sudan, the black African southerners feared the domination of the Khartum government of the Arab north. In all four cases, to varying degrees, there was conflict. In none could independence be postponed. In three there was violence after independence was granted, and in two—Nigeria and the Sudan—wars have devastated large regions of the state. If, in Surinam, there had been such an ethnic regionalism—for example, if the Creoles had been concentrated in the central parts of the country and the Indians on the coast—the course of events surely would have been different. Certainly the issues exist, but the foci, happily, are lacking.

CONCLUSIONS

To the four questions posed in the introduc-

Table 3—SURINAM ELECTION RESULTS, 1967 and 1969[13]

	1967	Per Cent	1969	Per Cent
Dominantly Creole-Supported Parties				
Nationale Partij Suriname	30,135	31.5	26,557	28.0
Progressieve Nationale Partij	8,506	9.0	22,142	24.0
Progressieve Surinaamse Volkspartij	5,373	5.5		
Surinaamse Democratische Partij	7,242	7.6	1,462	1.6
Dominantly Indian-Supported Parties				
Verenigde Hitkarie Partij	20,725	21.7	33,460	36.0
Actie Groep	11,614	12.2		
Partij Nationale Republiek	2,396	2.5	7,383	8.0
Dominantly Indonesian-Supported Parties				
Kaum Tani Persatuan Indonesia	5,825	6.0		
Sarakat Rakjat Indonesia	3,064	3.2	1,617	1.8

[13]Table drawn up from election data in *Surinaams Nieuws*, Vol. 19, No. 43, November 1969, p. 1.

tion to this paper, we have now partial answers. Surinam's cultural pluralism has its origins in Dutch colonial policy; the sparse indigenous population base has for all practical purposes been swept away. Surinam's multiracialism has only slight regional overtones; compared to other former and remaining dependencies this regionalism is a negligible factor at present. If an index of regional stress could be established, Surinam would rank near the lower end of any scale. The decolonization process has, for several reasons, been slow; as a result the interval between the postwar "new deal" and the

approaching date of independence is already long and still lengthening. In the interim Surinam is getting what other, more rapidly decolonized states have missed: a measure of return by investment and development for centuries of exploitation. These developments can indeed be read off the map of Surinam, now undergoing a transformation from a neglected backwater to a truly developing country. And the process has a crucial by-product: the gradual political maturing of a polity whose political maturity may prove to be the key to the successful advent of independence.

REFERENCES

Abbas, Mikki, *The Sudan Question: The Dispute over the Anglo-Egyptian Condominium, 1884–1951*, New York, F.A. Praeger, 1952.

Balogh, Thomas, "The Mechanism of Neo-Imperialism: The Economic Impact of Monetary and Commercial Institutions in Africa," *Oxford Univ. Inst. Statistics, Bulletin, 24*, 3 (August, 1962), 331–346.

Berard, Victor, *British Imperialism and Commercial Supremacy*. New York, Longmans, 1906.

Best, A.C.G., "South Africa's Border Industries: the Tswane Example," *Annals, A.A.G., 61*, 2 (June, 1971), 329–343.

Braine, Bernard, "Storm Clouds over the Horn of Africa," *Internat. Affairs, 34*, 4 (October, 1958), 435–443.

Brausch, Georges, *Belgian Administration in the Congo*. London, Oxford University Press, 1961.

Bretton, H.L., *Power and Stability in Nigeria. The Politics of Decolonisation*. New York, F.A. Praeger, 1962.

Cakste, Mintauts, "Latvia and the Soviet Union," *J. Central European Affairs, 9*, 1 (April, 1949), 32–60.

Catroux, Georges, "The French Union: Concept, Reality and Prospects," *Internat. Conciliation*, No. 495 (November, 1953), 195–256.

Church, R.J. Harrison, *Modern Colonization*. London, Hutchinson's University Library, 1951.

Cockram, Ben, "The 'Protectorates'—An International Problem," *Optima, 13*, 4 (December, 1963), 176–184.

Coleman, James S., *Nigerian: Background to Nationalism*. Berkeley and Los Angeles, University of California Press, 1958.

Coulter, John Wesley, *The Pacific Dependencies of the United States*. New York, Macmillan, 1957.

Crocombe, R.G., "Development and Regression in New Zealand's Island Territories," *Pacific Viewpoint, 3*, 2 (September, 1962), 17–32.

Crowder, Michael, *Senegal; A Study in French Assimilation Policy*. London, Oxford University Press, 1962.

Davis, William Columbus, *The Last Conquis-tadores; The Spanish Intervention in Peru and Chile, 1863–1866*. Athens, Ga., University of Georgia Press, 1950.

Deutsch, K.W., *Nationalism and Social Communication*. New York, John Wiley & Sons, 1953.

Duffy, James, "Portugal in Africa," *Foreign Affairs, 39*, 3 (April, 1961), 481–493.

———, *Portuguese Africa*. Cambridge, Mass., Harvard University Press, 1959.

Dunlop, John Stewart, "The Influence of David Livingstone on Subsequent Political Developments in Africa," *Scot. Geog. Mag., 75*, 3 (December, 1959), 144–152.

Emerson, Rupert, and others, *America's Pacific Dependencies*. New York, American Institute of Pacific Relations, 1949.

Fawcett, Charles B., "Geography and Empire," in *Geography in the Twentieth Century*, Griffith Taylor (ed.). New York, Philosophical Library, 1951, pp. 418–432.

Frank, Dorothea Seelye, "Pakhtunistan—Disputed Disposition of a Tribal Land," *Middle East J., 6*, 1 (Winter, 1952), 49–68.

Frankel, S. Herbert, *The Concept of Colonization*. Oxford, Clarendon Press, 1949.

Furnivall, J.S., *Colonial Policy and Practice; A Comparative Study of Burma and Netherlands India*. New York, New York University Press, 1956.

Goldblatt, I., *The Mandated Territory of South West Africa in Relation to the United Nations*. Cape Town, C. Struik, 1961.

Hammer, Ellen J., *The Struggle for Indochina*. Stanford, Calif., Stanford University Press, 1954.

Hancock, W.K., *Wealth of Colonies*. Cambridge, Cambridge University Press, 1950.

Harrison, Tom, "Sarawak in the Whirlpool of Southeast Asia," *Geog. Mag., 31*, 8 (December, 1958), 378–385.

Hensinkveld, H.M., "Separatist Tendencies in the Yucatan Peninsula," *Prof. Geog. 19*, 5 (September, 1967), 258–260.

Houphouet-Boigny, Felix, "Black Africa and the French Union," *Foreign Affairs, 35*, 4 (July, 1957), 593–599.

Huxley, Elspeth, "West Africa in Transition," *Geog. Mag.*, 25, 6 (October, 1952), 310–320.

Jennings, Sir Ivor, *Nationalism and Political Development in Ceylon*. New York, International Secretariat, Institute of Pacific Relations, 1950.

Kautsky, J.H. (ed.), *Political Change in Underdeveloped Countries; Nationalism and Communism*. New York, John Wiley & Sons, 1962.

Kerr, J.R., "The Political Future of New Guinea," *Australian Outlook*, 13, 3 (September, 1959), 181–192.

Kleinpenning, J.M.G., "Road Building and Agricultural Colonisation in the Amazon Basin," *Tijdschrift Economische Sociale Geografie*, LXII, 5 (October, 1971), 285–289.

Kolarz, Walter, *Russia and Her Colonies*. London, G. Philip and Son, Ltd., 1952.

Kretzmann, Edwin M.J., "Oil, Water, and Nationalism," *Inst. World Affairs, Proc.*, 33 (1959), 175–183.

Lattimore, Owen, *Nationalism and Revolution in Mongolia*. New York, Oxford University Press, 1955.

Legge, J.D., *Australian Colonial Policy; A Survey of Native Administration and European Development in Papua*. Sydney, Angus & Robertson, 1956.

LeVine, Victor T., *The Cameroons: From Mandate to Independence*, Berkeley, University of California Press, 1965.

Lewis, I.M., "Pan-Africanism and Pan-Somalism," *J. Modern African Studies*, 1 (1963), 147–162.

McColl, R.W., "A Political Geography of Revolution: China, Vietnam, and Thailand," *Jour. Conflict Resolution*, xi, 2 (June, 1967), 153–167.

———, "The Insurgent State: Territorial Bases of Revolution," *Annals, A.A.G.*, 59, 4 (December, 1969), 613–631.

McGee, T.G., "Aspects of the Political Geography of Southeast Asia," *Pacific Viewpoint*, 1, 1 (March, 1960), 39–58.

McKay, Vernon, "Nationalism in British West Africa," *Foreign Policy Rep.*, 24, 1 (March 15, 1948), 1–11.

Madariaga, Salvador de, *The Rise of the Spanish American Empire*. New York, Macmillan, 1947.

Meadows, Martin, "The Philippine Claim to North Borneo," *Political Sci. Quart.*, 77, 3 (September, 1962), 321–335.

Meinig, Donald W., "The American Colonial Era; A Geographic Commentary," *Proc. Roy. Geog. Soc. Australia, South Australia Branch*, 59 (1957–1958), 1–22.

Morrell, W.P., *Britain in the Pacific Islands*. Oxford, Clarendon Press, 1960.

Nuseibeh, H.Z., *The Ideas of Arab Nationalism*. Ithaca, N.Y., Cornell University Press, 1956.

Padmore, George, *Africa: Britain's Third Empire*. London, D. Dobson, 1949.

———, *Pan-Africanism or Communism? The Coming Struggle for Africa*. New York, Roy Publishers, 1956.

Palmier, Leslie H., *Indonesia and the Dutch*. London, Oxford University Press, 1962.

Pratt, Sir John T., *The Expansion of Europe into the Far East*. London, Sylvan Press, 1947.

Pratt, R. Cranford, "The Politics of Indirect Rule: Uganda, 1900–1955," in *Buganda and British Overrule; two studies by D. Anthony Low and R. Cranford Pratt*. New York, Oxford University Press, 1960, pp. 163–316.

Riggs, Fred W., "Wards of the U.N.: Trust and Dependent Area," *Foreign Policy Rep.*, 26, 6 (June 1, 1950), 54–63.

Rivlin, Benjamin, *The United Nations and the Italian Colonies*. New York, Carnegie Endowment for International Peace, 1950.

———, "Unity and Nationalism in Libya," *Middle East J.*, 3, 1 (January, 1949), 31–44.

Robinson, K.E., "French West Africa," *African Affairs*, 50, 199 (April, 1951), 123–132.

———, "Political Development in French West Africa," in *Africa in the Modern World*, Calvin W. Stillman (ed.). Chicago, University of Chicago Press, 1955, pp. 140–181.

Roucek, Joseph S. (ed.), "Moscow's European Satellites," *Ann. Amer. Ac. Pol. & Soc. Sci.*, 271 (September, 1950), 1–253.

Rupen, Robert A., "Mongolian Nationalism," *Royal Central Asian J.*, 45, Pt. 2 (April, 1958), 157–178.

Shaudys, Vincent K., "The External Political Geography of Dutch New Guinea," *Oriental Geography*, 5, 2 (July, 1961), 145–160.

Smith, C.G., "Arab Nationalism; A Study in Political Geography," *Geography*, 43, 202, Pt. 4 (November, 1958), 229–242.

Smogorzewski, K.M., "The Russification of the Baltic States," *World Affairs*, 4, 4 (October, 1950), 468–481.

Steel, R.W., "Land and Population in British Tropical Africa," *Geography*, 40, 187, Pt. 1 (January, 1955), 1–17.

Strachey, John, *The End of Empire*. London, Gollancz, 1959.

Strausz-Hupe, Robert, and Harry W. Hazard (eds.), *The Ideas of Colonialism*. New York, F.A. Praeger, 1958.

Teague, Michael, "Portugal's Permanence in Africa," *Geog. Mag.*, 28, 9 (November, 1955), 326–336.

Thompson, Virginia, and Richard Adloff, *French West Africa*. Stanford, Calif., Stanford University Press, 1958.

Tomasek, Robert D., "British Guiana; A Case Study of British Colonial Policy," *Political Sci. Quart.*, 74, 3 (September, 1959), 393–411.

Touval, Saadia, *Somali Nationalism*. Cambridge, Mass., Harvard University Press, 1963.

Treadgold, Donald W., "Siberian Colonization and the Future of Asiatic Russia," *Pacific Historical Rev.*, 25, 1 (February, 1956), 47–54.

Tregonning, K.G., "The Partition of Brunei," *J. Tropical Geography*, 11 (April, 1958), 84–89.

VanderKroef, Justus M., "Society and Culture in Indonesian Nationalism," *Amer. J. Sociol., 58*, 1 (July, 1952), 11–24.

Wainhouse, David Walter, *Remnants of Empires: The United Nations and the End of Colonialism.* New York, Council on Foreign Relations, Harper and Row, 1964.

Walker, Eric A., *Colonies.* Cambridge, England, The University Press, 1944.

Wigny, Pierre, "The Belgian Plan for Democracy in Africa," *Optima, 8*, 1 (March, 1958), 23–31.

Wurfel, D., "Okinawa: Irredenta on the Pacific," *Pacific Affairs, 35*, 4 (Winter, 1962–1963), 353–374.

Young, C., *Politics in the Congo: Decolonization and Independence.* Princeton, N.J., Princeton University Press, 1965.

CHAPTER
18
SUPRANATIONALISM:
FROM STATES TO BLOCS

Territorial units—tribal, national, colonial —are constantly changing. The change may not be unilineal, from clan to tribe to nation; it may not be cyclic either. But there is always adjustment. While European states seek to unify and there is talk of a United States of Africa, the federal state of Pakistan fragments into what was West Pakistan (now Pakistan) and Bangladesh. Irish irredentism intensifies an already bitter struggle between Protestants and Catholics in Ulster; many want to see the entire island of Eire united under one flag. But Biafra seeks to break away from Nigeria soon after the colonial yoke has been thrown off. Can trends really be discerned with such current contradictions?

States and nations over many centuries have attempted associations of various kinds, and about as often as these efforts succeeded, they failed. The ancient city-states of Greece formed leagues; so did the Hanseatic ports. Kings and princes joined their realms and then fought battles for renewed independence. Thus efforts toward international unity as they occur in the twentieth century must be viewed in the light of several thousand years of progress and reversal. Hence the question arises, Are present attempts at international unity in various parts of the world something new—or just another ill-fated version of one of man's ancient failings?

The question is relevant because the signs are unmistakable; the post-World War II era has been one of unprecedented activity in the field of supranationalism. In virtually all parts of the world and in practically every conceivable sphere states are seeking alliances, treaties, and other forms of association. And there is something new in this; in their determination to associate, states are doing something they have not been willing to do on such a scale previously. They are giving up some of their sovereignty in return for the security, economic advantage, cultural strength, or whatever benefit they perceive to accrue from their involvement.

As these supranational bodies emerge, the world political pattern changes. This appears to be the beginning of the period of the superstate, and although previous efforts of this sort, notably those of the interwar period, have failed and collapsed, the effort is much more universal and vigorous now than it was then. The United Nations is a far more representative body than the League of Nations was. The prestige and power of the International Court of Justice are greater. Military alliances are stronger. Economic agreements are more effective.

WORLD ORGANIZATIONS

Many of the past and present international bodies have been and are regional in nature. Some have been given names to indicate which region is involved, such as the North Atlantic Treaty Organization and the Southeast Asia Treaty Organization. Others are known simply as the Common Market or the Warsaw Pact. Equally significant, however, is the effort at worldwide (as opposed to local) cooperation in those spheres where such cooperation is feasible. In this, the forerunner was the ill-fated *League of Nations*, the fundamentals of which had emerged during the years of the first World War. In 1919 agreement was reached among the Allies concerning the text of the Covenant, and the League began operating in 1920.

The League of Nations was primarily designed to curb aggressive war, and was designed to act as an instrument of collective security through joint repudiation of any aggressor. The horrors of the first World War contributed to a general desire for such an agency, and the United States was among those countries that participated in discussions that were to lead to its establishment.

But the League received its first setback at the very beginning: in the United States, the proposal to join the organization was defeated, mainly through the hostility of Republican Senators to the efforts of President Wilson, who had strongly championed U.S. participation. The members had hoped that the threat of total economic boycott would stifle any would-be aggressor; the absence of the United States from the organization eliminated that possibility and dealt a severe blow to the confidence of the membership. In all, sixty-three states were members of the League of Nations, though in fact the total membership at any single time did not reach sixty-three: the Soviet Union joined in 1934, after Germany had withdrawn in 1933. Costa Rica and Brazil had departed as early as 1925 and 1926, respectively. Some eligible countries never joined. Others remained critical of the Covenant. But despite these troubles, the League of Nations represented a tremendous leap forward in international relations, for it embodied a principle that up until that time had been a matter only for theoretical discussion among political scientists and historians.

Among the achievements of the League of Nations have been the solution of the problem of Germany's colonies, which were placed under mandate, the erection of the Permanent Court of International Justice, the protection of minorities, the settlement of frontier and boundary disputes, the provision of avenues for discussion of sensitive areas such as Danzig and the Saar, and the establishment of a number of international agencies and bodies in such fields as health, communications, finance, and intellectual exchange. Among its failures were an inability to progress in the field of disarmament, a similar inability to stop the Italian attack on and annexation of fellow member Ethiopia, and that of Japan upon China. In fact the League began to crumble by 1933, when Germany and Japan left it; the years from 1933 to 1939 were a period of almost continuous crisis during which states either withdrew (Italy, 1937, Spain, 1939, etc.) or failed to adhere to the Covenant (as did Britain and France in their independent dealings with Italy and its victim, Ethiopia).

The League of Nations naturally ceased to have effect in 1939, when the outbreak of the second World War marked the final destruction of the hopes upon which it had been built; it was officially terminated in 1946, after the

United Nations had begun to function. Its contribution to the latter organization in terms of principles and practices is such that the United Nations in many ways is a renewal of the same aspirations possessed by the League.

The United Nations began its operations in 1945, the main forces behind its establishment having been the United States, the U.S.S.R., the United Kingdom, China (the "Nationalist" government then still in contention for control of the mainland), and France. More than fifty states joined as founding members of the organization, and the membership has more than doubled since then. As in the case of the League of Nations, the United Nations is not all-inclusive, although the admission of the Peoples Republic of China (1971) greatly increased its representativeness. But in 1972, neither the Federal Republic of Germany nor the German Democratic Republic were members of the U.N., and North and South Korea, North and South Viet Nam, Switzerland, and the microstates likewise do not participate. Some colonial peoples are represented only through their colonial masters, such as the peoples of Angola and Mozambique; problems loom in Rhodesia and South West Africa, the former colony and the latter a League of Nations mandate in the process of absorption by the mandate power, South West Africa.

Again, the importance of the United Nations lies in large measure in its subsidiary organizations. Some, such as the International Monetary Fund and the International Bank for Reconstruction and Development, are not subscribed to by the Communist states. Others, like the important Food and Agricultural Organization (F.A.O.), hav incomplete membership. But all these organizations are evidence of a growing international cooperation, as are the successful World Health Organization, the International Labor Organization, the Universal Postal Union, and the International Telecommunications Union. The International Law Commission has attempted—albeit unsuccessfully—to propose acceptable laws governing the seas. The United Nations Educational, Scientific and Cultural Organization has performed countless functions in those fields. The International Refugee Organization dealt with the problem of postwar European refugees.

Like the League of Nations before it, the United Nations has helped settle crises which might have led to world involvement. The

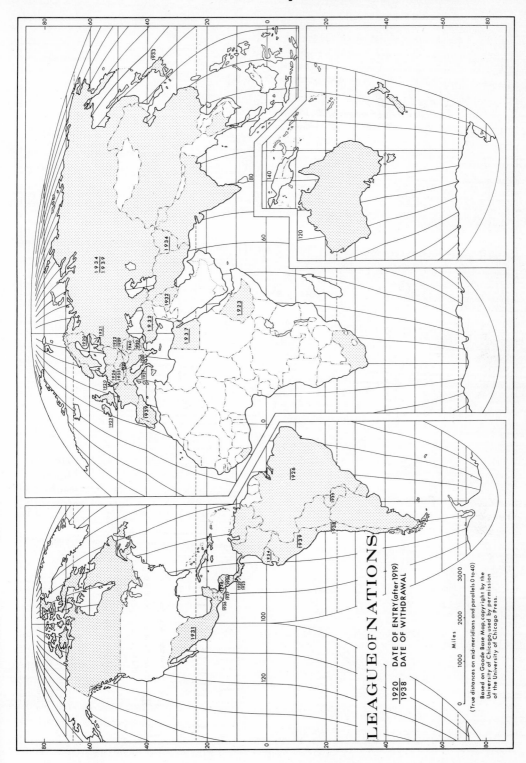

LEAGUE OF NATIONS

| 1920 | DATE OF ENTRY (after 1919) |
| 1938 | DATE OF WITHDRAWAL |

Miles

0   1000   2000   3000

(True distances on mid-meridians and parallels 0 to 40)

Based on Goode Base Map, copyright by the
University of Chicago, used by permission
of the University of Chicago Press.

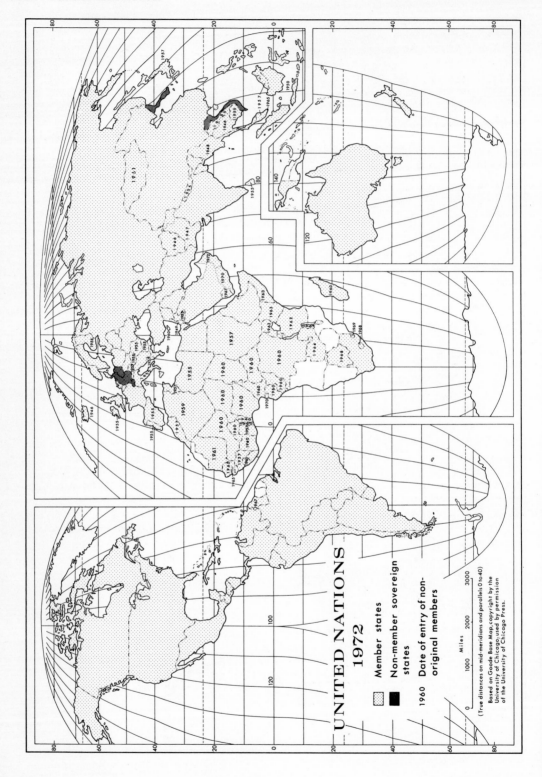

UNITED NATIONS
1972

Member states

Non-member sovereign
states

1960   Date of entry of non-
original members

(True distances on mid-meridians and parallels 0 to 40)

Based on Goode Base Map, copyright by the
University of Chicago, used by permission
of the University of Chicago Press.

Miles
0   1000   2000   3000

warfare that accompanied the Indonesian struggle for independence from the Netherlands was halted through United Nations mediation. United Nations forces have acted in the Congo, in the Suez Canal Zone, in Cyprus, and elsewhere. The major military effort has been in the repudiation of Communist aggression in Korea. These activities, however, are a severe drain on the limited resources of the United Nations, it has been necessary repeatedly to curtail the peace-keeping operation.

The significance of the United Nations, in the present context, lies in the fact that it reflects, however imperfectly, the continued desire on the part of states for mutual action, open communications, and a maintenance of international peace and security. States that have faced the censure of the United Nations nevertheless continue to participate and contribute. That attitude is an indication that the states of the world are beginning to be prepared to give up a small bit of sovereignty—however minimal—in the interest of international collaboration. This is a completely new phenomenon on the politicogeographical scene.

The *International Court of Justice* is worthy of separate mention, though a part of the United Nations Organization. In effect, the World Court, as it is often called, is a continuation of the Permanent Court of International Justice, an organ of the League of Nations. The Permanent Court had been one of the League's most effective agencies, and the new World Court, founded in 1945, became virtually a copy of its predecessor. Its offices also are located in The Hague, and the statute governing its operations reads almost completely like that of the former Permanent Court.

The Court consists of fifteen justices, with no more than one justice being designated by any single state represented. There is no veto power. When a case is being heard involving a country that is not represented in the Court, that country may designate an additional justice either of its own nationality or that of another state. The Court hears cases involving two or more of the member states of the United Nations, and has even heard cases involving the United Nations as a whole, for example, when U.N. mediator Bernadotte was assassinated by Jewish terrorists and the Israel government was ordered to make reparations to the organization. Perhaps its most impor-

tant task has been in the arbitration of the United Nations Charter, which has been strengthened as a result. It has been least effective in dealing with recalcitrant states which sometimes indicated, even before the case was actually heard, that they would not consider the Court's judgment binding.

The International Court of Justice represents the first step toward international legislation and an international order of law. Naturally, the Court has no executive power, and when it found against Albania in the Corfu Channel case (involving Britain), and against South Africa in the South West Africa case, those countries did not adhere to the Court's findings, and there was no force that could make them do so. But the Court has had some real success in what may be described as intrabloc disputes. The quarrel between Britain and Iceland over fishing rights in North Sea waters was settled by the Court, as was the argument between Nicaragua and Honduras over the location of their mutual boundary. Frequently, the states involved in such disputes have abided by the Court's decision. Again, this involves giving up a certain amount of sovereignty in the interest of international law and order.

The day is obviously far off when really effective world organizations arise which may properly be described as forerunners of a world government. In the major struggles in the presentday world, that of capitalism versus communism and that of colonialism versus independence for all peoples, the United Nations and the World Court have not managed to play dominant roles, although they certainly have had an impact in specific areas. But apart from the General Assembly and certain other bodies that form part of the U.N., the organization's membership remains one-sided (for example in the Monetary Fund and the International Bank) and is far from worldwide. But the world organizations of today mark the greatest achievements of a desire on the part of states to collaborate, a desire that is also reflected by the numerous regional organizations of international cooperation that have recently sprung up. The world organization incorporates the widest possible range of interests of member states. The regional organizations, based upon states that are often contiguous and share many historical and cultural experiences and attitudes, have gone farther. They may be indications of the political world to come.

INTERNATIONAL ORGANIZATIONS

Regionalism is a modern phenomenon in political geography. Interstate associations have existed in the past, but at no time has the idea of regionalism taken hold in so many parts of the world—or so effectively. By regionalism is understood the voluntary grouping or association of three or more states with the ultimate purpose of forming a unified political entity. That ultimate goal, complete unity, is far distant in most of the groupings to be discussed here. But the progress in some cases is remarkable and, from all appearances, permanent. Quite rapidly, thus, a new politicogeographical map is being created.

Basically, there are two views of regionalism among the proponents of the concept. Some have preferred the federal process, whereby states join in a federal framework, rendering the decisions of the federal government binding upon the member units. Others have felt that this is putting the cart before the horse; that political unity follows, not precedes, economic, social, cultural, and perhaps military cooperation. This is the "functional" (as opposed to the "federal") school, and there are indications that the functional approach produces the most tangible results.

Several distinct types of regional associations can be distinguished. Many, however, though begun in order to foster collaboration in one specific sphere, have produced cooperation in other spheres also. The North Atlantic Treaty Organization, for example, was initially devised as a defensive arrangement, but it has developed cooperation in other areas as well. Thus when these international organizations are classified, it is often necessary to remember that while the major function of a certain organization may be in a specific field (such as collective military security), its effects are felt in other fields also. On occasion, in fact, the whole emphasis has shifted.

1. Strategic Groupings

Probably the most frequently discussed type of association is the strategic alliance, and the most famous is the North Atlantic Treaty Organization. The preamble reads as follows:[1]

The parties to this Treaty reaffirm their faith in the

[1]*The North Atlantic Treaty Organization Handbook,* N.A.T.O. Information Service, Paris, 1961, p. 8.

purposes and principles of the Charter of the United Nations and their desire to live in peace with all peoples and all Governments.

They are determined to safeguard the freedom, common heritage and civilization of their peoples, founded on the principles of democracy, individual liberty and the rule of law.

They seek to promote stability and well-being in the North Atlantic area.

They are resolved to unite their efforts for collective defence and for the preservation of peace and security.

The first five articles of the treaty include the following undertakings on the part of the signatories: 1. Peaceful settlement of disputes and abstinence from force or threat of force. 2. Economic collaboration. 3. Strengthening of the means for resisting aggression, both by individual national efforts and by mutual assistance. 4. Consultation in the event of any signatory being threatened. 5. Mutual assistance in case of aggression.

Thus the organization is more than a defensive alliance. By the very fact that member states enjoyed the advantages of collective security, they could in times of need focus their attention upon the development of their resources in a way that would have been impossible had each been compelled to act individually. Hence the military organization has had considerable effect upon the Western European economy.

The United States policy of containment is evident from the location of the member states of alliances in which the United States participates. Subsequent to the formation of N.A.T.O., three other states entered the organization: Greece, Turkey, and the Federal Republic of Germany. Turkey also became a member of the now-defunct Baghdad Pact, formed in 1955 and including Iraq, Pakistan, Iran, as well as the United States and the United Kingdom. In 1959 Iraq withdrew from the pact, and since its headquarters had been in the city of Baghdad, a shift and reorganization became necessary. A new alliance, the Central Treaty Organization, was founded and headquartered in Turkey.

Another alliance furthering the United States aim of containment is the Southeast Asia Treaty Organization. Founded in 1954, the treaty included Pakistan, Thailand, and the Philippines, Australia and New Zealand, as well as the United States, United Kingdom, and France. Some of Southeast Asia's most important countries preferred to retain a

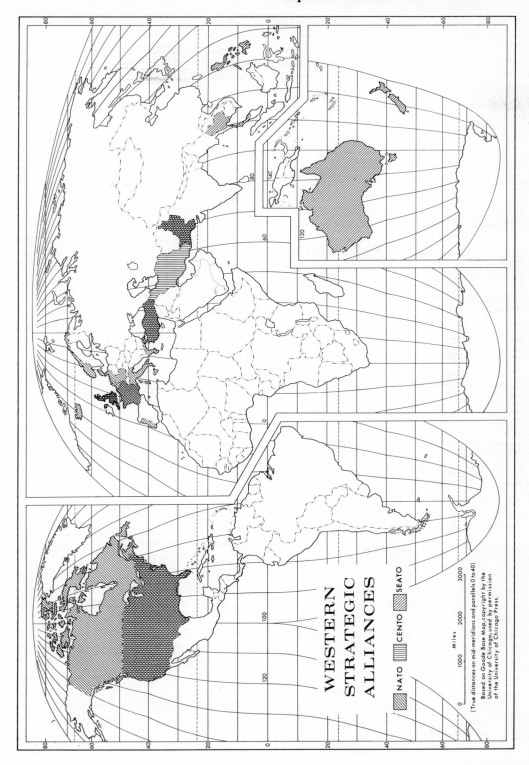

WESTERN
STRATEGIC
ALLIANCES

NATO   CENTO   SEATO

Miles

0   1000   2000   3000

(True distances on mid-meridians and parallels 0 to 40)

Based on Goode Base Map, copyright by the
University of Chicago, used by permission
of the University of Chicago Press.

policy of nonalignment and therefore refused to join the treaty, while others, mainly those of former French Indo–China, remained outside of it because of the Geneva agreements of 1954. Unlike N.A.T.O., S.E.A.T.O. does not have standing forces and relies upon the power of the individual member states for its collective security. S.E.A.T.O. also functions in certain cultural and economic spheres.

While N.A.T.O., C.E.N.T.O., and S.E.A.T.O. are Western strategic groupings, such groupings exist in the Communist orbit also. The most effective is the Warsaw Treaty Organization, known as the Warsaw Pact, signed in 1955 and dominated by the U.S.S.R. just as the above-mentioned alliances are dominated by the U.S.A. In effect the Warsaw Pact is a twenty-year defense treaty among the U.S.S.R., Albania, Bulgaria, Czechoslovakia, the German Democratic Republic, Hungary, Poland, and Rumania. The Warsaw Pact was partly a reaction to the admission of West Germany to the North Atlantic Treaty Organization. Its immediate effect was twofold. Allowing for the presence of Soviet armed forces on satellite soil, it greatly increased the effectiveness of Soviet control (as witnessed by the rapid termination of the Hungarian–Polish uprisings of 1956), and it also improved the Soviet bargaining position in Europe. Shortly after having erected the treaty, the Soviet leadership began to suggest the mutual dissolution of N.A.T.O. and the Warsaw Pact.

2. Political Groupings

Comparatively few truly political groupings exist. In fact, the borderline between political organizations and those with cultural overtones or those with economic bases is often very difficult to define. Perhaps the most significant development in this field is the Council of Europe. In 1948, deliberations began with the goal of establishing an embryo European "parliament." The result was a deliberative body which in reality is little more than a forum for the exchange of ideas, but which may in the future be recognized as the beginning of a European government. Initially there was some friction between those who wished to vest considerable powers in the Council and the participating governments that did not wish to give up any sovereignty. Meeting for the first time in Strasbourg in 1949, the Council consists of two organs: the Council of Ministers and the

Consultative Assembly. In both organizations, all members are represented.

The Council of Europe has no political power today, but it is attended by several states that otherwise are not politically aligned through international organizations: Austria, Ireland, and Finland. Many of its conclusions and suggestions have in fact influenced the policies of Western European countries despite the absence of executive authority.

In some ways, the former Central African Federation may be seen as a political grouping; although the economic argument was stressed by those who favored that union between Southern Rhodesia, Northern Rhodesia, and Nyasaland, the main object quite obviously was political. Another African union, the Mali Federation, was based largely upon political considerations, and it, too, failed. The ex-Federation of the West Indies and the present Federation of Malaysia both represent efforts to establish political units first, with integration in other spheres to follow.

3. Cultural-Political Organizations

In several parts of the world, states with certain cultural ties (ethnic, linguistic, historical) have established organizations designed to promote unity, coordinate policy, disseminate information, share information and funds, and foster strength. At times these organizations also take joint political action. Some of them have grown out of the empires of former colonial powers, while others have arisen as a result, at least in part, of a common enemy. Five examples will be given here: the Organization of American States, the Arab League, the Commonwealth, the French Community, and the embryo Organization of African Unity.

The *Organization of American States* had several predecessors, including the Pan-American Union and its organ, the International Union of the American Republics. American unity has strong foundations, for many of the republics of Latin America fought themselves free of Spanish domination; all except Brazil and Haiti share the heritage of Spanish language and culture (and Brazil is Portuguese-influenced, and therefore closely related in these respects), and the United States is the strongest trading and investment partner to most. The Organization of American States is but a recent expression of the

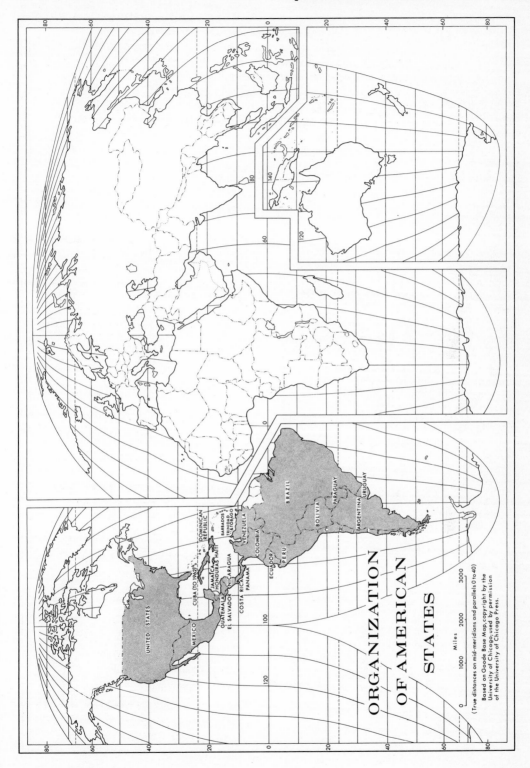

ORGANIZATION
OF AMERICAN
STATES

Miles
0   1000   2000   3000

(True distances on mid-meridians and parallels 0 to 40)

Based on Goode Base Map, copyright by the
University of Chicago, used by permission
of the University of Chicago Press.

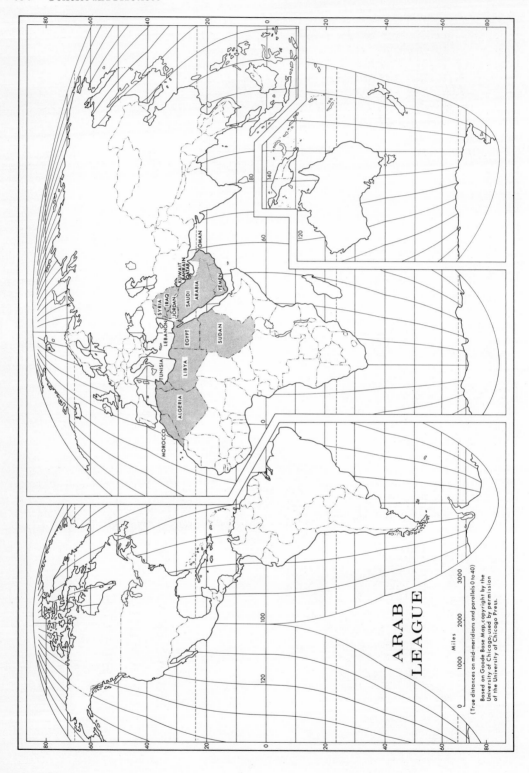

MOROCCO
ALGERIA
TUNISIA
LIBYA
EGYPT
SUDAN
LEBANON
SYRIA
JORDAN
IRAQ
KUWAIT
BAHRAIN
QATAR
SAUDI ARABIA
YEMEN
OMAN

ARAB LEAGUE

Miles

0   1000   2000   3000

(True distances on mid-meridians and parallels 0 to 40)

Based on Goode Base Map, copyright by the
University of Chicago, used by permission
of the University of Chicago Press.

mutual interests of the Americas, and moves in this direction have been going on for nearly a century. The Pan-American Union developed out of the 1890 Washington Conference aimed at greater unity, and the next important steps were taken at the 1933 Montevideo Conference. Subsequent events in Europe led to a general concern over the possibility of German–Italian war efforts in Latin America, and conferences held in 1939 and 1940 called for joint action to ward off that danger. Then in 1948 the Bogota Conference resulted in the formation of the O.A.S. At present (1973) only Canada is not a member of the organization, while Cuba no longer participates. Political action on the part of the members of the organization was taken in the form of sanctions against Cuba, but the more important work of the Washington-based O.A.S. involves cooperation in cultural, economic, social and legal spheres.

The *Arab League*, founded in 1945, also is based upon the cultural unity of the states that subscribe to it. The peoples of the Arab would have several things to unite them: the Arabic language, the Islam religion, the history of colonial subjugation. But there are also many things that continue to divide the Arab peoples. Feudalism still rears its head, and there is disapproval in certain Arab states of the government that rules in others. Perhaps the greatest unifying element of all is the general hostitlity to the state of Israel and the forces of Zionism in the Arab midst.

With the breakup of the Ottoman Empire and the elimination of Turkish control in the Middle East, the European colonial powers were put in charge of mandates over various parts of the Arab world. Arab nationalism arose after World War I just as African nationalism did after World War II: the French were ousted from Syria, the British from Iraq. Opposition to a British-sponsored Jewish state grew. Arab unity was beginning to develop. By the end of the second World War, some Arab leaders actually hoped for the establishment of a great Arab state, but they saw their hopes destroyed by the many divisive forces that still prevail there: tribalism, poverty, illiteracy, vested interest. Still, the Arab League was forged, with high ideals. The reality has been different: the League has been a loose and rather ineffective organization whose only real unifying factor, some observers have stated, remains the common opposition to Israel. Nevertheless, since the formation of the League, much has changed in the Arab world: Egypt has attained representative government, Algeria has rid itself of French control, the Suez invasion was warded off, the Sudan became independent. The Arab League, the unity of Arabic and Islam notwithstanding, consists of very diverse elements. When the long-standing differences among Arabs diminish in intensity, its effect will be felt more strongly.

The *British Commonwealth* has been created out of the vast colonial empire of Britain. In many ways this is the most nearly ideal of cultural-political organizations, for the Commonwealth is multiracial in character, has representatives on several continents, existed prior to the postwar period of decolonization, and incorporates many of the countries that waged a struggle for independence from the British. Despite this struggle, most emergent, British-influenced states availed themselves of the opportunity to join the Commonwealth, and the full-scale participation of such new states as full and sovereign members of the organization greatly enhanced their status and prestige. But the Commonwealth is not built on images. There are very real advantages to participation: preferential trade agreements, aid of a financial nature, loans, and other benefits come to the member states.

Several of the present members of the Commonwealth have long been independent —even during the days of the Empire, before the Commonwealth was founded. Canada, Australia, and South Africa (now no longer a member) all were self-governing dominions, in effect, sovereign states before the Commonwealth concept was implemented. The 1926 Imperial Conference formally brought the organization into being, but the years after the second World War saw many changes in the original concept. Initially, the independent Commonwealth states were all controlled or solely occupied by whites. Australia's heritage is undeniably British, that of Canada largely so, and South Africa's 1910 Union was the creation of a coalition between British and Boers, without the consultation of the vast majority of the country's nonwhites. Thus, though Britain gradually relinquished what little control was left in those states, there appeared no reason to fear any total breakaway from the British cultural, political, and economic sphere. But when, after 1945, the emancipation of the rest of the colonial empire became a matter of time, that picture changed.

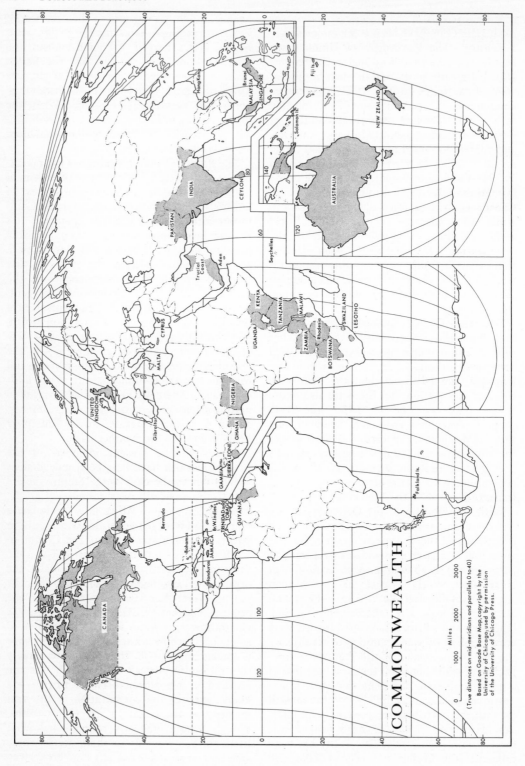

COMMONWEALTH

Miles
0   1000   2000   3000
(True distances on mid-meridians and parallels 0 to 40)

Based on Goode Base Map, copyright by the
University of Chicago, used by permission
of the University of Chicago Press.

Many of the newly independent states possessed institutions and practices introduced by the British, but the question was whether they would wish to continue to associate themselves on a voluntary basis with the former colonial ruler. All were given the opportunity; most took it. India, Pakistan, Ghana, Nigeria, Malaysia, Tanganyika (now Tanzania), and Jamaica are but a few of the new additions. Some refused: the Republic of Sudan is among these, and one of the original Commonwealth members, the Union (now Republic) of South Africa, departed after other Commonwealth states voiced criticism of its racial policies. Other absentees are the Republic of Ireland and Burma. However, even countries in which bitter wars were waged betwen British and rebels have stayed with the organization. Kenya is the prime example: less than ten years after the most violent days of Mau Mau, when all hope for future cooperation seemed lost, it is a Commonwealth member today.

Each year, the Commonwealth Prime Ministers and Presidents meet for informal discussions of mutual problems. In the Commonwealth the emphasis is on the informal, and there are no plans for united political action. Some of the most important members of the Commonwealth, in fact, are nonaligned or "neutral" states. What brings the leaders together each year is not an allegiance to the British Crown or any other political reason, but the fact that the countries of the Commonwealth all share the assets (and admitted liabilities) of a lengthy period of British domination during which certain British imprints were made which will not soon be eradicated. The spread of the English language is but one aspect of that impact. Most of the British-influenced emergent states have judiciary, educational, and governmental institutions that were, and are continuing to be, modeled along British lines.

The *French Community* has a very different history. It was born with the Fifth Republic, itself largely the product of the series of disasters that befell France in its efforts to retain a hold over its far-flung colonial empire. Prior to the Community the French Empire consisted of a very complex organizational structure known as the French Union, in which overseas but self-governing territories possessed a certain amount of representation in the Paris government. However, so many changes took place in the empire during and after World War II that almost constant revision was necessary, and confusion reigned. In 1958, the crisis in Algeria having dragged on for several years and the wind of change having an impact in other parts of Africa, the Community was erected and French overseas possessions were given a choice: to become

The founder of a supranational organization: monument to President De Gaulle in Brazzaville. De Gaulle founded the French Community by offering African dependencies of France a choice between continued colonial status, complete and detached sovereignty, and participation as an autonomous unit within an aid-providing greater French framework. Among the remaining dependencies only Guinea opted for sovereignty outside the new French Community; all others heeded the advice De Gaulle gave at the time he made his offer and joined the organization (Harm J. de Blij).

independent outside any French Community, to attain independence within the Community framework, or to continue as dependencies as before. Prior to the vote, De Gaulle traveled through Africa to outline his concept of the Community, indicating that considerable economic benefits would derive from Community participation. When the vote was taken, all African territories except Guinea chose membership in the Community and sovereignty. Guinea chose complete independence outside the French sphere.

While the economic promises inherent in Community participation obviously enhanced the Community's prospects in Africa, there can be no doubt concerning the cultural impact made by France in its former and present colonial realm. Almost every one of the new republics has an elite that is totally French oriented. Thousands of present-day leaders were trained in France at French universities; educational institutions in French Africa were based on the French example. French African pride in French cultural achievements is in many places intense and genuine. The cultural justification of the Community is beyond argument.

Under the Fifth Republic, independent states that are members of the Community do not enjoy the representation in the French Parliament formerly possessed by self-governing French overseas territories. In turn the French President does not have the powers in the member states once enjoyed by the parliament. Thus the Fifth Republic and its decentralization of power are a long way from the high degree of centralization that has marked French and French colonial politics for so long. Still, France continues to have considerable influence in its former empire. By virtue of its contribution to the economies of the French-influenced emergent state, it is in a position to dictate, to some extent, the policies of the new governments. Under Article 78 of the Constitution of the Fifth Republic, certain decisions regarding foreign policy, defense, economic relations, and the exploitation of strategic raw materials remain the province of the common organs of the Community rather than the sole responsibility of the individual governments. This means, of course, that the French President (who is President of the Community, and who is chosen by French overseas dependencies as well as France itself) has considerable power in French-influenced Africa despite the independence of the republics.

THE COMMUNITY
President of the Community
Executive Council
Court of Arbitration   Senate of the Community
Members

A. The French Republic
1. The 90 Departments of France
2. Overseas Departments (French Guiana, Reunion, Guadaloupe, Martinique)
3. Overseas Territories (St. Pierre, Miquelon, Oceania, Afars and Issas, New Caledonia, the Comoros)

B. Member States
Republics: Upper Volta, Dahomey, Ivory Coast, Mali, Mauritania, Senegal, Niger, Chad, Central African, Gabon, Congo, Malagasy

C. Associated States
None

Finally, the *Organization of African Unity* is an example of the various Pan-movements that have arisen in various parts of the world since the end of World War II. Headquartered in Addis Ababa, the organization, like the Arab League, is viewed optimistically as the embryo out of which an eventual all-African government may grow. A United States of Africa is the ideal of a number of African politicians, among whom Nkrumah of Ghana has been especially vocal. The organization has concerned itself with such matters as the persistent crisis in the Congo, action in the still-dependent territories of Africa, notably Portuguese Angola and Mozambique, and joint sanctions against South Africa (for example, the barring of overflights by South African aircraft). The organization presently enjoys the unifying influence of anticolonialism, but divisive elements already have appeared. While some wish to see the rapid implementation of a United States of Africa project, others desire to maintain their total sovereignty and are reluctant to enter political unions. The whole argument is not entirely dissimilar from that which attended the birth of the Council of Europe, and ultimately it goes back to the basic question of whether political unification should precede or follow collaboration in other spheres.

The O.A.U. does fit the present category, however, for although many of its actions and discussions have been related to political problems, its organs also deal with the spread

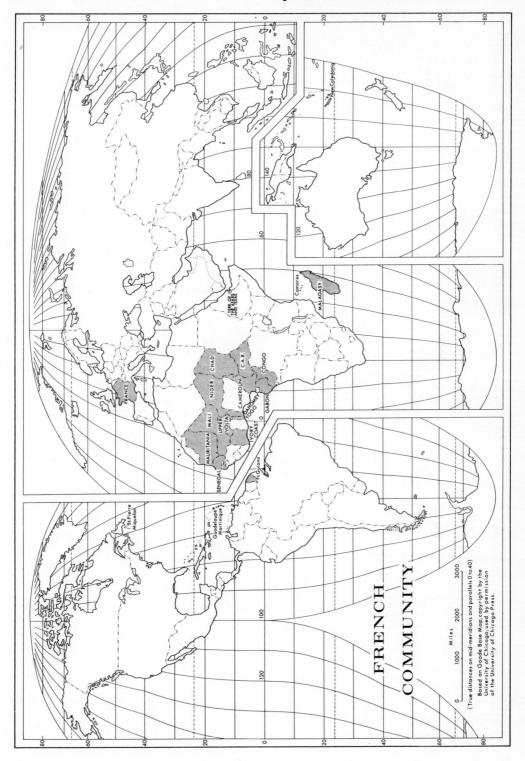

FRENCH COMMUNITY

Miles

0   1000   2000   3000

(True distances on mid-meridians and parallels 0 to 40)

Based on Goode Base Map, copyright by the
University of Chicago; used by permission
of the University of Chicago Press.

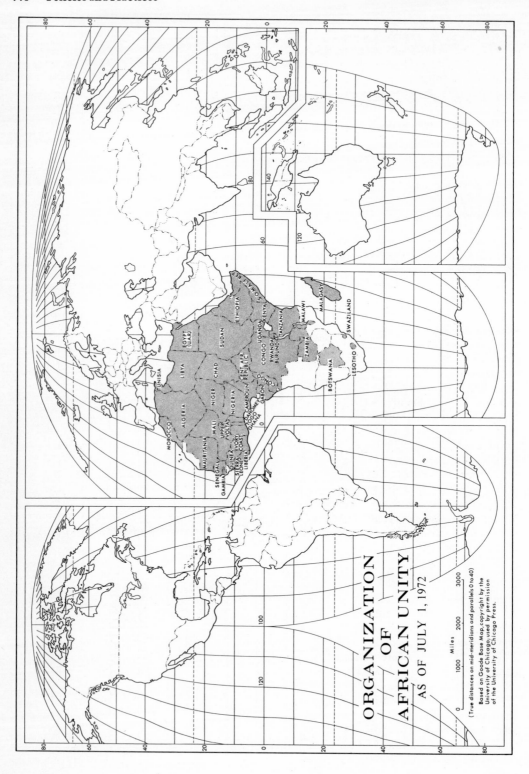

ORGANIZATION
OF
AFRICAN UNITY
AS OF JULY 1, 1972

Miles
1000   2000   3000

(True distances on mid-meridians and parallels 0 to 40)

Based on Goode Base Map, copyright by the
University of Chicago, used by permission
of the University of Chicago Press.

of education and the elimination of illiteracy, improvement of health standards, cultural exchange programs, and the like. In view of the youthfulness of the participant states, the survival of the O.A.U. is a matter for satisfaction on the part of those who want to see political divisions and barriers eliminated rather than strengthened.

ECONOMIC SUPRANATIONALISM

The last—and in many ways the most significant—phenomenon to be discussed in relation to supranational organization among states is that of the economic grouping. A host of economic unions and associations exist today, and in some of them there is evidence of growing political solidarity.

The most impressive developments in this sphere have taken place in Europe. Actually, Pan-European movements of one kind or another have existed in Europe for centuries: The Holy Roman Empire, the efforts of Erasmus in the early 1500's, Cruce's writings in the 1600's, those of Rousseau and Kant in the 1700's, Victor Hugo's work in the 1800's, and that of Condenhove-Kalergi in the first half of the present century all exemplify the permanent ideal of a united Europe. Condenhove published, in 1923, his *Pan Europa,* and he was the main organizer of the Vienna Pan-European Congress. But not until after the end of World War II did any really effective unifying movements develop, and when they did, they were of an economic rather than a political, cultural, religious, or ideological nature.

Benelux

Agreements for the establishment of an economic union of Belgium, the Netherlands, and Luxembourg were signed even before the end of the war, in London in 1944. Benelux was to become the forerunner of economic cooperation in Western Europe, although the original London agreements were revised a number of times and Benelux did not formally begin to function until 1948.[2] Common tariffs were established for many goods, and plans were made for the gradual elimination of import licenses and quotas. Interest in this new organization was great, but it was soon to

be superseded by other and larger unions. Also in 1948, the O.E.E.C., Organization for European Economic Cooperation, was established, with the specific object of coordinating the Marshall Plan funds contributed by the United States to speed the recovery of Europe from the ravages of the second World War. This organization, in which most non-Communist European states participated, administered the aid given to Europe, and it also scrutinized European needs. Thus the representatives of the various member states became very well acquainted with the needs of their neighbors and fellow Europeans. This eventually led to continued consultation, even after the O.E.E.C. had served its purpose and had been replaced.

The European Economic Community

Even closer cooperation than that envisaged by the O.E.E.C. was initiated by six O.E.E.C. members: France, West Germany, Italy, the Netherlands, Belgium, and Luxembourg. That collaboration came about through a series of steps, one of which was the "Schuman Plan." This plan, drawn up by French foreign minister Robert Schuman, was aimed at the expansion and integration of coal and steel production in the member states, while costs were lowered. Thus the E.C.S.C., the European Coal and Steel Community, proposed in 1950, drafted in 1951, and ratified in 1952, represented the most important step toward union yet to be taken in Europe, for each member state agreed to abide by the decisions of a supranational High Authority and a Court of Justice. Gradually (but rapidly) obstacles to the rapid flow of the necessary raw materials were removed, as were hindrances to the flow of labor and investment capital. Here, again, we see sovereign states willing to yield some sovereignty in the interests of common, regional progress.

The E.C.S.C. was only the beginning of cooperation among the six states. Through continued negotiation and planning, they agreed in 1958 to join in the European Economic Community (E.E.C.), also known as the Six, the Inner Six, and the Common Market. A common market was, in effect, what was being established. Tariffs and other restrictions to trade were to be gradually removed over a period of twelve to fifteen years, while the flow of labor and capital was to be freed completely as well. And the E.E.C.

---

[2]In 1921, Belgium and Luxembourg formed an economic union which continued to exist after the creation of Benelux.

was to be no closed club; other states could apply for entry under negotiable terms.

The European Economic Community today still constitutes one of the most significant examples of supranationalism in existence. After more than a decade of progress, the early 1970's saw a momentous development: the United Kingdom sought admission to the Community. At conferences in Luxembourg in the first half of 1971, Britain and the E.E.C. members worked out the essentials of an agreement that would enable the British leaders to persuade their houses of parliament to approve entry. This was no small achievement; apart from Britain's traditional aloofness to the continent and the considerable latent resistance to any major involvement with mainland countries, Britain's ties with its Commonwealth partners posed enormous problems. Britain had to secure preferential markets in the Community for its Caribbean, African, and Asian associates; countries in the Commonwealth whose economies depend heavily on sugar sales also needed guarantees of that sort. New Zealand, which sells a large part of its dairy production in Britain, needed guarantees that it would not lose its favored position in this respect.

But there were other problems—problems relating to British agriculture and to the industrial tariff system. Formulas were worked out whereby Britain would, in stages over several years, enter the Community farm price system. Since this would entail rising prices for farm products in Britain, that was a touchy matter for those who must "sell" entry to the public. A multiyear program also was created for the gradual . application of the Community's external tariff system in Britain; at the same time, British producers would, over a three-year period, gain unencumbered access to the markets of the E.E.C. countries.

Although Britain's negotiators came out of the Luxembourg Conference with conditions that were clearly favorable to the United Kingdom, the British Parliament and public did not exactly rush into membership with blind enthusiasm. The Labor Party strenuously opposed the terms of membership, and was joined by the Trades Union Congress in this opposition. But in the vote of October 28, 1971, many Laborites broke ranks and voted with the Conservative members of Parliament to approve the E.E.C. Agreement by 356 to 244. No major obstacles were encountered, Britain's entry into the Common Market took place formally on January 1, 1973.

Nor was the United Kingdom alone in seeking E.E.C. membership. While the negotiations were going on in Luxembourg, three other states announced their intention to apply for entry: Ireland, Denmark, and Norway. The signs of movement toward a united Europe were unmistakable in the first years of the decade, although the Norwegian electorate negated Norway's entry.

The European Free Trade Association (The Seven)

Those states that did not initially participate in the Common Market, most important among which was the United Kingdom, were naturally concerned over the future of their trade with E.E.C. countries, and sought ways to soften any blows that might be sustained. Seven of these states—the United Kingdom, Norway, Denmark, Sweden, Switzerland, Austria, and Portugal—decided in 1959 to create E.F.T.A., the European Free Trade Association. This association, though less populous and generally poorer than its contiguous counterpart, nevertheless possessed decided advantages, mainly because of the participation of Britain with its Commonwealth ties.

The objectives of the Seven were less farreaching than those of the Six. While there also was the goal of elimination of tariff barriers among member states, there was no intention to erect a common external tariff, so that each member state retained the power to handle non-E.F.T.A. external trade in its own manner. This permitted Britain to retain its normal trade relations with the Commonwealth, while creating an economic block in Europe in which it dominated.

With the developing relationship between the leading state in E.F.T.A., Britain, and the E.E.C., it is likely that the former will disintegrate and that members will seek some form of association with the expanded E.E.C. Thus E.F.T.A. will become part of the record of European supranational integration—not a lasting part, but an important one nevertheless.

The Organization for Economic Cooperation and Development

The United States, vitally interested in the progress of unification in Europe, viewed with some concern the division of the Western continent into two rival economic blocs, the

Six and the Seven. Having been instrumental in providing much of the aid that set Europe out in the direction of unprecedented prosperity, and having thus provided the impetus for the O.E.E.C., it was now felt by the United States that a revision of the O.E.E.C. might again promote unity. Hence a committee was constituted to suggest ways to improve the organization, and in 1960 that committee (in which all eighteen O.E.E.C. members were represented) published a report. It was proposed that the O.E.E.C. be remodeled into a twenty-member O.E.C.D., the United States and Canada becoming full members. In 1961, the organization was ratified by all the member states.

The O.E.C.D. has broader objectives than those of the O.E.E.C. Indeed, its function is a very different one in some ways. The O.E.E.C. was formed to administer to a recovering Europe; the O.E.C.D. is concerned with economic stability, aid and support to developing countries, and the expansion of world trade. From the European point of view, it may be argued that the O.E.C.D. represents a step backward and not forward in the struggle for European unity. Indeed, it is true that the O.E.E.C. possessed a certain degree of power, with an executive authority whose unanimous decisions were binding upon the member states. The O.E.C.D. has no such authority, and there were some questions whether a unifying Europe really needed an Atlantic organization that is somewhat weaker (if broader) than the former European one. Certainly the O.E.C.D. did not initially appear to provide any answers to the growing division between the Outer Seven and the Inner Six.

Whatever the outcome of the matter, the unification movement in Europe is gathering strength each year. In the military sphere, N.A.T.O. and the Western European Union are powerful alliances. In the political areas, the Council of Europe is an impressive start. In the economic sphere, so much has changed in Europe that the process may now be described as unique and irreversible. Monnet's ideal of a United States of Europe may be far from realization, but in two decades European unity has progressed more than in two previous centuries.

The Council of Economic Mutual Assistance (COMECON)

Economic cooperation is not confined to the capitalist part of Europe, although the Com-

munist counterpart of the Western economic unions, C.E.M.A., operates in very different fashion. Established in 1949, C.E.M.A. was to centralize and administer trade agreements as well as credit and technical assistance within the Sino–Soviet bloc and involving the Soviet Union and one or more of the members of the Communist world. Soviet trade systems were outdated and consisted of stop-gap, short-term arrangements; C.E.M.A. provided opportunities for national planning and long-term trade agreements.

C.E.M.A., however, bears little resemblance, to, for example, the Common Market. This is not to deny that considerable progress has been made in the economic development of the Soviet Union and its satellites, the transit of raw materials and finished products, and so on. But the Communist organization serves the government and their planning agencies, while the Common Market and E.F.T.A. are there to serve free enterprise.

Economic cooperation is by no means confined to Europe, and neither have the significant consequences of supranationalism been visible in Europe alone. Europe's unity is of world importance because of the power of the states involved and the strategic aspects of the region in the face of Communist expansionism. Economic collaboration has produced good results also in the Americas, in Africa, and in Asia.

America: The Alliance for Progress

The Alianza is, in a sense, the American equivalent of the old O.E.E.C. in Europe, designed to coordinate and administer the use of American aid, loans, and other forms of assistance in the Americas. Established in 1961, the ten-year program of the Alliance provided for the distribution of some $20 billion in financial and other aid throughout Latin America. As in the case of the European counterpart, the governments of the participating states are expected to use these funds to shore up their economies, and among the stipulations of the Alliance is the requirement that these states shall initiate reform programs in those spheres where reform is necessary—and in Latin America, that includes much. Land reform, tax reform, efforts to halt inflation, all are part of the duties of recipient states. The states are also expected to produce a program of their economic development, based upon the funds they will receive and the resources at their own disposal. One of

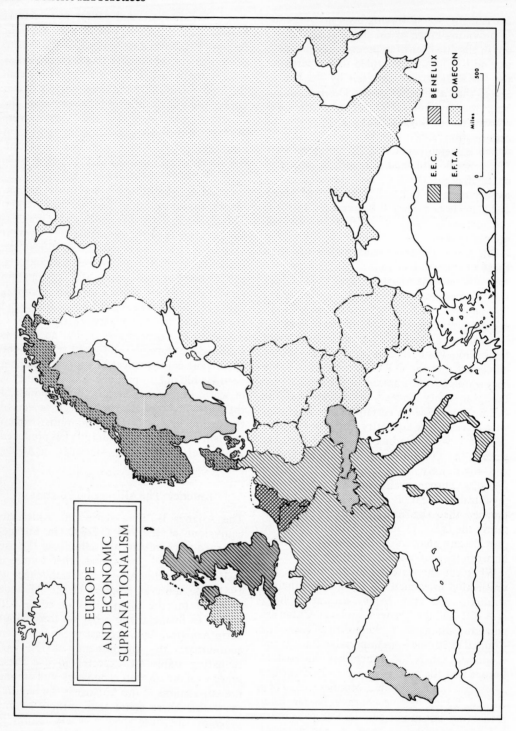

EUROPE
AND ECONOMIC
SUPRANATIONALISM

E.E.C.

E.F.T.A.

BENELUX

COMECON

0   500
Miles

the early disappointments of the Alliance was the fact that relatively few states seemed willing to make the necessary effort in the interests of obtaining Alliance funds. This is not so surprising, though, in view of the manner in which the United States has at times dispensed aid to various other countries, almost without any strings attached, and in greater amounts than some of the Latin American neighbors could expect to receive. The giant of the north easily arouses nationalist sentiments among the Middle and South American republics, and some of the requirements of the Alliance have had this effect.

Nor has the Alliance escaped the image of economic imperialism and neocolonialism so easily associated with a great power whose commerce dominates a foreign region. Latin American leaders whose political positions are predicated on a platform of independence from U.S. influence find it difficult to endorse programs of the Alliance. And the Alliance failed in a number of ways, rendering it an easy target; in agriculture and population control, for example, it fell far short of expectations.[3]

Asia: The Colombo Plan

The Plan for Cooperative Economic Development in South and Southeast Asia was developed in the late 1940's and formally established in 1950, when the interested states sent representatives to a conference at Colombo, capital of Ceylon. Britain took the lead in this organization, which was designed to combat poverty, illiteracy, and backwardness, and to promote human welfare. Britain was in a good position to forge this alliance, for several of the most important states to participate in it were under British colonial rule until very few years previous, and then were members of the Commonwealth. Although primarily economic and nonpolitical in nature, the Colombo Plan was in fact of political interest to those Western states that joined in the effort, for as in the case of Europe, it was felt that the greater economic development would be, the less was the chance for communism to succeed. Hence the Colombo Plan states included the United States, the United Kingdom, Canada, Australia, and New Zealand. The number of Asian states that

joined the organization at one time or another was considerable: British Borneo, Cambodia, Ceylon, India, Laos, Malaya, Pakistan, Singapore, and Viet Nam (later South Viet Nam only) were the original members, and Burma, Nepal, Indonesia, Japan, and the Philippines joined between 1952 and 1954.

It would be unreasonable to expect the Colombo Plan to have had the same salutary effect that the Marshall Plan had in Europe. In the case of Europe, the problem was one of recovery and return to prosperity and wealth; in Asia, the population to be assisted was far greater, resources fewer, health conditions much worse, food supply a matter for constant concern. Europe had the infrastructure and the means; South and Southeast Asia had neither. Hence the vast sums of money poured into the Colombo Plan had far less visible effect than the Marshall Plan appeared to have in Western Europe. But the very fact that the food situation improved somewhat was a great achievement, and many of the Colombo Plan states have irrigation works, cement factories, and other industrial concerns to show for their participation.

Africa: The Entente

Panafricanism in the political sphere has had its problems and will no doubt continue to have them, but in the economic sphere several successful interstate organizations have developed. One, the East African Common Services Organization, which joins Uganda, Kenya, and Tanzania in a loose economic union, is actually a legacy of British-dominated colonial days: the British saw the advantages of close cooperation between the territories they ruled, and the African leaders subsequently have seen the wisdom of continued cooperation. Another economic union is the so-called Entente in West Africa, which was founded in 1959 and whose original members were Ivory Coast, Upper Volta, Dahomey, and Niger.

The Entente states have similar constitutions, military and governmental arrangements; they have a common currency and a common official language. The total population of the four states is perhaps 13 million. The basic purpose of the Entente is the coordination of the members' economic (and to some extent political) activities. For example, in 1960 a common labor convention was established to regularize the salaries of workers and functionaries. Furthermore, a Solidari-

---

[3]For a view of the Alliance that emphasizes the positive but identifies the liabilities as well, see J.W. Nystrom and N.A. Haverstock, *The Alliance for Progress*, Van Nostrand, Princeton, 1966.

ty Fund was established, to which each member makes an annual contribution proportional to its revenues, and out of which the poorest state may draw the largest amount.

The Entente served as an example to other African states, for cooperation was extended to a number of other areas, notably the common military authority, joint overseas representation (again cutting expenditures), and elections timed within a few days of one another. A joint airline was created, and cooperation also was started in the field of education. Soon after the formation of the Entente, other states followed suit: in 1960, at conferences held in Abidjan and Brazzaville, an Abidjan Group was formed, including Senegal, Cameroun, Mauritania, and the four states of former French Equatorial Africa. The Group, which followed many of the guidelines of the Entente, is now associated loosely with that organization.

Supranationalism, thus, has come to virtually all parts of the world. The time of the blocs, the alliances, and the unions has arrived. Inevitably, the progress of politicoterritorial organization always having been an oscillating one, there will be breakups and setbacks. But the trend appears to have all the earmarks of permanency, and a new politicogeographical map is indeed being forged.

REFERENCES

Aderbigde, A.B., and others, "Symposium on West African Integration," *Nigerian J. Econ. and Social Studies, 5,* 1 (March, 1963), 1–40.

Akzin, Benjamin, *New States and International Organizations.* Paris, U.N.E.S.C.O., 1955.

Bailey, S.D., *The General Assembly of the United Nations.* New York, F.A. Praeger, 1964.

Benoit, Emile, *Europe at Sixes and Sevens; The Common Market, The Free Trade Association and the United States.* New York, Columbia University Press, 1962.

Bernstein, R.A., and P.D. Weldon, "A Structural Approach to the Analysis of International Relations," *Jour. Conflict Resolution, XII,* 2 (June, 1968), 159–181.

Bonn, M.J., *Whither Europe—Union or Partnership?* New York, Philosophical Library, 1952.

Boutros-Ghali, B.Y., "The Arab League, 1945–55," *Internat. Conciliation,* No. 498 (May, 1954), 387–448.

Brandt, Karl, "The Unification of Europe," *Vital Speeches of the Day, 19,* 6 (January 1, 1953).

Caplow, T. and K. Finsterbusch, "France and Other Countries: A Study of International Interaction," *Jour. Conflict Resolution, XII,* 1 (March, 1968), 1–15.

Catroux, G., "The French Union: Concept, Reality

and Prospects," *Internat. Conciliation,* No. 495 (1953), 195–256.

Coplin, W.D., "International Law and Assumptions about the State System," *World Politics, XVII,* 4 (July, 1965), 615–634.

Costanzo, G.A., "The Association of Overseas Countries and Territories with the Common Market," *Civilizations, 8* (1958), 505–526.

Desmond, Annabelle, "The Common Market," *Population Bull., 18,* 4 (July, 1962, 65–90.

Deutsch, K., and others, *Political Community and the North Atlantic Area.* Princeton, N.J., Princeton University Press, 1957.

Diebold, William, *The Schuman Plan; A Study in Economic Cooperation, 1950–1959.* New York, F.A. Praeger, 1959.

East, W. Gordon, *The Political Division of Europe.* London, Birkbeck College, University of London, 1948.

Efron, Reuben, and Allan S. Nanes, "The Common Market and Euratom Treaties: Supranationality and the Integration of Europe," *Int. and Comp. Law Quart., 6,* 4 (October, 1957), 670–684.

Etzioni, Amitai, "European Unification: A Strategy of Change," *World Politics, 16,* 1 (October, 1963), 32–51.

——, "A Paradigm for the Study of Political Unification," *World Politics, 15,* 1 (October, 1962), 44–74.

Fenwick, Charles G., *The Inter-American Regional System,* New York, D.X. McMullen Co., 1949.

Florinsky, Michael T., *Integrated Europe?* New York, Macmillan Co., 1955.

Franck, T.M., *East African Unity through Law.* New Haven, Conn., Yale University Press, 1964.

Gigax, William R., "The Central American Common Market," *Inter-American Economic Affairs, 16,* 2 (1962), 59–77.

Goormaghtigh, John, "European Coal and Steel Community," *Internat. Conciliation,* No. 503 (May, 1955), 343–408.

Haas, Ernst B., "Regionalism, Functionalism, and Universal Interantional Organization," *World Politics, 8,* 2 (January, 1956), 238–263.

Hallstein, Walter, *United Europe: Challenge and Opportunity.* Cambridge, Harvard University Press, 1962.

Harvey, Heather Joan, "The British Commonwealth: A Pattern of Cooperation," *Internat. Conciliation,* No. 487 (January, 1953), 1–48.

Hoffman, George, "Toward Greater Integration in Europe: Transfer of Electric Power Across International Boundaries," *J. Geography, 55,* 4 (April, 1956), 165–176.

Hudson, M.O., *The Permanent Court of International Justice.* New York, Macmillan, 1934.

Hurewitz, J.C., "Unity and Disunity in the Middle East," *Internat. Conciliation,* No. 481 (May, 1952), 197–260.

Issawi, Charles, "The Bases of Arab Unity," *Internat. Affairs, 31,* 1 (January, 1955), 36–47.

Kitzinger, U.W., "Europe: The Six and the Seven," *Internat. Organization, 14,* 1 (Winter, 1960), 20–36.

——, *The Politics and Economics of European Integration.* New York, F.A. Praeger, 1963.

Lepawsky, Albert, "International Development of River Resources," *Internat. Affairs, 39,* 4 (October, 1963), 533–550.

Lichtheim, George, *The New Europe: Today—and Tomorrow.* New York, F.A. Praeger, 1963.

Loewenstein, Karl, "Sovereignty and International Cooperation," *Amer. J. Internat. Law,* 48, 2 (April, 1954), 222–244.

Longrigg, S.H., "New Groupings Among the Arab States," *Internat. Affairs, 34,* 3 (July, 1958), 305–317.

Mayne, R., *The Community of Europe.* London, Gollancz, 1962.

Meinig, Donald W., "Cultural Blocs and Political Blocs: Emergent Patterns in World Affairs," *Western Humanities Quart., 10,* 3 (Summer, 1956), 203–222.

Myrdal, G., *Rich Lands and Poor: the Road to World Prosperity.* New York, Harper & Bros., 1957.

Neres, P., *French-Speaking West Africa.* London, Oxford University Press, 1962.

Nystrom, J.W., and Peter Malof, *The Common Market.* Princeton, N.J., Van Nostrand, 1962.

Owens, W.H. "International Roads for West Africa," *New Commonwealth, 40,* 6 (June, 1962), 363–366.

Padelford, Norman J., and Rupert Emerson (eds.), "Africa and International Organization," *Internat. Organization,* 16, 2 (Spring, 1962), 275–464.

Palmer, Norman D. (ed.), "The National Interest—Alone or With Others?" *Ann. Amer. Ac. Pol. & Soc. Sci.,* 282 (July, 1952), 1–118.

Panikkar, K.M., and others, *Regionalism and Security.* New Delhi, Indian Council of World Affairs, 1948.

Patterson, Ernest Minor (ed.), "Looking Toward One World," *Ann. Amer. Ac. Pol. & Soc. Sci.,* 258 (July, 1948), 1–123.

——, (ed.), "NATO and World Peace," *Ann. Amer. Ac. Pol. & Soc. Sci.,* 288 (July, 1953), 1–237.

——, (ed.), "World Government," *Ann. Amer. Ac. Pol. & Soc. Sci.,* 264 (July, 1949), 1–123.

Pollard, V.K., "A.S.A. and A.S.E.A.N. 1961–1967: Southeast Asian Regionalism," *Asian Survey, X,* 3 (March, 1970), 244–255.

Pounds, Norman J.G., *A Historical and Political Geography of Europe.* London, G.G. Harrap, 1949.

——, and William N. Parker. *Coal and Steel in Western Europe.* Bloomington, Indiana University Press, 1957.

Pryce, Roy, *The Political Future of the European Community.* London, Marshbank and Federal Trust, 1962.

Root, Franklin R., "The European Coal and Steel Community," *Studies in Business and Economics,* University of Maryland, Bureau of Business and Economic Research, 9, 3 (December 1955), 1–19; and 10, 1 (June, 1956), 1–16.

Russett, B.M., "Components of an Operational Theory of International Alliance Formation," *Jour. Conflict Resolution, XII,* 3 (September, 1968), 285–301.

Smith, C.G., "Arab Nationalism, a Study in Political Geography," *Geography,* 43 (1958), 229–242.

Smith, Howard K., *The State of Europe.* New York, Knopf, 1949.

Soward, F.H., and A.M. Macaulay, *Canada and the Pan American System.* Toronto, Ryerson Press, 1948.

Stamp, L. Dudley, *The British Commonwealth.* London, Longmans, Green, 1951.

Thomas, Anna Van Wynen, and A.J. Thomas, Jr., *The Organization of American States.* Dallas, Texas, Southern Methodist University Press, 1963.

Thompson, Dennis, "The European Economic Community: Internal Developments since the Breakdown of the British Negotiations," *Int. and Comp. Law Quart.,* 13, (July, 1964), 830–853.

Triska, Jan F., and Howard E. Koch, Jr., "Asian–African Coalition and International Organization: Third Force or Collective Impotence?" *Rev. Politics,* 21 (1959), 417–455.

Whitaker, Arthur P., "Development of American Regionalism; The Organization of American States," *Internat. Conciliation,* No. 469 (March, 1951), 121–164.

——, *The Western Hemisphere Idea: Its Rise and Decline.* New York, Cornell University Press, 1954.

Whitaker, P., *Political Theory and East African Problems.* New York and London, Oxford University Press, 1964.

Wolfe, Alvin W., "The African Mineral Industry: Evolution of a Supranational Level of Integration," *Social Problems,* 11, 2 (Fall, 1963), 153–164.

Wright, Esmond, "The 'Greater Syria' Project in Arab Politics," *World Affairs, 5,* 3 (July, 1951), 318–329.

CHAPTER
19
EMERGING POLITICOGEOGRAPHICAL REALITIES

The world politicogeographical scene, as we have noted, is one of constant change and adjustment. The state itself, as one of the stages in the evolving political world, has undergone several alterations and adaptations—and may well be superseded in the new, modern age of global contact. That this is not impossible is suggested by J.H. Herz in an article reproduced at the conclusion of this chapter; the pace of change appears even to have accelerated since this paper was published.[1] The time may not be too distant when even the global view of political geography will not suffice, and when the impact of the permanent use of space and extra-terrestrial bodies will be felt upon the world political order. In many ways the "modern" state, like the city-state and feudal fortress before it, is no longer capable of functioning in the manner for which it was originally intended. Technology has overtaken it. The inviolability of its boundaries, the impregnability of its heartland—these are lost desires as artificial satellites inspect the terrain from above and missiles halfway around the globe are poised to strike at the sources of power.

And yet, while the struggle for power now truly embraces the world and for the first time the actual and obtainable prize is world domination, vast colonial empires have just made way for political entities which are but trying to achieve that which may well have served out its usefulness elsewhere: the nation-state. Many of these emergent states have joined in groups, hoping to gain in strength. Others find themselves in the path of the great power struggle of the present-day world, and face subjugation or destruction. Will the surviving states of the developing world enjoy stages of consolidation and maturity, or will they be swept up under the pressure of the ever increasing quest for world power waged by ideological adversaries?

Naturally, political geographers try to make

[1]J.H. Herz, "The Rise and Demise of the Territorial State," World Politics, Vol. IX, No. 4. 1957.

predictions. Mackinder argued that his Heartland concept was not in fact a prediction, but an examination of his ideas shows that there was little, in 1904, to root it in the past. When power analysis is attempted and comparisons between states or power cores derived, one cannot help but think about the meaning of such analyses for the future of the world. Hence it may be profitable to attempt, in this final chapter, to identify major and current trends in the world political scene, trends that my lead us to a greater understanding of the changes that will occur in the next decades. These changes, it must be remembered, are superimposed upon those of which we are all constantly aware: the rapid increase in world population and its concentration in east and south Asia; the widening technological gap between the world powers of today and the developing countries; and the demise of colonial empires and the presence of many emergent, weak states.

Seven major trends appear to be of paramount significance, of which four refer to world patterns and three to specific regions:

1. The emergence of world ideological/ethnic regions and regional cores.

2. The development of supranational entities and alliances.

3. The evolution and rapid decay of buffer zones.

4. The rise of regionalism and national/tribalism within states.

5. The eastward development of the Soviet power core.

6. The ascent of China to world power and the rise of Japan.

7. The growing significance of the Pacific Ocean.

THE EMERGENCE OF WORLD IDEOLOGICAL/ETHNIC REGIONS AND REGIONAL CORES

Because of the growing strength of Communist ideology and the elimination of colonial empires, the peoples of many states are united—either through outside imposition or free will—in largely contiguous regional groupings which often coincide with racial-cultural areas. The demise of colonialism and the rise of nationalism have thrown this significant series of events into sharp focus, and common-usage words refer to the ethnic properties of these groups. The "Western" world is constituted mainly by those states in which white peoples are in the numerical majority or play dominant political roles. Within the Western world a number of regional groupings have emerged in the form of economic (E.E.C.), strategic (N.A.T.O.), and cultural (O.A.S.) associations, and in Western Europe a movement toward unity and independent power appears to be emerging.

The Communist ideological power core of Eurasia, too, is presently divided, but on more fundamental grounds. Significantly, the fracture is along racial lines: "Chinese" Communism distinguishes itself from "Soviet" Communism by something in addition to dogma. Soviet absorption of the Baltic states and control over the East European satellites produces a dividing line in Europe which generally coincides with one based on other criteria.[2] The Chinese themselves have justified their incorporation of Tibet on ethnic grounds and have argued boundary matters with India on the basis of racial affinity (see Chapter 8).

Arab and African nationalism likewise have produced regional strongholds which are generally, and in places quite specifically, circumscribed by racial transition zones. The Kurds in Iraq and the Nubas in Sudan are not Arabs and do not subscribe to Arab nationalism, their residence in Arab League countries notwithstanding.[3] The African sector of the Afro–Asian bloc in the United Nations is represented on the map by the vast region of tropical Africa. African nationalism and Arab nationalism, though sharing an aversion for colonialism, have given evidence of considerable hostility in such areas as Zanzibar and Kenya. Southward, as we have seen, African nationalism faces entrenched white nationalism in another ideological confrontation.

The foci of these world ideological-ethnic regions are, in many ways, the capitals in which decisions on policy and dogma are made. Washington and Moscow, in this context, have for two decades been virtual synonyms for the capitalist and Soviet Communist world. Recent years have witnessed the emergence of Peking as a distinct Communist focus in East Asia and Paris as an aspiring European headquarters. The Arab World's ideological center is unquestionably Cairo, although a widening (and possibly temporary) breach between Egypt's capital and Algiers can currently be observed. A regional focus for African nationalism can possibly be identified in West Africa, but despite the efforts of Ghana's Nkrumah and Ethiopia's Haile Selassie, black Africa has not as yet produced a strong and permanent ideological headquarters. Perhaps the strongest ideological core in Africa (both in terms of political intensity and tenacity and economic-power resources) lies, not in black, but in white Africa between Salisbury and the Orange Free State.

A number of states and regions are not encompassed by any of the five aforementioned ideological-ethnic regions: India, Indonesia, Cambodia, and other countries still adhere to no such unit. India, for example, is politically nonaligned; it is a member of the Commonwealth, votes with the Afro–Asian bloc in the United Nations, wars with S.E.A.T.O. member Pakistan over Kashmir, and has engaged in armed hostilities against Communist China over border questions. Indonesia temporarily left the United Nations, acted to destroy the Malaysian Federation as a "tool of Western Imperialism," but has kept the huge domestic Communist party out of the government—while producing a foreign policy that was almost exactly that prescribed by Chinese Communism.

What will become of these states? There are several possibilities: (1) they will ultimately be absorbed by the expanding world power cores; (2) they will permanently constitute a non-contiguous but effective "uncommitted" or "neutral" bloc in world politics; (3) among them one state will rise to world power status to form the focus for a sixth ideological region. In view of the power realities of the present-day world, and considering also the multiracial character of any such association, the last possibility appears least likely. The first possibility has been illustrated by events in

[2]See, for example, R. Murphey's division of the continent into Europe "A" and Europe "B" in *An Introduction to Geography*, Chicago, Rand McNally, 1961, p. 179.

[3]For a brief account of the Kurds' struggle for identity see D. Kinnane, *The Kurds and Kurdistan*, London, Oxford University Press, 1964. For an account of the Sudanese problem see J. Oduho and W. Deng, *The Problem of the Southern Sudan*, London, Oxford University Press, 1963.

Viet Nam, which has become a battlefield between ideological forces, but in what certain observers have described as China's "sphere of influence." The inescapable fact is that Westerners, mainly whites, are fighting a war in support of one Asian population sector against another, on the doorstep of Asia's greatest power.

THE DEVELOPMENT OF SUPRANATIONAL ENTITIES AND ALLIANCES

The period after the second World War has witnessed an unprecedented movement, on the part of states, toward international cooperation in a wide variety of spheres. In some cases, such cooperation is still very superficial and associations very loose: the Council of Europe is as yet very ineffective, the Alliance for Progress faces formidable, unattempted tasks, the Sino-Soviet ideological union has fallen apart, the United Arab Republic seems doomed to failure, the East African Federation's hopes for success have apparently disappeared. But for every failure there are several successes. At the beginning of 1973 there were no less than forty supranational organizations of world or regional membership, not counting a number of local trade, tariff, "solidarity," and ideological unions.[4]

More significant than the actual organizations and participants is the world manifestation of the trend toward supranationalism. Such participation, as we have seen in previous chapters, involves the voluntary relinquishing of a small or perhaps even considerable part of the state's sovereignty. To a large extent it may well be the direct result of the new world power situation, the global capacities of military equipment, the fading chances of the single state, however powerful and resource-wealthy, in the economic and ideological "cold" war of today and the threatening armed conflict of tomorrow. The Atlantic strategic alliance involving the United States and Western European countries is without doubt the mightiest force the world has ever seen; joint military operations and exercises by N.A.T.O. member armies require the permanent stationing (and acceptance by member states) of neighbors' armies on "sovereign" soil. Thus the participating states have

[4]For example, the Nordic Council, the South African Customs Union, the "Entente," the Casablanca and Monrovia "groups," Benelux, etc.

decided that their future is most secure in such a supranational arrangement, and are prepared to contribute accordingly.

When the functions of the state system change as the state commits itself to an ideological, economic, cultural, or strategic bloc, the functions of individual parts of the state system also change. Economic union in Western Europe has helped reduce the divisive nature of Western European boundaries, and the movement of people and goods (as well as ideas) has been greatly facilitated. Consider the nature and functions today of the boundary between N.A.T.O. partners Canada and the United States and that between Greece and Albania or Bulgaria! Thus we can observe the intensification of the divisive functions of certain boundaries and their reduction in others. That intensification or reduction is not necessarily related directly to the nature of the adjacent states, but is a consequence of their participation in opposed or allied supranational unions. Boundaries such as those between Greece and Albania, Turkey and the U.S.S.R., South and North Korea, and Rhodesia and Zambia are in fact boundaries between ideological world power regions, not merely borders between individual states.

THE EVOLUTION AND RAPID DECAY OF BUFFER ZONES

The rise of the major powers of today has been attended by the rather rapid development of modern buffer zones. The final disposition of these areas may to a large extent determine the course of world events in the next several decades. They may themselves result from evolving supranational patterns, although others have developed in the classic fashion, lying between expanding power cores.

Buffer zones which have resulted from the formation of supranational unions can best be recognized in Southeast Asia, where Laos, Viet Nam, and possibly Cambodia and Burma are positioned between the Chinese power core and the Southeast Asia Treaty Organization states. This buffer zone may shift southward, as adherents to the domino theory believe, until all of South and Southeast Asia have been absorbed by Maoism. The Federal State of Malaysia has fragmented under the stresses prevalent in this region. While United States–Western influence continues in this part of the Rimland, territories such as Laos (and possibly Cambodia, in the event of

Communist control in Viet Nam) will temporarily function as cushions, but the likelihood of their ultimate involvement (barring major change of policy in Washington) is great.

While the fortunes of the second World War and United States activity in the Pacific ultimately brought about the power arrangements and buffers in Southeast Asia, the evolution of a buffer zone within interior Eurasia is wholly the result of local conditions. In Chapter 3 we made mention of the Soviet effort to stimulate an eastward migration of population; in Chapter 13 we considered the eastward growth of the Soviet Heartland—the growth of the Volga–Baikal Region. In discussing core areas, the westward growth of the Chinese core region was described, as well as the increasingly effective organization of the Chinese state as a whole. We have made the point, in the present chapter, that ethnic considerations are of great importance in the evolution of world power regions. Soviet–Chinese border regions are marked by ethnic transition zones; both sides have made attempts to secure the allegiance of the peoples of the interior areas.[5] Mongolia has been the scene of this rivalry, which may yet be only in its initial stages. The possibility of the development of a major intra-Communist contest for certain parts of interior Asia exists.

Elsewhere, the existence—and continuing decay—of a Southern African buffer zone contains the ingredients for a serious international confrontation. South Africa, like China, may be said to possess a sphere of influence in several adjacent territories. It shares many interests with Rhodesia and with Portuguese Mocambique and Angola, while the African nationalist countries of tropical Africa become increasingly restive and threaten joint action to end white domination in the south.

THE RISE OF REGIONALISM AND NATIONALISM/TRIBALISM WITHIN STATES

Although the preceding discussion has indicated that worldwide trends toward international association prevail today, it is important not to lose sight of a recurrent movement in the opposite direction. In a number of states, both young and old, regionalism, tribalism, provincialism, and local nationalism have come to the fore and constitute

major internal problems. That this is so in many developing countries, such as Zaïre, Kenya, and Sudan, comes as no surprise. The equalizing effect of colonial control has disappeared, and with it went the major common enemy of local peoples who may well be divided by deep and permanent hostilities. In other words, historic centrifugal forces are getting the upper hand over temporary centripetal forces whose origins lie in the colonial period. The federal states of the developing, postcolonial world, for example, are almost all superimposed and without exception face divisive stresses. The Federation of Malaysia, which all but succumbed to these stresses in 1965, when Singapore was the first unit to leave the state, is the creation of British colonialism. Not only were there many opponents of the system within the state, but external pressure was put on the country as well. Pakistan, whose internal ethnic, religious, and economic differences were accentuated by its fragmented territory, succumbed to the forces of division in 1972. The Federation of the West Indies failed to survive more than a matter of months; the Central African Federation lasted just a decade. Fears may with good reason be expressed for the future of federal Aden, Uganda, Cameroun, and Nigeria; the fears expressed for the Congo at the time of independence have become reality. The federal union of India has recently been shaken by a language crisis, and there are other divisive features in that country which will test the strength of the state.

Indeed, it may be argued that federalism does not suit the emergent, new states, and that it militates against the other requirements of these political entities. The forging of a nation and the planning of economic development may well be best carried out by a strong centralized government. Certainly the internal rivalries and jealousies that disrupted the West Indies Federation also have consumed much energy in Nigeria and Pakistan, and their ultimate effect may be the same. And yet the recognition of tribal and national entities in the former colonial world and its consequent balkanization would surely constitute a backward step in the world's politicogeographical evolution. When, among the "nations" of today, there are the Singapores and the Gambias, the Maltas and the Jamaicas, the possibility of similar fragments seceding from dozens of tribally constituted emergent states would surely threaten world order.

[5]For an analysis of some of the ethnic problems in the Soviet realm see G. Wheeler, *Racial Problems in Soviet Muslim Asia*, London, Oxford University Press, 1962.

And yet the prospect exists, and some states are actively supporting it. South Africa's Bantustan scheme is nothing less than a retribalization of the population: the possibility of ultimate total independence is acknowledged, so that out of one state there would emanate perhaps a dozen or more. The alarming feature is not so much the actual existence of the phenomenon; it is nothing new in the political world. What *is* new is its ubiquitous aspect—in Guyana, in Cyprus, in Malaysia, in Pakistan, in Northern Ireland.

Regionalism, nationalism, provincialism —whatever the appropriate connotation—also is not confined to the developing world. While nationalism, predictably, is again on the rise in the East European Soviet satellite states, the phenomena of Quebec in Canada, Bahia in Brazil, and Flanders in Belgium, to identify several but by no means all such cases, continue to pose problems for "mature" states as well. Provincialism such as that of Quebec may have received new impetus as a result of the successes of anticolonial movements elsewhere, movements with which minorities have been quick to identify themselves. Hence, there is at present the paradoxical situation of a political world moving toward supranationalism, on the one hand, and intensified regionalism, on the other.

THE SOVIET EASTWARD MARCH, THE RISE OF CHINA AND JAPAN, AND THE PACIFIC OCEAN

The last three of the seven major trends listed earlier in this chapter are so closely related that they are here discussed under a single heading. Various recent discussions of the Soviet Heartland have suggested that the sources of Soviet power are found to an ever greater extent eastward of the "original" Moscow core area.[6] Industrial decentralization has doubtlessly lessened Soviet vulnerability in the event of attack; the Volga–Baikal area contains crucial new petroleum fields, rapidly

growing cities, expanding primary industries, and a rapidly developing transport network. As Meinig has pointed out, here lies the corridor through which communications between eastern and western Soviet regions will be channeled. Furthermore, the area points significantly toward the Chinese border, and

. . . the "open spaces" of Siberia have often been viewed covetously by the congested people of China, like the "empty lands" of Australia to the South. The massive build-up of industry and transfer of several million Chinese to Sinkiang, against the Soviet frontier, in the last few years, may now be seen less as a friendly gesture than as the provocative staking out of a claim to an area which has recently been under strong Russian influence. Similarly, it would not be surprising if the Soviet reaction to Chinese provocation was to try to fill up its open spaces and develop its resources, rather than beat a retreat, especially if a general dispersal of industry were considered desirable on other strategic grounds.[7]

Coupled with a Soviet eastern push, then, is the westward development of Chinese power. China's core area lies against the country's eastern seaboard, and in that sense this westward growth is inevitable. The fact is that the Soviet Union and China share the Asian heartland, and that increasing territorial competition is likely to occur. The present ideological disagreement between the Soviet Union and China may (however unlikely this now seems) be temporary, but the ethnic differences between Moscow and Peking are permanent. We have noted the apparent increase in regional political association among states of similar ethnic content, and we have also seen the growing number of ethnic confrontations in the postwar political world. Prominent among the internal problems of Guiana, Cyprus, Sudan, Iraq, and the United States are racial antagonisms; Chinese–Indian, Arab–Israeli, Ethiopian–Somali, Rhodesia–Zambian conflicts also are dominated by ethnic identifications. Is it reasonable to assume that Soviet–Chinese ethnic differences will not play a role in Eurasia's future?

We now appear to be at the threshold of a new political situation involving the Eurasian heartland which Mackinder himself may not have foreseen. China, the one rimland state to possess an avenue into the very heartland, is rapidly attaining the capacity to challenge the power position of the Soviet Union. Compari-

---

[6]See, for example, D.W. Meinig's map (p. 561) of the new heartland of Eurasia in "Heartland and Rimland in Eurasian History," *Western Political Quart., 9* (1956), 553–569, and D.J.M. Hooson's article suggesting "A New Soviet Heartland," *Geog. J., 128* (1962), 19–29. Also note Hooson's earlier article, "The Middle Volga—An Emerging Focal Region in the Soviet Union," *Geog. J., 126* (1960), 180–190. A summary of the contribution made by the eastern regions to Soviet power can be found in Hooson's recent volume, *A New Soviet Heartland?*, Princeton, Van Nostrand, 1964; see especially the maps on pp. 17, 40, and 64.

[7]Hooson, op. cit., 1964, p. 125.

sons with Germany's challenge from the west cannot be escaped: but Germany's thrust was directly into the Soviet heartland. We must not forget that the Soviet eastward march, while impressive, is yet in its formative stages. The focus of Soviet power and population, while shifting eastward, is still in the west—west, indeed, of the Urals. Thus the emerging situation is one in which race, ideology, power and resources are all at stake—and, possibly, an avenue toward world domination.[8]

Indeed, we should not overlook the fact that this is the first time in modern world history that European, "white" power (after all, Russians are, in this context, whites) is facing an effective nonwhite challenge. The other world power cores, counting not only the American but also any possible emerging united European bloc, are white, Western. The Japanese challenge of the second World War clearly does not fall into the same category; modern warfare and population resources have rendered Chinese capacities vastly more significant.

Nevertheless, the modern rise of Japan constitutes a crucial development in this last one-third of the twentieth century. Japan has overcome the disaster of its second World War defeat and has made an almost incredible recovery. Its economic power is enormous; Japan's military capacity, if the country's energies were focused in that direction, would be very great. In fact, there are pressures in Japan to create once again a superior military machine, and undoubtedly the Japanese could attain an important position in East Asia in a very short time by so doing. The momentous events involving China in the early part of 1972 and the apparent end of a quarter of a century of nearly total seclusion there have crucial ramifications for Japan. Japan was a colonizing power in China, but today China could be one of Japan's chief economic partners, with its enormous market and its raw materials. A new age of involvement between Japan and China may lie ahead. Such involvement will have economic foundations, but the potential for power conflict clearly exists.

These developments in the eastern parts of the Eurasian landmass have greatly added to the importance of the Pacific Ocean and the islands in it. While China was docile and stagnant, it only reinforced the rimland-harness around the heartland state. But with the rise of China to world power, the Pacific has taken on the role history also allotted to the Mediterranean and later the Atlantic: adversaries face each other across its waters. Again, this is not the first time that the Pacific has been an actual or potential theater for conflict. But the strength and capabilities of the powers now confronting each other is unmatched. Furthermore, the two most hostile of the ideological forces of today, China and the United States, are the two "effective" Pacific powers (possessing major population concentrations and installations on Pacific shores); the Soviet Union's northern Pacific coasts harbor proportionately much less.

Has modern war equipment reduced the significance of the ocean as a protective agent? It obviously has, but not to the point that bases and fleets no longer play their roles. H.J. Wiens has described the continued importance of the United States' island bases within the Pacific; recent events in Viet Nam have underlined the usefulness of such facilities as Guam and Okinawa.[9] China's modern capabilities are yet limited, and those hostilities in which it has been directly or indirectly involved have required "conventional" methods of combat. Furthermore, United States responsibilities within the Pacific region include Japan and the Philippines as well as Australia and New Zealand; with the last three states the U.S. has strategic alliance obligations. On the Asian shores of the Pacific lie territories in which the United States has already resisted Chinese-supported armed activities (Korea, Viet Nam) and others where it would doubtlessly do so (Thailand, Laos). Obligations to Taiwan and the Ryukyu Islands add to the long list of United States Pacific concerns.

On the Pacific, and in the airspace over it, the future of the politicogeographical world may well be determined.

[8]See W.A. Douglas Jackson, *Russo–Chinese Borderlands*, Princeton, Van Nostrand, 1962.

[9]H.J. Wiens, *Pacific Island Bastions of the United States*, Princeton, Van Nostrand, 1962.

RISE AND DEMISE
OF THE TERRITORIAL STATE

John H. Herz

Students and practitioners of international politics are at present in a strange predicament. Complex though their problems have been in the past, there was then at least some certainty about the "givens," the basic structure and the basic phenomena of international relations. Today one is neither her nor there. On the one hand, for instance, one is assured—or at least tempted to accept assurance—that for all practical purposes a nuclear stalemate rules out major war as a major means of policy today and in the foreseeable future. On the other hand, one has an uncanny sense of the practicability of the unabated arms race, and a doubt whether reliance can be placed solely on the deterrent purpose of all this preparation. We are no longer sure about the functions of war and peace, nor do we know how to define the national interest and what its defense requires under present conditions. As a matter of fact, the meaning and function of the basic protective unit, the "sovereign" nation-state itself, have become doubtful. On what, then, can policy and planning be built?

In the author's opinion, many of these uncertainties have their more profound cause in certain fundamental changes which have taken place in the structure of international relations and, specifically, in the nature of the units among which these relations occur. This transformation in the "statehood" of nations will be the subject of this article.

I. BASIC FEATURES OF THE MODERN STATE SYSTEM

Traditionally, the classical system of international relations, or the modern state system, has been considered "anarchic," because it was based on unequally distributed power and was deficient in higher—that is, supranational—authority. Its units, the independent, sovereign nation-states, were forever threatened by stronger power and survived precariously through the balance-of-power system. Customarily, then, the modern state system has been contrasted with the medieval system, on the one hand, where units of international relations were under higher law and higher authority, and with those more recent international trends, on the other, which seemed to point toward a greater, "collective" security of nations and a "rule of law" that would protect them from the indiscriminate use of force characteristic of the age of power politics.

From the vantage point of the atomic age, we can probe deeper into the basic characteristics of the classical system. What is it that ultimately accounted for the peculiar unity, compactness, coherence of the modern nation-state, setting it off from other nation-states as a separate, independent, and sovereign power? It would seem that this underlying factor is to be found neither in the sphere of law nor in that of politics, but rather in that substratum of statehood where the state unit confronts us, as it were, in its physical, corporeal capacity: as an expanse of territory encircled for its identification and its defense by a "hard shell" of fortifications. In this lies what will here be referred to as the "impermeability," or "impenetrability," or simply the "territoriality," of the modern state. The fact that it was surrounded by a hard shell rendered it to some extent secure from foreign penetration, and thus made it an ultimate unit of protection for those within its boundaries. Throughout history, that unit which affords protection and security to human beings has tended to become the basic political unit; people, in the long run, will recognize that authority, any authority, which possesses the power of protection.

Some similarity perhaps prevails between an international structure consisting of impenetrable units with an ensuing measurability of power and comparability of power relations, and the system of classical physics with its measurable forces and the (then) impenetrable atom as its basic unit. And as that system has given way to relativity and to what nuclear science has uncovered, the impenetrability of the political atom, the nation-state, is giving way to a permeability which tends to obliterate the very meaning of unit and unity, power and power relations, sovereignty and independence. The possibility of "hydrogenization" merely represents the culmination of a development which has rendered the traditional defense structure of nations obsolete through the power to by-pass the shell protecting a two-dimensional territory and thus to destroy—vertically, as it were—even the most powerful ones. Paradoxically, utmost strength now coincides in the same unit with utmost vulnerability, absolute power with utter impotence.

This development must inevitably affect traditional power concepts. Considering power units as politically independent and legally sovereign made sense when power, measurable, graded, calculable, served as a standard of comparison between units which, in the sense indicated above, could be described as impermeable. Under those conditions, then, power indicated the strategic aspect, independence the political aspect, sovereignty the legal aspect of this selfsame impermeability. With the passing of the age of territoriality, the usefulness of these concepts must now be questioned.

Thus the Great Divide does not separate "international anarchy," or "balance of power," or "power politics," from incipient international interdependence, or from "collective security"; all these remain within the realm of the territorial structure of states and can therefore be considered as trends or stages *within* the classical system of "hard shell" power units. Rather, the Divide occurs where the basis of territorial power and defensibility vanishes. It is here and now. But in order to understand the present, we must study more closely the origin and nature of the classical system itself.

II. THE RISE OF THE TERRITORIAL STATE

The rise of the modern territorial state meant that, within countries, "feudal anarchy" of jurisdictions yielded to the ordered centralism of the absolute monarchy, which ruled over a pacified area with the aid of a bureaucracy, a professional army, and the power to levy taxes, while in foreign relations, in place of the medieval hierarchy of power and authority,

there prevailed insecurity, a disorder only slightly attenuated by a power balance that was forever being threatened, disturbed, and then restored. Such has been the customary interpretation.

It is possible to view developments in a somewhat different light. Instead of contrasting the security of groups and individuals within the sovereign territorial state with conditions of insecurity outside, the establishment of territorial independence can be interpreted as an at least partially successful attempt to render the territorial group secure in its outward relations as well. Especially when contrasted with the age of anarchy and insecurity which immediately preceded it, the age of territoriality appears as one of relative order and safety.

Indeed, the transition from medieval hierarchism to modern compartmentalized sovereignties was neither easy, nor straight, nor short. Modern sovereignty arose out of the triangular struggle among emperors and popes, popes and kings, and kings and emperors. When the lawyers of Philip the Fair propounded the dual maxim according to which the king was to be "emperor in his realm" (rex est imperator in regno suo) and was no longer to "recognize any superior" (superiorem non recognoscens), it was the beginning of a development in the course of which, in McIlwain's words, "Independence de facto was ultimately translated into a sovereignty de jure."[1] But centuries of disturbance and real anarchy ensued during which the problems of rulership and security remained unsettled. The relative protection which the sway of moral standards and the absence of highly destructive weapons had afforded groups and individuals in the earlier Middle Ages gave way to total insecurity when gunpowder was invented and common standards broke down. Out of the internal and external turmoil during the age of religious and civil wars, a "neutralist" central power eventually managed to establish itself in and for each of the different territories like so many *rochers de bronze*.

The idea that a territorial coexistence of states, based on the power of the territorial princes, might afford a better guarantee of peace than the Holy Roman Empire was already widespread at the height of the Middle Ages, when the emperor proved incapable of

[1]Charles H. McIlwain, *The Growth of Political Thought in the West*, New York, 1932, p. 268.

enforcing the peace.[2] But territoriality could hardly prevail so long as the knight in his castle (that medieval unit of impermeability) was relatively immune from attack, as was the medieval city within its walls. Only with a developing money economy were overlords able to free themselves from dependence on vassals and lay the foundations of their own power by establishing a professional army. Infantry and artillery now proved superior to old-style cavalry, firearms prevailed over the old weapons.

As in all cases of radically new developments in military technology, the "gunpowder revolution" caused a real revolution in the superstructure of economic, social, and political relationships because of its impact on the units of protection and security. A feeling of insecurity swept all Europe.[3] Though a Machiavelli might establish new rules as to how to gain and maintain power, there still followed more than a century of unregulated, ideological "total" wars inside and among countries until the new units of power were clearly established. Before old or new sovereigns could claim to be recognized as rulers of large areas, it had to be determined how far, on the basis of their new military power, they were able to extend their control geographically.[4]

The large-area state came finally to occupy the place that the castle or fortified town had previously held as a unit of impenetrability. But the new unit could not be considered consolidated until all independent fortifications within it had disappeared and, in their place, fortresses lining the circumference of the country had been built by the new central power and manned by its armed forces.[5] If we contrast our present system of bases and similar outposts surrounding entire world regions with what are today small-scale nation-states, perhaps we can visualize what the hard shell of frontier fortifications consolidating the then large-scale territorial states meant by way of extending power units in the age of absolutism. They became, in the words of Frederick the Great, "mighty nails which hold a ruler's provinces together." There now was peace and protection within. War became a regularized military procedure; only the breaking of the shell permitted interference with what had now become the internal affairs of another country.

In this way was established the basic structure of the territorial state which was to last throughout the classical period of the modern state system. Upon this foundation a new system and new concepts of international relations could arise. And as early as the second half of the seventeenth century a perspicacious observer succeeded in tying up the new concepts with the underlying structure of territorial statehood.

III. THE NATURE OF TERRITORIALITY

It was hardly a coincidence that this connection was established shortly after the end of the Thirty Years' War, when formal sanction had been given to territorial sovereignty in the Westphalian Peace. For here was the turning point, the Great Divide between what were still partially medieval situations reflecting a certain permeability of the rising nation-state (when, for instance, outside powers could still ally themselves with *frondes* within a country against that country's sovereign) and the modern era of closed units no longer brooking such interference.[6]

The clarification of the nature of territoriality to which we referred above is found in a little and little-known essay by Leibniz, written for an entirely pragmatic pur-

---

[2]F.A. von der Heydte, *Die Geburtsstunde des souveränen Staates*, Regensburg, 1952, pp. 103ff., 277, 293ff.

[3]Ariosto expressed the feeling of despair which invaded the "old powers" of chivalry when gunpowder destroyed the foundations of their system, in terms reminding one of present-day despair in the face of the destructive forces loosed upon our own world:

> "Oh!curs'd device! base implement of death!
> Framed in the black Tartarean realms beneath!
> By Beelzebub's malicious art design'd
> To ruin all the race of human kind."

Quoted from *Orlando Furioso* by Felix Gilbert, in Edward M. Earle, ed., *Makers of Modern Strategy*, Princeton, N.J., 1943, p. 4.

[4]On this, see Garrett Mattingly, *Renaissance Diplomacy*, Boston, 1955, pp. 59ff., 121ff., 205ff.

[5]See Friedrich Meinecke, *Die Idee der Staatsraison in der neueren Geschichte*, Munich and Berlin, 1925, pp. 241ff.

[6]The emergence of "non-intervention" as a legal concept illustrates this transition. A complete change in the meaning of the term occurred in the brief period between the time of Grotius and that of Pufendorf. Grotius, writing during the last phase of the pre-modern era of religious and "international civil" wars and still thinking in terms of "just" and "unjust" wars, considered a ruler entitled to intervene in the affairs of another sovereign if it was necessary to defend oppressed subjects of the latter; Pufendorf, barely fifty years later, rejected such interference in the "domestic affairs" of another sovereign as a violation of the sovereign's exclusive jurisdiction over his territory and all it contained. See Walter Schiffer, *The Legal Community of Mankind*, New York, 1954, pp. 34f., 56.

pose—namely, to prove the right of legation of the territorial ruler (the Duke of Hanover) in whose service the philosopher then was.[7] Leibniz' problem derived directly from the situation created by the Peace of Westphalia. This settlement, for all practical purposes, had conferred sovereign independence upon those princes who formally were still included in the Empire; yet it had not abolished the long-established, essentially feudal structure of the Empire itself, with its allegiances and jurisdictions, its duties of membership, and even its clumsy and scarcely workable framework of government. Thus some of the factually sovereign territorial rulers in Europe were somehow still under a higher authority. Were they now "sovereign" or not? What accounted for sovereignty?

Leibniz' contemporaries failed to see the problem in this light. The muddled state of affairs was made to order for those jurists and others who argued fine points perennially with the aid of sterile or obsolete concepts. Leibniz, instead, proceeded to study "what actually happens in the world today," and as a result could boast of being "the first to have found the valid definition of sovereignty."[8]

As he saw it, the first condition for sovereignty was a minimum size of territory. Minuscule principalities, at that time still abundant, could not claim to be on a par with those that recognized each other as equally sovereign in respect to peace and war, alliances, and the general affairs of Europe, because, not possessing sufficient territory, they could at best, with their garrisons, only maintain *internal* order.[9] But there remained the chief problem: how to define the status of those rulers who, because of their membership in the Empire, were subjects of the emperor. Could one be "sovereign" and "subject" at the same time? If not, what was the status of these "subject" rulers as compared with that of their "sovereign" European brethren? If so, what did their subjection to the emperor amount to? These questions were further complicated by the fact that at every European court, and in the Empire as well, there were certain high dignitaries, often called "princes," "dukes," etc., who customarily held the rank of "sovereign." It was through this maze of

relationships that Leibniz arrived at his definitions.

He elaborated his concept of sovereignty by distinguishing it from "majesty." Majesty, the authority which the emperor has *qua* emperor over the Empire's members, consists of a number of jurisdictions that confer the right to demand obedience and involve duties of fealty, but it is not sovereignty. Why not? Simply because, with all its supreme authority, majesty does not involve an "actual and present power to constrain" subjects on their own territories. Their territory, in other words, is impermeable. The subject, on the other hand, if he is a territorial ruler, is sovereign because he has the power to constrain *his* subjects, while not being so constrainable by superior power. The decisive criterion thus is actual control of one's "estates" by one's military power, which excludes any other power within and without. Contrariwise, the absence of such forces of his own on his subjects' territories accounts for the absence of "sovereignty" in the emperor's "majesty." He can enforce his authority or rights only by applying his own or other sovereigns' forces from the outside, "by means of war." But in doing so, his condition is no different from that of any other sovereign vis-à-vis *his* fellow-rulers, for war is a contest which can be inaugurated not only by majesties but by any sovereign ruler. And force of arms may constrain a sovereign outside the Empire quite as well as one inside; in fact, war constitutes the only way in which even sovereigns can be constrained.[10] By perceiving that the emperor's power to enforce his authority was actually reduced to means of war, Leibniz was in a position to demonstrate that any and all rulers of impermeable territory, whatever their status in regard to imperial authority, were equal in their sovereign status.

This capacity also distinguished them from those dignitaries who were sovereigns in name only. Leibniz, by way of example, referred to the non-sovereign status of certain papal "princes," contrasting it with that of sovereign princes: "Should His Holiness desire to make . . . [the papal princes] obey, he has merely to send out his 'sbirros' [bailiffs], but in order to constrain . . . [the sovereign princes]

---

[7]"Entretiens de Philarète et d'Eugenè sur le droit d'Ambassade"; quoted here from *Werke*, 1st series, III, Hanover, 1864, pp. 331ff.

[8]*Ibid.*, pp. 340, 342.

[9]*Ibid.*, p. 349.

[10]"La souveraineté est un pouvoir légitime et ordinaire de contraindre les sujets à obéir, sans qu'on puisse être contraint soy même si ce n'est par une guerre" (*ibid.*, p. 352).

he would need an army and cannon."[11] Similarly, if the Empire wants to constrain a sovereign member, "what would begin as court procedure in an imperial Tribunal, in execution would amount to a war."[12] In the new age of territoriality, those superior in law no longer could use the machinery of government (courts, etc.) to enforce claims against territorial rulers.[13] In more recent times, this has come to be the relationship between sovereign nation-states as members of international organizations (like the League of Nations or the United Nations) and the organizations as such.

IV. THE TERRITORIAL STATE IN INTERNATIONAL RELATIONS

From territoriality resulted the concepts and institutions which characterized the interrelations of sovereign units, the modern state system. Modern international law, for instance, could now develop. Like the international system that produced it, international law has often been considered inherently contradictory because of its claim to bind sovereign units. But whether or not we deny to it for this reason the name and character of genuine law, it is important to see it in its connection with the territorial nature of the state system that it served. Only then can it be understood as a system of rules not contrary to, but implementing, the sovereign independence of states. Only to the extent that it reflected their territoriality and took into account their sovereignty could international law develop in modern times. For its general rules and principles deal primarily with the delimitation of the jurisdiction of countries. It thus implements the *de facto* condition of territorial impenetrability by more closely

[11]*Ibid.*, p. 354.
[12]*Ibid.*, p. 358.
[13]Leibniz' emphasis on constraint as a primary prerequisite of sovereignty might strike later observers as over-materialistic. But one should remember that the *rocher de bronze* of sovereignty was only then being established, not only against outside interference but also against still recalcitrant feudal powers within the territorial ruler's realm, and even in the latter case frequently by force of arms and armed forces which to the defeated may well have appeared as something very much like occupation forces. As a matter of fact, "garrisoning" is a key word in Leibniz' arguments: "As long as one has the right to be master in one's own house, and no superior has the right to maintain garrisons there and deprive one of the exercise of one's right of peace, war, and alliances, one has that independence which sovereignty presupposes (*liberté requise à la Souveraineté)*" (*ibid.*, p. 356).

defining unit, area, and conditions of impenetrability. Such a law must reflect, rather than regulate. As one author has rightly remarked, "International law really amounts to laying down the principle of national sovereignty and deducing the consequences."[14] It is not for this reason superfluous, for sovereign units must know in some detail where their jurisdictions end and those of other units begin; without such standards, nations would be involved in constant strife over the implementation of their independence.

But it was not only this mutual legal accommodation which rendered possible a relatively peaceful coexistence of nations. War itself, the very phenomenon which reflected, not the strength, but the limitations of impermeability, was of such a nature as to maintain at least the principle of territoriality. War was limited not only in conduct but also in objectives. It was not a process of physical or political annihilation but a contest of power and will in which the interests, but not the existence, of the contestants were at stake. Now that we approach the era of absolute exposure, without walls or moats, where penetration will mean not mere damage or change but utter annihilation of life and way of life, it may dawn on us that what has vanished with the age of sovereignty and "power politics" was not entirely adverse in nature and effects.

Among other "conservative" features of the classical system, we notice one only in passing: the balance of power. It is only recently that emphasis has shifted from a somewhat one-sided concern with the negative aspects of the balance—its uncertainty, its giving rise to unending conflicts and frequent wars, etc.—to its protective effect of preventing the expansionist capacity of power from destroying other power altogether.[15] But at the time of its perfection in statecraft and diplomacy, there were even theories (not lived up to in practice, of course) about the *legal* obligations of nations to form barriers against hegemony power in the common interest.[16]

More fundamental to the conservative structure of the old system was its character as

[14]François Laurent, as quoted by Schiffer, *op. cit.*, p. 157.
[15]See my *Political Realism and Political Idealism*, Chicago, 1951, pp. 206–21.
[16]J. von Elbe, "Die Wiederherstellung der Gleichgewichtsordnung in Europa durch den Wiener Kongress," *Zeitschrift für ausländisches öffentliches Recht und Völkerrecht*, IV (1934), pp. 226ff.

a community. Forming a comparatively pacified whole, Europe was set off sharply against the world outside, a world beyond those lines which, by common agreement, separated a community based on territoriality and common heritage from anarchy, where the law of nature reigned and no standards of civilization applied. Only recently have the existence and role of so-called "amity lines" been rediscovered, lines which were drawn in the treaties of the early modern period and which separated European territories, where the rules of war and peace were to prevail, from overseas territories and areas.[17] There was to be "no peace beyond the line"; that is, European powers, although possibly at peace in Europe, continued to be *homo homini lupus* abroad. This practice made it easier for the European family of nations to observe self-denying standards at home by providing them with an outlet in the vast realm discovered outside Europe. While the practice of drawing amity lines subsequently disappeared, one chief function of overseas expansion remained: a European balance of power could be maintained or adjusted because it was relatively easy to divert European conflicts into overseas directions and adjust them there. Thus the openness of the world contributed to the consolidation of the territorial system. The end of the "world frontier" and the resulting closedness of an interdependent world inevitably affected this system's effectiveness.

Another characteristic of the old system's protective nature may be seen in the almost complete absence of instances in which countries were wiped out in the course of wars or as a consequence of other power-political events. This, of course, refers to the territorial units at home only, not to the peoples and state units beyond the pale abroad; and to the complete destruction of a state's independent existence, not to mere loss of territory or similar changes, which obviously abounded in the age of power politics.

Evidence of this is to be found not only in a legal and political ideology that denied the permissibility of conquest at home while recognizing it as a title for the acquisition of territorial jurisdiction abroad.[18] For such a

doctrine had its non-ideological foundation in the actual difference between European and non-European politics so far as their territoriality was concerned. European states were impermeable in the sense here outlined, while most of those overseas were easily penetrable by Europeans. In accordance with these circumstances, international politics in Europe knew only rare and exceptional instances of actual annihilation through conquest or similar forceful means.

Prior to the twentieth century, there were indeed the Napoleonic conquests, but I submit that this is a case where the exception confirms the rule. The Napoleonic system, as a hegemonial one, was devised to destroy the established system of territoriality and balanced power as such. Consequently, Napoleon and his policies appeared "demonic" to contemporaries,[19] as well as to a nineteenth century which experienced the restoration of the earlier system. During that century occurred Bismarck's annexations of some German units into Prussia in pursuance of German unification. As in Napoleon's case, they appeared abnormal to many of his contemporaries, although the issue of national unification tended to mitigate this impression.[20] Besides these, there was indeed the partition of Poland, and considering the lamentable and lasting impression and the universal bad conscience it produced even among the ruling nations in a century used to quite a bit of international skulduggery, again one may well claim an exceptional character for that event.[21]

What, in particular, accounts for this remarkable stability? Territoriality—the establishment of defensible units, internally pacified and hard-shell rimmed—may be called its foundation. On this foundation, two phe-

[17]See Carl Schmitt, *Der Nomos der Erde*, Cologne, 1950, pp. 60ff.; also W. Schoenborn, "Über Entdeckung als Rechtstitel völkerrechtlichen Gebietserwerbs," in D.S. Constantinopoulos and H. Wehberg, eds., *Gegenwartsprobleme des internationalen Rechts und der Rechtsphilosophie*, Hamburg, 1953, pp. 239ff.

[18]On this, see M.M. McMahon, *Conquest and Modern International Law*, Washington, D.C., 1940; M.F. Lindlay, *The Acquisition and Government of Backward Territory in International Law*, London, 1926; and Robert Langer, *Seizure of Territory*, Princeton, N.J., 1947.

[19]As witness the impression made on contemporaries by the destruction of the first ancient European unit to fall victim to these policies—Venice.

[20]See Erich Eyck, *Bismarck*, II, Zurich, 1943, pp. 305ff.

[21]Except for these cases, we find only marginal instances of complete obliteration. The annexation of the Free City of Krakow by Russia eliminated a synthetic creation of the Vienna settlement. British conquest of the Boer Republics, if considered as an instance of annihilation of European politics in view of the European origin of the inhabitants, happened at the very rim of the world, as it were, remote from the continent where the practice of non-annihilation prevailed.

nomena permitted the system to become more stable than might otherwise have been the case: the prevalence of the legitimacy principle and, subsequently, nationalism. Legitimacy implied that the dynasties ruling the territorial states of old Europe mutually recognized each other as rightful sovereigns. Depriving one sovereign of his rights by force could not but appear to destroy the very principle on which the rights of all of them rested.

With the rise of nationalism, we witness the personalization of the units as self-determining, national groups. Nationalism now made it appear as abhorrent to deprive a sovereign nation of its independence as to despoil a legitimate ruler had appeared before. States, of course, had first to become "nation-states," considering themselves as representing specific nationality groups, which explains why in the two regions of Europe where larger numbers of old units stood in the way of national unification their demise encountered little objection. In most instances, however, the rise of nationalism led to the emergence of *new* states, which split away from multinational or colonial empires. This meant the extension of the European principle of "non-obliteration" all over the world. It is perhaps significant that even in our century, and even after the turmoil of attempted world conquest and resulting world wars, a point has been made of restoring the most minute and inconsiderable of sovereignties, down to Luxembourg and Albania.[22]

This hypertrophy of nation-states presented new problems—above all, that of an improved system of protection. For by now it had become clear that the protective function of the old system was only a relative blessing after all. Continued existence of states as such was perhaps more or less guaranteed. But power and influence, status, frontiers, economic interests—in short, everything that constituted the life and interests of nations beyond bare existence—were always at the mercy of what power politics wrought. Furthermore, much of the relative stability and political equilibrium of the territorial states had been due to the extension of Western control over the world. When what could be penetrated had been subjugated, assimilated, or established as fellow "sovereign" states, the

old units were thrown back upon themselves. Hence the demand for a new system which would offer more security to old and new nations: collective security.

I propose to view collective security not as the extreme opposite of power politics, but as an attempt to maintain, and render more secure, the impermeability of what were still territorial states. To an age which took territoriality for granted, replacing power politics with collective security would indeed appear to be a radical departure. From the vantage point of the nuclear age, however, a plan to protect individual sovereignties by collective guarantees for continuing sovereignty appears questionable not because of its innovating, but because of its conservative, nature. Its conservatism lies in its basic objective: the protection of the hard-shell territorial structure of its members, or, as the core article of the Covenant of the League of Nations put it, its guarantee of their "territorial integrity and political independence" against external aggression. The beginning of air war and the increasing economic interdependence of nations had indicated by the end of World War I that the old-style military barriers might be by-passed. If territorial units were to be preserved in the future, it would be accomplished less by reliance on individual defense potentials than by marshaling collective power in order to preserve individual powers.

But since the idea of organizing a genuine supranational force—an international police force—was rejected, the League had to cling to classical arrangements insofar as the procedures of protection were concerned. The guarantee to the individual states was to be the formation of the "Grand Coalition" of all against the isolated aggressor, which presupposed the maintenance of a certain level of armed strength by the member states. A member without that minimum of military strength would be a liability rather than an asset to the organization—in Geneva parlance, a "consumer" and not a "producer" of security.[23] Thus classical concepts (the sovereignty and independence of nation-states) as

---

[22]Cf. also the remarkable stability of state units in the Western Hemisphere *qua* independent units; unstable as some of them are domestically, their sovereign identity as units appears almost sacrosanct.

[23]In League practice, therefore, membership applications of countries without this minimum were rejected (for instance, that of Liechtenstein; cf. Walther Schücking and Hans Wehberg, *Die Satzung des Völkerbundes*, 2nd ed., Berlin, 1924, pp. 252ff.). The decline of genuine collective security in our time is apparent from the fact that, in contrast to this practice, the United Nations pays hardly any attention to the question of defensibility, particularly in connection with membership applications.

well as classical institutions (in particular, hard-shell defensibility) were to be maintained under the new system.

Whether there ever was a chance for the system to be effective in practice is beside the point here. It is sufficient to realize how closely it was tied to the underlying structure as well as to the prevailing concepts and policies of the territorial age.

V. THE DECLINE OF THE TERRITORIAL STATE

Beginning with the nineteenth century, certain trends became visible which tended to endanger the functioning of the classical system. Directly or indirectly, all of them had a bearing upon that feature of the territorial state which was the strongest guarantee of its independent coexistence with other states of like nature: its hard shell—that is, its defensibility in case of war.

Naturally, many of these trends concerned war itself and the way in which it was conducted. But they were not related to the shift from the limited, duel-type contests of the eighteenth century to the more or less unlimited wars that developed in the nineteenth century with conscription, "nations in arms," and increasing destructiveness of weapons. By themselves, these developments were not inconsistent with the classical function of war. Enhancing a nation's defensive capacity, instituting universal military service, putting the economy on a war footing, and similar measures tended to bolster the territorial state rather than to endanger it.

Total war in a quite different sense is tied up with developments in warfare which enable the belligerents to overleap or by-pass the traditional hard-shell defense of states. When this happens, the traditional relationship between war, on the one hand, and territorial power and sovereignty, on the other, is altered decisively. Arranged in order of increasing effectiveness, these new factors may be listed under the following headings: (a) possibility of economic blockade; (b) ideological-political penetration; (c) air warfare; and (d) atomic warfare.

(a) Economic Warfare

It should be said from the outset that so far economic blockade has never enabled one belligerent to force another into surrender through starvation alone. Although in World War I Germany and her allies were seriously endangered when the Western allies cut them off from overseas supplies, a very real effort was still required to defeat them on the military fronts. The same thing applies to World War II. Blockade was an important contributing factor, however. Its importance for the present analysis lies in its unconventional nature, permitting belligerents to by-pass the hard shell of the enemy. Its effect is due to the changed economic status of industrialized nations.

Prior to the industrial age, the territorial state was largely self-contained economically. Although one of the customary means of conducting limited war was starving fortresses into surrender, this applied merely to these individual portions of the hard shell, and not to entire nations. Attempts to starve a belligerent nation in order to avoid having to breach the shell proved rather ineffective, as witness the Continental Blockade and its counterpart in the Napoleonic era. The Industrial Revolution made countries like Britain and Germany increasingly dependent on imports. In war, this meant that they could survive only by controlling areas larger than their own territory. In peacetime, economic dependency became one of the causes of a phenomenon which itself contributed to the transformation of the old state system: imperialism. Anticipating war, with its new danger of blockade, countries strove to become more self-sufficient through enlargement of their areas of control. To the extent that the industrialized nations lost self-sufficiency, they were driven into expansion in a (futile) effort to regain it. Today, if at all, only control of entire continents enables major nations to survive economically in major wars. This implies that hard-shell military defense must be a matter of defending more than a single nation; it must extend around half the world.

(b) Psychological Warfare

The attempt to undermine the morale of an enemy population, or to subvert its loyalty, shares with economic warfare a by-passing effect on old-style territorial defensibility. It was formerly practiced, and practicable, only under quite exceptional circumstances. Short periods of genuine world revolutionary propaganda, such as the early stages of the French

Revolution,[24] scarcely affected a general practice under which dynasties, and later governments, fought each other with little ideological involvement on the part of larger masses or classes. Only in rare cases—for instance, where national groups enclosed in and hostile to multinational empires could be appealed to—was there an opening wedge for "fifth column" strategies.

With the emergence of political belief-systems, however, nations became more susceptible to undermining from within. Although wars have not yet been won solely by subversion of loyalties, the threat involved has affected the inner coherence of the territorial state ever since the rise to power of a regime that claims to represent, not the cause of a particular nation, but that of mankind, or at least of its suppressed and exploited portions. Bolshevism from 1917 on has provided the second instance in modern history of world revolutionary propaganda. Communist penetration tactics subsequently were imitated by the Nazi and Fascist regimes and, eventually, by the democracies. In this way, new lines of division, cutting horizontally through state units instead of leaving them separated vertically from each other at their frontiers, have now become possible.

(c) Air Warfare and (d) Nuclear Warfare

Of all the new developments, air warfare, up to the atomic age, has been the one that affected the territoriality of nations most radically. With its coming, the bottom dropped out—or, rather, the roof blew off—the relative security of the territorial state. True, even this new kind of warfare, up to and including the Second World War, did not by itself account for the defeat of a belligerent, as some of the more enthusiastic prophets of the air age had predicted it would. Undoubtedly, however, it had a massive contributory effect. And this effect was due to strategic action in the *hinterland* rather than to tactical use at the front. It came at least close to defeating one side by direct action against the "soft" interior of the country, by-passing outer defenses and thus foreshadowing the end of the frontier —that is, the demise of the traditional impermeability of even the militarily most

powerful states. Warfare now changed "from a fight to a process of devastation."[25]

That air warfare was considered as something entirely unconventional is seen from the initial reaction to it. Revolutionary transition from an old to a new system has always affected moral standards. In the classical age of the modern state system, the "new morality" of shooting at human beings from a distance had finally come to be accepted, but the standards of the age clearly distinguished "lawful combatants" at the front or in fortifications from the civilian remainder of the population. When air war came, reactions thus differed significantly in the cases of air fighting at the front and of air war carried behind the front. City bombing was felt to constitute "illegitimate" warfare, and populations were inclined to treat airmen engaging in it as "war criminals."[26] This feeling continued into World War II, with its large-scale area bombing. Such sentiments reflected the general feeling of helplessness in the face of a war which threatened to render obsolete the concept of territorial power, together with its ancient implication of protection.

The process has now been completed with the advent of nuclear weapons. For it is more than doubtful that the processes of scientific invention and technological discovery, which not only have created and perfected the fission and fusion weapons themselves but have brought in their wake guided missiles with nuclear warheads, jet aircraft with intercontinental range and supersonic speed, and the

---

[24]See my article, "Idealist Internationalism and the Security Dilemma," *World Politics*, II, No. 2 (January 1950), pp. 157ff.; in particular, pp. 165ff.

[25]B.H. Liddell Hart, *The Revolution in Warfare*, New Haven, Conn., 1947, p. 36. Suspicion of what would be in the offing, once man gained the capacity to fly, was abroad as early as the eighteenth century. Thus Samuel Johnson remarked: "If men were all virtuous, I should with great alacrity teach them all to fly. But what would be the security of the good, if the bad could at pleasure invade them from the sky? Against an army sailing through the clouds, neither walls, nor mountains, nor seas, could afford security" (quoted in J.U. Nef, *War and Human Progress*, Cambridge, Mass., 1952, p. 198). And Benjamin Franklin, witnessing the first balloon ascension at Paris in 1783, foresaw invasion from the air and wrote: "Convincing Sovereigns of folly of wars may perhaps be one effect of it, since it will be impracticable for the most potent of them to guard his dominions. . . . Where is the Prince who can afford so to cover his country with troops for its defense, as that ten thousand men descending from the clouds, might not in many places do an infinite deal of mischief before a force could be brought together to repel them?" (from a letter to Jan Ingelhouss, reproduced in *Life Magazine*, January 9, 1956).

[26]See Julius Stone, *Legal Controls of International Conflicts*, New York, 1954, pp. 611ff.

prospect of nuclear-powered planes or rockets with unlimited range and with automatic guidance to specific targets anywhere in the world, can in any meaningful way be likened to previous new inventions, however revolutionary. These processes add up to an uncanny absoluteness of effect which previous innovations could not achieve. The latter might render power units of a certain type (for instance, castles or cities) obsolete and enlarge the realm of defensible power units from city-state to territorial state or even large-area empire. They might involve destruction, in war, of entire populations. But there still remained the seemingly inexhaustible reservoir of the rest of mankind. Today, when not even two halves of the globe remain impermeable, it can no longer be a question of enlarging an area of protection and of substituting one unit of security for another. Since we are inhabitants of a planet of limited (and, as it now seems, insufficient) size, we have reached the limit within which the effect of the means of destruction has become absolute. Whatever remained of the impermeability of states seems to have gone for good.

What has been lost can be seen from two statements by thinkers separated by thousands of years and half the world; both reflect the condition of territorial security. Mencius, in ancient China, when asked for guidance in matters of defense and foreign policy by the ruler of a small state, is said to have counseled: "Dig deeper your moats; build higher your walls; guard them along with your people." This remained the classical posture up to our age, when a Western sage, Bertrand Russell, in the interwar period could still define power as something radiating from one center and growing less with distance from that center until it finds an equilibrium with that of similar geographically anchored units. Now that power can destroy power from center to center, everything is different.

VI. OUTLOOK AND CONCLUSION

It is beyond the compass of this article to ask what the change in the statehood of nations implies for present and future world relations; whether, indeed, international relations in the traditional sense of the term, dependent as they have been on a number of basic data (existence of the nation-state, measurable power, etc.) and interpreted as they were with the aid of certain concepts (sovereignty,

independence, etc.), can survive at all; and, if not, what might take their place.[27] Suffice it to remark that this question is vastly complex. We cannot even be sure that one and only one set of conclusions derives from what has happened or is in the process of happening. For, in J. Robert Oppenheimer's words, one of the characteristics of the present is "the prevalence of newness, the changing scale and scope of change itself. . . ."[28] In the field of military policy, this means that since World War II half a dozen military innovations "have followed each other so rapidly that efforts at adaptation are hardly begun before they must be scrapped."[29] The scientific revolution has been "so fast-moving as to make almost impossible the task of military men whose responsibility it is to anticipate the future. Military planning cannot make the facts of this future stay long enough to analyze them."[30]

If this applies to military planning, it must apply equally to foreign policy planning, and, indeed, the newness of the new is perhaps the most significant and the most exasperating aspect of present world relations. Hardly has a bipolar world replaced the multipower world of classical territoriality than there loom new and unpredictable multipower constellations on the international horizon. However, the possible rise of new powers does not seem to affect bipolarity in the sense of a mere return to traditional multipower relations; since rising powers are likely to be nuclear powers, their effect must be an entirely novel one. What international relations would (or will) look like, once nuclear power is possessed by a larger number of power units, is not only extremely unpleasant to contemplate but almost impossible to anticipate, using any familiar concepts. Or, to use another example: We have hardly drawn the military and political conclusions from the new weapons developments, which at one point seemed to indicate the necessity of basing defense on the formation and maintenance of pacts like

[27]Some of the pertinent questions are discussed in a more comprehensive manuscript, "Reflections on International Politics in the Atomic Age," from whose initial chapters the preceding pages were adapted.

[28]The Open Mind, New York, 1955, p. 141.

[29]Roger Hilsman, "Strategic Doctrines for Nuclear War," in William W. Kaufmann, ed., Military Policy and National Security, Princeton, N.J., 1956, p. 42.

[30]Thomas K. Finletter, Power and Politics: US Foreign Policy and Military Power in the Hydrogen Age, New York, 1954, p. 256.

NATO and the establishment of a network of bases on allied territory from which to launch nuclear weapons "in case" (or whose existence was to deter the opponent from doing so on his part), and already further scientific and technological developments seem to render entire defense blocs, with all their new "hard shells" of bases and similar installations, obsolete.

To complicate matters even more, the change-over is not even uniform and unilinear. On the contrary, in concepts as well as in policies, we witness the juxtaposition of old and new (or several new) factors, a coexistence in theory and practice of conventional and new concepts, of traditional and new policies. Part of a nation's (or a bloc's) defense policy, then, may proceed on pre-atomic assumptions, while another part is based on the assumption of a preponderantly nuclear contest. And a compounding trouble is that the future depends on what the present anticipates, on what powers now think and how they intend to act on the basis of their present thinking; and on the fact that each of the actors on the scene must take into consideration the assumptions of the others.[31]

There then evolves the necessity of multilevel concepts and of multilevel policies in

[31]The expectations connected with the situation of nuclear deterrence may serve as an illustration. Each side, so we may assume, wants to act "rationally"—that is, avoid resort to a war which it knows would be suicidal; in this, in fact, is grounded the widespread present belief in the obsoleteness of major—i.e., nuclear—war. However, not knowing for sure that the other side can be trusted to behave rationally, each feels that the possibility of irrational behavior by the opponent must be included in its own calculations. For instance, assuming that rationally the United States would not permit itself to be provoked into nuclear action, can it rely on Soviet abstention from nuclear attack for similarly rational reasons? Or can the Soviets, who may actually believe that the "imperialist" powers are ready to inflict the worst on them, rely on Western rationality? And if, knowing that the other side may be swayed by considerations like these, one side takes these amended calculations as yardsticks for its own, what rational considerations remain? Policies then become so dependent on considerations of what you believe the other side believes, etc., ad infinitum, that no sane calculations are any longer feasible. One is caught here in the vicious circle inherent in the problem of the effects of assumptions (in behaviorist parlance, the problem of "anticipated reactions"), of what David Easton has called the possibility of an "infinite regress of effects" (The Political System, New York, 1953, p. 27). It may be doubted that even the theory of games as applied to international relations can cope with this one. And suppose that, sometime in the future, more than two major units "play"? In the face of this prospect, as Herbert Butterfield says, "The mind winces and turns to look elsewhere" (History and Human Relations, New York, 1952, p. 23).

the new era. In this we have, perhaps, the chief cause of the confusion and bewilderment of countries and publics. A good deal in recent foreign policies, with their violent swings from one extreme to another, from appeasement or apathy to truculence and threats of war, and also much in internal policies, with their suspicions and hysterias, may be reflections of world-political uncertainties. Confusion, despair, or easy optimism have been rampant; desire to give in, keep out, or get it over with underlies advocacy of appeasement, neutralism, or preventive war; mutually exclusive attitudes follow each other in rapid succession.

One radical conclusion to be drawn from the new condition of permeability would seem to be that nothing short of global rule can ultimately satisfy the security interest of any one power, and particularly any superpower. For only through elimination of the single competitor who really counts can one feel safe from the threat of annihilation. And since elimination without war is hardly imaginable, destruction of the other power by preventive war would therefore seem to be the logical objective of each superpower. But—and here the security dilemma encounters the other great dilemma of our time—such an aim is no longer practical. Since thermonuclear war would in all likelihood involve one's own destruction together with the opponent's, the means through which the end would have to be attained defeats the end itself. Pursuance of the "logical" security objective would result in mutual annihilation rather than in one unit's global control of a pacified world.

If this is so, the short-term objective must surely be mutual accommodation, a drawing of demarcation lines, geographical and otherwise, between East and West which would at least serve as a stopgap policy, a holding operation pending the creation of an atmosphere in which, perhaps in consequence of a prolonged period of "cold peace," tensions may abate and the impact of the ideologies presently dividing the world diminish. May we then expect, or hope, that radically new attitudes, in accordance with a radically transformed structure of nationhood and international relations, may ultimately gain the upper hand over the inherited ones based on familiar concepts of old-style national security, power, and power competion? Until recently, advocacy of policies based on internationalism instead of power politics, on substituting the observance of universal interests for the prevalence of national interests, was considered utopian, and correctly so. National interests were still tied up with nation-states as units of power and with their security as impermeable units; internationalist ideals, while possibly recognized as ethically valid, ran counter to what nations were able to afford if they wanted to survive and prosper. But the dichotomy between "national self-interest" and "internationalist ideals" no longer fits a situation in which sovereignty and ever so absolute power cannot protect nations from annihilation.

What used to be a dichotomy of interests and ideals now emerges as a dichotomy between two sets of interests. For the former ideal has become a compelling interest itself. In former times, the lives of people, their goods and possessions, their hopes and their happiness, were tied up with the affairs of the country in which they lived, and interests thus centered around nation and national issues. Now that destruction threatens everybody, in every one of his most intimate, personal interests, national interests are bound to recede behind—or at least compete with—the common interest of all mankind in sheer survival. And if we add to this the universal interest in the common solution of other great world problems, such as those posed by the population-resources dilemma (exhaustion of vital resources coupled with the "population explosion" throughout the world), or, indeed, that of "peacetime" planetary pollution through radio-active fallout, it is perhaps not entirely utopian to expect the ultimate spread of an attitude of "universalism" through which a rational approach to world problems would at last become possible

It may be fitting to conclude this article by quoting two men, one a contemporary scientist whose words on nuclear problems may well apply to other problems of world relations, the second a philosopher whose statement on the revolutionary impact of attitude changes seems as valid today as when it was first made: "It is a practical thing to recognize as a common responsibility, wholly incapable of unilateral solution, the complete common peril that atomic weapons constitute for the world, to recognize that only by a community of responsibility is there any hope of meeting the peril. It would seem to me visionary in the extreme, and not practical, to hope that methods which have so sadly failed in the past to avert war will succeed in the face of this far greater peril. It would in my opinion be most dangerous to regard, in these shattering times, a radical solution less practical than a conventional one" (J. Robert Oppenheimer).[32] And: "Thought achieves more in the world than practice; for, once the realm of imagination has been revolutionized, reality cannot resist" (Hegel).

REFERENCES

Alexander, L.M., "Major Trends in the World Political Patterns," Inst. Indian Geographers, Pub. No. 1 (1954), 6–12.

Cole, J.P. Geography of World Affairs (4th ed.), Baltimore, Penguin Books, 1972.

Deutsch, K.W., and W.J. Foltz (ed.), Nation-Building. New York, Atherton Press, a Division of Prentice-Hall, Inc., 1963.

———, and J. David Singer, "Multipolar Power Systems and International Stability," World Politics, 16, 3 (April, 1964), 390–406.

Eyre, J.D., "Japanese–Soviet Territorial Issues in the Southern Kurile Islands," Prof. Geog. 20, 1 (January, 1968), 11–15.

Hartshorne, Richard, "The Politico-geographic Pattern of the World," Ann. Amer. Ac. Pol. & Soc. Sci., 218 (1941), 45–57.

Herz, J.H., "The Rise and Demise of the Territorial State," World Politics, 9, 4 (July, 1957), 473–493.

Jones, Stephen B., "Views of the Political World," Geog. Rev., 45, 3 (July, 1955), 309–326.

Nijim, B.K., "Israel and the Potential for Conflict," Prof. Geog. 21, 5 (September, 1969), 319–323.

Pye, Lucian W., "The Non-Western Political Process," J. Politics, 20, 3 (August, 1958), 468–486.

Spengler, J.J., "Economic Development: Political Preconditions and Political Consequences," J. Politics, 22, 3 (August, 1960), 387–416.

Sprout, Harold and Margaret, "Geography and International Politics in an Era of Revolutionary Change," J. Conflict Resolution, 4, 1 (March, 1960), 145–161.

———, Man-Milieu Relationship Hypotheses in the Context of International Politics. Princeton, N.J., Princeton University Center for International Studies, 1956.

[32]"Atomic Weapons," Proceedings of the American Philosophical Society, xc (January 29, 1946), pp. 9f.

Author Index

Abbas, M., 422
Abel, W., 101
Abuetan, B., 381
Ackerman, E. A., 77
Acquah, I., 125
Adami, V., 143-144, 156, 165, 174
Adams, D. K., 292
Adams, G. B., 174
Adams, R. M., 34
Aderbidge, A. B., 446
Adloff, R., 423
Ahmad, K. S., 174
Ahmad, N., 186
Ahmed, A., 52
Aitken, H. G. J., 77
Akzin, B., 446
Alcock, N. Z., 77
Alexander, I. M., 84
Alexander, L. M., 156, 186, 195, 199, 218, 265, 296, 465
Alford, R. R., 339
Alger, C. F., 125
Allan, S. N., 446
Alland, A., 339
Allen, E. W., 199
Amador, F. V. G., 199, 217
Amery, 283
Anderson, A. T., 156
Andrews, J., 292
Angell, N., 77
Anninos, P. C. L., 199
Apter, D. E., 324
Apthorpe, R., 77
Archdale, H. E., 199
Archer, J. C., 340
Archibald, C. H., 381
Arciszewski, F., 156
Arden-Clarke, C., 156
Ardrey, R., 337-339
Armstrong, H. F., 156, 292
Arnade, C. W., 381
Arora, S. K., 381
Ashford, D. E., 324
Atkinson, W. C., 99
Augelli, J. P., 125, 292
Austin, D. G., 156

Awa, E. O., 381
Ayearst, M., 381
Azikiwe, N., 360, 381

Bailey, S. D., 324, 446
Baldoria, P. L., 324, 381
Ball, S. S., 84, 87-103
Balogh, T., 422
Banks, A. L., 34
Baradez, J., 166, 174
Baratz, M. S., 381
Barbour, N., 381
Barker, J. E., 174
Barnett, H. J., 77
Barnett, J. R., 339
Barton, R. F., 163, 173
Barton, T. F., 230
Barton, W., 156
Bascom, W., 115
Baty, T., 199
Bavarski, G., 94
Beard, C. A., 324
Becker, L., 218
Beloch, J., 101
Bemis, S. F., 174
Benians, E. A., 320
Bennett, G., 156
Benoit, E., 446
Bentwich, N., 324
Berard, V., 422
Berber, F. J., 230
Bernstein, R. A., 446
Berry, B. J. L., 334
Best, A. C. G., 69, 121, 125, 422
Best, H., 381
Betts, R. R., 156
Bianchi, R. L., 231
Bianchi, W. J., 156
Billington, M., 156, 186
Bindoff, S. T., 230
Binns, B. O., 320
Birch, A. H., 370
Bird, J., 125
Birdsall, S. S., 326-339
Birdwood, C. B. B., 156
Blalock, H. M., 328

467

Blij, de, H. J., 307-317
Bloch, M., 166, 174
Blood, H., 381
Bloomfield, L. M., 186, 218
Boateng, E. A., 125
Boggs, S. W., 133, 143, 156, 170-171, 173, 186, 190, 199, 206, 218, 257-258, 292
Bogue, D. J., 52
Bolin, R. L., 236
Bone, R. C., 52
Bonn, M. J., 446
Boots, B. N., 339
Bose, N. K., 381
Bouchez, L. J., 187
Boulding, K. E., 339
Boutros-Ghali, B. Y., 446
Bowman, I., 34, 244, 265, 292
Bradford, S., 381
Braine, B., 422
Brainerd, G. W., 34
Brams, S. J., 125
Brandt, K., 77, 446
Brausch, G., 422
Brecher, M., 156
Bretton, H. L., 422
Briggs, H. W., 144
Brigham, A. P., 34
Brittin, B. H., 199
Broek, J. O. M., 167, 174
Brown, D. J. L., 156
Brown, W. N., 381
Brunn, S. D., 326, 339
Brunskill, G. S., 230
Bryce, J., 34, 369
Buchanan, K., 381
Buday, L., 156
Bunsen, De, B., 78
Burghardt, A., 84, 86, 88, 326, 339
Burke, F., 307
Burke, W. T., 199
Burns, A., 381
Bushman, D. O., 156
Busk, C. W. F., 156
Butterfield, H., 464
Bywater, H. C., 292

Cagle, M. W., 218
Cahnman, W. J., 156
Cakste, M., 422
Campbell, J. C., 230
Campbell, M. J., 125
Campbell, R. D., 265, 382
Canaway, A. P., 382
Caplow, T., 446
Capone, D. L., 216-218, 307-317
Carlson, L., 266
Caroe, O., 52, 156
Carr, E. H., 77
Carrington, C. E., 52
Carr-Saunders, A. M., 52
Catroux, G., 422, 446

Cervin, V., 324
Chakrabongse, C., 34
Chandrasekhar, S., 382
Chang, S., 125
Chapin, H. B., 125
Chapin, M., 382
Chapman, B., 125
Chaput, M., 352
Chatterjee, S. P., 382
Chaudhuri, M., 292-293
Chairelli, G., 125
Chidell, F., 52
Child, C. J., 156
Childe, V. G., 98
Christie, E. W. H., 156
Chubb, B., 293
Church, R. J. H., 382, 422
Clark, C., 376
Clark, J. G. D., 98
Clarke, J. I., 34, 52
Classen, H. G., 187
Clement, D. B., 218
Clemns, J., 53
Cobban, A., 168, 174
Cockram, B., 422
Codding, G. A., Jr., 199
Cohen, S. B., 218, 266, 296, 317, 324, 386
Colborn, P. A., 199
Cole, J. P., 266, 465
Cole, M. M., 115
Coleman, J. S., 77, 411, 422
Collingwood, R. G., 34
Colombos, C. J., 199
Conditt, G., 125
Condominas, G., 52
Connell, J., 156
Copland, D., 377
Coplin, W. D., 446
Cornish, V., 122, 125, 304
Corti, W. R., 157
Costanzo, G. A., 446
Couglan, R., 174
Coulborn, R., 34
Coulter, J. W., 422
Cowan, L. G., 382
Cox, K. R., 326, 339
Crary, D. D., 230
Crawshaw, N., 52
Cressey, G. B., 77
Crisler, R. M., 325, 339
Crocombe, R. G., 422
Crowder, M., 382, 422
Cumming, D. C., 382
Cumpstom, J. H. L., 187
Cunningham, J. K., 34, 52, 382
Currie, D. P., 382
Curzon, G. N., 143, 157, 168-170, 174

Dahl, R. A., 324
Dale, E. H., 125, 382
Darby, H. C., 90-91

Das, G. S., 352
Das, T., 382
Davies, A., 376
Davis, K., 52
Davis, W. C., 422
Davis, W. M., 237
Day, W. M., 157, 187
Dayan, M., 187
Dean, A. H., 199, 218
Dean, V. K., 325, 339, 382
Dearden, A., 324
de Blij, H. J., 307-317
De Bunsen, B., 78
de Lapradelle, P., 140, 143, 146
de Leon, P. C., 27
Delf, G., 78
de Madariaga, S., 423
De Mille, J. B., 78
Deng, W., 383, 447
Dening, B. H., 382
Denz, E. J., 218
de Planhol, X., 53
De Seversky, A. P., 287, 289, 293
Deshpande, C. D., 382
Desmond, A., 446
de Somogyi, J., 219
Deutsch, H. J., 187
Deutsch, K. W., 34, 78, 88, 302, 422, 446, 465
Dickenson, R. E., 115, 125, 157
Diebold, W., 446
Dikshit, R. D., 293, 382
Dobby, E. H. G., 382
Donald, R., 230
Dorpalen, A., 293
Drysdale, J., 411
Duffy, J., 394, 422
Dugdale, J., 382
Duncan, O. D., 115
Dunlop, E. W., 382
Dunlop, J. S., 422
Dunn, F. S., 305
Dunn, J. M., 78
Dvorin, E. P., 324

Eason, W. W., 52
East, W. G., 115, 157, 212, 230, 243, 266, 289, 293, 446
Easterlin, R. A., 324
Easton, D., 464
Edison, S. S., 308
Efron, R., 446
Elegant, R. S., 78
Emeny, B., 34, 266
Emerson, R., 422, 447
English, P. W., 337
Etzioni, A., 446
Evensen, J., 218
Eyck, E., 459
Eyre, J. D., 165, 174, 465

Fagen, 318

Fair, T. J. D., 115, 312
Fairfield, R. P., 52
Fairgrieve, J., 30, 89, 266, 293
Faisol, S., 125
Faladreau, J., 52
Fall, B. B., 157
Falls, C., 293
Farran, C., 52
Faucett, C. H., 143, 157, 422
Febvre, L. P. V., 34, 87
Feer, M. C., 157
Fenwick, C. G., 187, 446
Fesler, J. W., 301
Fifer, J. V., 231
Fifield, R., 157
Finkelstein, L. S., 382
Finletter, T. K., 463
Finsterbusch, K., 446
Fischer, E., 157, 163, 187, 302
Fishel, W. R., 157
Fisher, C. A., 266, 293, 324, 382
Fisher, M. W., 157
Fiske, C., 157
Fiske, Mrs. C., 157
Fitzgerald, G. F., 218
Fitzpatrick, B., 372
Fleure, H. J., 34
Florinsky, M. T., 446
Floyd, B. N., 34
Flugal, R. R., 52
Foltz, W. J., 465
Foran, W. R., 125
Forde, C. D., 162, 173
Foulkes, C. H., 187
Franck, T. M., 446
Frank, D. S., 187, 422
Frank, T., 34
Frankel, S. H., 386, 422
Franklin, H., 382
Fraser-Tytler, W. K., 157
Frazier, E. F., 78
Freeman, T. W., 231
Freshfield, D. W., 157
Friters, G. M., 157
Fryer, D. W., 125, 266
Fulton, T. W., 199
Furber, H., 382
Furnivall, J. S., 382, 422

Gangal, S. C., 382
Gann, L. H., 52
Gathorne-Hardy, G. M., 382
Gerbrandy, P. S., 382
German, F. C., 60-66, 78, 265
Gerson, L. L., 231
Getis, A., 339
Gigax, W. R., 446
Gilbert, E. W., 382
Gilbert, F., 456
GilFillan, S. C., 187
Gilliard, C., 93

Gilliland, H. B., 78
Gillin, J., 382
Ginsburg, N. S., 52, 382
Goad, H. E., 34
Goblet, Y. M., 236, 266, 293
Goetzmann, W. H., 187
Golay, J. F., 382
Goldblatt, I., 422
Goode, 38
Goodwin, H. L., 218
Goormaghtigh, J., 446
Gorbold, R., 382
Gottmann, J., 115, 174, 266, 293, 297, 299-301, 303-304, 317, 324, 337
Gould, P. R., 339
Green, L. P., 115
Greenidge, C. W. W., 382
Greenwood, G., 376
Gregory, J. W., 52
Grey, 100
Grey, A. L., 187
Griffiths, P., 359
Groom, S. M., 199
Gross, L., 218
Grzybowski, K., 199
Guill, J. H., 218
Gyorgy, A., 171, 293

Hass, E. B., 446
Hadawi, E., 324
Hagen, E. E., 78
Hagen, T., 157
Haig, R. M., 115
Hale, R. W., Jr., 187
Hall, A. R., 187, 289, 293
Hall, E. T., 338-339
Hall, H. D., 157
Hallowell, A. I., 34
Hallstein, W., 446
Hammer, E. J., 422
Hammond, T. T., 157
Hance, W. A., 78, 125, 382
Hancock, W. K., 374, 422
Hanessian, J., Jr., 157
Hanna, A. J., 157
Happe, E. D., 125
Harbeson, R. W., 78
Harding, J., 53
Hardy, L. R., 200
Hardy, W. G., 382
Hargreaves, R., 199
Harris, M., 394
Harrison, J. A., 157
Harrison, R. E., 295
Harrison, T., 422
Hart, B. H. L., 462
Hart, J. F., 325, 340
Hartshorne, R., 59, 77, 143-144, 146, 157, 174, 185, 187, 223, 240-267, 293, 296, 299-301, 303-305, 317, 324, 337, 465
Harvey, H. J., 446

Hassinger, H., 9-10, 251-252
Haupert, J. S., 53, 125, 157
Hauser, P. M., 53
Haushofer, K., 140, 143, 145, 147, 168, 170-171, 175, 268, 337, 386-387
Haverstock, N. A., 445
Hay, R., 157, 187
Hayton, R. D., 78, 157
Hazard, H. W., 423
Heenan, L. D. B., 53
Hegel, 465
Held, C. C., 157
Helin, R. A., 78, 231
Henning, R., 293
Hensinkveld, H. M., 422
Herman, T., 53, 173, 339, 382
Herskovits, F. S., 416
Herskovits, M. J., 416
Hertslet, E., 157
Hertz, F., 53
Herz, J. H., 454-465
Heslinga, M. W., 187
Hill, J. E., Jr., 157
Hill, N., 231
Hilsman, R., 463
Hinsley, F. H., 78
Hirsch, A. M., 187, 231
Hodgkins, J. A., 78
Hodgkiss, A. G., 187
Hoffman, G. W., 78, 157, 187, 324, 382, 446
Hoffman, W. L., 326
Hogarth, 284
Holdich, T. H., 143, 157, 169, 282-283
Holford, W., 125
Holmes, J. M., 377
Hookham, M., 125
Hooson, D. J. M., 115, 290, 293, 452
Horne, A., 78
Horton, F. E., 339
Horvath, R. J., 125
Houphouet-Boigny, F., 422
House, J. W., 157, 187
Houten, P. H. J. M., 420
Howe, M., 324
Howells, W. W., 34
Huang, T. T. F., 231
Hudson, M. O., 446
Huke, R. E., 382
Humphreys, R. A., 157
Huntington, E., 48, 53
Hurewitz, J. C., 446
Hutchinson, B., 187
Huttenback, R. A., 157
Huxley, E., 53, 423
Hyde, C. C., 157
Hyde, G. E., 34

Ingrams, H., 324
Inlow, E. B., 151, 157
Innis, H. A., 157
Ireland, G., 157

Isard, W., 115
Issawi, C., 446
Iwata, K., 266

Jackson, W. A. D., 157, 187, 266, 293, 296, 324, 453
Jamws, P. E., 103, 106, 125
Janowsky, O. I., 78
Jarrett, H. R., 125
Jefferson, M., 119, 125, 304, 382
Jenkins, W., Jr., 324
Jennings, I., 423
Jesman, C., 382
Jessup, P. C., 199, 218
Joesten, J., 218
John, I. G., 158
Johnson, G. R., 199
Johnson, J. H., 382
Johnston, R. J., 339
Jones, C. F., 230
Jones, E., 53
Jones, S. B., 58, 78, 135, 143, 145, 158, 161-175, 187, 269, 293, 297-306, 308, 310, 317, 321, 337, 465
Jose, A., 371

Kaganovich, L. M., 148
Kain, R. S., 231
Kalijarvi, 266
Kantorowicz, H. U., 294
Kapil, R. L., 158
Kaplan, A., 78, 303
Karan, P. P., 156, 187, 294, 324
Karnes, T. L., 382
Kasperson, R. E., 236-237, 326, 336, 339
Kates, R. W., 336, 339
Kaufmann, W. W., 463
Kautsky, J. H., 403, 423
Kawakami, K., 199
Keith, B., 125
Kelly, J. B., 187
Kelman, H. C., 340
Kent, H. S. K., 190, 199
Kephart, C., 34
Kerner, R. J., 94, 158, 231
Kerr, J. R., 423
Key, V. O., Jr., 328
Keyser, C. F., 218
Khadduri, M., 324
Khan, F. R., 158
Khrushchev, N. S., 78
Kieffer, J. E., 78
Kimble, G. H. T., 382
King, F. H. H., 383
King, L. J., 331
Kingsbury, P., 158
Kingsbury, R. C., 158, 187
Kinnane, D., 383, 449
Kirchheimer, O., 383
Kirk, G., 266
Kirk, W., 158
Kirk-Green, A. H. M., 125

Kish, G., 294
Kissinger, H. A., 78
Kitzinger, U. W., 446
Kjellen, R., 147, 171, 267, 269, 337
Kleinpenning, J. M. G., 423
Klineberg, O., 340
Knight, D. B., 125
Knopf, A. A., 328
Knorr, K., 78
Koch, H. E., Jr., 78, 447
Kohn, H., 158
Kolarz, W., 423
Kostelski, Z., 34
Kozicki, R. J., 158
Krebheil, E., 325, 340, 383
Krengel, R., 78
Krenz, F. E., 53
Kretzmann, E. M. J., 423
Kriesel, K. M., 266
Krishan, R., 294
Kristof, L. K. D., 127, 129, 135-140, 173, 266-267, 294
Kruijer, G. J., 418, 420
Kruszewski, C., 294
Kuehnelt-Leddihn, E. R. V., 231
Kuhn, D., 158
Kuhn, F., 158
Kumar, C. K., 218
Kumar, M., 324
Kunz, J. L., 199
Kureshi, K. U., 125, 158
Kurganov, I., 53
Kusielewicz, E., 187

Lamb, A., 158
Lambert, R. D., 53
Landheer, B., 78
Langlands, B. W., 231
Lapradelle, de, 140, 143, 146
Larus, J., 34
Laswell, H. D., 78, 303
Lattimore, O., 34, 145, 148, 158, 164, 173, 423
Laylin, J. G., 231
Lee, D. R., 53
Legge, J. D., 423
Leibniz, 456-458
Leistikow, G., 218
Leith, C. K., 78
Lenczowski, G., 158
Leon, de, P. C., 27
Leonard, L. L., 199
LePage, R. B., 53
Lepawsky, A., 447
Lessing, O. E., 158
Levi, W., 158
LeVine, V. T., 423
Lewin, K., 324
Lewis, I. M., 158, 423
Lewis, P. F., 326, 340
Lewis, W. A., 78
Lichtheim, G., 447

Lijphart, A., 53
Lincoln, G. A., 78
Linge, G. J. R., 126
Linke, L., 383
Litt, E., 319
Little, T., 383
Livermore, S., 78
Livingstone, W. S., 383
Lloyd, T., 187
Loewenstein, K., 447
Longnon, A., 89
Longrigg, S. H., 447
Lonsdale, R. E., 115
Lord, R. H., 187
Lorenz, K., 338, 340
Lorimer, F., 53
Losch, A., 53, 115, 129
Lot, F., 89
Low, D. H., 158
Lowenthal, D., 53, 124-126, 336, 383
Lower, A. R. M., 353
Lowie, R. H., 162-163, 173
Lowry, M., 53
Lyde, L. W., 145
Lydolph, P. E., 383

Maas, A., 78
Macartney, C. A., 95, 158
Macaulay, A. M., 447
Macdonald, M. M., 231
Mackay, J. R., 129
Mackinder, H. J., 171-172, 175, 267-286, 289-292,
    294, 386-387, 448
MacKintosh, J. P., 383
MacKirdy, K. A., 383
Macmahon, A., 383
Madariaga, de, S., 423
Maddick, H., 383
Mahan, A. T., 171, 268-269, 278, 286, 386-387
Maillart, E., 158
Malcolm, G. A., 383
Mallows, E. W. N., 115
Malof, P., 447
Mance, O., 231
Mansergh, N., 383
Marble, D. F., 334
Margary, I., 35
Markham, S. F., 48, 53
Maron, S., 53
Marquis, R. V., 34
Martin, G. J., 34, 294
Martin, H. H., 53
Martovych, O. R., 53
Martz, J. D., 115
Masai, Y., 115
Mason, P., 383
Mathews, D. R., 116, 335
Mattern, 171
Mattingly, G., 456
Maull, O., 143, 168, 243, 251
Mayfield, R. C., 158, 337

Mayne, R., 447
Mazour, A. G., 158
McCarty, H. H., 328
McColl, R. W., 423
McCune, S., 187
McDougal, M. S., 199
McFee, W., 199
McGee, T. G., 423
McIlwain, C. H., 455
McKay, J. R., 187
McKay, V., 423
McKee, J. O., 324
McMahon, M. M., 459
McManis, D. R., 115
McNee, R. B., 266
McWhinney, E., 383
Mead, W. R., 158
Meadows, M., 423
Meinecke, F., 456
Meinig, D. W., 151, 158, 289, 294, 423, 447, 452
Melamid, A., 53, 78, 200, 218, 294, 324
Mellor, R., 78
Merriam, A. P., 384
Merrill, G., 383
Mikerji, A. B., 158
Mille, De, J. B., 78
Miller, J. D. B., 369
Miller, J. M., 126
Mills, D. R., 294
Minghi, J. V., 158, 213, 236, 296
Mings, R. C., 340
Mirot, A., 89
Misra, S. D., 158
Missakian, J. A., 158
Moll, K. L., 269, 294
Monroe, E., 158
Montagu, M. F. A., 340
Moodie, A. E., 32, 158, 176, 187, 200, 212, 218, 266,
    289, 294, 296
Mookerjie, S., 266
Morgan, J. C., 159
Morgan, R., 200
Morley, S. G., 34
Morrell, W. P., 423
Morris, D., 340
Morris, K. W., 231
Morrison, J. A., 94
Moscoso Cardenas, A., 126
Mosely, P. E., 187
Mouton, M. W., 200
Mudd, S., 53
Munger, E. S., 231
Murdoch, R. K., 158
Murphey, R., 115, 126, 449
Murray, R. A., 53
Myrdal, G., 447

Nachtegaal, C., 417
Nadan, R., 158
Nazzaro, A. A., 308
Nef, J. U., 462

Nel, A., 53
Neres, P., 447
Neumann, F. L., 78
Newbigin, M. I., 53, 231
Newcombe, A. G., 77
Newton, A. P., 320
Nicholson, N. L., 187, 266
Niebuhr, R., 34
Nijim, B. K., 158, 465
Nithard, 88
Noel, H. S., 218
North, D., 115
North, G., 78
North, R. C., 78
Nowland, J. L., 115
Nugent, W. V., 158
Nuseibeh, H. Z., 423
Nystrom, J. W., 445, 447

Oda, S., 200
Odell, C. B., 53
Oduho, J., 383, 449
Ogilvie, A. G., 158
Oppenheimer, J. R., 463, 465
Orchard, J. E., 78
O'Reilly Sternberg, H., 383
Organski, A. F. K., 53, 78
Organski, K., 53, 78
Orico, O., 126
Orr, D. M., Jr., 340
Osborne, H., 53
Owens, W. H., 447

Padelford, N. J., 447
Padmore, G., 423
Padwa, D. J., 218
Pakatas, K., 53
Palmer, N. D., 447
Palmier, L. H., 423
Panda, B. P., 294
Panikkar, K. M., 383, 447
Pankhurst, E. S., 383
Pankhurst, R. K. P., 383
Park, R. L., 383
Parker, A., 78
Parker, M., 53
Parker, R. S., 370
Partridge, P. H., 377
Paterson, J., 252
Patten, G. P., 383
Patterson, E. M., 447
Pattison, W. D., 175
Paullin, C. O., 175
Pearcy, G. E., 200, 206, 218, 266, 294
Pearson, N., 115
Peattie, R., 135
Pelham, H. F., 166, 174
Pelzer, K. J., 158, 303
Pendle, G., 231
Perham, M., 53, 383
Perlmann, M., 383

Petterson, D. R., 115
Petty, W., 235-236, 240
Philbrick, A. K., 103, 106, 115, 340
Pike, W., 382
Pillai, R. V., 324
Pitts, F. R., 187
Planhol, de, X., 53
Platt, R. A., 103-104, 106
Platt, R. S., 115, 126, 158-159, 225, 231, 258
Poidebard, A., 174
Polisk, A. N., 294
Pollard, V. K., 447
Porter, P. W., 383
Portus, G. V., 373
Pospisil, L., 173
Potter, E. B., 78
Pounds, N. J. G., 38, 78, 84, 87-103, 111, 159, 162,
    166-167, 173, 188, 230-231, 266, 294, 296, 447
Powers, R. D., Jr., 200
Pratt, J. T., 423
Pratt, R. C., 383, 423
Prescott, J. R. V., 71-72, 188, 266, 294, 325, 340,
    383
Price, A. G., 294
Prochazka, T., 188
Proctor, J. H., 383
Prothro, J. W., 335
Pryce, R., 447
Pye, L. W., 79, 465

Radin, G., 324
Randall, R. R., 324
Rao, K. K., 159
Ratzel, F., 147, 162-163, 168, 173, 236-237, 240,
    242-243, 247, 251-252, 267-268, 337
Raup, P. M., 159
Ravenholt, A., 383
Rawlings, E. H., 159
Read, M. H., 79
Reilly, B., 159
Reischauer, J., 174
Reischauer, R. K., 174
Reitzel, W., 303
Renier, G. J., 87, 100
Renner, G. T., 219
Reyner, A. S., 188
Reynolds, D. R., 328, 339-340
Rich, M., 330
Richards, J. H., 79, 159
Riggs, . W., 79, 423
Ripley, W. Z., 276
Ritter, K., 236
Rivlin, B., 423
Roberts, M. C., 326, 340, 383
Roberts, W. A., 126
Robertson, J., 383
Robinson, E. A. G., 53
Robinson, G. W. S., 43, 53, 393
Robinson, K. W., 350, 369-381, 383
Rollins, A. A., 175
Romsa, G. H., 326

Root, F. R., 447
Rose, A. J., 294, 380, 383
Rose, J. H., 320
Rose, L. E., 157
Rosenthal, L. D., 317, 324
Rotchild, D. S., 345
Roucek, J. S., 159, 266, 294, 423
Rowley, G., 340
Roxby, P. M., 34, 53, 115
Roys, R. L., 35
Rubenstein, A. Z., 199
Rubin, A. P., 159
Ruddock, G., 126
Ruiz Cardenas, A., 126
Rumage, K. W., 326, 340
Runciman, S., 100
Rupen, R. A., 423
Rushton, G., 340
Russell, F. M., 159
Russell, J. C., 115
Russell, R. J., 241, 244
Russett, B. M., 447
Ryan, A. F., 216-218
Ryan, C., 53, 383

Sage, W. N., 383
Saller, G. T., 53
Salter, P. S., 340
Sauer, C. O., 241, 266
Savelle, M., 175, 188
Schiffer, W., 456, 458
Schiller, A. A., 383
Schmieder, O., 115
Schmitt, C., 459
Schoenborn, W., 459
Schucking, W., 460
Schurr, S. H., 79
Scoenrich, O., 159
Scofield, J., 53
Scott, J., 159
Seawall, F., 53
Segal, A., 307
Selak, C. B., 218
Semmell, B., 294
Semple, E. C., 168, 174, 237, 248
Sen, D. K., 159
Serle, G., 376
Setson-Watson, R. W., 96
Seversky, De, A. P., 287, 289, 293
Shabad, T., 79, 383
Shalowitz, A. L., 200, 217, 219
Sharp, R. L., 162, 173
Sharp, W. R., 266
Shaudys, V. K., 383, 423
Sheean, V., 383
Shimkin, D. M., 79
Shreevastava, M. P., 266
Shuman, F. L., 266
Shute, J., 159
Siddall, W. R., 126
Sieger, R., 143

Siegfried, A., 79
Silberman, L., 383
Sills, D. L., 321
Silver, L., 316
Silvert, K. H., 382
Simey, T. S., 126
Simon, R., 125
Simonds, F. H., 266
Simpich, F., 126
Singer, J. D., 465
Singh, U., 126
Sjoberg, G., 115
Smailes, A. E., 35, 126, 304
Smetham, D. J., 91
Smit, P., 188
Smith, C. G., 423, 447
Smith, H. A., 192, 200, 231
Smith, H. K., 447
Smith, H. R., 325, 340
Smith, J. B., 324
Smith, R. A., 219
Smith, S. G., 188
Smith, W. C., 53
Smogorzewski, C., 231
Smogorzewski, K. M., 423
Smyth, W. J., 340
Snyder, E. E., 116, 126
Soja, E. W., 338-340
Solch, J., 143
Solomon, R. L., 159-160
Solly, M. B., 383
Sombart, W., 294
Somerville, J. J. B., 384
Sommer, R., 338, 340
Somogyi, de, J., 219
Sonnenfeld, J., 337, 340
Sorel, A., 88
Sorenson, M., 200, 219
Soward, F. H., 447
Spate, O. H. K., 53, 119, 122-124, 126, 159, 165,
    174, 304
Spengler, J. J., 465
Sprout, H., 35, 79, 172, 175, 266, 294, 324, 465
Sprout, M., 35, 79, 172, 175, 266, 324, 465
Spykman, N. J., 79, 150, 159, 170-172, 175, 286,
    289, 294
Stacey, C. P., 159, 188
Stahl, R., 79
Stamp, L. D., 447
Stanislawski, D., 115, 384
Stanley, W. R., 339
Stantchett, S., 100
Stauffer, R. B., 384
Stea, D., 340
Steel, R. W., 115, 187, 423
Stefansson, V., 261, 294
Steiner, H. A., 79
Stenberger, M., 91
Stephenson, G. U., 54
Stern, H. P., 159
Stevens, G. G., 79

Stewart, C., 99
Stoessinger, J. G., 55, 59, 387
Stokes, W. S., 384
Stone, J., 462
Stoneman, E. A., 159
Strachey, J., 423
Straker, E., 35
Strang, W., 159
Strausz-Hupe, R., 171, 294, 423
Stryberg, O., 219
Sukhwal, B. L., 384
Sullivan, W., 159
Sulzberger, C. L., 377
Sundstrom, H. W., 219
Sutherland, M., 126
Swan, M., 54
Swann, R., 159
Sweet, J. V., 54
Sweet-Escott, B., 384
Symonds, R., 384
Szaz, Z. M., 159

Tarlton, C. D., 266, 269
Taubenfeld, H. J., 218
Taylor, A., 384
Taylor, A. R., 324
Taylor, G., 159, 294, 369
Tayyab, A., 159
Teague, M., 423
Teal, J. J., Jr., 159
Thomas, A. J., Jr., 447
Thomas, A. V. W., 447
Thomas, B. E., 188, 302
Thomas, E. M., 18
Thomas, E. N., 334
Thomas, F., 54
Thomas, H. B., 159
Thomas, O. J., 54
Thomas, S. B., 79
Thompson, D., 447
Thompson, J. E. S., 35
Thompson, J. H., 115
Thompson, V., 423
Thorndike, J. J., Jr., 175
Tomasek, R. D., 423
Touval, S., 423
Toynbee, A. J., 101, 124, 305
Treadgold, D. W., 423
Tregonning, K. G., 423
Triska, J. F., 447
Troll, C., 247, 294
Trueblood, L. W., 123
Tuan, Y., 340
Tuori, H., 219
Turner, F. J., 54, 159

Ullman, E. L., 115

Vaillant, G. C., 35
Valkenier, E. K., 384
Van Bynkershoek, C., 191-192, 212

Vance, J. E., Jr., 115
Van Cleef, E., 231
VanderKroef, J. M., 54, 424
Van Donger, I. S., 125
van Hamel, J. A., 231
Van Heerden, W., 54
Van Valkenburg, S., 55, 237-239, 266, 294, 386-387
Varma, S. N., 384
Verlag, K. V., 143
Vevier, C., 159
Villard, H. S., 384
Volacic, M., 188
Von der Heydte, F. A., 456
Von Elbe, J., 458
von Glahn, G., 195
von Humboldt, A., 236

Wahl, N., 384
Wainhouse, D. W., 424
Walhen, F. T., 157
Walker, E. A., 424
Walker, P. C. G., 54
Walker, R. G., 384
Walker, R. L., 384
Walker, W. L., 192
Walsh, 171
Ward, F. H., 174
Ward, M., 159
Ward, R. D. C., 54
Waterman, T. T., 35
Wehberg, H., 460
Weigend, G. G., 159, 188
Weigert, H. W., 171, 174, 261, 266, 294-295
Weihl, A., 54
Weldon, P. D., 446
Welensky, R., 384
Welles, S., 175
Wheare, K. C., 384
Whebell, C. F. J., 54
Wheeler, G., 54, 384, 451
Wheeler, R. H., 54
Whetten, N. L., 384
Whitaker, A. P., 447
Whitbeck, R. H., 54
White, H. L., 126
Whiteman, M. M., 200, 219
Whittam, D. E., 188
Whittlesey, D., 5, 54, 59, 83-84, 87, 101, 115-116,
    120-121, 144, 168, 171, 174, 240, 243, 245, 248,
    265-267, 295, 299, 302, 305, 317, 319, 384
Wiens, H., 79, 164, 173, 295, 453
Wigmore, J. H., 245
Wigny, P., 424
Wilber, D. N., 159
Wiley, S. C., 159
Wilkinson, S., 278, 282
Wilson, C. M., 79
Wilson, T., 384
Williams, M. H., 159
Willson, B., 126
Winch, M., 126

Windmiller, M., 384
Wirt, F., 340
Wiskermann, E., 126, 159
Withington, W. B., 115
Wittfogel, K. A., 79, 164-165, 173-174
Wolbers, J., 415
Wolf, E., 25, 27
Wolfe, A. W., 447
Wolfe, R. I., 79
Wolff, H. J., 415
Wolpert, J., 336, 340
Woodley, F. W., 316
Wooldridge, S. W., 91
Woytinsky, E. S., 54
Woytinsky, W. S., 54
Wriggins, W. H., 384

Wright, E., 447
Wright, J. K., 245, 295, 325, 340, 384
Wright, L. A., 225, 231
Wrong, D. H., 49, 54
Wurfel, D., 424

Young, C., 424
Young, M. C., 307
Young, R., 199-200, 384

Zaidi, I. H., 384
Zartman, I. W., 159
Zarur, J., 384
Zelinsky, W., 54
Zinnes, D. A., 78

Subject Index

Africa, armed forces, 59
  boundaries, 131
  British colonial policies in, 400-401
  buffer zone, 154
  capital, 120-121
  core areas, 107-111
  corridors, 225
  education, 67
  Entente, 445-446
  French colonial policies in, 396-398
  landlocked states, 228
  natural resources, 67-68
  Organization of African Unity, 438-441
  Portuguese colonial policies in, 392-394
Age of Reason, 167
Age-Sex Pyramid, 49-52
  defined, 49
Agriculture, in South America, 24
Algeria, core area, 108
  French colonial policies in, 396
Aircraft, 215
Alliance for Progress, 443-445
Alloys, in steel production, 69
America, boundaries, 169-170
American Independent Party, 327-335
Ancient Greece, 28
Ancient States, factors in growth of, 18
  relative location of, 22
Antarctic Treaty, 130
Antarctica, claims in, 128
Antecedent boundaries, 180-182
Anthropogeographic boundaries, 178
Anticolonialism, 404
Ar Rivad, 118
Arab League, 2, 435
Argentina, core area, 107
  ranked in world power, 65
  as world power, 63
Aristotle, 28, 235
Asia, boundary concepts and practices, 163-165
  Colombo Plan, 445
  core areas, 111-112
Attenuated state, defined, 39
Australia, 352-353, 369-381
  boundaries, 370, 380
  capital, 120

core area, 113-114
Federal Constitution as geographical expression, 370-373
federation in, 369-381
interstate relationships, changes in, 374-375
occupational structure, 379-380
railroads in, 37
ranked in world power, 65
states, changes in, 373-375
  and the Commonwealth, changes in, 375-377
  as geographical regions, changes in, 377-378
  specialisms, 378-379
urban settlement, patterns of, 378
as world power, 63
Australian aborigines, compared to Bushmen, 19
Austria, core area, 98
Autostrade, 11
Aztec, human sacrifice, 27
  state, 25

Balkan Peninsula, 99
Bamako, 118
Bangladesh, 366
Barcelona Conference, 228
Baselines, 201-204
Bathurst, 118
Bavaria, 101
Belgium, colonialism, 394-396
  formation of, 100
  ranked in world power, 65
  as world power, 63
Belgrade, 124
Benelux, 441
Bogota, 106
Bohemia, 95
Bolivia, 229-230
  capitals, 122
  core area, 106-107
Boundary, 129-137
  antecedent, 180-182
  anthropogeographic, 178
  Asian, 163-165
  of clans, 19
  classification, 175-186
  compared to frontier, 137-138
  concept and classification, 160-186

477

concepts, and imperialism, 168-169
    and nationality, 167-168
contractual concept of, 169-170
criteria, 132-133
defenses, 9
as defense, 133-134
definition, 129-131
delimitation, 131
demarcation, 131
displacements, 9
emergence of, 17
function of, 133-135
geometrical, 178-179
    concept of, 170-171
indeterminate, 179
international, 8, 257-258
lake as, 176-178
legal function of, 134-135
as legal-political phenomena, 139-140
Liechtenstein-Austria, 134
maritime, 3, 192-195, 201-218, 258
median-line, 206-207
mountain as, 133
natural, concept of, 167
Papal Line of Demarcation, 13
physiographic, 175-176
physiographic-political, 176
of political map, 17
relic, 185-186
river as, 133, 176
security of, 8-9
as separating factor, 138
since second World War, 172-173
special features of, 8-10
of state, 3, 36
subsequent, 182
superimposed, 182-185
territorial relations, 257-258
tribal concepts, 162-163
voting behavior, due to, 328-330
zone, replacement by boundary line, 9
Brandenburg, 92, 101
Brazil, capital, 120
    core area, 107
    fishing industry, 214
    iron reserves, 69
    ranked in world power, 65
    as world power, 63
Brasilia, 117
Britain, British Commonwealth, 435-437
    buffer zone, 154
    Colombo Plan, 445
    colonialism, 398-403
    core areas of, 91
    nationalism, response to, 405-407
    supranationalism, 442
British Commonwealth, 435-437
Bronze Age, 21
Buenos Aires, 107
Buffer states, 141
Buffer zone, 148-156

evolution and rapid decay of, 450-451
    in history, 154-156
Bulgaria, core area, 99-100
Bushman clan, organization of, 18

Calanque, 8
Canada, 352-353
    core area, 103
    language, 46-47
    ranked in world power, 64
    as world power, 63
Canberra, 121
Capital, cities (map), 118
    divided, 121-122
    function of, 116-119, 122-123
    government spending for, 12
    head-link function, 122-125
    introduced, 120-121
    location of, 12
    permanent, 119-120
    of states, 116-125
    types, 117-119
Caribbean, natural resources, 67-68
Caribbean Sea, 216-218
Carolingians, 89
Carthage, 31
Cayenne, 118
Central Andes, 27
Central Authority, 10
    defined, 6
    distribution of funds, 11
Central place, as stimulus, 20
Chad, 108
Charlemagne, 30
Chile, 229-230
    core area, 106
    as elongated state (map), 41
Ch'in Dynasty, expansion during, 23
China, boundary, 141, 163-165
    buffer zones, 149-154
    coal production, 69
    core area, 111
    Hwang Ho, 21
    industrialization, 70
    and Mongol Empire, 138
    ranked in world power, 64
    rise of, 452-453
    Shang (Yin) Dynasty, 21
    Wei River, 21
    as world power, 63
Clan, 18-20
    Bushman, 18
    Hottentots, 19
Climate, relationship to behavior, 47-48
Closed Sea, The, 191
Coal, in industry, 69
Colombia, core area, 106
Colombo Plan, 445
Colonial administration, 413-414
Colonialism, 385-403
    defined, 386

economic motive, 389-391
geopolitics, 385-387
methods, 391-403
motives, 387-391
Netherlands in the New World, 414-415
results, 391-403
rewards, 387-391
Communist, ideological power core, 449
  countries, foreign trade, 73
    industry in, 62-63
Community development, 18
Congo, Belgian colonial policies in, 394-396; *see also*
    Zaire
Contiguous zone, 195
Continental shelf, 193, 194, 196-199, 210-211
Continental slope, 193
Contraception, in restrictive population policy, 50
Core, contempory, 84
Core area, Africa, 109
  Asia, 112
  Australia, 114
  Britain, 91
  concept of, 255
  in Danube Valley, 95
  defense, 99
  definitions of, 84-86
  development of the European State System, 87-103
  ephemeral, 92
  Europe, 85, 92
  European cases, 84
  France, 90
  functional value, 86
  Italy (in Roman times), 97
  North America, 104
  peripheral, 92
  primary, 85, 104
  secondary, 85, 104
  state, 1, 83
  South America, 105
  trade, 98-99
Corridors, 223-225
Costa Rica, shelf-locking, 217
Council of Economic Mutual Assistance, 443
Council of Europe, 432
  Consultative Assembly, 432
  Council of Ministers, 432
Creoles, 417-418
Cultural plurism, 414-422
Cultural-political organization, 432-441
Cuzco, 27
  roads of, 27
Cyprus, boundaries, 132
Czechoslovakia, capital, 124
  ranked in world power, 65
  as world power, 63

Danes, territorial waters, 190
Danish Straits, 73
Danube, 100
Danube Valley, 94
  core areas in, 95

Danzig, boundary displacement of, 10
Dar es Salaam, 110
Decision making, in political geography, 335-336
Declaration of Santiago, 207
Defense, boundaries, 133-134
Delimitation, 131
Demarcation, 131
Democracy, compared to dictatorship, 56
Denmark, core area, 92
Diet, 45
Diffusion, of state-idea, 22
Divided capitals, 121-122
Domaine royale, 89
Dominance behavior, 338
Dutch, territorial waters, 190-191

East Africa, land, 307-308
  landlocked states, 228
  wildlife conservation areas, 307-317
East Asia, 21-23
East Germany, ranked in world power, 65
  as world power, 63
Economic, organization, 57-59
  relations, state, 258-260
  strength, 57
  supranationalism, 441-446
Ecuador, core area, 86, 106
Education, 67
  in the state, 45
Egypt, 108
  change from theocratic to militaristic state, 21
  impact upon politicogeographic world, 20-21
  innovations of, 21
Electoral geography, 2, 325-326
Elongated state, defined, 39
Emotional nationhood, components of, 33
England, territorial waters, 190
English Common Law, 13
Entente, 445-446
Environmental determinism, defined, 47
Environmentalism, 47-48
Ephemeral core area, 92
Equatorial Africa, 108
Ethiopia, core area, 110
Europe, Asiatic influence upon, 272-282
  closing of Suez Canal, 74
  colonialism, 387-403
    methods and results, 391-403
  consequences of political evolution, 32
  core areas of, 85, 92
  Council of, 432
  economic community, 441-442
  international relations, 459
  landlocked states, 220-222
  Organization for Economic Cooperation and
      Development, 442-443
  Organization for European Economic Cooperation,
      441
  trade, 28
  unitary states, 344
  unity of peoples, 32

European civilization, Greek influence upon, 28
European Coal and Steel Community, 441-442
European Economic Community, 441-442
European Free Trade Association, 442
European influence, upon world, 18
Europeanization, 3
Exclave, defined, 42-43
    normal, 44
    pene-, 43-44
    quasi-, 43-44
    temporary, 43-44
    virtual, 43

Farmsteads, compared to farm villages, 6
Federal states, 348-350, 360-364
    Boer War, 355-357
    compromise, 355-360
    imposed, 364-366
    mutual interest, 352-355
    territorial morphology, 366-368
    territory, 349
    types, 350-366
Federation, idea of, 369-370
Feudal Europe, 30-32
Feudalism, in Europe, 30
    powers of, 30
Field theory, 296-305, 308-309
    application of, 307-317
    utility of, 305-306
Finland, Arctic Corridor, 223
    core area, 97-98
Foreign trade, 72-74
    maritime, 73
    Panama Canal, 74
    Suez Canal, 74
France, colonialism, 396-398
    core area, 88-90
    Fifth Republic, 438
    French Community, 437-438
    nationalism, reaction to, 404-405
    Paris, 4
    political geography of, 243
    ranked in world power, 64
    as world power, 63
Franconia, 101
Free Sea, The, 191
Freedom of Transit Conference, 225-226
French Community, 437-438
French-Swiss boundary, 140
French West Africa, 396-398
Frontier, 127-129
    compared to boundary, 129, 137-138
    in contemporary world, 140-142
    defined, 127
    as integrating factor, 138
    origin, 136

Gangtok, 118
GATT (map), 75
Gdynia, boundary displacement of, 10
General Agreement on Tariffs and Trade, 73

General multilateral policy, 71
General unilateral policy, 71
Geneva Conference, 215, 227-228
Geneva Convention, 197, 202-204
    contiguous zone, 195
Geometric boundaries, 170-171, 178-179
Geopolitics, 4, 267-270
Geopolitik, 171
Geography, government and regional, 14
Germany, boundaries, 172
    formation of, 100-102
    heartland, 270
Ghana, 23, 108, 347
    irrendentism in, 411-412
Government activity, expressions of, 10-12
Government agencies, location of, 12
Government aid, misdirected, 11-12
    from taxes in the U.S. and Australia, 11
Great Britain, control of ports, 73
    dependence upon Suez Canal, 74
    fishing industry, 213-214
    foreign trade, 73
    "June War," 74
    as world power, 63
Great Wall, 164
Greece, core area, 96
Grid, examples of, 10
Guatemala, shelf-locking, 217
Guayaquil, 106
Gulf of Aqaba, shipping, 74
Gulf of Mexico, 216-218

Hadrian's Wall, 31
Hague Conference, 201-202, 204-205
Han Dynasty, growth during, 23
Heartland debate, 286-292
Hellenic civilization, 28
High seas, 196
Historic waters, 204
Hottentots, compared to Bushmen, 19
Hungary, 88
    as compact state (map), 41
    core area, 95-96

Iceland, fishing industry, 213-214
Icon, defined, 297
Iconography, 297, 300
Ifugaos, 163
Imperialism, and boundary concepts, 168-169
Inca Empire, 25
    contrasted to Roman society, 28
    organization of, 27
Indeterminate boundaries, 179
India, boundaries, 165
    compromise federation, 357-359
    core area, 111
    iron reserves, 69
    ranked in world power, 64
    as world power, 63
Indonesia, core area, 113
Industry, development of, 67-70

in relation to world power, 62-63
Internal waters, 195, 201-204
International Court of Justice, 429
International organizations, 430-441
  cultural-political organizations, 432-441
  political groupings, 432
  strategic groupings, 430-432
International relations, territorial state in, 458-461
International rivers, 222-223
Introduced capitals, 120-121
Iron, in industry, 69
Irredentism, 407-412
Israel, armed forces, 59
  "June War," 74
Italy, colonialism, 389
  core areas, 96
  ranked in world power, 65
  as world power, 63
Ivory Coast, 108

Japan, boundaries, 164-165, 172
  core area, 111-113
  fishing industry, 213
  ranked in world power, 64
  rise of, 452-453
  steel production, 69
  as world power, 63
Jefferson, Thomas, 170-171
Jural law, 139
Jylland, 92

Kabul, 118
Kalahari Desert, as Bushman habitat, 18
Kalingas, 163
Kenya, 307-310, 312, 314, 317
  British colonial policies in, 400-401
  core area, 108
Khrushchev, Nikita, 52
Kiev, 68
Kremlin, the, 113

Lakes, as boundaries, 176-178
Land, in relation to world power, 61-66
Landholdings, laws restricting size, 14
  size, 11, 13
Landlocked states, 220-230
  transit, 228-229
Landscape modifications, laws resulting in, 12-14
Language, and boundaries, 167-168
  differences within the state, 46-47
Law of nature, 139
Law of the Sea Conference, 227-228
League of Nations, 425-426
  achievements of, 426
  failures of, 426
Legal nationhood, components of, 33
Liberia, core area, 108
Liechtenstein-Austria boundary, 134
Lima, core area, 106
Limes, defined, 166
London, function as capital, 123

Low-tide elevation, 202
Lower Vistula Valley, boundary displacement of, 9-10

Mafia, Sicily, 6
Magyar, 95
Malaysia, as fragmented state (map), 41
Mali, 24
  Federation, 42
Managua, 118
Maps, electoral, 326
  information derived from, 1
Maritime boundaries, 192-195, 201-218
  envelope method, 204-205
  fishing disputes, 212-215
  procedures and methods, 204-205
  replica method, 204
  straight baseline method, 204
Maritime trade, 73
Masai, 309, 312, 316
Mauritania, 121
Mayan civilization, 25
Mayapan, 25
McMahon Line, 151-154
Mean low water, 202
Median-line boundary, 206-207
  defined, 206
Medieval Europe, boundary concepts of, 166-167
Mediterranean Ocean, 189
Mercantilism, 71
Mercantilist period, trade, 72
Mesopotamia, innovations of, 21
Mexico, core area, 103
Microstates, defined, 38
Middle America, 24-25
Middle East, corridors, 225
  early progress of, 20
  natural resources, 67-68
Military, of Aztec State, 25
  organization, 59
  power, 61-66
Ming Dynasty, 164
Ministates, defined, 38
Mongol Empire, 138
Mongol invasions, 276-277
Mongols, Chinese influence upon, 23
Moravia, 94
Morocco, core area, 108
Moscow, 113
Muscovy, 94
Mwanza, 110

Nassau, 118
Nation, communications in, 33
  concept of, 253-255
  defined, 32-33, 253
  -state, 33-34
    defined, 33-34
National economy, 61-66
National power, studies of, 303-304
Nationalism, anticolonialism, 404
  effects of, 460

irrendentism, 407-412
  response to, 403-407
  rise in Europe, 32
  tribalism, rise of, 451-452
Nationality, and boundary concepts, 167-168
Nationhood, emotional and legal, 33
Natural boundaries, concept of, 167
Natural law, 139
Natural resources, balance of, 70
  use of, 67-69
Negro, voting behavior in 1968, 330-331, 334-335
Netherlands, capital, 121-122
  formation of, 100
Nicaragua, shelf-locking, 217
Nigeria, 24
  compromise federation, 359-360
  core areas, 86, 110-111
Normal exclaves (map), 44
Norman invasion, 30
North America, core area, 103-104
North Atlantic Treaty Organization, 2, 430
North China Plan, 111
Northern Ireland, conflict in, 46
Northwest Europe, core area, 90
Norway, core area, 98
  fishing industry, 214
Novgorod, archaeological site, 26
Nuclear core, 84
Nuclear weapons, 61, 63
Nyasaland, imposed federation, 364

Organizations, international, 430-441
  international, cultural political organizations, 432-
      441
    political groupings, 432
    strategic groupings, 430-432
  world, 425-430
Organization of African Unity, 2, 438-441
Organization of American States, 432-435
Organization for Economic Cooperation and Develop-
    ment, 442
Organization for European Economic Cooperation,
    441
Original core, 84

Pacific Ocean, 452-453
Pacific War, 229-230
Pakistan, as fragmented state, 40
  territorial morphology, 366-368
Pampa, contrasted to the United States and Canada,
    13
Panama, resentment toward United States, 74
Panama Canal, 76
  control of, 74
Paraguay, core area, 107
Paramaribo, 118, 417-418
Paris, as focus, 4
Pene exclaves (map), 44
People of Han, 23
Peripheral core area, 92
Permanent capitals, 119-120

Peru, 229-230
  core area, 105
Philippines, core area, 113
Plato, 28
Pnom Penh, 118
Poland, core area, 93
  foreign trade, 73
  ranked in world power, 64
  as world power, 63
Policy, state, 71-72
Polish Corridor, 223
Political action area, 321
  area, 310, 321
  behavior, study of, 3
  counteraction area, 321
  geographers, function of, 2
  geography, 241-264, 296-306
    approaches, 296-297
    boundaries, 304
    capitals, 304
    centrifugal forces, 248-251
    circulation, 300
    cities, 304
    decision making, 335-336
    defined, 1, 264, 296, 299, 317-318
    dynamic fields, 304-305
    economic relations of states, 258-260
    field theory, application of, 307-317
    functional approach, 59-60
    historical approach, 59, 242, 265
    idea-area chain, 300-302
    kinetic fields, 304-305
    major trends, 448-453
    model, 321-324
    morphological approach, 59, 244, 264-265
    movement, 297, 301
    nation, concept of, 253-255
    political relations, 260-261
    power analysis, 59-60, 265
    progress of, 241-244
    relation of territorial, economic, political and
        strategic relations, 262-263
    in schools, 242
    spatial aspect, 2
    spatial attributes, 320-321
    spatial perception, 336-337
    state-area, 299-300
    state-idea, 251-253, 255-256
    strategic relations, 261-262
    unified field theory, 298-306
    voting behavior, 325-326
  groupings, 432
  interaction, 321-324
  power, 61-66
  process, 318-320
  region, 297
  relations, in the state, 260-261
  science, 252, 298-299
  system, concerning states, 1
    defined, 318
Population, census, 49

cycles in growth, 48-49
eugenic policy, 50
expansive policies, 50
growth, 48-49
policies, 50
in relation to world power, 61-66
restrictive policy, 50
of states, 43-54
world, 17
Portugal, colonialism, 392-394
core area, 99
nationalism, reaction to, 404
Power, analysis, 59-60
defined, 303
measurement of, 67
in transportation, 74-77
Prague, 124
Primary core area, 85, 104
Prussia, boundaries, 167

Quality, of states, 45-49
Quasi exclaves (map), 44
Quito, 106

Racial diversity, 45-46
Radio Cairo, 67
Radio Free Europe, 67
Radio South Africa, 67
Regionalism, defined, 430
rise of, 451-452
Relic boundaries, 185-186
Republic of Ireland, core areas, 97
Resources, 57
categories of, 58-59
as power, 59
Resurgent nationalism, 403-412
Revolutions, of state and nation, 32-34
Rhineland, 101
Rhodesia, core area, 108
imposed federation, 364
Rimland, continental, 289-290
maritime, 289-290
Rio de Janeiro, 107
Rivers, as boundaries, 176
international, 222-223
Roman Empire, 29-30
communications, 30
map of, 31
organization of, 29-30
provinces of, 31
reasons for advances, 29-30
social and economic advances of, 29
Roman-Hellenic civilization, 29
Roman State, 300-200 B.C., 97
Romania, core area, 96
Rome, 97, 123
Russia, 273-275, 279-282
buffer zone, 154
centralized federation, 360-364
core area, 93-94
and Mongol Empire, 138

Warsaw Pact, 432

Sao Paulo, 107
Saxony, 101
Scandinavia, core area, 91-93
Secondary core area, 85, 104
Security, expressions of, 6-8
product of effective central authority, 6
Seigneurial system, 13
Senegal, 108
Shape, of states, 38-43
Shatter belt, 149
Size, of states, 37-38
Sjaelland, 92-93
Social science, territoriality, 337-339
Social geography, 249-250
Somali Republic, irrendentism in, 411
Songhai, 24
South Africa, Capitals, 122
core area, 107-108
corridors, 225
decay of buffer zone, 451
eugenic policy, 50
frontier, 128
industrialization, 70
landlocked states, 228
as perforated state (map), 41
policy, 72
South America, 24-25
core areas of, 105
corridors, 225
South West Africa, corridors, 225
Southeast Asia, buffer zones, 149, 450-451
Southeast Asia Treaty Organization, 430-432
Sovereignty, 457-458
Soviet Union, 142
airspace, 215
core area, 111, 290-292
buffer zone, 149, 151
coal production, 69
eastward march, 452-453
heartland, 270
policy, 71
population, 50
ranked in world power, 64
steel production, 69
transportation, 67
Spacecraft, 215
Spain, core area, 99
Spatial perception, 336-337
Specific multilateral policy, 71
Specific unilateral policy, 71
Stalin, Joseph, personality cult, 68
State, adolescence, 238
anatomy of, 3
ancient, 20-28
factors in growth of, 18
as approach to political geography, 2
boundaries, 129-131
buffer, 141
capitals, 3, 116-125

centrifugal forces, 240, 249-250
centripetal forces, 240, 250-251
claims to territorial waters, 207-212
compact, 39
components, 1
concept of, 17-18
core area, 83
defined, 6
degree of development, 50
density of population, 43-45
distribution of population, 43-45
economic organization, 57-59
economic relations, 258-260
elements of organization, 55-59
European, 28-32, 87-103
evolution of, 18
external functions, 257-263
federal, 348-350
  defined, 343
foreign trade, 72-74
fragmented, 40
governmental organization, 55
idea, 299-300
  in political geography, 255-256
internal organization, 47, 256-257
internal transport network, 77
landlocked, 42, 220-230
location, 38
maturity, 238
military organization, 59
military power, 261-262
natural resources, 67
old age, 238-239
organization, 3, 67, 247-248
  of power, 55
perforated, 40
pillars of, 3
policy, 71-72
political relations, 260-261
politicogeographical framework, 56
population, 43-54
problem of quality, 45-49
prorupt, 38-39
regional differences, 247-248
relative location, 42
resources, 57
self-sufficiency, 70
shape, 3, 38-43
size, advantages and disadvantages, 37-38
strategic relations, 261-262
system, 17
  basic features of, 454-455
territorial, air warfare, 462-463
  decline of, 461-463
  economic warfare, 461
  in international relations, 458-461
  nuclear warfare, 462-463
  psychological warfare, 461-462
  relations, 257-258
  rise of, 455-456
  rise and demise of, 454-465

unifying forces in, 47
unitary, 5, 343-344
  defined, 343-344
youth, 237-238
Steel Industry, 69
Strabo, 235-236, 240
Strategic groupings, 430-432
Strategic relations, state, 261-262
Strategic waters, 204
Streets, European and Asiatic, 8
  Japanese, 8
Strength, in transportation, 77
Subsequent boundaries, 182
Sudan, 345
  core area, 108
  size, 37
Suez Canal, 76
  closing of, 74
  control of, 74
Superimposed boundaries, 182-185
Surinam, British influence upon, 415
  cultural plurism, 414-417
  decolonization, 418-420
  East Indian cultural influence upon, 416
  economic progress of, 419-420
  Ethnic regionalism in, 417-418
  Dutch administration in, 416-417
  political modernization, 420-421
Supranationalism, 148-149, 425-446
  development of supranational entities and alliances,
    450
  economic, 441-446
  international organizations, 430-441
  world organizations, 425-430
Swabia, 101
Swaziland, boundary of, 131
Sweden, core area, 91-92
  ranked in world power, 65
  as world power, 63
Switzerland, 353-355
  core area, 93

Tanzania, 307
  core area, 110
Tariffs, compared to free trade, 12-13
  determined by economic geography, 12-13
Technology, development in Americas, 24
Tenochititlan, organization of state, 25
Territory, of states, 36-43
Territorial sea, concept of, 189-199
Territorial state, air warfare, 462-463
  decline of, 461-463
  economic warfare, 461
  in international relations, 458-461
  nuclear warfare, 462-463
  psychological warfare, 461-462
  rise of, 455-456
  rise and demise of, 454-465
Territorial waters, 195
  development of claims to, 190-192
Territoriality, 337-339

nature of, 456-458
Temporary exclaves (map), 44
Thailand, core area, 86
  as proprut state, (map), 41
Thalweg, 207
Tibet, boundaries, 164
Tirane, 118
Togo, irredentism in, 411-412
Tokyo, as capital, 119-120
Toltec society, 25
Totalitarianism, aspects of, 56
Township and Range System, 56
Trade, 8
Transportation, merchant marine, 77
  organization of, 67
  power of, 74-77
  in the state, 67, 77
  in war, 77
Treaty of Panama, 194
Treaty of Tordesillas, 156
Tribe, 18-20
  central place, 19-20
  concept of, 19
  Hottentots, 19
  organization of, in Americas, 24-25
Tribal states, growth of, 20
Truman Declaration of 1945, 207, 212
Truman, Harry S., 196
Tunisia, core area, 108
Turkish Straits, 73-74

Uganda, 307
  core area, 108
Ulan Bator, 118
Union of South Africa, ranked in world power, 65
  as world power, 63
Unitary states, 343-344
  adjusted, 347-348
  centralized, 346
  Communist, 347
  evolution of, 344-346
  highly centralized, 346-347
  present distribution, 344-346
United Kingdom, 347-348
  compared to France, 5
  core area, 90-91
  ranked in world power, 64
  steel production, 69
  as world power, 63
United Nations, 426-429
United States, airspace, 215
  armed forces, 59
  capital, 123
  coal production, 69
  core area, 86, 103
  education, 67
  growth, 237-238
  North Atlantic Treaty Organization, 430
  Organization of American States, 432-435
  Organization for Economic Cooperation and

Development, 443
  Organization for European Economic Cooperation,
    442-443
  Panama Canal, 74
  ranked in world power, 64
  Southeast Asia Treaty Organization, 430-432
  steel production, 69
Upper Volta, 108
Urganization, 83
Uruguay, 107

Valley of Mexico, relating to Aztecs, 25-27
Venezuela, core area, 106
  shelf-locking, 217
Verulamium, 91
Via Appia, 30
Viet Nam, buffer zone, 150-151
Village chief, in South America, 24
Voice of America, 67
Voting behavior, 325-326
  support regions, 332-335
  1968 Wallace vote in the Southeast, 327-335

Walachia, 95
Wallace, George, 327-335
Warsaw Pact, 2, 432
West Africa, 23-24
  core area, 108
  early trade, 23
  formation of city-state, 23
  "savanna belt," 20
West Berlin, as exclave (map), 44
West Germany, ranked in world power, 64
  steel production, 69
  as world power, 63
West Indies Federation, 124-125
Western Europe, commercial competition in, 32
  maritime boundaries, 193-194
Western Nigeria, 116
Wildlife conservation, Convention of 1900, 309-312
  in East Africa, 307-317
  licensing of hunters in East Africa, 309
William the Conqueror, 30
Wilson, Woodrow, 168
World organizations, 425-430
World power, evaluation of, 61-66

Yaounde, 118
Yerevan, 68
Yugoslavia, capital, 124
  centralized federation, 364

Zaire, 40
  Belgian influence upon, 394-396
  core area, 108-110
  see also Congo
Zimbabwe, construction of, 7
Zomba, 121
Zone of diffusion, 195-196
Zones, maritime, 195-196